VARIORUM COLLECTED STUDIES SERIES

Reason and Belief
in the Age of
Roscelin and Abelard

Dr Constant J. Mews

Constant J. Mews

Reason and Belief
in the Age of
Roscelin and Abelard

Ashgate
VARIORUM

Published in the Variorum Collected Studies Series by

Ashgate Publishing Limited
Gower House, Croft Road,
Aldershot, Hampshire GU11 3HR
Great Britain

Ashgate Publishing Company
131 Main Street,
Burlington, Vermont 05401–5600
USA

Ashgate website: http://www.ashgate.com

ISBN 0–86078–866–0

British Library Cataloguing-in-Publication Data
Mews, Constant J.
  Reason and Belief in the Age of Roscelin and Abelard. -
  (Variorum Collected Studies Series: CS730)
  1.Theology – France – History – Middle Ages, 600–1500 2.Faith 3.Reason
  I.Title
  230'.0944'09021

US Library of Congress Cataloging-in-Publication Data
Reason and Belief in the Age of Roscelin and Abelard/Constant J. Mews.
      p. cm. – (Variorum Collected Studies Series: CS730)
  Includes Bibliographical References and Index.
  1. Theology–History–Middle Ages, 600–1500 2.Philosophy, Medieval.
  3. Roscelin, of Compiègne, ca. 1050–ca. 1125? 4. Abelard, Peter, 1079–1142.
  I. Mews, C. J. II. Collected Studies: CS730.

BT26.R43 2002
230'09021–dc21

2002018200

The paper used in this publication meets the minimum requirements of the
      American National Standard for Information Sciences – Permanence of
      Paper for Printed Library Materials, ANSI Z39.48–1984. ∞ ™

Printed by TJ International Ltd, Padstow, Cornwall

VARIORUM COLLECTED STUDIES SERIES CS730

CONTENTS

This volume contains xviii + 332 pages

ACKNOWLEDGEMENTS

Grateful acknowledgement is made to the following institutions and publishers for their kind permission to reproduce the papers included in this volume: Pegasus Press, Asheville, NC (I); Le Léopard d'Or, Paris (II); Institut d'Études augustiniennes (III); Fordham University Press, New York (IV); Publicacions de l'Abadia de Montserrat, Barcelona (V); Vrin, Paris (VI, IX, X); Brill Academic Publishers, Leiden (VII); University of Sheffield Press, Sheffield (VIII).

PUBLISHER'S NOTE

The articles in this volume, as in all others in the Collected Studies Series, have not been given a new, continuous pagination. In order to avoid confusion, and to facilitate their use where these same studies have been referred to elsewhere, the original pagination has been maintained wherever possible.

Each article has been given a Roman numeral in order of appearance, as listed in the Contents. This number is repeated on each page and quoted in the index entries.

INTRODUCTION

Peter Abelard (1079–1142) is such a well-known personality from the twelfth century that his immediate predecessors and contemporaries are easily passed over in silence within general surveys of the period. The papers in this volume all serve, in one way or another, to explore wider issues of reason and belief in the age of Peter Abelard, focusing on the achievement of both his peers, and his little known teacher, Roscelin of Compiègne (c. 1050–c. 1125?). In a previous volume of papers (*Abelard and his Legacy*), my focus was on Abelard's evolution as a writer and thinker, both in logic and in theology. In this volume, I seek to present a larger picture of the world to which both Abelard and Roscelin made such significant and controversial contributions. For many students of the period, Abelard's *Historia calamitatum* provides the standard introduction to the intellectual and religious history of the twelfth century. The papers in this volume synthesise my research into the dynamism of thinking about reason and belief in northern France from the time of St Anselm (1033–1109) until the mid twelfth-century, when scholastic thought seems to reach a new stage of stability and acceptance within wider society. Scholasticism is a concept that often evokes images of sterile argument over textual minutiae. My aim in these papers is to show that the intellectual culture of the schools in the age of Roscelin and Abelard cannot be dissociated from broader cultural developments during the period 1070–1150. Rational questioning of belief took place, not just within the schools, but within monastic as well as 'heretical' communities. The monastic context of so many surviving scholastic manuscripts itself throws into question the notion of a strict division between monastic and scholastic environments. While Abelard was certainly the most spectacular and controversial figure to emerge in the first half of the twelfth century, his importance has to be measured against a broader ferment that had started to gain momentum in northern France in the second half of the eleventh century.

Too often the history of scholasticism in the twelfth century has been approached as if it were a simply a preparation for the great synthesis of Thomas Aquinas in the thirteenth century. This at least has been the legacy of Joseph de Ghellinck and a school of research into twelfth-century scholastic literature long associated with the *Recherches de théologie ancienne et médiévale*, when it was published from the Abbaye de Mont-César in Leuven. In their vision, scholasticism was understood to refer to a particular way of teaching and debating theology, through the technique of the *quaestio*. Peter Lombard was viewed as a forerunner of St Thomas, providing the most effective synthesis of reason and belief in the twelfth century. In this neo-scholastic vision, Peter Abelard tended to be recognised as a logician, who endeavoured unsuccessfully to apply reason to catholic belief, rather than as a theologian in his own right. This was a mirror image of the passing comments that might be made about Roscelin of Compiègne as the nominalist logician who was much less successful than St Anselm in using philosophical reason to expound the doctrine of the Trinity. Perhaps the most eloquent recent exposition of this perspective on twelfth-century religious thought is that of Richard W. Southern, in *Scholastic Humanism and the Unification of Europe*, vols. 1–2 (Oxford: Blackwell, 1995–2001). It presupposes that there was an ideal synthesis of scholastic and humanist culture in the twelfth century, represented by some scholars better than others. In this perspective, Christian orthodoxy is either challenged or strengthened by intellectuals of the period. Less attention is given to philosophical systems in themselves, than to their contribution or challenge to Christian belief.

There is another perspective on scholastic culture in the twelfth century which focuses not on theology, but on secular philosophy. This is a tradition of enquiry that can be traced back to the pioneering research of Victor Cousin in the early nineteenth century into the contribution of Abelard as a logician to 'the scholastic method'. He was interested in Abelard as a nominalist and as someone who applied his questioning mind to religious belief, but not as a theologian proper. As John Marenbon has so well shown in *The philosophy of Peter Abelard* (Cambridge: Cambridge University Press, 1997), this image of Abelard as 'a critical thinker' was profoundly selective in that it ignored his contribution to ethical thought. Abelard was not just a logician and ethicist, however. He was a theologian, whose interpretation of many aspects of Christian belief, disturbed a number of his contemporaries. A similar claim can be made for his first teacher, Roscelin of Compiègne, one of the first logicians to develop the theme that categories are words of human invention that were applied to an individual thing or *res* (a term that provoked particular difficulty when he applied it to the persons of the Trinity). My interest in these papers is to show that the period between 1070 and 1150 was one of great dynamism in thinking about both logic and theology, a discipline which emerged from applying the tools of reason to Christian belief. The fact that there was no clear definition of catholic orthodoxy in the first half of the twelfth century certainly provoked St Anselm and Bernard of Clairvaux into arguing against the particular theologies offered by Roscelin and Abelard. It would be misleading, however, to assume that Roscelin and Abelard were inspired by commitment to reason, while St Anselm and Bernard were driven by love of catholic belief. All of these individuals were seeking to interpret Christian belief in a way that conformed to their own vision of the world and of human nature. In these and other cases, the charges of heresy thrown up in the heat of debate testify to the vibrancy of contemporary desire to find meaningful ways of understanding Christian doctrine both within and outside the schools, rather than to any concerted assault on Christian orthodoxy.

In 'Orality, Literacy and Authority in the Twelfth-Century Schools' (I), I consider a feature of pedagogical experience that is very difficult for a historian to reconstruct, but that I believe is essential to understanding the sense of excitement and controversy of the twelfth-century schools, the role of the spoken word. My intention in this paper is to show that collections of theological *sententiae*, gathered by students, often recorded heated arguments and original perspectives with a freshness that is sometimes concealed by more formal written treatises. At the same time, there was a profound pressure, felt by Abelard among others, for innovative theological argument to be buttressed by the authority of the written word. Even between the original version of his treatise on the Trinity, the *Theologia 'Summi boni'* and its most mature revision, the *Theologia 'Scholarium'*, we can see this growing tendency to quote and discuss specific passages from scriptural, patristic and philosophical tradition. Abelard was at the forefront of promoting a critical attitude towards the textual authorities of the past, most clearly evident within his *Sic et Non*. Yet Abelard's theological teaching was communicated first of all through oral presentations that were taken down by his students. It was this oral quality that made reports of his teaching such controversial documents during the 1130s. By the 1150s, however, the teaching of theology had come to be dominated by greater reverence for the written word, as Robert of Melun observes in the prologue to his book of sentences. Peter Lombard, by contrast (who certainly used Abelard's *Theologia* as a source of patristic quotations, even if he disagreed with many of its arguments) was much more careful to structure his argument around specific texts. This ultimately made Lombard's *Four Books of Sentences* much more useful as a foundation for teaching theology than the equivalent treatise of Robert of Melun.

My survey of philosophy and theology 1100–1150 (II) endeavours to provide an overview of the major intellectual developments in the schools during this period. While Peter Abelard is well known to us through the *Historia calamitatum*, a number of his contemporaries were no less daring in their willingness to create a synthesis of secular and sacred learning, each with its own particular emphasis. By the mid twelfth-century Aristotle had come to be known as 'the philosopher' par excellence. There were many different ways, however, in which scholars sought to combine the insights of Plato, Aristotle and contemporary science. For all the new ideas and authors introduced into twelfth century thought, Augustine continued to exercise fascination on many. Rather than classifying thinkers into Augustinians, Platonists, and Aristotelians, we need to be sensitive to the multitude of ways in which scholars sought to create their own particular synthesis of the path to wisdom.

No discussion of ideas in twelfth-century France can ever detach itself from consideration either of cultural context or of the manuscripts through which they are transmitted. A number of studies in this volume bear the fruit of close study of manuscripts that provide a rich window into the past. Scrutinizing manuscripts, even those that have been noticed by scholars, often rewards the scholar with new insights into familiar episodes. A manuscript, for example, that contained an unusual copy of the heretical propositions attributed to Peter Abelard, also transmits the passage of Guibert of Nogent about the so-called 'Manichaean' heretics of Soissons, here appended to a copy of Augustine's *De haeresibus* (III). In itself this might not seem so important, given that the text of Guibert's autobiography is already known through a seventeenth-century transcription. Yet if we look more closely at this passage, rich in patristic stereotypes about heretics (themselves taken over from pagan rumours about Christians), we realise that Guibert has added this passage to his original narrative. Guibert imagined that Clement and Everard of Bucy were illiterate rustics, with no understanding of Scripture, who encouraged gross indecency and fornication among their disciples. Reading this passage more closely enables us to appreciate that these so-called 'heretics' were in fact responding in their own way to the call of the *vita apostolica*, but outside formal clerical control. While not scholastics, they were endeavouring to interpret Christian faith in a way that they felt fully rational–creating their own version of a quasi-monastic community that involved both women and men. Guibert refused to accept that their understanding of the apostolic life could be anything other than an assault on both reason and belief.

Another illustration of how a small anecdote preserved within a manuscript can reveal much about how events become reshaped through rumour and hearsay is provided by a story reported about Abelard and Thierry of Chartres (IV). My initial curiosity was provoked by a minor, but irritating detail about Abelard, the multitude of ways in which his name has been spelt, both in manuscripts and in modern publications. There became no doubt in my mind that the correct spelling was *Abaelardus*, pronounced as five syllables (*ae* being two vowel sounds, as in *Israel*). This provided a clue for deciphering two layers in an anecdote that had clearly been transmitted orally rather than in writing: there was an original story about Abelard's unsuccessful attempt to learn mathematics from Thierry, onto which a quite fictitious story had been laid about Abelard's supposed skill in the quadrivium (probably based on confusion with the name of Adelard of Bath). Whatever the exact truth of the first anecdote, it does highlight what we know from other sources about Abelard, that knowledge of the quadrivium was never his strong point. The story provides telling insight into the exaggerated reputation that always surrounded Abelard. His enthusiasm for learning was such that he became a mythic symbol of superhuman intelligence, who peered over his contemporaries. While such stories may have been much embellished in the re-telling, they provide valuable insight into the way masters like Thierry and Abelard were perceived as breaking the boundaries of tradition in their zeal for knowledge.

Manuscripts themselves, even those copied after the twelfth century, provide fascinating witness into the changing image of an author across the centuries. In the case of Abelard, a figure whose writings were never copied in large number by contemporaries, the abbey of the Paraclete played an important role in the diffusion of one aspect of his literary *oeuvre*. In a sense my study of the library of the Paraclete, from the thirteenth century to the French Revolution (V) might not seem to fit into the general theme of the other papers, on reason and belief in the age of Abelard. Yet the story of the transmission of his writings can throw important insight on the way we perceive his importance. For too long, the scholastic aspect of his achievement has been considered simply in terms of ideas, without appreciating the fact that the abbey of the Paraclete was one of the few places which preserved his memory. Yet even at the abbey that he founded, Abelard's influence was never as sustained as has sometimes been imagined. My study of the most important manuscript of the letters of Abelard and Heloise (Troyes, Bibliothèque municipale 802) led me to conclude that it had been given to the abbey of the Paraclete, sometime before the late fifteenth century. The image of the Paraclete and its various daughter houses all faithfully preserving the memory of Abelard from the twelfth-century to the Revolution is a fanciful hypothesis, but without foundation in manuscript evidence. Even if some writings of Abelard had been preserved at the Paraclete from the twelfth century, war and destruction took its toll on the abbey in the fourteenth century, demanding a major programme of restoration over the next century. The Counter Reformation was even more damaging to the abbey, as it provoked a new abbess to abandon usage of all manuscripts, and to distance herself from memory of the abbey's controversial founders. When the nuns of the Paraclete reclaimed interest in Abelard and Heloise in the eighteenth century, they had effectively lost all firm links with their founders, who had now become mythical figures, no longer part of the monastic milieu in which they had once lived out their lives.

The second half of this volume is devoted to a range of texts that reveal a great deal about the dynamic intellectual environment in which the young Abelard was raised. I had always been driven by curiosity about his debt to Roscelin of Compiègne, never mentioned in the *Historia calamitatum*, but clearly a major influence on Abelard's intellectual development. While a letter from Roscelin to Abelard had been identified in a manuscript from Benedictbeuern (now in the Bavarian State Library in Munich) in the middle of the nineteenth century, it had always been assumed that nothing more could be known about the teacher reported by Otto of Freising to have been the first to institute the *sententiam vocum* (the teaching of words or utterances) in logic, and accused of being a dangerous heretic by St Anselm. In a series of papers, published between 1991 and 1998, I argued that a number of anonymous texts preserved in twelfth-century manuscripts could tell us much more about Roscelin's theological teaching, and the world in which the young Abelard was raised, than we had previously realised.

My first paper in this series (VI) was provoked by my discovery of a hitherto unnoticed version of St Anselm's treatise against Roscelin, the *De incarnatione verbi* within a twelfth-century copy of St Anselm's writings, apparently from the Augustinian abbey of Lantony, near Gloucester. While the learned Fr Schmitt had produced an exemplary edition of two recensions of this text, he had not realised that an intermediary version survived that provided fascinating insight into Anselm's anxious desire to find an intellectually satisfactory response to the very logical question that Roscelin had raised: if the Father and the Son were of a single substance, why did the Father not become incarnate with the Son? Was it not necessary to say that the three persons of the Trinity were separate things? The draft enables us to see passages that were excised from the much more polished final version of the *De incarnatione verbi*, given wide circulation in the twelfth-century as an authoritative refutation to Roscelin's argument. While

Anselm claimed to be preserving catholic tradition, the manner in which he argued, from reason alone, was quite new. The draft reveals quite clearly how Anselm was using rational argument, such as Roscelin had himself deployed, to defend catholic belief. I was also intrigued to find that this manuscript contained a number of other texts not reproduced in standard collections of St Anselm's writings. The most interesting of these was a dialogue between a Gentile philosopher and a Christian about belief in the incarnation. The only other comparable such dialogue from the period, prior to the *Collationes* of Peter Abelard is by Gilbert Crispin. While the issue of whether or not this dialogue is by St Anselm still needs to be explored, it provides valuable insight into new ways of thinking about applying reason to belief from the late eleventh or early twelfth century, even before Abelard applied himself to creating a theology.

An even larger text that testifies to a new level of philosophical reflection about language in the late eleventh century is a commentary or *Glosule* on Books I–XVI of the *Grammatical Institutes* of Priscian, that Margaret Gibson discovered was printed by Arrivabenus in incunable editions of Priscian from the late fifteenth century (VII). While the *Grammatical Institutes* are in themselves more concerned with describing than analysing various categories of word, the *Glosule* author is fascinated by a desire to find the causes behind words, or in his terminology the things (*res*) to which words refer. He is aware that words can be considered both as utterances and as the things which they name. Compared to Abelard, this author is very crude in his terminology. Yet in explaining that a noun names a substance, while signifying a quality (as distinct from Priscian's bald statement that a noun signifies a substance with a quality), this commentator appreciates that a noun or name is applied first of all to a specific thing, that may share a common quality with other things. I argue that this way of thinking helps explain what Roscelin was talking about when he referred to the three persons as separate things that could not be identified with each other. According to one chronicler from the period, Roscelin was only one of a number of teachers who followed a certain John, in holding that logic was an *ars vocalis*, a discipline to do with words. In traditional historiography, nominalists have been portrayed as philosophical heretics, radically opposed to philosophical realists. Roscelin has in consequence been constructed as a rather deluded dialectician, whose refusal to recognise the existence of a universal substance led him to teach that the three divine persons must be three separate things. In the same way as Guibert of Nogent distorts the ideas of Clement and Everard of Bucy, so St Anselm turns Roscelin into an insane dialectician, intent on imposing his perverse reasoning on the most sacred issues of Christian belief. Philosophically, the *Glosule* on Priscian are neither specifically vocalist nor specifically realist. Nonetheless, they help elucidate Roscelin's desire to explain the doctrine of the Trinity in rational terms that he could understand. Roscelin's description of the three divine persons as three things was not theologically elegant, and appeared outrageous to many (including both St Anselm and Peter Abelard), but it did highlight the point that what was said about God the Father was not the same as what was signified by God the Son. Theological language needed to take into account these basic rules of grammar.

In a third paper relating to Roscelin (VIII), I concentrate on the political circumstances surrounding the accusations made against his teaching by St Anselm, initially in 1090, and then again in 1092/93. Intellectual history needs to be aware of the profound impact of sometimes petty local politics on the way in which philosophical and theological argument can be framed. Roscelin is too often identified simply as a philosophical nominalist, when he was first of all a teacher, both of the *artes* and of sacred Scripture. My point of departure is a fascinating list of books bequeathed by a certain *Roscelinus grammaticus* to the cathedral of Beauvais. Is this *Roscelinus*, apparently a canon of St-Étienne, Beauvais, the same Roscelin as taught Peter Abelard in the Loire valley between 1093 and 1100? Questions first were raised about Roscelin's theological teaching by a former monk of Bec then employed in seeking to establish Fulco, as bishop of Beauvais, against a previous bishop, who had promoted collegiate churches within the city. St Anselm's letters give strong indication that Roscelin of Compiègne was one of those many clerics at Beauvais, who apparently resisted this extension of the influence of a Norman abbey into the kingdom of France. Political rivalries between different factions of the Church, each claiming to represent the cause of ecclesiastical reform, are just as important as philosophical differences of opinion in provoking accusations of heresy. In this particular case, St Anselm was supporting the cause of Fulco, a monk whose father was an ambitious local magnate, strongly suspected of buying the bishopric from the king of France, for his son. The short-lived episcopate of Fulco seems to have been rather an embarrassment for St Anselm, but it served to highlight the radical gulf between a Norman Church, in which reformed monasticism played an important role, and a French Church, in which non-monastic clerics were becoming increasingly important.

The last two papers in this volume consider two theological texts that articulate characteristic themes of Roscelin of Compiègne. The first (IX) develops the theme that Roscelin's understanding of the doctrine of the Trinity was shaped by his desire to consider the doctrine from the point of view of the different meanings generated by different words (*voces*) applied to God. In particular, I look at a short treatise occuring alongside Roscelin's letter to Peter Abelard, that clearly reflects all the same arguments as Roscelin makes to his former disciple. Roscelin may have been unusually vituperative towards Abelard in that letter, but he was a theologian, attempting to speak logically about a doctrine that many have thought impossible to submit to reason. Roscelin did not imagine that there were three gods, as his critics charged. This essay confirms what we learn from his letter to Abelard, that he understood God to be single and undivided. Difference within God is a consequence of the different ways in which we speak of *Father*, *Son* and *Holy Spirit*. The fact that each of those words refers to something different, does not mean that the unity of the divine essence is impugned.

The same themes are expounded in more length in a treatise on the unity and trinity of the divine essence found alongside Abelard's *Theologia christiana* (X). This essay similarly takes pains to explain why it is that the three divine persons cannot be identified with each other. Perhaps the most remarkable feature of this treatise is that in many ways it parallels St Anselm's *Monologion*, also a supremely rational investigation of why it is legitimate to speak of a trinity of divine persons within a single divine unity. St Anselm himself came under criticism from Lanfranc for presenting a familiar Christian doctrine in a new way, by appealing to reason rather than to Scriptural authority. Roscelin, I suggest, was pursuing the same underlying goal as St Anselm in seeking to find a philosophically acceptable way of arguing that there could be three distinct identities to God, as *Father*, *Son* and *Holy Spirit* that could not be identified with each other, even though each of these persons was divine. I argue that labels of 'nominalist' and 'realist', thrown up by contemporary argument between masters, disguise the extent to which all these teachers were grappling with the meaning of words when applied to God. St Anselm was troubled by Roscelin's literal concern to identify the meaning or 'thing' behind individual words. There can be little doubt that St Anselm was the more imaginative thinker, more skilled than Roscelin in showing how words could change their meaning when placed in different situations. Nonetheless, Roscelin put more emphasis than St Anselm on the difference between God the Father and God the Son. Peter Abelard was very aware of the limitations of Roscelin as a teacher, with his strict concentration on the meaning of individual words applied to God. Abelard's solution to the doctrine of the Trinity was to define the three divine persons not as things, but as attributes of God, the supreme good. Much of the argument of the initial version of Abelard's treatise on the Trinity was directed against Roscelin's thesis that the three persons were as separate from each other as three things. Abelard was dissatisfied with the way St Anselm had sought to rebut Roscelin simply by reverting to imagery of the Trinity previously suggested by Augustine. Yet although Abelard argued so fiercely with Roscelin, there was much that he imbibed from his first teacher. Above all, Abelard imbibed from Roscelin a passion for analysing words and their meaning. In a paradoxical way, Abelard owed much as well to Roscelin's critic, St Anselm, for moving forward the larger project of exploring Christian belief through the tools of reason.

A final word needs to be offered about a confusing matter, touched on in one of these papers (IV), the variety of ways in which Abelard's name is spelt. When researching the material about the spelling of Abelard's name in medieval manuscripts, I became convinced that its correct form was *Abaelardus*, and that *Abelardus* was quite incorrect. In a number of studies, I preferred to use the spelling Abaelard, in the interests of authenticity. For practical reasons, however, not least the ubiquity of *Abelard* in computerised library catalogues, I eventually decided to revert to Abelard as the most common form of the *cognomen* of master Peter.

CONSTANT J. MEWS

Monash University
March 2002

Orality, Literacy, and Authority

in the twelfth-century Schools

the growth of scholasticism" is one of those clichés of twelfth-century cultural history that are often used all too loosely of the period in order to cover an immense range of intellectual and educational activity.[1] The names of Peter Abaelard, Gratian and Peter Lombard are commonly cited as authors who paved the way for the great scholastic *summae* of the thirteenth century by applying reason to the subject matter of religious faith. According to this interpretation the defining characteristic of scholasticism is taken as the quest to frame answers to philosophical or theological *quaestiones* within a systematic framework, so creating a unified whole. Abaelard is conventionally seen as a key figure in this process, his *Sic et non* a seminal document in the search for synthesis.[2]

Scholasticism thus has tended to be discussed in predominantly literary terms, other forms of communication (like the oral) being treated as peripheral to the written word. Another interpretative framework suggested more recently is Brian Stock's hypothesis that the eleventh and twelfth centuries witnessed an underlying shift towards more "textual" modes of thinking, a consequence of the growth of literacy in the period.[3] Stock sees Abaelard as only one of several writers who bring consciousness of ideas as "text" to the forefront of their reflection. Yet this is still an argument based on the written word. What role does oral communication play in the formation of scholastic literature? Is oral discourse textualised to a new degree in the scholastic milieu of the twelfth century? Does the written word acquire in this period a new authority?

The history of spoken discourse may seem, by virtue of its transient nature, impossible to reconstruct. Are not all speech acts distorted, consciously or otherwise, when recorded in script? We can gain some idea of what may have been said in an early medieval classroom through glosses to the standard *auctores*. In both secular and sacred subjects the most familiar pattern of education was for a master to read aloud a text and to explain individual words as they were encountered. The writings of the Fathers assisted in providing an armoury of explanation to shape the pattern of spoken discourse.

What needs to be investigated is the extent to which the growth of analytical writing about aspects of Christian faith in the eleventh and twelfth centuries was fostered through public debate within — and perhaps also beyond — an expanding clerical and literate elite. To focus on literary modes of communication is to neglect the importance of face to face contact in the transmission of ideas. It is on the level of interaction between individuals in a specific social environment that we need to locate the emergence of "scholastic literature" and thus of new canonical texts in the educational curriculum.

Perhaps the most original of eleventh-century thinkers was Anselm of Bec, later to become archbishop of Canterbury. Although he insisted that he wanted only to complement the writings of Augustine, not to oppose ideas that had been formulated by the bishop of Hippo, he felt no need to buttress his ideas by critical discussion of other people's writings.[4] The meditative quality of his language springs in part from the relative absence of direct quotation from the Fathers of the Church. St Anselm was a refreshingly innovative thinker, unconcerned by any need to search out words of authority.

The originality of his thought notwithstanding, Anselm's influence on twelfth-century theology was remarkably limited.[5] Although praised by Abaelard as an outstanding doctor of the Church, Anselm was only named once by him in his *Theologia* and then in order to be criticised for reproducing an Augustinian image too closely.[6] One simple explanation for this is that Anselm never occupied a position of *magister* in a public school. His teaching activity was confined to the abbey school of Bec and perhaps to a small circle of devotees at Christ Church, Canterbury. The meditative, non-controversialist tone of his writing was partly a consequence of the restricted milieu with which he wished to communicate. If there is evidence of his influence on such disciples it is in the formulation of numerous *dicta* containing his teaching on both logic and sacred matters such as have been closely studied by Schmitt and Southern.[7] The literary historian and cataloguer of manuscripts whose eye is narrowly focussed on "authenticity" has perhaps been too apt to label these works "spurious" or "pseudo-Anselm," and thus potentially less reliable than those writings judged to be "genuine."[8] Their rejection from an *Opera omnia* to a volume entitled *Memorials* creates a conceptual division which Anselm may not have anticipated.

The distinction between "authentic" and "of a disciple" becomes quite blurred when we consider the traditional process of writing employed in a monastic environment where time was available to produce fine copy. Documents were composed (*dictare*, also meaning to dictate) on wax tablets and then copied out neatly onto good parchment. A notary or scribe customarily took down the composition (*dictamen*) from its actual author. When does a talk become a composition? Anselm's *Proslogion*, first drafted on wax tablets, reads as a meditation delivered without recourse to any book beyond what lay in his memory.[9] The monks of Bec were able to memorise the *Monologion*, similarly unencumbered by patristic quotation, in its entirety.[10]

Two teachers who had a greater impact on the development of theology in the twelfth century—or at least were more often cited in its sentence and gloss literature—were Anselm of Laon and William of Champeaux.[11] Unlike Anselm of Bec, they came into contact with a large number of students. Considerable debate has surrounded the numerous writings, such as the *Sententie Anselmi*, associated with their "school."[12] The difficulty scholars have had in attributing specific writings to either of these authors may result from pursuing a distinction between "author" and "disciple of his school" irrelevant to their teaching activity. In these sentence collections, patristic texts are often alluded to rather than quoted verbatim. They provide crucial evidence for the growth of discussion of theological ideas in a public context in the twelfth century and are thus of much wider than purely literary significance.

A good illustration of the way in which scholastic literature could be generated by public disagreement is given by the Benedictine monk, Rupert of Deutz:

I had a most vexatious conflict concerning the body and blood of the Lord with a master of great repute, although a monk, who,

among other ways in which he tried to lessen the majesty of such
a great sacrament, objected to me that the Lord gave that sacrament to Judas, his betrayer, just as to the other apostles. . . . He
claimed for this and other things the authority of blessed Augustine.
Necessity forced me to say that the writings of blessed Augustine
were not in the canon and that he could not be trusted in everything like the canonical books.[13]

Rupert avoided being condemned for heresy at Liège in 1116 only when
his abbot Cuno unexpectedly demonstrated that Hilary of Poitiers held
the opinion questioned by Augustine, an opinion that implied that only
the morally pure received Christ's body in the eucharist.

A similar confrontation took place five years later at Soissons. Alberic
of Rheims insisted that Abaelard provide an authority to support his
claim that God could not beget himself. In the *Historia calamitatum* Abaelard conveys the impression that he could locate an appropriate quotation from Augustine's *De Trinitate* through his own natural genius. In fact
Abaelard had quoted it in his *Theologia* in exactly the same truncated form
as Roscelin had used in his letter to Abaelard.[14] Textual sparring of the
kind engaged in orally by Roscelin, Rupert of Deutz and Abaelard was
a technique foreign to Anselm of Bec. Monks and secular masters alike
were being affected by this trend to a more aggressive kind of literacy,
sign of a breakdown of consensus on the interpretation of a wide range
of Christian doctrines. Arguments about belief could even take place outside the school environment.[15]

   Ideas and texts were debated aloud. One often misinterpreted passage of the *Historia calamitatum* confirms the impression which we gain from
the text of the *Theologia "Summi boni"* that the treatise was written to be
read in public:

For they said that it ought to be sufficient for the book to be condemned that I had presumed to read it in public when it had not
been commended either by the Roman pontiff or the Church and
had allowed it to be transcribed by many, and that it would be useful for the Christian faith if by my example such presumption in
many were forestalled.[16]

Abaelard is not saying that a book needed an official imprimatur before
it could be copied, as some have thought. His critics objected to the public
reading of an independent treatise (as distinct from a reading with com-

mentary on a safe text, like writings of Boethius) and wished that it were illegal.[17] The phrase *librum legere* can have the meaning "to lecture on a book," in the sense of reading aloud and then glossing a text, but I am inclined to think that here *legere* means simply to read aloud and paraphrase or expand in the process. When Abaelard says that he allowed his treatise to be copied by many, he uses the same word (*transcribendum*) as he uses in connection with his glosses on Ezekiel to mean "to be taken down from oral delivery."[18] The habit of reading aloud one's own composition in a university context is well documented in the thirteenth century.[19] There is no reason to assume that the same technique did not also apply in the twelfth.

Reading aloud a treatise was an effective way of reaching a wide audience. The *Theologia* caused Alberic and Lotulph alarm, not because of the work itself (they had long been agitating to have him silenced as a master), but because it furthered Abaelard's reputation as a public speaker.[20] The burning of the treatise at the council of Soissons was a symbolic attempt to silence an individual whose charismatic authority presented a threat to other masters. Only six years earlier in the same city, Clement of Bucy had been accused of spurning the sacraments and establishing illegal gatherings outside the Church. While awaiting sentence, he and a few followers were seized from the episcopal prison by a crowd and burnt to death.[21] Abaelard and his disciples faced similar physical violence from a crowd at Soissons. Needless to say, he was protected by his status as a master and a measure of ecclesiastical sympathy (notably from the bishop of Chartres) such as Clement never enjoyed.

Nowhere in the *Historia calamitatum* does Abaelard define himself as a *scriptor* or an *auctor*; his self-image in both scholastic and monastic milieux is that of *magister*, master or man of authority. When Abaelard does mention a literary composition in the autobiography (twice only: the glosses on Ezekiel and the original version of his writing on the Trinity) it is only within the context of his teaching. He is silent about those glosses on logic, the *Dialectica*, the *Sic et non* and the *Theologia Christiana*, to which modern scholars give such attention. The relatively small number of manuscripts which survive of these works reinforces the impression conveyed by the *Historia calamitatum* that people knew more about Abaelard from hearsay than through his writing.[22]

The atmosphere of academic debate was changing even within Abaelard's lifetime. Increasing emphasis was being placed on the need to justify one's argument by written quotation. The change is evident from even a cursory comparison of the *sententie* of Anselm of Laon to the technically much more sophisticated and precise *Libri IV sententiarum* of Peter Lombard. It can also be glimpsed by comparing successive versions of Abaelard's *Theologia*. His original text (*Theologia "Summi boni"*) contains much direct appeal to the reader or listener in the second person singular. This is particularly true of a long and rather involved passage in the third book probably added to the treatise after its initial completion.[23] Placed after a triumphant assertion that the ancient philosophers understood the generation of the Word from the Father better than the prophets of the Old Testament, it begins with an admission that the solutions proposed still left many questions unanswered. The subsequent argument is unstructured, devoid of direct quotation and conversational in style. There are even bad jokes about whether God can be said to be in a latrine if he is everywhere and the sexual meaning of the word *cognoscere* in the Bible.[24] Here more than anywhere we listen to Abaelard speak. In the *Theologia Christiana* the humorous tone disappears; the phrase *quod dicis* is regularly replaced by *quod dictum est*.

Abaelard's attitude to quotation also changes. In the *Theologia "Summi boni"* he is relatively casual in his citation of authorities. There are many more remembered allusions to the writings of Aristotle, Cicero and Boethius than quotation from the Christian Fathers. He could expect his audience to recall a quotation simply by citing a few key words of a text learnt at school.[25] In the *Theologia Christiana* these passages are swamped by extensive extracts copied from patristic texts. Often they correct and extend a vaguely remembered quotation from Augustine in the original treatise. He is seeking to impress with the written word.

Sometime after he had drafted the initial version of his treatise on the Trinity Abaelard began to compile a collection of sometimes contradictory *sententie* from the Fathers, first on the nature of God and of Christ, later expanded to cover questions of faith, the sacraments and morality.[26] In the prologue to his *Sic et non* Abaelard defines with great clarity a technique which was not in itself original: apparent discord among the sayings of the Fathers had to be resolved through rational investigation. The canonists of the eleventh century — Burchard of Rheims, Bernold of Constance and Ivo of Chartres, to name but a few — had long sought to establish an underlying order in apparently conflicting texts.[27] Roscelin had emphasised the significance of reconciling apparently conflicting doctrines relating to the Trinity.[28] In his prologue to the *Sic et non* Abaelard provided formal justification for a technique already being practiced in the schools. It was never quoted by his critics as proof of heresy.

The originality of the *Sic et non* lay rather in the range and importance of the questions it raised. Many touched on fundamental points of Christian doctrine. Through judicious selection of patristic authorities Abaelard sometimes hinted at his own answer to a problem without ever adding his own voice.[29] It was a common practice to compile personal dossiers or florilegia of patristic texts in order to help with teaching or preaching. The *Sic et non* differed from many of these florilegia not in simply presenting traditional *sententie* to given problems, but rather in raising the possibility of an alternative solution.

The manuscript traditions of the *Sic et non*, the *Theologia* and collections of *sententie* attributed to Abaelard himself are of enormous complexity, being subject to extension and revision by author and scribe alike. Nonetheless a pattern does emerge through all the different manuscripts, an underlying search for answers to an ever-widening range of questions on aspects of Christian belief. To understand the evolution of a written work we have to appreciate the oral context in which it is conceived.

One of the barometers of change which we can apply to different versions of the *Theologia* is that of literary style. The original version of the treatise, the *Theologia "Summi boni,"* is free and often colloquial in tone. After the council of Soissons (1121) Abaelard transformed the work into the *Theologia Christiana* by incorporating a great deal of commentary on patristic texts as well as by revising significant parts of his argument. Whereas the original work reads, like Anselm's *Monologion*, as if it had been composed aloud (which of course we can never know for certain), the *Theologia Christiana* is tortuous to read aloud in the same way. Certain errors in its manuscript tradition are difficult to explain unless Abaelard himself was correcting a manuscript of his text; copyists often consistently misunderstand a correction.[30] The pressure placed on him at Soissons to justify controversial theological arguments with long and learned marginal notes changed a treatise which could easily be delivered aloud to a work of reference accesible only to an educated elite. This in itself rendered the *Theologia* less dangerous as a work of theology.

One example may suffice to illustrate Abaelard's attitude to written quotation. In the first version of the *Theologia* he had misquoted a passage from the *De doctrina Christiana*. Where Augustine had praised the capacity of dialectic "to penetrate and dissolve questions about sacred scripture," Abaelard made the bishop praise dialectic for its capacity "to penetrate and discuss questions." As if the mistake had been pointed out to him Abaelard omitted the faulty "and discuss" in the *Theologia Christiana* without replacing it by the correct "and dissolve" or acknowledging the different context of his own argument. When it came to drafting the *Theologia "Scholarium,"* Abaelard, forestalling any pedant who might quote him the exact text, prefaced the quotation with a comment that Augustine wanted to dissolve doubt about difficult questions.[31] Criticism forced him to adopt a more careful attitude to the written word.

In the same way as dispute over the eucharist in the preceeding century had forced masters to take careful note of what the Fathers had said on the subject, so debate about the Trinity provoked exploration of patristic teaching on this more abstract doctrine. The master of theology who wielded the greatest influence in Paris, while Abaelard was teaching there in the 1130s, was Hugh of St. Victor. His *De Sacramentis* contains numerous allusions, always critical, to ideas expounded by Abaelard, although never any references to specific writings.[32] Hugh never felt as obliged to buttress his arguments with quotations from the Fathers. In this respect his writing is similar to that of Anselm, although he was more concerned to place a wider range of topics within a systematic whole. Abaelard came to quote much more rigorously from the Fathers because he had to defend the legitimacy of ideas which in fact parted much further from patristic teaching, under the influence of his vision of Aristotelian dialectic. The compiler of the immensely popular *Summa sententiarum* drew extensively from the teaching of Hugh of St. Victor (so much so that the work was often attributed to Hugh), while also incorporating a few of the patristic quotations used by Abaelard in the *Theologia "Scholarium"* and in his sentences.[33] The *Summa sententiarum* simplified the ideas of Hugh and buttressed them with a new patristic foundation. The zest for such quotation within this new type of theological writing concealed a growing uncertainty about the authority of tradition.

The changes which Abaelard made to the *Theologia* have to be understood within the context of his spoken teaching. Unlike the two earlier versions of the work (*"Summi boni"* and *Christiana*), which begin with definition of the Trinity as the supreme good, the *Theologia "Scholarium"* opens with a brief summary of all the elements essential to salvation — faith, charity and the sacraments. The fact that the treatise proceeds with discussion of only one of these issues — faith in God as a Trinity — has long perplexed scholars. Did Abaelard ever go on to discuss these subjects? A number of sentence collections survive, which begin in the same way as the *Theologia "Scholarium"* but then go on to discuss those topics (redemption, the sacraments, charity) not dealt with in that work.[34] When William of St. Thierry and Bernard detected numerous heresies in one such sentence collection, Abaelard denied that this particular "book of sentences" was one of his *scripta* even though it reproduced his mature teaching down to the finest detail.[35]

Scholarship on the issue has been bedevilled by an obsession with the written, as distinct from the spoken word. In an endeavour to excuse Abaelard from the taint of heresy, Ostlender assumed that all these sentence collections were composed by disciples who extended the thought of their master, often beyond the limits of orthodoxy.[36] His elaborate hypothesis that all known sentence collections derived from a missing *liber sententiarum* could not explain why different sentences recorded Abaelard's thought at different stages of development. The only way that these sentences differ from Abaelard's writings is in their literary form. Their sentence structure is nowhere as complicated, arguments are given simply and boldly without extensive caveat, patristic texts are alluded to or remembered vaguely rather than quoted in extenso. These texts, which display many characteristics of oral delivery, have often been understood as written documents, each by a different author.[37] One consequence of this interpretation was to postulate the existence of a large number of highly creative, but otherwise unknown disciples. The most important, presumed author of a widely copied text, consistently titled in manuscripts "the Sentences of Peter Abaelard" was given the name Hermann (on very thin textual grounds) and the work renamed "the Sentences of Hermann".

As I have argued elsewhere, the hypothesis does not stand up to close scrutiny.[38] It is much easier to interpret these sentence collections as records of Abaelard's lectures on faith, the sacraments and charity. For the introductory part of his course, in which he set out the framework of his discussion, he put together notes which also served to introduce the new *Theologia "Scholarium."* The sentences, which have long languished under erroneous attribution to a disciple, provide a far more accessible point of entry into Abaelard's thought than his more formal writings. Certainly a student must have assisted in the recording of these sentences, but this does not mean that the student was their author. All of the new ideas in the *Theologia* are sketched out more briefly, though with no less originality, in these sentences. Ideas first delivered within an oral context are only subsequently given textual form.

Although Abaelard used a written text as an aid when delivering his lectures, he frequently departed from his script to make a particular point. A vivid picture of his teaching style is provided by the *Sententie Parisienses*, a *reportatio* copied in a minute and untidy script on a very scrappy piece of parchment.[39] The initial discussion about whether the pagan philosophers had knowledge of God is far more outspoken than anything in the *Theologia*. Yet when he comes to discuss the sacraments the text is at times identical to the the equivalent section of the *Sententie Petri Abaelardi*, a document which seems to have the status of an official set of lectures.[40] As Abaelard never wrote a treatise on the sacraments (unlike Hugh of St. Victor), his lectures on the subject remained substantially the same. There are passages in the *Sententie Parisienses* where the flow of delivery is interrupted by a series of questions and answers. For example:

> It is asked if God can love someone whom God has not always loved. Reply. No.
> It is asked if a man whom God does not love can love God? Reply. Yes. If you answer back with "I love those who love me" (Prov. 8:17) etc., the reply is that this is about love which endures.[41]

The brevity of these answers suggests that the interjection was raised by a student, as the flow of Abaelard's argument is interrupted. Such questions raised in public might later be incorporated into a more formal treatise, with more carefully nuanced and less dogmatic answers. Arguments from remembered verses of scripture would be buttressed by quotation from the Fathers. But the questions and answers in the *Sententie*, much more than those in the *Theologia*, help us to understand why Abaelard had such a reputation as a master and why he was so feared by some of his contemporaries. He was skilled in the art of repartee.

Bernard of Clairvaux emphasised the public danger presented by his teaching in a letter to cardinal Guido:

> We have in France one Peter Abaelard, a monk without a rule, a prelate without responsibility, an abbot without discipline, who argues with boys and consorts with women. He puts "stolen waters and hidden bread" before his household in his books, and in his discourses he introduces profane novelties of phrase and meaning. He approaches the dark cloud which surrounds God, not alone as Moses did, but with a whole crowd of his disciples. Catholic faith, the childbearing of the Virgin, the sacrament of the Altar, the incomprehensible mystery of the Holy Trinity, are being discussed in the streets and the market places.[42]

Such language should not be dismissed as mere rhetoric. The phrase "arguing with boys and consorting with women" is a direct allusion to his involvement with his students and with the nuns of the Paraclete. Of course Abaelard did not initiate the questioning of orthodox belief in the Trinity, Christ and the sacraments referred to by the archbishop.

He had merely given a degree of academic respectability to ideas and questions raised by his audience. He rejected the extremist fringe of popular heresy.[43] Nonetheless, in his public teaching he did bring to bear his knowledge of scripture, the Fathers and the ancient philosophers on questions about God, Christ, the sacraments and ethics increasingly being debated in some sections of society.

His mature thoughts about the nature of sin may well have been influenced by Heloise. In the *Problemata Heloissae* Abaelard provided solutions to forty-two questions put to him by Heloise and her fellow nuns at the Paraclete. While most relate to scriptural passages (often concerning women in the Bible or questions of guilt and innocence), her last question is a general one, the meaning of which was clear to Abaelard: whether one could sin doing something ordained or permitted by God.[44] He understood the question to mean whether sexual intercourse (enjoined on Adam and Eve by God) could be sinful in itself. His answer here is largely based on a string of passages from Augustine, all to the effect that Jerome was wrong in damning sex as impure in its own right. In the *Ethics*, Abaelard formulates a much more subtle argument explaining why intercourse (among other examples) was not sinful in itself. Only consent to an evil will, in contempt of God, was wrong.[45] This was an argument which Abaelard had not formulated in his earlier writings, even though Heloise in her personal letters had insisted on her own innocence with regard to their past relationship.

Only once these ideas had been aired in lectures and formulated in a treatise did they acquire a certain measure of authority, and thus notoriety. The doctrine that sexual desire was morally neutral was one that was picked up from a book of Abaelard's sentences by his critics early in 1140. Only subsequently was the same argument detected in the *Ethics*. Invariably Abaelard's arguments were more subtle than the simplistic assertions made by his opponents. He refused to allow discussion of his teaching to be based on the book of his sentences currently in circulation, and insisted on being judged only on his writing. After the council of Sens, held 2 June 1140, Abaelard rewrote the offending passages of his *Theologia* as part of a compromise arrangement worked out with Bernard of Clairvaux, and the papal sentence of excommunication was lifted.[46]

Studies of the influence of Abaelard's thought have tended to treat the subject as a matter of literary history. Thus a number of authors are said to have been influenced by the *Theologia "Scholarium"* when there is no solid evidence for this. Certainly a number of writers, such as Omnebene, Roland, Robert of Melun and the compilers of some anonymous sentence collections all reproduce key elements of Abaelard's teaching on the Trinity, but their common source cannot be identified with any single version of the *Theologia*. It seems more likely that they drew on a public reading of a draft version of the *Theologia*, delivered — perhaps several times — before the work had been completed.[47] Such exposure to students affected its final form in the same way as delivery to a monastic audience influenced the final text of Bernard's sermons on the Song of Songs.

The contrast between listening to Abaelard and reading his *Theologia* is well illustrated by comparison of the *Sentences* of Robert of Melun with those of Peter Lombard. Both men taught in Paris from the mid 1130s, when Abaelard and Hugh of St. Victor were at the height of their fame, until 1159–60, when Robert left for England subsequently to become bishop of Hereford and Peter Lombard was consecrated bishop of Paris. Although Robert never quotes directly from the *Theologia*, his understanding of Abaelard's trinitarian theology is deep and all-pervasive.[48] Peter Lombard quotes extensively from a complete copy of the *Theologia "Scholarium"* which he owned (one without the emendations made by Abaelard after June 1140), yet ultimately owes more in points of doctrine to the teaching of Hugh of St. Victor, mediated through the *Summa Sententiarum*. John of Cornwall says that Peter Lombard often had a copy of the *Theologia* in his hand.[49] He reproduced many of the scriptural and patristic authorities unearthed by Abaelard (though not those from the pagan philosophers), without ever adopting the most controversial aspects of Abaelard's trinitarian doctrine.[50]

Robert introduces his own book of sentences with an important preface "on various ways of reading sacred scripture," in which he ridicules a contemporary trend of giving more weight to glosses on scripture than to scripture itself.[51]

> A new kind of teaching has arisen lately, a puerile concern for recitation. . . . For they do not study, but seek to be considered studious, nor do they read to understand, because they prefer not understanding to not reading.[52]

Reading had become an end in itself. Robert is protesting against the veneration accorded to the *Glossa ordinaria*, which had acquired an authoritative status in its own right.

How many people are there and have there been who have never
listened to or inspected glosses who yet have gained a full knowledge
of the text?[53]

Robert is insistent that the sacred text can be understood without glosses. Did not its author and the glossator both arrive at understanding
without these glosses to help them? Robert does not mince his words:

For those whom fame now extolls to the stars plunge all into the
murky darkness of ignorance by their public speech. It is clear that
the masters of the glosses — for this is the name by which they are
known — lack understanding of the glosses as much as of their text,
even though they can distinguish glosses and divide them with full
stops and assign a gloss to the text to which it belongs.[54]

Throughout this preface Robert emphasises the importance of grasping the *sententia*, the thought or opinion behind a text. A book of *sententie*
or thoughts about issues raised by scripture he thought of more value
than simple glosses on the scriptural text.

No-one is competent in reading who is not capable of discussion
of sentences. . . . For this is said to be the case where reading or
rather recitation of glosses holds center stage. For there the text is
spurned, the gloss is worshipped with devout veneration, the text
is read for the gloss and the gloss not explained for the sake of the
text.[55]

Robert's insistence that only the comments of the Fathers were necessary for understanding of scripture echoes Abaelard's own criticism of
the adulation given to Anselm of Laon.[56] The young dialectician had
similarly asserted that only the writings of the Fathers were necessary
for commentary on scripture. However, where Abaelard had questioned
the authority of a living master, Robert of Melun objected to adulation
of the written word.

Robert's long diatribe is intended to explain why he prefers to study
a different kind of treatise about the Bible:

Among those treatises which deal with sacred scripture I find particularly useful those which are given the name of sentences, since
in them there is a clear sparseness of words and a rich wealth of
sentences, expressed not obscurely but clearly. There are few authors
of such treatises, but of them there are two in particular who have
made rational enquiry about the sacraments of faith as about faith

itself and charity, who in everything outshine all subsequent commentators of scripture in the judgement of all; it happened that they did not keep to the same paths in everything; in fact it rarely or never happened, even though they dealt with and taught the same matters. For what is dealt with by one more briefly than it ought to be or said more diffusely than necessary is dealt with in a different order by the other.[57]

The two authors to whom Robert is referring are Hugh of St. Victor and Peter Abaelard. Both intended their teaching and writing to introduce sacred scripture, even though they did not imitate the line by line technique of the gloss. They taught and wrote about the problems of belief, sacraments and morality posed by the Bible.

Robert insisted that it was dangerous to place excessive trust in the written word:

For what is writing other than a kind of image and obscure figure of the will of the writer himself? Neither does it represent only those things which a writer wants to be understood through it, but sometimes other things which are, not just diverse, but completely contradictory, equally evidently and perhaps even more evidently. . . . Those therefore who have heard the authors of the above mentioned treatises *viva voce*, as is said, expounding their own opinion in person are more to be believed than those who opine what they thought from their writings and twist what was written to their own sense rather than to the intellect of those who wrote it. For they are certainly not able to say what was in the mind of the author; as a result they do not know or, as I say, they only conjecture.[58]

This scepticism towards the written word recalls Abaelard's own observation that an utterance did not signify everything which it could signify; rather it signified what was in the *sententia vocis*. It was irrational to imagine the contrary.[59] Robert reacted similarly against any tendency to objectify and give intrinsic authority to the written word. Despite its evident partisan spirit, this preface sheds much valuable light on trends in the teaching of theology in mid twelfth-century Paris. Robert did not see scriptural commentary and systematic theology as two separate fields of endeavour. His ire was directed against a tendency, evident within Abaelard's own lifetime, to elevate comments made by recent masters, such as Anselm of Laon, into a normative gloss on the Bible. Like Abaelard, Robert preferred discursive commentary on selected parts of the

Bible (notably the letters of St. Paul), focussing on major theological themes, to glosses on the specific significance of individual verses. Books of sentences seemed to Robert a compact way of arranging discussion of major doctrinal questions raised by scripture. Abaelard himself saw his *Theologia "Scholarium"* as no more than an introduction to the sacred text.[60]

But by 1150 Anselm of Laon, Abaelard and Hugh of St. Victor were no more than names remembered from the past. Only writings and sentences attributed to them remained. Glosses on individual books of the Bible delivered by Anselm of Laon and others had hardened into a normative *Gloss*, itself the subject of commentary. Robert's argument that only the writings of the Fathers should be accorded respect in commenting on the Bible was a wistful and ultimately unrealistic lament for a generation which had passed away.

If one excludes collections of Abaelard's *sententie* as proof of the existence of independent masters (as distinct from students taking down lectures of Abaelard), Robert of Melun stands out as one of the few teachers in Paris in the mid twelfth century to continue to advocate theological doctrines harshly condemned in the writings of Bernard of Clairvaux. Even Abaelard's writings on logic had become out of date with the translation of many new logical texts from the Greek in the 1130s and 1140s. The writings of Aristotle acquired an authority those of Abaelard had never gained.

Abaelard's influence on the teaching of theology in the mid twelfth century was indirect.[61] Unlike Robert of Melun or Peter Lombard, he never composed a book of sentences. The task of recording the opinions which he delivered orally in his lectures was one he left to his students. In some ways Abaelard was closer to Anselm in preferring to confine his written treatises to specific investigation of aspects of doctrine. For all his respect for Abaelard and his nostalgia for the oral teaching of his masters, Robert of Melun belonged to a different generation. Students preferred useful textbooks to impressive oratory. Robert devoted his major literary effort towards a convenient compendium of Christian faith in the form of books of sentences, a genre which he thought far superior to yet more glosses on scripture.

Robert's *sententie* never achieved great renown. By contrast, the *Sentences* of Peter Lombard, his frequent opponent in theological debate, soon came to join the *Gloss* as an encyclopaedia of orthodox belief, becoming the standard text for commentary in the medieval curriculum of the next three centuries. His writing acquired an authority next to that of the

Bible itself. Even Luther commented on the *Sentences*. The reason behind the Lombard's success lies in his precise and methodical technique and provision of clearly defined answers to disputed matters of belief.[62] Where Robert preferred to allude to opinions of the Fathers and (without direct acknowledgement) more recent masters, notably Abaelard, the Lombard quotes his authorities verbatim. Thus many scriptural and patristic texts which Abaelard had incorporated into the *Theologia "Scholarium"* passed unrecognised into the common vocabulary of scholastic dispute, although stripped of the doctrinal framework into which they had been set. Unlike Robert, Peter Lombard used Abaelard more as a source of reference than as a fount of inspiration.

Gratian's exploitation of the *Sic et non* in his *Concordia discordantium canonum* was similar to that of Peter Lombard, although directed towards a synthesis of canon law rather than of theology.[63] The idea for such a systematic concord of conflicting canons went back to Ivo of Chartres and other great canonists of the late eleventh century. Gratian drew extensively on the *Sic et non* among other sources, but where Abaelard had left the opinions of the Fathers open to question, the Bolognese monk endeavoured to ensure that the same Church Fathers provided definitive answers to disputed points of ecclesiastical belief and practice. In matters of doctrine they are often poles apart.[64] As with the *Sentences* of Peter Lombard, the *Concordia* gave the impression that all the major difficulties that a student might raise had been solved. The struggle of subsequent commentators to persuade their audience that this was in fact so is a separate story.

Abaelard's theological writings cannot be put into the same category as the encyclopaedic *summae* of later generations. Their originality lies in the questions they raise, questions raised by students, by Heloise and her nuns, or simply by Abaelard's own reflection on difficulties inherent in Christian doctrine. They served as a useful point of departure for scholars, who might follow one of his questions in order to reproduce a firm answer quite at odds with the thinking which had inspired its original formulation.

The arguments he raised were more aggressive than the ruminating thoughts voiced by Anselm because the environment in which they were given voice, the classroom rather than the cloister, was more turbulent. Yet both men brought new issues to the attention of their literate milieu. The pressure to systematise arguments into the framework of a *summa* came from students who wanted easily accessible manuals of doctrine. This happened with the teaching of Anselm of Laon.[65] Abaelard allowed students to take down his *sententie*, but was unwilling to take responsibility for what they contained. Only towards the middle of the century did the trend to personally written books of Sentences gain ground, and with it a tendency to clear-cut solutions, based on precisely quoted patristic documentation for their authority. Increasingly scribes paid attention to page layout, headings and subheadings in order to facilitate speedy access to information.[66] As the *Sentences* of Peter Lombard, rather than those of say Robert of Melun, gradually acquired an authoritative status in the teaching of theology, so discussion became increasingly focussed around the precise wording of a canonical text. Arguments about religion conducted in an academic milieu and without reference to these texts soon acquired the taint of heresy.[67]

Renaissance criticism of scholastic literature as a meaningless jumble of irrelevant questions about the *Sentences* was perhaps not so different from Robert of Melun's complaint that excessive veneration was accorded to written glosses rather than to the Bible and the Fathers. A hundred years later Thomas Aquinas lamented similarly in the prologue to his *Summa theologiae* the profusion of "meaningless questions" dealt with in no systematic order by commentators on existing texts.[68] As Leonard Boyle has so masterfully demonstrated, it was his growing frustration at Orvieto in the years 1261–65 (where he was Lector at a provincial *studium*) with the inadequacy of existing texts in the Dominican curriculum to answer questions put to him that led to his planning the *Summa theologiae* on the model of existing educational and pastoral manuals for clergy.[69] He was able to draw on his early lectures on the *Sentences* of Peter Lombard.

The situation of excessive commentary on existing texts about which Thomas was complaining in the introduction to his own synthesis of theology had mushroomed out of an explosion of written material the previous century. By the end of the twelfth century certain texts had established themselves as normative in the teaching of theology. Every question a student might raise was thought to be anticipated in Lombard's *Sentences*. While oral discourse continued to provide an essential mode of communication within the learned community, it became shaped and formalised by the written word to a new degree. Stock's argument that the eleventh and twelfth centuries witness the extension of written modes of thought into a predominantly oral culture perhaps only catches part of the truth. The normative texts of Western culture were changing. Where Priscian and Augustine had previously held sway in the fields of language

I

and theology, now Aristotle and Peter Lombard became established as new authorities. The use of rational method in twelfth-century scholasticism is part of the much wider effort of a literate elite to establish its authority in a society increasingly unsure of its cultural foundations. Abaelard belonged in spirit to an older world, one in which it was possible to write speculative monographs for a minority audience. By the mid twelfth century, attitudes were changing. The schools of Paris were becoming as institutionally stable as monasteries had been in the previous century. Education in the schools of Paris became a necessary prerequisite for a successful ecclesiastical career. The book trade flourished. Masters of the ilk of Peter Lombard felt an obligation to provide firm, easily understood teachings for a less certain world.

NOTES

1. This paper was originally presented to the Fourteenth Australia-New Zealand Conference of Medieval and Renaissance Studies, University of Sydney, February 1988. I am grateful for helpful comments made by various colleagues at that conference, in particular by Brian Stock, and to the Advisor who read this paper for *Exemplaria*.

2. Joseph de Ghellinck defined the foundations for this "classic" approach in *Le Mouvement théologique du XIIe siècle: Sa Préparation lointaine avant et autour de Pierre Lombard, ses rapports avec les initiatives des canonistes*, 2e édition considérablement augmentée, Museum Lessianum — Section historique no. 10, 2 (1948; reprint Brussels: Culture et Civilisation, 1969), especially chapter 2, 133–277. The first edition, published in 1914, followed on closely from Martin Grabmann's *Die Geschichte der Scholastischen Methode* (Freiburg i.B.: Herder, 1909-11). H. Cloes examined systematisation as the fruit of applying dialectic to faith in "La Systématisation théologique pendant la première moitié du XIIe siècle," *Ephemerides Theologicae Lovanienses* 34 (1958): 277-329. Artur Landgraf, *Introduction à l'histoire de la littérature théologique de la scolastique naissante*, 2d rev. ed. (Montréal: Institut d'Études Médiévales, 1973) provides a useful and concise survey of the literature within a similar interpretative framework. More recently Gillian R. Evans has provided a general introduction to the subject in *Anselm and a New Generation* (Oxford: Oxford University Press, 1980) and *Old Arts and New Theology* (Oxford: Oxford University Press, 1980).

3. Brian Stock, *The Implications of Literacy: Written Language and Models of Interpretation in the Eleventh and Twelfth Centuries* (Princeton: Princeton University Press, 1983). The transition from oral to written culture in England is well documented by Michael

T. Clanchy, *From Memory to Written Record: England 1066–1377* (Cambridge: Harvard University Press, 1979). For a general survey of this theme, see Walter J. Ong, *Orality and Literacy: The Technologizing of the Word* (London: Methuen, 1982) and the essays edited by Stephen Knight and S.N. Mukherjee, *Words and Worlds: Studies on the Social Role of Verbal Culture* (Sydney: Sydney Association for Studies in Society and Culture, 1983). Paul Zumthor has written extensively on the oral context of medieval literature, notably *La Poésie et la voix dans la civilisation médiévale* (Paris: Presses Universitaires de France, 1984) and *La Lettre et la voix de la littérature médiévale* (Paris: Éditions du Seuil, 1987).

4. Cf. *Monologion*, Prologus, ed. Franciscus S. Schmitt, *S. Anselmi Opera*, 6 vols. (Edinburgh: T. Nelson, 1946–68), 1:8:

> Quam ergo saepe retractans nihil potui invenire me in ea dixisse, quod non catholicorum patrum et maxime beati Augustini scriptis cohaereat.

5. De Ghellinck does not offer an explanation for general ignorance of Anselm's thought prior to the thirteenth century in *Le Mouvement théologique*, 83–86.

6. Abaelard, *Epist. XIV*, in *Peter Abelard: Letters IX–XIV*, ed. Edmé Smits (Gronigen: Rijksuniversiteit, 1983), 280 (PL 178:357–58): "illum magnificum ecclesiae doctorem Anselmum." Abaelard's criticism comes in *Theologia Christiana* 4.83, in *Petri Abaelardi Opera Theologica* 2, ed. Eligius Marie Buytaert, CCCM 12 (Turnhout: Brepols, 1969); *Theologia "Scholarium"* 2.120, in *Petri Abaelardi Opera Theologica* 3, ed. Buytaert and Mews, CCCM 13 (Turnhout: Brepols, 1987). These comments are not found in the *Theologia "Summi boni,"* the original version of the work (CCCM 13:85–201). Reference to the three versions of the *Theologia* will henceforward be to *TSum, TChr* and *TSch,* quoted by their book and paragraph number alone. David E. Luscombe plays down Abaelard's criticism of Anselm in "St. Anselm and Abelard," *Anselm Studies. An Occasional Journal,* 1 (New York, 1983): 207–229; see my comments in CCCM 13:46–47.

7. *Memorials of St. Anselm*, ed. Franciscus S. Schmitt and Richard W. Southern (London: Oxford University Press for the British Academy, 1969).

8. I myself fell into this trap in description of the *De beatitudinibus* in a fifteenth-century manuscript that contained Anselm's complete works in CCCM 13:240, a slip Southern graciously pointed out to me in a private communication.

9. Eadmer, *Vita Sancti Anselmi*, ed. Richard W. Southern (London: T. Nelson, 1962), 30–31:

> Reputans ergo apud se hoc ipsum et aliis si sciretur posse placere, livore carens rem ilico scripsit in tabulis, easque sollicitus custodiendas uni ex monasterii fratribus tradidit. . . . Reparat Anselmus aliud de eadem materia dictamen in aliis tabulis, et illas eidem sub cautiori custodia tradit custodi. [Wax tablets were first lost, then broken]: Adunat ipse ceram, et licet vix scripturam recuperat. Verens autem ne qua incuria penitus perditum eat, eam in nomine Domini pergamenae jubet tradi. Composuit ergo inde volumen parvulum, sed sententiarum ac subtilissimae contemplationis pondere magnum, quod *Proslogion* nominavit.

Orderic Vitalis describes his use of wax tablets in his *Historia ecclesiastica* 6.3--see the *Ecclesiastical History*, ed. Marjorie Chibnall, 6 vols. (Oxford: Clarendon Press, 1966–80), 3:218.

10. *Monologion*, in *S. Anselmi Opera*, ed. Schmitt, 1:8:

nescio tamen quo pacto sic praeter spem evenit, ut non solum praedicti fratres, sed et plures alii scripturam ipsam quisque sibi eam transcribendo in longum memoriae commendare satagerent.

11. Sentences attributed to them have been gathered together by Odo Lottin in *Psychologie et morale aux XIIe et XIIIe siècles*, 6 vols. (Louvain: Abbaye du Mont César, 1942-60, and Gembloux: J. Ducolot, 1959), vol. 5 (Gembloux, 1959).

12. The issues are well documented and explained by Valerie I. Flint, "The School of Anselm of Laon: A Reconsideration," *Recherches de théologie ancienne et médiévale* 43 (1976): 89-110.

13. Rupert, *Commentarius in Regulam S. Benedicti* 1 (PL 170:496AB):

Habueram quippe cum aliquo magni nominis magnaeque aestimationis scholastico licet monacho certamen permolestum de sacramento corporis et sanguinis Domini, qui inter caetera quibus deprimere conabatur maiestatem tanti sacramenti, illud mihi obiecerat, quia sacramentum illud Iudae quoque traditori suo Dominus dedit sicut et caeteris apostolis . . . Quod autem illi, uidelicet Iudae proditori, dedisset simul cum caeteris in promptu erat illi astruere auctoritate beati Augustini. Eius rei necessitas me compulit ut dicerem non esse in canone scripta beati Augustini, non esse illi per omnia confidendum sicut libris canonicis.

See John Van Engen, *Rupert of Deutz* (Berkeley: University of California Press, 1983), 142-76.

14. *Historia calamitatum*, ed. Jacques Monfrin (Paris: J. Vrin, 1959), 84:

Revolvi ad locum quem noveram, quem ipse minime compererat aut qui non nisi nocitura mihi querebat; et voluntas Dei fuit, ut cito occurreret mihi quod volebam.

The same episode is recounted in *TChr* 4.78. The quotation from Augustine, *De Trinitate* 1.1, is quoted in the same truncated form by Roscelin in his *Epistola ad Abaelardum*, ed. J. Reiners, *Der Nominalismus in der Frühscholastik*, Beiträge zur Geschichte der Philosophie des Mittelalters, Bd. 8 (Münster: Aschendorffsche Buchhandlung, 1910): 69, 74, and by Abaelard, *TSum* 2.62 and *TChr* 3.109.

15. This is argued by Artur Landgraf in "Zur Technik und Überlieferung der Disputation," *Collectanea franciscana* 20 (1958): 173-88. He cites examples from manuscripts he has seen (n37), such as from a gloss on Job about a priest who recites the psalms in order not to appear to his parishioners to be beaten in debate with a layman (MS Paris, Mazarine lat. 178, fol. 22):

Respondens autem. Glosa: qui contra veritatis verba defeciunt (!), sepe etiam nota replicant, ne tacendo victi videantur, ut sacerdos disputans contra secularem dicens psalmos, ne coram parochianis victus videretur.

16. *Historia calamitatum*, ed. Monfrin, 87:

Dicebant enim ad dampnationem libelli satis hoc esse debere quod nec romani pontificis nec Ecclesie auctoritate eum commendatum legere publice presumpseram, atque ad transcribendum jam pluribus eum ipse prestitissem;

et hoc perutile futurum fidei christiane, si exemplo mei multorum similis presumptio preveniretur.

17. The passage was interpreted as an allusion to pre-censorship of books by G. B. Flahiff, "The Censorship of Books in the Twelfth Century," *Mediaeval Studies* 4 (1942): 1–22, at 4, and subsequently by Hubert Silvestre, in "L'Idylle d'Abélard et Héloïse: La Part du roman," in *Bulletin de la classe des lettres et des sciences morales et politiques*, 5e série 71.5 (1985): 183–84. Silvestre's paraphrase —

le livre d'Abélard est jugé condamnable de manière rédhibitoire pour la seule raison qu'il n'ait pas reçu l'approbation des autorités compétentes

— does not specify that his critics thought this *ought* to be sufficient for its condemnation. Abaelard's statement does not imply that this was the legal situation. Silvestre translates *commendatum* as approved when its principal meaning is simply that of "commended," in the manner that the writings of the Fathers had been commended by the Church. The text does not imply a notion of pre-censorship as thought by Flahiff.

18. *Historia calamitatum*, ed. Monfrin, 69:

Quo quidem audito, hii qui non interfuerant ceperunt ad secundam et terciam lectionem certatim concurrere et omnes pariter de transcribendis glosis quas prima die inceperam in ipso earum initio plurimum solliciti esse.

19. Ruth Crosby, "Oral Delivery in the Middle Ages," *Speculum* 11 (1936): 88–110. See too Gerald of Wales, *De rebus a se gestis* 16, in *Giraldi Cambrensis Opera*, ed. J. S. Brewer, 8 vols., RS Rerum Britannicarum Medii Aevi Scriptores (London: Longman, 1861–91), 1:72–73:

apud Oxoniam, ubi clerus in Anglia magis vigebat et clericatu praecellebat, opus suum [*Topographia Hibernica*] in tanta audientia recitare disposuit. Et quoniam tres erant in libro suo distinctiones, qualibet recitata die tribus diebus continuis recitatio duravit; primoque die pauperes omnes oppidi totius ad hoc convocatos hospitio suscepit et exhibuit. In crastino vero doctores diversarum facultatum omnes et discipulos famae majoris et notitae. Tertio die reliquos scolares cum militibus oppidanis et burgensibus multis. Sumptuosa quidem res et nobilis, quia renovata sunt quodammodo authentica et antiqua in hoc facto poetarum tempora; nec rem similem in Anglia factam vel praesens aetas vel ulla recolit antiquitas.

20. *Historia calamitatum*, ed. Monfrin, 82.

21. Guibert of Nogent, *De vita sua* 3.17, ed. Edmond-René Labande, *Autobiographie* (Paris: Belles Lettres, 1981), 428–34. I have emended the text of this passage and discussed the nature of this movement in "An Excerpt from Guibert of Nogent's *Monodiae* (III, 17) appended to Augustine's *De haeresibus*," *Revue des études augustiniennes* 33 (1987): 113–27.

22. William of St.-Thierry commented that copies of Abaelard's writing were hard to find, *Epist. ad Bernardum*, ed. Jean Leclercq, "Les Lettres de Guillaume de Saint-Thierry à S. Bernard," *Revue bénédictine* 79 (1969): 378. On the manuscript tradition of his writing, see Julia S. Barrow, Charles F. Burnett and David E. Luscombe, "A Checklist of the Manuscripts containing the Writings of Peter Abelard and Heloise

and Other Works closely associated with Abelard and his School," *Revue d'histoire des textes* 14-15 (1984-85): 183-302. I discuss an interesting example of an orally transmitted anecdote based on Abaelard's name (strictly speaking, to be pronounced *Abaëlard*) in "In Search of a Name and of its Significance: A Twelfth-century Anecdote about Thierry and Peter Abaelard," *Traditio* 44 (1988).

23. *TSum* 3.68-105; see my introduction to *TSum* in CCCM 13:66-71.

24. *TSum* 3.79.

25. John of Salisbury comments on the importance of memory in *Metalogicon* 1.11 and 24, ed. C. C. J. Webb (Oxford: Clarendon Press, 1929), 29 and 54. On the role of memory, see Pierre Riché, "Le Rôle de la mémoire dans l'enseignement médiéval," in *Jeux de mémoire: Aspects de la mnémotechnie médiévale*, ed. Bruno Roy and Paul Zumthor (Paris: J. Vrin, 1985), 133-46.

26. *Peter Abailard. Sic et non*, ed. Blanche Boyer and Richard McKeon (Chicago: University of Chicago Press, 1976-77); cf. Mews, CCCM 13:52.

27. Burchard, dedicatory letter to the *Liber decretorum*, PL 140:537A; Bernold, *De excommunicatis vitandis*, MGH *Libelli de lite*, 2:139; Ivo, *Decretum* or *De consonantia canonum*, PL 161:47 et seq. See too de Ghellinck, *Le Mouvement théologique*, 56-78.

28. Cf. Roscelin, *Epistola ad Abaelardum*, ed. Reiners, 72:

> Neque vero dicendum est, quod in fide trinitatis errent triplicando substantiam, quia licet aliter dicant quam nos, id tamen credunt quod nos, quia sicut Graeci triplicare solent substantiam. Neque vero dicendum est, quod in fide trinitatis errent triplicando substantiam, quia licet aliter dicant quam nos, id tamen credunt quod nos, quia sicut diximus sive persona sive substantia sive essentia in deo prorsus idem significant. In locutione enim tantum diversitas est, in fide unitas. Alioquin iam non esset apud Graecos ecclesia. Si autem ipsi sic loquendo verum dicunt, quare nos idem dicendo mentiamur, non video.

29. For example, on the first question of the *Sic et non*, "Quod fides humanis rationibus sit astruenda," Abaelard had virtually declared his position in the Prologue. He presents first negative answers, then affirmative ones with which he agrees and which he quotes elsewhere in the *Theologia*. On the questions whether or not Christ suffered like a man and wanted to die (q. 80, 81, 83), the texts chosen overwhelmingly emphasise the humanity of Christ. The doctrinal aspect of the *Sic et non* deserves further study.

30. For detailed discussion of the complex textual problems presented by manuscripts of the *Theologia*, see my comments in CCCM 13:66-69.

31. *TSum* 2.5; *TChr* 2.117; *TSch* 2.19. The text of Abaelard's *Epist. XIII* (ed. Smits, 272; a tract in defence of the use of dialectic in theological discussion known only through Duchesne's 1616 edition of Abaelard's *Opera Omnia*) reproduces the revised prefatory passage first introduced in *TChr CT* 2.117-a (drafting *TSch* 2.19), but is followed by a correct version of the Augustinian text, even though at the end of *Epist. XIII*, Abaelard seems to allude to his own modification of this passage. Duchesne's text (reproduced without criticism by Smits) seems to incorporate a silent correction of Abaelard's reading of Augustine, as certainly happened in the case of Abaelard's quotation of Jerome in *Epist. IX*; see Mews CCCM 13:50-51 and 214-15n7.

32. Roy J. Deferrari has translated Hugh's *De sacramentis* (PL 176), *On the Sacraments of the Christian Faith* (Cambridge: Medieval Academy of America, 1958). David

E. Luscombe has admirably documented the extent of this criticism in *The School of Peter Abelard* (Cambridge: Cambridge University Press, 1969), 183-97.

33. *Summa sententiarum*, PL 176:41-174; Luscombe, *The School*, 198-213.

34. The most important of these is the *Sententie Abaelardi*, edited by Rheinwald under the title *Epitome Theologiae Christianae Petri Abaelardi* (PL 178:1697-1758). They have been re-edited by Sandro Buzzetti, *Sententie Petri Abelardi (Sententie Hermanni)* (Florence: La Nuova Italia Editrice, 1983). See also the *Sententie Florianenses*, ed. Heinrich Ostlender, Florilegium Patristicum 19 (Bonn: P. Hanstein, 1929) and *Sententie Parisienses*, ed. Artur Landgraf, in his *Écrits théologiques de l'école d'Abélard* (Louvain: Spicilegium Sacrum Lovaniense, 1934), 1-60.

35. *Confessio fidei* 18, ed. Charles S.F. Burnett, "Peter Abelard, *Confessio fidei 'Universis'*. A Critical Edition of Abelard's Reply to Accusations of Heresy," *Mediaeval Studies* 48 (1986): 138:

> Quod autem capitula contra me scripta tali fine amicus noster concluserit ut diceret: hec autem capitula partim in libro theologie magistri Petri, partim in libro sententiarum eiusdem, partim in libro cuius titulus est Scito te ipsum reperta sunt, non sine admiratione maxime suscepi, cum nusquam liber aliquis qui sententiarum dicatur a me scriptus repperiatur.

See also Abaelard's *Apologia*, ed. Buytaert, CCCM 11 (Turnhout: Brepols, 1969): 360-61. I have edited the surviving fragments of this *liber sententiarum* and discuss the relationship between the different sentence collections in "The *Sententie* of Peter Abelard," *Recherches de théologie ancienne et médiévale* 53 (1986): 130-84. On the sequence of events leading up to Bernard's list of Abaelard's heresies, see my study "The Lists of Heresies imputed to Peter Abelard," *Revue bénédictine* 95 (1985): 73-110.

36. Ostlender, "Die Sentenzenbücher der Schule Abaelards," *Theologische Quartalschrift* 117 (1936): 208-252.

37. David E. Luscombe interprets these collections as works of different authors (*The School*, 143-72).

38. Mews, "The *Sententie*," 138-49.

39. Paris, MS Bibliothèque Nationale lat. 18108, fols. 70-75v. See Landgraf's detailed description in *Écrits théologiques*, xiii-xxvi.

40. *Sententie Parisienses*, ed. Landgraf, 37-48.

41. *Sententie Parisienses* 49; cf. *Sententie Parisienses* 21-22, for a similar dialogue.

42. *Epist. 332*, ed. Jean Leclercq, *S. Bernardi Opera*, 8 vols. (Rome: Editiones Cistercienses, 1957-77), 8:271:

> Habemus in Francia monachum sine regula, sine sollicitudine praelatum, sine disciplina abbatem, Petrum Abaelardum, disputantem cum pueris, conversantem cum muilierculis. Aquas furtivas et panes absconditos domesticis suis apponit in libris, et in sermonibus suis profanas vocum novitates inducit et sensuum. Accedit non solus, sicut Moyses, ad caliginem in qua erat Deus, sed cum turba multa et discipulis suis. Per vicos et plateas de fide catholica disputatur, de partu Virginis, de Sacramento altaris, de incomprehensibili sanctae Trinititatis mysterio.

The reference to "streets and market places" is an allusion to the Song of Songs 3:2.

43. *TSch* 2.62, alluding to Peter of Bruys and Tanchelin of Utrecht.

44. *Problemata Heloissae* 42, PL 178:723A. See my study, "Un lecteur de Jérôme au XIIe siècle: Pierre Abélard," in *Jérôme entre Occident et Orient*, ed. Yves-Marie Duval (Paris: Études Augustiniennes, 1988), 429–44, in which I argue that Berengar is reproducing Abaelard's own mature thought on this opinion of Jerome in commenting on how a celebrated writer could sometimes err; cf. *Apologia contra Bernardum*, ed. Rodney M. Thomson, in his "The Satirical Works of Berengar of Poitiers: An Edition with Introduction," *Medieval Studies* 42 (1980): 89–138, at 129.

45. *Ethics*, ed. David E. Luscombe (Oxford: Clarendon Press, 1971), 12–14.

46. For fuller details on these changes, see my comments in CCCM 13:283–92.

47. Mews, CCCM 13:276–77.

48. *Oeuvres de Robert de Melun*, ed. R. M. Martin, 4 vols., 13, 18, 21, 25 (Louvain: Spicilegium Sacrum Lovaniense, 1932–52), vol. 3 [21] (1947): *Sententie*, 2 vols.

49. John of Cornwall, *Eulogium ad Papam Alexandrum III*, ed. Nikolaus Häring, *Mediaeval Studies* 13 (1951): 265.

50. Martin notes parallels in an appendix, but they are rarely direct quotations (Robert de Melun, *Oeuvres*, 324–25).

51. *Sententie*, ed. Martin, 1:3–56. Beryl Smalley argues that Robert's criticism of the masters of the Gloss was unjust in *The Study of the Bible in the Middle Ages* (Notre Dame: University of Notre Dame Press, 1964), 215–216, 228–30.

52. *Sententie* 1:4, 6:

Est vero preter hec novum docendi genus nuper exortum, immo puerile recitandi studium, populari favore quorundam folia fructum tegentia querentium inmoderate elevatum. . . . Nam non student, sed studiosi haberi appetunt, neque legunt ut intelligant, quia malunt non intellexisse quam non legisse.

53. *Sententie* 1:10:

Quot namque sunt et multo plures fuerunt quos constat glosas nec audisse nec inspexisse, qui tam plenam textus doctrinam sunt consecuti?

54. *Sententie* 1:10–11:

quoniam quos nunc fama in talibus usque ad astra extollit, eosdem in caliginosissimis ignorantie tenebris publica voce inmergit. Cuius quam impudens, quam fallax, quam sibi sit iudicium adversum, nullum latet qui intelligit quanto favore ad sedem cathedralem eos sublevat quibus adeo manifeste docendorum intelligentiam tollit. Predicat namque glosarum magistros — hoc quidem nomen nunc adepti sunt — intelligentia tam glosarum quam textus carere, licet eis concedat glosas distinguere et per puncta dividere ac cuique textui queque subserviat assignare.

55. *Sententie* 1:12:

Indubitanter ergo tenendum est nullum utilem esse in lectione qui in sententiarum non valet discussione. Qui enim scitur, si sententia nescitur, aut quid docetur ubi sententia non explicatur. Nec ibi aliquid addiscitur ubi sententia omnino incognita preteritur. Hoc autem ibi fieri fatendum est, ubi lectioni glosarum, immo recitationi, tota incumbitur intentione. Nam ibi textus spernitur, glosa cum devota veneratione colitur, textus propter glosam legitur et non glosa causa textus exponitur.

56. *Historia calamitatum*, ed. Monfrin, 68:

sed me vehementer mirari quod his qui litterari sunt ad expositiones sanctorum intelligendas ipsa eorum scripta vel glose non sufficiunt, ut alio scilicet non egeant magisterio.

Robert, like Abaelard, did not question that the writings of the Fathers could be considered a source of authority—*Sententie*, ed. Martin, 1:24.

57. *Sententie* 1:45-46:

His vero omnibus in illis sacre scripture tractatibus precipue consultum invenio, qui sententie nomine inscribuntur, quoniam in eis est parcitas verborum aperta et sententiarum conpendiosa fecunditas, non obscure sed evidenter expressa. Horum autem tractatuum auctores pauci inveniuntur, sed ex illis tamen duo precipui, qui tam de sacramentis fidei quam de ipsa fide ac caritate ratione inquirenda ac reddenda, omnibus qui post illos sacre scripture expositores extiterunt, omnibus omnium iudicio prepollent; quos tamen non per omnia eadem tenuisse itinera contigit; quod raro vel nunquam contingere solet, licet res eadem tractetur et doceatur. Nam que aput istum brevius quam oporteret, vel diffusius quam necesse esset dicta sunt, ordine converso tractata ab illo inveniuntur.

58. *Sententie* 1:47-48:

Quid enim scriptura aliud est quam quedam imago et obscura figura voluntatis ipsius scriptoris? Nec ea solum representat que ipse scriptor per eam intelligi voluit, sed alia quandoque, non tantum diversa, sed penitus aversa, eque evidenter aut forsitan non parvo evidentius. . . . Eis ergo qui auctores predictorum tractatuum viva voce, ut dici solet, suam exponentes sententiam presentes audierunt magis credendum est in eorundem tractatuum expositione, quam illis qui ex scripturis eorum quid senserint opinantur, et scripturam ad suum retorquent potius sensum quam ad intellectum eorum qui eam composuerunt. Nam quem eius auctores in ea intellectum habuerint, certo modo dicere non possunt, eo quod nesciunt, sed, ut dixi, solum conitiunt. Hii ergo verius coniectores voluntatis auctorum sunt habendi quam expositores.

59. Abaelard was not the first to make the distinction; cf. *Dialectica*, ed. Lambert Marie de Rijk, 2nd ed. (Assen: Van Gorcum, 1970), 112:

Alii enim omnia quibus vox imposita est, ab ipsa voce significari volunt, alii vero ea sola que in voce denotantur atque in sententia ipsius tenentur. Illis quidem magister noster V. favet, his vero Garmundus consensisse videtur; illi quidem auctoritate, hi vero fulti sunt ratione. Quibus enim Garmundus annuit rationabiliter ea sola que in sententia vocis tenentur ⟨significari, sustinentur⟩ iuxta diffinitionem "significandi," que est intellectum generare; de eo enim vox intellectum facere non potest de quo in sententia eius non agitur.

60. *TSch*, Prefatio 1:

Scolarium nostrorum petitioni prout possumus satisfacientes aliquam sacre eruditionis summam quasi diuine scripture introductionem conscripsimus.

61. Luscombe maintains however that Abaelard's influence was still considerable; cf. *The School*, 310: "he provoked much of the keenest thinking which appears in scholastic writing for some twenty years after his death."

62. This point is made briefly by Tina Stiefel in a book concentrating on scientific thinking, *The Intellectual Revolution in Twelfth Century Europe* (New York: St. Martin's Press, 1985), 104–5.

63. *Decretum*, in *Corpus Juris Canonici*, ed. A. Friedberg (Leipzig: B. Tauchnitz, 1879–81). Considerable debate surrounds the additional material or *paleae* which accrued to Gratian's work, much of it embedded in Friedberg's edition. For recent commentary, see Stanley Chodorow, *Christian Political Theory and Church Politics in the Mid-Twelfth Century: The Ecclesiology of Gratian's Decretum* (Berkeley: University of California Press, 1972), 11–15.

64. Luscombe, *The School*, 214–33. Stephan Kuttner emphasises Gratian's textual dependence (for quotation of patristic texts) on both Hugh of St. Victor and Abaelard in "Zur Frage der theologischen Vorlagen Gratians," *Zeitschrift der Savigny-Stiftung für Rechtsgeschichte, Kan. Abt.* 23 (1934): 243–68, reprinted with many other valuable studies in his *Gratian and the Schools of Law 1140–1234* (London: Variorum Reprints, 1983).

65. Valerie I. Flint, "The School of Anselm of Laon: A Re-consideration," *Recherches de théologie ancienne et médiévale* 43 (1976): 89–110.

66. Richard H. Rouse and Mary A. Rouse, "*Statim invenire*: Schools, Preachers, and New Attitudes to the Page," in Robert L. Benson and Giles Constable, *Renaissance and Renewal in the Twelfth Century* (Oxford: Oxford University Press, 1982), 201–28. See also Malcolm Parkes, "The Influence of the Concepts of *Ordinatio* and *Compilatio* on the Development of the Book," in *Medieval Learning and Literature: Essays presented to Richard William Hunt*, ed. J. J. G. Alexander and M. T. Gibson (Oxford: Clarendon Press, 1976), 115–41.

67. R. I. Moore raises questions about the growth of "labelling" in society between the eleventh and thirteenth centuries, which could profitably be extended to the study of scholastic literature, in *The Formation of a Persecuting Society. Power and Deviance in Western Europe 950–1250* (Oxford: Basil Blackwell Press, 1987).

68. *STh* 1. Prol. 1a:

> Consideravimus huius doctrinae novitias in his quae a diversis conscripta sunt plurimum impediri, partim quidem propter multiplicationem inutilium quaestionum, articulorum et argumentorum; partim etiam quia ea quae sunt necessaria talibus ad sciendum non traduntur secundum ordinem disciplinae, sed secundum quod requirebat librorum expositio, vel secundum quod se praebebat occasio disputandi; partim quidem quia eorundem frequens repetitio et fastidium et confusionem generabat in animis auditorum.

69. Leonard E. Boyle, *The Setting of the "Summa theologiae" of Saint Thomas*, The Etienne Gilson Series, 5 (Toronto: PIMS, 1982). I am grateful to Peter Howard for pointing this study out to me, as also for showing me proofs of his penetrating article on Antoninus, which echoes similar concerns with the oral and social context of scholasticism within a fifteenth-century milieu: "'Non parum laborat formica ad colligendum unde vivat': Oral Discourse as the Context of the *Summa Theologica* of St. Antoninus of Florence," *Archivum Fratrum Praedicatorum* 60 (1990), forthcoming.

II

PHILOSOPHY AND THEOLOGY 1100-1150 : THE SEARCH FOR HARMONY

Between 1100 and 1150 intellectual life in the Latin West underwent a profound transformation (1). For centuries scholarly effort had been primarily devoted to preservation of and commentary upon a canon of texts largely stabilised between the fourth and early sixth centuries. Augustine had been particularly influential in moulding the direction of philosophy and theology. In the *City of God*, he had surveyed various philosophical schools and pronounced 'followers of Plato, coming to a knowledge of God, have come closest to understanding the cause of the organised universe', but then argued that for all their insight, Platonists lacked knowledge of the true salvation taught by the Christian religion. (2) Within a monastic milieu, Augustine's neoplatonist assumptions about the transcendence of an ideal form over the world of matter overshadowed attitudes to philosophy. Boethius had preserved a more overthy sympathetic attitude towards Aristotelian tradition, but interpreted it within a Platonizing metaphysics. The cultural flowering of the ninth century under Charlemagne, Louis the German and Charles the Bald was, by and large, the activity of a small monastic elite, more concerned to rescue the past from oblivion than to question its legitimacy.

By the mid twelfth century, intellectual attitudes forged in Late Antiquity were being questioned at a profound level. Demographic growth coupled with economic prosperity extended educational opportunity, and thus literacy. (3) Students sought rational answers to their questions about the legitimacy of received wisdom. The brief glosses explaining difficult words and phrases of classical and scriptural texts, customary in the eleventh century, had to compete with in depth commentaries from the most famous masters. After 1100 it became increasingly common for teachers to compose independent treatises for their students which synthesised the issues raised by these texts, whether dealing with the trivium, the quadrivium or theology, into a systematic whole. (4) Philosophical attitudes were also changing. In the more urbanised and politically stable regions of Europe, Augustine's polemical contrasts between pagan and Christian religion, the worldly city and the City of God, pagan *theologia* about the gods and authoritative sacred scripture, were giving way to a tendency to emphasise the harmony between pagan and Christian pursuit of wisdom, between the natural and the spiritual world, or simply between reason and faith. Aristotle, barely mentioned in the *City of God*, was being referred to as 'the philosopher'. (5) Aristotelian analysis of language as a human instrument was forcing scholars to re-think the arguments of grammar and dialectic, as well as of theology. In the 1130s enthusiasm for Aristotle's *Categories* and the *Periermeneias*, began to extend to the previously ignored *Sophistical Refutations, Prior Analytics* and *Topics*. (6) Sometime between 1130 and 1159, James of Venice translated these works anew from the Greek, as well as the *Posterior Analytics*. He also translated other Aristotelian texts on science and metaphysics, destined to have a profound impact in the schools, so helping establish a new philosophic canon for the Latin West. (7)

The attitudes of Augustine could not be challenged without provoking debate. The first half of the twelfth century witnessed a number of sharp conflicts between teachers offering different strategies to steer their students through the variety of alternative positions being offered in a competitive environment. Scholars influenced by Bernard of Chartres combined interest in Aristotle with a Platonist philosophical tradition, mediated through the *Timaeus* and the writings of Chalcidius, Macrobius and Boethius, to provide an alternative to Augustinian neoplatonism in quite a different way from Peter Abelard. By the mid twelfth century, John of Salisbury was sufficiently troubled by the multiplicity of opinions in circulation and by fear that excessive specialisation and argument could bring into disrepute genuine advances in learning, that he composed the *Metalogicon*, his own summary of *Logica*, paying particular attention to its branches of grammar and dialectic. (8) Enthusiasm for Aristotelian identification of dialectic with logic led, he thought, to a mistaken devaluing of *grammatica*, the study of both language and literature. For better or worse, a pattern of intellectual specialisation had emerged that would characterise academic life for centuries to come.

The first scholar to analyse philosophical developments in the early twelfth century was Victor Cousin. From the opening pages of his pioneering study of early scholasticism, Cousin made clear that the hero of his narrative was Peter Abelard. (9) He understood Abelard's principal contribution to philosophy to be his decisive intervention in the debate between realists and nominalists, while to theology the establishment of 'what today one calls rationalism'. (10) His editions of the *Dialectica* and *Sic et Non* substantiated for him an image of Abelard as the questioning innovator in philosophy and theology. (11) An undisguised national pride animated Cousin's historical vision, in which philosophy before Abelard was little more than unthinking exposition of sacred dogma. Abelard became 'the principal founder of medieval philosophy', a system eventually overthrown by Descartes. (12) Even before Cousin, Abelard had become familiar as an emblem of philosophical enlightenment in the eighteenth century. (13) Such attitudes derived from the controversial literature which Abelard had himself generated in the twelfth century. Bernard of Clairvaux had propagated an influential image of Abelard as an arrogant intellectual, inflated by a love of questioning for its own sake, opposed to everything Christian society considered sacred. Through the *Historia calamitatum* Abelard had conveyed the impression that he was a solitary genius persecuted by mediocre rivals. (14) Cousin gave scientific credibility to the assumption that Abelard was the central force behind a scholastic challenge to an overwhelmingly monastic tradition.

Since the time of Cousin, it has become very clear that the first half of twelfth century was not just the age of Abelard. Through critical editions of hitherto unknown or little studied texts, a broader picture has emerged of the intellectual vitality both of his generation, and that of his teachers. L.M. De Rijk has greatly extended our knowledge of the evolution of dialectic in the twelfth century. (15) N. Häring's editions of the commentaries of Thierry of Chartres and of Gilbert of Poitiers on the Boethian *Opuscula Sacra* have opened up the creative role of Platonic traditions in the twelfth century. (16) É. Jeauneau has pioneered the study of William of Conches, some of whose writings still await critical edition. (17) Lesser known figures like Honorius Augustudonensis are coming out of obscurity. (18) Cistercian writers, above all St Bernard, are much better understood than in the nineteenth century, not least through the research of Dom Jean Leclercq. (19) After a long period of neglect, the creativity of Benedictine authors like Rupert of Deutz and Hildegard of Bingen in their attitude to scripture and the natural world is becoming appreciated. (20) St Anselm has been studied for the originality of his thought about language as about theology. (21) There are still many aspects of the intellectual achievement of the late eleventh and early twelfth century remaining to be explored. Most philosophical and theological texts and glosses from the period remain anonymous, and largely unread. Any attempt at a synthesis must remain provisional. Nonetheless, it is clear that Abelard, far from being the first original thinker, issued from over half a century of vigorous intellectual debate. He lived at a time of great competition between a host of distinguished masters. While Abelard attracted more controversy than most of his contemporaries, in part because of his personality and the unusual circumstances of his career, it is misleading to understand the development of philosophy and theology in the first half of the twelfth century simply in terms of his achievement alone.

Philosophy and theology before 1100

Dialectic, the art of distinguishing truth from falsehood by rational argument, had been enthusiastically studied in the schools long before Abelard. (22) Even before the year 1000, a Benedictine monk, Gerbert of Aurillac, had established at Rheims an educational curriculum which gave particular priority to the *Categories* and *On Interpretation* of Aristotle, texts which had been available in good monastic and cathedral libraries since the time of Charlemagne. (23) In Gerbert's curriculum, as reported by Richer, these two core Aristotelian texts were studied alongside Porphyry's *Isagoge* or *Introduction* to the *Categories*, and four treatises of Boethius, *On the Categorical Syllogism*, *On the Hypothetical Syllogism*, *On Division*, as well as his *On Topical Differences*. (24) The manuscript evidence, however, suggests that for most of the eleventh century these texts never attracted more than very brief glosses. Other authors studied in the Carolingian period, were still being used, albeit less frequently : the *Categoriae Decem*, a paraphrase of the *Categories* attributed to Augustine, treatises *De Dialectica* of Augustine and of Alcuin, the *On Interpretation* of Apuleius, and the fourth book of Martianus Capella's, *On the marriage of Philology and Mercury*. (25)

By the eleventh century Boethius had come to enjoy a privileged position over these other interpreters as one who transmitted Greek wisdom. In a didactic poem on the seven liberal arts copied in the early twelfth century at the abbey of Saint-Évroul, Normandy (Alençon, Bibl. mun. 10), the liberal arts are described as rivers flowing from a Greek spring, here identified as philosophy's table. (26) Pythagoras taught physics, Socrates and Plato expounded ethics, while Aristotle betrothed himself to 'loquacious Logic', which embraced grammar, dialectic and rhetoric. (27) This wisdom flowed from Athens to the West. As Rome was mighty in war, thus it shone in philosophy. Vergil, Cicero and Severinus (Boethius) were the outstanding representatives of Latin learning. After listing twenty-three Latin authors (playwright, poets and historians) studied within *grammatica*, the poem praised Priscian as the *restaurator strenuus* of this first art. Grammar was the foundation, preparing the way for other arts as an instrument. While rhetoric discussed and settled disputes, dialectic enjoyed a pre-eminent role : 'Common by genus to this [rhetoric] is dialectic, which by nature exists prior to grammar ; while the latter binds and separates all things, it does not know how to penetrate ; the former [dialectic] defines and discerns, divides and asserts, powerful to think, an invincible conqueror, which illuminates the lamps of Manlian light [i.e. of Boethius]. He transmitted it [dialectic] by resolving the two *Analytics*, introducing the *Isagoge* with two commentaries, and explaining the *Categories* with the *Periermeneias*, the *Topics* with the Syllogisms and the Differences, the book of Definitions with the Divisions, adding one on the Propositions.' (28) After a briefer explanation of the quadrivium, the poem concluded with praise of Boethius for enriching all these subjects. It was probably in circulation by the mid eleventh century, when it prompted a parody in praise of Vergil, comic poets and satirists. (29) The curriculum of dialectic advocated in the poem, identical to that used by Gerbert at Rheims, was still used by Abelard over a century later. As the poem was copied at St-Évroul during the period that John of Rheims was its most famous luminary (1076/77-1126), we may presume that it reflects the educational programme John brought with him from Rheims to Normandy. Orderic Vitalis praised John for his mastery of the grammatical art, and for his understanding of the ancients. (30) It reflected a more overtly classicizing ethos than that encouraged by St Anselm at Bec.

While Boethius was respected for transmitting the philosophical wisdom of ancient Greece, his authority as a commentator on dialectic was being questioned by the late eleventh century. Hermann of Tournai spoke with alarm about teachers like Reimbert of Lille who favoured teaching dialectic *in voce*, 'reading their own inventions' into the texts of Porphyry and Aristotle, rather than the commentary of Boethius and other authorities. (31) One of the most controversial of these teachers was Roscelin of Compiègne (c. 1045/50-1120/25), a product of the school of Rheims. (32) Roscelin was accused of teaching heresy by John, a monastic disciple of St Anselm seconded by Pope Urban II from Rome to Beauvais to assist another Bec monk, Fulco, as its new bishop during the year of 1089/90. Fulco was then facing widespread criticism from non-monastic clergy over his appointment, possibly the context of the argument with Roscelin. (33) According to a contemporary chronicle, Roscelin was one of a number of teachers influenced by a certain John, who taught dialectic to be an *ars vocalis*. (34) Even in 1093, Roscelin had been described by St Anselm as one of a number of 'heretics of dialectic, who

do not think universal substances to be anything but the puff of an utterance *(flatum vocis)*, who cannot understand colour to be other than a
body, or the wisdom of man different from the soul'. (35) St Anselm
considered such reasoning to be so wrapped up in corporeal images, that
it could not distinguish those universals it ought to contemplate – an
allusion to Boethius' discussion in the fifth book of the *Consolation of
Philosophy* of universals as comprehensible to a mind that had risen above
sense and imagination. (36)

St Anselm's invective confirmed Hermann's impression that teachers
of dialectic could be divided into those who were reliable and taught
their subject *in re*, that is with a basis in reality, and those superficial
innovators who taught *in voce*, that is as relating to words rather than
reality. Hermann's model teacher was Odo of Tournai, who defended
the Augustinian doctrine of original sin on the grounds that there was
a common universal man shared by individuals of that species. (37)
Contemporary glosses on Porphyry's *Isagoge* confirm the observations of
St Anselm and Hermann that the issue of whether a generic category
like *homo* was a thing or a vocal utterance, raised by Porphyry, had become a matter of dispute. (38) Some teachers defined Porphyry's five
categories as vocal utterances because Aristotle was dealing with *voces* in
the *Categories*. (39) They did not deny that genus could designate things,
but maintained that universal *voces*, since they were names imposed *ad
placitum*, were not necessarily the same for all people. One text to adopt
a 'vocalist' approach was the *Dialectica* of Gerlandus of Besançon, from
the early twelfth century (not the mid eleventh, as thought by De
Rijk). (40) Gerlandus analysed issues of dialectic, like universals or categorical and hypothetical propositions, simply as to do with *voces*. (41)
While writings of Roscelin on dialectic have not yet been identified with
certainty, it is clear from his letter to Abelard that he also analysed the
theological terms, Father, Son and Holy Spirit, in an Aristotelian sense,
as *voces* of human imposition. Whether one used *persona* like the Latins,
or *substantia* like the Greeks, the same thing was being referred to. 'In
speech there is diversity, in faith unity.' (42) One could not be predicated of another. This was the essence of his argument that 'Father', 'Son'
or 'Holy Spirit' were distinct vocal utterances, standing for non-equiva-
lent things, a term he used in Augustine's rather crude sense of that of
which a word was a sign. They were eternally plural, like three eternal
things. (43) Nowhere in his letter to Abelard did he assert that they signified separate things.

A key influence on discussion of *voces* in the late eleventh and early
twelfth century was the *Glosule* on Books I-XVI of Priscian's *Grammati-*

cal Institutes. (44) The earliest known copy (Cologne, Dombibl. 201) is from the late eleventh century, while another extended version belonged in the early twelfth century to Chartres cathedral (Chartres MS 209), in a volume which had some connection to St-Évroul. (45) The *Glosule*, widely influential by the early twelfth century, played a centrol role in the Priscian commentary of William of Conches. (46) No manuscript copy carries the identification of an author, if we exclude Arrivabenus' 1488 edition of Priscian, in which the *Glosule* is printed from an unknown manuscript as the work of 'Johannes de Aingre' (probably a misreading of *Johannes Dei gratia*). (47) Although Priscian had been commented upon since the ninth century, the *Glosule* provided a much more systematic discussion than ever before on the 'causes' of language. (48) Those passages of the *Grammatical Institutes* I-XVI in which Priscian had used Aristotelian categories like 'substance' and 'quality' to identify parts of speech, were of particular interest to the commentator. He glossed only books I-XVI, in which Priscian had documented all the individual *voces* of the Latin language so as to provide a grammatical framework for Latin comparable to that furnished by Greek grammarians. Priscian's opening thoughts on the fount of Greek wisdom, 'from whose springs the teaching of all eloquence and every kind of study derive', provoked reflection on the role grammar played in the understanding of Logic : 'I say grammatically as different from dialectic, which teaches speaking according to truth and falsehood and from rhetoric, which teaches speaking according to the decoration of words and phrases. Of these arts grammar comes first, because one ought to know how to make appropriate joining of words before truth or falsehood or the decoration of eloquence is learnt.' (49) The commentator wanted to place grammar within the overall framework of philosophy, from which different streams flowed. (50) Grammar was a part of Logic, a subject which embraced what was *sermocinalis* (to do with language) and what was *disertiva* (to do with finding arguments). 'Through this linguistic part, grammar was led back to Logic as if to its genus.' (51) These were the same themes as had been raised in the poem on the seven liberal arts in the St-Évroul manuscript, perhaps an influence on the *Glosule*'s prologue. (52)

The *Glosule* author expanded enthusiastically on the introductory comment of Priscian, *quanto iuniores, quanto perspicatiores*, 'the younger, the more perspicacious' to justify reflection that study enabled the faults of earlier writers to be improved upon. Originally Adam knew only four letters, but a subsequent generation extended the capacity for human speech. (53) Not content with a purely descriptive approach to language, the commentator wanted to determine the causes behind voces. Priscian's definition that 'a noun signified substance with quality' he clarified to specify that a noun signified by imposition, or by 'naming' a substance, while it signified a quality. (54) He was here working out the implications of Aristotle's remark in the *Categories* that *album* did not signify anything other than a quality. (55) A noun first of all was applied properly to specific individuals. Only subsequently was a noun like *homo* applied through appellation to discrete things to indicate what they shared in common. A predicate term like *albus* in *homo est albus* signified a quality and not a substance. Used as a noun it signified principally a quality, and only secondarily a body. The *Glosule* thus clarified a conceptual ambiguity latent in the Latin language, which, unlike Greek or French, lacks the modifying precision of a definite article.

The commentator defined the 'causes' of *voces* as things. (56) Thus, when talking about the first, second and third persons of a verb, he distinguished between a *persona realis*, namely the thing which *persona* designated and a *persona vocalis*, namely a vocal utterance. (57) Within grammatical discourse, 'person' was a *vox* which referred either to the one who spoke, the one to whom one spoke, or the one about whom an action was performed. A grammatical person with a purely notional existence had to be distinguished from the actual person or *res* to which the utterance might apply. Although the *Glosule* was not specifically concerned with universal categories as such, its use of Aristotelian classifications to analyse the meaning of names had profound implications for a subject also discussed in dialectic. (58) Its significance and relationship to wider grammatical tradition deserves further examination.

St Anselm was also concerned with the meaning of such categories in his *De grammatico*, written perhaps between 1080 and 1085. In the *Categories* Aristotle had used the example of *grammaticus* as a category that could ambiguously refer to a substance or a quality. (59) At issue was the relationship between a quality (that of being literate) and a substance (the literate person). Like the author of the *Glosule*, Anselm wanted to improve upon Priscian's definition by taking into account Aristotle's comment that *album* signified 'only a quality'. He resolved the problem by arguing that *grammaticus* could signify in two ways, *per se* the quality of being a grammarian, but *per aliud* the man who is a grammarian, in contrast to the more overtly Aristotelian 'primary'/'secondary' distinction of the *Glosule* with its distinction between *voces* and *res*. Anselm remarked at the close of the *De grammatico* that he hoped he had resolved the problem raised by 'modern dialecticians', possibly referring to debates inspired by the *Glosule*. St Anselm distanced himself from discussion which depended too much on explicit quotation from Aristotle or Priscian, just as he avoided direct citation from the Fathers in his theological writing. The solution was no less original.

St Anselm's strategy to a semantic problem in the *De grammatico* was similar to that which he adopted in his theological writing, namely to solve a question 'from reason alone' rather than from a written authority, like that of Priscian. In his first major treatise, the *Monologion*, Anselm had argued from reason alone that within a single divine essence, there co-existed three *nescio quid*, called 'persons' in Latin tradition or 'substances' by the Greeks. (60) It was a treatise *De trinitate* which avoided direct citation of the writings of Augustine or Boethius, even though it was profoundly influenced by both. When criticised by Lanfranc for not defending his argument from authority, Anselm quoted the passage from Augustine's *De trinitate* which admitted that Latin definition of three 'persons' was used by convention to refer to what Greeks defined as three 'substances'. (61) Anselm was not questioning that there were three divine persons in one substance, but elucidating for an enquiring mind what the doctrine signified. Anselm emphasised that understanding flowed out of faith. He wanted to demonstrate the true meaning of a catholic doctrine, without adhering unnecessarily to a particular verbal formulation.

Roscelin of Compiègne also wanted to explain the essentials of Christian doctrine in terms acceptable to human reason. St Anselm reported Roscelin's justification for his method : 'The pagans defend their Law, the Jews defend their Law, therefore we Christians must defend our faith.' (62) Roscelin's argument that the three persons were as separate as three things flowed from a desire for consistency between his attitudes to language and to theology. He defended his definition of plurality in the Trinity by adducing the same passage from Augustine's *De Trinitate* about the equivalence of Greek and Latin definitions as St Anselm used to defend the *Monologion* to Lanfranc. (63) He went further, however, in believing that *voces* were vocal utterances imposed to refer to things. (64) In a very crude way, Roscelin was trying to identify what was particular to 'Father', 'Son' and 'Holy Spirit'. The accusation that he preached division in the divine essence was quite unfounded, as his argument related to divine names of human imposition, rather than God himself. Like Anselm, Roscelin wanted to provide a convincing defence of Christian doctrine in terms which conformed to reason, although working from rather different semantic assumptions. Anselm's invective against 'modern dialecticians' was sharpened by contemporary rivalry between canons and monks. He translated the contrast into one between those who focussed on *voces* and those who remained faithful to a tradition established by Boethius. Anselm was, nonetheless, himself an original exegete of tradition.

William of Champeaux and Peter Abelard

In the *Historia calamitatum*, Peter Abelard passed over in silence his long period of study under Roscelin of Compiègne. (65) Over a decade earlier, he had been chastised by Roscelin for not recognizing the debt which he owed to his former master, with whom he studied at Loches 'from being a boy to being a young man', perhaps from around 1093 to 1100. (66) Abelard implied that he decided to give up the privileges of the eldest son to devote himself to learning of his own accord. Howe-ver, if he had been sent to Loches by his father at about fourteen or fifteen to become a *miles litteratus* under the aegis of the Counts of An-jou, it must have been Roscelin who inspired Abelard to abandon a seigneurial vocation. From Roscelin he inherited a passion for Aristote-lian argument as an instrument for challenging traditional definitions of both dialectic and theology. At some point their relationship soured. According to a contemporary anecdote, Abelard became bored and frus-trated with his teacher. (67) Nonetheless, the attitudes he absorbed from Roscelin undoubtedly shaped his approach to intellectual life.

Sometime around 1100, Abelard came to Paris to study under William of Champeaux, then teaching dialectic as well as theology at the cathe-dral school of Notre-Dame. After attending William's lectures on dia-lectic, he established himself as a teacher in his own right at schools attached to the royal castles of Melun and Corbeil. He was probably helped in this by Stephen de Garlande, an archdeacon of Paris and a powerful figure in the royal court bitterly resentful of William, appointed fellow archdeacon by the reforming bishop Galo in 1104. (68) In the *Historia calamitatum*, Abelard focussed on William's resentment towards him as the root of his troubles, without appreciating the wider political rivalries involved. In 1108, William left Notre-Dame to establish a com-munity of regular canons at the abbey of St-Victor, where he continued to maintain a public school. Abelard was meanwhile established at the abbey school of Ste-Geneviève, of which Stephen de Garlande had been appointed dean by the young king Louis VI by 1111 (a position he held until he withdrew to St-Victor after 1137, year of the king's death). (69)

William shared the opinion of Odo of Tournai that a universal was a thing essentially the same in individuals. He modified this to 'indifferently the same thing' after a public disputation with Abelard. (70) Certain *In-*

troductiones dialecticae secundum Wilgelmum provide a hitherto neglected source for understanding William's teaching. The treatise, dealing with various parts of speech, propositions and inferential references, is the earliest known example of a genre still influential in the mid twelfth century. (71) It began with definition of how dialectic differed from grammar and rhetoric. (72) Its opening discussion of *vox* presented an opinion that Abelard resisted : that as a universal, an utterance like 'animal' signified a universal thing, namely that thing shared in all animals. (73) Much of the treatise is taken up with defining arguments from topics. He defined the topics, John of Salisbury later recalled, as 'the science of finding a middle term, and of thence constructing an argument.' (74) William was particularly interested in defining topics, sometimes going beyond those mentioned by Boethius. (75) Although Abelard did not mention William by name in the long discussion of topics in his *Dialectica*, his comments here on the multiplicity of senses of a maxim are closer to those of William than his argument in his later commentary on the *De differentiis topicis*, in which he denies such multiplicity. (76)

William left St-Victor in 1113 to become bishop of Châlons-sur-Marne, a position he held until his death in 1121. Abelard was invited to teach at the cathedral school of Notre-Dame. Probably sometime before 1120, Abelard began work on his *Dialectica*. (77) In the first of its five tractates, dealing with various parts of speech, there are frequent discussions with the opinions of 'our teacher' or 'our teacher V.', once identified as 'our teacher W.', undoubtedly William of Champeaux. (78) The section which might have dealt with universal categories is missing from the manuscript. The criticisms of 'our teacher' relate not to universal categories as such, but to the question of whether or not a noun signified everything on which it was imposed. This is the debate he presents as between Garmundus, who held 'rationally' that an utterance signified only what was *in sententia vocis*, and his teacher who held that it signified whatever that on which the *vox* was imposed, supposedly on the authority of Priscian's definition that a noun signified a substance with a quality. (79) Abelard's insistence here that *album* principally signified a quality, only secondarily a substance, restated the Aristotelian argument emphasised by the *Glosule* on Priscian. He was contradicting William's definition in the *Introductiones* that an utterance like 'animal' signified a thing. (80) Abelard also rejected William's idea that a thing like 'race' inhered in a verb, like 'he runs', which meant no more than 'he is running'. (81) The verb 'is' did not carry any substantive significance itself in 'Socrates is white' (as distinct from its meaning in 'Socrates is').

Abelard's criticisms in the first tract of the *Dialectica*, the 'book of parts', were directed against assertions that an utterance or a proposition signified something in itself, independently of the particular sense engendered by its imposition. Discussion of universal categories, he insisted, should not divorced from their predicative function. He was extending the argument of the *Glosule* in maintaining that a term like *homo* in Socrates est *homo* signified a quality of Socrates rather than an entity in itself. Abelard rebuked his teacher for holding that in 'Homer is a poet', the accidental predication was not achieved through the verb but through the figurative and improper expression of the construction as a whole. (82) Abelard insisted that the meaning of a phrase was not to be sought in individual words, but in its sense as a whole. (83) Similarly he criticised his teacher for denying that 'a not white man', which could be imposed infinitely, was an infinite expression because its construction was not infinite. In the *Introductiones* William had interpreted a non-animal as a thing, like an animal. (84) In his glosses on the *De Differentiis Topicis* Abelard expanded more fully on his disagreement with *magister Wilhelmus* and his followers that the grammatical sense of a proposition was different from its logical sense. (85) This is the same criticism as Abelard makes against 'our teacher' or 'our teacher V.' in the *Dialectica*. Like his argument about the substantive verb, such ideas flowed not so much from a theory about universals as from a semantic theory about discourse as not in itself committed to extra-linguistic reality. In subsequent sections of the *Dialectica*, Abelard developed the implications of these ideas for analysis of propositions and arguments. The truth of a conditional depended not on any external state of affairs, but on the sense of the consequent being contained in the antecedent (86).

Abelard's glosses on Porphyry and Aristotle, known as the *Logica 'Ingredientibus'*, frequently explore individual issues in more detail than the *Dialectica*. (87) In glossing the *Isagoge*, Abelard developed the thesis for which he would become famous, that the categories defined by Porphyry were not just *voces* or vocal utterances, but *nomina*, names applied to any subject as a result of human imposition. (88) To argue that universal categories were things was to fly against physical reality. They signified an understanding of what they predicated. Although he was not the first teacher to reject the idea that 'man' was necessarily a thing, his formulation focussed more on its predicative function in generating *intellectus* than Roscelin's rigid emphasis that *voces* applied to discrete things. A universal was not a common thing, but a noun predicated of a subject to signify a common status, such as 'being a man'. When revising his commentary on Porphyry in the 1120s, he moved further from Roscelin by re-defining a universal category as a *sermo*, a spoken word rather than a simple sound. (89) The question of universals was only one of many issues about predication and meaning, which he explored in commentaries on Porphyry and Aristotle remarkable for their independence from the Platonizing tendencies of the commentaries on these texts by Boethius.

Abelard's frustration with Roscelin's insistence that *voces* signified discrete entities came to a head in disagreement about the meaning of 'Father', 'Son' and 'Holy Spirit'. In his treatise on the Unity and Trinity of God (*Theologia 'Summi boni'*), first composed c. 1120, revised as the *Theologia christiana* c. 1122-26 and again as the *Theologia* (or *Theologia 'Scholarium'*), Abelard argued that they were *nomina*, names or nouns predicated of God, signifying discrete attributes of God : divine power, wisdom and benignity. (90) This sort of speculative discussion assumed much greater understanding of contemporary linguistic debate than conventional in the theological teaching of Anselm of Laon, whose lectures Abelard had found so wanting in 1113. Although Abelard was familiar with the *De trinitate* of Boethius, he preferred to present his own logical arguments for understanding Trinitarian doctrine without referring extensively to that text. He argued with renewed insistence in the *Theologia christiana* against those who maintained that a divine attribute was a thing, insisting that it was a name predicated of God to signify some quality or aspect of his being. Like St Anselm, Abelard wanted to explain the doctrine of the Trinity by arguing from reason. Unlike Anselm, however, he supported his case from authority, pagan and scriptural, as well as from rational argument. Familiar doctrines about the relationship of the Son to the Father, and of the Holy Spirit to the Father and the Son could be understood in terms of the relationships between these properties, each of which was predicated of God rather than being a fixed entity in itself. Abelard explained in the *Theologia christiana* that he was adopting philosophical analogies because he thought them superior to a Trinitarian analogy used by St Anselm in his treatise against Roscelin, which he identified as Augustinian in origin. (91)

Abelard was not innovative in using Romans 1, 19-20 to argue pagan philosophers had glimpsed the doctrine of the Trinity. An influential commentary on the Pauline epistles dated to 1101/2 had commented at length about philosophers' natural knowledge of God through their understanding of creation. (92) His thesis that the divine persons were the divine power, wisdom and goodness that sustained creation was not unique to his teaching. Similar analogies were used in the teaching of the school of William of Champeaux, whose own theological *sententie* employed rational analogies and arguments more freely than those of

Anselm of Laon. (93) Abelard's discussion focussed in more detail, however, on the doctrine of the Trinity and relied explicitly on the authority of pagan authors, a practice not found at all in William's *sententie*. His analogies disturbed William of St-Thierry and Bernard of Clairvaux, who considered them to diminish divine omnipotence, by focussing on the goodness and rationality of the created world, and on philosophic capacity to understand divine order.

Abelard's understanding of the redemption achieved by Christ, first formulated in his commentary on St Paul's Epistle to the Romans, also provoked alarm. He argued that the Devil did not hold anyone prisoner by legitimate right because of Adam's sin, except as a jailer through God's permission. (94) Although St Anselm had already rejected the idea of a legitimate right of the Devil over man in the *Cur Deus homo*, Abelard took the argument a step further by questioning whether humans had inherited equally the guilt of Adam, as St Anselm's logic tended to imply. Rather than teaching that our redemption had been achieved through the sacrifice of a sinless God-man substituting himself for a sinful humanity, he argued that we were redeemed through the supreme love manifested in the passion of Christ. This perfect love freed us from the slavery of sin and led us to the love of God. St Bernard construed Abelard's rejection of the Devil's yoke as challenging the doctrine of the redemption. The wider context of his remarks suggests that Abelard was rejecting not the redemption as such, but a view of the redemption based on an anthropology that he did not accept.

Abelard never composed a systematic synthesis of his teaching in the manner of Hugh of St-Victor. Nonetheless, he integrated these ideas about God and the incarnation into his theological lectures, recorded in collections of his *sententie*, which brought together his thoughts about faith in God, the incarnation, the sacraments and ethics, subsumed under the theme of charity, in a sequence he had already laid out in his *Sic et Non*. (95) This collection of contrary quotations from the Fathers provided a manual by which students could formulate their own syntheses of Christian doctrine, by reflecting rationally on the legacy of Christian tradition. The sentence collection seen by William of St-Thierry included thoughts about the definition of sin he had developed in the *Ethica or Scito teipsum* in the late 1130s, perhaps prompted by discussion with Heloise. Instead of defining sin simply as an evil will, as he had done in the past, he qualified it as consent to an evil will, in contempt of God. (96) Sin was not a concrete action in itself. In the *Historia calamitatum* Abelard had assumed that his castration had been for the good as he had now been purged of the opportunity to sin. Heloise by contrast complained that she could not feel true remorse for her past behaviour, in which her intentions had been pure. The intense ethical concern in her letters is paralleled by the subject matter of various *Problemata* she addressed to Abelard. The last had direct personal relevance : she asked whether one could sin doing something ordained by God, a question Abelard understood to be about whether the injunction 'go forth and multiply' could be sinful.97 In the spirit of the *Sic et Non*, Abelard moved away from Jerome's strict condemnation of sex to explore more affirmative texts of Augustine about the *bonum nuptiale*. His ideas in the *Scito teipsum* are much more nuanced than those in response to Heloise, in which he is mostly discussing patristic testimony. They testify to his desire to integrate into his teaching a more sympathetic understanding of human nature than conventional in much ascetic tradition.

Bernard of Chartres and his school

Abelard is more visible to us as a personality than most of his contemporaries. Nonetheless he was far from unique in the value which he attached to the testimony of pagan writers. Some of the most celebrated of the Christian humanists of the twelfth century are those associated in one way or another with the school of Chartres Cathedral, most famously Bernard and Thierry of Chartres, William of Conches and Gilbert of Poitiers. The exact connection of all of these individuals to Chartres has been much debated. (98) What matters is that they formed a distinct intellectual tradition, which looked back to the teaching of Bernard of Chartres. In very different ways, they were all interested in integrating Aristotelian thought into a Platonic and Christian framework. Abelard focussed more single-mindedly on the implications of Aristotle's thought about language, distancing himself from talk about abstract forms. Enthusiasm for classical authors was not an innovation of the school of Chartres. The school of Rheims in the eleventh century boasted a tradition of study of classical authors that went back to Gerbert of Aurillac and beyond. The significance of these 'Chartrian' masters lay in their effort to effort to create a harmony from different intellectual traditions, Platonic, Aristotelian and, in the case of William of Conches, scientific.

John of Salisbury singled out Bernard of Chartres as 'the greatest font of learning in Gaul in recent times', 'the foremost Platonist of our time', a *grammaticus* endowed with uncommon skill in introducing students to Latin authors (99). Little is known about his life other than that he was a master at Chartres by 1112, its chancellor in 1124 and that he probably died around 1126. Bernard's impact seems to have been more that of a teacher who inspired reverence for the ancients than a major author in his own right. This sense of reverence to the past was encapsulated in his apothegm : 'We are dwarves sitting on the shoulders of giants ; we see more and farther than our predecessors, not because we have keener vision or greater height, but because we are lifted up and borne aloft on their gigantic stature.' (100). Inspired by Plato's *Timaeus* and the *De Trinitate* of Boethius, Bernard believed in a hierarchy of forms descending from ideas which existed eternally in God (although not co-eternally, like the three divine persons), to their images, native forms enmeshed in matter. Glosses on the *Timaeus* formulating these principles have plausibly been attributed to Bernard himself. (101) Bernard combined Platonism with an interest in Aristotelian categories. In discussion of *albedo, albet* and *album*, he relied on Aristotle's assertion that '*album* signifies only a quality' to argue that *album* signified a quality, corrupted as it were by the subject of whiteness, which it stood for. (102) Given the presence of the *Glosule* at Chartres in the early twelfth century, it is likely that Bernard was also influenced by its interpretation of Priscian's definition of a noun, while preserving a Platonizing emphasis about qualities as forms. John was guarded about Bernard's attempts to harmonise the thought of Aristotle and Plato in this way. (103)

William of Conches

Little is known about William of Conches' career other than that that he was Bernard's student at Chartres. (104) William was, however, a wide ranging thinker. He used the *Glosule* on Priscian extensively in his own commentary on the *Grammatical Institutes*. (105) Like the *Glosule* commentator, he was interested in establishing the causes behind the imposition of parts of speech. At the end of his *Philosophia mundi* (written in the 1120s), he explicitly criticised commentaries on Priscian for not assigning them systematically. (106) His interest in *causae inventionis* took him beyond grammar to the causes behind the composition of a text like the *Timaeus*, and indeed the causes behind the images which Plato used. (107) Plato in turn was investigating the causes behind the natural world. In some of his earliest glosses, on the *Consolation of Philosophy* of Boethius, William explicitly identified the Holy Spirit with the world soul, 'a natural vigor' in the universe. (108) Such claims were not unique to the school of Chartres. In the late eleventh century Manegold of Lautenbach had reproached a Rhineland abbot for reading too much into Macrobius.

Peter Abelard similarly questioned the literal identification of the world soul with the Holy Spirit both in the *Dialectica* and the *Theologia*. (109) In later writings, William became more guarded in his comments about the world soul, perhaps under Abelard's influence.

William differed from Abelard in being interested in physical as well as linguistic issues. His fascination with the *Timaeus*, inspired by Bernard of Chartres, provoked William to relate its contents to what *physici* said about substances. He made extensive use of the writings of Constantinus to reflect on the nature of the elements as the building blocks of nature and on the basic forces within the natural world. These scientific authors enabled William to understand the Genesis account as a presentation of the balance of the natural world, disturbed by disease and death. The *Dragmaticon* contained the most mature expression of this vision of the cosmos, first formulated in his *Philosophia mundi*. (110)

Thierry of Chartres

Thierry, identified by Otto of Freising as brother of Bernard, was a teacher of the same generation as William of Conches. (111) Again very little is known for certain about where Thierry taught before succeeding to Gilbert of Poitiers as chancellor at Chartres in 1141. Abelard descri-bes Thierry as present at Soissons in 1121 as an established *magister sco-larum*. In 1149 he embarked on a voyage to Frankfurt, with Gerland of Besançon and archbishop Albero of Trier. Like William, his interests embraced both the trivium and the quadrivium, the sciences of language and of nature. John of Salisbury implied that he was very learned in every subject, 'a very assiduous investigator of the arts', but confessed that he had not learnt a great deal from his lectures on rhetoric. (112) Thierry's range of learning is evident in the fifty odd texts which make up the *Heptateuchon*, a vast encyclopaedia of the seven liberal arts, prefaced with a reflection on the pursuit of philosophy as a union of the trivium and quadrivium. (113) These included scientific translations from the Arabic, as well as rare Boethian translations of the *Prior Analytics* and the *Sophistical Refutations*, texts which he was reportedly the first teacher to use. (114) Thierry was more knowledgeable about the Aristotelian tradi-tion than Abelard, who had cited the *Prior Analytics* only briefly in his *Dialectica* (according to Thierry's text) and once mentioned having seen a copy of the *Sophistical Refutations* in his *Logica 'Ingredientibus'*. (115) Ac-cording to a humorous anecdote recorded in the second half of the twelfth century, Abelard once tried to listen to Thierry lecture on mathematics, but became despondent at finding the subject hard to follow. This fits in with Abelard's admission in his *Dialectica* that he had listened without profit to lectures on Boethius' *Arithmetica*. (116) Although Thierry spoke up for Abelard at Soissons in 1121, there may have been subtle rivalry between the two men. The author of the *Metamorphosis Goliae* remembered his tongue as one 'which cut like a sword'. Thierry's acerbic criticisms in his commentary on Cicero's *De inventione* of both fawning admirers and jealous rivals suggests that his was not an easy personality.

Thierry's known literary output is much smaller than that of Abelard : apart from the commentaries on the *De inventione* and *Rhetorica ad Herennium*, we know only of a *Tractatus* on the first six days of creation and various commentaries on the *De Trinitate* of Boethius. (117) Like Abelard and William of Conches, Thierry sought to identify the common basis of philosophical and scriptural insight into the nature of the universe. He matched comments of Augustine to arguments about an ultimately ineffable cosmic divinity attributed to the older, and hence more venerable, authorities of Hermes Trismegistus and Denis the Areopagite. Thierry's understanding of God was shaped by a sense of the order and rationality of the universe, whose complexity was the result of the unfolding of a primal unity. Unlike Abelard, however, Thierry's metaphysical categories were profoundly influenced by the Boethian idea that all being emanated from form. Names existed in the divine mind, before being imposed by human beings. This was a Platonism which Abelard rejected. While Thierry did not believe in the eternity of the world (an accusation Abelard directs against one of two famous 'brothers' that he knew), he was fascinated by the idea of a primordial matter which subsequently received forms through the unfolding of a natural process. (118) He identified without qualification the spirit or world soul animating creation with the Holy Spirit and read the book of Genesis as a narrative of this physical process, so breaking with the traditional Augustinian emphasis on the moral and allegorical truths behind its text. (119) Thierry, like William, was more innovative than Abelard (who also wrote a commentary on the Hexaemeron) in understanding the physical process of creation.

Gilbert of Poitiers

Slightly more is known about the background of Gilbert of Poitiers, although again he is a figure who is much less visible than Peter Abelard.

Born around 1075, he studied liberal arts under a master Hilary at Poitiers, Bernard at Chartres, and then sacred scripture at Laon under Anselm and his brother Raoul, at about the same time as Abelard came into open competition with Anselm, around 1113-14. (120) After a spell in Poitiers, Gilbert became canon at Chartres, succeeding Bernard as chancellor in 1126. According to Everard of Ypres, he certainly taught at Chartres, although to only four students, compared to classes of three hundred in Paris. (121) In 1142 he became bishop of Poitiers, remaining there until his death in 1154. A disagreement with two of his archdeacons provoked accusations of heresy against Gilbert, unsuccessfully pressed by St Bernard at the council of Rheims in 1148. (122) Apart from still unpublished commentaries on the Psalms delivered at Laon in Anselm's presence (i.e. before 1117) and on the Pauline epistles, the only major writings we have of Gilbert are a collection of commentaries on the *Opuscula Sacra* of Boethius, composed at an unknown date. (123) Gilbert's teaching on dialectic is only known from a work emanating from his school. (124) John of Salisbury described him as unequalled in his knowledge of secular learning, as well as being fully conversant with the Fathers of the Church. (125)

Like Thierry of Chartres, Gilbert believed that the truths of orthodox Christian doctrine were fully consistent with the truths taught by secular philosophy. In choosing to structure his thought in the form of commentary upon the *Opuscula Sacra* rather than as an independent treatise, Gilbert avoided giving the impression of deliberate innovation. Nonetheless his commentaries were highly innovative, and extended the arguments of Boethius in a quite new direction. John commented appositely of his teaching that it 'seemed obscure to beginners, but all the more compendious and profound to advanced scholars'. (126) His genius, John observed, was to make use of every discipline as occasion demanded, while respecting the particular boundaries of each.

The central distinction Gilbert used in his theological analysis was that between that which is (*quod est*) and that by which something is (*quo est*). A man is a man by his humanity. Gilbert's distinction was one which Priscian had touched on more crudely in defining a noun as that which signified substance with quality. He followed the Aristotelian insight of the *Glosule* on Priscian, as interpreted by Bernard of Chartres, that a noun like 'man' strictly speaking signified a quality (i.e. humanity), while denoting a particular substance (a man) by imposition. (127) This defining quality was not so much a predicate of human imposition, as for the more rigorously Aristotelian Abelard, but a *subsistentia* actualised in a particular individual 'concreation' of matter and form. The *quo est* could not exist apart from a *quod est* except on a notional level. There were many different subsistent forms by which something came to be a single individual. The conformity of a form common to two individuals was of a different nature, however, from the *id quod est*. The universal was not a common essence in the manner that William of Champeaux held prior to his debate with Abelard. According to John of Salisbury, Gilbert expanded on Bernard's idea of universals as 'native forms', 'sensible in things perceptible by the senses, but insensible as conceived in the mind.' (128) Gilbert adapted typically Chartrian Platonic themes, transmitted through Chalcidius' translation of and commentary on the *Timaeus*, of *yle* as that first matter shaped by those forms or *ideas*, which in turn descended from a Creator. (129) The Platonism of Boethius also provided Gilbert with a framework for considering that all subsistents derived from form. (130)

Like Thierry, Gilbert was inspired by Boethius' argument in his *De Trinitate* that plurality in God was of a completely different nature from that in creation to emphasise the contrast between the plurality of forms in creation and the utter simplicity of God. However, where Thierry was interested in understanding the rationality of God from the creation which unfolded from the divine simplicity, Gilbert focussed more on the metaphysical structure of being, both material and spiritual. The distinction between *deus* and *divinitas*, which so alarmed his critics, did not imply any division within the divine nature. *Divinitas* was in the Father as essence was in that which truly is. (131) Gilbert's explanation of the doctrine of the Trinity hinged on recognition that what the Father, Son or Holy Spirit was as a distinct person, each with properties (like 'paternity' etc.), had to be distinguished from that 'divinity' which provided God with the quality of being God (132). The co-existence of two natures, human and divine, in Christ could similarly be understood by applying such distinctions. Whatever the problem, Gilbert insisted that heretical opinions about God or Christ flowed from faulty or inaccurate thinking. (133) A 'person' in the theological sense was certainly different from 'person' in a physical sense. Care had to be taken that the limits of each discipline were respected.

The complexity of Gilbert's thought was notorious even to contemporaries. His commentaries on the *Opuscula Sacra* represent only one application of his thought to a particular problem, rather than a complete synthesis of his philosophy. His commentaries on the Pauline Epistles, still unedited, reveal that in his understanding of faith, sin and grace, Gilbert was loyal to patristic tradition. Thus he taught that pagan philosophers could come to know God through creation as a result of grace, but that they selfishly rejected recognition of divine glory. (134) Faith was granted by divine grace. (135) Human beings grew in knowledge of God through the gift of the Holy Spirit. (136)

Gilbert used the language of Platonic forms to distinguish what was individual from what was universal. Abelard by contrast disapproved of the tendency of certain contemporaries, 'counted as true catholics, who have obtained the position of master through assiduous study of divine books', to distinguish properties like 'paternity', 'filiation' or 'procession' as separate things from God. (137) Ulger of Angers was just one such master who used Priscian's definition that a noun signified substance and quality to argue that a divine quality like justice or strength was a thing distinct from God. Abelard charged that this was an unnecessary reification of what Augustine and Boethius had taught to be relations. (138) Whether Gilbert was among those masters whose doctrine Abelard was criticising is not certain. In his commentaries on Boethius Gilbert never goes so far as to say that a *quo est* like divinity or paternity is a separate 'thing', but he did describe any such quality as a subsistent, distinct from the quod est it informed. Abelard resisted any tendency to impute reality to what was a predicate. His fidelity to Aristotle made him uncomfortable with notions of autonomous abstract forms. His report that some educated contemporaries described 'paternity' as a 'thing' may have been no more than a caricature to denigrate those who separated in Platonic fashion a quality from the substance it informed.

Disciples of Gilbert used use the term *res* to distinguish what was particular to a person. Otto of Freising, an enthusiastic admirer of his, defined as 'orthodox doctrine' (against Abelard) that three divine persons were three things, each separate with its own property. (139) Otto deliberately contrasted the orthodoxy of Gilbert, a loyal student of Anselm of Laon, with the arrogance of Peter Abelard, who 'incautiously' applied the teaching of Roscelin about *voces* to the doctrine of the Trinity. In Otto's eyes, Abelard's heresy was to deny the specificity of the three persons of the Trinity. Adhemar of St-Ruf defended Gilbert's theology by arguing that the three names, Father, Son and Holy Spirit, did not name a single thing, but each its own thing (*suam rem*) as subsisting individually (*singulariter subsistentem*). (140)

Whether or not Gilbert ever described subsistents as 'things', it is certain that his strategy for understanding individuality was very different to that Peter Abelard. Gilbert was the more detached analyst, faithful to the Platonizing tradition of Bernard of Chartres, while Abelard focussed on the more subjective process of predication to analyse both language itself and language about God. In very different ways, the commitment of both to seeking a harmony of secular and religious wisdom provoked the suspicion of St Bernard that each both used secular philosophy to undermine religious truth. Gilbert's more overt respect for tradition, however, made it more difficult for accusations of heresy to stick.

Adam of Balsham, Alberic and Robert of Melun

Not all masters taught both secular and religious subjects. The expanding student population of Paris in the second quarter of the twelfth century made it possible for masters to specialize in grammar, dialectic or theology. One such teacher, possibly deceased before John wrote his *Metalogicon*, was Adam of Balsham or *Parvipontanus*, an influential figure known for his innovative treatise of dialectic, the *Ars disserendi*, written in 1132. (141) Complaining of the incompleteness of so many textbooks on the subject, he set out to compose a treatise that was complete. It was the first to use both Aristotle's *Sophistical Refutations* and *Topics*. (142) He was able to correct a faulty reading in Thierry's rare copy of the *Refutations* (in the translation of Boethius). Although John of Salisbury admired Adam as a devoted student of Aristotle, he had some harsh words to say about the technicality of his presentation, implying that good things he had to say were obscured by excessive fidelity to detail. (143) Adam analysed different kinds of sophisms, explaining how they arose from using a similar term for different reasons. He claimed to provide a key for detecting sophistical arguments based on a strict theory of appellation, inspired by Aristotle, distinguishing words from the things for which they stand. The teacher from whom Adam drew his inspiration is not known. His theory of reference as a property of terms used within a proposition marks him out as an innovator within a tradition that looked back to Gerlandus of Besançon (the only author before Adam known to have used Aristotle's *Topics* in a textbook). (144)

Alberic was another master active in the 1130s and 1140s of whom little is known, except that he was a vigorous opponent of the *nominales*, a label not recorded in academic literature before the mid twelfth century. (145) There is little doubt that he used the term to refer pejoratively to the students of Peter Abelard, with whom the *sententia nominum* was particularly associated, replacing the earlier label of vocales, used of masters like Roscelin of Compiègne. The large number of surviving texts from Alberic's school on the Mont Sainte-Geneviève testify to his influence, as well confirm that he frequently criticised positions of Abelard. (146) The *Introductiones Montane Minores* from his school analysed weaknesses in Abelard's theory of conditionals. (147) A *Categories* commentary from his school maintained that Aristotle's predicaments referred both to terms and to things. (148) A criticism Alberic made of Abelard's comprehension of the *Sophistical Refutations* in a rare mention of the work in his gloss on the *Periermeneias* encapsulates the advance that the study of dialectic had made in the second quarter of the twelfth century. (149) When Abelard wrote that commentary, probably in the early 1120s, he had to rely on recollection of a text that he had once seen. By the 1130s, new texts of Aristotle were changing the agenda of logical debate. Abelard's achievement in dialectic, once so innovative, was now seeming out of a date to scholars more informed about the texts of Aristotle.

A teacher of both dialectic and theology whose thought deserves further exploration is Robert of Melun. He taught in Melun and Paris between the late 1130s and 1160, when he returned to England, becoming bishop of Hereford 1164-67. John of Salisbury, who studied under both Robert and Alberic on the Mont Ste Geneviève after Abelard's departure from Paris in 1137, characterised Robert as 'ever ready with answers', unlike the ever questioning Alberic. (150) The loyalty Robert commanded as a teacher of dialectic is witnessed by the fact that his students were known as *Meludinenses*, a distinct sect from the *Parvipontani* (followers of Adam), the *Porretani* (followers of Gilbert) and *Montani* (followers of Alberic ?). Robert argued against Gilbert at the council of Rheims in 1148. (151) Godfrey of St-Victor, reserved some mocking lines of his *Fons philosophiae* for them, describing them as the *turbae Robertinae*. (152) The major synthesis of the dialectic of this school is the *Ars Meliduna*, a treatise De Rijk has characterized as of 'outstanding importance' for our understanding of twelfth-century logic. (153) Continuing a theme of Abelard, it analyzes terms by emphasizing the primary role of appellation of a subject term as distinct from the signification of a predicate term, which could vary not in itself, but through differences in context. (154) Its teaching may have had an influence on terminist logic in the thirteenth century, but this is not certain.

Robert was certainly closer to Abelard in spirit than Alberic. In his theological sentences and commentary on Romans, he defended Abelard's understanding of the Trinity at length against the criticisms made of it by St Bernard. (155) In the prologue to his sentences he lamented the contemporary tendency for teachers to become famous for their knowledge of glosses on scripture rather than for their understanding of scripture itself. He warned against excessive reliance on the authority of the written word : 'For what is writing other than a kind of image and obscure figure of the will of the writer himself ? Neither does it represent only those things which are not just diverse, but other things sometimes completely contradictory, equally obviously or perhaps not a little more obviously.' (156) The danger was that a teacher could twist words to his own meaning rather than to the author's understanding. Robert's awareness of the dependence of language on context in these theological writings deserves to be compared to the semantic arguments of the *Ars Meliduna*. (157) Robert was not a pale imitator of Abelard. He differed on certain points of doctrine. Nonetheless, Robert shared with Abelard a conviction that gentile philosophers understood the Trinity, a perspective that Peter Lombard did not include in his book of sentences, and they also shared a common tendency to focus on the importance of sense rather than of words. Unlike Peter Lombard, Robert tended to allude to his authorities, rather than quote and discuss them in precise detail. Robert's books of sentences never became a canonical text in theology in the manner of Lombard's *Libri IV Sententiarum*. Nonetheless, they were of great originality in examining questions of meaning as applied to sacred doctrine.

Criticism of the schools

The growing enthusiasm for Aristotle in the first half of the twelfth century, in particular discussion about correct discourse, provoked criticism from those who felt that linguistic discussion left unanswered spiritual questions about the direction one should take with one's life. A good illustration of this fear is provided by an account of Goswin's decision to abandon academic life for the monastery. His biographer was relating an event which took place around 1110, not long after Goswin had dared dispute with Abelard on the Mont Sainte-Geneviève. It reveals that before Abelard had established himself as a major author, a grammatical commentary (the *Glosule* on Priscian ?) was being fêted as innovative in its content.

'At that time, a very famous grammarian had produced commentaries on the works of Priscian seized on everywhere by everyone as much for the depth of meanings as for the elegance of its diction, particularly because many people accept new things more, throw out old things for the sake of new things coming in, soak themselves in new things and preach novelty. Master Azo, most skilled and reputed of *physici* at the time recommended these commentaries to beloved Goswin, not as a whole, but in parts, so that he could send back a copied section and accept another to copy out. So that this task could be done more quickly, he asked his brother, who was speedy in his job and thus ready to follow his will. On a certain day, when he had written one quaternion and gave it to him, he [Goswin] said : "What use is it to gain eternity to know the rules of speaking correctly and not to keep the rule of living correctly ? Surely he who speaks skillfully and lives without direction, should be considered not skilled, but lost ? If Priscian holds the key to secular wisdom, are we not lost ? It shall not be asked by the supreme judge whether we have read Priscian, but if have kept to Christian behaviour." (158)

Goswin subsequently embraced the monastic life. As prior of St-Médard, Soissons, he adopted a friendly attitude to Abelard when he was detained there in 1121. (159) Throughout his life he preserved a strong interest in what was going on in the schools, building up a library at Anchin of the works of all the major figures of his day. (160)

Not all monks were as sympathatically inclined to intellectual developments in the schools. Bernard of Clairvaux (1090-1153) was the most articulate representative in the twelfth century of a tradition of thought suspicious of the pursuit of wisdom through secular learning, which claimed the authority of Augustine. (161) Professed a monk of Cîteaux in 1112, and ordained a priest as abbot of Clairvaux only three years later by William of Champeaux, Bernard never received more than a basic training in secular philosophy. His approach to opinions with which he disagreed was more that of an orator than that of an analyst. The framework of his thought was that of a reforming monk, imbued with an Augustinian pessimism about the frailties of human nature and man's need for grace. The monastic order provided the safest path to eternal salvation, when purified from the material luxuries by which it had grown fat. Bernard was quite innovative, however, in being interested in the psychology of the human soul. His guide was Augustine the spiritual writer rather than the dogmatic theologian. He was fascinated not by the structure of the universe, or the relative role of the sciences and theology, but by the process by which the individual came to understand and know the *Verbum*, the divine Word incarnate in Christ. His language was rooted in the cadences of the Latin Bible, as well as of Augustine and Gregory. Through the physical imagery of the Song of Songs, Bernard sought to describe the process by which soul encountered the Word and was transformed through love. Wisdom was arrived at through self-knowledge. In *On Loving God*, Bernard defined the stages of growth in the search for wisdom, from loving oneself to understanding the love of God. The intensity of his language appealed to those who felt that Aristotelian discourse had lost contact with psychological truth.

Bernard's friend, William of St-Thierry (c. 1075-1148), was also profoundly influenced by Augustine's Platonism, but in a more speculative fashion than Bernard of Clairvaux. (162) William developed Augustine's teaching about the process of spiritual purification, leading to the vision of God, as a process of participation in divine being through grace. While it has been suggested that William drew extensively on Greek Platonic tradition, notably through Origen and Gregory of Nyssa, many of his themes of restoration, image and likeness can be traced to a particularly close reading of Augustine. (163) William understood divine attributes, like charity and goodness, not as terms predicated of God by human imposition, but as eternal realities inseparable from God. The rational soul, created in the image of God may be only dimly aware of these realities, but it can return to God through recollection of its true nature. Like Bernard, he was interested in defining the stages of love from will, to love, to charity and then to wisdom. However, where Bernard followed Augustine in constructing his theology around the Word, William of St-Thierry focussed on illumination through participation in the Holy Spirit and the unity of spirit by which the soul was joined to God, and thus shared in the understanding of God.

William of St-Thierry, then a monk at St-Nicasius of Rheims, was present at the council of Soissons in 1121 when Abelard was asked to defend himself against charges of heresy by Alberic, master of the school of Rheims, but he was not directly involved in the trial. (164) The argument then was between rival *magistri*. By 1140, the situation had changed. The masters of Paris did not take an active role in the second condemnation of Abelard. Rather, the initiative for acting against Abelard came from William of St-Thierry, now a Cistercian abbot at Signy, in the diocese of Rheims. William was perturbed by the contents of Abelard's *Theologia* and a summary of his teaching on faith, the sacraments and charity, which reported essentially similar ideas. The treatise he sent to Bernard quoted from these two texts in considerable detail. William construed Abelard's theological definitions of faith, the Trinity, the redemption, the sacraments and ethics as giving too much weight to subjective definitions and too little to transcendent realities. (165) In his eyes Abelard's analogies implied diminution of the power of God the Son and elimination of the power of the Holy Spirit, by their stress on wisdom and goodness. William feared that Abelard's philosophical emphasis on the temporality of human speech about God challenged the eternal realities on which the Christian faith was founded.

Bernard of Clairvaux was largely dependent on William's critique of Abelard's theology when he wrote his own, more rhetorical and also more influential critique (Letter 190) to Pope Innocent II in 1140. (166) He presented Abelard as an arrogant upstart, a *theologus* (a word he never used in any other context) who claimed transcendent knowledge of divine mysteries that he did not understand. Bernard shared William's concern that Abelard enjoyed favour in some sections of the curia, most significantly Cardinal Guido di Castello, who personally owned copies of Abelard's writings and eventually succeeded Innocent II as Pope Celestine II in 1143-44. He painted an apocalyptic picture of schism within the Church provoked by arguments which seemed to question the omnipotence of God and the achievement of Christ's redemption. The fact that a popular preacher, Arnold of Brescia, notorious in Italy for his association with urban communes and for his criticism of the political power of the papacy, was aligning himself with Abelard in France, gave added reason for Bernard to fear that the existing ecclesiastical order was gravely threatened. By focussing on Abelard as the source of all danger, Bernard created the impression that he was unique among the masters of France in his arrogance and presumption. Because of his influence, the catholic faith, the Virgin birth, the eucharist, the Trinity were being debated 'through towns and market places' (Song of Songs 3,2). Abelard was an easy target. He was an outsider to France, politically tainted in Bernard's eyes by his past association with Stephen de Garlande. The scandal of his past private life undoubtedly made him easy prey for common rumour. Abelard became a scapegoat for all that Bernard considered wrong with the Church. Abelard was far from being the only teacher to apply an original philosophical framework to understand the language of religious belief. In fact the questioning of religious doctrines to which Bernard took exception was provoked by a far more complex set of factors than the inspiration of a single individual.

The School of St-Victor

More nuanced attitudes towards intellectual life in the schools were developed at the abbey of St-Victor, founded by William of Champeaux. Its regular canons maintained a public school not far from the schools of Notre-Dame, the Petit-Pont, and the abbey of Ste-Geneviève, while preserving the contemplative traditions of the monastic life. The most famous recruit to the abbey was Hugh, a canon from Saxony. Hugh, arrived at St-Victor with his uncle probably around 1115. (167) Over the next twenty-five years, Hugh transformed the abbey school into an innovative force in the teaching of theology. When he died in February 1141, Richard of Poitiers remembered Hugh with Peter Abelard as one of the two great luminaries of the Latin world. (168) In terms of survival of manuscripts, Hugh's influence far outstripped that of any of his contemporaries, with the possible exception of St Bernard.

The central theme of Hugh's teaching was that of the restoration of divine wisdom in the soul through the pursuit of both the liberal arts and the study of scripture. He opened his *Didascalicon*, a synthesis of his ideas on education written perhaps in the late 1120s, with an affirmation of faith that owed much to Platonic tradition as mediated by Augustine and Boethius : 'Of all things to be sought, the first is that wisdom in which the form of the perfect good stands fixed'. (169) Everything existed according to a divine model in the mind of God. Through meditation on creation and the sacraments, the mind can arrive at understanding of God. Like Augustine, Hugh focussed on the psychological significance of the pursuit of wisdom, ultimately achieved through the contemplation of truth revealed in divine scripture and through the practice of virtue. Hugh wanted to provide a framework with which students could place their studies within an overall structure. He warned against a contemporary trend to reject tradition for the sake of worldly knowledge : 'For the vice of an inflated ego attacks some men because they pay too much fond attention to their own knowledge, and when they seem to themselves to have become something, they think that others whom they do not even now can neither be nor become as great. So it is that in our days certain peddlars of trifles come fuming forth ; glorying in I know not what, they accuse our forefathers of simplicity and suppose that wisdom, having been born with themselves, with themselves will die. They say that the divine utterances have such a simple way of speaking that no one has to study them under masters, but can sufficiently penetrate to the hidden treasures of Truth by his own mental acumen.' (170) Hugh's comment may well allude directly to a suspicion of the bold claims of Abelard to be breaking with tradition.

Despite the influence of Augustine, Hugh parted from him on significant points. He adopted an Aristotelian analysis of wisdom as theoretical and practical, logical and mechanical, rather than the traditional Platonic classifications of Logica, Ethica and Physica. Logic was a *scientia sermocinalis* which embraced the three arts of the trivium, grammar, dialectic and rhetoric. The *Didascalicon* provides relatively scanty information about the secular texts to be read in Hugh's ideal curriculum. On grammar, he recommended the student to read Donatus, Servius,

Isidore's *Etymologies*, Priscian's *De accentibus, De duodecim versibus Vergilii* and *De barbarismo*. Significantly he does not mention the *Grammatical Institutes*. There is no influence of the famous *Glosule* on this text either here or in Hugh's *De grammatica*. (171) Hugh did not identify a single text of dialectic or rhetoric in his discussion of these arts, confining himself to a general account of their principles. He emphasised the importance of an appreciation of all seven liberal arts as essential to the study of philosophy, rather than specialisation in any one subject. (172) Unlike Augustine, Hugh wanted to find a place for practical skills – 'mechanical' (in the sense of practical) arts like fabric making, commerce or theatrics – within the framework of philosophy. All subjects, correctly understood in their context, provided a path to the love of wisdom. Whereas Augustine in his *De doctrina christiana* sought to select those subjects from a pagan education that could profit a Christian, Hugh placed a larger range of both practical as well as theoretical human activities within a universalizing framework. The price of such comprehensiveness was generality. Hugh did not depart from the psychological focus of Augustine's thought as radically as did some of his contemporaries. He did not enter directly the discussions of nomination and signification provoked by the *Glosule* on the *Grammatical Institutes* of Priscian. His teaching of the trivium and quadrivium was encyclopaedic without being specialised. (173) Hugh appealed to those who wanted to cope with the intellectual and practical concerns of a more optimistic society than Augustine knew without overtly breaking from tradition.

Hugh's most original reflections were directed to answering questions which arose from interpreting the text of sacred scripture. He undoubtedly helped transform the abbey of St-Victor into a leading centre of scholarship into the scriptural text, far outstripping the cathedral school of Laon. (174) Hugh synthesised his theological teaching within his *De sacramentis christianae fidei*. (175) Anselm of Laon and William of Champeaux had both presented their solutions to doctrinal questions raised by scripture within systematic collections of *sententie*, taken down perhaps by a student or an amanuensis from the master's teaching. In the *De Sacramentis*, Hugh did more than answer individual questions. He explored a central theme, that of God's progressive revelation to humankind within two categories, the *opus conditionis* and the *opus restaurationis*. The first book dealt with divine revelation prior to the incarnation, the second with the task of restoration through Christ and the sacraments of the Church. Whereas Augustine had focussed on the idea of an uncomfortable co-existence between two cities, which would be separated only at the end of time, Hugh concentrated on the legitimacy of the sacramental order which had been introduced into society, first through the Jews, and then through Christ and his Church. Everything in creation, in scripture and in the Church had a significance in the order of things. He gave primacy to the literal or historical sense of scripture, before moving to its allegorical meaning. Hugh extended the notion of the mystical body of Christ to refer not just to the eucharist, but to the Church itself. (176) Hugh did not argue from any written authority other than scripture. His synthesis was intended to be pleasing to reason. He incorporated Abelard's definition of the three divine persons as power, wisdom and benignity into his account, while questioning many of his more controversial arguments, such as his denial that God could do other than he did. (177) Hugh's philosophic vision was shaped by St Augustine, but with a more positive attitude to rational enquiry about the natural world. In his commentary on the *Celestial Hierarchy* Hugh sought to relate the ideas of pseudo-Denis about the spiritual life as the path of return to an ineffable divinity to more familiar Augustinian notions of sin and grace.

While Hugh's synthetic vision lacked the speculative subtlety of Gilbert of Poitiers or Peter Abelard, it exercised a profound influence on theology in the twelfth century. Perhaps the most significant pupil he influenced towards the end of his life was Peter Lombard, commended to Hugh's abbey by Bernard of Clairvaux. He had come there from a spell in Rheims, where Abelard's old antagonist, Alberic of Rheims had been teaching until 1136. He became a master of Notre Dame by 1145, testimony to the ever expanding influence of St-Victor within the Parisian Church. (178) After preparing commentaries on the Psalms and the Pauline Epistles which extended glosses initiated by Anselm of Laon, he embarked in the 1150s on his major work of synthesis, the *Libri IV Sententiarum*. He was much more careful than Hugh of St-Victor in presenting the specific patristic texts on which individual theological debates depended. Often he culled them directly from Abelard's *Theologia 'Scholarium'*, a text with which he was intimately familiar, according to John of Cornwall. (179) The Lombard's rigorously analytic theological method borrowed much in style from Abelard, although his conclusions often sided with those of Hugh of St-Victor. (180) Robert of Melun, who explicitly mocked 'the masters of the gloss', often criticised the Lombard's opinions on individual matters, such as Christology. Robert also alluded to both Hugh and Abelard as his mentors in the formulation of theological *sententie*, but tended to draw more closely to Abelard in the conclusions he drew. By comparison, the Lombard's synthesis was more faithful to Augustinian tradition, but it had the great merit of laying out very precisely the arguments and proof texts on every major theological issue under debate.

Bernard of Clairvaux lamented what seemed to be the loss of consensus in society about the definition of belief within its educated elite. In 1140 he blamed Abelard for stirring up dangerous questions about faith, in 1148 – with much less success – Gilbert of Poitiers. Yet masters in different schools had been constructing a wide variety of philosophical and theological syntheses in response to questions being put to them by their students ever since the late eleventh century. Augustine no longer provided the only intellectual structure by which individuals could interpret their world. Within urban schools, Aristotle often provided an exciting new avenue to rethinking the traditional definitions of grammar, dialectic

and theology. Some preferred to focus on texts like Plato's *Timaeus* to provide a vision of philosophy. Bernard of Clairvaux himself preferred to avoid academic writings, using instead holy scripture, above all the Song of Songs, to create for a wider audience a framework for understanding the search for wisdom.

By the mid twelfth century, the babble of competing voices within the schools of Paris only served to reinforce the arguments of critics of the educational system that it encouraged empty debate rather than the pursuit of wisdom. Monasteries still provided an outlet for those who preferred the path of meditation or who had completed their course of study in the schools. Otto of Freising and Everard of Ypres were two such students of Gilbert of Poitiers who became Cistercian monks after completing their studies, without renouncing any of their passion for intellectual enquiry. Many scholastic texts, including those of Abelard and Gilbert, were preserved in monastic libraries. They issued, however, from an educational environment divided by competing loyalties. John of Salisbury was just one former student of the schools who sought to steer an even path through the educational curriculum to demonstrate the true value of both grammar and dialectic. He closed his *Metalogicon* with a meditation on divine reason and truth. Augustine was his guide in spiritual matters, but he chose to conclude with a comment that effectively undermined every affirmative assertion of theology : 'No small part of our knowledge of God consists in knowing what he is not, as it is absolutely impossible to know what he is.' (181)

II

NOTES

(1) It is impossible here to give anything like a complete bibliographical survey on twelfth-century philosophy and theology. Classic essays of M.-D. Chenu were assembled in *La théologie au douzième siècle*, Paris, 1957, translated in part by J. Taylor and L.K. Little, *Nature, Man and Society in the Twelfth Century*, Chicago, 1968. Still useful is A.-M. Landry's French edition of A.M. Landgraf, *Introduction à l'histoire de la littérature théologique de la scolastique naissante*, Montreal-Paris, 1973. On philosophy, see *A History of Twelfth-Century Western Philosophy*, ed. P. Dronke, Cambridge, 1988, as well as individual chapters within *Renaissance and Renewal in the Twelfth Century*, ed. R.L. Benson and G. Constable, Oxford, 1982. The issue of *Vivarium*, 30.1, 1992 is devoted to twelfth-century nominalism. Recent literature relating to St Anselm (H. Kohlenberger), Peter Abelard (J. Jolivet and C.J. Mews) and the school of St Victor as well as some other twelfth-century figures (J. Châtillon and M. Lemoine) is reviewed in *Contemporary Philosophy. A new survey*, ed. G. Fløstad vol. 6/1, Dordrecht, 1990. There is also a useful survey of twelfth-century thought in A. de Libera, *La philosophie médiévale*, Paris, 1993, pp. 307-54.

(2) *De civitate Dei* VIII, 10 (CCSL 47, 227).

(3) Some of the intellectual consequences of the expansion of literacy in the eleventh and twelfth centuries are analysed by B. Stock, *The Implications of Literacy : written language and models of interpretation in the eleventh and twelfth centuries*, Princeton, 1983.

(4) Commentaries on Aristotle are studied by J. Marenbon, 'Medieval Latin Commentaries and Glosses on Aristotelian Texts, Before c. 1150 A.D., *Glosses and Commentaries on Aristotelian Logical Texts. The Syriac, Arabic and Latin Traditions*, ed. C. Burnett, Warburg Institute Surveys and Texts XXIII, London, 1993, pp. 77-127 (incorporating a working catalogue of Commentaries on the *Isagoge, Categories* and *De interpretatione*). On syntheses of dialectic, see L.M. De Rijk, *Logica Modernorum : a Contribution to the History of Early Terminist Logic*, II.1, Assen, 1967, pp. 127-76. Comparable syntheses of *Grammatica* and *Rhetorica* have been less studied. On the development of new scientific treatises, see G. Beaujouan on 'The Transformation of the Quadrivium' in *Renaissance and Renewal*, pp. 463-87. The growth of theological syntheses is studied by H. Cloes, 'La systématisation théologique pendant la première moitié du XIIᵉ siècle, *Ephemerides Theologicae Lovanienses*, 34, 1958, pp. 277-329.

(5) John of Salisbury, *Metalogicon II*, 16, ed. J.B. Hall, CCCM 98, Turnhout, 1991, p. 80.

(6) On the use of new Aristotle, see nn. 114, 115, 142 below.

(7) The translations of James are examined by L. Minio-Paluello, 'Iacobus Venetus grecus, Canonist and Translator of Aristotle', *Traditio*, 8, 1952, pp. 265-305, and 'Giacomo Veneto e l'Aristotelismo Latino', *Venezia e l'Oriente fra tardo Medioevo e Renascimento* rept. in his *Opuscula : The Latin Aristotle*, Amsterdam, 1972, pp. 189-228 and 565-86. On stylistic grounds, Minio-Paluello suggests that James also translated the *Physics*, the *De anima*, parts of the *Parva Naturalia*, and the *Metaphysica vetustissima* (only partially preserved). James may have come into contact with Byzantine scholars in 1136, in particular Michael of Ephesus (author of a commentary on the *Sophistical Refutations*), when he heard Anselm of Havelberg debate with Greek theologians in Constantinople. The patronage of Aristotelian scholars by Anna Comnena is documented by R. Browning, 'An unpublished funeral oration on Anna Comnena', *Aristotle Transformed. The ancient commentators and their influence*, ed. R. Sorabji, London, 1990, pp. 393-406 ; see too S. Ebbesen, 'Philoponus, 'Alexander' and the origins of medieval logic' on pp. 445-61 of the same volume.

(8) John describes contemporary enthusiasm for systematic treatises, and Abelard's cautious comments about their utility, in *Metalogicon III*, 4, ed. Hall, p. 116. John places grammar

and dialectic under the genus Logic (henceforward capitalised in this chapter to distinguish its broader sense) in I, 10, 13, ed. Hall, pp. 28, 32.

(9) *Fragments philosophiques. Philosophie scolastique*, Paris, 1836, 2nd ed. 1840, pp. 1-2 : 'L'université de Paris est au Moyen Age la grande école de l'Europe. Or, l'homme qui par ses qualités et par ses défauts, par la hardiesse de ses opinions, l'éclat de sa vie, la passion innée de la polémique et le plus rare talent d'enseignement, concourut le plus à accroître et à répandre le goût des études et ce mouvement intellectuel d'où est sortie au treizième siècle l'université de Paris, cet homme est Pierre Abélard. Ce nom est assurément un des noms les plus célèbres ; et la gloire n'a jamais tort : il ne s'agit que d'en retrouver les titres.'

(10) *Ibid.*, p. 3.

(11) Published incomplete within *Ouvrages inédits d'Abélard pour servir à l'histoire de la philosophie scolastique*, Paris, 1836, pp. 171-503 and 1-163 respectively.

(12) *Fragments philosophiques*, p. 5.

(13) On Cousin's Abelard, see M. de Gandillac, 'Sur quelques figures d'Abélard au temps du roi Louis-Philippe', *Abélard en son temps. Actes du colloque international organisé à l'occasion du 9ᵉ centenaire de la naissance de Pierre Abélard (14-19 mai 1979)*, ed. J. Jolivet, Paris, 1981, pp. 197-209, and on his antecedents, M. Lemoine, 'Un philosophe médiévale au temps des Lumières : Abélard avant Victor Cousin', *L'art des confins : Mélanges offerts à Maurice de Gandillac*, ed. A. Cazenave, J.-F. Lyotard, H. Gouhier, Paris, 1985, pp. 571-84.

(14) *Historia calamitatum [HC]*, ed. J. Monfrin, Paris, 1959.

(15) *Logica Modernorum : a Contribution to the History of Early Terminist Logic [LM]*, 2 vols. Assen, 1962, 1967.

(16) *Commentaries on Boethius by Thierry of Chartres and his School*, ed. N.M. Häring, PIMS Studies and Texts 20, Toronto, 1971 ; *The Commentaries on Boethius by Gilbert of Poitiers*, ed. N.M. Häring, PIMS Studies and Texts 13, Toronto, 1966.

(17) See n.104 below.

(18) On Honorius Augustodunensis, see the studies of V.I.J. Flint gathered in *Ideas in the Medieval West*, London, 1988.

(19) See his enormously influential *L'Amour des lettres et le désir de Dieu*, Paris, 1957, and many detailed studies gathered in *Receuil d'études sur S. Bernard et le texte de ses écrits*, 4 vols. (Storia e letteratura 92, 104, 114, 167), Rome, 1962, 1966, 1969, 1987.

(20) See for example J. van Engen, *Rupert of Deutz*, Berkeley, 1983, and on Hildegard, S. Flanagan, *Hildegard of Bingen : A Visionary Life*, London, 1989, and B. Newman, *Sister of Wisdom : St Hildegard's Theology of the Feminine*, Berkeley, 1987.

(21) D.P. Henry, *The De Grammatico of St Anselm. The Theory of Paronymy*, Notre-Dame, 1964 and *The Logic of St Anselm*, London, 1967.

(22) A full investigation of the 11th century schools is still needed ; cf. J.R. Williams, 'The Cathedral School of Rheims in the Eleventh Century', *Speculum*, 29, 1954, pp. 661-77, and P. Riché, *Ecoles et enseignement dans le Haut Moyen Age, Fin du Vᵉ -milieu du XIᵉ siècle*, 2e ed. Paris, 1989.

(23) P. Riché, *Gerbert d'Aurillac, le pape de l'an mil*, Paris, 1987.

(24) Richer, *Historiarum libri IIII*, ed. G. Waitz, Hannover, 1877, p. 101.

(25) A. van de Vyver, 'Les Etapes du développement philosophique du haut moyen âge', *Revue belge de philologie et d'histoire*, 8, 1929, pp. 425-53 must now be supplemented by J. Marenbon, "Medieval Latin Commentaries and Glosses on Aristotelian Texts, Before c. 1150 AD", *Glosses and Commentaries on Aristotelian Logical Texts*, pp. 77-127. See also the census of MSS assembled by O. Lewry, "Boethian Logic in the Medieval West", in *Boethius. His Life, Thought and Influence*, ed. M. Gibson, Oxford, 1981, pp. 90-134.

(26) F. Ravaisson edited the poem in *Rapports sur les bibliothèques des départements de l'Ouest*, Paris, 1841, pp. 404-6, reprinted in PL 151, 729-32 and by K. Strecker as an appendix to *Die Cambridger Lieder*, MGH, 3rd ed. Berlin, 1955, pp. 113-5.

(27) *PL* 151, 729 : 'Ad mensam philosophiae sitientes currite / Et saporis tripertiti septem rivos bibite / Uno fonte procedentes, non eodem tramite / Quem Pithagoras rimatus

excitavit phisicae / Inde Socrates et Plato honestarunt ethicae / Aristotiles loquaci despon-savit logicae.'

(28) *PL* 151, 731-2 : 'Prime sedis fundamento presidens grammatica / preter denas atque ternas partes <est> dividua, / in primis quinque pertita, per bis quaternaria. / Huic secunda sociatur civilis rethorica / et verbosa super omnes, partibus quinaria, / genera causarum tria cuius <sunt> materia. / Hec forenses lites sedat, causas agit, clamitat, / discernendo, recu-sando, defendendo iudicat / et quo vult leges retorquet, dicit, negat, implicat. / Cujus genere communis hinc est dialectica / Quae natura prior extat etiam grammatica ; / Dum cunctas ligat et solvit, pervideri nescia, / Hec diffinit et discernit, dividit et asserit / Ratiocinari po-tens, vincens invincibilis / Quam lampas clarificavit Manliani luminis. / Transtulit hanc re-solvendo binis Analeticis / Introducens Isagogas binis commentariis / Et idem Kategorias cum Perierminiis / Topica cum Sillogismis atque Differentiis / Diffinicionum librum cum Divisionibus / Explicavit, addens unum Propositionibus.'

(29) *Die Cambridger Lieder*, ed. Strecker no. 37, pp. 91. Strecker argued that the stanza is more likely to be excerpted from the longer poem than to be its original form. The first three stanzas also occur with a common variant in its opening line within the *Carmina burana* (s. XIII) and, with an additional line, within the Fulda MS, C 11, f. 329 (s. XV).

(30) Cf. Orderic Vitalis, *Ecclesiastical History*, ed. M. Chibnall, 6 vols., Oxford, 1972-80, 3, p. 164, 'gramaticae artis peritus' and pp. 168-70, 'in indagandis librorum abditis misteriis uehementer laborauit... maiorum scripta legebat. Commoda priscorum carpens documenta uirorum...' Orderic recalled Gerbert's secular and sacred learning in *EH* 1, p. 155. He implies that John was already a significant *scholasticus* when he left Rheims in 1077 (*EH* 3, pp. 118, 164), probably at the same time as Bruno of Cologne, following conflict with archbishop Manasses, cf. J.R. Williams, 'The Cathedral School of Rheims in the Eleventh Century', p. 669. Chibnall comments on the study of the liberal arts at St-Évroul in *EH* 1, pp. 15-23. The impact of John's teaching still needs to be studied from the many surviving MSS of St Évroul, recorded by G. Nortier, *Les Bibliothèques médiévales en Normandie*, Caen, 1966, pp. 98-123. Dom Bellaise (Paris, BN lat 13073 f. 53v-54v ; Chibnall, 1, p. 20 n.7) described a MS containing works of John of Rheims, including poetry, a history of St-Évroul, a theological anthology based on the Fathers, a treatise *De modo intelligendi, imo et tractandi s. scripturam et de tropis quae ibidem reperiuntur*, and excerpts from Virgil and other poets. The quality of gram-matical study at St-Évroul during John's time may be gleaned from discussion of relative categories added to the margin of the *Scalprum Prisciani* (e.g. Rouen, Bibl. mun. 1407, ff. 250-250v, 253v). Among the copies of Priscian recorded by Dom Bellaise is Paris, BN n.a.l. 1824, containing interlinear glosses and some marginal glosses to the prologue, book I, some on II and book VIII on the verb. Other twelfth-century patristic and theological miscellanies needing examination include Rouen, Bibl. mun. 661, 662, 665, 1407.

(31) *Narratio restaurationis abbatiae S. Martini Tornacensis*, ed. G. Waitz, Hannover, 1883, MGH.SS 14, 275 : 'Sciendum tamen de eodem magistro, quod eandem dialecticam non iuxta quosdam modernos in voce, sed more Boetii antiquorumque doctorum in re discipulis legebat. Unde et magister Rainbertus, qui eodem tempore in oppido Insulensi dialecticam clericis suis in voce legebat, sed et alii quam plures magistri ei non parum invidebant et detrahebant suasque lectiones ipsius meliores esse dicebant... [A deaf mute was then asked to judge who was the better teacher ; his reply was to criticise those...] qui nichil aliud querentes nisi ut dicantur sapientes, in Porphirii Aristotelisque libris magis volunt legi suam adinventitiam novitatem, quam Boetii ceterorumque antiquorum expositionem. Denique dominus Ansel-mus Cantuariensis archiepiscopus in libro quem fecit de *Verbi incarnatione* non dialecticos huiusmodi clericos, sed dialectice appellat hereticos : Qui nonnisi flatum, inquit, universales putant esse substantias, dicens eos de sapientium numero merito esse exsufflandos.'

(32) Roscelin mentions that he was 'raised and educated in the dioceses of Soissons and Rheims, *Epistola ad Abaelardum*, ed. J. Reiners, *Der Nominalismus in der Frühscholastik. Ein Bei-trag zur Geschichte der Universalienfrage im Mittelalter*, Beiträge zur Geschichte der Philosophie [und der Theologie] des Mittelalters Bd. 8.5, Münster, 1910, p. 65.

(33) Ep. 128 among the letters of Anselm, ed. Schmitt 3, 270-271 ; cf. Mews, 'Nominalism and Theology before Abaelard : New Light on Roscelin of Compiègne', *Vivarium*, 30.1, 1992, pp. 4-33, esp. p. 24 n.52. There is no evidence that Roscelin was a canon of Compiègne, his birthplace. In 1072 a Roscelin, precentor of Beauvais, and Nevelon of Compiègne, helped establish St-Vaast as a collegiate church in 1072 on behalf of Guido, the bishop of Beauvais who was ousted from his position by Lancelin, father of Fulco, St Anselm's protégé. The independence of St-Vaast from episcopal contral was reinforced in 1095, after Fulco was forced to resign the see in the face of widespread criticism of the behaviour of his family. According to a marginal addition in the St-Pierre martyrology (dated to around 1120 by F. Gasparri), a *Roscelinus grammaticus* bequeathed to the cathedral property and fourteen books of grammar, dialectic and theology (including a seventh-century uncial copy of Augustine's homilies on John), as well as a *troparium* – suggesting that this was Roscelin the precentor. Although Roscelin of Compiègne subsequently acquired canonries at Loches, Tours and Besançon, there is no record of his remaining until his death at St-Martin of Tours.

(34) *Historia Francica,* ed. M. Bouquet, *Recueil des historiens des Gaules et de la France,* 12, Paris, 1781, 3. This is probably more accurate than Otto of Freising's claim that Roscelin had established the *sententia vocum* in Logic, *Gesta Friderici I,* I, 48, ed. G. Waitz and B. von Simson, Hannover-Leipzig, 1912, p. 69.

(35) Anselm, *De incarnatione verbi,* ed. F.S. Schmitt, *Anselmi Opera Omnia,* 6 vols., Rome-Edinburgh, 1938-68, 2, 9.20-10.1, with the earlier version in 1, 285.4-6.

(36) Boethius, *Philosophiae Consolatio* V, 4, 27-37, ed. L. Bieler, CCSL 94, Turnhout, 1957, p. 97. The allusion is identified by J. Jolivet, 'Trois variations sur médiévales sur l'universel et l'individu : Roscelin, Abélard, Gilbert de la Porrée', *Revue de Métaphysique et de Morale,* 97, 1992, p. 125 (111-55).

(37) *De peccato originali, PL* 160, 1071-1102 ; cf. I.M. Resnick, 'Odo of Tournai on Original Sin', *Medieval Philosophy & Theology,* 1, 1991, pp. 18-38.

(38) Y. Iwakuma, "Vocales', or Early Nominalists', *Traditio,* 47, 1992, pp. 37-111, esp. 42-45, discussing the pseudo-Rabanus commentary, the commentaries in Munich, Clm 14458, ff. 83-93 and in Paris, BN lat. 17813, ff. 1-16v (Marenbon, 'Medieval Latin Commentaries', p. 19, P3, P16 and P14 respectively).

(39) According to an addition to the pseudo-Rabanus commentary, discussed by Iwakuma, pp. 43-44 (Paris, BN lat. 13368, f. 214) : 'Quorundam tamen sententia est Porphyrii intentionem fuisse in hoc opere non de quinque rebus, sed de quinque vocibus tractare, i.e. Porphyrium intendere naturam generis ostendere, generis dico in vocum designatione accepti. ... Non tamen genus in rerum designatione accipi posse negant.'

(40) Ed. L.M. de Rijk, *Garlandus Compotista, Dialectica,* First Edition of the Manuscripts with an *Introduction on the Life and Works of the Author and on the Contents of the Present Work,* Assen, 1959. Y. Iwakuma argues for the authorship of the later Gerland from a re-dating of Paris, BN lat. 6438 to the first half of the twelfth century, "Vocales', or Early Nominalists', pp. 47-54. Such dating also makes sense of Gerlandus' use of Aristotle's *Topics,* identified by I. Rosier, 'Note sur une surprenante citation des *Topiques* d'Aristote au XIᵉ siècle', *Bulletin de philosophie médiévale,* 28, 1986, pp. 178-84. As Roscelin was also a canon of Besançon, the possibility arises that he may have taught Gerlandus.

(41) M.M. Tweedale, 'Logic : to the time of Abelard', in *A History of Twelfth-Century Western Philosophy,* pp. 198-205. Certain common themes in the treatises on *Dialectica* of both Gerlandus and Abelard, such as the doctrine that the copula is part of the predicate, and that in *homo animal est, animal* was predicated principally, est secondarily (cf. Iwakuma, pp. 52-53) could be explained in terms of the common influence of Roscelin, rather than as consequent on Abelard being influenced by Gerlandus.

(42) *Epist. ad Abaelardum,* ed. Reiners, p. 72. For further discussion of this letter and of other texts attributable to Roscelin, see 'Nominalism and Theology' (n.33 above).

(43) *Epist. ad Abaelardum,* ed. Reiners, p. 76.

(44) The complete text of the *Glosule* was identified by M. Gibson in the 1488 Arrivabenus edition (reprinted several times until 1520) in 'The Collected Works of Priscian : the Printed Editions 1470-1859', *Studi Medievali*, ser. 3a 18, 1977, pp. 249-60. Its importance was first signalled by R.W. Hunt in 'Studies on Priscian in the Eleventh and Twelfth Centuries I', *Mediaeval and Renaissance Studies*, 1, 1941-43, 194-231, reprinted in his *Collected Papers on the History of Grammar in the Middle Ages*, Amsterdam, 1980, pp. 1-38 and subsequently by M. Gibson, 'The Early Scholastic 'Glosule' to Priscian, 'Institutiones Grammaticae' : the Text and its Influence', *Studi Medievali*, 20, 1979, pp. 235-54. I. Rosier, to whom I am grateful for seeing a draft, presents a critical edition of its discussion of *vox* in 'Le commentaire des *Glosulae* et des *Glosae* de Guillaume de Conches sur le chapitre *De Voce* des *Institutiones Grammaticae* de Priscien', *Cahiers de l'Institut du Moyen Age Grec et Latin de Copenhague*, 63, 1993, pp. 115-144.

(45) Possibly it came from St-Père. Although destroyed in 1944, a microfilm of the *Glosule* in the Chartres MS is preserved at the IRHT, Paris, but not the list of books sent from St-Évroul to another abbey, mentioned in Omont's 1889 catalogue. Artistic connections between St Évroul and St-Père at Chartres are noted by F. Avril, 'Notes sur quelques manuscrits bénédictins normands du XIe et du XIIe siècle', *Mélanges d'archéologie et d'histoire. Ecole française de Rome*, 77, 1965, p. 245 (209-48). I am indebted to P. Stirnemann for this reference. In 'The Early Scholastic 'Glosule' to Priscian', Gibson also notes one manuscript of the prologue (Brussels, Bibl. roy. 3920, fol. 12ra-vb ; s. xii[1]) which belonged in the 15th century to Nicholas of Cusa (d. 1464) and then to the church of St Nicholas, Cusa. Early twelfth-century copies also survive in Paris, BN nouv. acq. lat 1623, fols. 1-54v from Fleury, and Metz, Bibl, mun. 1224, fols. 1ra-110rb from the East of France.

(46) Cf. É. Jeauneau, 'Deux rédactions des gloses de Guillaume de Conches sur Priscien', *Recherches de théologie ancienne et médiévale*, 27, 1960, pp. 212-47 and K.M. Fredborg, "The dependence of Petrus Helias 'Summa super Priscianum' on William of Conches 'Glose super Priscianum'", *Cahiers de l'Institut du Moyen Age Grec et Latin de Copenhague*, 11, 1973, pp. 1-57. Fredborg discusses a treatise based on the *Glosule* in 'Tractatus glosarum Prisciani in MS Vat. lat. 1486', *Cahiers de l'Institut du Moyen Age Grec et Latin de Copenhague*, 21, 1977, pp. 21-44. Gibson notes its influence on other commentaries of the late eleventh or early twelfth century from across Europe – in England at the Augustinian house at Lanthony, Gloucestershire, and the Benedictine houses of Durham, St Augustine's Canterbury, and at St. Emmeram, Regensburg ; cf. 'The Early Scholastic 'Glosule'", pp. 242-6. The Durham Cathedral Library MS C.IV.29, fols. 2ra-136rb cites many individual masters : G., Anselmus, Stephanus, R., Guar., Menegaldus, A. and Guillelmus. See too Hunt, 'Studies on Priscian', 196-210. Masters G. and M. (sometimes MA and MANIG) are cited in the St Emmeram commentary (Munich, Clm 14459, fols. 1ra-48vbr). A leaf summarizing the preface of the Glosule is found within Manegold's commentary on Cicero's *De inventione* in Cologne, Dombibl. 197, fol. 20r-v. The Lanthony MS (London, Lambeth Palace Lib. 196, ff. 1-119v) contains glosses on Priscian influenced by the *Glosule*, as does the St Augustine's MS Cambridge Univ. Lib. Ii.2.1, fols. 3-126. Gibson also notes the influence of the Glosule on Priscian glosses in a manuscript from northern France (Vienna, Nationalbibl. lat. 220, fols. 1-150v) which carries a pledge note (fol. 151v) in money of Beauvais and in another (Vatican, Bibl. Apost. Vat. Reg. lat. 251, fol. 1r-v) from S. Benigne, Dijon.

(47) A similar reference to an author whose name meant 'by the grace of God' [i.e. John] is given as the rubric to the best manuscript of an influential *glosule* on the Pauline epistles in Paris, BN lat. 14442, carrying a dateable reference to 1101/2. Like the *Glosule* on Priscian it is very concerned with investigating the 'causes' behind words, in this case of St Paul ; cf. 'Nominalism and Theology', p. 14 n.29.

(48) For an overview of the Priscian tradition, see M. Gibson, 'Milestones in the Study of Priscian, circa 800-circa 1200', *Viator*, 23, 1992, pp. 17-33 and on speculative grammar in the late eleventh and twelfth centuries, the chapter of K.M. Fredborg in *A History of Twelfth-Century Western Philosophy*, pp. 177-95.

II

(49) This proemium was not included in the printed edition. *Glosule*, ed. Gibson, *Studi Medievali*, 20, 1979, p. 249 : 'Grammatice dico ad differentiam dialectice, que docet loqui secundum ueritatem et falsitatem, et rethorice, que docet loqui secundum ornatum uerborum et sententiarum. Quibus artibus prior est grammatica, quia prius scire oportet facere conuenientem coniunctionem dictionum quam ueritas uel falsitas uel ornatus eloquentie addiscatur.'

(50) *Ibid.*, p. 251.

(51) *Ibid.*, pp. 249-50 : 'Nec dubitandum quin *logice* supponatur, cuius est ipsa grammatica tercia pars. Logice alia pars est sermocinalis, alia disertiua. Disertiua partes habet inuentionem et iudicium, que solis dialecticis et rethoricis conueniunt. Sermocinalis uero grammaticorum est ; ac per eam ad logicam uelut ad suum genus grammatica reducitur.'

(52) In 'Nominalism and Theology', (n. 33 supra) I have argued that the author of the *Glosule* is the John who taught dialectic to be an *ars vocalis*. One possible John needing investigation is John of Rheims, a skilled grammarian according to Orderic, who left Rheims in 1076/77 for St-Évroul (n.30 above), with which the Chartres copy of *Glosule* had a connection. Place names mentioned in the *Glosule* include Rheims and Paris, suggesting that the Cologne MS travelled there from northern France. Bruno of Cologne returned for a while to his native city in 1077 after a political crisis in Rheims at the same time as John left for St-Évroul. Could this explain the presence of an early version of the *Glosule* in Cologne ?

(53) *Inst. Gram. I 2 K* [Cologne, Dombibliothek 201] 1rb-2va e [ed. Arrivabenus, Milan, 1502] 2v : '[Cuius auctores quanto iuniores [quanto perspicatiores]. Arguitur inquam scilicet a iunioribus. Et bene a iunioribus potuerunt redargui, quia sunt perspiciatiores, et vere sunt perspicatiores, quia et ingenio florent et diligentia id est arte valent, quia sicut fructus ex flore procedit, sic ex ingenio scientia. Ideo post floruisse addit diligentia studii valet, quia nihil prodest per ingenium florere, nisi studium faciat florem ad maturitatem venire. Et hoc, id est perspicatiores eos esse comprobatur omnium auctoritate. Non debet mirum videri si iuniores grammaticae artis dicuntur perspiciatiores in inventione : cum primus inventor per totam viam suam in quattuor forsitan litteris elaborasset inveniendis : iuniores in solo die poterunt eas addiscere, et post ex sua parte alias reperire. Ita per additionem successorum ad perfectionem ista ars increvit, sed postquam consummata est non arbitror iuniores esse perspicatiores.

(54) Priscian, *Inst. Gramm.* II, 4, 18, ed. H. Keil 1, p. 55. The significance of the *Glosule's* definition for the history of the theory of supposition was observed by De Rijk, who edits the passage in *LM* II, 1, p. 522-3 and further on p. 228 n.1 : 'Notandum est tamen quod nomen non significat substantiam et qualitatem insimul nuncupative, scilicet ita ut utriusque coniuncti sit nomen vel utriusque per se nomen sit, sed substantiam nominat tantum, quia ei fuit impositum, qualitatem vero significat non nuncupative, immo representando et determinando circa substantiam, propter quam tamen notandam substantiae fuit impositum. Quare omne nomen duas habet significationes : unam per impositionem in substantia, alteram per representationem in qualitate ipsius substantie, ut homo per impositionem significat rem Socratis et ceterorum hominum, id est nominando, determinans circa illa rationalitatem et mortalitatem et hec representando.' See too Mews, 'Nominalism and Theology', p. 37 nn.37-38.

(55) *Categoriae* 5, transl. Boethii, ed. L. Minio-Paluello, p. 5.

(56) *Glosule* VIII 101 K 41 e 123v, 'Res enim est causa uocis', quoted in 'Nominalism and Theology', p. 16 n.35.

(57) *Glosule* VIII 101 K 40vb e 123v, quoted in 'Nominalism and Theology', p. 15 n. 33.

(58) C.H. Kneepkens, 'Nominalism and Grammatical Theory in the Late Eleventh and Early Twelfth Centuries. An Explorative Study', *Vivarium*, 30.1, 1992, pp. 34-50, points out the role of theory of *nominatio* for discussion of universals, esp. pp. 46-49, without tracing a specific link between grammatical theory and nominalism although he does note its importance for both Abelard and William of Conches.

(59) See above n.21.

195

(60) *Monologion* c.79, ed. Schmitt, 1, p. 85.

(61) *Monologion*, Prol., ed. Schmitt, 1, p. 8, quoting Augustine, *De Trinitate* VII, 4, 7 (CCSL 50, 259) ; cf. *Ep. 77*, 3, pp. 199-200 and more explicitly Ep. 83, 3, pp. 207-8 to abbot Rainald of Séez in which uses the same passage of Augustine to refute criticism of his argument.

(62) *De inc. Verbi*, ed. Schmitt 2, 10.

(63) See above nn. 42, 61.

(64) The analysis of a *vox* as a sign of a thing is made in a gloss on Ps. 18 :4 *Non sunt loquelae, neque sermones quorum non audiantur voces eorum* attributed, with good reason, to Roscelin by Stegmüller (*Repertorium Biblicum* 7516) in : Paris, BN lat. 436, fols. 58v-59, Paris, BN lat 547, 62vb-63rb, Paris, Arsenal 83, fols. 65v-66, Troyes, Bib mun. 1507, fols. 88-88v : 'Notandum quod constructio ista quibusdam intransitiue facta videtur, quia *quorum* ad loquelas et ad sermones refertur, quae nihil aliud quam voces esse videntur, sed cum *loquelae* et *sermones* et *voces* in se contineant et ipsae voces sint signa rerum – aliud est enim vocem esse in natura sui, aliud signum, cum eadem vox sit et signum ; alioquin omnis vox significativa esset--cum, inquam, loquelae et sermones ex vocibus cum significatione constent, et minus mirandum esset scire quid voces significent quam habere scientiam proferendi et etiam proferre. Ipsi non solum sciunt quarum rerum voces signa sint, sed ipsas voces proferre sciunt et proferunt ita ut *audiantur* esse *eorum* et multorum testimonio id comprobari possit.' Cf. Jolivet, 'Trois variations sur l'universel et l'individu', p. 126.

(65) *HC* ll. 24-25 : 'Martis curie penitus abdicarem ut Minerve gremio educarer'. It is not clear if the statement about wandering through many provinces (ll. 28-30) refers to a period before going to Paris in 1100, or whether it summarizes the peripatetic nature of Abelard's studies prior to becoming established at Notre-Dame. The fact that Roscelin says he remained a pupil until being a *iuvenis* (normally at least twenty-one), suggests that the travels could refer to his subsequent studies within and outside the Ile-de-France.

(66) *Epist. ad Abaelardum*, ed. Reiners, p. 63. On Loches, and the church of the Counts of Anjou within its fortified site, see *Actes du Colloque Médiéval de Loches* (1973), Mémoires de la Société archéologique de Touraine t. IX, Tours, 1975.

(67) The first part of the anecdote about Abelard in the Munich MS Clm 14160 is of greater authority than the second part ; cf. Mews, 'In Search of a Name and its Significance : a Twelfth Century Anecdote about Thierry and Peter Abaelard', *Traditio*, 44, 1988, pp. 171-200.

(68) *HC* ll. 32-57 ; R.-H. Bautier, 'Paris au temps d'Abélard', *Abélard en son temps. Actes du colloque international organisé à l'occasion du 9e centenaire de la naissance de Pierre Abélard (14-19 mai 1979)*, Paris, 1981, pp. 21-77 and 'Les origines et les premiers développements de l'abbaye St-Victor de Paris', *L'abbaye parisienne de St-Victor au Moyen-Age*, Bibliotheca Victorina 1, Paris-Turnhout, 1991, p. 33 (23-52).

(69) Cf. J. Châtillon, 'De Guillaume de Champeaux à Thomas Gallus : chronique d'histoire littéraire et doctrinale de l'Ecole de Saint-Victor ; I, Guillaume de Champeaux et les origines de Saint-Victor', *Revue de Moyen Age Latin*, 8, 1952, pp. 141-6, and the studies of Bautier (n.68 above).

(70) *HC* ll. 85-91 ; cf. J. Jolivet, 'Données sur Guillaume de Champeaux dialecticien et théologien', *L'abbaye parisienne de Saint-Victor au Moyen Age*, pp. 235-51.

(71) Partially edited by De Rijk, *LM*, II.1, pp. 13046 from Vienna, VPL 2499. His identification of the treatise as reporting the teaching of William of Champeaux has been corroborated by Y. Iwakuma, to whom I am indebted for communicating drafts of forthcoming publications. He has discovered an essentially similar text (with some variant passages) in MS Escorial, e IV 24, described as *Introductiones dialecticae artis secundum magistrum G. paganellum*, edited in 'Introductiones dialecticae secundum Wilgelmum and secundum magistrum G. Paganellum : An Edition', *Cahiers de l'institut du moyen âge grec et latin*, 63, 1993, pp. 45-114. He discusses their content, noting subsequent forms of the genre in the *Introductiones Montanae minores, Abbreviatio Montana, Introductiones dialecticae Berolinenses, Introductiones Montanae maiores*, in 'William of Champeaux and the *Introductiones*', *Acts of the 10th European Symposium on Mediaeval*

Logic and Semantics, ed. H.A.G. Braakhuis and C.H. Kneepkens (forthcoming). Iwakuma has also suggested that the glosses on Porphyry in Paris, BN lat. 17813, f. 1-16v may be by William, because it espouses the argument that different things are one thing per *indifferentiam*, "Vocales', or Early Nominalists', p. 43 n.24 and 45 ; cf. Marenbon, 'Medieval Latin Commentaries', P14 and H3, pp. 106, 116.

(72) Ed. Iwakuma, 57 : 'Ars ista dialectica, quam Peripatetici loycen appellabant, propter discretionem veri et falsi inventa est. Quae non potest fieri nisi per voces. Et ita, dum tractant de voce, ut quidem grammatici et rhetorici tractant, sed diverso modo. Grammatici ut doceant casum cum casu construere, tempus et personam regere ; rhetorici docent ornate et acute loqui ; dialectici verum a falso per voces discernunt.' [73-4] : Aliquod dicendum ut competenter veniamus, trinum finem logicae breviter colligamus. Cuius tota intentio est agere de vocibus, sed hoc diversis finibus. Habet enim logica alium finem in grammatica, alium in rhetorica, alium in dialectica. In grammatica habet hunc finem ut reddat lectorem peritum loquendo grammatice, ita scil. ut casum cum casu, numerum cum numero, et alia quae pertinent ad ipsam artem sciat competenter adaptare. In rhetorica autem habet hunc, ut qui peritus fuerit rhetor sciat loqui persuasorie, ita scil. quod attentos sibi possit reddere audientes. In dialectica hunc finem dicitur habere ut qui dialecticus fuerit, veritatem a falsitate sciat discernere et ut audita aliqua re sciat eam probare categorice vel hypothetice, quae discretio veritatem et falsitatem vocibus et syllogismorum ratione firmissimam manifesta[n]t.'

(73) *Ibid.* 58-9 : 'Vox universalis dicitur, quae rem universalem significat, ut haec vox 'animal' ; haec enim 'animal' significat illam rem universalem, quae est substantia animata sensibilis, quae diffusa est in omnibus animalibus. Singularis vero vox dicitur, quae rem singularem significat, ut haec vox 'Socrates'.'

(74) *Metalogicon* III, 9, ed. Hall, p. 129.

(75) On William's teaching as reported in a Fleury manuscript, N.J. Green-Pedersen, 'William of Champeaux on Boetius' Topics according to Orléans Bibl. Mun. 266', *Cahiers de l'Institut du Moyen Age grec et latin*, 13, 1974, pp. 13-40 ; K.M. Fredborg, 'The Commentaries on Cicero's De inventione and Rhetorica ad Herennium by William of Champeaux', *ibid.*, 17, 1976, pp. 1-39 ;

(76) Cf. N.J. Green-Pedersen, 'The Doctrine of 'maxima propositio' and 'locus differentia' in Commentaries from the 12th Century on Boethius' Topics', *Studia Mediewistyczne*, 18, 1977, pp. 125-63 ; Tweedale, in *A History of Twelfth-Century Western Philosophy*, pp. 213-14.

(77) The dating of this work has been disputed. References in the prologues to tracts 2 and 4 refer to hostility to Abelard such as correspond to the difficulties he experienced in his early years at St Denis. Abelard could however have started the treatise before becoming a monk. I argue that the *Dialectica* precedes the *Logica 'Ingredientibus'* in 'On dating the works of Peter Abelard', *AHDLMA*, 52, 1985, pp. 73-134 and 'Aspects of the evolution of Peter Abaelard's thought on signification and predication', *Gilbert de Poitiers et ses contemporains. Aux origines de la Logica Modernorum*, ed. J. Jolivet and A. de Libera, Naples, 1987, pp. 15-41.

(78) Magister V. is identified with William of Champeaux rather than Ulger of Angers (as suggested by De Rijk), by Jolivet, *Arts du language*, p. 66 n.22 and 'Quelques données sur Guillaume de Champeaux', pp. 239-40, Fredborg, 'Tractatus Glosarum Prisciani', p. 34 n.77 and Iwakuma, 'William and the Introductiones', n.14, who notes the following references in the *Dialectica* as all about the same master : ed. De Rijk : pp. 105.16, 112.26, 123.29, 168.11, (169.25) ; *magister V.* 141.27 ; *magister noster W.* 541.32 ; *magister noster* 57.2, 59.6, 64.16, 67.5, 82.7, 116.5, 135.28, 136.19, 195.12 & 27, (200.7), 201.2, 271.38.

(79) *Dial.*, pp. 112-3.

(80) See n.73 above. The absence of any influence here or in the subsequent discussion of *nomen* of the *Glosule's* definition of a noun, argues against the suggestion that William might have been its author, made by L. Reilly, Petrus Helias, *Summa super Priscianum*, Toronto, 1993, 1, pp. 22-26 (publication of a 1978 D.Phil. thesis), and reiterated by Fredborg, *A History of Twelfth-Century Western Philosophy*, p. 178. Given the widespread influence of the *Glosule* by 1100 noted by Gibson, it may not be surprising if William eventually came to

accept some opinions of the *Glosule*. One would need to find a total coherence of perspective, however, to argue for William's authorship. Tweedale, in *A History of Twelfth-Century Western Philosophy*, p. 212 n.69, rejects Fredborg's suggestion ('Tractatus glosarum Prisciani', pp. 33-39) that the master W. or G. whose *Glosule*-related comments are appended to the Vatican treatise, is William of Champeaux, suggesting rather Guido d'Étampes. Cf.'Nominalism and Theology', p. 23 n.48.

(81) *Dial.*, p. 123.

(82) *Dial.*, p. 135.

(83) *Dial.*, p. 136.

(84) *Dial.*, p. 141-2, referring to certain *Glossule* on the *Periermeneias*. William does not use the infinite category when he discusses *non animal* and *non homo* in the *Introductiones dialecticae*, where he defines them as terms which signified 'animal' and 'man', but 'in a different way from *animal* and *homo*, because the latter signify these things (*ipsas res*) by placing, the former non-animal and non-man by removal', *LM* II.1, pp. 131-2. Cf. *Introductiones* ed. Iwakuma, 62 : 'Affirmativa enim est, si sic intelligatur : omne non animal est non homo, i.e. omnis illa res quae est non animal est illa res quae est non homo, ita quod per has voces *non animal* et *non homo* ponatur aliquid de rebus existentibus. Ut autem plus dicam, secundum hoc quod *non homo* ponit aliquam rem existentem, potest probari ex *omnis homo est animal omnis lapis est* modo supradicto.'

(85) *Super Topica Glossae*, ed. M. Dal Pra, *Scritti di Logica*, Florence, 1970, pp. 271-4.

(86) Abelard's theory of conditionals and the subsequent criticism it attracted are expounded by C.J. Martin in 'Embarrassing Arguments and Surprising Conclusions in the Development of the Theories of the Conditional in the Twelfth Century', *Gilbert de Poitiers et ses contemporains. Aux origines de la Logica Modernorum*, ed. J. Jolivet and A. de Libera, Naples, 1987, pp. 377-400 and 'The Logic of the *Nominales*, or, The Rise and Fall of Impossible *Positio*', *Vivarium*, 30.1, 1992, pp. 110-26.

(87) *Peter Abaelards Philosophische Schriften. 1. Die Logica 'Ingredientibus'*, ed. B. Geyer, BGPTMA, 21.1-3, pp. Münster 1919-27, of which the gloss on the *Periermeneias* is completed by L. Minio-Paluello, *Twelfth Century Logic, Texts and Studies II Abaelardiana Inedita*, Rome, 1958, pp. 3-108. From the large literature on Abelard's philosophy of language, we may single out J. Jolivet, *Arts du langage et théologie chez Abélard*, Paris, 1969, and many of his essays reprinted in *Aspects de la pensée médiévale : Abélard. Doctrines du langage*, Paris, 1987.

(88) *Logica 'Ingredientibus'*, ed. Geyer, p. 2. Marenbon traces the Boethian roots of this usage in 'Vocalism, Nominalism and the Commentaries on the *Categories* from the Earlier Twelfth Century', *Vivarium*, 30.1, 1992, pp. 51-61.

(89) *Logica 'Nostrorum petitioni sociorum'*, ed. B. Geyer, BGPTMA 21.4, Münster, 2nd ed. 1970, pp. 522-4. I argue that Abelard introduced related refinements of his thought in his *Grammatica* or 'reconsideration of the predicaments' (a revised version of the *liber partium* of the *Dialectica*), to which he refers in his *Theologia christiana*, 'Aspects of the evolution of Peter Abaelard's thought' (n.77 above).

(90) The *Theologia 'Summi boni'* and *Theologia 'Scholarium'* are edited by E.M. Buytaert and C.J. Mews, *Petri Abaelardi Opera Theologica III*, CCCM 13, Turnhout, 1987, the *Theologia christiana* by E.M. Buytaert, CCCM 12, Turnhout, 1969. Abelard only introduces the term *Theologia* as a title in *Tchr.* See too U. Niggli, ed. and trans., *Peter Abaelard. Theologia Summi boni. Tractatus de unitate et trinitate divina. Abhandlung über die göttliche Einheit und Dreieinigkeit*, Philosophische Band 395, Hamburg, 1988 and J. Jolivet, trans., *Du bien suprême*, Cahiers d'études médiévales 4, Montreal-Paris, 1978.

(91) *Theologia christiana* IV, 83, ed. Buytaert, p. 304. M. Clanchy emphasises this criticism of Anselm in 'Abelard's Mockery of St. Anselm', *Journal of Ecclesiastical History*, 41, 1990, pp. 1-23.

(92) Cf. Paris, BN lat 14442, f. 2 : 'Philosophi per celum et terram et quasdam alias creaturas quas magnas quas immensas ac perpetuas esse intellexerunt, ipsum conditorem incorporabile, magnum inmensum eternum esse mente conspexerunt. Qua cognitione simi-

les nobis erant, cognoscebant enim sicut nos que deus sit et quid non sit, quid autem sit a nemine comprehendi potest, et bene potest haberi cognitio de deo per creaturas.' On this commentary, attributed to a teacher 'whose name means grace of God' (i.e. John), see n.47 above.

(93) William's *sententie* are edited by O. Lottin, *Psychologie et morale au XIIe et XIIIe siècles* 5, Gembloux, 1959, pp. 190-227 ; see too no. 522 (p. 338-41).

(94) *Commentaria in Epistolam Pauli ad Romanos* (3 :26), ed. E.M. Buytaert, CCCM 11, Turnhout, 1969, pp. 114-18 ; cf. R.E. Weingart, *The Logic of Divine Love. A Critical Analysis of the Soteriology of Peter Abelard,* Oxford, 1970.

(95) S. Buzzetti, ed., *Sententie Petri Abelardi (Sententie Hermanni),* Florence, 1983 ; see my study 'The Sententie of Peter Abelard', *Recherches de théologie ancienne et médiévale,* 53, 1986, pp. 130-84.

(96) *Peter Abelard's Ethics,* ed. D.E. Luscombe, Oxford, 1971, pp. 14-16.

(97) *PL* 178, 723-30 ; see further C.J. Mews, 'Un lecteur de Jérôme au douzième siècle', *Jérôme entre l'Occident et l'Orient,* ed. Y.-M. Duval, Paris, 1988, pp. 431-44.

(98) For discussion of the debate surrounding the school of Chartres, see J. Verger on pp. 00-00 of this volume.

(99) *Metalogicon* I, 24, ed. Hall, p. 52 : 'exundatissimus modernis temporibus fons litterarum in Gallia' ; cf. IV, 35, p. 173 : 'perfectissimus inter Platonicos saeculi nostri'.

(100) *Metalogicon* III, 4, ed. Hall, p. 116 ; also cited by William of Conches, 'Deux rédactions des gloses de Guillaume de Conches sur Priscien', p. 235.

(101) *The « Glosae super Platonem » of Bernard of Chartres,* ed. P.E. Dutton, Toronto, 1991.

(102) *Metalogicon* III, 2, ed. Hall, pp. 106-7. ; J. Jolivet observes the close connection between Bernard's grammatical theory and Platonism within 'Eléments pour une étude des rapport entre la grammaire et l'ontologie au moyen age', reprinted in *Aspects de la pensée médiévale,* pp. 204-8.

(103) *Metalogicon* II, 17 and III, 2, ed. Hall, pp. 83, 107.

(104) On William of Conches, a valuable and full bibliographical survey is given by É. Jeauneau in *Dictionnaire des Lettres Françaises. Le Moyen Age,* Paris, 1992, pp. 610-12. His earlier studies are collected in *« Lectio philosophorum » : Recherches sur l'École de Chartres,* Amsterdam, 1973.

(105) É. Jeauneau, 'Deux rédactions des gloses de Guillaume de Conches sur Priscien', *Recherches de theologie ancienne et médiévale* 27, 1960, pp. 212-47 ; cf. De Rijk, *LM* II, 1, pp. 221-8. The revised version from the 1140s also covered Books XVII-XVIII on syntax.

(106) Fragment edited by Jeauneau, *art. cit.,* p. 218.

(107) *Glosae super Platonem,* ed. É. Jeauneau, Paris, 1965, p. 58.

(108) See the texts cited by Jeauneau in his note (c) to *Glossae in Timaeum* 34B, p. 145 : 'Hunc spiritum dicunt quidam esse Spiritum Sanctum, quod nec negamus.' Cf. T. Gregory, *Anima mundi. La filosofia di Gugliemo di Conches e la scuola di Chartres,* Florence, 1955.

(109) *Dial.,* pp. 558-9 ; cf. *TSum* I, 56, ed. Buytaert-Mews, p. 106.

(110) Full bibliographical details on William's scientific background are given by D. Elford in her chapter on William in *A History of Twelfth-Century Western Philosophy,* pp. 308-27.

(111) Biographical details about Thierry are assembled by K.M. Fredborg's introduction to her edition of *The Latin Rhetorical Commentaries by Thierry of Chartres,* Toronto, 1988.

(112) *Metalogicon,* I, 5 and II, 10, ed. Hall, pp. 20, 72 ; cf. IV, 24, p. 162.

(113) É. Jeauneau, 'Le Prologus in Eptateuchon de Thierry de Chartres', *Mediaeval Studies,* 16, 1954, pp. 1-12, reprinted in *Lectio Philosophorum,* Amsterdam, 1973, pp. 37-39, 87-91.

(114) A. Vernet, 'Une épitaphe inédite de Thierry de Chartres', *Mélanges Clovis Brunel,* t. 1, Paris, 1955, pp. 660-70, reprinted in *Etudes médiévales,* Paris, 1981, pp. 160-70 ; cf. S. Ebbesen, 'Medieval Latin Glosses and Commentaries on Aristotelian Logical Texts of the Twelfth and Thirteenth Centuries', *Glosses and Commentaries on Aristotelian Logical Texts,* pp. 149-50 and (on the *Prior Analytics*), 'Analyzing Syllogisms or Anonymus Aurelianensis III –

II

The (Presumably) Earliest Extant Latin Commentary on the Prior Analytics, and Its Greek Model', *Cahiers de l'Institut du moyen âge grec et latin*, 37, 1981, pp. 1-20.

(115) Abelard alludes to the *Prior Analytics* for the definition of a syllogism and, inaccurately, on certain modal propositions (ed. De Rijk, p. 232, 233, 245) ; cf. L. Minio-Paluello, 'I « Primi Analytici » : la redazione carnutense usata da Abelardo e la « Vulgata » con scolii tradotti dal greco', *Opuscula : The Latin Aristotle*, pp. 229-41. Abelard similarly refers loosely to the *Sophistical Refutations* in his gloss on the *Periermeneias*, ed. Geyer, p. 400 ; see too p. 489 (= ed. Minio-Paluello, *Twelfth Century Logic* II, p. 13). However, when distinguishing dialectical from sophistical reasoning in *Epist. XIII* (written in the early 1130s ?), ed. E.R. Smits, *Peter Abelard. Letters IX-XIV*, Groningen, 1983, p. 273, Abelard singled out the *Sophistical Refutations* as his authority.

(116) The first part of the anecdote about Thierry and Abaelardus is more accurate in this respect than the second part, based on a confusion with the name of Adelard of Bath, 'In Search of a Name and its Significance : a Twelfth Century Anecdote about Thierry and Peter Abaelard', *Traditio*, 44, 1988, pp. 171-200 ; cf. *Dial.*, p. 59.

(117) See above n.16 and 111. For what follows, I am indebted to the chapter on Thierry by P. Dronke within his *A History of Twelfth-Century Western Philosophy*. S. Gersh discusses the *Commentum or Librum hunc* on Boethius, attributed to Thierry's pupil, Petrus Helyas in one MS, in 'Platonism – Neoplatonism – Aristotelianism. A Twelfth-Century Metaphysical System and Its Sources', in *Renaissance and Renewal*, pp. 512-34.

(118) *Tchr* IV, 80, ed. Buytaert, p. 302.

(119) *Tractatus* 26-27, in *Commentaries on Boethius by Thierry of Chartres*, ed. Häring, pp. 566-7.

(120) Otto of Freising, *Gesta Friderici* I, 53, p. 236. On Hilary and the educational tradition of Poitiers, see N.M. Häring, 'Zur Geschichte der Schulen von Poitiers', *Archiv für Kultur-Geschichte*, 47, 1965, pp. 23-47. On Gilbert, see Marenbon's chapter in *A History of Twelfth-Century Western Philosophy*, several papers in *Gilbert de Poitiers et ses contemporains. Aux origines de la Logica Modernorum*, ed. J. Jolivet and A. de Libera, Naples, 1987, the comparative study of Jolivet, 'Trois variations sur l'universel et l'individu' (n.36 above), H.C. Van Elswijk, *Gilbert Porreta. Sa vie, son oeuvre, sa pensée*, Louvain, 1966, B. Maioli, *Gilberto Porretano. Dalla grammatica speculativa alla metafisica del concreto*, Rome, 1979, and L.O. Nielsen, *Theology and Philosophy in the Twelfth Century. A Study of Gilbert Porreta's Thinking and the Theological Expositions of the Doctrine of the Incarnation during the Period 1130-1180*, Leiden, 1982.

(121) Ed. Häring, 'A Latin Dialogue on the Doctrine of Gilbert of Poitiers', *Mediaeval Studies*, 15, 1953, p. 252 (243-89).

(122) John of Salisbury, *Historia Pontificalis*, ed. M. Chibnall, 2nd ed. Oxford, 1986, pp. 15-41 ; Otto of Freising, *Gesta Friderici* I, 49, pp. 222-5 ; cf. Nielsen, pp. 30-39.

(123) See n.16 above. Two works of his school are edited by Häring as 'Die Sententie magistri Gisleberti Pictavensis episcopi', *AHDLMA*, 45, 1978, pp. 83-180 and *AHDLMA*, 46, 1979, pp. 45-105.

(124) S. Ebbesen, K.M. Fredborg, L.O. Nielsen, 'Compendium Logicae Porretanum ex Codice Oxoniensi Collegii Corporis Christi 250 : A Manual of Porretan Doctrine by a Pupil of Gilbert's', *Cahiers de l'Institut du Moyen Age Grec et Latin*, 46, 1983, pp. 1-113.

(125) *Historia Pontificalis*, ed. Chibnall, p. 27.

(126) *Historia Pontificalis*, ed. Chibnall, p. 27.

(127) *Commentaries*, ed. Häring, p. 302, 73 : 'Hec enim est sola ratio qua cuiuslibet nomnis appellatio naturaliter est communis : si uidelicet qualitas – secundum quam est nomen – illis, quorum est nomen, tota forme substantia est communis : ut homo uel album ; cf. p. 163, 2-4 : QUERO AN PATER ET FILIUS ET SPIRITUS SANCTUS, i.e. horum nominum illa significata que diuersis rationibus grammatici 'qualitates', dialectici 'cathegorias', hoc est predicamenta uocant.' Cf. *Compendium Logicae Porretanum* I, 11, p. 6.

(128) *Metalogicon* II, 17, ed. Hall, p. 83.

(129) *Commentaries*, ed. Häring, p. 85, 97-100.

(130) *Ibid.*, p. 88, 76-79.

(131) *Ibid.*, p. 99, 4-5.

(132) *Ibid.*, p. 147, 41-48.

(133) *Ibid.*, pp. 58, 40-62, 30.

(134) Nielsen, p. 129-30 nn.41-43, quoting from Gilbert's Commentary on Romans 1 :19-20. Gilbert's understanding on natural knowledge of God lays more emphasis on philosophers' blindness than that in Paris, BN lat. 14442, quoted in n.92 above.

(135) Nielsen, p. 117.

(136) Nielsen, pp. 120-8.

(137) *Tchr* III, 166-70, ed. Buytaert, p. 301.

(138) *Tchr* IV, 77, 154-8, ed. Buytaert , p. 301, 342-4.

(139) *Gesta Friderici I*, I, 48, p. 69.

(140) A. Dondaine, *Ecrits de la « petite école porrétaine »*, Montreal-Paris, 1962, pp. 28-29, quoted by Jolivet, 'Trois variations médiévales sur l'universel et l'individu', p. 154.

(141) Cf. L. Minio-Paluello, 'Adam of Balsham and his Ars Disserendi', *Mediaeval and Renaissance Studies*, 3, 1953, pp. 116-69 and his edition of this work in *Twelfth Century Logic I*, Rome, 1956 ; see too De Rijk, *LM* 1, pp. 62-81 and 2, pp. 206-9. Minio-Paluello thinks that John's references to him imply that he had died before 1159.

(142) The *Topics* were used by Gerlandus of Besançon in the early twelfth century (see n.40 above) and are otherwise first known in the West through an early twelfth-century MS (Oxford, Trinity College 47) and Thierry's *Heptateuchon*, compiled before 1140 ; cf. L. Minio-Paluello, 'The Text of Aristotle's *Topics* and *Sophistici Elenchi*', *The Classical Quarterly* N.S. V, 49, 1955, 108-18, reprinted in *Opuscula : The Latin Aristotle*, Amsterdam, 1972, pp. 299-309.

(143) *Metalogicon* IV, 3, ed. Hall, p. 142 ; cf. II, 10, p. 72 and III, 3, p. 114.

(144) Abelard refers to an unidentified work of his on fallacies, the *Liber fantasiarum* in his *Dialectica*, p. 448, that could have provided a stimulus. The important *Fallacie Parvipontane* from the school of Adam occur in the same twelfth-century MS (Munich, Clm 4643) as contains the letter of Roscelin to Abelard ; ed. De Rijk, LM 1, pp. 134-52, 551-609.

(145) *Metalogicon* II, 10, ed. Hall, p. 71. All uses of the term *nominales* are recorded in the list of Iwakuma and Ebbesen (n.152 below) ; none can be verified as having been used before 1150.

(146) L.M. De Rijk, 'Some New Evidence on Twelfth Century Logic : Alberic and the School of Mont Ste Geneviève (*Montani*)', *Vivarium*, 4, 1966, pp. 1-57.

(147) Ed. De Rijk, LM 2, 2, pp. 11-71 ; see the studies of C.J. Martin, n.86 above. Iwakuma (cf. n.71 above) notes that this work follows the structure of the *Introductiones dialecticae* of William of Champeaux, a possible influence on Alberic. Another text from Alberic's school is the *Abbreviatio Montana*, ed De Rijk, *LM* 2, 2, pp. 77-107.

(148) F. Bottin, 'Quelques discussions sur la transitivité de la prédication dans l'école d'Alberic du Mont', *Gilbert de Poitiers et ses contemporains*, pp. 57-72.

(149) *LM* I, pp. 60, 620.

(150) *Metalogicon* II, 10, ed. Hall, p. 71. John explains that 'of Melun' was a cognomen used in the schools, although Robert was English by birth. Presumably he taught at both Melun and the Mont Ste-Geneviève, both incidentally centres of royal influence where Abelard taught at different times.

(151) *Historia pontificalis*, ed. Chibnall, p. 16.

(152) The references of Geoffrey and of all other known texts to groups of students are usefully presented by Y. Iwakuma and S. Ebbesen, 'Logico-Theological Schools from the Second Half of the Twelfth Century : A List of Sources', *Vivarium*, 30.1, 1992, pp. 173-210. Godfrey's text is translated and presented by E.A. Synan, *The Fountain of Philosophy*, Toronto, 1972.

(153) Studied and edited in part by De Rijk, *LM* 2, 1, pp. 76-77, 264-390.

(154) Cf. the complementary papers of H.A.G. Braakhuis, 'Signification, Appellation and

Predication in the *Ars Meliduna'* and of Joël Biard, 'Sémantique et ontologie dans l'*Ars Meliduna', Gilbert de Poitiers et ses contemporains,* pp. 107-20 and 121-44.

(155) R.M. Martin, 'Pro Petro Abaelardo. Un plaidoyer de Robert de Melun contre saint Bernard', *Revue des sciences philosophiques et théologiques,* 12, 1923, pp. 308-33 ; cf. *Œuvres de Robert de Melun,* ed. R.M. Martin, 4 vols. 13, 18, 21, 25, Louvain, 1932-52.

(156) *Sententiae,* Praef., ed. Martin, *Œuvres* 2, 47-8.

(157) Paradoxically, De Rijk's pioneering study of the *Ars Meliduna* makes no reference to Robert's theological output. D.E. Luscombe does not mention the *Ars Meliduna* in his chapter on Robert in *The School of Peter Abelard,* Cambridge, 1969. A detailed comparison might establish whether the *Ars Meliduna* is in fact a treatise of Robert, whose name is cited in some extra notes by way of example (*LM* 2, 1, p. 77).

(158) *Vita Goswini,* ed. Bouquet, *Recueil* 14, 1877, p. 444 : 'Eo temporis, grammaticus quidam famosissimus commenta quaedam exaraverat super opera Prisciani, quae passim ab omnibus raptabantur, tam pro altitudine sensuum quam pro eloquii venustate, maxime quod plerique nova plus acceptant, novis supervenientibus vetera projiciunt, novis insudant, praedicant novitatem. Haec commenta magister Azo, peritissimus et opinatissimus illius temporis physicorum, unice dilecto commodaverat Gosvino, non ex integro sed par partes, ut cum remitteret partem transcriptam, aliam acciperet transcribendam. Quod opus ut celeriter expleretur, fratri suo injunxerat, eo quod in opere suo velox esset, et ita promptus ad imperium eius suscipiendum. Die vero quadam, cum quaternionem unum perscripsisset et ei porrexisset, ait ille : 'Quid proficit ad aeternitatem promerendam recte loquendi regulas scire, et recte vivendi regulam non tenere ? Numquid qui perite loquitur et perdite vivit, haberi non debet pro perito, sed pro perituro ? Si Priscianus clavem tenet scientiae saecularis, non desertores [sumus ?], nec a judice summo requiretur utrum legerimus Priscianum, sed si morem tenuerimus christianum'. Deposita igitur rerum sarcinam mundanarum, suscepit jugum domini suave et onus leve et una cum germano suo Bernardo ad aratrum Domini obedientiae loris adstrictus, paratus fuit deinceps subsequendi quocumque se voluntas rectoris inclinasset, habens obsequendi quidem scientiam, sed ignorantiam culcitrandi.'

(159) *Ibid.* 14, p. 445 ; cf. *HC* ll. 910-13.

(160) Besides having copied the complete works of Peter the Venerable and Bernard of Clairvaux, he may also have collected MSS of Abelard in 1142 ; cf. my introduction to Abelard's *Theologia 'Scholarium',* CCCM 13, pp. 254-6.

(161) Recent studies are gathered in *Bernard de Clairvaux : histoire, mentalités, spiritualité : colloque de Lyon-Cîteaux-Dijon,* Sources chrétiennes 380, Paris, 1992 ; see too n.19 above.

(162) A survey of William's life, with full bibliography, is provided by P. Verdeyen in the introduction to his edition of William's *Expositio super Epistolam ad Romanos,* CCCM 86, Turnhout, 1989, pp. v-li.

(163) The Augustinian roots are emphasised by D.N. Bell, *The Image and Likeness. The Augustinian Spirituality of William of Saint-Thierry,* Kalamazoo, 1984, questioning some of the assumptions of J.M. Dechanet recapitulated in *Guillaume de saint-Thierry, aux source d'une pensée,* Paris, 1978.

(164) A detail pointed out by J. Benton, 'Fraud, Fiction and Borrowing in the Correspondence of Abelard and Heloise', *Pierre Abelard. Pierre le Vénérable. Les courants philosophiques, littéraires et artistiques en occident au milieu du XII' siècle,* Paris, 1975, p. 486 n.41.

(165) J. Jolivet, 'Sur quelques critiques de la théologie d'Abélard', *AHDLMA,* 30, 1963, pp. 7-51, reprinted in *Aspects,* pp. 7-51.

(166) On Bernard's involvement in the affair, see my 'The lists of heresies imputed to Peter Abelard', *Revue Bénédictine,* 95, 1985, pp. 73-110.

(167) Details of Hugh's life and thought are given by P. Sicard, *Hugues de Saint-Victor et son École,* Turnhout, 1991. Sicard notes (p. 45 n.101) that his commonly assigned date of birth (c.1100) is based on no more than supposition.

(168) *Chronicon,* ed. Bouquet, *Receuil* 12, p. 415 ; MGH.ss XXVI, 81.

(169) *Didascalicon* I, 1, translated with useful notes by J. Taylor, *The Didascalicon of Hugh of St Victor*, New York, 1961, pp. 175-6.

(170) *Didascalicon* III, 13, trans. Taylor p. 96.

(171) *Didascalicon* II, 29, trans. Taylor, p. 80 ; cf. *Hugonis de Sancto Victore Opera Praedeutica*, ed. R. Baron, Publications in Mediaeval Studies. The University of Notre Dame XX, Notre-Dame, 1966, pp. 66-163.

(172) *Didascalicon* III, 4, trans. Taylor, p. 89.

(173) Hugh's *Practica Geometriae* is edited by Baron in *Opera Propedeutica*, pp. 3-64 ; see too *La Descriptio mappe mundi de Hugues de Saint-Victor*, ed. P. Gautier-Dalché, Paris, 1988.

(174) See the study of Stirnemann in this volume.

(175) *PL* 176, 173-618.

(176) Sicard, *Hugues de Saint-Victor*, pp. 115-19.

(177) Cf. *De Sacramentis* I.ii.24 (*PL* 176, 214-16) and I.iii.26-27 (*PL* 176, 227-30). Hugh's indirect questioning of ideas of Abelard is examined by D.E. Luscombe, *The School of Peter Abelard*, Cambridge, 1969, pp. 183-97.

(178) I. Brady, 'Peter Lombard : Canon of Notre-Dame', *Recherches de theologie ancienne et médiévale*, 32, 1965, pp. 277-95. Two years later in 1147, the canons of St-Victor took over Ste-Geneviève.

(179) N.M. Häring, 'The Eulogium ad Alexandrum Papam tertium of John of Cornwall', *Mediaeval Studies*, 13, 1951, p. 265 ; cf. my comments on Lombard's use of Abelard in CCCM 13, pp. 264-67.

(180) The Lombard's criticisms of Abelard are analysed by Luscombe, *The School of Peter Abelard*, pp. 261-80 and M. Colish, 'Peter Lombard and Abelard : The *Opinio Nominalium* and Divine Transcendence', *Vivarium*, 30.1, 1991, pp. 139-56 ; on his critical attitude to Gilbert, see her study, 'Gilbert, the Early Porretans, and Peter Lombard. Semantics and Theology', *Gilbert de Poitiers et ses contemporains*, pp. 229-50.

(181) *Metalogicon* IV, 40, ed. Hall, p. 181 ; cf. Augustine, *De Trinitate* VIII, 2, 3 (CCSL 50, 270).

III

Guibert of Nogent's *Monodiae* (III, 17) in an appendage to the *De haeresibus* of Augustine[*]

In a well known passage of his *Monodiae* (or *De vita sua*), written *c.* 1115 Guibert of Nogent describes how he interrogated two brothers, Clement and Everard of Bucy. They had been summoned by the bishop of Soissons for questioning « because they were making *conventus* outside the Church and were accused by kinfolk of being heretics[1] ». Guibert was perplexed by their refusal to admit to any unorthodox doctrine until he remembered a comment of Augustine in his *De haeresibus* that Priscillianists used to say to each other : « *iura, periura, secretum prodere noli*[2] ». Realising that further interrogation was pointless, Guibert recommended to the bishop that they be tried by ordeal. Once their guilt had been established in this way, they were incarcerated. Before the council of Beauvais had decided on their fate, they and two other ' heretics ' present at the interrogation were seized by a mob and burnt to death.

Immediately preceeding this account occurs a digression in which Guibert informs us of those beliefs to which the accused would not admit : that they denied the incarnation and condemned child baptism, the eucharist, marriage

* I would like to express my gratitude to François Dolbeau, secretary of this journal, R.I. Moore of the Department of History, University of Sheffield and A.J. Piper of the Department of Palaeography and Diplomatic, University of Durham, for discussion of a number of points in this paper.

1. *Guibert de Nogent : Autobiographie* III, 17, ed. E.-R. Labande, Paris, Les Belles Lettres, 1981 (Les Classiques de l'Histoire de France au Moyen Age, 34), p. 428-432. Guibert indicates that *Monodiae* is the correct title to his « Memoirs » in the *De pignoribus sanctorum* (see below n. 15).

2. Augustine, *De haeresibus* LXXI.1, ed. R. Vander Plaetse and C. Beukers, *Aurelii Augustini Opera* Pars XIII, 2, CC. SL 46, Turnhout, 1969, p. 333 (*periura* occurs in some MSS as a variant for *peiera*, the reading retained by the editors). Guibert's debt to Augustine is commented upon by R.I. MOORE, *Guibert of Nogent and his World*, in *Studies in Medieval History presented to R.H.C. Davis*, ed. H. Mayr-Harting and R.I. Moore, London, 1985, p. 107-118.

and procreation[3]. He provides a lurid description of their practice of indiscriminate intercourse and consumption of a eucharist baked with the ashes of any baby conceived in their midst. Guibert concludes this passage by noting how closely their beliefs and practices resemble those attributed to the Manichaeans by Augustine in the *De haeresibus*. This passage (ed. Labande, p. 428, 18-430, 28) occurs without any of the surrounding narrative, immediately after the *De haeresibus* of Augustine in a manuscript copied *c.* 1300 (Durham Cathedral Library B. III. 7 = *Dur*). As we have no medieval witness to the text of this passage, the fragment is potentially valuable. We re-edit this particular fragment of the *Monodiae*, and examine both Guibert's possible sources and the context in which it was written.

Dur is made up of two separate sections. The first (f. 1-312) is largely taken up by the *Excerptiones* of Eugippius, a compilation extracted from various works of Augustine, while the second contains his *Retractationes* (f. 313-348ᵛ) and *De haeresibus* (f. 348ᵛ-364)[4]. Sandwiched between the *De haeresibus* and a list of Augustine's works (f. 365-369) occur three separate texts : f. 364ʳᵇ-365ᵛᵃ the extract (III, c. 17) of Guibert's *Monodiae* mentioned above ; f. 365ᵛᵃ⁻ᵛᵇ eighteen heretical capitula, titled *errores petri abailardi* ; f. 365ᵛᵇ-366ʳᵃ the series of texts collected by Geoffrey of Auxerre concerning the errors of Gilbert of Poitiers, titled *Errores gisleberti pictauensis episcopi in remensi concilio dampnati sub papa eugenio*[5]. The single hand which copied these texts, as indeed all of the accompanying works of Augustine, is English. The manuscript was presented to the monastic library of Durham cathedral during the time that Robert Fossor was prior (1342-74) by Robert of Hexham, a student in Oxford *c.* 1317 and prior of St Leonard's, Stamford, 1346-52[6].

---

3. *Autobiographie* III, 17, ed. Labande, p. 430 ; see below p. 123-124 for a new edition of this passage.

4. *Dur* is described by T. Rud, *Codicum MSS Ecclesiae Cathedralis Dunelmensis Catalogus*, Durham, 1825, p. 150-151, and further by C.J. Mews, *The lists of heresies imputed to Peter Abelard*, in *Revue Bénédictine*, 95, 1985, p. 73-110, especially p. 79. *Dur* is cited without being used by A. Mutzenbecher, *Retractationum libri II*, CC.SL 57, Turnhout, 1984, p. XXIII. The *De haeresibus* in *Dur* concludes with the additional chapters *De Nestorianis* (II) and *De Eutychianis* (IIIA), *De haeresibus*, ed. Vander Plaetse-Beukers, p. 349-351.

5. These texts were commented on briefly by J. Leclercq, *Notes abélardiennes*, in *Bulletin de philosophie médiévale*, 13, 1971, p. 69-70, the manuscript having been pointed out to him by J. Benton. The *errores petri abailardi* in *Dur* are discussed by Mews, *The lists...*, p. 83-86. N. Häring edited the texts about Gilbert a number of times, but never from *Dur* : *Das sogenannte Glaubensbekenntnis des Reimser Konsistoriums von 1148*, in *Scholastik*, 40, 1965, p. 55-90 (edition, p. 86-90) ; *The Writings against Gilbert of Poitiers by Geoffrey of Auxerre*, in *Analecta Cisterciensia*, 22, 1966, p. 3-83 (edition, p. 31-35) and *Texts concerning Gilbert of Poitiers*, in *Archives d'histoire doctrinale et littéraire du moyen âge*, 37, 1970, p. 169-203 (edition, p. 174-176).

6. I am very grateful to A.J. Piper for informing me that a caution-note for the Burnel Chest in Oxford, dated 2 May 1317 is found with Robert of Hexham's name in the Durham Cathedral MS B.I.10. Robert of Hexham is mentioned as prior of St Leonard's in *Victoria County History. Lincolnshire*, London, 1908, vol. II, p. 128.

A complete manuscript (*X*) of the *Monodiae* belonging to the cathedral of Laon, was in the possession of a local antiquary, Georges de Y (d. 1641), when it was studied both by Jacques Sirmond and André Duchesne in the first half of the seventeenth century. Luc d'Achery could not locate the manuscript, however, when he set to work on his edition of the *Monodiae* (published in 1651) and had to be content with a transcription (Paris, BN *Baluze* 42, f. 30-107^v = *P*) of *X*, lent to him by François Duchesne[7]. Other seventeenth-century transcriptions of excerpts from *X* survive in Bibliothèque nationale, *Dupuy* 34, f. 72-74^v (= *Dp*) and *Duchesne* 64, f. 138-141^v (= *Du*). *P* has remained the basis for subsequent editions of the *De vita sua*, notably of both Bourgin and Labande. Nonetheless the manuscript, which also contained the *De miraculis beatae Mariae Laudunensis* of Hermann of Tournai, was recorded as present at Laon by Montfaucon in his catalogue, published in 1739[8].

Our knowledge of the text of the *Monodiae* has been greatly extended by Dolbeau's analysis of a transcription of book III (Berlin, Deutsche Staatsbibliothek Phillipps 1690, f. 93-120^v = *S*), copied for Jacques Sirmond from *X*, and a fifteenth-century legendary (Vatican, *Reg. lat.* 583, f. 4-20^v = *V*) which includes long extracts from books III and I, 8-14[9]. Dolbeau has been able both to correct many faulty readings in *S* and to deduce from the medieval abbreviations common to *P* and *S*, that *X*, far from being Guibert's autograph as d'Achery had speculated, probably dated to the fourteenth or fifteenth century. By contrast, the compiler of the legendary, who occasionally extended or modified Guibert's text with information from other sources, notably Hermann's *De miraculis beatae Mariae Laudunensis*, seems to have used an exemplar occasionally more correct than *X*. The fragment of the *Monodiae* found in *Dur* was not used by the fifteenth-century compiler of *V*, so we can only compare its text with that of *PS*. In the following discussion phrases are cited by the line number of the edition at the end of this study.

---

7. The edition of L. d'Achery, *Venerabilis Guiberti abbatis B. Mariae de Novigento opera omnia*, Paris, 1651, p. 456-525 was reprinted by Migne, PL 156, 837-962. It was succeeded by that of G. BOURGIN, *Guibert de Nogent : Histoire de sa vie (1053-1124)*, Paris, 1907 (Collection de textes pour servir à l'étude et à l'enseignement de l'histoire 40). A small fragment of the *Monodiae* in a thirteenth-century obituary, Laon, Bibl. mun. 341, f. 96-97 was edited by Bourgin as an appendix to his edition (p. 235-238).

8. The identity of Georges de Y (previously misnamed Dey) is discussed by L. CAROLUS-BARRÉ, *Georges de Y, antiquaire († 1640), et le manuscrit de Guibert de Nogent, De Vita sua*, in *Bibliothèque de l'École des Chartes*, 142, 1984, p. 317-24. The *Monodiae* (here *libri Guiberti de Nogento de vita sua*) and the *De miraculis Ecclesiae Laudunensis* occurred together at Laon according to B. DE MONTFAUCON, *Bibliotheca bibliothecarum MSS nova*, Paris, 1739, vol. II, p. 1298 (no. 309, 14.X). Hermann's text, followed by his prefatory letter to the bishop of Laon, is copied on f. 108-134 of Baluze 42, according to a note on f. 108 : *Historia Combustionis et restaurationis Ecclesiae Laudunensis. E qua et Gesta Bartholemei episcopi complectitur. Auctore Hermanno Monacho, ex codice MS Ecclesiae Laudunensis.* D'Achery edited this work as an appendix to the *Monodiae*.

9. F. DOLBEAU, *Deux nouveaux manuscrits des « Mémoires » de Guibert de Nogent*, in *Sacris Erudiri*, 26, 1983, p. 155-176.

One of the most difficult readings in *PS* within Guibert's digression about heresy is « *Conventicula faciunt in ypogeis aut pennalibus abditis* » (l. 15). D'Achery suggested that *pennalibus* could be a corruption of either *penetralibus* (Labande's preferred reading) or *penatibus*. *Dur* supplies the equally meaningless *penualibus*, but also has a gloss to this word in the margin « *id est cellatiis* » ; *ypogeis* is glossed « *id est subintaneis* ». These annotations have probably been copied blindly from an exemplar in which these words were glossed « *id est cellariis* » and « *id est subterraneis* » respectively. The gloss tends to confirm Labande's preference for *penetralibus*. The copyist of *Dur* may have read *penualibus* from a similar abbreviation as gave rise to *penna-libus* in *PS*, perhaps *pen<etra>libus* without an abbreviation sign. The glossator's comment that they met in underground cellars conforms fully to the sense of the passage, in particular since lighted candles had to be used. Benton used this gloss in *Dur* to correct his earlier rather free translation of *penetralibus abditis* as « secret cobwebby places » to « unfrequented cellars », not unlike Labande's « endroits souterrains bien dissimulés[10] ». Whether these glosses were originally added by Guibert himself we do not know.

The miscopying of these annotations and of other words in *Dur* suggests that its copyist did not pay great attention to the sense of his text. One notes the omission of small words and the confusion of similar letters (*s* for *f*, *c* for *t* etc.). The initial *autem* (l. 2) may have been omitted because the passage was part of a wider narrative. The use of *obtuitu* (l. 16) in *Dur* is as legitimate as *obtutu* given by *PS*. The reading *doctioribus* (l. 24), found in *P* and accepted by the editors, is supported by *Dur* against *doctoribus* in *S*. Both *conspersi* and *cum sparsi* may be corruptions of *consparsi* (l. 10) in *S*, but this does not change Guibert's sense.

Nonetheless, there are three important words or phrases where *Dur* can be used to improve Labande's text. *Dur* and *S* combine to support the reading *sentencia* (« teaching ») against *summa* in *P* (l. 2). Another improvement is the fuller version of l. 6 in *Dur*. The omission of *quo dotatu* in *PS* places *nescio* in a peculiar adjectival status. The clause is translated by Labande as « par je ne sais quelle longue répétition de paroles » and by Benton as « by some long rig-marole of talk ». *Dur* contains a complete subordinate clause which translates much more easily as « by a long repetition of words, from I do not know what source ». Guibert thus contrasts *nescio quo dotatu* with *suum verbum dei* (l. 5). The accidental omission of *quo dotatu* could have occurred through confusion with *rotatu* in *X*, the exemplar of *PS*.

The third improvement we suggest does not depend particularly on *Dur*. All three witnesses agree in reading « ... *nam viri apud eos in feminam nefas est* » (l. 13). Labande suggested that *coitus* should be added before *nefus*, although this involves a contradiction in sense which does not seem to have been obser-

---

10. Labande, *ed. cit.*, p. 431. Benton provided this correction from *Dur* in his translation reproduced by E. PETERS, *Heresy and Authority in Medieval Europe*, London, 1980, p. 72-74. Otherwise this is a reprint of Benton's translation *Self and Society in Medieval France. The Memoirs of Abbot Guibert of Nogent (1064?-c. 1125)*, New York, 1970, p. 212-214.

ved.   Guibert leaves no doubt that these supposed heretics indulged willingly
in heterosexual intercourse.   If « *et certe cum per latinum consparsi sint
orbem, uideas uiros mulieribus cohabitare... femine cum feminis cubitare
noscantur* » is a lengthy aside added later rather than a new sentence, then
« *et fructificare coitibus... viri* » becomes the subject of *nefas est* rather than the
grammatical complement of *dampnant* (l. 9).   It becomes unnecessary to insert
coitus, while much greater sense is made of the subsequent sentence about their
elimination of everything procreated by physical union.

   Guibert's account of the orgy and of the murder of babies is very similar to
that given by Paul, monk of St-Père of Chartres, in relation to the heretics tried
at Orleans in 1022[11].   Paul's account, erroneously described by d'Achery as
the « Acts of the council of Orleans », was written sometime after 1078.   No
other witness to the events of 1022 provides this story, which may itself have
been interpolated into an earlier record.   Comparison of the two passages
reveals the extent of Guibert's debt to an existing tradition.   Both authors say
that meetings were held by candle-light (Paul, in a house at night ; Guibert, in a
cellar) and that there was some lengthy incantation.   According to Paul they
invoked the names of devils and a devil then appeared in the form of a small
beast.   Guibert says that they invoked their own ' Word of God ', but when
they assembled they sodomised a female victim.   Both agree that when the
candles or lanterns were extinguished, each copulated with whoever was to
hand.   If a baby was born from such a union, it was thrown into a fire (Paul,
in the manner of the pagans ; Guibert, from hand to hand through the flames
until it died).   According to Paul the ashes were turned into a viaticum, kept
with the same devotion as the eucharist ; Guibert held that the ashes were
turned into a eucharist.   Both agreed that whoever shared in this sacrament
would never abandon the heresy.

   The simplest explanation for the parallelism in the two accounts is that either
Guibert or his source reported the same story as told by Paul, embellishing it in
the process.   Guibert makes clear from his subsequent narrative about the
interrogation that he did not obtain any information from Clement or Everard
which could be used in any way to impugn their orthodoxy or their
morals.   We can only conclude that Guibert drew on this story about their
behaviour, not found in this form with regard to any other heretical group,
in order to supplement a narrative which might otherwise convey the impression that he had acted hastily in recommending trial by ordeal.   Guibert goes
further than Paul in observing that these heretics resemble the Manichaeans

---

11. Thus BENTON, *Self and Society*, p. 212. R.I. Moore (to whom I grateful for pointing out
the references which follow) translates Paul's account and notes the similarity with stories told
about early Christians, *The Birth of Popular Heresy*, London, 1975, p. 10-15. Paul's account is
edited in the *Cartulaire de l'abbaye de Saint-Père de Chartres* I, éd. B. Guérard (Collection de
documents inédits sur l'histoire de France. Collection des cartulaires de France I), Paris, 1840,
p. 108-15 and cited in part, p. 124 below. The erroneous description of this document as the
Gesta synodi Aurelianensis and the unreliability of its account are exposed by R.-H. BAUTIER,
L'hérésie d'Orléans et le mouvement intellectuel au début du XIᵉ siècle, in *Actes du 95ᵉ Congrès
national des sociétés savantes. Reims 1970. Philosophie et histoire*, Paris, 1975, I, p. 63-88.

described by Augustine in the *De haeresibus*, with the difference that those of Soissons were rustics rather than learned men. The label ' Manichaean ' is not used by Paul of St-Père, although it is used in passing of the heretics of Orleans by Adhemar of Chabannes[12].

As a good Augustinian scholar, Guibert recognised that the rumours which he had heard echoed distantly a relatively matter-of-fact account within the *De haeresibus*. Augustine recalls a trial at which a Manichaean nun called Eusebia admitted that Margarita, a twelve year old girl, had been violated at a Manichaean gathering over a bed of flour which was then used to make eucharistic bread[13]. By the time it reaches Paul of St-Père, Augustine's account has been so embellished that the flour mixed with human seed has become the ashes of a cremated child. Guibert's version is closer to that of Augustine in that a single woman is raped and that a sacrilegious eucharistic bread is consumed. Although Guibert says that he is simply reporting what is said (l. 16), one cannot avoid the suspicion that he deliberately changed the devil from a *bestiola* (as in Paul's account) to a *muliercula*, perhaps imagined as a succubus, so as to make the story echo more closely Augustine's account in the *De haeresibus*. The doctrines which Guibert attributes to these heretics, of denial of the incarnation and refusal of child baptism, the eucharist and conventional cemeteries, are not the defining characteristics of Manichaean doctrine as described by Augustine, but are rather common accusations made by unreliable chroniclers about those who dissent from orthodoxy. There is no evidence that they reflect accurately the views of those clergy and laity tried at Orleans in 1022[14]. The account which Guibert provides is intended to shock readers, not to give a report of his findings as an inquisitor.

In his account of the interrogation Guibert never refers to the accused as Manichaeans, only as *heretici*. Paradoxically, when writing the *De pignoribus sanctorum* towards the end of his life (*c.* 1125), he refers back to this passage of the *Monodiae* as an account of the punishment meted out to ' Manichaeans '[15]. At the time of conducting his interrogation he only knew for certain that they held *conventicula* outside the Church. They would not admit to anything other than orthodox catholic doctrine and were familiar with scripture. Guibert's comment that Clement misunderstood the verse *Beati eritis* (Jn. 13, 17) as « Blessed are the heretics or heirs (*hereditarii*) » is probably a

---

12. Adhemar de Chabannes, *Chronique*, ed. Chavanon, Paris, 1897 (Collection de textes pour servir à l'étude et à l'enseignement de l'histoire), p. 194.

13. *De haeresibus* XLVI.9 (*ed. cit.*, p. 315).

14. Bautier summarises these doctrines from various surviving sources, *L'hérésie d'Orléans*, p. 72-75.

15. *De pignoribus sanctorum* I, 3 (PL 156, 622B) : « Reliquiae Manichaeorum pridem Suessionis zelo dei plebis arserunt, sed extorres a iusta causa, solummodo addemnatis corporibus sibi damno fuerunt, super quibus in libris Monodiarum mearum laciniosius dixi. » By *laciniosius* Guibert seems to mean « in more detail », *lacinia* literally meaning a lappet or flap. Cf. *Gesta Dei per Francos* VIII, 4 (PL 156, 807C) : « Sed quo, per verborum lacinias allegoriae libertas excurrit, cum historialis nos veritas, ne per opiniones passim evagari videamur, astringat ? »

false imputation[16]. The verse refers to the reward given those who carry out Christ's mandate. Convinced that the two brothers harboured seditious beliefs, Guibert insisted that only an ordeal would establish their guilt. It may only have been after he had written the narrative part of this chapter that he heard rumours about the doings of ' heretics ' and that it occurred to him that he may have been interrogating Manichaeans. He had long been convinced that all heresy stemmed either from Africa or from the East, so the reports which he had heard seemed to him quite plausible[17].

The passage reproduced in *Dur* corresponds exactly to a digression within Guibert's narrative, concerned otherwise with his fruitless interrogation of Clement and Everard. In the previous chapter Guibert had been describing the ' infamous behaviour ' of the count of Soissons and had been led to discuss this trial because count John once declared that no-one was wiser than Clement. The climax of Guibert's story is that the accused were put to death by the local population, a sure sign of divine retribution. If the passage found in *Dur* is read as a later addition to the *Monodiae*, the action of the bishop of Soissons in summoning the two brothers to an investigation follows logically after the assertion of the count that he considered no-one wiser than Clement. The digression serves to ridicule the count's assertion and to justify Guibert's conduct of the interrogation, but it disrupts the flow of his narrative.

We have ample evidence that Guibert would often revise his own writings. He tells us that he would always commit his thoughts directly to the written page in their final form, without using drafts prepared on wax tablets[18]. In the preface to his *Tropologiae* on Osee, Amos and the lamentations of Jeremiah (*c.* 1121-25) he acknowledges that he frequently used to revise his own work[19]. His autograph copy of the *De pignoribus sanctorum* and *Epistola de bucella Iudae* contains a number of long additional passages either in the margin or at the foot of the page[20]. It is thus quite possible that he added the passage found in *Dur* at any time between the initial writing of the

---

16. *Monodiae* III, 17, ed. Labande, p. 432.

17. *Gesta Dei per Francos* I, 2 (PL 156, 686D-687C).

18. *Monodiae* I, 17, ed. Labande, p. 144 : « Opuscula enim mea haec et alia nullis impressa tabulis dictando et scribendo, scribenda etiam pariter commentando immutabiliter paginis inferebam. »

19. *Ad Tropologias in prophetas Osee et Amos ac lamentationes Ieremiae Prooemium* (PL 156, 340B) : « Hactenus enim non tam perpetuitate legendi quam nimia continuatione scribendi, utpote qui non solum dictator exstiteram, sed et laboris indefessi notarius... In quo pii moderatio lectoris attendat ut, si insolito mihi modo dictantem minus aliqua competenter dixisse repererit, eo mihi intuitu indulgere non differat, quo minus alienae dum mea scribi manui, quam meae quondam facere consueveram institisse cognoscit. Dum enim mea manu propria scriptitarem, et crebro contuitu inter scribendum eadem dicta reviserem, facillimum mihi erat et omissa retexere, et dum notarii mei fastidia nulla ex mora revereor, verborum curialitati secure mihimet ipsi morosus intendo. »

20. Paris, Bibl. nat. lat. 2900, f. 37ᵛ, 60, 69ᵛ, 115ᵛ etc. For a detailed study of this MS as of lat. 2502 (*Tropologiae in Osee, Lamentationes Jeremiae et Amos*) and lat. 2500 (*Moralia in Genesim*), both of which have been corrected by Guibert, see M.-C. GARAND, *Le Scriptorium de Guibert de Nogent*, in *Scriptorium*, 31, 1977, p. 3-29.

Monodiae (1115) and the *De pignoribus sanctorum* (c. 1125). A reader may have noticed the annotation in the autograph copy or alternatively Guibert himself added this passage to his copy of the *De haeresibus*. The fact that he refers explicitly to the *De haeresibus* in the digression lends credence to this possibility.

The most puzzling aspect of *Dur* is the introductory rubric : *De hereticis qui gallica lingua dicuntur telier uel deimait*[21]. It is unlikely to have been invented by the scribe of *Dur*. The only remotely similar word used of heretics in this period is *textores* or tistres, the Old French equivalent of weavers. The letters *st* might conceivably have been separated into *li*. Geoffrey of Auxerre uses the term of the heretics known to be in the region of Toulouse : *Paucos quidem habebat civitas illa, qui heretico faverent : de textoribus, quos Arianos ipsi nominant, nonnullos*[22]. The word « *deimait* » vaguely resembles one label used by Hughes of Poitou to describe individuals believed to espouse the same doctrines as those of Soissons : « *quidam heretici qui dicuntur Deonarii seu Populicani*[23] ». The most significant feature of the rubric in *Dur* is the phrase « *qui gallica lingua dicuntur* ». These people were known by a French name.

Even if Guibert is elaborating unsubstantiated rumours, the question remains as to the nature of the sect led by Clement of Bucy. His accusation that they spurned the sacraments is contradicted by his subsequent admission that the two brothers insisted that they shared fully the faith of the Church : « *Nos omnia quae dicitis credimus* » (ed. Labande, p. 432). His key statement is that they claimed to be leading the apostolic life and that they concentrated their attention on the Acts of the Apostles (l. 24-25). How are we to interpret Guibert's comment, not made by Paul of St-Père, that « since they are scattered through the latin world, you can see men and women living together without being married, so that a man does not remain loyal to his wife, rather men are known to lie with men, women with women » (l. 10-12) ? What is meant by the *conventus* to which Clement and Everard admitted ?

Guibert's comments become clear if we examine similar accusations of sexual misconduct made against a number of other preachers and reformers of the period, many of whom established religious communities for both women and men. Some earned widespread censure, even though their motivations follow those of the Gregorian reform, such as Tanchelm, a preacher who was murdered by a priest of Antwerp in 1115, the year Guibert wrote his

21. The last word is difficult to read. Rud (*Catalogus*, p. 151) erroneously reads *Deiamait*. Earlier I had transcribed this as *deimart* (MEWS, *The lists...*, p. 79), but I now correct this to *deimait*.

22. PL 185, 411D. *Textores* is also used of heretics of Cologne by Bernard of Clairvaux, *Sermones in Cantica* 65, 5 (PL 183, 1092B) and by Eckbert of Schönau, *Sermones contra catharos* I, 1 (PL 195, 13C). Much has been written on the terms *textores* and *arriani*. Extensive bibliography on the term is cited by R.I. MOORE, *St Bernard's Mission to the Languedoc in 1145*, in *Bulletin of the Institute of Historical Research*, 47, 1974, p. 1-10.

23. *Chronique* IV, 3542, ed. R.B.C. Huygens, *Monumenta Vizeliacensia*, CC. med. 42, Turnhout, 1976, p. 606.

Monodiae[24]. Robert d'Arbrissel, who founded a community of both women and men at Fontevrault in 1100, was more successful in obtaining ecclesiastical patronage, but he would still earn much criticism from those who felt that it was impossible for men and women to live chastely together[25]. Roscelin of Compiègne comments that husbands accused Robert of breaking up marriages, taking women away from their rightful masters[26]. Norbert of Xanten, who first established religious communities for women and men in the diocese of Laon in 1120, was one of the most successful of these preachers. Hermann of Laon was very impressed by the way Norbert's approach differed from that of Bernard of Clairvaux in attracting a following of women, but took care to emphasise that they still preserved their modesty in dealings with men. He also noted that many of Norbert's followers came from a lower social class, « *multoties quos in priori vita novimus aut rusticos fuisse aut pauperes, in religionis habitu quasi fastuose cernimus equitantes ; feminis autem mox ut conversae fuerint perpetua deinceps lex manet, semper intra domus ambitum clausas retineri*[27] ». The same term *rustici* is used of Clement and Everard of Bucy by Guibert, but in a pejorative tone very different from that of Hermann of Laon.

Guibert does not elaborate on the accusations of heresy made against these brothers *ab affinibus* — by kinfolk or explain why they were lynched by the local population. However, if we use Roscelin's comments about Robert d'Arbrissel as a guide, then the accusations may have been made by husbands who felt that their wives had been ' stolen ' by a religious sect, dedicated to pursuing the apostolic life. The doctrinal accusations made by Guibert are clearly gross exaggerations intended to horrify the reader, but it is possible that Clement's followers may well have spurned marriage, have buried their dead in

---

24. *Vita Norberti*, MGH.SS 12, p. 691 : « Et cum filias in matrum praesentia sponsasque maritis videntibus corrumperet, opus spirituale esse asserebat, in tantum ut infelicem se diceret, quae huic coniunctioni nefariae misceri non meruisset. » Similar charges were made against Henry of Lausanne by Bernard of Clairvaux, *Epist.* 241, ed. J. Leclercq, *S. Bernardi Opera* VIII, Rome, 1980, p. 127. On Tanchelm's reforming inspirations, see for example M.D. LAMBERT, *Medieval Heresy*, London, 1977, p. 55-59.

25. Marbodus of Rennes, *Epist.* 6 to Robert (PL 171, 1484C) : « Videmus turbas ad te undique confluentes, tibi tuisque honores, quos propriis debent pastoribus, impendentes. Quos tamen, ut manifestum est, non religionis amor, sed ea quae semper vulgo familiaris est curiositas, et novorum cupiditas ducit... Iam vero et illud qua ratione defendi potest quod cuiuslibet conditionis aut aetatis mares et feminas qui, te predicante, sicut fit, ad horam compunguntur, passim admittas, et statim ad religionem profitendam improbatos compellas. » Similarly Geoffrey of Vendome, *Epist.* 47 to Robert (PL 157, 182 A) : « Feminarum quasdam, ut dicitur, nimis familiariter tecum habitare permittis, quibus privata verba saepius loqueris, et cum ipsis etiam, et inter ipsas noctu frequenter cubare non erubescis. »

26. Roscelin of Compiègne, *Epist. ad Abaelardum* (PL 178, 361D) : « Vidi enim dominum Robertum feminas a viris suis fugientes, viris ipsis reclamantibus, recepisse et, episcopo Andegaviensi ut eos redderet praecipiente, inobedienter usque ad mortem obstinanter tenuisse. Quod factum quam irrationabile sit considera. Si enim uxor viro debitum negat, et ob hoc ille moechari compellitur, maior culpa est compellentis quam agentis. Rea ergo adulterii est femina virum dimittens postea ex necessitate peccantem. »

27. Hermann, *Liber de miraculis S. Mariae Laudunensis* III, 7 (PL 156, 996C).

an unknown cemetery, and have followed Gregorian precedent in spurning sacraments from ' unworthy ' clergy. Clement of Bucy was rendered suspect in the eyes of Guibert simply because he enjoyed the support of count Jean. This in itself contributed to his downfall. While we have no independent testimony of Clement's activity, Guibert's comments suggest that he was a preacher not unlike Tanchelm, Ramihrdus of Douai or Otfried of Watten, all of whom attracted a following among both sexes[28]. Norbert of Xanten shared a similar desire to recreate the enthusiasm of the early Church, but he differed from Tanchelm and Clement in obtaining episcopal approval. Guibert was not alone at feeling outraged at the establishment of religious communities for both sexes. Having heard wild stories about blasphemous doctrines and practices in connection with these groups, Guibert was quite prepared to believe that they were a new manifestation of the Manichaean heresy.

Seen in this context, Guibert's statement that the two brothers were summoned by the bishop « quod conventus praeter ecclesiam facerent et heretici ab affinibus dicerentur » may mean more than « le fait de tenir des réunions en dehors de l'église, rappelant que, autour d'eux, on les qualifiait d'hérétiques », as translated by Labande (p. 433). If conventus are understood as communities rather than as meetings, then it is understandable why accusations should be made by kinfolk and husbands in particular, who felt that traditional family ties were being undermined. The reference to unmarked cemeteries suggests that he was talking about permanent communities. Guibert's use of conventicula to describe the place where orgies took place may be a forced effort to link a story which he had heard with the facts of the situation. His lengthy aside about the practice found « throughout the latin world » of men living with women in an unmarried state makes sense if it is an allusion to mixed religious communities. By conventus he means « convents » in the traditional religious sense. Refusing to believe that men and women could live together chastely, he accused them irrationally both of homosexuality and of suppressing children born to them.

The fragment of Guibert of Nogent's Monodiae (III, 17) found in Dur is thus a valuable witness to the development of new religious communities at the beginning of the twelfth century, not to the survival of the Manichaean religion in this period. Guibert is quite likely to have added the passage to his narrative of the trial of Clement and Everard of Bucy only after its initial redaction. We are unable to tell for certain who originally added the passage to a copy of the De haeresibus. It is not impossible that it was Guibert himself, but if this is so, somebody else must have added the texts about Abaelard and Gilbert of Poitiers also found in Dur. The fragment, which clarifies certain otherwise obscure sentences in Guibert's text, needs to be interpreted in the light of a very similar account given of heretical beliefs and behaviour by Paul

---

28. Ch. Dereine examines the evidence about these other preachers of the period in a region north-west of Soissons, Les prédicateurs « apostoliques » dans les diocèses de Thérouanne, Tournai et Cambrai-Arras durant les années 1075-1125, in Analecta Praemonstratensia, 59, 1983, p. 171-189.

of St-Père of Chartres, in the late eleventh century. Neither author is providing a factual account. If the rhetoric is stripped away from Guibert's description, Clement of Bucy emerges as a reforming preacher, who was, as not unusual in the period, intent on founding religious communities for women as well as men. Their espousal of a life of chastity led Guibert to imagine that they condemned marriage and murdered all babies conceived in illicit intercourse. Deeply influenced by the pessimistic strain in Augustine's thought, he perceived social change as a sign of the sinfulness of the world. Guibert's criticisms of a movement of reform thus became another entry in a catalogue of heresies originally drawn up by the bishop of Hippo.

Monodiae (De vita sua) III, 17

We provide here an edition of the passage based on *Dur, P* and *S* with indication of significant variants. We also supply extracts from a similar description by Paul of St-Père of Chartres about heretics tried at Orleans in 1022. The orthography chosen is that of *Dur* except where it seems corrupt. The punctuation has been modernised so as to make the sense clear. Because the passage found in *Dur* may have been added only subsequently to Guibert's original text, we indicate the preceeding and subsequent sentences as given by Labande.

Dur	Durham, Cathedral Library B. III. 7, f. 364rb-365va
P	Paris, Bibliothèque nationale Baluze 42, f. 101^v
S	Berlin, Deutsche Staatsbibliothek Phillipps 1690, f. 114^v-115
Ach	d'Achery, *De vita sua, Guiberti... Opera*, p. 519-520.
Bo	Bourgin, *Histoire de sa vie*, p. 212-213.
Lab	Labande, *Autobiographie*, p. 428-432.
edd.	agreement of d'Achery, Bourgin and Labande.

<At quoniam hereticorum, quos hic nefandus amabat, meminimus, quidam rusticus, Clementius nomine, cum fratre Ebrardo, apud Buciacum, proximam Suessioni villam, commanebat qui, ut vulgabatur, de primoribus suae haereseos erat. De hoc ferebat impurissimus ille comes, quod sapientiorem eo neminem comprobasset.>

De hereticis qui gallica lingua dicuntur telier uel deimait[a]

Heresis <autem[b]> ea est, non que palam suum dogma defendat, sed que perpetuis dampnata susurris clandestina serpat. Eius vero talis dicitur esse sentencia[c] : dispensationem Filii Virginis phantasma fatentur ; baptisma parvulorum non intelligentium sub patrinis quibuscunque adnullant[d] ; suum autem appellant verbum Dei, quod fit, nescio quo dotatu[e], rotatu longo sermonum ; mysterium quod fit[f] in altari nostro ita exhorrent, ut ora sacerdotum omnium os inferni appellent et, si pro velamine sue hereseos aliquotiens inter alios nostra sacramenta suscipiant, sic pro dieta habent, ut ea die nil amplius edant ; sacra cimiteria a reliqua terra comparatione non dividunt ; coniugia dampnant, et fructificare coitibus[g] — et certe cum[h] per latinum consparsi[i] sint orbem, videas viros mulieribus cohabitare sine mariti coniugisque nomine, ita ut vir cum femina, singulus cum singula, non moretur, sed viri cum viris, femine[j] cum feminis cubitare noscantur — nam viri apud eos in feminam nefas[k] est ; edulia[l] omnium que ex coitu nascuntur eliminant.

Conventicula faciunt in ypogeis[m] aut penetralibus[n] abditis, sexus simul indifferens, qui candelis accensis, cuidam muliercule sub obtuitu[o] omnium, retectis ut dicitur natibus, procumbenti eas a tergo offerunt. Hiisque mox extinctis, chaos undecunque conclamant, et cum ea que ad manum venerit persona quisque coit. Quod si inibi femina gravidetur, partu demum fuso in idipsum reditur, ignis multus accenditur, a circumsedentibus puer de manu in manum per flammas iacitur donec exstinguitur ; deinde in cineres redigitur, ex cinere panis conficitur, cuique pars pro eukharistia tribuitur, qua assumpta numquam pene ab heresi ipsa resipiscitur. Si relegas hereses ab Augustino digestas, nulli magis quam manicheorum reperies convenire. Que olim coepta a doctioribus[p], residuum demisit ad rusticos qui vitam se apostolicam tenere iactantes, eorum actus solos legere amplectuntur.

<A domino ergo Suessorum pontifice, viro clarissimo Lisiardo, praefati duo ad examen urgentur. Quibus cum ab episcopo ingereretur, quod conventus praeter ecclesiam facerent et heretici ab affinibus dicerentur, respondit Clementius : « Num legistis, domine, in evangelio ubi dicitur : ' Beati eritis ' ? » ... >

a De hereticis... deimait] Dur ; om. PS edd. ‖ b autem] om. Dur ‖ c sentencia] Dur S ; summa P edd. ‖ d adnullant] Dur ; anullant PS edd. ‖ e nescio quo dotatu] quo nescio PS edd. ‖ f fit] sit Dur ‖ g coitibus] coicibus Dur ‖ h cum] om. Dur ‖ i consparsi] S ; cum sparsi Dur ; conspersi P edd. ‖ j femine] femina Dur ‖ k nefas] PS Dur Ach Bo ; coitus nefas Lab ‖ l edulia] edula P ‖ m ypogeis] id est subintaneis mg add. Dur ‖ n penetralibus] Lab ; penetralibus vel penatibus proposuit Ach ; pennalibus PS Bo ; penualibus Dur, id est cellatiis (!) mg add. Dur ‖ o obtuitu] obtutu PS edd. ‖ p doctioribus] Dur P ; doctoribus S

Lines 4-6 : Cf. Paul of St-Père, Chronicon, ed. Guérard, p. 111 : «... dicentes Christum de virgine Maria non natum, neque pro hominibus passum, nec vere in sepulchro positum, nec a mortuis resurrexisse ; addentes in baptismo non esse ullam scelerum ablutionem, neque sacramentum corporis Christi in consecratione sacerdotis. »

Lines 15-22 : Cf. Paul of St-Père, Chronicon, ed. Guérard, p. 112 : « Congregabantur siquidem certis noctibus in domo denominata, singuli lucernas tenentes in manibus, et, ad instar letaniae demonum nomina declamabant, donec subito demonem in similitudine cuiuslibet bestiolae inter eos viderent descendere. Qui statim ut visibilis illa videbatur visio, omnibus extinctis luminaribus, quamprimum quisque poterat, mulierem quae ad manum sibi ueniebat, ad abutendum arripiebat, sine peccati respectu et utrum mater aut soror aut monacha haberetur, pro sanctitate et religione eius concubitus ab illis estimabatur. Ex quo spurcissimo concubitu infans generatus, octava die, in medio eorum copiose igne accenso piebatur per ignem more antiquorum paganorum, et sic in igne cremabatur. Cuius cinis tanta veneratione colligebatur atque custodiebatur, ut christiana religiositas corpus Christi custodire solet, aegris dandum de hoc seculo exituris ad viaticum. Inerat enim tanta vis diabolicae fraudis in ipso cinere, ut quicumque de praefata heresi imbutus fuisset et de eodem cinere, quamvis sumendo parum praelibavisset, vix umquam postea de eadem heresi gressum mentis ad viam veritatis dirigere valeret. »

Lines 22-23 : Cf. De haeresibus XLVI, 9, ed. Vander Plaetse-Beukers, Aurelii Augustini Opera XIII, 2 (CC. SL 46), p. 314-15.

APPENDIX. MANUSCRIPTS OF AUGUSTINE AT OURSCAMP

How could this passage of the *Monodiae* come to be copied into a late thirteenth-century manuscript of Augustine's *De haeresibus,* belonging to Durham cathedral ? Either Guibert or a subsequent reader of the work must have added it to his copy of the *De haeresibus.* The two texts which follow in *Dur,* about the errors of Peter Abaelard and of Gilbert of Poitiers, may both have been drawn up by Geoffrey of Auxerre, secretary to Bernard of Clairvaux from late 1139. He was quite likely present at the meeting between Bernard, Thomas of Morigny and William of St Thierry held to compose a definitive list of heretical capitula from the writings of Abaelard, which would then be appended to Bernard's *Epist.* 190, on the errors of Abaelard[29]. In his life of Bernard, Geoffrey groups together the heresies of Abaelard, Gilbert and the « textores » or « arriani » of Toulouse as similar manifestations of a demonic spirit[30].

The list of Abaelard's errors in *Dur,* a draft version of the much more widely publicised list of nineteen capitula, found at the end of Bernard's *Epist.* 190, also survives in one other manuscript, Paris, Bibliothèque de l'Arsenal 248 (= *Ar*)[31]. Unlike *Dur,* this manuscript was copied in the second half of the twelfth century. One small error in its text of the *errores petri abaielardi* (phonetically more correct than *errores petri abailardi* in *Dur*) shows that it cannot be the source of *Dur.* Both must derive from a common exemplar. As in *Dur,* the list follows the *Retractationes* (f. 2-49ᵛ) and *De haeresibus* (f. 50-70ᵛ), while preceding a list of the works of Augustine (f. 71-75) : *Incipiunt capitula opusculorum siue sermonum beati Augustini ypponeis episcopi et doctoris.* Only the absence of the fragment from the *Monodiae* and Geoffrey of Auxerre's collection of texts about Gilbert of Poitiers distinguishes *Ar* from the second section of *Dur.* Because the copyist of *Ar* has indicated which works of Augustine mentioned in the *Retractationes* are owned by the Cistercian monks of Ourscamp, in the diocese of Noyon, we may presume that this is where *Ar* was copied. Ourscamp, founded from Clairvaux in 1129, is only twenty-five kilometres from Guibert's monastery of Nogent. There is thus a possibility that the manuscript of the *De haeresibus,* to which the fragment of the *Monodiae* had been appended, may come from the region of Ourscamp.

There is another connection between Ourscamp and Durham, which, though remote, may be more than a coincidence. The second abbot of Ourscamp was an Englishman, Gilbert of Stamford (1143-63), who later became abbot of Citeaux (1163-68). Sometimes called Gilbertus Magnus, he knew Bernard of Clairvaux personally. A chance discovery in a Peterborough ritual has led Gransden to identify Gilbert as a former monk of that Cathedral, and his native Stamford as the town on the ancient high road to the North, where Peterborough had a dependent cell[32]. Between

29. MEWS, *The lists of heresies,* p. 83-86, 96-103.

30. *Vita prima,* liber III, 5-6 (PL 182, 310B-314C).

31. H. MARTIN, *Catalogue des manuscrits de la Bibliothèque de l'Arsenal* 1, Paris, 1885, p. 137-138. I was unaware of the list in *Ar* at the time of writing the study mentioned in n. 29, but its text corresponds so closely to that of *Dur* that the arguments there presented still hold.

32. On Gilbert of Stamford (Gilbertus Magnus), see Br. BRARD, *Catholicisme,* vol. 5, Paris,

1266 and 1334 Stamford would become an important university city, as the result of the temporary exodus of masters from Oxford. One of its many religious houses was St Leonard's, a dependency of Durham cathedral, to where young monks were sent for their studies. Robert of Hexham, the earliest known owner of *Dur*, was its prior between 1346 and 1352[33]. Robert subsequently bequeathed the manuscript, which he may have bought, to Durham cathedral. We can suggest as a hypothesis that Gilbert of Stamford sent a copy of the *Retractationes* and *De haeresibus*, containing additional information about major heresies of the day, to the region of Stamford and that *Dur* may derive from this manuscript. Only the identification of other Ourscamp manuscripts in English houses connected to Stamford would confirm this possibility.

In the hope that such connections between French and English manuscripts might be found, we list here those manuscripts of Augustine held at Ourscamp in the twelfth century, according to the annotations made by a monk of Ourscamp to the list of the works of Augustine at the beginning of the *Retractationes* in *Ar*. The copyist has added « *Hunc habent monachi sancte marie de ursicampo* », followed by « *Et hunc* », « *Et hunc* » etc. by twenty-nine works of Augustine. A number of Ourscamp manuscripts would later come into the possession of archbishop Laud and thus into the Bodleian library, Oxford, but the source of Laud's collection is not known[34]. In the hope that further Ourscamp manuscripts may be identified, perhaps in English libraries, we list here all those works of Augustine thus annotated in *Ar* :

De immortalitate anime
De moribus ecclesie catholice
De libero arbitrio
De genesi aduersum manicheos
De uera religione
De utilitate credendi (Oxford, Bodl. Laud Misc. 343, f. 2-43).
De sermone domini in monte
De mendacio
Contra epistolam manichei que dicitur fundamenti
De agone christiano
De doctrina christiana
Confessionum
Contra epistolam manichei que dicitur fundamenti
De natura boni
De trinitate
De consensu euangelistarum
De opere monachorum

1957, p. 8-9 ; *Dictionnaire de spiritualité ascétique et mystique*, 6, Paris, 1965, col. 377-8 ; A. GRANSDEN, *The Peterborough Commentary and Gilbert de Stanford*, in *Revue Bénédictine*, 70, 1960, p. 625-638 ; J. LECLERCQ, *Le Commentaire de Gilbert de Stanford sur le Cantique des Cantiques*, in *Analecta monastica* 1, Vatican City, 1948, p. 209-230.

33. R.B. Dobson documents the close connection of Durham monks with Oxford from the 1280's and the richness of the Durham library in this period in *Durham Priory 1400-1450*, Cambridge, 1973, p. 342-378. A mark on the inside flyleaf of *Dur* suggests that it might have been bought from a bookseller. See above n. 6.

34. R.W. Hunt notes the presence of a collection of twenty-seven manuscripts of French origin, including those from Ourscamp (Laud, Misc. 398, lat. 89, Misc. 343, 449), although had not succeeded in identifying from which source they entered the collection of archbishop Laud, H.O. COXE, *Bodleian Library Quarto Catalogues, II. Laudian Manuscripts. Reprinted from the edition of 1858-1885, with corrections and additions, and an historical introduction by R.W. Hunt*, Oxford, 1973, p. XVI-XVII.

De bono coniugali
De sancta uirginitate
De genesi ad litteram (Arras, Bibl. mun. 80 or perhaps Oxford, Bodl. Laud lat. 89, f. 1-153)
De unico baptismo conta petilianum ad constantinum
De gratia <noui> testamenti ad honoratum (Oxford, Bodl. Laud Misc. 343, f. 2-43)
De uidendo deo
De natura et gratia
De ciuitate dei
Ad horosium probum contra priscillianistas
Ad iheronimum probum
De nuptiis et concupiscentia ad ualerium
De anima et eius origine
Ad Laurentium de fide et spe et caritate, id est enchiridion (Oxford, Laud Misc. 398, f. 84-99)
De cura pro mortuis gerenda ad paulinum episcopum.

Not mentioned in this list are the two works occurring in *Ar* itself, the *Retractationes* and *De haeresibus*, which passed into the hands of a master of the Sorbonne in the fifteenth century[35]. One manuscript of Ourscamp which ended up in the Bodleian library, Oxford is Laud Misc. 449 containing the letters of Gregory the Great, while another, containing the sermons of St Bernard, came to Aberdeen, University Library 156. Most of the manuscripts of Ourscamp would find their way into the municipal library of Arras, at the Revolution : Arras, Bibl. mun. 70, 76, 80, 85, 114, 116, 117, 120, 615, 649, 715, 758, 797. Others passed to the cathedral library of Cambrai : Cambrai, Bibl. mun. 211, 304, 335, 358, 487, 548, 554, 561, 563, 602. Some followed an independent path, such as Paris, Bibl. nat. lat. 1879 and Vatican, Reg. lat. 185 or Troyes, Bibl. mun. 1771, which had passed from Ourscamp to the mother house of Clairvaux[36]. Many of its manuscripts of Augustine have either disappeared or are still to be identified. To discover that one might contain another fragment of the writing of Guibert of Nogent is more than one could hope for.

SUMMARY : Immediately following Augustine's *De haeresibus* in the MS Durham Cathedral Library B.III.7 (*c.* 1300) occurs Guibert of Nogent's description of the beliefs and practices of a sect in the region of Soissons. The fragment, edited here, enables us to improve our text of this part of the *Monodiae*. Guibert probably added this passage to his narrative after he had learnt of rumours told by Paul of St-Père of Chartres about heretics burnt at Orleans *c.* 1022. Those of Soissons were not Manichaeans, as Guibert thought, but followers of a local preacher, Clement of Bucy, who established religious communities for both sexes according to a common pattern in the period. In an appendix, a possible link between the Durham MS and Ourscamp is discussed.

35. Martin (*Catalogue... Arsenal*, p. 137-8) reproduces some of the extensive annotations on the flyleaves of this manuscript, relating to accounts of the university as well as biographical information about its possessor. On f. 76ᵛ in a fifteenth-century hand is written « hunc librum habui a Dionisio ...lleri precio unius libre Parisiensis. The only monk of Ourscamp recorded in the *Chartularium Universitatis Parisiensis*, ed. H. Denifle, Paris, 1897, is Robert de Ourscamp, a bachelor in the faculty of theology 1431-32 (no. 2415, p. 543) and licentiate in 1437 (no. 2517, p. 602). The Arsenal manuscript passed into the possession of the discalced Carmelites of Paris in the seventeenth century.

36. This information comes from the files of the « Institut de Recherche et d'Histoire des Textes », to whose staff I am grateful.

IV

IN SEARCH OF A NAME AND ITS SIGNIFICANCE: A TWELFTH-CENTURY ANECDOTE ABOUT THIERRY AND PETER ABAELARD

'Abaelard,' 'Abelard,' 'Baiolard'... ? Twelfth-century scribes were as uncertain of the exact spelling and pronunciation of the famous philosopher's cognomen as scholars have been in more recent centuries.[1] Trivial as it might seem, correct pronunciation provides the key to understanding a short anecdote copied onto the opening folio of a twelfth-century manuscript (MS Munich, Bayerische Staatsbibliothek Clm. 14160 = **M**), formerly belonging to the Benedictine abbey of St. Emmeran, Regensburg.[2] It tells the reader that the peripatetic philosopher wanted to supplement his studies of the trivium by

---

[1] D. E. Luscombe lists thirty-seven medieval forms of the name in *The School of Peter Abelard* (Cambridge 1969) 315. More recent spellings are commented on in an epilogue to this study. The following supplementary abbreviations will be used:

AHDLMA — *Archives d'histoire doctrinale et littéraire du moyen âge*

BGPTMA — *Beiträge zur Geschichte der Philosophie und der Theologie des Mittelalters*

Commentaries — *Commentaries on Boethius by Thierry of Chartres and his School* (ed. N. Häring; Toronto 1971)

Commentum — *Commentum super Boethii librum de trinitate*, ed. N. Häring, *Commentaries* 57–116

MABK — *Mittelalterliche Bibliothekskataloge Deutschlands und der Schweiz*, ed. P. Lehmann (Munich 1918—)

RTAM — *Recherches de théologie ancienne et médiévale*

Tchr — *Theologia christiana* (ed. E. M. Buytaert, CCL CM 12; Turnhout 1969)

TSch — *Theologia 'Scholarium'* (edd. E. M. Buytaert and C. J. Mews, CCL CM 13; Turnhout 1987).

I would like to thank J. S. Barrow, C. S. F. Burnett, and D. E. Luscombe for being able to draw on the extensive microfilm collection built up at the University of Sheffield under the aegis of the Leverhulme Trust. They summarise the fruits of their research in 'A Checklist of the Manuscripts Containing Writings of Peter Abelard and Heloise and of Other Works Closely Associated with Abelard and his School,' *Revue d'histoire des textes* 14–15 (1984–85) 183–302. Further information on all the manuscripts mentioned in this article can be found in this checklist. I am also grateful to C. S. F. Burnett for his comments on many parts of this paper and for information concerning Adelard of Bath.

[2] An incomplete form of the text was first published by B. Pez, *Thesaurus anecdotorum novissimus* III.1 (Paris 1721) xxii, in turn copied by J.-A. Fabricius, *Bibliotheca mediae et infimae Latinitatis* (Hamburg 1734) 232, by J.-P. Migne in PL 178.57–58, and with discussion by R. L. Poole, *Illustrations of the History of Medieval Thought and Learning* (London 1884) 363–66; (2nd ed. London 1920) 313–15. L. Hödl published a complete text without any commentary in *Die Geschichte der scholastischen Literatur und der Theologie der Schlüsselgewalt*, pt. 1 (BGPTMA 38.4; Münster 1960) 78.

IV

following the lectures of master Thierry on mathematics, but then found the
subject too difficult. Thierry gave Peter the name 'Baiolard' because he was
like a greedy dog who had eaten his fill yet still wanted to lick (given as the
meaning of *baiare*) lard, here used as an image of the quadrivium. The word
lardum may itself be a pun on *artium*. The story-teller goes on to claim that
Peter changed 'Baiolard' ('lick-lard') to 'Abelard' ('have-lard') because he
came to master geometry and arithmetic. The patent absurdity of a number of
details in this anecdote — such as, that Abelard was an Englishman or that he
wrote on geometry and arithmetic — has led most scholars to dismiss the story
as a spurious invention.[3] In this study I shall examine whether there are any
historical insights to be gained from the anecdote, the text of which is given
here with an attempt at a translation. The full flavour of the Latin is best
appreciated if the story is read aloud:

> Petrus qui abelardus. a plerisque baiolardus dicitur. natione anglicus. pri-
> mum grammatice et dialetice. hinc diuinitati operam dedit. Sed cum esset
> inestimande subtilitatis. inaudite memorie. capacitatis supra humanum
> modum. auditor aliquando magistri Roscii. cepit eum cum exfestucatione[4]
> quadam sensuum illius audire. attamen imperauit sibi ut per annum lectioni-
> bus ipsius interesset. Mox ergo socios habere. et parisiis palam dialetice
> atque diuinitatis lectiones dare cepit. et facile omnes francie magistros in
> breui superuenit. Qui cum de quadriuio nichil audisset. clam magistro Tirrico
> in quasdam mathematicas lectiones aures dabat. in quibus supra quam existi-
> maret optentu difficultatis intellectus resiliebat audientis. Cui semel afflicto et
> indignanti per iocum magister tirricus ait. Quid canis plenus nisi lardum
> baiare consueuit. Baiare autem lingere est.[5] Exinde baiolardus appellari cepit.
> Quod nomen tanquam ex defectu quodam sibi impositum cum abdicaret. sub
> literatura non dissimili habelardum se nominari fecit. quasi qui haberet ar-
> tium apud se summam et adipem. Nam processu temporis se usque adeo [de][6]

---

[3] The episode has been alluded to by R. W. Southern in 'Humanism and the School of
Chartres,' in *Medieval Humanism and Other Essays* (Oxford 1971) 61–85 at 81–82, and R.
Klibansky, 'The School of Chartres,' in *Twelfth-Century Europe and the Foundations of
Modern Society*, edd. M. Clagett, G. Post, and R. Reynolds (Madison 1961) 3–14 at 12.
Scepticism regarding its value was expressed by A. Vernet in 'Une épitaphe inédite de Thierry
de Chartres,' in *Recueil de travaux offerts à Clovis Brunel* 2 (Paris 1955) 660–70 at n. 2, repr. in
his *Études médiévales* (Paris 1981) 160–70, and by David Luscombe in *Peter Abelard's Ethics*
(Oxford 1971) xliv n. 4.

[4] Literally 'renunciation' or 'abandonment.'

[5] This is the only use of *baiare* cited by Du Cange 1.522. The nearest term given by J. F.
Niermeyer is *bajulare*, meaning 'to care for' or 'to watch over,' in *Mediae Latinitatis lexicon
minus* (Leiden 1976) 77; *baiula* is defined as a nurse in *Mittellateinisches Wörterbuch* I (Munich
1967) 1313.

[6] The *de* seems redundant here. A dative rather than an ablative *lardo* makes more sense.
The additional *de* might have been copied mistakenly by misreading the preceding *adeo* or
have been taken down from faulty dictation; alternatively it may hide another pun on *Adelardus*.

lardo quadriuio potenter intromisit. ut nos opera illius de geometricis et arithmeticis subtilitatibus usque hodie plura uideamus.

Peter, who is called 'Abelard' and by many 'Baiolard' and is English by birth,
first applied himself to grammar and to dialectic, and then to divinity. But
since he was someone of an unbelievable intelligence, an unsurpassed memory,
and superhuman capacity, being at one time a pupil of master Roscius [Rosce-
lin of Compiègne], he began to listen to him with a certain lack of concentration. Nevertheless, he [Roscelin] ordered him to attend his lectures for a whole
year. As a result, he [Peter] soon began to have pupils of his own and to give
lectures on dialectic and divinity openly in Paris, and in a short time he easily
outstripped all the teachers of France. Since he had heard nothing about the
quadrivium, he secretly followed certain mathematical lectures of master
Thierry, from which the intellect of the listener recoiled, under the guise that
it was more difficult than imagined. Master Thierry once said as a joke to him
when he [Peter] was disheartened and put out: 'What has a full dog been used
to other than to lick [baiare] lard?' For baiare is to lick. From then on he
[Peter] began to be known as 'Baiolard' [= 'lick-lard']. Since he rejected this
name, given to him as if from a failing, he had himself called 'Habelard' [=
'have-lard'], not dissimilar in letters, as he had mastered the entirety and the
fat [adipem, word play on apicem or peak] of the arts. For in the course of
time, he introduced himself mightily to the lard of the quadrivium to such a
great extent that we see many works of his on the subtleties of geometry and
arithmetic right up to the present day.

How much of this story is based on historical fact? The first detail needing
to be elucidated is the correct spelling and pronunciation of Peter's cognomen.
The habit among English-speaking scholars of referring to him as 'Abelard'
unfortunately weakens the force of the joke about 'Baiolard.'

Twice within the Dialectica Peter comments on his cognomen to argue that a
word is a human construct with no intrinsic meaning beyond that established
by convention: 'Only those utterances are to be considered [as part of logic]
which signify by convention, that is, according to the will of the imposer, and
which, having been formed at will by men, are retained for constituting human
expressions and imposed for designating things, as the word "Abaelardus" has
been allocated to me so that through it, my substance can be referred to.'[7]
Elsewhere in the Dialectica he observes that until the present 'Abaelardus'
referred by convention to himself alone, and not to any common substance.[8]

---

[7] Petrus Abaelardus. Dialectica (ed. L. M. de Rijk; 2nd ed. Assen 1970) 114: 'Eas [sc. voces]
igitur solas oportet exequi que ad placitum significant, hoc est secundum voluntatem impo-
nentis, que uidelicet prout libuit ab hominibus formate ad humanas locutiones constituendas
sunt reperte et ad eas res designandas imposite, ut hoc vocabulum Abaelardus michi ideo
collocatum est ut per ipsum de substantia mea agatur.'

[8] Ibid. 566: 'Quod autem "commune" supposuit [Boetius] voces unius tantum singularis
substantie designativas separavit, ut Abaelardus, quod michi uni adhuc convenire arbitror.'

In the single surviving manuscript of this text (MS Paris, BN lat. 14614, fols. 127ᵛ and 196ᵛ), 'Abaelardus' is spelt with *a* and *e* as separate vowels, as in *aer*, Michael or Israel. This is the spelling of his signature in a copy of a charter of Notre-Dame du Ronceray, Angers, drawn up in his presence on 15 March 1128.[9]

'Abaelardus' is the most frequently found spelling in the manuscript tradition, as both Duchesne and Geyer observed.[10] It is never spelt with a cedilla underneath the *e*. One finds '[magistri] Petri Abaelardi' with *ae* as a double vowel in rubrics to manuscripts of his glosses on Porphyry and Aristotle,[11] the *De intellectibus*,[12] the *Sic et Non*,[13] the *Theologia*,[14] his commentary on the Epistle to the Romans,[15] the *Expositio in Hexameron* (in a manuscript probably copied in part by Abaelard himself),[16] the *Problemata Heloissae*,[17] the *Historia calamitatum* and correspondence with Heloise,[18] and a number of smaller works.[19]

---

[9] The signature is reproduced on the front cover of *Abélard en son temps. Actes du colloque international organisé à l'occasion du 9ᵉ centenaire de la naissance de Pierre Abélard (14–18 mai 1979)* (ed. Jean Jolivet; Paris 1981) from Loire-Atlantique, Archives départementales H 351, pièce 1. The charter is edited by P. Marchegay, *Archives d'Anjou* III (Angers 1854) 289 no. 453.

[10] A. Duchesne, *Notæ ad Historiam Calamitatum*, in *Petri Abaelardi... et Heloissæ coniugis eius... Opera* (Paris 1616) 1141–42, repr. in PL 178.113AB. The printers of PL 178 changed Duchesne's 'Abaelardus' into 'Abælardus' by mistake. B. Geyer comments on the correct spelling in *Peter Abaelards philosophische Schriften* 1. *Die Logica 'Ingredientibus'* (BGPTMA 21.1; Münster 1919) v n. 1.

[11] MS Milan, Biblioteca ambrosiana M 63 sup., fols. 1, 15ᵛ, 16, 43ᵛ, 44; see also the briefer glosses in MS Paris, BN lat. 13368, fols. 128, 146, 156. All manuscripts cited are of the twelfth century unless otherwise stated.

[12] MS Avranches, Bibl. mun. 135, fol. 64, from Mont-St-Michel. The authenticity of this work has been reaffirmed and its text re-edited by Lucia Urbani Ulivi, *La psicologia di Abelardo e il 'Tractatus de intellectibus'* (Rome 1976) 103–27.

[13] MSS Brescia, Civica Biblioteca Queriniana A.V.21, fol. 17; Cambridge University Library Kk 3.24, fol. 67ᵛ, from Christ Church, Canterbury; Montecassino, Archivia della Badia 174, p. 277 (saec. XIII); London, British Library, Royal 11 A.V, fol. 73, from Merton, Surrey.

[14] MS Berlin, Staatsbibliothek Preussischer Kulturbesitz, theol. lat. oct. 95, fol. 64, from Hautmont, diocese of Cambrai (*Theologia 'Summi boni'*).

[15] MS Angers, Bibl. mun. 68, fol. 36.

[16] MS Avranches, Bibl. mun. 135, fol. 75, from Mont-St-Michel. Mary Romig argues that one of the three hands which copied the *Expositio in Hexameron* is that of Abaelard: 'A Critical Edition of Peter Abelard's Expositio in Hexameron' (diss. University of Southern California 1981) lxxxv–cxviii.

[17] MS Paris, BN lat. 14511, fol. 44ᵛ (saec. XV).

[18] MSS Troyes, Bibl. mun. 802, fol. 1 (saec. XIII/XIV); Paris, BN lat. 2923, fol. 1 (saec. XIII); Oxford, Bodleian Library, Add. C 271, fol. 76 (saec. XIV). See J. Monfrin, *Pierre Abélard, Historia calamitatum* (Paris 1959) 1–24.

[19] E.g., *Confessio fidei 'Universis'* in MS Oxford, Bodleian Library, Canon. Pat. lat. 171, fol. 222ᵛ; letter 11 (on the identity of St. Denis) in MSS Paris, BN lat. 2445A, fol. 35; BN lat. 1447,

It is the spelling given in the largest extant collection of his theological writings (MS Oxford, Balliol College 296), containing the *Theologia, Scito teipsum, Collationes*, and commentary on Romans.[20] The best manuscript of the correspondence of William of Saint-Thierry and Bernard of Clairvaux relating to Abaelard preserves the same orthography.[21] The great majority of manuscripts with the spelling *ae* come from northern France.

That an *ae* in twelfth-century manuscripts indicates two distinct syllables is evident from the way in which poets scan Abaelard's name in verse, as noted by both Poole and Geyer. The example of the *Metamorphosis Goliae* is only one of many which could be quoted:

> Celebrum theologum uidimus Lumbardum
> cum Yvone, Helyam Petrum, et Bernardum
> quorum opobalsamum spirat os et nardum
> et professi plurimi sunt Abaelardum.[22]

Sometimes a consonantal *i* is used to divide the *a* and *e*, but this does not affect the scansion.

The pronunciation suggested by poetic testimony is corroborated indirectly by the myriad variations of spelling in manuscripts from outside northern France. The variations in orthography reflect different ways of transcribing the same underlying phonetic structure. A brief excerpt from Abaelard's *Sententie* in a late twelfth-century manuscript from Göttweig (MS Vienna, ÖNB cvp 998, fol. 177) is introduced as 'Petrus abaielardus in theologia sua.' 'Abaielardus' is also the spelling in a thirteenth-century manuscript of the *Sic et Non* from Tegernsee (MS Munich, Bayerische Staatsbibliothek Clm. 18926, fol. 14ᵛ) and in a fourteenth-century fragment of that work. 'Abaialardus' occurs in twelfth-century copies of the *Sententie* (MS Pavia, Biblioteca Universitaria, Aldini 49, fol. 73), of the *Sic et Non* and five sermons from Einsiedeln (MS Einsiedeln, Stiftsbibliothek 300, pp. 1, 74), and in two related late twelfth-century manuscripts of the *Theologia 'Scholarium'* from the abbey of Anchin (MS Douai, Bibl. mun. 357, fol. 108) and an unknown English house (MS Lon-

---

fol. 17; BN nouv. acq. lat. 1509, fol. 16; *Planctus Jephta* in MS Vatican, Biblioteca Apostolica, Reg. lat. 288, fol. 63ᵛ; *Carmen ad Astralabium* in MS London, British Library, Burney 216, p. 199.

[20] Fols. 61, 80, 161 (saec. XIV). The opening page of the MS, which might have carried an attribution for the *Theologia 'Scholarium,'* is missing.

[21] MS Charleville-Mezières, Bibl. mun. 67, fols. 72ᵛ–132, from William's abbey of Signy.

[22] '*Metamorphosis Goliae episcopi*, Mitteilungen aus Handschriften,' ed. R. B. C. Huygens, *Studi Medievali* 3ᵉ ser. 3 (1962) 764–72 at 771. The two MSS of the poem differ in their spellings: *ab aelardum* O [sic]; *abaielardum* H. See Poole, *Illustrations* 313–15 and Geyer, *Philosophische Schriften* v n. 1.

IV

don, British Library, Royal 8 A.I, fol. 3).[23] Some manuscripts read 'Abailardus,' but these do not match those with 'Abaelardus' in authority or number.[24] The consonantal *i* is replaced with an *h* ('abahelardus') in the title of certain verses on the Blessed Virgin in MS Mons, Bibliothèque publique 25/118 (fol. 52ᵛ).[25]

A similar pronunciation is intended by the form 'petri AbaGelardi,' found in a mid-twelfth-century manuscript of the *Expositio in Hexameron* (MS Copenhagen, Køngelige bibliotek e don. var. 138 4°, fol. 9), belonging to the Cistercian house of Herrevad, in the diocese of Lund.[26] The majuscule *G* here indicates the same guttural sound as used for 'Apulegius,' the spelling consistently used in this manuscript. In a *reportatio* of Abaelard's ethical teaching added in the first half of the twelfth century to the margin of an Anglo-Saxon text (MS London, British Library, Cotton Faustina A X, fol. 151), master P. is qualified variously as 'abag.,' 'abagel.,' and 'abagelardus.' Its copyist follows a practice of English scribes of the early twelfth century who use a *g* to denote the sound

---

[23] On the Turin fragment, see J. S. Barrow, 'Tractatus Magistri Petri Abaielardi de Sacramento altaris,' *Traditio* 40 (1984) 328–36. *Abaielardus* introduces a comment made after q. 141 of the *Sic et Non, Quod opera misericordie non prosunt infidelibus*, found only in a Montecassino MS (Archivio della Badia 174) of the *Sic et Non* (edd. B. Boyer and R. McKeon; Chicago 1976–77) 609–10. The Turin fragment is related textually to this MS, as well as to those from Tours, Brescia (to which it is the closest), and Einsiedeln. The common exemplar of these MSS seems to have been Abaelard's personal workbook, containing heavily annotated copies of the *Sic et Non* and *Theologia christiana*, a copy of which was brought to Italy by Cardinal Guy of Castello, friend of Abaelard and later Pope Celestine II. See Mews, 'Peter Abelard's Theologia Christiana and Theologia "Scholarium" Re-examined,' *RTAM* 52 (1985) 111–59 at 148–49.

[24] MSS Tours, Bibl. mun. 85, fol. 106, introducing the *Sic et Non*; Paris, BN lat. 7493, fol. 168, introducing glosses on the *De differentiis topicis*; Heidelberg, Universitätsbibliothek 71, fol. 145ᵛ (a letter against Bernard); Bloomington, Indiana University Library, Poole MS fragment 99 (two lines from the *Carmen ad Astralabium*); London, British Library, Add. 22287, fol. 128 ('versus magistri Petri Abailardi de sancta maria vergine'). The oldest manuscripts (group B) of Otto of Freising's *Gesta Frederici I Imperatoris* 1.48 (edd. G. Waitz and B. de Simson; Hannover 1912) 68 read 'Abaiolardus,' but the editors adopted 'Abailardus' from a later recension.

[25] The poem was edited by V. Cousin from this 13th-century MS and MS Paris, BN lat. 16565, fol. 59 in *Petri Abaelardi Opera* I (Paris 1849) 330. Both are from the region of Cambrai. The same poem has the attribution 'abellardi' in MS Douai, Bibl. mun. 825, fol. 140 (from Anchin) and 'abailardi' in MS London, British Library Add. 22287, fol. 128 (from the Celestine priory of Sainte-Croix, Offemont, diocese of Soissons). The entry 'a.d. MCXLII obiit Petrus Abahelardi perypateticus' occurs at the end of a late 13th- or early 14th-century copy of Abaelard's correspondence (MS Paris, BN lat. 2544) belonging in the mid-fourteenth century to master Jacobus de Gantis; see Monfrin, *Historia calamitatum*, 20.

[26] On the Herrevad MS, see Romig, *Expositio* lviii–lxv. The reading *Apulegius* occurs twice on fol. 14 (PL 178.752c).

previously denoted by the Anglo-Saxon 3, for which there was no direct equivalent in continental script.[27]

Another form of the cognomen occurs in manuscripts from Germany and
Austria. A mid-twelfth-century copy of the *Theologia 'Summi boni'* from the
Cistercian abbey of Heilsbronn in the diocese of Eichstätt (MS Erlangen, Universitätsbibliothek 182, fol. 27 = **E**) begins with lavish praise of its author in
the opening rubric: 'Incipiunt capitula librorum de trinitate magistri petri,
clarissimi atque doctissimi uiri, cognomento adbaiolardi.'[28] In a catalogue of
the library of Prüfening, Regensburg, drawn up in 1165, Wolfger noted that
'Petrus Baiolardus' was one of the many modern authors represented in the
library — alongside Hugh of Saint-Victor, Gratian, Rupert of Deutz, and Peter
Lombard, among many others.[29] Wolfger specified that the library owned a
codex containing 'Sententie Petri baiol. et liber eius qui dicitur Scito teipsum
et sent. m. Hugonis in uno uolumine.' This manuscript was very similar to,
though cannot be identified with, Clm. 14160 (**M**), which contains the anecdote
cited at the beginning of this study.[30] The same scribe who copied this anecdote composed the rubrics 'sentencie magistri Petri Abelardi' (fol. 1ᵛ) and 'liber
magistri Petri Abelardi qui dicitur Scito teipsum' (fol. 39ᵛ).[31] The script and

---

[27] On the Cotton MS, see N. R. Ker, *Catalogue of Manuscripts Containing Anglo-Saxon*
(Oxford 1957) 194–96, who dates the hand to the first quarter of the twelfth century. I am
grateful to David Luscombe and Charles Burnett for a transcription of this gloss. For philo-
logical commentary on these changes, see Cecily Clark, 'L'Angleterre anglo-normande et ses
ambivalences socio-culturelles: Un coup d'œuil de philologue,' *Les mutations socio-culturelles
au tournant des xɪᵉ–xɪɪᵉ siècles*. Actes du colloque international du CNRS. Études Anselmien-
nes (ɪᵛᵉ session) (Spicilegium Beccense 2; Paris 1984) 99–110, where further references are
given.

[28] H. Fischer, *Katalog der Handschriften der Universitätsbibliothek Erlangen*. Neubearbeitung I. *Die lateinischen Pergamenthandschriften* (Erlangen 1928) I 202–203.

[29] G. Becker, *Catalogi bibliothecarum antiqui* (Bonn 1885) 209 and MABK 4 (ed. C. E.
Ineichen-Eder; Munich 1977) 422. These entries are re-edited and discussed in detail by H.-G.
Schmitz, *Kloster Prüfening im 12. Jahrhundert* (Miscellanea Bavarica Monacensia; Munich
1975) 74, 91–92.

[30] Both MSS are listed in a catalogue of 1347 (MABK 4.1.431 and 4.1.157). **M**, mentioned
again in catalogues of 1449/52 (MABK 4.1.172) and 1500 (MABK 4.1.193), is described in
detail by Luscombe, in *Peter Abelard's Ethics* xli–xliv. Uncertainty over the spelling of the
cognomen crept into the opening rubric of a 15th-century copy from Tegernsee (MS Munich,
Bayerische Staatsbibliothek Clm. 28363, fol. 4): 'Incipit liber magistri petri abelardi uel baiolardi.'

[31] Under the heading 'Sententie magistri Hugonis' **M** groups together on fols. 68–157 the
Summa Sententiarum, extracts from works of Hugh of St-Victor, Ivo of Chartres, and the *De
claustro animae* of Hugh of Fouilloy († 1172/73), here entitled 'Liber domini Hugonis de
claustralibus.' The latter text, not mentioned by Wolfger as found within the MS containing
works of Baiolard and Hugo, occurs in another manuscript cited in the catalogue: Schmitz,
Kloster Prüfening 91–92. H. Weisweiler reported the opinion of L. Ott that Wolfger could not
be referring to **M** in *Das Schrifttum der Schule Anselms von Laon und Wilhelm von Champeaux
in deutschen Bibliotheken* (BGPTMPA 33.1–2; Münster 1936) 27.

IV

decoration of **M** suggest that it was copied at Prüfening in either the late third or the early fourth quarter of the twelfth century.[32] **M** had passed to the neighbouring abbey of St. Emmeran by the late twelfth century, when the inscription *Emmerammum* was added over an erasure on its flyleaf.

The spelling 'Baiolardus' or a variant on this is often found in manuscripts belonging to Benedictine houses in Austria. Admont owned a copy (MS Princeton, University Library, R. Garrett 169 = **A**) of Abaelard's *Sententie* textually superior to that in **M**, bearing on fol. 83 the title given by Wolfger: 'Sententie magistri Petri Baiolardi.'[33] The Erzabtei St. Peter, Salzburg, possessed a manuscript containing 'Sententie Petri Bailardi,'[34] as did the canons of St. Nicolas, Passau (MS Munich, Bayerische Staatsbibliothek Clm. 16085, unattributed). The rubric 'Dialogus Petri Baiolardi' introduces Abaelard's *Collationes* or dialogue of a philosopher with a Jew and a Christian in a manuscript from Klosterneuburg (MS Vienna, ÖNB cvp 819, fol. 151).[35] The initial *a* is not elided, but the *B* is enlarged in a rubric introducing some unpublished 'Versus Petri aBaiolardi in laudem crucis' in a twelfth-century manuscript (now MS Vienna, ÖNB cvp 143, fol. 12). Another copy of these verses is mentioned in a catalogue of Walderbach (diocese of Regensburg) compiled in 1511/12.[36] The

---

[32] A. Boeckler observed the similarities between **M** and other manuscripts of Prüfening in *Die Regensburger–Prüfeninger Buchmalerei des XII.–XIII. Jahrhunderts* (Munich 1924) 81, 120, although he was mistaken in identifying **M** with Wolfger's MS (and hence datable to before 1165). He compared the decoration of initials in **M** to that in two other Prüfening MSS, now Munich, Clm. 14042 and Clm. 14051. The latter was copied by one Ysingrinus, under the abbacy of Adalbert (1149–77). The script of **M** is not unlike that of an important scientific MS of Prüfening (Munich, Clm. 13021; see n. 72 below), which because of its contents (the Toledan Tables in particular) was probably copied not before 1170.

[33] Its script is similar to that of another Admont MS, now Oxford, Bodleian Library, Lyell 49 (**L**), descended from the same exemplar as **E**. The *Sententie* in **M** and **A** were attributed to a supposed disciple of Abaelard called Hermann by H. Ostlender, 'Die Sentenzenbücher der Schule Abaelards,' *Theologische Quartalschrift* 117 (1936) 208–52, on the grounds that 'Hermannus' is cited as a name within examples of future propositions (where 'Petrus' occurs in another recension, in better MSS). I argue that the *Sententie* report the lectures of Abaelard, not of any Hermann, in 'The *Sententie* of Peter Abaelard,' *RTAM* 53 (1986) 131–84. The work has been re-edited by Sandro Buzzetti, *Sententie magistri Petri Abelardi (Sententie Hermanni)* (Florence 1983).

[34] Becker, *Catalogi* 237 n. 211.

[35] See too an 'Epitaphium Petri Baiolardi a semet compositum,' MS Zürich, Zentralbibliothek C 58, fol. 5ᵛ, discussed by Peter Dronke, *Abelard and Heloise in Medieval Testimonies* (Glasgow 1976) 37, 47–50.

[36] 'Versus magistri Petri Baiolardi valde boni' are listed at Walderbach in MABK 4.1.561. On the diffusion of Abaelard's writings in this part of the Empire, see Peter Classen, 'Zur Geschichte der Frühscholastik in Österreich und Bayern,' *Mitteilungen des Instituts für Öster-*

abbey of Engelberg (diocese of Constance) owned certain 'Excerpta auctorita-
tum a Petro Baiulardo collecta,' presumably the *Sic et Non*, according to a
catalogue drawn up before 1178.[37]

This survey of different twelfth-century spellings of the cognomen shows
that in northern France the most widely used form was 'Abealardus.' Outside
this region scribes rendered a name pronounced as *'Aba'elardus'* in a variety of
ways. The form 'Baiolardus,' attributed in the anecdote to master Thierry,
occurs mainly in manuscripts from religious houses along the Danube and its
tributaries. To my knowledge, no twelfth-century manuscript other than **M**
supplies the form 'Abelardus.'

The function of the anecdote is ostensibly to explain the derivation of two
imagined forms of the cognomen, 'Baiolard' and 'Abelard.' The story also
hints at certain aspects of Peter's personality — notably that he was ambitious, yet easily frustrated and at times depressed. The information that Abaelard began to get bored as a pupil of Roscelin introduces a similar story about
his inability to follow the lectures of Thierry. The comparison of 'Baiolard' to
a well-fed dog used to licking up more lard than necessary is a caustic comment
on an insatiable intellectual appetite which seemed to over-run natural capacity. The pun on 'have-lard' itself contains another play on words, impossible
to translate, which suggests that he mastered the sum and the 'fat' of the arts
(*artium apud se summam et adipem*). If the Latin is read aloud, it become
apparent that *adipem* is used to evoke *apicem*, so as to refer to both fat or lard
(namely, the quadrivium) and a physical summit. There may also be another
play on *artium* and *lardum*. Peter's achievement in mastering these disciplines
is quoted as proof of his outstanding intelligence, mentioned at the beginning
of the anecdote. Can any historical credence be attached to the text, which
relates episodes not mentioned at all in the *Historia calamitatum*, or is it to be
confined to the realm of unsubstantiated fantasy?

We know from Roscelin's only surviving letter that Abaelard had been his
pupil 'from boyhood to early manhood,' but not that the friction between the

---

reichische Geschichtsforschung 67 (1959) 249–77, repr. in *Ausgewählte Aufsätze von Peter Classen* (Sigmaringen 1983) 279–306.

[37] MABK 1.32. An early list 'He sunt hereses petri baylardi pauce de multis' occurs in MS
Vienna, ÖNB cvp 998, fol. 173 from Göttweig; a 14th-century attribution 'Theologia Petri
Baylardi' to 12th-century extracts of the *Sententie* is almost totally erased in MS Cologne,
Historisches Archiv W 4° 137, fol. 1.

two men went back to this early period.[38] According to the anecdote, Abaelard started to teach in reaction to his master's demand that he remain a student for another year. This kaleidoscoping of events is not so far from the truth. In the *Historia calamitatum* Abaelard minimises any debt to other teachers, because this is not part of his theme: 'I began to travel about in several provinces disputing, like a true peripatetic philosopher, wherever I heard there was a keen interest in dialectic.' He then came to Paris to study with William of Champeaux, but after a while started to question the opinions of his master and began to teach himself.[39] Like Otto of Freising, the author of the anecdote recognised that Abaelard's principal teacher was Roscelin.[40] Their testimony corrects the misleading perspective provided by the *Historia calamitatum*.

Although no other evidence confirms that Abaelard had had a serious argument with Roscelin in his youth or that he had left his teacher after refusing to remain for another year, such an episode helps explain the evolution of Abaelard's early career and thinking about logic. He went to study in Paris, having mastered the subject matter under a teacher known to be quite opposed to William's realist views. Such initial tutelage would inevitably have made Abaelard critical of William from the outset. Whereas in the *Dialectica* Abaelard expressed frequent disagreement with the realist opinions of 'our teacher' (likely to be William), only once did he allude to Roscelin, and he did so then to mock him for holding an 'insane opinion' about the relationship between parts and a whole.[41] The tone which Roscelin adopts towards his former pupil, whom he charges with gross ingratitude, is no less vitriolic. His criticism of

---

[38] *Epistola ad Abaelardum*, ed. J. Reiners, *Die Nominalismus in der Frühscholastik* (BGPTMA 8; Münster 1910) 63: 'Si christianae religionis dulcedinem, quam habitu ipso praeferebas, vel tenuiter degustasses, nequaquam tui ordinis tuaeque professionis immemor et beneficiorum, quae tibi tot et tanta a puero usque ad iuvenem sub magistri nomine et actu exhibui, oblitus . . .'; (p. 65:) 'Neque vero Turonensis ecclesia vel Locensis, ubi ad pedes meos magistri tui discipulorum minimus tam diu resedisti, aut Bizuntina ecclesia, in quibus canonicus sum, extra mundum sunt, quae me omnes et venerantur et fovent et, quae dico, discendi studio libenter accipiunt.'

[39] *Historia calamitatum*, ed. Monfrin 64; see n. 43 below.

[40] *Gesta Frederici I Imperatoris* 1.48 (edd. Waitz and de Simson 69).

[41] *Dialectica*, ed. de Rijk 554–55. A similar criticism of Roscelin's logic is made in letter 14 to the bishop of Paris, *Peter Abelard, Letters IX–XIV* (ed. Edmé Smits; Groningen 1983) 279–80. The best study on Roscelin is still F. Picavet, *Roscelin philosophe et théologien, d'après la légende et d'après l'histoire* (2nd ed. Paris 1911). I argue that 'magister noster' (often identified as V. and once as W.) is the same person, namely William of Champeaux, in 'On Dating the Works of Peter Abelard,' *AHDLMA* 53 (1985) 73–134 at 85. In the gloss on Porphyry '*Ingredientibus*,' Abaelard weighs up two major possible interpretations of universals, concluding firmly that they were *voces* (ed. Geyer 22). In a later gloss '*Nostrorum petitioni sociorum*' he changes his terminology to *sermones* so as to criticise definition of universals as *voces* and so distance himself from Roscelin's approach (ed. Geyer 522).

Abaelard's theological teaching provoked an angry letter, since lost, to the
church of St. Martin of Tours where Roscelin was a canon. Roscelin's virulent
reply certainly influenced, if it did not prompt the composition of, the *Theologia 'Summi boni.'*[42] In this treatise Abaelard attacked the arrogance of un-
named 'pseudo-dialecticians' while asserting that their arguments had to be
answered in their own terms, namely of logic. The conflict between master and
former pupil was as much personal as doctrinal in nature.

Abaelard's silence about Roscelin in the *Historia calamitatum* does not prove
the inauthenticity of the latter document, as has been claimed.[43] Roscelin
himself accused Abaelard of ingratitude towards his former teacher. Nowhere
in his writings does Abaelard acknowledge any intellectual debt to the famous
nominalist logician. When drafting the *Theologia 'Scholarium'* in the early
1130s (the apparent date of the *Historia calamitatum*) he deliberately deleted
from the *Theologia christiana* a hostile allusion to Roscelin, who was no longer
the target of his argument.[44] In the short autobiographical account which
prefaces the *Theologia 'Scholarium'* Abaelard described the circumstances
behind the initial composition of the *Theologia* without referring to Roscelin by
name.[45] Although he did not want to be remembered as the pupil of a teacher
who had been condemned for heresy, contemporaries did not dissociate the two
men so easily. The brief allusion in the anecdote to the argument with Roscelin provides valuable insight into a period of Abaelard's youth about which he
was unwilling to speak.

---

[42] The sequence of events must be reconstructed from Roscelin's description of Abaelard's
letter, itself a reaction to comments of Roscelin in his *Epistola ad Abaelardum*, ed. Reiner
63–68. Once Roscelin had seen Abaelard's treatise, he tried to have it condemned for heresy.
This led Abaelard to write letter 14 to the bishop of Paris. Smits devotes a long discussion to
establishing the authenticity and the circumstances behind the redaction of this letter and the
Theologia 'Summi boni' in *Letters IX–XIV* 189–202.

[43] Hubert Silvestre argues that the absence of any mention of Roscelin in the *Historia
calamitatum* is proof of its inauthenticity, in 'Pourquoi Roscelin n'est-il pas mentionné dans
l' "Historia calamitatum"?,' in *RTAM* 48 (1981) 218–24 and with other arguments in
'L'idylle d'Abélard et Héloïse: la part du roman,' *Académie royale de Belgique. Bulletin de la
classe des lettres et des sciences morales et politiques* 5th ser. 71 (1895) 157–200. His argument
depends on the assumption that Abaelard can only be expected to give a completely full and
accurate account of his past and that any inconsistencies must be mistakes of a forger rather
than the result of colouring by Abaelard himself.

[44] In version CT of *Tchr* 3.132 (ed. Buytaert 244), Abaelard has revised the text as it stood
in the recension R. The manuscripts CT include *Tchr* 3.131, although from *TSch* 2.89 (edd.
Buytaert and Mews 262) it is evident that Abaelard intended to omit this paragraph with its
direct appeal to Roscelin: 'Responde tu mihi, acute dialectice seu [not *aut* as Buytaert]
uersipellis sophista. . . .'

[45] *TSch* Prol. 2 (ed. Buytaert; CCL cm 12.401): 'Quo enim fides nostra, id est christiana,
inquiunt, difficilioribus implicita questionibus uidetur et ab humana ratione longius absistere,
ualidioribus utique munienda est rationum presidiis, maxime uero contra impugnationes
eorum qui se philosophos profitentur.'

IV

The story-teller mentions Abaelard's inability to concentrate on Roscelin's lectures to introduce the account of his difficulty in following the mathematical lectures given by Thierry. Is there any truth to this part of the anecdote? Abaelard may allude to this very episode in his *Dialectica*:

> Although I have heard many solutions [to a certain objection] offered by arithmeticians, I judge that I should not offer any, as I recognise that I am completely ignorant of this subject.[46]

In the *Theologia christiana*, written ca. 1122–25, Abaelard asserts:

> We also know two brothers, who number themselves among the most outstanding teachers, one of whom attributes such efficacity to the words uttered over the eucharist that they could be uttered validly by a woman; the other is so involved in philosophical texts that he asserts that God could not have existed before the world.[47]

Since Otto of Freising says that Thierry had an equally famous brother called Bernard, we may presume that these are the brothers to whom Abaelard is alluding in the *Theologia christiana*.[48] Although Thierry never taught that the world was eternal, he did argue in his commentary on the *De trinitate* of Boethius that the forms of all things existed eternally in the divine mind. Abaelard was suspicious of any literal interpretation of Plato.[49] Thierry by contrast

---

[46] *Dialectica*, ed. de Rijk 59: 'Cuius quidem obiectionis, etsi multas ab arithmeticis solutiones audierim, nullam tamen a me proferendam iudico, quem eius artis ignarum omnino recognosco.' Good comments on Abaelard's attitude to the quadrivium are made by Jean Jolivet, *Arts du langage et théologie chez Abélard* (Paris 1969) 13–19.

[47] *Tchr* 4.80 (ed. Buytaert 302): 'Nouimus et duos fratres qui se inter summos connumerant magistros, quorum alter tantam uim diuinis uerbis in conficiendis sacramentis tribuit, ut a quibuscumque ipsa proferantur aeque suam habeant efficaciam, ut etiam mulier... sacramentum altaris conficere queat. Alter uero adeo philosophicis innitatur sectis, ut profiteatur deum priorem per existentiam mundo nullatenus esse. Est et quidam eorum patriota, inter diuinos celeberrimos magistros, qui in tantam prorumpit insaniam, ut corpus dominicum eiusdem longitudinis seu grossitudinis in utero Virginis fuisse adstruat cuius et in prouecta aetate exstitit.'

[48] Otto, *Gesta Frederici* 1.48 (edd. Waitz and de Simson 68). Whether the Bernard mentioned by Otto and alluded to by Abaelard is Bernard of Chartres is a separate matter. M.-D. Chenu suggested that the belief in the intrinsic efficacy of the sacramental formula imputed by Abaelard to one of the brothers reflects a Platonist approach to language such as Bernard espoused: 'Un cas de platonisme grammatical du xiie siècle,' *Revue des sciences philosophiques et théologiques* 51 (1967) 666–68. The writer of letter 18 in a letter book of Chartres asks for news 'de gente nostra' (other Bretons?) from a brother of master Bernard, ed. L. Merlet, 'Lettres d'Ives de Chartres et d'autres personnages de son temps 1087–1130,' *Bibliothèque de l'Ecole des Chartes* 4th ser. 1 (1855) 443–71 at 460. The main argument that Thierry and Bernard of Chartres are not brothers is that John of Salisbury mentions them both in one sentence without indicating that they were related, *Metalogicon* 1.5 (ed. C. C. J. Webb [Oxford 1929] 16); see nn. 63 and 66 below.

[49] The criticism of Thierry's teaching may have been based on misinterpretation of statements such as 'Est enim rerum uniuersitas in deo,' *Commentum* 4.7 (ed. Häring 97).

was interested in scientific cosmological questions inspired by the *Timaeus*, as well as in issues of theology.[50]

There is further evidence in the *Dialectica* that Abaelard might have had prior contact with Thierry. Minio-Paluello has pointed out that the only direct quotation from the *Prior Analytics* supplied in the *Dialectica* follows the same text incorporated by Thierry into his *Heptateuchon*.[51] Within his gloss on the *Peri hermeneias* Abaelard commented that he had seen a manuscript purporting to contain the *Sophistical Refutations* of Aristotle, but said he was not fully convinced that this was the genuine text because its contents did not correspond fully to the description of its argument given by Boethius.[52] His text of the *Peri hermeneias* is itself closely related to that included within the *Heptateuchon*.[53] The copy of the *De trinitate* of Boethius quoted in every recension of the *Sic et Non* belongs to the same group of manuscripts as that used by Thierry and is quite different from that commented upon by Gilbert of Poitiers.[54] Abaelard's knowledge of works of Boethius and Aristotle was not as encylopaedic as that of his great contemporary. That he made only superficial use of the *Prior Analytics* and *Sophistical Refutations* is itself a comment on the nature of their relationship.

While Abaelard was not hostile to the subjects of the quadrivium, his scientific assumptions were more traditional than those of Thierry. In every version of the *Theologia* he praised arithmetic as 'the mother and mistress of the arts,' an expression taken from the *De arithmetica* of Boethius. He also included in his text an extensive quotation from the *De musica* to demonstrate that the ancient philosophers perceived the soothing effect of music as an echo of

---

[50] Stimulating studies of Thierry's thought published by Edouard Jeauneau between 1954 and 1964 are collected in his *Lectio philosophorum: Recherches sur l'école de Chartres* (Amsterdam 1973) 5–23, 75–99. Klibansky claimed to have found a commentary of Thierry on the *De arithmetica* of Boethius, but has not published any more about this; cf. 'The School of Chartres' 5 (see n. 3 above).

[51] L. Minio-Paluello, 'I Primi Analitici: la redazione carnutense usata da Abelardo e la "Vulgata" con scolii tradotti dal greco,' *Rivista di filosofia neo-scolastica* 46 (1954) 211–23, repr. in *Opuscula: The Latin Aristotle* (Amsterdam 1972) 229–41.

[52] *Logica 'Ingredientibus,'* ed. Geyer 400: 'Memini tamen quendam libellum vidisse et diligenter relegisse, qui sub nomine Aristotelis de sophisticis elenchis intitulatus erat, et cum inter cetera sophismatum genera de univocatione requirerem; nil de ea scriptum inveni.'

[53] Minio-Paluello, *Twelfth-Century Logic* II. *Abaelardiana inedita* (Rome 1958) xxxii–xxxiv.

[54] The Boethian *De trinitate* is mentioned in *Tchr* 3.74, 85–86 and 4.10, 33 (ed. Buytaert 225, 270, 280) but is cited much more fully in the *Sic et Non* qq. 8.7–16 and 9.1–2 (edd. Boyer and McKeon; Chicago 1976–77) 130–31, 136. There is one significant crux where the MS tradition of the *De trinitate* divides: Abaelard agrees with Thierry in reading 'praeter id quod est' (*Sic et Non* 8.7; *Commentum* 2.59, ed. Häring 86), against Gilbert, who reads 'praeter id quo est' in his own *Commentary*, ed. Häring, *The Commentaries on Boethius by Gilbert of Poitiers* (Toronto 1966) 372.

IV

heavenly harmony, the fruit of divine goodness.[55] These works of Boethius provided support for Abaelard's argument about harmony as a manifestation of the Holy Spirit, not the core of his trinitarian theology. He had no interest in the mathematical analogies of unity, connection, and equality mentioned briefly by Augustine in the *De doctrina christiana* and expanded by Thierry into a key argument. Thierry and the young William of Conches had both asserted that the world soul was the Holy Spirit.[56] Abaelard never went this far. Insisting on a theological interpretation of the *Timaeus* he did not hesitate to criticise those who adopted (in his eyes) an excessively literal approach to Plato's doctrine of the world soul. Full of praise for pagan wisdom in general as proof of God's self-revelation through reason, Abaelard concentrated with little apology on only one branch of that learning — dialectic — for the opportunity which it gave to reflect on the Trinity.

The difference in their attitudes towards natural science is apparent in their contrasting interpretations of the first chapters of Genesis. Faithful to a scientific perspective inherited from Augustine, Abaelard could not accept, as he says some argued, that the waters placed by God above the firmament 'where they praise the name of the Lord' (Gen. 1.6; Ps. 148.4) fell to the earth at the time of the Flood. Thierry held a contrary, more original opinion: that this water slipped to the earth to give life to creation.[57] Quite traditional attitudes lie behind Abaelard's suspicion of those *astronomi* who use their discipline to pronounce on future contingents, which can never be known. Nonetheless, he did recognise that in studying the nature of the stars and the regions of heaven, astronomers are justified in making climatic and medical pronouncements about the future. Abaelard described Moses as an outstanding example of 'astronomical discipline.'[58] It was legitimate to be concerned with natural as

---

[55] *Tchr* 1.80–82 (ed. Buytaert 104–106). In *Tchr* 1.79 Abaelard comments that number was the most perfect exemplar of all things: 'Omnis quippe ordo naturae et concinna dispositio numerorum proportionibus uestigatur atque assignatur, et omnium perfectissimum exemplar occurrit qui rebus congruit uniuersis. Quod quidem eos [eos omitted by Buytaert] non latet qui philosophiae rimantur arcana.' Thierry developed arithmetical imagery much further along not dissimilar lines, but stressed that number was created by unity, in which all things participated; cf. *Tractatus de sex dierum operibus* 34–36 (ed. Häring, *Commentaries on Boethius by Thierry of Chartres* 69–70).

[56] *Dialectica*, ed. de Rijk 558–59; *Tchr* 1.123 (ed. Buytaert 124). For further references, see Mews, 'On Dating' 98–102.

[57] Thierry's discussion in *Tractatus de sex dierum operibus* (ed. Häring, *Commentaries* 558–60) can be compared with that of Abaelard, *Expositio in Hexameron* (ed. Romig 28–34, with discussion on xxxv–xl; PL 178.742A–45D).

[58] On *astronomia* and its dangers, see Abaelard's *Expositio in Hexameron* (ed. Romig 55–60; PL 178.753D–56A). M.-T. d'Alverny compares his reserved attitude to that of Raymond of Marseilles (author of the *Liber cursuum planetarum*, composed in 1141) in 'Abélard et l'astrologie,' *Pierre Abélard — Pierre le Vénérable: Les courants philosophiques, littéraires et artistiques en Occident au milieu du xiiᵉ siècle. Abbaye de Cluny, 2 au 9 juillet 1972 (Paris 1975) 611–28.

distinct from contingent events in the future. He claimed the authority of
Aristotle for doing so. Heir to the predominantly linguistic bias of Roscelin
and William of Champeaux, Abaelard had a superficial enthusiasm for the
natural sciences without ever being profoundly influenced by their subject
matter. The pun on Abaelard's name — 'lick-lard' — was funny because it
touched on a core of truth.

Just when Abaelard might have attempted to study mathematics under
Thierry is difficult to determine. If Thierry is the teacher alluded to in the
Dialectica, it is likely to have been before Abaelard became a monk at Saint-
Denis.[59] Estimates of Thierry's age in relation to that of Abaelard vary considerably. Abaelard's allusion to 'two brothers' in the *Theologia christiana* suggests that Thierry had already gained a considerable reputation by the early
1120s. At the Council of Soissons (1121) Thierry, described by Abaelard as a
magister scolarum, quoted the Athanasian Creed in such a way as to ridicule a
remark of the papal legate.[60] Thierry is last heard of in 1149 and had probably
died by 1156.[61] He may thus not have been much younger than Abaelard, if at
all. From the standpoint of their relative ages it is not impossible for the
famous logician to have heard Thierry lecture on arithmetic.

With the evidence at our disposal, no firm judgement can be made about
where Thierry was teaching before the 1130s, when he surfaces as a teacher in
Paris.[62] The issue has provoked considerable debate. Briefly put, there is no
firm proof that he taught at Chartres prior to becoming its chancellor in 1142.
His name is not found in any early charters of the cathedral, although he may
have been archdeacon of Dreux in the 1130s.[63] In his account of the Council of

---

[59] I have argued that the single surviving copy of the *Dialectica* was probably completed
after he had become a monk at Saint-Denis (ca. 1117), but before he wrote the *Theologia
'Summi boni'*: see Mews, 'On Dating' 74–104.

[60] *Historia calamitatum*, ed. Monfrin 88: 'Quo audito Terricus quidam, scolaris magister,
irridendo subintulit illud Athanasii "Et tamen non tres omnipotentes, sed unus omnipotens".'

[61] William of Tyre, who studied in Paris between 1144 and 1163, described Thierry as an
old man in his *History*: R. B. C. Huygens, 'Guillaume de Tyr étudiant: Un chapitre (XIX, 12)
de son "Histoire" retrouvé,' *Latomus* 21 (1964) 822. Thierry is last heard of in 1149, when he
made a journey to Frankfurt as a guest of Albero, archbishop of Trier (1131–52); see Balde-
rich, *Gesta Alberonis* 26, MGH SS 8.257. He subsequently took the Cistercian habit. Otto of
Freising, writing in 1157, speaks of Thierry in the past tense in *Gesta Frederici* 1.48 (edd.
Waitz and de Simson 68). Ward does not justify the late dates which he gives in his title 'The
Date of the Commentary on Cicero's *De inventione* by Thierry of Chartres (ca. 1095–1160?)
and the Cornifician Attack on the Liberal Arts,' *Viator* 3 (1972) 263–66. Vernet's estimation
('Une épitaphe inédite' 662) that Thierry would have been about sixty in 1149 is only a guess.
Thierry could have been up to ten years or so older than this.

[62] Adalbert studied with Thierry in Paris 1132–37, according to the *Vita Adalberti* 684–788,
ed. Ph. Jaffé, *Bibliotheca rerum Germanicarum* 3 (Berlin 1866) 589–92.

[63] Much has been written about the vexed issue of 'the school of Chartres' since R. W.
Southern questioned its importance in 'Humanism and the School of Chartres,' published in

Soissons Abaelard does not make clear whether or not Thierry owed obedience at the time to the bishop of Chartres. No manuscripts have been found which combine writings of Thierry with the works of Gilbert of Poitiers, chancellor of Chartres 1126–42, or with those of William of Conches, often associated with its cathedral school. By contrast, Thierry's writings do sometimes occur alongside works of Abaelard and other Parisian masters.[64] Even if Thierry's brother was Bernard of Chartres, it does not automatically follow that Thierry taught at Chartres in his early years. Chartres did not have a monopoly over teaching the arts of the quadrivium.

The pun on 'Baiolard' or 'lick-lard' reported by the story-teller sums up Abaelard's attitude to the quadrivium rather neatly. Could Thierry in fact have made the joke with which he is credited? The cutting power of his tongue is commented on by the author of the *Metamorphosis Goliae*.[65] John of Salisbury, who reports unfavourably an obscure joke of Thierry slighting the *Topics* of Aristotle 'as the work of Drogo of Troyes,' confesses that he had tried to study rhetoric with Thierry, but understood little. He found one of Thierry's pupils, Peter Helias, a much better teacher of the subject. By contrast, John could not learn enough from Abaelard, whom he describes as a master of

---

Medieval Humanism and Other Essays (Oxford 1970) 61–85. He reviewed the debate in 'The Schools of Paris and the School of Chartres,' in *Renaissance and Renewal in the Twelfth Century* (edd. R. L. Benson and G. Constable; Oxford 1982) 113–37. Southern reported in his 1970 essay (70) that he could not find any text to substantiate the claim of A. Clerval in *Les écoles de Chartres* (Paris 1897) 160, that Thierry's name was mentioned in a charter from Chartres 1119–24, based 'on the authority of B. Hauréau, 'Mémoire sur quelques chancelliers de l'église de Chartres,' *Mémoires de l'Academie des Inscriptions et Belles-Lettres* 31.2 (1884) 80. Häring followed Clerval's claim without verification, in *Life and Works of Clarenbald of Arras* (Toronto 1965) 23. In a thoroughly documented reply to Southern, Häring was unable to identify Thierry positively in any such charter: see 'Chartres and Paris Revisited,' in *Essays in Honour of Anton Charles Pegis*, ed. J. R. O'Donnell (Toronto 1974) 268–329.

[64] Thierry's *Expositio in Hexameron* occurs with works attributed to Hugh of Saint-Victor and his school in MS Tours, Bibl. mun. 85, fols. 181–83ᵛ, a MS which also contains Abaelard's *Theologia christiana*. A fragment of Thierry's *Expositio* occurs in the Heiligenkreuz MS Stiftsbibliothek 153, fol. 110ᵛ; see Häring, *Commentaries* 52, and Southern, *Platonism, Scholastic Method and the School of Chartres* (Stenton Lecture; Reading 1979) 33–34. While this fragment is more likely to have been copied from the *Expositio* than to be an oral report, as thought by Southern, the context in which it occurs suggests that it may have come from a student's notebook compiled in Paris in the 1130s. Besides works of the school of Hugh of Saint-Victor, the Heiligenkreuz MS also contains a copy of an early draft of the *Theologia 'Scholarium'* and a commentary on the Apocalypse by an unknown master who taught in Paris ca. 1125–50. This latter commentary also occurs in MS Paris, BN lat. 17251 after Abaelard's own *Expositio in Hexameron*; see Mews, 'Peter Abelard's *Theologia Christiana* and *Theologia "Scholarium"* Re-examined,' *RTAM* 52 (1985) 140 n. 70.

[65] *Metamorphosis Goliae*, ed. Huygens 771: 'Ibi doctor cernitur ille Carnotensis / Cuius lingua vehemens truncat velut ensis.'

clear exposition.[66] Thierry himself tells us that he preferred to exclude 'the common herd' from his classes.[67] Although not opposed to the educational values which Thierry represented, John was more interested in the study of letters as expounded by Bernard of Chartres than in Thierry's goal of linking the quadrivium to the trivium. With characteristic shrewdness, he describes Thierry as 'that most studious investigator of the arts.' He qualifies the peripatetic of Le Pallet as one 'who outshone his contemporaries in the teaching of logic to such an extent that he alone was thought to converse with Aristotle.'[68] The contrast which John draws between a learned master of all the arts endowed with an acerbic tongue and a teacher whose reputation was that of a logician is not unlike that drawn between Thierry and Peter 'Baiolard' in the first part of the anecdote.

The unknown story-teller is definitely wrong in asserting that Peter was English and wrote much on geometry and arithmetic. An original joke about 'Baiolard' seems to have been overlaid by another about 'Abelard.' An Englishman who did write about geometry and arithmetic was Adelard of Bath, whose name may have been confused with that of the logician either out

---

[66] *Metalogicon* 4.24 (ed. Webb 191): 'Satis ergo mirari non possum quid mentis habeant (si quid tamen habent) qui hec Aristotilis opera carpunt, que utique non exonere propositum fuerat sed laudare. Magister Theodericus, ut memini, Topica non Aristotilis sed Trecassini Drogonis irridebat; eadem tamen quandoque docuit. Quidam auditores magistri Rodberti de Meliduno librum hunc fere inutilem esse calumniantur.' D. McGarry follows Clerval's translation of this passage, deliberately favourable to Thierry ('. . . derided the *Topics* of Drogo of Troyes rather than of Aristotle . . .') in *The Metalogicon of John of Salisbury* (Gloucester, Mass. 1971) 240; see Clerval, *Les écoles* 170 and 245. The context of John's statement leaves no doubt that Webb was quite correct in believing it to mean that Thierry was deriding the *Topics* as worthy only of Drogo rather than of Aristotle. John's comment in *Metalogicon* 2.10 (ed. Webb 80) is similarly unfavourable: 'Relegi quoque rethoricam, quam prius cum quibusdam aliis a magistro Theoderico tenuiter auditis paululum intelligebam.' Compare his praise for Abaelard, *ibid.* 2.10 and 3.1 (ed. Webb 78 and 120).

[67] In his commentary on the *De inventione*, ed. P. Thomas, 'Un commentaire du moyen âge sur la rhétorique de Cicéron,' *Mélanges Graux: Recueil de travaux d'érudition classique* (Paris 1884) 41–45, Thierry says of himself: 'Ut ait Petronius, nos magistri in scolis soli relinquemur nisi multos palpemus et insidiis auribus fecerimus. Ego uero non ita. . . . Ecce Theodericus Brito, homo barbaricae nationis, verbis insulsus, corpore ac mente incompositus, mendacem de se te vocat. . . . Sic tamen consilium meum contraxi ut vulgum profanum et farraginem scolae petulcam excluderam. . . . Talibus Invidiae verbis Fama permota alas concutit, sonos multiplicat, urbes et nationes duce Invidia peragat, rumoribus implet, Theodoricum ubique accusat, ignominiosis nominibus appellat.' These passages are discussed by Häring in 'Thierry of Chartres and Dominicus Gundissalinus,' *Mediaeval Studies* 26 (1964) 271–86.

[68] *Metalogicon* 1.5 (ed. Webb 16): 'Sed et alii uiri, amatores litterarum, utpote magister Theodericus, artium studiosissimus inuestigator; itidem Willelmus de Conchis, gramaticus post Bernardum Carnotensem opulentissimus; et Peripateticus Palatinus, qui logice opinionem pretulit omnibus coetaneis suis, adeo ut solus Aristotilis crederetur usus colloquio, se omnes opposuerunt errori.'

of ignorance or out of a desire to make another joke. There is a redundant *de* in the last sentence of the anecdote which may hide yet another pun: 'Nam processu temporis se usque *de* lardo quadriuii potenter intromisit ....' Possibly the person who invented the pun 'Abelardus' as 'have-lard' knew the spelling 'Adelardus.' We cannot tell for certain.

As far as is known, Adelard never studied in Paris, reputed more for the study of linguistic than of scientific subjects. He preferred to travel extensively in southern Italy and perhaps further East in search of 'the wisdom of the Arabs,' before returning back to England. A recent survey of Adelard's writings and translations shows that in the twelfth century they mainly circulated within the ambit of England and northern France.[69] One rare exception to this is a manuscript of the Erzabtei St. Peter, Salzburg (a.V.2), which contains on fols. 35ᵛ–63ᵛ the *Quaestiones naturales* of Adelard and on fols. 82–101 the best of four known copies of his *De opere astrolapsus*. Hitherto unidentified in this Salzburg manuscript is a quotation on fol. 105 from Abaelard's *Theologia*, placed among various theological notes. It concerns the difficulties inherent both in accepting and in denying that God cannot do more or less than he does.[70] The combination of texts of Adelard and Abaelard in this manuscript parallels the conflation of two separate stories in the anecdote.[71]

---

[69] C. S. F. Burnett, 'The Introduction of Arabic Science into Northern France and Norman Britain: A Catalogue of the Writings of Adelard of Bath and Petrus Alfonsi and Closely Associated Works, Together with the Manuscripts in which They Occur,' *Adelard of Bath: An English Scientist and Arabist of the Early Twelfth Century*, ed. C. S. F. Burnett (London 1987). I am indebted to the author for showing me proofs of this catalogue prior to publication.

[70] The Salzburg MS (Sa) is no. 114 of the Catalogue (n. 69 above). The text of the *Theologia* is identical to that in *Tchr* 5.29–30 (ed. Buytaert 358) and *TSch* 2.27, 29 in the manuscripts BMAP (edd. Buytaert and Mews 321–22): 'Querendum arbitror utrum plura facere possit deus uel meliora quam faciat aut ab his etiam que facit ullo modo cessare ne ea umquam uidelicet faceret. Quod siue concedamus siue negemus multa fortassis inconuenientie [-tium *Tchr TSch*] anxietates incurremus. Si enim ponamus ut plura uel pauciora facere possit uel ab his que facit cessare [cessare facit *Tchr TSch*] profecto [Sa adds multa] multum summe eius bonitāte derogabimus [derostrabimus Sa]. Constat eum quippe [quippe eum *Tchr TSch*] nonnisi bona facere posse. < space where *Tchr TSch* BMAP read: Si autem bona cum possit non faciat, et ab aliquibus que facienda essent se retrahat, quis eum tamquam emulum > uel iniquum non arguat (?) presertim cum nullus labor eum in faciendo aliquid grauet cuius eque omnia uoluntate subiecta sunt.' The Salzburg MS contains a copy of Bernard's letter 190 on the errors of Abaelard (without the final list of 19 articles) on fols. 72–80. An unidentified text on the soul's journey through the zodiac found on fols. 64–67 concludes 'Explicit liber Alardi.' The names of Abaelard and Adelard could easily be confused by someone who did not know them personally.

[71] The disparate notes on fols. 67–71ᵛ of Sa about the body and life of the soul, the classification of numbers (based on the *De arithmetica* of Boethius), the elements, virtues and vices, and scriptural exegesis include comments on creation similar to ideas of Thierry of Chartres: (fol. 70) 'Dicunt etiam quidam quod inpotens uidetur deus si successiue et per interualla opus suum distinxisset. Tercio loco opponunt de auctoritate qui manet in eternum omnia creauit

The abbey of Prüfening possessed one manuscript (now MS Munich, Bayerische Staatsbibliothek Clm. 13021), written in a late twelfth-century hand similar to that of **M**, of particular scientific interest. It contains a translation of Euclid's *Elements* and the *Liber ysagogarum Alchorismi*, a synthesis of much new learning about arithmetic. An abbreviated form of the later text occurs in another Prüfening manuscript (now MS Vienna, ÖNB cvp 275).[72] While it is unlikely that either this particular translation of Euclid or the *Liber ysagogarum* was written by Adelard, these could have been the works of geometry and arithmetic mistakenly attributed to 'Abelardus' in the anecdote.[73]

The story reported in **M** seems to have originated as an oral tradition which included a reference to Roscelin as well as Thierry's pun on 'Baiolard.' It was then elaborated upon by someone who thought or pretended that Baiolard and Adelard, here called 'Abelard,' were the same person. While the pun on 'Abelard' as 'have-lard' is weak and inaccurate, the first part of the anecdote does express a core of truth about Abaelard's relationship to both Roscelin and Thierry. How can we explain the presence of this anecdote in a manuscript from the abbey of Prüfening? Regensburg is a long way from Paris.

One possibility is that the story was transmitted by the student who brought to Prüfening the copy of Abaelard's *Sententie* and *Scito teipsum* from which **M** derives. Both works, however, belong to a relatively late date in his career.

---

simul. Ad oppositionem de inperfectione primum eis respondemus eos ignorare quomodo perfectum siue inperfectum accipiatur'; (fol. 70ᵛ) 'Vnde illi probantur errare qui supernam igneam esse dicunt. Nota etiam quod non oportuit elementa equa esse in pondere, quia illa in quibus est uis consumptiua ut ignis, alia omnino superaret, sed in potentiis tantum liberata sunt'; see n. 57 above. The author adopts a critical approach to patristic testimony: (fols. 70ᵛ–71) 'Non est inconueniens si sancti dicant contraria in exponendo secundum licitam estimationem, in qua non credere est superbum, sicut in uera assertione hereticum. Non enim semper habent spiritum sanctum in exponendo, sed ubi de eis agunt que pertinent ad fidem catholicam.' The authorship of these notes will be examined in a future study.

[72] Burnett, 'Catalogue' no. 74. MS Vienna ÖNB cvp 275 was copied sometime after 1143, not in that year, according to H. Fichtenau, 'Wolfger von Prüfening,' *Mitteilungen des Instituts für Österreichische Geschichtsforschung* 51 (1937) 313–57 at 320. On the *liber ysagogarum*, see A. Allard, *Les plus anciennes versions latines du XIIᵉ siècle de l'arithmétique d'Al-Khwarizmi: Histoire des textes suivis de l'édition critique des traités attribués à Adélard de Bath et Jean de Seville* (Louvain 1975). The only attribution of this work is to a 'master A.' in MS Paris, BN lat. 16208, fols. 76–83ᵛ, of the late twelfth century.

[73] Among other examples of confusion of the names of Abaelard and Adelard may be noted in the catalogue of Richard of Fournival, 'Petri Abadelardi liber de pugna numerorum qui dicitur Rychmimachya'; see L. Delisle, *Le cabinet des manuscrits de la Bibliothèque nationale* II (Paris 1874) 526. Master John Erghome gave to the Augustinian friars of York, ca. 1373, a 'liber sacratus petri abellardi' and a 'philosophia petri abelardi': see M. R. James, *The Catalogue of the Library of the Augustinian Friars at York*, in *Fasciculus Ioanni Willis Clark dicatus* (Cambridge 1909) 55 and 64.

IV

The *Sententie* provide a summary of Abaelard's lectures on faith, the sacraments, and charity as delivered in the mid-1130s. The *Scito teipsum* was written not long before 1140. There is another path of transmission which deserves to be considered: one that leads through the Benedictine abbey of Michelsberg in Bamberg. Various clues point in this direction.

That Wolfger of Prüfening, who died sometime after 1173, was familiar with the names of many teachers in France—Peter Baiolard among them—is evident from the catalogue which he produced in 1165. He had entered the abbey of Michelsberg by 1103, to move to its daughter house of Prüfening (founded in 1109) by 1130.[74] Under the abbacies of Wolfram I (1112–23) and Gottfried I (1123–46) Michelsberg acquired a large number of philosophical as well as sacred texts. Many of its books were copied by Cistercian monks from Ebrach (founded in 1127), who in turn established a house at Heilsbronn in 1132.[75] One mid-twelfth-century manuscript of Heilsbronn (**E**) contains marginal and interlinear glosses on the Boethian *Opuscula sacra* perhaps by Remigius of Auxerre, the continuous gloss or *Commentum* on these texts by Thierry of Chartres, and the *Theologia 'Summi boni,'* here the attributed work 'magistri Petri, clarissimi atque doctissimi Viri, cognomento adbaiolardi.'[76] A closely related copy of the *Commentum* on Boethius occurs in a manuscript (MS Munich, Bayerische Staatsbibliothek Clm. 2580) from Aldersbach, a house settled in 1146, again by Cistercians from Ebrach. Almost identical to **E** is a manuscript from Admont (MS Oxford, Bodleian Library, Lyell 49 = **L**) which includes two versions of the Carolingian gloss, the *Commentum* (here attributed to 'Helias, a certain French master'), and an unattributed copy of the *Theologia 'Summi boni.'* **L** was transcribed late in the third quarter of the twelfth century from the same defective exemplar as **E**.[77]

---

[74] On Wolfger's early career, see Fichtenau, 'Wolfger von Prüfening' 341–50 and Schmitz, *Kloster Prüfening* 234ff.

[75] Fischer, *Katalog* 541, 547–51.

[76] See n. 28 above. Marginal and interlinear glosses on the *Opuscula sacra* (I, II, III, V) close to those edited by E. K. Rand, *Johannes Scotus ihm zugeschriebenen Glossae zu Boethius' 'Opuscula Sacra'* (Quellen und Untersuchungen 1.2; Munich 1906) 30–80, are found on fols. 1–25ᵛ. These were attributed to Remigius of Auxerre by M. Cappuyns, 'Le plus ancien commentaire des "Opuscula Sacra" et son origine,' *RTAM* 3 (1931) 243. The *Commentum* of Thierry (ed. Häring, *Commentaries* 57–116) occurs on fols. 66–103ᵛ. It includes the so-called 'Stavelot' commentary on the Athanasian Creed on fols. 103–106. Abaelard's treatise (fols. 27–65ᵛ) was originally copied separately but by the same person who copied the Boethian glosses. This scribe also copied another Heilsbronn MS (Erlangen 216), containing works of Anselm of Canterbury.

[77] **L** is described in detail by A. C. de la Mare, *Catalogue of the Collection of Medieval Manuscripts Bequeathed to the Bodleian Library Oxford by James P. R. Lyell* (Oxford 1971) 131–33. As well as the marginal and interlinear gloss on the *Opuscula sacra* found in **E**, **L** contains on fols. 59–79ᵛ these glosses written out in continuous form with the Boethian text. The third part of **L** (fols. 81–99ᵛ) contains the *Commentum* introduced as *Commentum Helye*

The contents of **L** correspond to those of one codex mentioned in a Michels-berg library catalogue of 1140, detailing books which entered the house under the abbacy of Wolfram I — that is, between 1112 and 1123: 'Boecii tres, unus ex his glosatus cum continuis glosis.' This may be the same codex as the 'Glose super Boecium' given by a monk Berenger to Michelsberg at an unspecified date in the early twelfth century.[78] Could this lost codex have been the common ancestor of **E** and **L**? Thierry's *Commentum* differed from earlier glosses on the *De trinitate* precisely because it offered a continuous commen-tary on its major themes rather than literal glosses on individual words. That Abaelard's treatise is not mentioned in the Michelsberg catalogue is not a sufficient counter-argument. It is not cited either in medieval descriptions of **E** and **L**. Irimbert, abbot of Admont 1172–77, had previously been abbot of Michelsberg (1160–72), following in the footsteps of his brother Gottfried (abbot 1138–52).[79] The connection between the two abbeys was close.

If **E** and **L** both derive from the Michelsberg codex, then it contained Caro-lingian glosses on the *Opuscula sacra* of Boethius, a continuous commentary by Thierry on the *De trinitate*, and Abaelard's own attempt at a treatise on the same subject. A monk had given it to the abbey sometime before 1123. Could he also have brought back from his student days in France a funny and rather biting joke which had been attributed to Thierry about the name 'Baiolard'?

---

cuiusdam magistri gallicani super Boetium de trinitate and, by the same author, the beginning of a commentary on the *De hebdomadibus*, edited by Häring as the *Fragmentum Admuntense* (*Commentaries* 119–21). Häring discusses **L**'s text of Abaelard's treatise (the best surviving witness) in 'A Third Manuscript of Peter Abelard's Theologia "Summi boni" (MS. Oxford, Bodleian Lyell 49, ff. 101–28"),' *Mediaeval Studies* 18 (1956) 215–24. On the authenticity and date of the *Commentum* see n. 80 below.

[78] Edd. P. Lehmann and P. Ruf, MABK 3.1 (Munich 1939) 358 and again by K. Dengle-Schreiber, *Scriptorium und Bibliothek des Kloster Michelsberg in Bamberg* (Studien zur Biblio-theksgeschichte 2; Graz 1979) 15 'L 41'. The librarian Burckhardus († 14 Sept. 1149) records of abbot Wolfram I: '...ita fuit in augmentandis libris promptus et alacer. Nam cum ipse liberali polleret sciencia, in discipulis suis liberalium studiorum maxime diligebat exercicia.' Berenger's gift of the *Glose super Boecium* along with scriptural glosses, *Commentum Ammonii super Analetica*, *Albricus de radiis dictaminum*, *Epistole Ivonis*, and *Derivationes* are listed separately, MABK 3.1.365 and Dengle-Schreiber, *Scriptorium* 204. L 41 is mentioned after patristic texts, but before a number of glosses on Porphyry and Aristotle (L 44–47).

[79] Dengle-Schreiber does not identify L 41 and doubts that Michelsberg owned any MSS of Abaelard, because of the 'conservative' nature of its collection, as compared to that of Prüfe-ning, *Scriptorium* 86 and 92. This presumes that a library catalogue would always document the most 'modern' authors. Yet **E** is mentioned in a thirteenth-century Heilsbronn catalogue only as *Boetius de trinitate in duobus*, ed. Fischer, *Katalog* 566 n. 92; **L** was described in 1376 as 'Boecius glosatus de S. Trinitate, commentum super Boecium et magister Helyas super Boecium,' ed. G. Möser-Mersky, *Mittelalterliche Bibliothekskataloge Österreichs. 3 Steiermark* (Graz 1961) 30. On the abbots of Admont, see Möser-Mersky, *MABK Österreichs 3.2*.

IV

If the *Commentum* on the *De trinitate* of Boethius did exist in the Michelsberg codex, then Thierry may have written it at about the same time as Abaelard composed the *Theologia 'Summi boni'* (ca. 1120) rather than over twenty-five years later, as has been thought. This re-dating also helps explain why Thierry had established a reputation by the early 1120s.[80] The impression Abaelard indirectly conveys in the *Historia calamitatum* that he was the only outstanding teacher of his day is not wholly accurate. He wrote the *Theologia 'Summi boni'* for students accustomed to extensive commentary on the *De trinitate* of Boethius such as found in the Heilsbronn and Admont manuscripts. An early date for the *Commentum* also gives indirect support to the picture presented by the anecdote of Thierry and Abaelard as contemporaries of equal stature. If a secondary and fictitious layer to the story, based on a confusion of Abae-

---

[80] The attribution *Commentum Helye cuiusdam magistri gallicani super Boetium de trinitate* in **L** has led some scholars to suggest that the gloss was written not by Thierry, as had hitherto been believed, but by his pupil Peter Helyas, who taught grammar and rhetoric between the late 1130s and the early 1150s — notably, L.-J. Bataillon, 'Bulletin d'histoire des doctrines médiévales,' *Revue des sciences philosophiques et théologiques* 43 (1959) 692 and under the same rubric *ibid.* 46 (1962) 508 and 51 (1967) 69–72; M.-T. d'Alverny, *Alain de Lille. Textes inédits* (Paris 1965) 176 n. 62; K. M. Fredborg, 'The Dependence of Petrus Helias' Summa super Priscianum on William of Conches' Glose super Priscianum,' *Cahiers de l'Institut du Moyen Age grec et latin* 11 (1973) 1–57 at 51–54. Fredborg argues that the close affinity between the *Commentum* and Thierry's known thought could be explained by Thierry's influence on Helias without excluding that Thierry was its author. The views of Batallion are discussed by Häring in *Commentaries* 20–23. The authenticity of the *Commentum* was reaffirmed in a detailed study by E. Maccagnolo, *Rerum Universitas (Saggio sulla filosofia di Teoderico di Chartres)* (Florence 1976) 4–7. No critic has noted any doctrinal inconsistencies with other works attributed to Thierry or indeed any close connection of the *Commentum* to Helias' glosses on Priscian. Clarenbald of Arras, who quotes from the *Commentum*, says in a prefatory letter that he was imitating the lectures of Thierry (as well as of Hugh of Saint-Victor): *Life and Works of Clarenbald of Arras* (Toronto 1965) 64. Häring never modified his opinion that the *Commentum* was earlier than the *Lectiones* and *Glosa* on Boethius, but was less clear regarding the date. In 'Two Commentaries on Boethius (*De Trin.* and *De Hebd.*) by Thierry of Chartres,' *AHDLMA* 27 (1960) 75, he held that it had been written 'ca. 1135 or even earlier,' but changed this to a date of ca. 1148 in *Commentaries* (1971) 24. He was influenced in part by an argument of d'Alverny (*Alain de Lille* 176 n. 62) that the Sibylline prophecy quoted in the *Commentum* 2.34 (ed. Häring 79) 'only became known around 1148 but did not remain current for long because it was disproved by the failure of the second Crusade.' Otto of Freising, *Gesta Frederici* Proemium (edd. Waitz and de Simson 10–11) says that this prophecy was widely respected in France, not that it suddenly appeared at this time. There is no evidence that the prophecy was invented in 1146 for political ends. Häring's second argument for dating the *Commentum* after 1148 was based on its criticism of a doctrine imputed to Gilbert of Poitiers at the Council of Reims, *Commentum* 4.2 (ed. Häring 95): 'Et peccat et desipit qui quemadmodum homo dicitur ab humanitate sic deum dici estimat a deitate.' Writing ca. 1122–25, Abaelard made a similar accusation about another teacher (Ulger of Angers?) in *Tchr* 3.167 and 4.77 (ed. Buytaert 257 and 301). Arguments for a late date for the *Commentum* are not based on any firm evidence.

lard's name with that of Adelard of Bath, is disregarded, the anecdote has much to say. It presents Abaelard as a restless individual who could not submit for long to the tutelage of others. In subjects such as mathematics he was not as competent as Thierry, whose lectures he apparently had tried to follow. Given that our picture of Abaelard's career is so influenced by his own version of events, this little text deserves respect.

Even if there is a grain of truth in the pun on 'Baiolardus,' Thierry certainly did not invent Peter's cognomen. Where did the name 'Abaelardus' come from?

In a short note published in 1870 Ernest Renan said that 'Petrus Abaelardus' meant 'Petrus filius Alardi.' He noted that *Ab* was a Gallic word meaning 'son' like *Mab* in Breton and that it occurred quite frequently in his home region of lower Brittany.[81] This contradicts Abaelard's own testimony about the name of his father, Berengar, as Renan himself acknowledged. We may safely assume that Abaelard's parents were responsible for choosing the cognomen of their first-born son, in the same way that Abaelard and Heloise chose to call their child 'Astralabe' ('Petrus Astralabius' according to the necrology of the Paraclete).[82] 'Astralabe' and 'Abaelard' were intimate names, used to differentiate one Peter from another.[83]

Renan may have been too eager to suggest a link between his own Breton roots and those of Abaelard. Nonetheless, at least one regional connection escaped the notice of the great philologist. A contemporary of Peter Abaelard was also called 'Abaielardus' ('Abaielart' in the vernacular): the son of Humphrey, count of Apulia, the nephew of Robert Guiscard and grandson of Tan-

---

[81] E. Renan, 'Sur l'etymologie du nom d'Abélard,' *Revue celtique* 1 (1870) 265–68. He was led to this idea by his discovery of an allusion to Abaelard's *Carmen ad Astralabium* in Guibert of Tournai's *De modo addiscendi* (MS Paris, BN lat. 15451, p. 227; saec. XIII): 'Habetis enim et habere potestis ad manum Boecium ... Quintilianum ... Petrum filium Alardi quem Abaelart vocant Ad filium.' Renan also remembered seeing a reference 'Abaelardus, id est filius Alardi' on the first page of a 13th-century glossary, but could not recall the shelfmark of this MS.

[82] *Historia calamitatum*, ed. Monfrin 74: '... apud sororem meam tam diu conversata est donec pareret masculum quam Astralabium nominavit'; cf. *Recueil des historiens de la France: Obituaires de la province de Sens* IV (Meaux–Troyes) (edd. A. Boutillier du Retail and P. Piétrisson de Saint-Aubin; Paris 1923) 425. D'Alverny, 'Abélard et l'astrologie' 611, notes that the scientific instrument is sometimes called *astrolapsus* and suggests that the child might thus have 'fallen from the stars.'

[83] Heloise addresses Peter simply as 'Abaelardus' in her first letter (ed. Monfrin 111) in the same way that Abaelard refers to his child simply as 'Astralabius' in the *Historia calamitatum* and the *Carmen ad Astralabium*. By contrast, scribes almost always include 'Petrus' when attributing a work to him.

cred de Hauteville, founder of the dynasty which was to hold such influence in southern Italy.[84] This family came from Hauteville, eight miles north of Coutances and not far from the ill-defined border between Brittany and Normandy. Tancred and his son Humphrey were born at Hauteville, as Abaielard may also have been. The family, relatively obscure locally, were unable to satisfy territorial ambitions in their own region and turned instead to military adventures in southern Italy.

While it is most unlikely that the two Aba(i)elards were linked by kin, the fact that the cognomen was used by a Norman is significant. Peter Abaelard did not consider himself a *brito*, even though he had been born within the borders of Brittany. The province had been overrun by Normans in the tenth century, when Nantes had become one of their strongholds. While the late eleventh-century chronicle of Nantes affirms that the invading Normans had been driven out, some of these Norman knights established themselves in the region as a new local aristocracy pitting itself against other Normans.[85] An ethnic divide between Normans and Bretons within the court of Hoelus, count of Nantes, is apparent in a charter of 1085, drawn up in his presence. A list divides people into two groups: 'Daniel de Palatio [Le Pallet], Gaufridus Normannus, Warinus dapifer ceterique Namnetenses; de Britonibus, Iestin filius Daniel, Alan filius Guegon, Gurmahelon filius Glevian.' The witnesses all have celtic names: David, Mab Gulchuen, Mab Tanki.[86] The antagonism between the *Namnetenses* and the *Britones* is a major theme of the chronicle of Nantes. Its clerical author was very hostile to the Breton faction, then dominant in local politics.[87]

That Abaelard did not speak Breton is evident from his admission that he was unable to understand the language of the monks of Saint-Gildas.[88] Unlike

---

[84] 'Abagelardus, filius Unfredi principis Normannorum,' is mentioned by William of Apulia, writing ca. 1111, in *Gesta Roberti Wiscardi* 2.451, 536–656 and 3.289, MGH SS 9.263, 276–78, 289. Amatus, whose *Historia Normannorum* is known only through a late translation, *Y Istoire de li Normant* 5.4 (ed. O. Delarc; Rouen 1892), implies that it was a cognomen: 'Rogier-Toute-Bone liquel se clamait autres, Balarde. . . . Et Balalarde pour ce qu'il avoit este filz de lo frere.' 'Abaielardus' is the form used by Robert de Monte in his chronicle for 1129, MGH SS 6.489.

[85] J. Le Patourel comments on this process in *The Norman Empire* (Oxford 1976) 7. Our major source for the invasion is the *Chronicon Namnetense*, ed. R. Merlet, *La chronique de Nantes* (Paris 1896) 80–96, 110–12. N.-Y. Tonnerre describes the political tensions in the region in 'Le comté nantais à la fin du xie siècle,' *Abélard en son temps* (ed. J. Jolivet; Paris 1981) 11–20.

[86] G. A. Lobineau, *Histoire de Bretagne* (Paris 1707) 2.119; cf. Tonnerre, 'Le comté nantais' 13.

[87] Merlet, *La chronique de Nantes* xxxix–xl.

[88] *Historia calamitatum* (ed. Monfrin 98): 'Terra quippe barbara et terre lingua mihi incognita erat, et turpis atque indomabilis illorum monachorum vita omnibus fere notissima, et gens terre illius inhumana atque incomposita.' Abaelard mentions that he once stayed with

Thierry, he never described himself as a Breton. He preferred the sobriquet *palatinus*, a pun combining the word for courtier with the name of his native village, *Palatium* or Le Pallet.[89] The hostility which Abaelard encountered at Saint-Gildas was directed against a reformer from the East whose vernacular tongue and political loyalties differed from those of the local population. In the *Dialectica* he did not hesitate to make abusive references to Bretons in discussing the etymology of *brito*. When arguing that Aristotle used 'infinite' in a particular context to refer to an infinite multitude because of its affinity to what was infinite, he commented:

> Such reasons are often given in etymologies, where for example *brito* is said to be 'like a brute.' For granted that they are not all or the only ones to be stupid, the person who composed the name *brito* according to its affinity with the name 'brute' had in mind that the greatest number of Bretons were unintelligent.[90]

Near the end of his *Dialectica* Abaelard came back to this example to distinguish the meaning of a word from its etymology: 'as Britons are said to be quasi-brutes in so far as they seem brutish and irrational out of folly.'[91] While denying that 'Breton' meant 'a brute,' he accepted that the name originated in an individual's judgement that the Bretons were brutish. Abaelard, no *brito*

---

his brother when visiting the count and that he then narrowly avoided being poisoned: *Historia calamitatum* 106. This brother could have been Porcarius, a canon of Nantes, who, according to a cartulary of Buzé (ed. H. Morice, *Mémoires pour servir à l'histoire de Bretagne* [Paris 1742] 1.587), had a nephew called Astralabius, also a canon of the cathedral. The assassination attempt was probably provoked by friction between Breton and Nantais factions in the city. Otto of Freising, *Gesta Frederici* 1.48 (edd. Waitz and de Simson 68) identified Abaelard as a native of Brittany like the brothers Bernard and Thierry. The assumption that Abaelard was a Breton is widespread in scholarly literature: see, e.g., P. Lasserre, 'Deux hommes: Deux races,' in his *Un conflit religieux au xiiᵉ siècle* (Paris 1930) 69–96. Lasserre places Abaelard in the same noble Breton tradition as Chateaubriand, Lamennais, and Renan.

[89] For Thierry's mocking description of himself as 'a Breton, a man of a barbaric nation,' see n. 67 above. Clarembald identifies Thierry as 'Theodericus brito' in his commentary on the *De trinitate* 10 (ed. Häring, *Life and Works of Clarembald of Arras* 69). The epithet 'Peripateticus Palatinus,' used frequently by John of Salisbury, occurs within rubrics to Abaelard's logical glosses, the *Dialectica*, and the Berlin copy of the *Theologia 'Summi boni,'* cited in nn. 11 and 14 above.

[90] *Dialectica*, ed. de Rijk 128: 'quales quidem cause sepe in ethimologiis redduntur, ut "Brito" dictus est "quasi-brutus." Licet enim non omnes vel soli sint stolidi, hic tamen qui nomen "Britonis" composuit secundum affinitatem nominis "bruti," in intentione habuit quod maxima pars Britonum fatua esset, atque hinc hoc nomen illi affine in sono protulit.'

[91] *Dialectica*, ed. de Rijk 583: 'Sed has quidem non inveni interpretationes appellari, sed forte ethimologie vocis ipsius sonum maxime consequuntur, sive sint orationes, ut supraposita, sive dictiones, ut Britones quasi-brutones dicti sunt, eo quod bruti et irrationabiles ex insipientia videantur.'

IV

himself, was as inclined as the unknown humorist of Prüfening to use the etymology of a name as an argument that there could be a rational reason for its imposition. The anecdote found in **M** is of more than passing interest for understanding the way in which two outstanding teachers of the twelfth century, Thierry and Peter Abaelard, appeared to contemporaries. The brief picture it presents of Abaelard's personality and relationship to both Roscelin and Thierry fits in with what is already known about these figures. The pun on 'Baiolard' attributed to Thierry hides a barbed comment on Abaelard's attitude to the quadrivium. It is of much greater force than a second pun in the anecdote, based on confusion of the names of Abaelard (correctly pronounced as 'Aba'elard') and Adelard of Bath. While it is possible that Thierry may have made such a pun on 'Abaelard' in the circumstances described in the anecdote, the cognomen itself was a familiar name probably chosen by his parents. Not all the details in the anecdote are meant to be taken seriously. Nonetheless, like all good humour, the story contains a grain of truth.

EPILOGUE: THE HISTORY OF ABAELARD'S NAME

If twelfth-century scribes were uncertain about the correct spelling of Abaelard's name, more recent scholars have not fared much better. It is to the great credit of André Duchesne that he should have established 'Abaelardus' as the reading of the best manuscripts. He took care that in the edition of 1616 the a and the e were printed as separate vowels, and not as æ as conventional in typography of his day.[92] Seventeenth-century scholars tended to remain fairly close to an authentic spelling. Sébastien Rouillard, writing in French in 1628, used 'Pierre Abaielard.' Before the 1616 edition appeared he had read the correspondence of Abaelard and Heloise in a manuscript, since lost, belonging to the library of Saint-Victor.[93] The anonymous Maurist author of a

---

[92] See n. 10 above.

[93] *Histoire de Melun* (Paris 1628) 331–51. This is one of the first accounts of Abaelard's life in French to appear after the 1616 edition. Rouillard notes (348): 'Et ayant sceu qu'il y en avoit de manuscripts en la Bibliothèque de S. Victor, je les ay curieusement demandé par communication; ce qu'ayant obtenu, je me mis a les lire et les relire, avec un ardeur non pareille.' Rouillard says (334) that he first read the MS before 1616: 'elle me fut baillée manuscripte, de la Bibliothèque de S. Victor, du depuis elle ha esté imprimé avec les aultres œuvres.' This may have been the lost MS of Saint-Victor GGG 17, mentioned in Claude de Grandru's Catalogue as containing on fols. 1–57 *Epistole Petri Abaelardi*. These folios had been cut from the MS when Jean Picard annotated the Catalogue (probably in 1604). The remainder of the MS, containing texts of Gerson and Petrarch inter alia, disppeared after 1706. Monfrin gives these details without mentioning Rouillard, in *Historia calamitatum* 42–43.

major history of the monastery of Saint-Gildas, written in 1668 (MS Paris, BN fr. 16822), preferred 'Pierre Abaelard.' L. E. Dupin preserved the correct pronunciation by using the form 'Pierre Abaëlard' throughout a long essay on his doctrine. E. Martène and U. Durand followed a similar practice in printing 'Petrus Abaëlardus' throughout their editions of the *Theologia christiana* and *Expositio in Hexameron*.[94]

These orthographical standards slipped with reprintings of the *editio princeps*. Richard Rawlinson was not only quite unscrupulous in adding fictitious manuscript readings to Duchesne's text so as to pass it off as a new edition, but he adopted the form 'Abælard'us' throughout.[95] The practice was followed by Dom Gervaise in his 1723 edition of the letters, again pirated from Duchesne's text, and by Victor Cousin in the following century.[96] For the PL volume 178, J.-P. Migne reprinted the editions of Duchesne and Martène without modification, apart from corrupting the spelling of Abaelard's name in the same way as Cousin had done, to conform to popular convention.

Its pronunciation had already been shortened to four syllables by 1662 when L. Bertaud (sometimes called Berthault) and P. Cusset published a history of Chalon-sur-Saône. They generally used 'Abelard,' but sometimes it was 'Abélard.' These are the earliest writers that I have been able to trace to venture an etymological explanation of one other form, 'Abailard':

> D'autres l'ont appellé Abailardus et on tire l'Etymologie et l'origine de ce nom de la langue française, qui signifie une petite abeille, ce qui fut sans doute un augure et un presage (si les noms peuvent estre les charactères et les images des choses) de la prudence de son esprit, et de la profondeur de sa doctrine, qui l'on signalé en son siècle.[97]

---

[94] L. E. Dupin, *Histoire des controverses, des matières ecclésiastiques traités dans le XIIe siècle* (Paris 1696) 360–409; *Thesaurus novus anecdotorum* 5 (edd. E. Martène and U. Durand; Paris 1717) 1155–1416.

[95] *PETRI ABÆLARDI, Abbatis Ruyensis et HELOISSÆ Paraclitensis EPISTOLÆ a prioribus Editionis Erroribus purgatæ et cum Cod. MS. Collatæ cura Ricardi Rawlinson, A.M.* (London 1718). Monfrin exposes the fraud involved, in *Historia calamitatum* 46–50. The claim of Gervaise that his translation was based not only on the 1616 edition 'mais de plus anciens Manuscrits que j'aye pû trouver dans les Bibliothèques les plus curieuses' is as false as that of Rawlinson; see Gervaise, *Les veritables lettres d'Abeillard et d'Heloise, tirées d'un ancien Manuscrit Latin trouvé dans la Bibliothèque de François d'Amboise Conseiller d'Etat* (Paris 1723) xiii.

[96] *Ouvrages inédits d'Abélard pour servir à l'histoire de la philosophie scolastique* (ed. V. Cousin; Paris 1836). Charles de Rémusat argued that 'Abœlardus' was the correct spelling in a long note on the problem, *Abélard* (Paris 1845) 1.14 n. 1.

[97] *L'illustre orbandale ou l'histoire ecclésiastiqie de la ville et cité de Chalon-sur-Saône* (Paris 1662) 2.2–3. Bertaud adds here: 'J'ay trouvé ce dernier nom dans la chronique du sçavant Historien Jean Crespin,' but I have been unable to locate this reference. In his *L'Estat de l'église* (Bergues sur le Zoom 1605) 333, Crespin only mentions 'Pierre de Balard.'

The belief that names were images of what they signified lasted long into the modern period. Even though the seventeenth-century etymology of 'Abailard' was quite spurious, this spelling was widely used for over two centuries subsequently.

'Abailard' became particularly popular through a highly imaginative history, *Les amours d'Abailard et d'Heloïse*, apparently first published by Jacques Alluis, a notary of Grenoble, in 1675.[98] His essay was reprinted in Amsterdam in 1693 along with a free translation of part of the correspondence. The same text of Alluis was published in The Hague in 1693 (and reprinted many times subsequently) with the title *Histoire d'Eloïse et d'Abélard*. The only change to the original text made by the rival publishing house was to replace 'Abailard' by 'Abélard.' The fact that the spelling 'Abelard' has come to prevail in the English-speaking world is largely due to the fact that in 1710 John Hughes relied on the French translation of the correspondence published in The Hague for his own English version. 'Abelard' was popularised by Alexander Pope in his poem *Eloisa to Abelard*, written in 1717.[99] Another translation had been prepared in 1687 by Roger de Rabutin, comte de Bussy, with the spelling 'Abeilard' (by analogy with 'abeille'), but was not printed until 1697.[100] 'Abaillard' appeared in a translation supposedly published at the Paraclete in 1696.[101]

The question of the correct spelling of the philosopher's name became a matter of considerable learned debate in the early eighteenth century. Dom Gervaise argued in the first major biography (1720) that 'Abeillard' was the correct form. He cited an unidentified tradition:

> Que sa mère lui donna ce nom au sortir de son sein par un pressentiment de sa future éloquence, et de cet amas des plus belles connoissances, dont il découleroit un miel plus délicieux que celui de l'Abeille. En s'attachant à cette étymologie, il faut dire Abeillard et non pas Abélard, ni Abalard, ni Abaillard. C'est en la suivant que saint Bernard l'appelle Apis de Francia.[102]

---

[98] Allard, *La Bibliothèque du Dauphiné* (Paris 1680) 9, identifies Alluis († 1688) as the author, but there are no surviving editions in the major Parisian libraries from earlier than 1693. The complex bibliographical history of the free translations of Rémond des Cours (and of other translators) has been documented by Charlotte Charrier, *Héloïse dans l'histoire et dans la légende* (Paris 1933) 406–32. The Hague and Amsterdam translations, both of which are anonymous, are conveniently bound into a single volume in the British Library copy, 1085.a.12.

[99] On Pope's source and the reception of his poem, see *Pope: The Critical Heritage* (ed. J. Barnard; London 1973) 140–42.

[100] *Les Lettres de Messire Roger de Rabutin, comte de Bussy* (Paris 1697) II 116.51.

[101] *Le philosophe amoureux, histoire gallante, contenant une Dissertation curieuse sur la vie de Pierre Abaillard et celle d'Héloïse*, ed. F.-N. Du Bois (Au Paraclet 1696).

[102] Dom F.-A. Gervaise, *La vie de Pierre Abeillard, abbé de Saint-Gildas-de Ruis, de l'ordre de Saint-Benoist, et celle d'Héloïse, son épouse, première abbesse du Paraclet* (Paris 1720) 3. His

Where Bertaud and Cusset had used the 'abeille' pun to emphasise Abaelard's prudence and depth of wisdom, Gervaise used it as an augury of his eloquence. La Monnoye invoked the authority of the Académie Française to establish 'Abailard' as the correct form.[103] He in turn was countered by the abbé Papillon, who argued in an essay published within Nicéron's *Mémoires*:

> Mais il me semble que la prononciation d'Abélard est plus douce et plus conforme au génie de notre langue. Quelques Anciens d'ailleurs avec Vincent de Beauvais, ont mis en œuvre cette orthographe. Au reste, ce qui décide l'affaire en ma faveur, c'est que les Bretons n'admettent point d'autre prununciation que celle que j'ai adopté.[104]

The transformation of Abaelard's regional identity had become complete.

Pierre Bayle did much to popularise 'Abélard' through his article in the *Dictionnaire historique*, again dependent on the translation published in The Hague in 1693.[105] Bayle may also have been influenced by the grossly inaccurate 'Abelardus,' used by Christian Thomasius in a Latin summary of his life published in 1693 without the aid of Duchesne's edition.[106] Although most translations in the eighteenth and early nineteenth centuries used 'Abailard,' Victor Cousin adopted Bayle's 'Abélard' for his edition of the philosophical works in 1836. Since this time 'Abélard' has prevailed in French scholarship and literature.

Writing in 1884, Reginald Lane Poole used poetic testimony to re-establish the correct pronunciation, if not the correct spelling, of the name.[107] Having at hand only limited manuscript evidence, Poole suggested that the correct form might be 'Abaielardus,' from a thirteenth-century Tegernsee manuscript (MS Munich, Bayerische Staatsbibliothek Clm. 18926), but opted for 'Abailardus' on the authority of another, of the twelfth (MS Tours, Bibl. mun. 85). He maintained that it was only a coincidence that this spelling was also used by French translators. Poole thus broke with a tradition established by John Hughes. The first scholar to return to the exact spelling selected by Duchesne

---

acknowledged source may have been Bertaud (see n. 92 above). His claim that Bernard relied on this tradition in letter 189 (ed. J. Leclercq, *S. Bernardi Opera* VIII [Rome 1977] 14) is not made by Bertaud.

[103] La Monnoye, in his notes to A. Baillet, *Jugements des savants sur les principaux ouvrages des auteurs* (Amsterdam 1725) I 326: 'Plusieurs ont écrit Abaillard, mais on prononce et l'on devait toujours écrire Abailard.'

[104] Nicéron, *Mémoires pour servir à l'histoire des hommes illustres dans la république des lettres* IV 1 (Paris 1728) 1. The reference to Vincent of Beauvais is based on a remark of Duchesne in his notes (see n. 10 above). In the 1624 Douai edition of the *Speculum naturale* (col. 2468DE) the spelling 'Abailardus' is given.

[105] P. Bayle, *Dictionnaire historique et critique* (Rotterdam 1697) I 23–31; (2nd ed.; Rotterdam 1702) 17–23.

[106] C. Thomasius, *Vita Abelardi*, in *Historia sapientiae et stultitiae* (Halle 1693) I 75–112.

[107] See n. 2 above.

IV

was Bernhard Geyer. Relying on his excellent knowledge of the manuscripts, Geyer pointed out that the correct spelling was 'Abaelardus,' pronounced with five syllables. His practice of writing 'Abaelard' has been followed by most German scholars, although not often by those from other countries. Sikes, writing in 1932 in apparent ignorance of Geyer's important footnote, repeated the argument of Poole in favour of 'Abailardus.'[108] Geyer's spelling of 'Abaelardus' is, however, the more accurate. By being aware of its correct pronunciation, we can come a little closer to the peripatetic of Le Pallet — if only through understanding a joke made about his name.

---

[108] J. G. Sikes, *Peter Abailard* (London 1932) I 108.

V

LA BIBLIOTHÈQUE DU PARACLET DU XIIIe SIÈCLE À LA RÉVOLUTION

Le renom du Paraclet, couvent fondé par Pierre Abélard pour Héloïse en 1129, n'a pas rejailli sur sa bibliothèque, dont le contenu reste très mal connu. Nous ignorons les ouvrages d'Abélard qui s'y trouvaient au moment de la dissolution de la communauté en 1792. Quels écrits d'Abélard et d'Héloïse les religieuses ont-elles conservés durant ces six siècles et demi?[1] Aucun catalogue de la bibliothèque n'a survécu à la Révolution. Il nous a fallu, dans notre enquête, rassembler les témoignages de plusieurs visiteurs du couvent durant les XVIIe et XVIIIe siècles, et analyser les indices laissés par les rares manuscrits subsistants. Nous essayerons d'évaluer la date des pertes, et de comprendre leurs raisons. L'histoire de cette bibliothèque est significative du changement des attitudes des soeurs envers Abélard et Héloïse, à travers les siècles.

I. LES MANUSCRITS CONNUS

Sur les cinq manuscrits conservés dont la provenance est connue, un seul (MS Chaumont, Bibliothèque municipale 31) transmet des écrits d'Abélard — les hymnes et d'autres prières composées pour la

° Je remercie vivement les conservateurs des Bibliothèques municipales de Verdun et de Troyes, Mme M.-P. Laffitte de la Bibliothèque nationale, M. C.S.F. Burnett et surtout F. Chrysogonus Waddell O. Cist. (Trappiste) de l'abbaye de Gethsemani pour l'aide qu'ils ont eu l'obligeance de m'apporter. Je ne veux pas oublier Mlle C. Rengot et M. M. Lejbowicz qui ont revu mon texte.
1. Voir D. E. LUSCOMBE, *The School of Peter Abelard*, Cambridge, 1969, p. 65: «Only the Paraclete under Heloise appears to have been a major repository for copies of Abelard's writings and was still such a repository in early modern times when D'Amboise and Duchesne and Camuzat read, used and printed writings by Abelard. But those manuscripts are now lost». N. Häring doute de son importance, «Abelard yesterday and today», *Pierre Abélard - Pierre le Vénérable. Les courants philosophiques, littéraires et artistiques en occident au milieu du XIIe siècle. Abbaye de Cluny 2 au 9 juillet 1972*, Paris, 1975, p. 362.

liturgie du Paraclet. Nous condensons ici le contenu et l'histoire de chacun d'eux:

CHAUMONT, BIBLIOTHÈQUE MUNICIPALE 31 (saec, XV^ex)

Fol. 2-7v	Calendrier du Paraclet
Fol. 8-245	Bréviaire (incomplet à cause de l'absence de la plupart des textes de l'Office de nuit, mais cependant, plus complet qu'un *Diurnale*)
Fol. 245v	Epitaphe d'Abélard: *Petrus in hac petra...*; formule d'absolution de Pierre le Vénérable; épitaphe d'Héloïse *Hoc tumulo...*

On relève au fol. 1 la signature de Dame Loyse de Saumery (cantrix du Paraclet, morte le 12 déc. 1581) et au-dessus: *Le bréviaire d'Abailard, donné par le Père Cerizier, en l'an 1640. Filsi*. Devenu la propriété des Oratoriens de Langres en 1640, il est entré à la Bibliothèque de Chaumont à la Révolution. [2]

PARIS, BIBLIOTHÈQUE NATIONALE FR. 14410 (saec. XIII²)

Fol. 5-28	Livre des sépultures (nécrologe du Paraclet)
Fol. 29-116v	Ordinal du Paraclet
Fol. 117-123	Incipits des chants processionnels [3]

Aux fol. 1-3v se trouvent des notes relatives au manuscrit lui-même, de la main de Dom Charles Cajot (1731-1807), dernier aumônier

---

2. J. CARNANDET, *Notice sur le bréviaire d'Abailard conservé à la bibliothèque de Chaumont (Haute-Marne)*, Paris, 1851, qui se trouve aussi, sous une forme abrégée et anonyme, dans *Portefeuille archéologique de la Champagne*, éd. A. GAUSSEN, Bar-sur-Aube, 1861, p. 40-44. G. M. Dreves a utilisé ce manuscrit, ainsi que celui de Bruxelles, Bibliothèque royale 10147-10158, pour son édition *Petri Abaelardi... Hymni Paraclitensis sive Hymnorum libelli tres ad fidem codicum Bruxellensis et Calmontani*, Paris, 1891; de même, J. SZÖVERFFY, *Peter Abelard's Hymnarius Paraclitensis*, Albany N. Y.- Brookline Mass., 1975. C. Waddell, qui prépare une édition critique de tous les textes dans le bréviaire, décrit le manuscrit dans «Peter Abelard as creator of liturgical texts», *Petrus Abaelardus (1079-1142). Person, Werk und Wirkung*, éd. R. THOMAS, Trier, 1980, p. 267-80, surtout p. 268. Sur les épitaphes, voir l'appendice à cette article.

3. *Le livre des sépultures*, éd. C. LALORE, *Collection des principaux obituaires et confraternités du diocèse de Troyes*, Paris, 1862, p. 446-60, et aussi éd. BOUTILLIER DU RETAIL et PIÉTRESSON DE SAINT-AUBIN, *Recueil des historiens de la France. Obituaires de la Province de Sens*, t. IV, Paris, 1923, p. 387-403; voir WADDELL, *art. cit.*, p. 268-269.

du Paraclet, de 1780 à 1792.[4] D'après Corrard de Breban, dans une étude publiée en 1861, il existait encore des notes de la main de Cajot tant au début qu'à la fin du volume; ces dernières ont depuis disparu. De fait, en 1861, le manuscrit avait 129 feuillets, mais aujourd'hui on n'en trouve que 125, chiffre indiqué à la première page de garde, avec la date du 6 mars 1875. Les fol. 1-4 ont été reliés à la fin du volume. Le fol. 4 a été ajouté au manuscrit; il s'intitule: *Nottes à joindre au manuscrit remis à Monsieur Capronnier* [sic]. Jean-Augustin Capperonnier a été conservateur à la Bibliothèque royale de 1795 à 1820.[5] Or l'auteur de ces notes parle du tombeau d'Abélard et d'Héloïse au Père Lachaise, où leurs cendres ont été transférées en 1817. On peut donc supposer que le manuscrit est entré à la Bibliothèque royale entre 1817 et 1820. Corrard de Breban cite une lettre du Dr. Colin de Nogent-sur-Seine, selon laquelle ce manuscrit «contenant les lois dictées aux saintes filles», faisait partie des livres donnés au père du Dr. Colin par les soeurs, lors de la fermeture de leur couvent. Le père du Dr. Colin travaillait au Paraclet. Le frère du Dr. Colin l'avait à son tour cédé à la Bibliothèque royale en échange d'un Rousseau en 18 volumes.[6]

PARIS, BIBLIOTHÈQUE NATIONALE LAT. 10582 (saec. XVII)

Pp. 1-46   *Cérémonial bénédictin pour les vestures et professions des religieuses du royal et célèbre monastère du Paraclet*

Nous ne savons pas avec certitude comment ce manuscrit est entré à la Bibliothèque royale, dont il porte, aux p. A et 46, l'estampille en usage de 1815 à 1831.[7] La même estampille se trouve aux fol.

---

4. C. CHARRIER, *Héloïse dans l'histoire et dans la légende*, Paris, 1933, p. 621 se trompe sur ces notes et de l'identité de Dom Cajot, qu'elle confond avec son frère Jean-Joseph Cajot (1726-79). Sur Dom Charles Cajot, voir plus loin, n. 70.
5. CORRARD DE BREBAN, *Les abbesses du Paraclet*, Troyes, 1861, p. 9 n. 1 et p. 31. Sur Jean-Augustin Capperonnier, voir V. de BERNVILLE, *Biographie montdidérienne*, Paris, 1875, p. 42-44. La Bibliothèque du roi s'est appelée la Bibliothèque nationale à partir de 1792, la Bibliothèque impériale à partir de 1804 et enfin la Bibliothèque royale à partir de 1815 jusqu'à 1848.
6. CORRARD DE BREBAN, *Les abbesses*, p. 30-31. Dr. Colin (ou Collin) a écrit «Notes historiques et statistiques sur le canton de Nogent-sur-Seine, département de l'Aube, *Annuaire administratif et statistique de l'Aube*, 2e partie, 1836, p. 122, qui contient une description du Paraclet, p. 102-107.
7. L'estampille correspond au no. 21 de l'article de P. JOSSERAND et J. BRUNS, «Les estampilles du Département des Imprimés de la Bibliothèque nationale», *Mélanges d'histoire offerts à Franz Calot*, Paris, 1960, p. 281-283.

5 et 193v du MS Paris, Bibl. nat. fr. 14410. Il est donc possible que ces deux manuscrits soient entrés en même temps à la Bibliothèque, et qu'ils aient, l'un et l'autre appartenu au père du Dr. Colin; mais ce n'est là qu'une hypothèse.

TROYES, BIBLIOTHÈQUE MUNICIPALE 2284 (saec. XIV^med)

Fol. 1-290v   Cartulaire du Paraclet

M. Coffinet, chanoine de la cathédrale de Troyes, et secrétaire de l'évêché, a fait don de ce manuscrit à la Bibliothèque de la ville, le 16 novembre 1851. Nous ignorons comment il l'avait eu en sa possession. [8]

TROYES, BIBLIOTHÈQUE MUNICIPALE 2450 (1770 a.d.)

Fol. 1-47v   Nécrologe du Paraclet, copié en 1770, avec additions.

Fol. 48-48v   *Catalogue des Dames Abbesses qui ont gouverné l'Abbaye Royale du Paraclet,* de la main de Dom Charles Cajot. Devenu la propriété du Dr. Colin de Nogent-sur-Seine, il a été ensuite acheté par la Bibliothèque de Troyes. [9]

ARCHIVES DÉPARTEMENTALES DE L'AUBE 24 H (saec. XII-XIII)

Les chartes, bulles, lettres patentes etc. du Paraclet sont les seuls documents que les administrateurs du district de Nogent-sur-Seine ont emportés du couvent, en 1792, et déposés ensuite aux Archives départementales. [10]

---

8. Ed. LALORE, *Collection des principaux cartulaires du diocèse de Troyes. I. Cartulaire de l'abbaye du Paraclet,* Paris, 1878.
9. Boutillier du Retail et Piétresson de Saint-Aubin ont édité le nécrologe, *Obituaires de la Province de Sens,* t. IV, p. 403-440. Charrier doute que le *Catalogue* soit de la main de Cajot, mais sans justification, *Héloïse,* p. 623.
10. Un inventaire dactylographié du fonds du Paraclet se trouve aux Archives départementales de l'Aube. Voir aussi, A. VALLET DE VIRIVILLE, *Les archives historiques du département de l'Aube,* Paris 1841, p. 79, 174 et 229 et, plus important, CORRARD DE BREBAN, «Rapport relatif aux archives du Paraclet», *Documents historiques inédits tirés des collections manuscrites de la Bibliothèque Royale et des archives ou des bibliothèques des départements,* ed. J. J. CHAMPOLLION-FIGEAC, t. I, Paris, 1841, p. 3-15.

MANUSCRITS MENTIONNÉS AU MS PARIS, BIBL. NAT. FR. 14410

L'Ordinal du Paraclet (Paris, Bibl. nat. fr. 14410, fol. 29-116v), qui mentionne les leçons, les hymnes et les sermons à lire ou à chanter pendant l'année, nous permet de dresser un inventaire sommaire de plusieurs livres du couvent au début du treizième siècle. Etant donné l'important travail que C. Waddell termine sur ce sujet, nous n'essayerons point d'analyser en détail le contenu de chaque livre. Nous nous bornerons à indiquer leur titre, en précisant les feuillets de l'Ordinal où il en est fait état. [11]

bible {en plusieurs tomes: Genèse, Isaïe, Evangiles, Epîtres de St Paul etc.}	(fol. 29v, 38-38v, 42, 43-43v, 45-45v, 48, 64v, 92v, 105, 106v)
breuiaire de couuent	(fol. 29v, 31, 32v, 36, 40v, 41v, 42, 42v, 43v, 57, 59, 66, 67, 69, 71v, 73v, 75, 76v, 83, 85, 88, 89, 96, 106, 111, 111v, 112v)
epistolaire {recueil des Epîtres et des Evangiles}	(fol. 42v, 47, 47v, 60v)
esmeraude {*neuue*} {commentaires sur les Epî- tres et les Evangiles pour Carême, Pâques et quelques fêtes}	(fol. 44v-45: *sermons de saint gregoire*; fol. 65v-66: *sermons de saint augustin*; fol. 46, 46v, 47, 48v-49, 52v, 54, 55, 55v, 56, 81, 84, 107)
espitre saint augustin {parmi une collection de textes divers?}	(fol. 63v)
expositions ezechiel, liure *uelu petit expositions de* *ysiaie*	(fol. 64v, 110; fol. 87: les sermons, liure petit) (fol. 30v)
leconnier	(fol. 34, 37v, 39, 54v, 55, 69v, 70, 72, 72v, 81, 82, 83v, 86, 93, 94v, 97 99, 99v, 100v, 101v, 102v, 103, 105, 105v, 106, 107, 107v, 108, 109v, 112)

---

11. Je suis très reconnaissant à C. Waddell des brèves précisions, ajoutées ici entre parenthèses. Une analyse critique de toutes les citations dans l'Ordinal doit attendre la parution de l'édition qu'il prépare.

messieux et greeux	(fol. 53v)
{missels et graduels}	
miracles de nostre dame	(fol. 52v, 65)
omelier	(fol. 61, 62v, 63, 78v, 100v, 107, 108v)
omelier neuf	(fol. 95, 104v)
omelier plat	(fol. 56, 58, 59v, 60, 60v, 61v, 77)
omelier plat viez	(fol. 98, 107v, 108)
Osculetur me, liure	(fol. 87-87v)
que len apelle {Ps - Jerome: *Cogitis me, O Paula et Eustochium...*}	
Pastoriaus, liure qui a non	(fol. 64)
{Gregory, *Liber pastoralis*}	
petit liuret, la benicon ou	(fol. 53)
{livre de bénédictions}	
sermons au mestre	(fol. 39v, 47v, 63v, 76; fol. 62v: *sermons*
{Pierre Abélard}	*maistre pierre*)
trinite, liure de la	(fol. 63v)
{sans indication d'auteur}	
uert, liure {commentaires sur les Epîtres et les Evangiles de l'Avent au Carême}	(fol. 30v, 36, 36v, 38, 41, 41v, 43v, 66-66v, 67, 69, 70, 70v)
Vite patrum	(fol. 65v; fol. 55, 60, 65v: *uie legyptienne*; fol. 71, 73v, 80v. 110: *uie des saints agathe, alexi, antoigne, brice, eugene, eustace, fabian, martin, mor, nicholas, sebastien, uincent*; fol. 71. *uita beati hylarii, beati antonii*)

Le *breuiaire de couuent* (*grant breuiaire* au fol. 29v) et le *leconnier* sont les deux livres les plus souvent cités dans cet Ordinal. Est-ce que ce *breuiaire* se rapprochait du manuscrit de Chaumont, copié à la fin du XVᵉ siècle, et connu au XVIIᵉ siècle comme *le bréviaire d'Abailard*? Les références au *breuiaire* faites dans l'Ordinal se rapportent toutes aux leçons de l'Office de nuit, qui manquent dans le bréviaire de Chaumont. [12] Ce dernier comprend les hymnes d'Abélard, des collectes et d'autres textes liturgiques, dont plusieurs sont peut-être

---

12. WADDELL, art. cit., p. 279-281.

aussi de sa main. [13] Le *leconnier* comprenait au moins vingt-cinq for-
mulaires, chacun de douze leçons, qui sont souvent très liés aux
hymnes et aux sermons d'Abélard. L'originalité du choix des textes
du leconnier nous incite à penser qu'Abélard lui-même les avait rassemblés. Les *sermons au mestre* sont des sermons d'Abélard qui se
retrouvent parmi ceux publiés par Duchesne dans son édition des
Opera Omnia de 1616. [14]

L'Ordinal ne précise que les livres employés pour la liturgie et
lus au chapitre (ou cloître) et au réfectoire. Il n'indique pas si la bibliothèque du couvent possédait des textes d'Abélard, en dehors de
ses hymnes, sermons et autres textes liturgiques. A supposer qu'elle
en ait eus, nous en avons perdu la trace.

II. LES MANUSCRITS PERDUS

D'Amboise, Duchesne et le Paraclet

Le premier témoignage formel des manuscrits d'Abélard au Paraclet, en dehors de celui de l'Ordinal, se trouve dans la *praefatio
apologetica* que François d'Amboise a ajoutée à l'édition de 1616.
Cette préface remplace celle de Duchesne, lequel avait fait la plus
grande partie du travail d'édition. [15] D'Amboise s'est rendu au Paraclet pour rechercher des manuscrits, et il affirme avoir obtenu un
manuscrit des lettres d'Abélard et d'Héloïse, ainsi qu'un autre (ou
d'autres) des sermons, hymnes et collectes, écrits «dans le style
d'Abélard»:

> Itaque unum exemplar Epistolarum nactus sum in Armorica...;
> Alterum ex Filippo Portaeo...; Tertium ex Monasterio Paraclitensi,
> ad quod profectus sum, ut quae ibi ex ejus operibus reperire pote-
> ram, in usum publicum convasarem, ibique comiter sum exceptus
> et ad contigua fundatoris et fundatricis sepulchra manu ductus
> benignitate reverendae D. Mariae Rupifocaldae Diaconissae sapien-
> tissimae cognatae meae: ejus enim paterna avia Antonia Amboesia,
> quae equiti Torquato Barbesio nupsit, Vidi Amboesii filia unica,

---

13. *Ibid.*, art. cit., p. 279-281.
14. *Petri Abaelardi Sancti Gildasii in Britannia abbatis et Heloissae conjugis ejus... Opera...*
Paris, 1616 (désormais cité *Opera* (1616), p. 726-971. L. Engels, de Groningen, prépare une nouvelle édition des sermons.
15. Monfrin discute les deux préfaces dans une analyse détaillée, *Abélard. Historia Calamitatum*, Paris. 1959, p. 31-46.

Karoli Calvimontis D. Franciae marescalli neptis et haeres totam vetustissimam familiam crevit, et primogenita nostra ad Rupifocaldos transtulit. Ea etiam mihi communicavit divini officii homilias toto anni curriculo legendas stylo Abaelardico exaratas cum collectis et hymnis, in quibus magna catholicae pietatis lux seu legenti affulget. [16]

Avant d'analyser en détail chacun de ces manuscrits, il faut rappeler la situation, à cette époque, du couvent (abbaye dans tous les documents). Les constitutions et le commentaire sur la règle de S. Benoît, publiés en 1632, nous donnent à cet égard de précieux éclaircissements. [17] Aucun auteur n'a signé l'ouvrage, mais nous pouvons raisonnablement supposer que Marie III de La Rochefoucauld, abbesse du Paraclet de 1593 à 1639, en est l'auteur, ou du moins l'inspiratrice. Dans la *Petition* qui préface les constitutions, elle explique que les soeurs avait décidé en 1610 de «quitter les traces de leurs devancieres» et ont mis dix ans pour mener à terme toutes les réformes:

> Les Abbesses et Religieuses du Paraclit... vous remonstrent tres humblement que leurs devancieres ont vescu pres de cinq cens ans faisans profession de Benedictines, toutesfois sans Constitutions aucunes suffisamment authorisées, exprimantes l'intention de sainct Benoist, qui bailla loy à son Ordre en Italie environ l'an cinq cens vinct six, ce qui les a menés l'an mil six cens dix à quitter les traces de leurs dites devancieres pour commencer la reforme qu'elles ont dix Ans apres embrassé tout à fait, ... Telles donc desirans de cueillir la moisson de leur essay, practiqué l'espace de douze ans, ont d'un commun accord compromis de l'obliger à certaines et determinées Constitutions, dressées sur le modelle que plusieurs Monasteres reformés observent, mais non autrement qu'apres une suffisante authorisation d'icelles. [18]

Le texte de 1632 codifie les réformes, soumises à l'approbation de l'évêque de Troyes, douze ans après leur achèvement. Pour notre étude sur les manuscrits du Paraclet, il est instructif de constater l'absence de toute référence à Abélard ou à Héloïse dans l'ouvrage. Dans le chapitre traitant de la liturgie, Marie de La Rochefould

---

16. D'AMBOISE, *praef. apol.*, fol. a iiij (*PL* 178, 75D-76A).
17. *La Regle de S. Benoist. Avec les declarations et constitutions sur icelle, authorisées et Confirmées par Monseigneur le Reverendissime Evesque de Troyes. Pour les Religieuses du Paraclet, Chef d'ordre et des Prieurez qui en dependent. A Paris chez Sebastien Hervé rue S. Iacques au Coeur-bon MDCXXXII.* Deux exemplaires de cet ouvrage sont connus, à la Bibliothèque municipale de Troyes (cote RR 200) et à Lubin, en Pologne. Voir J. D. BROEKAERT, *Bibliographie de la règle de Saint-Benoît*, Studia Anselmiana, t. 77, Rome, 1980, no. 245, t. I, p. 200-201.
18. *Regle*, fol. a ij-iij[v]

précise que l'ordre du Paraclet a commencé à utiliser le bréviaire Tridentin en 1609, abandonnant ainsi l'usage des manuscrits. [19] Les constitutions se caractérisent par un désir de se moderniser et d'embrasser l'orthodoxie de la Contre-Réforme. Le couvent du Paraclet n'était pas le seul à adopter de telles réformes à cette époque, ravagée par les guerres de religion. [20] La précédente abbesse, Jeanne III de Chabot (abbesse de 1560 à 1593), s'était convertie au protestantisme, et quand Marie de La Rochefoucauld a pris ses fonctions au Paraclet, il n'y restait plus que trois soeurs. [21] Les manuscrits liturgiques étant usés et difficilement lisibles, il était moins onéreux de les remplacer par des textes imprimés.

Le «Paraclitense» et le MS Troyes, Bibl. Mun. 802 (T)

Les réformes du début du XVII siècle peuvent nous aider à comprendre le sort du manuscrit des lettres d'Abélard et d'Héloïse (*Paraclitense*) que d'Amboise dit avoir obtenu de Marie III de La Rochefoucauld. D'Amboise et Duchesne ont utilisé ce manuscrit pour éditer les *Institutiones nostrae*, constitutions qu'ils ont attribuées à Héloïse, mais qui, en fait, datent du XIIIe siècle. [22] Le texte imprimé de ces *Institutiones* est si proche de celui du seul manuscrit connu qui les contient (Troyes, Bibl. mun. 802, fol. 89-94v), que toutes les divergences entre les deux textes peuvent provenir de l'inexactitude avec laquelle l'éditeur a transcrit le *Paraclitense*. [23] Comme dans l'édition imprimée, les *Institutiones* suivent, en *T*, la règle rédigée par Abélard pour les soeurs du Paraclet (*Epist.* VIII). [24] Toutes les notes laissées en marge d'*Epist.* VIII en *T* sont reproduites avec beaucoup de fidélité dans l'édition imprimée, excepté deux d'entre elles, qui sont difficiles à lire dans la marge intérieure de *T*. [25] S'il s'agit de deux manuscrits différents ils sont identiques au moindre détail.

L'identification du *Paraclitense* avec *T* fait difficulté pour Monfrin, qui discute le problème en détail, parce qu'il ne trouve aucune

19. *Regle*, p. 119-120.
20. Voir, par exemple, l'étude de C. WADDELL, «A reforming abbess "manquée": Françoise de Nerestang 1591-1652», *Citeaux Commentarii Cistercienses*, t. II, 1981, p. 215-36.
21. A. ROSEROT, «Les Abbayes du département de l'Aube. Additions et Corrections à la *Gallia Christiana* tomes IV et XII», *Bulletin historique et philologique*, 1903, p. 122-126.
22. *Opera*, 1616, p. 198-213 (=*PL* 178, 313-326).
23. MONFRIN, p. 17, n. 28.
24. L'*Epist.* VIII comporte une lettre d'envoi et le texte de la *regula*, MONFRIN, p. 11.
25. J. BENTON, «Fraud, Fiction and Borrowing in the Correspondence of Abelard and Heloise», *Pierre Abélard - Pierre le Vénérable*, p. 482, n. 34.

40

preuve de l'appartenance de *T* au Paraclet avant 1616.[26] Selon une note ajoutée à la dernière page de *T* (fol. 103v), Robert de Bardi, ami de Pétrarque et chancelier de la Sorbonne, a acheté le manuscrit au Chapitre de Notre-Dame de Paris *anno 1346 in die beati Benedicti abbatis* (= le 21 mars 1347).[27] Après la mort de Robert de Bardi en 1349, nous perdons toute trace du volume, jusqu'à sa mention en 1630 dans le catalogue des manuscrits de F. Pithou (1545-1621) légués à l'Oratoire de Troyes.[28] Monfrin doute de l'identification du *Paraclitense* avec *T* en prétendant qu'il est «peu vraisemblable qu'une telle abbesse ait aliéné un volume auquel s'attachaient de respectables souvenirs, au moment même où un livre savant en rappelait l'existence».[29] Il doute également que d'Amboise «ait poussé l'indélicatesse jusqu'à le céder de son vivant», ou que Pithou, mort le 25 janvier 1621, ait pu acquérir le volume auprès des héritiers de d'Amboise, mort en 1619.[30] L'hypothèse que nous propose Monfrin est que *T* et le *Paraclitense* ne sont que les épaves d'une série d'exemplaires identiques, faits tout exprès pour les filles spirituelles d'Héloïse et d'Abélard et que chaque prieuré du Paraclet ainsi que la maison mère de l'ordre en possédaient un exemplaire.[31]

Pourtant, il y a de graves difficultés à admettre cette hypothèse. Les constitutions de 1632 nous montrent que depuis 1609/10 les soeurs s'étaient engagées dans des réformes caractérisées par l'absence de toute référence à Abélard ou à Héloïse. Selon ces constitutions, l'abbesse seule gardait la clef de la bibliothèque et devait veiller à n'y faire entrer que des livres approuvés par l'Eglise.[32] Aucun intérêt pour Abélard ne se manifeste dans ces constitutions. Il faut rappeler qu'à cette époque les ouvrages d'Abélard étaient toujours inscrits à l'*Index librorum prohibitorum*; les théologiens de la Sorbonne ont dressé une *Censura Doctorum Parisiensium* en 1616 —critique détaillée des doctrines d'Abélard et d'Héloïse d'après l'édition de Duchesne.[33]

---

26. MONFRIN, p. 14-18.
27. *Ibid.*, p. 13.
28. *Ibid.*, p. 13-14. Le catalogue est édité par GROSLEY, *Vie de Pierre Pithou...*, Paris, 1756, p. 278.
29. MONFRIN, p. 15-16.
30. *Ibid.*, p. 16 n. 22.
31. *Ibid.*, p. 17.
32. *Regle*, p. 17-18.
33. *Index librorum... prohibitorum*, Rome, 1596, p. 84, reproduit dans l'édition de 1632 (p. 500). La *Censura Doctorum Parisiensium* fut ajoutée par D'Amboise à l'édition qui porte son nom, *Opera*, 1616, fol. °°°ij-iiij (=*PL* 178, 109-112). Duchesne a fait réimprimer l'édition en 1626 avec sa préface, mais sans la *Censura*. L'attitude critique de l'Église se voit dans un des premiers livres consacrés à Abélard, I. CARAMUEL LOBKOWITZ, *S. Bernardus Petrum Abailardum eiusque potentissimos sectarios triumphans*, Louvain, 1644.

Marie III de La Rochefoucauld aurait contrevenu à ses propres constitutions en conservant un manuscrit d'Abélard.

Bien que dans sa *praefatio apologetica* d'Amboise prétende être
un parent de l'abbesse du Paraclet, dont une tante était Antoinette
d'Amboise, il n'appartenait pas en réalité à la grande famille aristocratique qui portait ce nom. Il était un simple bourgeois, avocat par
profession, originaire du village d'Amboise.[3] Par le statut qu'il s'oc-
troyait, il aurait pu ne pas ressentir l'obligation sociale de rendre le
manuscrit. Ni d'Amboise ni Duchesne ne sont connus comme des
collectionneurs des manuscrits; l'un ou l'autre aurait pu le céder à
F. Pithou, un grand collectionneur de l'époque. Notons que F. Pithou
a eu des rapports étroits avec J. Sirmond, lequel a communiqué plusieurs manuscrits à Duchesne pour l'édition d'Abélard.[35] Duchesne,
à son tour, reconnaît avoir reçu de d'Amboise tous les manuscrits
d'Abélard lui ayant appartenus.[36]

Monfrin émet l'hypothèse, en en reconnaissant la fragilité, que
le *Paraclitense* est resté au Paraclet jusqu'à la Révolution.[37] Cependant, plusieurs visiteurs du couvent, amateurs de manuscrits, n'en
font jamais mention. Martène et Durand, lors d'une visite en 1709, ont
consulté les archives, mais n'ont pas remarqué un manuscrit des
lettres d'Abélard et d'Héloïse, tandis qu'à l'oratoire de Troyes ils
ont relevé avec intérêt la présence du manuscrit *T*.[38] Dom Charles
Cajot, dans une étude sur l'ordre de Saint-Benoît publiée en 1787,
mentionne plusieurs manuscrits de liturgie et d'homélies qui se trouvaient au Paraclet, mais, louant les soeurs pour leur connaissance du
latin, ne parle pas d'un manuscrit des lettres.[39] Q. Craufurd, un aris-
tocrate écossais très porté sur l'histoire, nous fournit une relation

---

34. *Dictionnaire de Biographie Française*, éd. BALTEAU, t. II, Paris, 1936, col. 479-80; voir
aussi les fiches de E. Picot, Paris, Bibliothèque nationale, nouv. acq. fr. 23193, nos. 196-225.
35. Grosley relate les efforts de F. Pithou pour acquérir ses manuscrits, *Vie de Pithou*,
p. 106-268, et sur Sirmond, p. 264. Un autre manuscrit appartenant à d'Amboise, qu'il appelle
Nanneticus, a été acquis par Baluze, qui lui a donné la cote 346. Le manuscrit est ensuite
entré à la Bibliothèque du roi (maintenant Paris, Bibl. nat. lat. 2545). La cote de Baluze se
trouve au fol. 1. Monfrin (p. 40) identifie ce manuscrit avec celui de d'Amboise, mais sans
parler de Baluze. Les autres manuscrits utilisés par d'Amboise et Duchesne, comme ceux
de sermons, du commentaire sur l'Epître aux Romains (qui provenait du Mont St Michel)
et d'autres lettres d'Abélard (*Epist*. X, XII, XIII) ont depuis disparu, ainsi qu'un manuscrit de St. Victor (cote GGG 17) que Duchesne aurait vu; voir MONFRIN, p. 42-45.
36. MONFRIN, p. 41.
37. *Ibid.*, p. 16-17.
38. E. MARTÈNE et U. DURAND, *Voyage littéraire de deux religieux bénédictins*, t. I, Paris,
1717, p. 84-86, 94.
39. C. CAJOT, *Recherches historiques sus l'esprit primitif et les anciens collèges de l'ordre
de Saint-Benoît, d'où résultent les droits de la Société sur les biens qu'il possède*, Paris, 1787,
t. I, p. 141; voir plus loin, n. 70.

de choix: il reproduit dans un livre de *Mélanges* le récit d'une visite du couvent faite en 1787, que lui a envoyé un ami dont il préserve l'anonymat.[40] Cet anonyme affirme qu'il n'existe pas de manuscrits des ouvrages d'Abélard et d'Héloïse mais seulement quelques manuscrits qui pouvaient leur avoir appartenus:

> J'ai vu aux archives quelques livres qui ont appartenu à Abeillard et à Héloïse, ce sont des évangiles grossièrement reliés avec des nerfs et des couvertures de bois de chêne de six ou huit lignes d'épaisseur. Les manuscrits particuliers et les lettres originales de ces deux amans existèrent pareillement dans les archives jusqu'au moment où l'abbesse Jeanne III de Chabot, ayant embrassé le calvinisme, abandonna son monastère dont elle fit enlever les effets les plus précieux; mais on y a conservé la tradition que les originaux des lettres d'Héloïse furent transportés et vendus en Angleterre, où des perquisitions soigneuses pourroient peut-être les faire retrouver.[41]

S'il existait au Paraclet un manuscrit des lettres, Dom Cajot l'aurait montré à l'ami de Craufurd. La tradition suivant laquelle Jeanne de Chabot aurait vendu le manuscrit des lettres en Angleterre est évidemment fausse, étant donné que Marie de La Rochefoucauld, allait le donner à d'Amboise. La tradition avait toutefois le mérite de disculper une abbesse réformatrice, en attribuant la perte du manuscrit à un prédécesseur, une hérétique notoire.

Il existe dans *T* l'indice d'une liaison directe entre ce manuscrit et le couvent du Paraclet, preuve possible que *Paraclitense* et *T* sont identiques: la série d'épitaphes d'Abélard et d'Héloïse, suivie par la formule d'absolution de Pierre le Vénérable, ajoutées à la dernière page de *T* (fol. 245v) à la fin du XVe siècle.[42] Le même copiste a entrepris d'inscrire soigneusement en rouge des titre courants sur les premières pages du manuscrit.[43] Le seul autre manuscrit subsistant qui contient toute cette série de textes, y compris la formule d'absolution, provient du Paraclet: Chaumont, Bibl. mun. 31, où ces textes se trouvent également ajoutés à la dernière page (fol. 245v) à la fin du XVe siècle.[44] L'ordre de ces textes dans *T* est un peu différent de celui de

---

40. Q. CRAUFURD, *Mélanges d'histoire, de littérature, etc. tirés d'une portefeuille*, s. l., 1809, p. 15-27 (2e éd., Paris, 1817). L'auteur du récit dit que Cajot, qui a connu son père, lui a montré la bibliothèque en compagnie de Madame de Roucy, *Mélanges*, p. 15. Il ajoute à sa lettre une traduction des lettres de Pierre le Vénérable à Héloïse (p. 27-38) et de plusieurs chartes du Paraclet (p. 67-77) et un catalogue des abbesses du couvent (p. 39-67) écrit par Dom Cajot.
41. CRAUFURD, *Mélanges*, p. 22-23.
42. MONFRIN, p. 13. Voir l'appendice.
43. Il faut lire XVe et non pas XVIe siècle à la p. 14 du texte de Monfrin.
44. Voir au-dessus, n. 2.

Chaumont: la formule d'absolution se trouve entre les épitaphes d'Abélard et d'Héloïse dans ce dernier, et non pas à la suite. La même série de textes se trouvait dans un autre manuscrit du Paraclet, depuis disparu, dont N. Camuzat a publié des extraits en 1610 sous la rubrique *Excerpta ex MS codice obituum Paraclitici*, dans l'ordre de *T*. [45] Duchesne les a publiées à son tour dans ses notes à la *Bibliotheca Cluniacensis* de 1614 et dans son introduction à l'édition des oeuvres d'Abélard de 1616. [46]

La formule d'absolution est sans aucune doute celle qu'Héloïse a sollicitée de Pierre le Vénérable pour le tombeau d'Abélard. [47] Les épitaphes de deux lignes pour Abélard (*Est satis in tumulo...*) et de quatre lignes pour Héloïse (*Hoc tumulo abbatissa iacet prudens Heloysa...*), qui datent du XIIᵉ siècle, se trouvaient aussi sur les tombeaux. [48] Les cendres ont reposé dans la chapelle de St Denis —l'ancien oratoire du Paraclet, connu sous le nom de Petit Moustier (petit monastère)— depuis le XIIᵉ siècle jusqu'au 2 mai 1497, date à laquelle Catherine de Courcelles les a fait transférer dans le choeur de l'église principale. [49] Or, à la même époque, l'on a ajouté les épitaphes et la formule d'absolution aux manuscrits de Chaumont et de Troyes. Une telle concomitance nous amène à penser que ce sont les soeurs ellesmêmes qui les ont copiées, précisément lors du transfert des corps. [50] La rédaction d'un nouveau bréviaire (MS Chaumont, Bibl. mun. 31) reflète l'activité de Catherine de Courcelles, qui a entrepris tout un programme de réforme de la vie religieuse au couvent. [51]

Nous ignorons la date de composition de l'épitaphe *Petrus in hac petra...*, transcrite avec la formule d'absolution et l'épitaphe pour

45. N. CAMUZAT, *Promptuarium sacrarum antiquitatum Tricassinae diocesis*, Troyes, 1610, fol. 348-348v. Sur ce manuscrit, voir plus loin, n. 87.
46. DUCHESNE, *Notae ad Bibliothecam Cluniacensem*, Paris, 1614, col. 148 et 155; *Opera*, 1616, p. 336, 345 et dans la préface de Duchesne, fol. i ijᵛ et dans celle de d'Amboise, fol. d i, e iiij.
47. *Epist. Heloissae Abbatissae ad Dominum Abbatem*, éd. G. CONSTABLE, *The Letters of Peter the Venerable*, Cambridge, Mass., 1967, t. I, p. 400-401.
48. Voir l'appendice.
49. Voir le rapport officiel rédigé le 2 mai 1497 (Archives de l'Aube 24 H), ed. VALLET DE VIRIVILLE, *Journal de l'Institut historique*, t. XII (1840), p. 255-258: «...fecit transportari ossa corporum seu cadaverum nunc defunctarum magistri Petri Abelardi, primi fundatoris predicte ecclesia de Paraclito, et Heloisse, prime abbatisse ipsius monasterii, a quodam loco humido et aquoso, scilicet in quadam capello in dicto monasterio in honore sancti Dionysii... et eadem ossa inhumari ac sepeliri fecerat et fecit separatim in duobus locis chori primo dicte ecclesie de Paraclito, uidelicet ossa dicti fundatoris a parte dextera, et ossa dicte defuncte prime abbatisse a parte sinistra, scilicet accedendo de dicto choro ad maius altare ipsius ecclesie».
50. On retrouve les mêmes formules *magistri Petri Abelardi fondatoris monasterii* et *Heloisse prime abbatisse* dans le rapport officiel et dans les manuscrits de Troyes (*prime om.*) et de Chaumont.
51. Sur Catherine de Courcelles, voir CORRARD DE BREBAN, *Les abbesses*, p. 61.

44

Héloïse dans les manuscrits de Troyes et de Chaumont et dans le nécrologe latin copié par Camuzat. Cette épitaphe se retrouve, dans le Ms Berne, Bürgerbibliothek 211, fol. 160v-161 (*B*). Le copiste de ce dernier est un humaniste qui peut-être s'est rendu au couvent voir les tombeaux. [52]

Tous ces indices nous incitent à penser que le manuscrit de Troyes est un témoin du regain d'intérêt au Paraclet à la fin du xve siècle, pour les fondateurs du couvent; et qu'il est identique au *Paraclitense*, cédé à d'Amboise par Marie de La Rochefoucauld, et dont la perte était ensuite attribuée à Jeanne III de Chabot.

Il reste à expliquer pourquoi *T*, écrit à la fin du xiiie ou au début du xiv siècle, est parvenu au Paraclet, après avoir appartenu au Chapitre de Notre-Dame et, ensuite, à Robert de Bardi. Il faut rappeler que les anglais avaient totalement détruit le couvent en 1359, et que l'évêque de Troyes ne l'avait fait reconstruire qu'en 1366. [53] Il est possible que *T* ait été donné au Paraclet à la suite de l'intérêt des humanistes pour Abélard et Héloïse au xive siècle. Pourtant les ouvrages aux fol. 89-102v de *T* (*Institutiones nostrae* et des extraits de la diète d'Aix relatifs à la vie des moniales) correspond bien à des textes rassemblés par des personnes vivant à l'intérieur d'un couvent. [54] Comment expliquer la présence de ces ouvrages dans un manuscrit qui appartenait au Chapitre de Notre-Dame avant 1347?

Monfrin propose de voir dant *T* et *Paraclitense* les rescapés d'une série d'exemplaires identiques destinés aux prieurés de l'ordre du Paraclet. Il n'existe, malheureusement, aucune preuve d'une telle diffusion. Le manuscrit des lettres le plus ancien connu (Paris, Bibl. nat. lat. 2923, la propriété de Pétrarque vers 1337) ne date que de la fin du xiiie siècle, la même époque que la traduction de Jean de Meun (vers 1300) et longtemps après celle de la fondation des prieurés. Il est bien possible que le manuscrit des lettres servant de modèle ait comporté les divers textes sur la vie religieuse de *T*, rassemblés au Paraclet. Est-ce que l'on a apporté ce manuscrit du couvent à Paris

---

52. H. HAGEN, *Catalogus codicum Bernensium*, Berne, 1875, p. 256-260. P. DRONKE les édite à partir de ce manuscrit, *Abelard and Heloise in Medieval Testimonies*, Glasgow, 1976, p. 49-50.

53. LALORE, *Cartulaire du Paraclet*, p. xxi-xxii.

54. MONFRIN, p. 57-61. Voir aussi son étude, «Le problème de l'authenticité de la correspondance d'Abélard et d'Héloïse», *Pierre Abélard - Pierre le Vénérable*, p. 409-424, surtout p. 409-424. Nous n'avons pas l'intention d'aborder ici le problème de l'authenticité des lettres, mise en question par BENTON, «Fraud, fiction and borrowing in the correspondence of Abelard and Heloise», *ibid.*, p. 469-506, puis acceptée en grande partie dans son étude, «A reconsideration of the authenticity of the correspondence of Abelard and Heloise», *Petrus Abaelardus*, ed. THOMAS, p. 41-52.

avant la fin du XIIIe siècle, peut-être en raison de l'intérêt des humanistes? Les certitudes manquent. Pourtant, nous constatons l'existence à Notre-Dame de Paris vers 1300 des manuscrits d'autres ouvrages d'Abélard, écrits spécialement pour Héloïse et ses moniales: les sermons et l'*Expositio in Hexaemeron* en deux exemplaires (Paris, Bibl. nat. lat. 17251, saec. XII; [2] Vatican, Bibl. apost. lat. 4214, saec. XII[2]). [55] Les *Problemata Heloissae* et l'*Epist. IX de studio litterarum* ne subsistent que dans un manuscrit de Saint-Victor de Paris (Paris, Bibl. nat. lat. 14511, saec. XIV[jn]). Il est donc concevable que le recueil des lettres ait été rassemblé au couvent, mais diffusé de Paris à partir de la fin du XIIIe siècle. [56] Du témoignage des manuscrits connus des lettres d'Abélard et d'Héloïse il ressort que Paris a joué un rôle beaucoup plus important que la maison-mère ou que les prieurés de l'ordre du Paraclet. [57]

La perte du manuscrit des lettres (*Paraclitense*) par le couvent au début du XVIIIe siècle doit être rapproché du transfert des cendres d'Abélard et d'Héloïse de leur emplacement à droite et à gauche de la grande grille, qui sépare le choeur du maître-autel, jusqu'au «charnier» souterrain, au-dessous du maître-autel, le 15 mars 1621. [58] Charrier, et les autres auteurs qui traitent de ce déplacement n'ont

---

55. *Sermones Petri Abalardi, qui incipiunt* «Ascendat puteus», selon le catalogue des livres légués par Pierre de Joigny au Chapitre de Notre-Dame, en 1297, éd. DELISLE, *Le Cabinet des MSS de la Bibliothèque nationale*, t. III, Paris, 1881, p. 4. Ce manuscrit est maintenant disparu. Le MS Paris, Bibl. nat. lat. 17251 porte un *ex libris* de Notre-Dame du XVIe siècle. Annibale de Ceccano, proviseur de la Sorbonne de 1320 à 1326 acheta le MS Vatican, Bibl. apost. lat. 4284 du Chapitre de Notre-Dame avant 1326, selon une note au feuillet de garde.
56. Selon Monfrin (p. 58), le manuscrit de Troyes, celui de Pétrarque (Paris, Bibl. nat. lat. 2923 s. XIII[ex]) et la traduction de Jean de Meun (Paris, Bibl. nat. fr. 920 s. XIV), remontent indépendamment au même archétype.
57. L'importance de Paris dans la diffusion des lettres est soulignée par Luscombe, dans une étude sur un recueil des extraits inconnu de Monfrin, «Excerpts from the Letter Collection of Heloise and Abelard in Notre Dame (Indiana) Ms 30», *Pascua Mediaevalia. Studies voor Prof. Dr. J. M. De Smet*, éd. R. LIEVENS, E. VAN MINGROOT et W. VERBEKE, Louvain, 1983, p. 529-544. En dehors du manuscrit de Troyes, aucun manuscrit des lettres ne provient d'une communauté monastique. Il n'est pas du tout certain que le cahier de 8 feuillets, qui contient le début de l'*Historia Calamitatum*, ajouté au 4e volume du *Speculum historiale* de Vincent de Beauvais (MS Douai, Bibl. mun. 797 (4), fol. 321-328v), provienne de l'abbaye de Marchiennes, comme le propose Monfrin (p. 22, où il cite la cote 794 (4) par erreur); selon toute vraisemblance, le cahier fut lui-même ajouté après l'inscription au fol. 320v: *Quintius Algambe est hujus libri possessor 1569*, écrit au-dessus *Ex libris bibliothecae religiosissimorum Marchenensium* (main du XIe siècle).
58. Voir la note ajoutée au nécrologe latin, éd BOUTELLIER I U RETAIL et PIÉTRESSON DE SAINT-AUBIN, *Obituaires de la Province de Sens*, t. IV, p. 410-411: *Ce jour d'huy 15 mars 1621 a eté fait la translation des corps de maître Pierre Abaillard et d'Heloise, lesquels ont eté enlevés d'un du coté dextre, l'autre senestre de la grande grille de l'eglise pour être transporté sous le grand autel en un charnier, et ce par le commande de... Marie de La Rochefoucault... .*

jamais expliqué les raisons du transfert de sépultures. [59] Catherine de Courcelles avait mis les tombeaux dans le choeur de l'église principale pour qu'ils soient plus visibles. Le caveau où ils ont été transférés en 1621 n'a plus que 1 mètre 50 de haut. [60] Catherine III de La Rochefoucauld, abbesse de 1675 à 1706 a fait enlever de cet endroit le 3 juin 1701 une statue représentant la Trinité et la placer dans le choeur des religieuses, pour que la statue soit plus visible. [61] Marie de La Rochefoucauld a fait enlever les tombeaux d'Abélard et d'Héloïse du regard des soeurs au moment même où elle terminait les réformes codifiées plus tard dans les *Constitutions* de 1632. C'est dans ce climat qu'elle a cédé le manuscrit des lettres des fondateurs à d'Amboise.

LES SERMONS D'ABÉLARD

Nous avons déjà observé que les sermons au mestre, les sermons d'Abélard, sont mentionnés plusieurs fois dans l'Ordinal. Est-ce que ce manuscrit des sermons est identique à celui qui contenait les *divini officii homilias* communiqué par Marie de La Rochefoucauld à d'Amboise? Les *incipits* des sermons dans l'Ordinal correspondent à ceux des sermons adressés aux soeurs du Paraclet et édités par Duchesne. [62] Monfrin interprète les mots de d'Amboise *homilias... cum Collectis et Hymnis* dans le sens d'un seul manuscrit, mais il pourrait y en avoir deux, dont l'un comporterait les sermons et l'autre les hymnes et collectes. [63] D'Amboise affirme avoir trouvé aussi des *homilias ex Sorbonico gymnasio celeberrimo*; sans doute s'agit-il du manuscrit légué à la Sorbonne en 1500 par Jean l'Huillier, évêque de Meaux, et cité par Papire Masson dans son *Annalium* de 1577. [64] De tous les ma-

---

59. CHARRIER, *Héloïse*, p. 309 parle d'un «leger regain de popularité des fondateurs» à cette époque, mais sans fournir aucune preuve. E. McLEOD, *Héloïse*, trad. Viollis, s.l. 1941, p. 196 avoue son ignorance.

60. Cette crypte se voit toujours au Paraclet. L'auteur de l'article dans la *Gallia Christiana*, t. XII, Paris, 1770, col. 576 affirme: *Sed iam pridem exinde extracta in subterraneo specu sub altari sanctae Trinitatis quod est pone chorum monialium quiescent*. Voir aussi le témoignage de M. Vincent, cure de Quincy, publié dans le *Mercure de France* d'octobre 1780, p. 138-143: *Les deux tombes furent déposées dans un caveau que l'on avoit pratiqué sous l'Autel de la Chapelle qui porte encore à présent le nom de Chapelle de la Trinité*.

61. Martène et Durand, qui ont visité le couvent en 1709, racontent l'histoire de la découverte de la statue, cachée dans ce caveau, *Voyage littéraire*, t. I, p. 85.

62. WADDELL, *art. cit.*, p. 277-279.

63. MONFRIN, p. 45.

64. D'AMBOISE, *praef. apol.* fol. a iiij (= *PL* 173, 76A). Voir L. THUASNE, «Jean l'Huillier, évêque de Meaux et la bibliothèque du Collège de Sorbonne», *Revue des bibliothèques*, 1897, p. 136: *Item aliud volumen Petri Abaelardi in quo continentur sermones ad virgines Para-*

nuscrits légués par Jean l'Huillier, c'est le seul qui ne se trouve plus parmi les manuscrits de la Sorbonne; est-ce parce que d'Amboise l'a emprunté? Duchesne précise qu'il n'avait utilisé qu'un manuscrit pour son édition des sermons, celui de d'Amboise. [65] Nous ignorons si ce dernier a restitué au couvent le manuscrit des sermons; mais puisqu'aucun visiteur du Paraclet n'a mentionné l'existence d'une telle pièce, nous inclinons à croire que d'Amboise l'a conservé.

Dom Charles Cajot affirme dans son étude de 1787 qu'il existait au couvent plusieurs manuscrits latins:

> Quant à la latine, on la cultivoit encore au commencement de ce même (XVIᵉ) siècle, comme le prouvent les cérémoniaux alors en usage, que prescrivent les lectures de l'Ecriture sainte, les Homélies des Pères, des Sermons du Maître, les vies des Saints qui se fesoient en latin soit au réfectoire soit au Chapitre, livres qui tous avoient été écrits par les Religieuses et qui se voient encore au Paraclet. Les livres de choeur, tels que Bréviaires, Martyrologes, sont remplis d'abbréviations si étranges, qu'il est impossible de les lire sans être guidé par l'intelligence du texte. [66]

On peut supposer que Dom Cajot a fondé cette description sur son analyse de l'Ordinal du Paraclet, étant donné les similitudes entre ce texte et les notes qu'il a ajoutées au manuscrit:

> L'Evangile et l'Epître se lisoient au réfectôire en latin, les livres de l'ancien testament étoient distribués dans les cours de l'année, les sermons des Pères de l'Eglise, parmi lesquels il est fait mention des Sermons du Maître (c'est à dire Abélard), les Vies des Saints se lisoient en communauté dans des MS latins que l'on conserve presque tous au Paraclet et qui fait juger que les Religieuses de cette maison ont longtemps cultivé la langue latine. [67]

Cajot a vu la mention des sermons du Maître dans l'Ordinal, mais il n'a pas signalé leur existence à l'ami de Craufurd, lequel ne parle que des livres utilisés par Abélard et Héloïse. Martène et Durant n'en parlent pas non plus après leur visite au couvent, en 1707. Il semble que le manuscrit ne se trouvait plus au Paraclet au XVIIIᵉ siècle.

---

clitenses. Le texte de la lettre d'introduction aux sermons, publiée par PAPIRE MASSON, Annalium libri quatuor, Paris, 1577, t. III, p. 260 est presqu'identique à celui de Duchesne.
65. Opera, 1616, p. 727.
66. CAJOT, Recherches, t. I, p. 141.
67. Bibl. nat. fr. 14410, fol. 2.

LES MANUSCRITS LITURGIQUES

Les deux livres les plus cités dans l'Ordinal sont le *breuiaire* et le *leconnier*. Duchesne savait qu'Abélard avait composé des *Hymnos etiam ecclesiasticos, qui reperiuntur in Breviario Paraclitensi*; nous ignorons s'il a consulté le manuscrit de Chaumont ou le *breuiaire* mentionné dans l'Ordinal, mais il est plus probable qu'il s'agissait de celui de Chaumont. [68] Les soeurs n'ont plus employé leurs manuscrits liturgiques après 1609, date à partir de laquelle elles ont utilisé le bréviaire Tridentin. Nous ne savons pas non plus comment le Père Cerizier (1609-1662) est entré en possession du manuscrit de Chaumont, avant de le donner à l'Oratoire de Langres en 1640.

Les témoignages de Cajot dans son étude de 1787 et dans les notes qui préfacent l'Ordinal, ainsi que ceux de l'ami de Craufurd, sont concordants: le Paraclet conservait à cette époque plusieurs manuscrits liturgiques, mais pas des écrits d'Abélard. L'ami de Craufurd décrit des manuscrits «en vélin contenant des évangiles, grossièrement reliés avec des nerfs et des couvertures de bois de chêne». [69] Nous ne pouvons pas, malheureusement, identifier les manuscrits qu'il a vus et ceux indiqués dans l'Ordinal, par manque de détail.

Dom Charles Cajot prit un des manuscrits du couvent en 1792, quand il retourna à Verdun, sa ville natale; il le légua à la Bibliothèque de Verdun, où il travaillait comme bibliothécaire, jusqu'à sa mort le 6 décembre 1808. [70] Dans un catalogue de ses livres laissés à

---

68. *Opera*, 1616, p. 1161 (= PL 178,143B).
69. CRAUFURD, *Mélanges*, p. 22.
70. Sur Dom Charles Cajot, voir l'excellente étude de J. E. GODEFROY, «Un précurseur de la Révolution: Dom Charles Cajot (1731-1807)», *La Révolution dans l'Aube, Bulletin d'histoire moderne et contemporaine*, t. IV, 1911, p. 1-18. Godefroy corrige l'attribution fautive, faite en premier lieu par Dom Lambelinot en 1788, des *Recherches historiques sur l'esprit primitif* à Dom Jean-Joseph Cajot, frère de Charles. Cette erreur est reprise dans le *Catalogue des livres imprimés de la Bibliothèque nationale*, t. XXII, Paris, 1905, col. 547 et perpétué par CHARRIER, *Héloïse*, Paris, 1933, p. 623, parmi d'autres. On trouve des notes biographiques sur Jean-Joseph aux fol. 175-176v du MS Paris, Bibl. nat. nouv. acq. fr. 22636, et une réponse de Charles Cajot au Dom Lambelinot aux fol. 50-56v du même manuscrit, inconnu de Godefroy. Aux écrits connus de Ch. Cajot, on peut ajouter: le début d'un catalogue des manuscrits de Verdun des textes sur sa nomination comme bibliothécaire et sur les premières années de la bibliothèque de Verdun (MS Paris, Bibl. nat. lat. nouv. acq. fr. 22638, fol. 5-12v); un catalogue des livres donnés à la bibliothèque par M. de Plaine (MS Verdun, Bibl. mun. 745); un éloge de l'historien l'abbé Fleury, avec des critiques adressées à Bossuet, attaché à un exemplaire de FLEURY, *Discours sur l'histoire ecclésiastique*, Paris 1720 (MS Verdun, Bibl. mun. 806); des annotations au *Rituel de Troyes*, un bréviaire qui appartenait à Cajot (Verdun, Bibl. mun. cote TF 31); les textes publiés par Craufurd (voir plus haut, n. 38). Des détails biographiques se trouvent ajoutés à son exemplaire des *Recherches* dans la même bibliothèque (cote TK 55). A. Gaillemin donne d'autres références, *Dictionnaire biographique des prêtres, religieux et religieuses en Meuse... pendant la révolution et au concordat (1789-1803)*, Bar-le-Duc, s. d., p. 57. Le catalogue des livres au MS Verdun, Bibl. mun. 745, auquel on a ajouté «Apparamant de la main de Dom Cajot (le jeune)», n'est pas de sa main, mais de la main de F. Clouet (bibliothécaire de 1822 à 1837).

la Bibliothèque de la ville on trouve la mention *MS. à l'usage d'Héloïse - 1 vol. in 4.°* [71] Il y figure deux autres manuscrits —un bréviaire de l'ordre des Prémontrés et un catalogue des plantes de la main de Cajot (MS Verdun, Bibl. mun. 285)— et les titres de 101 livres imprimés. Le catalogue des livres de Cajot est de la main de Dom Ybert, bibliothécaire de Verdun de 1805 à 1822. Ce dernier aurait fourni au *Narrateur de la Meuse* la description des deux pièces les plus précieuses, que Charlotte de Roucy, dernière abbesse du Paraclet, avait données à Cajot lors de la dissolution de la communauté:

> La première est un manuscrit latin in-4.°, revêtu d'une vieille couverture de bois, qui contient la distribution des évangiles selon la règle de Saint-Benoît, et qui, d'après la constante tradition du Paraclet, avait servi à l'usage d'HELOISE. Quelques personnes ajoutent même qu'il est de la main d'ABEILARD. — La seconde pièce est un miroir de métal, espèce seule connue des anciens, ayant près d'un double decimètre de hauteur, quinze centimètres de largeur. Il pèse un peu plus d'un demi-kilogramme, et n'a d'épaisseur qu'environ trois millimètres. Ce miroir, d'après la même tradition, passe pour avoir appartenu à Héloïse. Les personnes qui ont fréquenté Dom Cajot disent, ainsi que ses anciens confrères, que c'était un homme de grand sens, très versé dans les antiquités ecclésiastiques, et qui n'avait aucun intérêt d'en imposer. En conséquence, on ne révoque point en doute, d'après son témoignage, l'authenticité de l'origine des dits objets. [72]

On trouve les mêmes renseignements dans un article du même journal du 20 aout 1819, mais le manuscrit est désigné *un livre d'église écrit de la main d'Abeilard, et qui était à l'usage d'Héloïse.* L'attribution du manuscrit à Abélard est devenue définitive. [73]

Pareilles expressions se retrouvent dans la note ajoutée à l'Ordinal (fol. 4) et écrite après le transfert des cendres d'Abélard et d'Héloïse au Père Lachaise, en 1817:

> Les notes sont de la main de Dom Cajot, savant bénédictin qui desservit l'abbaye du Paraclet, époque de la destruction du couvent. Il a recueilli lui-même et conservé un livre d'heures écrit de la main d'Abeillard pour l'usage personnel d'Héloîse. Don Cajot vient de léguer ce précieux Manuscrit à la Bibliothèque de Verdun (voir les journaux de mois de juillet et août 1809).

---

71. MS Verdun 745. Je remercie M. Cary de la Bibliothèque de Verdun de l'avoir retrouvé. Il est cité par N. FRIZON, *Catalogue méthodique de la Bibliothèque Publique de la ville de Verdun. Histoire*, Verdun, 1884, p. xxv, xlvi, mais Godefroy, en 1912, n'a pas pu le retrouver.
72. *Le Narrateur de la Meuse*, t. XVIII, 1808, p. 107-108.
73. *Ibid.*, t. XXIX, 1819, p. 95.

50

L'inexactitude de la référence aux *journaux du mois de juillet et août 1809* peut s'expliquer par une confusion entre les deux articles du *Narrateur de la Meuse*, l'un du 14 février 1808 et l'autre du 20 août 1819. L'auteur de cette note, soit le Dr. Colin de Nogent-sur-Seine, soit son frère, décrit le manuscrit comme un *livre d'heures*, ce qui est loin de la description du février 1808, mais se rapproche du *livre d'église* de celle d'août 1819.

Malheureusement, ce manuscrit ne se trouve plus à la Bibliothèque municipale de Verdun.[74] Dom Ybert, successeur de Dom Cajot à la Bibliothèque de Verdun, n'a jamais dressé un catalogue des manuscrits de la Bibliothèque, mais affirme dans un rapport de 1812 (MS 745) qu'il y avait 272 manuscrits, presque tous théologiques ou liturgiques. Par contre, au moment où l'abbé L. Clouet (bibliothécaire de 1837 a 1871) dressait son catalogue des manuscrits, vers 1860-62, il n'y avait plus dans l'ancien fonds que 158 manuscrits.[75] Son père, F. Clouet (bibliothécaire de 1822 à 1837) avait commencé un catalogue des manuscrits en 1829, mais il n'y en a fait figurer que dix-sept. Corrard de Breban a écrit à l'abbé L. Clouet à propos du manuscrit légué par Dom Cajot, mais il n'a reçu qu'une réponse négative.[76] Qui est responsable de la perte des 114 manuscrits? F. Clouet avait transféré beaucoup de livres au séminaire de Verdun entre 1822 et 1837, et son fils, l'abbé L. Clouet, avait lui aussi pris beaucoup de livres de la Bibliothèque. Un procès fut intenté par l'Etat à la nièce de l'abbé Clouet, Mlle Buvignier, pour récupérer les livres et les manuscrits dérobés. L'abbé N. Frizon, bibliothécaire de 1877 à 1898 et historien de la Bibliothèque, ne parle pas de la perte des 114 manuscrits; son silence peut s'expliquer du fait qu'il était lui-même impli-

---

74. Des 158 manuscrits de l'ancien fonds de la bibliothèque, il n'y a que cinq manuscrits liturgiques dont la provenance est inconnue (MSS 101, 115, 132, 140, 142). Les MSS 121 et 122 proviennent de la Cathédrale de Verdun; les MSS 116, 117, 126 du couvent de St-Maur, Verdun; les MSS 86 1-2 de St. Paul de Verdun (ces provenances ne sont pas indiquées dans le *Catalogue général des MSS des bibliothèques publiques*, t. V, Paris, 1879). Il n'y a qu'un manuscrit qui puisse correspondre à celui de Cajot: le Ms 101, un lectionnaire, mais les *incipits* ne correspondent pas à ceux cités dans l'Ordinal. Waddell cite quelques *incipits* du *leconnier*, *art. cit.*, p. 275.

75. Voir FRIZON, *Catalogue méthodique*, t. I, p. xlv et 1, et l'introduction au *Catalogue général*, t. V, Paris, 1879, p. i et 422. En 1794, la Bibliothèque possédait 170 manuscrits, selon le catalogue dressé par Dom Cajot (Paris, Bibl. nat., nouv. acq. fr. 22638, fol. 5). Le catalogue de l'abbé L. Clouet servait de base à celui de M. Michelant, dressé en 1869 et imprimé avec un supplément en 1879. Dom Ybert n'a dressé qu'un catalogue des livres imprimés (MS Verdun, Bibl. mun. 383). Le début du catalogue, de sept pages seulement, dû à F. Clouet, a été détaché du MS 383, selon une mention au manuscrit de la main de Frizon, pour devenir MS 612.

76. *Les abbesses du Paraclet*, p. 31.

LA BIBLIOTHÈQUE DU PARACLET

qué dans l'affaire.[77] Le manuscrit conservé par Dom Cajot, après avoir survécu aux désordres de la Révolution, s'est perdu entre 1812 et 1861.

Le sort des autres manuscrits liturgiques du Paraclet reste également inconnu. Corrard de Breban cite un extrait d'une lettre du Dr. Colin qui parle des manuscrits et des lettres donnés par les soeurs du couvent à son père, lorsqu'il y travaillait:

> Don (*sic*) Cajot paraît avoir emporté une partie des plus précieux objets avec lui, et à sa mort il en a fait don à la bibliothèque de Verdun, sa patrie. J'ai vu aussi dans le grenier de mon père beaucoup de volumes que les soeurs lui avaient donnés en partant, de là vient le nécrologe latin que je possède. De là venait un écrit de la main d'Abélard, contenant les lois dictées aux saintes filles, volume que mon frère consentit à céder à la Bibliothèque impériale en échange d'un Rousseau en 18 volumes, qui est aujourd'hui dans ma bibliothèque.[78]

Le Dr. Colin ne précise pas dans cette lettre le nombre des manuscrits déposés dans le grenier de son père. Il donne des détails sur le nécrologe latin, maintenant Troyes, Bibl. mun. 2450, et sur l'Ordinal, maintenant Paris, Bibl. nat. fr. 14410. Il se peut que le cérémonial du XVIIe siècle (Paris, Bibl. nat. lat 10582), qui porte l'estampille de la Bibliothèque royale utilisée entre 1815 et 1831, soit arrivé à la Bibliothèque par le même chemin que l'Ordinal.[79]

Corrard de Breban avait écrit son premier rapport sur les archives du Paraclet en 1837 mais on ne l'a fait publier qu'en 1841. Dans ce rapport il ne fait pas mention du nécrologe latin. Sans référence au Dr. Colin, il parle d'un manuscrit qu'il croyait perdu, mais qui pourrait être l'Ordinal:

> L'ancienne liturgie aura aussi perdu un document précieux dans ce manuscrit du XIIe siècle sur les Ordonnances des saints et du service de tout l'an que l'on conservait dans cette abbaye.[80]

Puisque dans ce rapport Corrard de Breban ignore les renseignements donnés par le Dr. Colin, nous pouvons supposer que le Dr.

---

77. Les documents relatifs à cette affaire se trouvent aux archives de la Bibliothèque, MSS 617 et 748. Après le procès, la collection des MSS Clouet-Buvignier fut divisée entre les Bibliothèques de Verdun et de Bar-le-Duc et la Bibliothèque nationale. Le manuscrit de Cajot ne se trouve pas dans cette collection.
78. *Les abbesses du Paraclet*, p. 31.
79. Voir plus haut, n. 7.
80. CORRARD DE BREBAN, «Rapport relatif aux archives de l'abbaye du Paraclet», p. 5.

52

Colin l'informa par la suite de l'existence du nécrologe latin et de l'Ordinal. Selon une note ajoutée au nécrologe (Troyes, Bibl. mun. 2450), le Dr. Colin avait prêté ce manuscrit à Corrard de Breban, qui le lui rendit en 1839. Le Dr. Colin ne lui aurait pas caché l'existence d'autres manuscrits du Paraclet, s'il en avait eu connaissance.

Un autre manuscrit liturgique qui subsistait au Paraclet au XVIIIe siècle était un missel du XIIIe siècle, qui contenait des chants en langue grecque, mais rédigés en caractères latins. [81] Au début du XVIIe siècle N. Camuzat avait entendu les soeurs du Paraclet chanter l'office de la Pentecôte en langue grecque, peut-être pour la dernière fois avant le déroulement des réformes de 1609. [82] Courtalon-Delaistre, dans une étude publiée en 1784, est resté sceptique sur cette observance. Il n'en a pas trouvé mention dans un manuscrit que nous pouvons identifier avec l'Ordinal:

> ... et un ancien manuscrit du treizième siècle contenant ce qui doit se faire chanter et lire chaque jour, ne fait aucune mention du service en grec. [83]

Ce missel était sans doute un des manuscrits dispersés ou vendus à l'époque de la Révolution; il n'a jamais été retrouvé.

LES NÉCROLOGES DU PARACLET

Nous disposons de beaucoup plus de précisions sur les nécrologes que sur les manuscrits liturgiques. Dom Cajot nous décrit trois nécrologes dans une notice communiquée à l'ami de Craufurd:

> ... le plus ancien de ces nécrologes est en Gauloise. L'écriture primitive ne fait mention que d'Héloïse, Melesinde, Ermangarde et Marie, qui vivoit encore en 1263 sans parler d'Aliside, ou Alepide, troisième ou quatrième abbesse du Paraclet. Il doit avoir été rédigé sur la fin du XIIIe siècle. [84]

81. *Histoire littéraire de la France*, t. XII, Paris, 1763, p. 642 n. 1: «On conserve au Paraclet un Missel manuscrit de la fin du treizième siècle où elle se trouve écrite en caractères latins et notée en notes lozangées comme les nôtres. Elle commence par ces mots: *Exapostelis to pneuma sou, ke kticisonte, ke anakeniis tou prosopou tis gis. Ito doxa kyriou is tous eonas*».
82. CAMUZAT, *Promptuarium*, fol. 346-346v: *...quod etiam hodie sacri huius collegii velatae virginis, die Pentecostes, officium divinum Graecanico idiomate celebrant*. Camuzat ne précise pas si les soeurs ont chanté la messe en langue grecque, comme l'affirme la note de l'*Histoire littéraire*. Il peut s'agir d'un livre des chants et non pas un missel.
83. COURTALON-DELAISTRE, *Topographie historique de la ville et du diocèse de Troyes*, t. III, Troyes, 1784, p. 208.
84. CRAUFURD, *Mélanges*, p. 39.

Cajot remarque l'addition de passages à des époques différentes. Duchesne cite des passages de ce manuscrit, qu'il appelle *Un vieux Calendrier Francois intitulé le Mortologe du Paraclit*.[85] Le deuxième nécrologe que décrit Cajot contenait le texte latin du nécrologe, mais fut écrit plus tard:

> Le second nécrologe est en latin. Le premier rédacteur ne fait mention que d'Héloïse, Melesinde, Ermangarde, de Marie et de Catherine, morte en 1322, ce qui fait juger qu'il n'a été composé qu'après cette date.[86]

Il s'agit du *Calendarium aliud Coenobii Paraclitensis Latinum*, un manuscrit disparu depuis la Révolution, mais dont nous connaissons le texte à travers les citations de Camuzat et Duchesne.[87] Un anonyme l'a transcrit dans son entier en 1170 (Troyes, Bibl. mun. 2450), en ajoutant des passages du *Livre des sépultures* (Paris, Bibl. nat. fr. 14410, fol. 5-28v).[88] Cajot décrit ce nécrologe dans les notes ajoutées à l'Ordinal et dans la notice publiée par Craufurd:

> Le troisième obituaire se trouve à la fin d'un ritual. Le premier écrivain ne fait mention que des quatre abbesses contenues dans le rituel gaulois, et il a été complété avec ainsi que les autres.[89]

Dom Gervaise, auteur de la première biographie d'Abélard et d'Héloïse, publiée en 1720, affirme avoir vu les nécrologes latin et français.[90] L'auteur du compte-rendu de l'examen des ossements d'Abélard et d'Héloïse le 3 mars 1765 a également vu le nécrologe latin:

> Les Dames Prieure et Religieuses nous ont representé le Nécrologe de ladite abbaye du douzième ou treizième siècle en parchemin,

---

85. DUCHESNE, *Opera*, 1616, *praefatio* fol. 1 ij et p. 1887-1890 *passim*, où il le décrit: *Calendarium aliud vetus Gallico sermone scriptum*.
86. CRAUFURD, *Mélanges*, p. 70.
87. CAMUZAT, *Promptuarium*, fol. 348; DUCHESNE, *Notae ad Bibliothecam Cluniacensem*, Paris, 1614, p. 148 et *Opera*, 1616, fol, ij^v et p. 1141, 1142, 1149, 1187-1190. Les extraits du nécrologe latin au MS Paris, Bibl. nat. Baluze 46, p. 133-140, ainsi que ceux du nécrologe francais (p. 140-142) et *Ex chartulario Paraclitensi* (p. 113-119, 121-131) sont de la main de Duchesne, non pas de Baluze, comme le disent BOUTILLIER DU RETAIL et PIÉTRESSON DE SAINT-AUBIN, *Obit. de la Province de Sens*, t. IV, p. 387; voir aussi J.-L. LEMAÎTRE, *Recueil des historiens de la France. Répertoire des documents nécrologiques français*, Paris, 1980, p. 519-520. Ces notes au MS Baluze 46 ont servi de base de l'édition de 1616.
88. Notons que le copiste n'a pas transcrit les épitaphes et la formule d'absolution qui, selon Camuzat (*Promptuarium*, fol. 248-348v) se trouvaient dans le même livre que les citations du nécrologe latin.
89. CRAUFURD, *Mélanges*, p. 40; Paris, Bibl. nat. fr. 14410, fol. 1.
90. A. GERVAISE, *La vie de Pierre Abeillard, abbé de Saint-Gildas-de-Ruis, de l'ordre de Saint Benoist, et celle d'Héloïse, son épouse, première abbesse du Paraclet*, Paris, 1720, t. II, p. 65.

Ecriture gothique, Duquel a été extrait ce qui suit, qui établit en même tems les différentes translations faites dans cette Abbaye des corps ou ossements de Pierre Abélard et d'Héloïse. [91]

Ces nécrologes apportaient des renseignements précieux sur la date du décès des soeurs et sur leur lieu d'inhumation. D'un certain point de vue, ils possédaient plus de valeur que les manuscrits liturgiques: ils concernaient de plus près la vie et la mémoire collective de la communauté.

LA DISPERSION DES MANUSCRITS DU PARACLET

Le Paraclet au XVIIIe siècle, à la différence du siècle précédent, connaît un renouveau d'intérêt pour Abélard et Héloïse. Les ossements des fondateurs furent examinés en 1765 et remis en 1780 dans la crypte, pour qu'ils soient au-dessous de la statue de la Trinité, elle-même remise dans l'église principale depuis 1701. [92] La bibliothèque fait également l'objet d'un classement, ce qui participe du besoin de remise en ordre du couvent. Les soeurs ont même fait appel à un archiviste pour effectuer ce travail:

> Les archives étoient entrés mauvais ordre, il a fallu prendre plusieurs Mois un archiviste à qui on a donné six cent livres pour les arranger. [93]

Le travail de cet archiviste anonyme s'observe aujourd'hui dans les notes détaillées écrites au dos de plusieurs chartes et d'autres documents actuellement aux Archives départementales de l'Aube (24 H), ainsi que dans la transcription du nécrologe latin, faite en 1770 (Troyes, Bibl. mun. 2450).

Malheureusement, en dehors des documents pris par les administrateurs du district de Nogent-sur-Seine et des manuscrits donnés au père du Dr. Colin, les manuscrits du couvent ont été dispersés dans les directions les plus diverses. Corrard de Breban affirme que

---

91. Ed. O. GUELLIOT, «Charlotte de Roucy. Dernière Abbesse du Paraclet», *Revue historique ardennaise*, t. XVIII, 1911, p. 21.
92. *Mercure de France*, octobre 1780, p. 138-143.
93. Paris, Archives nationales G9 150 dossier 11. Les dossiers 11-12 (ancienne cote 0 150) sont des demandes de secours du 19 novembre 1775 et du 25 octobre 1782.

les administrateurs avaient trouvé 173 volumes au couvent, qu'ils ont vendus, mais n'indique pas sa source:

> Les agents du district ne trouvèrent au Paraclet que 173 volumes qui furent vendus en thermidor (an III) ... Ils avaient tous trait à la liturgie, missels, breviaires, rituels etc. à l'usage de Troyes, de Sens, des Bénédictins, des Capucins. [94]

Nous pouvons supposer qu'il n'y avait pas de manuscrits parmi ces volumes, étant donné que les administrateurs du département ont pris soin de consigner les manuscrits des communautés religieuses, comme celle de Clairvaux, à la Bibliothèque de Troyes. [95]

Dans l'introduction à son édition, avec traduction, des lettres d'Abélard et d'Héloïse, O. Gréard cite une note qu'il avait trouvée à la Bibliothèque impériale, mais n'en précise pas la source:

> D'après une note conservée à cette bibliothèque les administrateurs du district de Nogent-sur-Seine possédaient vers le milieu de l'an II (1793) un manuscrit qu'ils avaient retiré de la bibliothèque du Paraclet. On ne sait ce qu'il est devenu. [96]

Monfrin propose de voir dans ce manuscrit celui des lettres d'Abélard et d'Héloïse. Il remarque que la mairie de Nogent-sur-Seine a brûlé en 1814, entraînant la perte éventuelle de ce manuscrit. [97] En fait, il est peu probable que l'abbesse ait offert des manuscrits liturgiques à ses connaissances pour laisser aux administrateurs un manuscrit des lettres des fondateurs du couvent.

Du fait que les administrateurs du district n'ont relevé au Paraclet qu'un manuscrit (si nous faisons confiance à la note citée par Gréard), nous pouvons supposer que la dernière abbesse, Charlotte de Roucy, a donné les manuscrits les plus précieux à ses proches. Nous ne connaissons que les dons faits à Dom Cajot et au père du Dr. Colin. Il se peut qu'elle ait cédé le cartulaire à quelqu'un de la famille du chanoine Coffinet, qui à son tour, l'a cédé à la Bibliothèque de Troyes, en 1851. Cette Bibliothèque a acheté le nécrologe latin qui appartenait au Dr. Colin, entre 1839 et 1861. Les autres manus-

94. *Les abbesses du Paraclet*, p. 94.
95. BRUSLÉ, *Mémoire sur la statistique du département de l'Aube*, Troyes, An IX [1800], p. 9. Un compte rendu de la fermeture du couvent, rédigé en 1840 par un des administrateurs, n'apporte aucun éclaircissement sur le destin de manuscrits, «L'expulsion des Religieuses du Paraclet» (éditeur anonyme), *Almanach Est-Eclair*, 1952.
96. O. GREARD, *Lettres completes d'Abélard et d'Héloïse*, Paris, 1859 (2e éd. 1875), p. v n. 5.
97. MONFRIN, p. 16-17.

V

crits auraient disparu, faute d'intérêt pour leur valeur historique. Il n'est pas sans ironie qu'en 1819/20 la Bibliothèque royale ait obtenu du frère du Dr. Colin l'Ordinal du Paraclet en échange de 18 volumes de Rousseau. Les écrits de Rousseau avaient plus d'intérêt pour un honnête homme du début du XIXe siècle qu'un manuscrit liturgique attribué à Abélard.

III. LES LIVRES DU PARACLET

La bibliothèque du Paraclet possédait beaucoup plus de livres que les 173 vendus en 1794. Le Dr. Colin affirme avoir vu «beaucoup de volumes» dans le grenier de son père. Charlotte de Roucy emporta des livres du Paraclet à Reims, sa ville natale, en 1792.[98] Des 259 tomes légués par Dom Cajot à la Bibliothèque de Verdun, quelques-uns portent soit la signature de Charlotte de Roucy, soit l'*ex libris* de l'abbaye du Paraclet. Des livres imprimés du Paraclet nous pouvons identifier à la Bibliothèque de Verdun une *Biblia Sacra* (Paris 1653; la date 1689 est écrite sur le feuillet de garde; cote TA 131); Le Nain de Tillemont, *Mémoires pour servir à l'histoire ecclésiastique des six premiers siècles* (16 vols. Paris 1701-12; il porte la signature «de Roucy» au premier volume; cote TJ 36); A. Godeau, *Histoire de l'Eglise* (6 vols. Paris 1690; «A l'abbaye du Paraclet 1721» au feuillet de garde; cote TJ 41). Il y a d'autres livres qui figurent au catalogue des livres légués par Cajot qui pourraient provenir du Paraclet mais qui ne portent pas d'ex *libris*.[99]

Un des livres les plus précieux du couvent était l'édition des *Opera Omnia* d'Abélard et d'Héloïse de 1616, avec la préface de d'Am-

98. GUEILLIOT, «Charlotte de Roucy», p. 11.
99. En dehors des livres cités plus haut (p. 26) nous pouvons identifier dans la bibliothèque de Verdun les livres suivants du legs de Dom Cajot, qui pourraient provenir du Paraclet: *Acta Primorum Martyrum*, Paris, 1689. (TL 9). *Pastorale Parisiense*, Paris, 1786. (TF 27). LE NAIN DE TILLEMONT, *Histoire des Empereurs...*, Paris, 1701-1712 (TI 244). P. HELYOT, *Histoire des ordres monastiques...*, Paris, 1714-19 (72221). FLEURY, *Histoire Ecclésiastique*, Paris, 1750-1751 (TJ 42). BOSSUET, *Opuscules*, Paris, 1751 (TD 360). S. *Augustini Opuscula*, Paris, 1726 (TD 177). BOISSY, *Lettres sur les Spectacles...*, Paris, 1780 (18981). COLONIA ET PATOUILLET, *Dictionnaire des livres Jansenistes*, Paris, 1752 (TJ 399). *Regula S. Benedicti cum constitutionibus S. Mauri*, Paris, 1770. LONGUEVAL, *Histoire de l'Eglise Gallicane*, Paris, 1732-1749 (TJ 166). Cajot possédait aussi la *Bibliotheca Cluniacensis*, éd. DUCHESNE, Paris, 1614 (72214), et LEBRUN, *Explication... de la Messe*, Paris, 1716-26 (TE 141), mais les exemplaires de Verdun proviennent de St. Vannes. Les livres qui portent la cote *T* (Théologie) ne se trouvent pas au fichier de la Bibliothèque, mais au catalogue manuscrit de l'abbé Clouet, avec continuations de la main de Frizon (MS 385).

boise. L'exemplaire de la Bibliothèque de Verdun (cote 18608) porte au recto du dernier feuillet de garde l'inscription *Ex libris Paraclitensis* et au verso, *In Gratiam Religiosissimorum monialium illustrissimae domus paraclitensis in Campania.* Dom Cajot n'a pas inscrit son nom sur le livre, mais on reconnaît son écriture sur les feuillets de garde, qui comportent une longue série de notes sur les épitaphes d'Abélard et d'Héloïse. Il transcrit également le texte, avec traduction, de l'épitaphe gravée sur le tombeau par Charlotte de Roucy en 1779, de celle de Pierre le Vénérable et d'une «faite par un moderne». Cajot a annoté à plusieurs endroits le texte de l'édition, notamment à propos de la chronologie de la vie d'Abélard et d'Héloïse et des biens du Paraclet.

Nous voyons ici le travail d'un érudit qui s'intéressait aux problèmes scientifiques posés par les écrits des fondateurs et par les documents du Couvent. Dans son seul ouvrage publié, sur l'ordre de Saint-Benoît, Dom Cajot avance l'idée que les congrégations bénédictines ne peuvent justifier leur existence et les biens qu'elles possèdent que par leur utilité sociale, notamment dans l'éducation des jeunes. [100] Son intérêt pour l'histoire ecclésiastique, comme pour les manuscrits du Paraclet, était plus séculier que théologique: il portait sur les problèmes de chronologie, sur les possessions du couvent ou sur l'érudition des soeurs. Après 1792, Dom Cajot n'a plus écrit sur Abélard, sur le Paraclet ou sur l'ordre bénédictin. Il s'est consacré à son travail de bibliothécaire à Verdun, et à son autre grande passion, la botanique. Parmi les livres qui figurent au catalogue de sa bibliothèque, nous pouvons identifier une collection importante de livres sur la botanique et sur d'autres sujets scientifiques. [101] C'est un savant qui dans ses centres d'intérêt passe du monde médiéval à l'époque moderne.

---

100. Voir Godefroy, *art. cit.*

101. Les plus importants et les plus récents sont: Lamarcq, *L'Encyclopedie méthodique sur la Botanique,* Paris, 1783-1808 (10 tomes) et Valmont de Bomare, *Dictionnaire d'histoire naturelle,* Lyons, 1791, (15 tomes), auxquels Frizon, *Catalogue méthodique,* t. III, Verdun, 1896, donne les cotes 1740 et 1579. Parmi les livres scientifiques que nous pouvons identifier, il s'en trouve beaucoup également décrits par Frizon dans le tome III de son *Catalogue méthodique.* Nous rappelons ici la les cotes données par Frizon, mais en suivant l'ordre du catalogue des livres de Cajot: 1821/2; 1740; 2333 (?); 1737, 1775; 1744; 1743; 1784; 1741; 1759; 1510; 2238; 226/7; 2240; 2726; 7; 3741. Ses livres de langue et littérature (la plupart des auteurs latins) se trouvent au t. II du *Catalogue méthodique,* Verdun, 1888: nos. 2928, 2936; 1171; 1140; 902; 1090 (?); 947; 880; 857; 1025; 1463; 37; 173; 2432. Pour ses livres sur l'histoire du monde, voir t. I, nos. 38; 39; 85; 489; 32; 2799; 2449. Ces livres non-scientifiques ont ¿ous été publiés avant 1772.

V

CONCLUSIONS

Quelles sont les conclusions à tirer de cette étude de la bibliothèque du Paraclet? En premier lieu, il nous faut écarter l'hypothèse
que le couvent a joué un grand rôle dans la transmission des oeuvres
d'Abélard en dehors des hymnes, sermons et autres prières qu'il aurait
composés. Le transfert des cendres d'Abélard et d'Héloïse en 1497 de
l'ancien oratoire du Petit Moustier au choeur de l'église abbatiale et
l'ajout de leurs épitaphes à la fin d'un nouveau «bréviaire» (MS Chaumont, Bibl. mun. 31) signale l'intérêt des soeurs pour les fondateurs à
cette époque. Cependant, il ne subsiste aucune preuve que le couvent
ait possédé d'autres ouvrages théologiques du *mestre pierre*.

Le manuscrit le plus célèbre était sans doute celui qui contenait les
lettres d'Abélard et d'Héloïse, la règle du Paraclet et les *Institutiones
nostrae*. Marie III de La Rochefoucauld, l'abbesse réformatrice du couvent l'a communiqué a F. d'Amboise au début du XVIIᵉ siècle afin qu'il
l'utilise pour l'édition des *Opera Omnia*, en préparation avec A. Duchesne. Monfrin avance une hypothèse: ce manuscrit du Paraclet
(Paraclitense), bien que son texte soit très proche de celui du MS
Troyes, Bibl. mun. 802 (*T*), n'est pas identique à *T*; tous les deux
seraient des «épaves» d'une série d'exemplaires des lettres possédés
par tous les prieurés du Paraclet, et par la maison mère. Pourtant
des neuf manuscrits subsistants de la correspondance, il n'y en a pas
un dont nous pouvons dire avec certitude qu'il a été copié dans une
maison de l'ordre du Paraclet. Le manuscrit de Troyes, écrit au début
du XIVᵉ siècle, appartenait au Chapitre de Notre-Dame de Paris avant
son achat par Robert de Bardi en 1347. La similitude du texte imprimé des *Institutiones nostrae*, qui reprend celui du *Paraclitense*,
avec le texte de *T*; l'ajout des épitaphes au dernier feuillet de *T* à la
fin du XVᵉ siècle, qu'on trouve aussi dans le manuscrit de Chaumont,
originaire du Paraclet; la coïncidence entre la perte du *Paraclitense*
et l'apparition vingt ans après de *T* — tout cela amène à croire que le
Paraclitense et *T* sont le même manuscrit. La tradition courante au
couvent au XVIIIᵉ siècle, selon laquelle Jeanne III de Chabot avait
vendu à l'étranger le manuscrit des lettres d'Abélard et d'Héloïse,
n'est pas incompatible avec l'affirmation de d'Amboise, selon laquelle
il avait obtenu un manuscrit des lettres auprès de l'abbesse suivante,
Marie III de La Rochefoucauld. Il semble bien que d'Amboise n'ait
jamais rendu le manuscrit au couvent, et, au siècle suivant, on a
préféré attribuer cette perte à une protestante, plutôt qu'à une
abbesse réformatrice. Si on identifie le *Paraclitense* avec *T*, il faut re-

jeter l'hypothèse de la diffusion de la correspondance d'Abélard et d'Héloïse dans toutes les maisons de l'ordre du Paraclet. Il se peut que le couvent ait joué un rôle dans la collection des lettres et des règles sur la vie religieuse, mais il n'a pas diffusé la collection, comme les humanistes l'ont fait au début du XIVᵉ siècle.

La perte du manuscrit s'explique par les réformes introduites par Marie de La Rochefoucauld après une période de désordre dans la la communauté. Ces réformes sont caracterisées par l'abandon de plusieurs observances traditionnelles et l'adoption du bréviaire Tridentin. Dans les constitutions de 1632, on ne faisait aucune mention d'Abélard. Marie de La Rochefoucauld a fait déplacer les cendres des fondateurs du choeur de l'église à la crypte. Les manuscrits des sermons et des hymnes d'Abélard auraient également disparu à la même époque.

Il n'existe donc au Paraclet pendant les XVIIᵉ et XVIIIᵉ siècles que des manuscrits liturgiques et quelques nécrologes du couvent. Le couvent connaît un renouveau d'intérêt pour Abélard et Héloïse au XVIIIᵉ siècle, non comme fondateurs monastiques, mais comme individus et amants. En 1701 Charlotte de La Rochefoucauld remet dans l'église principale la statue représentant la Trinité, qui ornait leur sépulture; et, en 1768 la prieure, Geneviève du Passage a autorisé l'examen de leurs ossements. En 1780, le couvent publie la traduction des lettres d'Abélard et d'Héloïse due à Bussy-Rabutin et à d'autres auteurs. [102] Dans un esprit plus scientifique, Dom Cajot, aumônier du couvent de 1780 à 1792, étudie les manuscrits latins qui y subsistent et y annote un exemplaire des *Opera Omnia* de 1616.

A la dissolution de la communauté en 1792, Charlotte de Roucy, offre les livres les plus précieux à Dom Cajot, au père du Dr. Colin et sans doute à d'autres amis. Nous connaissons seulement quatre de ces manuscrits (Troyes, Bibl. mun. 2284, 2450; Paris, Bibl. nat. fr. 14410, lat. 10582), qui sont arrivés dans les bibliothèques publiques à la suite de don ou d'achat, tandis que nous avons perdu la trace de tous les autres. Le plus intéressant d'entre eux aurait peut-être été celui contenant 'la distribution des évangiles selon la règle de Saint-Benoît' que Dom Cajot avait reçu des soeurs, et qu'il a daté du temps d'Héloïse. Ce manuscrit a survécu à la Révolution, mais a disparu

---

102. *Lettres veritables d'Héloïse à Abeilard avec les réponses d'Abeilard à Héloïse, traduites librement d'après les lettres originales latines*, Paraclet, 1780; *Lettres et épîtres amoureuses d'Heloïse et d'Abeilard, traduites librement en prose et en vers par MM. de Bussy-Rabutin, Pope, Colardeau, Dorat, Dourxigné, C.°°° (Cailleau), Saurin et Mercier*, Paraclet, s. d.

pendant la première moitié du xixe siècle de la Bibliothèque de Verdun, à laquelle Dom Cajot l'avait légué.

L'histoire des manuscrits du Paraclet jette quelques lumières sur les attitudes de la communauté envers leurs fondateurs. La pire époque n'a pas été la Révolution, mais le début du xviie siècle quand le couvent a adopté les observances bénédictines. Au cours de ces années, les soeurs ont abandonné dans la liturgie l'usage des manuscrits au profit du bréviaire Tridentin; et d'Amboise et Duchesne ont publié la première édition des oeuvres d'Abélard. Ainsi, dans deux domaines différents, on assiste au passage du manuscrit à l'imprimé. Les manuscrits qui restaient encore au Paraclet n'étaient plus utilisés, sauf quelques nécrologes, auxquels on continuait à faire des additions. Les autres n'étaient plus que de vénérables vestiges. A la dissolution du couvent en 1792, la plupart d'entre eux ont disparu et n'ont jamais été retrouvés.

APPENDICE

LES ÉPITAPHES D'ABÉLARD ET D'HÉLOÏSE AU PARACLET ET AU PRIEURÉ DE
SAINT-MARCEL, À CHALON-SUR-SAÔNE

Abélard est mort le 21 avril 1142 au prieuré de Saint-Marcel, à
Chalon-sur-Saône. A la demande d'Héloïse et à l'insu des moines de
Saint-Marcel, Pierre le Vénérable fit enlever le corps du défunt pour
le faire transporter le 16 novembre au Paraclet. [1] Dans cette appendice,
nous donnons une nouvelle édition des épitaphes d'Abélard et d'Héloïse au Paraclet, ainsi que l'édition d'un texte inédit d'un manuscrit
de Saint-Marcel.

LES ÉPITAPHES SUR LES TOMBEAUX AU PARACLET

Les chroniques les plus anciennes —de Clarius, moine de Saint-
Pierre-le-Vif de Sens, le *Chronicon Turonense* et la chronique de Guillaume de Nangis— affirment que l'épitaphe du tombeau d'Abélard
au Paraclet était la suivante:

> Est satis in titulo: Petrus hic iacet Abaelardus,
> cui soli patuit scibile quicquid erat. [2]

L'épitaphe se trouve également dans deux manuscrits du XIIᵉ
siècle (Rouen, Bibliothèque municipale 1392, fol. 1 et Soissons, Bibliothèque municipale 24, fol. 1) et dans un manuscrit de la fin du
XVᵉ siècle (Berne, Bürgerbibliothek 211, fol. 160v-161). [3] Dans ce der-

---

1. HÉLOÏSE, *Epist. ad Dominum Abbatem, Rescriptum Domini Abbatis*, éd. G. CONSTABLE
(Epist. 167, 168), *The Letters of Peter the Venerable*, Cambridge, Mass., 1967, t. I, p. 400-401;
voir aussi la formule d'absolution de Pierre le Vénérable, ci-dessous, p. 65.
2. *La chronique de Saint-Pierre-le-Vif de Sens, dite de Clarius*, éd. R. H. BAUTIER et
M. GILLES, Paris, 1979, p. 198; *Chronique de l'Abbaye de St-Pierre-le-Vif de Sens par Geoffroy
de Courlon*, éd. G. JULLIOT, Sens, 1876, p. 472; *Chronicon Turonense*, extrait édité par P. DRONKE,
Abelard and Heloise in Medieval Testimonies, Glasgow, 1976, p. 51 à partir du MS Berlin,
Deutsche Staatsbibliothek, Phillipps 1852, fol. 204v (s. XIII); *Chronique latine de Guillaume
de Nangis de 1113 à 1300...* nouv. édn, éd. H. GÉRAUD, Paris, 1843, t. I, p. 33. Voir aussi le
Chronicon de ROBERT D'AUXERRE, éd. HOLDER-EGGER, *Monumenta Germaniae Historica, Scriptores*,
t. XXVI, Hannover, 1882, p. 235 et celui de WILLIAM GODELL, *Recueil des historiens des Gaules
et de la France*, t. XIII, Paris, 1869, p. 675.
3. L'épitaphe est éditée à partir du manuscrit de Rouen par B. KRUSCH, *Neues Archiv*,
t. XVIII, 1893, p. 613, de celui de Soissons par C. C. J. WEBB, *Joannis Sarisberiensis Policraticus*, Oxford, 1909, t. I, p. xiii, et de celui de Berne par DRONKE, *Medieval Testimonies*, p. 50.

nier, que nous désignons *B*, une rubrique précise qu'une sculpture d'Abélard tenant un livre à la main surmontait le tombeau et que l'épitaphe était gravée dans ce livre.[4] Le mot *titulo* est ajouté au-dessus du mot *tumulo* dans le texte de *B*.

Héloïse avait sollicité une formule d'absolution de Pierre le Vénérable afin de la placer sur la tombe d'Abélard. Cette formule se trouve non pas dans les manuscrits des lettres de Pierre le Vénérable mais avec les épitaphes d'Abélard et d'Heloïse ajoutées à la fin des manuscrits de Troyes (*T*: Bibliothèque municipale 802, fol. 102v) et de Chaumont (*C*: Bibliothèque municipale 31, fol. 245v).[5] Comme nous l'avons déjà montré, il est fort probable que l'on a ajouté ces épitaphes et la formule d'absolution à ces manuscrits à l'occasion du transfert de la chapelle du Petit Moustier au choeur de l'église principale, des ossements des fondateurs du Paraclet, le 2 mai 1497. Camuzat et Duchesne ont également trouvé le texte de la formule et de ces épitaphes dans un nécrologe latin du Paraclet.[6] Nous n'avons aucune raison de douter de son authenticité:

Ego Petrus Cluniacensis Abbas, qui Petrum Abaelardum in monachum Cluniacensem suscepi, et corpus eius furtim delatum Heloyse abbatisse et monialibus Pracliti concessi, auctoritate omnipotentis Dei et omnium sanctorum absolvo eum pro officio ab omnibus peccatis suis. Amen.

Abaelardum] Abailardum *Camuzat* suscepi] recepi *Duchesne 1616* Heloyse] Heloissae *Camuzat*, *Duchesne* Pracliti] Paracleti *Duchesne* Amen] *om*. *C*

L'épitaphe d'Héloïse suit cette absolution dans le manuscrit de Chaumont et le nécrologe latin (selon Camuzat), alors qu'elle la précède dans le manuscrit de Troyes. Selon P. Dronke, la forme métrique des versets (*trinini salientes*) permet de la dater du XIIe siècle.[7]

---

4. *Aliud quod est insculptum in libro quem ymago sua supra tumulum tenet*. Ce manuscrit comporte aux fol. 160v-161 les textes suivants: *Gallorum Socrates..., Est satis in titulo..., Petrus in hac petra...* (au sujet d'Abélard), *Feminei sexus...* et *Hoc tumulo...* (au sujet d'Héloïse). Voir H. HAGEN, *Catalogus codicum Bernensium*, Berne, 1875, p. 256-260. Ces épitaphes furent copiées vers 1492; on lit au fol. 162: *Sensuiuent les nons des notables personnages qui assistoient au baptesme de monsieur le daulphin, le samedi XIII jour doctobre lan mil CCCC quatre vintz et douze environ dix heures.*
5. La formule n'accompagne pas la réponse de Pierre le Vénérable à la demande d'Héloïse ni dans le seul manuscrit subsistant qui contient les deux lettres (Le Puy, Bibliothèque du Chapitre, sans cote, fol. 79-79v, s. xv) ni dans l'édition de Pierre de Montmartre, qui aurait utilisé un manuscrit de Cluny, *Petri Venerabilis... Opera*, Paris, 1522, fol. 99-100.
6. Voir au-dessus, n. 87.
7. DRONKE, *Medieval Testimonies*, p. 50.

L'épitaphe est également reproduite dans le manuscrit de Berne, contemporain des manuscrits *C* et *T*:

> Epitaphium Eloyse abbatisse Paracliti
> Hoc tumulo abbatissa iacet prudens Heloysa.
> Paraclitum statuit, cum Paraclito requiescit.
> Gaudia sanctorum sua sunt super alta polorum.
> Nos meritis precibusque suis exaltet ab imis.

Titre: Aliud *B*; Epitaphium Heloissae *Camuzat, Duchesne* [*voir titre à* Petrus in hac petra
...*C*] prudens] *om. CT* Heloysa] Heloyssa *B*. imis] Amen *add. C*.

L'ÉPITAPHE «GALLORUM SOCRATES» DE PIERRE LE VÉNÉRABLE

En dehors de la formule d'absolution, Pierre le Vénérable aurait également composé l'épitaphe *Gallorum Socrates...*, qui se trouve à la suite de sa lettre en éloge d'Abélard dans l'édition de Pierre de Montmartre, de 1522. Le manuscrit qu'utilisait Pierre de Montmartre, appartenait, selon toute vraisemblance, au monastère de Cluny.[8] François de Rivo, sous-prieur de Cluny, cite l'épitaphe dans sa chronique de Cluny, redigée vers 1500 (Paris, Bibl. nat. lat. 9875, fol. 34v), peut-être à partir du même manuscrit des lettres de Pierre le Vénérable.[9] L'épitaphe se trouve également dans une note marginale, ajoutée au XIIIᵉ siècle, à la chronique de Robert d'Auxerre (Auxerre, Bibliothèque municipale 145 (132), p. 297) et dans le manuscrit Berne, Bürgerbibliothek 211.[10] Tandis que l'épitaphe est absente du seul manuscrit subsistant qui contient la lettre de Pierre le Vénérable au sujet d'Abélard (Le Puy, Bibliothèque du chapitre, sans cote, fol. 61v-63), nous n'avons aucune raison de douter de son attribution à Pierre le Vénérable dans les manuscrits de Cluny et d'Auxerre.

Duchesne reprend le texte de l'épitaphe de l'édition de Pierre de Montmartre dans la *Bibliotheca Cluniacensis* de 1614 et dans l'édi-

---

8. *Petri Venerabili... Opera*, Paris, 1522, fol. 165v. Sur ce manuscrit de Cluny, qui a disparu au XVIᵉ siècle, voir CONSTABLE, *The Letters of Peter the Venerable*, t. II, p. 56. Un moine de Cluny a copié au début du XVII siècle un extrait de la lettre sur Abélard et l'épitaphe *Gallorum Socrates...* de cette édition, dans une histoire des hommes illustres de Cluny, maintenant Paris, Bibl. nat. lat. 9876. fol. 421-422v.

9. Paris, Bibl. nat. lat. 9875. fol. 34v. Sur François de Rivo, qui s'est servi du manuscrit des lettres de Pierre le Vénérable à Cluny, voir CONSTABLE, *The Letters of Peter the Venerable*, t. II, p. 17. L. Delisle décrit ce manuscrit et celui du fonds latin 9876, *Inventaire des MSS de la Bibliothèque nationale. Fonds de Cluni*, Paris, 1884, p. 218-219 et p. 229. La chronique est éditée par Marrier et Duchesne, mais l'épitaphe n'est citée que par ses premiers mots, *Bibliotheca Cluniacensis*, Paris, 1614, col. 553 (=*PL* 189, 35A).

10. L'épitaphe, ajoutée en marge dans le manuscrit d'Auxerre (l'autographe de Robert) n'est pas reproduite dans les autres manuscrits de la chronique, *MGH. Scriptores*, t. XXVI, p. 235. Sur le manuscrit de Berne, voir dessus, n. 4.

V

tion des oeuvres d'Abélard de 1616.[11] Dans cette dernière, l'épitaphe se trouve à la suite de la lettre de Pierre le Vénérable, comme dans l'édition de 1522.

D'Amboise reproduit l'épitaphe dans sa *praefatio apologetica*.[12] Selon l'étude de l'Abbé Philibert Papillon (1666-1738), imprimée dans les *Mémoires... des hommes illustres* de Nicéron, et suivie par Dom Clément dans l'*Histoire littéraire*, cette épitaphe se trouvait sur la muraille de l'aile droite de l'église de Saint-Marcel, près de la sacristie.[13] Cependant, le témoignage de Claude Perry en 1659 est formel: il affirme avoir vu l'église de Saint-Marcel, mais n'avoir trouvé aucune inscription au sujet d'Abélard dans l'église.[14] Baluze (1660-1723) dit qu'il y existait une inscription, mais illisible à son époque.[15] Il semble que Papillon reproduit le texte de l'épitaphe à partir de l'étude de Jacob, publiée en 1652, qui le prend à son tour de l'édition de Duchesne. Les mêmes fautes d'orthographe se trouvent dans les études de Jacob et de Papillon.[16]

Nous donnons ici le texte de l'épitaphe selon l'édition de Pierre de Montmartre (*Cl*), la chronique de François de Rivo (*Fr*), le MS Auxerre, Bibl. mun. 145 (132), p. 292 (*Au*) et le MS Berne, Burgerbibliothek 211, fol. 160v (*B*). Nous pouvons supposer que cette épitaphe se trouvait au Paraclet, comme les autres textes dans le manuscrit de Berne, mais la certitude manque. *Cl*, *Fr*, *Au* et *B* ne présentent aucune grande divergence dans le texte de l'épitaphe. Nous suivons la ponctuation de *Fr*, très proche de celle de *Cl* et plus complète que celle de *Au* ou de *B*.

11. *Bibliotheca Cluniacensis*, col. 1354 (=*PL* 189, 1022D-23A); *Opera* (1616), p. 342-343.
12. D'Amboise, *Opera* (1616), fol, e iiij^v. Cousin reproduit le texte de cette épitaphe, comme d'autres, à partir de l'édition de Duchesne, *P. Abaelardi Opera*, t. I, Paris, 1849, p. 717.
13. Papillon, éd. Niceron, *Mémoires pour servir à l'histoire des hommes illustres dans la république des lettres*, t. IV, Paris, 1728, p. 19, reproduit, sans référence à Papillon, dans l'*Histoire littéraire de la France*, t. XII, Paris, 1763, p. 102. Sur la vie et les oeuvres de l'Abbé Papillon, voir l'introduction de P. Marteret à l'ouvrage de Papillon, publié après sa mort, *Bibliothèque des Auteurs de Bourgogne*, Dijon, 1742. Marteret n'a pas inclu l'article sur Abélard dans cette édition.
14. Claude Perry, *Histoire civile et ecclésiastique ancienne et moderne de la ville et cité de Chalon-sur-Saône*, Chalon, 1659, p. 134. Sur le cénotaphe et son sort, voir Charrier, *Héloïse*, p. 334 n. 4.
15. Paris, Bibl. nat. Baluze 12, fol. 172-172v; voir dessous p. 36-37.
16. L. Jacob, *De claris scriptoribus cabilonensibus libri III*, Paris, 1652, p. 142. On constate d'autres inexactitudes dans l'article de Papillon comme l'attribution à Abélard d'un ouvrage, qui est en réalité de Pierre le Vénérable: *Dispositio rei familiaris facta a domno Petro abbate* «*ms in-folio à Cluni*» (Niceron, *Mémoires*, t. IV, p. 38). Papillon lit *Abael.* pour *abbate*. Il s'agit des statuts de Pierre le Vénérable au cartulaire de Cluny, maintenant Paris, Bibl. nat. nouv. acq. lat. 1497, fol. 4v-6, éd. Bruel, *Recueil des chartes de Cluni*, t. V. Paris, 1885, p. 475-482.

Epitaphium Abaelardi

Gallorum Socrates, Plato maximus Hesperiarum,
Noster Aristoteles; logicis quicunque fuerunt
Aut par, aut melior, studiorum cognitus orbi
Princeps. Ingenio varius, subtilis et acer,
Omnia vi superans rationis et arte loquendi;
Abaelardus erat. Sed tunc magis omnia vicit,
Cum cluniacensem monachum moremque professus,
Ad Christi veram transivit philosophiam.
In qua longeve bene complens ultima vite;
Philosophis quandoque bonis se connumerandum,
Spem dedit; undenas Maio renovante Kalendas.

Titre: philosophi sancti monasterii Cluniacensis *add. Fr;* Epytaphium petri abahelardi *B;*
Et Petrus Cluniacensis abbas de eodem sic ait *Au* vicit] *corr.* ex vicis *B* Maio] *corr.* ex Maii
B renouante] revocante *B, Duchesne (1616).*

ÉPITAPHES PLUS ÉLABORÉES D'ABÉLARD ET D'HÉLOÏSE

En dehors des épitaphes déjà mentionnées, on en trouve d'autres,
écrites au XIIᵉ et XIIIᵉ siècles, qui n'ont aucun rapport avec les tombeaux d'Abélard et d'Héloïse au Paraclet. [17] Quelquefois, l'épitaphe originale sert de base pour une épitaphe plus élaborée, comme dans le
MS Zurich, Zentralbibliothek C. 58, fol. 5v, du XIIᵉ siècle. [18] Dans les
manuscrits de Troyes, de Chaumont et de Berne, ainsi que dans le
nécrologe latin du Paraclet, maintenant disparu, se trouve une épitaphe
d'Abélard en dix vers, dont les deux derniers reprennent l'épitaphe
originale. Il peut s'agir de deux épitaphes différentes, copiées ensem-
ble dans tous les manuscrits, sauf dans celui de Berne, qui place l'épitaphe originale en tête. Notons que le mot *tumulus* et non pas *titulus*
est employé dans tous ces manuscrits, y compris dans celui de Berne.
Duchesne attribue cette épitaphe à Pierre le Vénérable, guidé sans
doute par la proximité constatée dans les manuscrits entre elle et
la formule d'absolution; rien n'indique pourtant qu'elle fût écrite
avant la fin du XVᵉ siècle.

Elle reprend quelques idées de celle de Pierre le Vénérable et de
l'épitaphe originale.

17. Sur ces épitaphes, voir J. BARROW, C. BURNETT et D. LUSCOMBE, «A Checklist of the
Manuscripts containing the Writings of Peter Abelard and Heloise and other works closely
associated with Abelard and his School», *Revue d'histoire des textes*, t. XIV, 1984.
18. Ed. DRONKE, *Medieval Testimonies*, p. 50; voir son étude, *Medieval Latin and the
Rise of the European Love-Lyric*, (2ᵉ édn) Oxford, 1968, t. II, p. 469-471.

Epitaphium magistri Petri Abelardi fondatoris monasterii Paracliti

Petrus in hac petra latitat, quem mundus Homerum
Clamabat, sed iam sydera sydus habent.
Sol erat hic Gallis, sed eum iam fata tulerunt,
Ergo caret regio Gallica sole suo.
Ille sciens quicquid fuit ulli scibile, vicit
Artifices, artes absque docente docens.
Undecime Maii Petrum rapuere kalende,
Privantes logices atria rege suo.
Est satis in tumulo, Petrus hic iacet Abaelardus
Cui soli patuit scibile quicquid erat.

Titre: Metra per modum epytaphii pro eodem *B*; Epitaphium Abailardi *Camuzat, Duchesne* (*add.* Petri); *début du titre coupé dans C*:... fundatoris et heloissae prime abbatisse petra] urna Duchesne (1614) Homerum] *om. C, lacuna Camuzat* Gallis] gallus *B* eum] cum *C* Gallica] gallia *B ante* vicit] st *in rasura B* Est satis... erat] *om. B* Cui] Huic *Camuzat*.

UNE ÉPITAPHE INÉDITE DE L'ÉGLISE DE SAINT-MARCEL

Comme nous l'avons déjà remarqué, on ne pouvait lire au XVIIe siècle aucune inscription concernant Abélard sur le cénotaphe érigé dans l'église de Saint-Marcel, à Chalon-sur-Saône.[19] Cependant, Baluze transcrit une épitaphe, devenue illisible à son époque, à partir d'un manuscrit de Saint-Marcel, maintenant disparu. L'auteur de cette épitaphe décrit le renom d'Abélard, la persécution qu'il a subie durant sa vie et la translation de son corps au Paraclet. Nous ne pouvons pas affirmer avec certitude si cette épitaphe date du XIIe siècle. Nous reproduisons ici le texte de l'inscription avec le commentaire de Baluze du MS Paris, Bibl. nat., Baluze 12, fol. 172-172v.[20]

Epitaphium Petri Abailardi aliud ab editis in Bibliotheca Cluniacensi et Gallia Christiana ampliori

Cum pie Abailardus vixisset in Coenobio Sancti Marcelli Cabilonensis die xxi aprilis anno 1143, ibidem sepelitus in sacello Sanctae Mariae in cornu evangelii iuxta altare et epitaphium quod habetur in *Bibliotheca Cluniacensi* tumulo inscribitur ibidem ad annum mclxii, quo petente Heloyssa olim coniuge iamdiu abbatissa ad Paraclitense coenobium defertur et ibi tumulatur cum epitaphio quod

19. Voir n. 14.
20. L. AUVRAY et R. POUPARDIN, *Catalogue des MSS de la Collection Baluze*, Paris, 1921, p. 28-31. Je remercie J. S. Barrow d'avoir transcrit le texte.

habes in *Gallia Christiana ampl.*, tomo 4, fo. 707.[21] Eo vero in sarco-
phago quod apud Sanctum Marcellum Cabilonensem iacuerat haec
inscripta videntur quae modo tantum in manuscripto codice leguntur.

D.O.M.

Hic quondam latuit Petrus abeylardus huius coenobii Monachus
incola, si tamen latere potuit quem totus orbis agnovit; inter philosophos solem, nec minus inter theologos sydus. Quamvis enim multorum sui temporis invidia nisi malueris eam zelum nimium appel-
lare deprimere eum tentaverit, tamen ille spiritus qui eum illumi-
naverat mortuum etiam et iacentem ut ipsum vindicaret suscitavit.
Siquidem Petrus Mauritius dictus venerabilis abbas Cluniacensis
annuens votis Heloyssae abbatissae quondam uxoris eius (*fol. 172v*)
quam inter feminas tum ob ingenii acumen tum ob litterarum abun-
dantiam iure phoenicem dixerit, ad paraclitenses moniales quas in
Christo genuerat corpus eius hic per aliquot tempus conditum transtulit anno mcxlii (mclxii *MS*), ut illud ipsum quod aliquando Elysaeo
Elya patris translati pallium postulanti sibi eveniret (Cf. *4 Reg. 2, 13*).
Sed discas, lector, quod si de corpore quod animae vestem Seneca
nominavit illae (illa *MS*) multum glorientur, sat nobis superest cum
sit post funera virtus.

Cenotaphium lapideum elevatum et satis cultum in quo olim
Abaylardus jacuit hactenus visitur in cornu evangelii sacelli Sanctae
Mariae Monasterii Sancti Marcelli Cabilonensis predicti, sed inscrip-
tio supradicta deleta est et reperitur tantum in manuscripto codice
dicti monasterii in quo nonnullae dicit monasterii cartae videntur
incertae.

---

21. *Notae ad Bibliothecam Cluniacensem*, Paris, 1614, p. 148; *Gallia Christiana qua series
omnium archiepiscoporum et episcoporum et abbatum per quatuor tomos deducitur*, éd. S.
et L. Sainte-Marthe, t. IV, Paris, 1656, p. 707. Un exemplaire de la *Gallia Christiana*, signé et
annoté de la main de Baluze se trouve dans la Bibliothèque nationale, Réserve Ld¹ 9.

ST ANSELM AND ROSCELIN: SOME NEW TEXTS AND THEIR IMPLICATIONS

I. THE *DE INCARNATIONE VERBI* AND THE *DISPUTATIO INTER CHRISTIANUM ET GENTILEM*

The solid reputation of St Anselm as thinker and saint could scarcely be more different from the few hazy details commonly remembered about Roscelin of Compiègne.[1] Was not St Anselm a deeply spiritual monk determined to explain his religious faith in terms of reason rather than of written authority? The contrast is often drawn between a saint who was also a sophisticated intellectual and a secular minded logician like Roscelin of Compiègne, whose attempt to apply secular reasoning to the doctrine of the Trinity resulted in nothing short of heresy. Was he not, as St Anselm implied, a leading exponent of the nominalist heresy that there were no eternal realities beyond the evanescent categories of human language? In any history of philosophy in which he is mentioned, Roscelin is remembered as someone who challenged philosophical and religious authority, but without anywhere near the success of his most famous pupil, Peter Abaelard.

These stereotypes owe much to the way St Anselm was able to commit his reflections on language and theology to writing and become quickly recogni-

(1) I am indebted to the Institut de Recherche et d'Histoire des Textes, whose fichier led me to the British Library manuscript with which this study is largely concerned, to the Institute for Advanced Study (Princeton) for enabling me to research and write this paper, and particularly to Giles Constable for his prudent comments. I am also grateful to Irène Rosier for checking my transcription of the Arsenal manuscript *in situ*.

zed as the outstanding intellectual of the Latin Church in the late eleventh and early twelfth century. He had the ear of the Pope when he wrote a treatise *De incarnatione uerbi,* condemning the absurd and dangerous argument of Roscelin of Compiègne, who was reported to maintain that the Father, Son and Holy Spirit had to be three separate things if the Father did not become incarnate with the Son in the person of Jesus Christ. Anselm reminded the Pope that as a logician Roscelin held the equally absurd belief that universal substances were in Roscelin's view no more than "the puff of an utterance"—*flatum uocis.* Anselm's rhetoric has been all the more persuasive given that Roscelin seems to have left us no major treatise to put his side of the argument. The only document so far successfully attributed to him is a letter to Peter Abaelard, accusing his former pupil in no uncertain terms not just of despicable ingratitude towards his master, but of heresy in the exposition of Christian doctrine.[2]

Despite an occasional attempt to re-evaluate the very scant and almost uniformly hostile surviving testimony about Roscelin as a thinker, no historian has been able to escape the opacity of the historical record with regard not just to Roscelin but to intellectual life in the late eleventh century in general. Anselm of Bec has been the only figure of the period to have a mind and feelings which we can explore with a degree of intimacy.[3] Much of our problem has to do with the stubborn anonymity of texts which may be significant, but which have hitherto eluded efforts at firm identification of their author and specific milieu. In the studies which follow we shall present some

(2) The letter was discovered by J. A. Schmeller in the Bavarian State Library, Munich Clm 4643, ff. 93ᵛ-99ʳ (s. xii) and published with arguments for its authenticity in the *Abhandlungen der philosophisch-philologischen Klasse der königlichen bayerischen Akademie der Wissenschaften,* 5 Bd. 3 Abt. (Munich, 1849), 187-210; it was re-edited by J. Reiners as an appendix to his study, *Der Nominalismus in der Frühscholastik. Ein Beitrag zur Geschichte der Universalienfrage im Mittelalter,* Beiträge zur Geschichte der Philosophie [und der Theologie] des Mittelalters, Bd 8.5 (Münster, 1910), pp. 62-80.

(3) By far the most important attempt to bring together the known testimony as it stood in 1911 was that of François Picavet, whose *Roscelin, philosophe et théologien d'après la légende et d'après l'histoire* (2nd revd ed. Paris, 1911) was a much enlarged version of a study of the same title published in Paris in 1896. The few other studies that have been produced since then rely on the same limited evidence and have been very lacking in historical context: cf. Heinrich Christian MEIER, *Macht und Wahnwitz der Begriffe. Der Ketzer Roscellinus* (Aalen, 1974); Eike-Henner W. KLUGE, "Roscelin and the Medieval Problem of Universals", *Journal of the History of Philosophy* 14 (1976), 405-14. Medieval nominalism has its own not inconsiderable literature; for most recent views, see Calvin G. NORMORE, "The Tradition of Medieval Nominalism", in *Studies in Medieval Philosophy,* ed. John F. WIPPEL, Studies in the Philosophy and the History of Philosophy 17 (Washington, 1987) and William J. COURTENAY'S "*Nominales* and Nominalism in the Twelfth Century" to appear a volume being published by Vrin in honour of Paul Vignaux. I am indebted to Courtenay for allowing me to see this article in typescript, as for the same reason to Yukio Iwakuma, who is preparing an article on "*Vocales,* or early nominalists".

new or relatively little studied texts relating to intellectual life in the late
eleventh century, making suggestions as to their provenance and authorship,
in the hope that they may deepen our understanding of a period of dramatic
intellectual ferment. We shall begin by looking more closely at Anselm's treatise against Roscelin, the *Epistola de incarnatione uerbi*, addressed to Pope
Urban II.

1. The *Epistola de incarnatione uerbi ad Urbanum Papam.*

Anselm's *De incarnatione uerbi* has never attracted the same critical attention as some of his more famous writings. Philosophers have long been fascinated by those chapters of the *Proslogion* which seem to offer a proof for the
existence of God, while theologians have admired the *Cur deus homo* for its
exposition of the redemption in terms of reason alone. Anselm is generally
remembered as a calm, meditative thinker whose natural environment was
that of the cloister, rather than as a disputatious polemicist of the schools like
Roscelin of Compiègne or Peter Abaelard. Among Anselm's writings the
small treatise is often seen as marking a short uncomfortable moment between
the philosophical tranquillity of over thirty years at Bec (1059-1092) and the
firm intellectual authority of his time as archbishop of Canterbury (1093-
1109). The polemical tone of the *De incarnatione uerbi*, first drafted in his last
years at Bec and then rewritten shortly after he had been appointed archbishop, fits awkwardly into an image of Anselm as a progressive and meditative thinker. Roscelin must have been a singularly unattractive figure to merit
such condemnation from a philosophical saint.

Anselm was, however, profoundly troubled by the ideas that he thought
Roscelin represented. As a result of the pioneering work of Dom André
Wilmart and Dom Franciscus Schmitt, we have learnt that five different versions survive of the *De incarnatione uerbi.*[4] The earliest *(DIV¹)* Anselm drafted sometime between 1090 and 1092 while he was still abbot of Bec, in

(4) André Wilmart edited the hitherto unknown initial version in "Le premier ouvrage de
saint Anselme contre le trithéisme de Roscelin", *Recherches de théologie ancienne et médiévale*
3 (1931), 20-36. Franciscus Salesius Schmitt edited both this text and the final version (*DIV*¹
and *DIV*², as the two major recensions will subsequently be referred to) quite independently
in the same year along with other relevant documents in *S. Anselmi Epistola de incarnatione
verbi; accedit prior eiusdem opusculi recensio nunc primum edita,* Florilegium Patristicum 28
(Bonn, 1931). He edited the two recensions again in *S. Anselmi Opera* vol. 1 (Seckau, 1938),
pp. 281-90 and vol. 2 (Rome, 1940), pp. 1-17, volumes reprinted as the first two of a six
volume series of the *Opera* (Edinburgh, 1946-61), reprinted again with an important *Prolegomena seu Ratio Editionis* and corrections in *S. Anselmi Opera* (Stuttgart-Bad Canstatt, 1968),
2 vols. Schmitt's editions of *DIV*¹ and *DIV*² have been photographically reproduced with
accompanying notes and translation into French by Alain GALONNIER in *L'œuvre de S.
Anselme de Cantorbéry,* vol. 3 (Paris, 1988), pp. 171-193 and 195-275 respectively. References
to Anselm's writing will be to the volume, page and line of the 1946-61 edition, retained in the
1968 reprint.

response to a report that Roscelin was arguing that the three persons of the Trinity had to be distinguished as three things. Apparently he claimed that if the divine persons were not three separate *res*, the Father must have become incarnate with the Son—and that Anselm would concede this in debate. The abbot of Bec initially prepared an open letter (known through only a single copy: London, Lambeth Palace 224, ff. 121^{v}-124^{v} *[W]*) for a forthcoming council at Soissons, where Roscelin was obliged to abjure all heretical views on the Trinity.[5] Soon after being appointed archbishop of Canterbury (6 March 1093) Anselm transformed and greatly lengthened his earlier text into a letter to Pope Urban II *(DIV²)*, countering ideas that Roscelin was continuing to propagate after supposedly abjuring heresy at this council, or so he explains in its revised introduction.[6]

Schmitt also argued intermediate recensions were preserved in three other manuscripts, all twelfth-century.[7] The Hereford Cathedral MS P.1.i, ff. 154^{v}-155^{v} *(H)* comprised in his view three fragments of the *De incarnatione uerbi*: the first two were of its introduction (the first closer to that of *DIV¹* as printed in 1, 281.3-283.25, the second identical to that in *DIV²* in 2, 7.5-9.11, almost identical to 1, 283.26-284.29), the third a preliminary version of chapters 8-10 in *DIV²* (2, 22.22-28.3). *DIV¹* had extended only as far as the beginning of ch. 6 in *DIV²*.[8] He also found a complete text of *DIV²* in Vatican, Reg. lat. 452, ff. 131^{r}-141^{r} *(V)* and Paris, Bibl. nat. lat. 2479, ff. 1^{r}-10^{r} *(P)* slightly earlier than the most widely disseminated version, and which may have been the one originally sent to Urban II.[9]

(5) The council is not specifically mentioned in *DIV¹*, but we know that in *Ep.* 136 (2, 279-81) he asked Fulco, bishop of Beauvais, asking to carry *has autem litteras* to the forthcoming council, as much as anything to disassociate himself from any opinion attributed to him by Roscelin. In the Lambeth MS (of which f. 122^{r} is reproduced by Schmitt facing 1, 282) the treatise is untitled, but addressed as an open letter "Dominis et patribus et fratribus omnibus catholicae et apostolicae cultoribus, qui hanc legere dignabuntur epistolam" (1, 282.3-4)

(6) *DIV²* 2, 4.5-5.6.

(7) "Cinq recensions de l'*Epistola de incarnatione verbi* de s. Anselme de Cantobéry", *Revue bénédictine* 51 (1939), 20-36, substantially unchanged as "Die verschiedenen Rezensionen der *Epistola de Incarnatione Verbi*", in the 1968 *Opera* 1, 78*-89*.

(8) Schmitt learnt about the Hereford MS from Richard Southern after having prepared the 1938 Seckau edition of *DIV¹*; consequently the variants to its text in *H* are to be found in the apparatus to *DIV²* in vol. 2 (Rome, 1940). On *H*, see A. T. Bannister, *A Descriptive Catalogue of the Manuscripts in the Hereford Cathedral Library* (Hereford, 1927), pp. 96-98. Rodney M. Thomson is preparing a new catalogue of the Hereford Cathedral Library. In none of the MSS of the *De incarnatione uerbi* are chapter divisions identified by number. Schmitt's numerical divisions are however based on dividing signs within the MS tradition, and consequently will be used for convenience; cf. his notes to *Opera* 1, 281 and 2, 3.

(9) *V* is our oldest copy (c. 1100, of unknown provenance) of *DIV²* (f. 133^{v} illustrated facing *Opera* 2, 12). The Greek associations of its contents lend weight to Schmitt's thought that this was the copy sent to the Pope, who used the work in his debate with the Greeks at

Schmitt did not notice another recension of chapters 10-11 of the *De incarnatione uerbi*, occurring in three other manuscripts (none of which he notes in his 1968 list of manuscripts surveyed):[10]

A Paris, Bibliothèque de l'Arsenal 269, ff. 107^r-108^r (s. xii), introduced with the rubric *Anselmus. Quod magis conuenit filio incarnatio quam patri uel spiritui sancto.*

B London, British Library, Royal 5 E xiv, ff. 81rb-82va (s. xiii), untitled, but within a collection of the works of St Anselm.

C Cambridge, U.L. Dd. 1.21, f. 147rb-147vb (s. xiv), untitled, but within a collection of the works of St Anselm.

The text begins in the same way as ch. 10 of *DIV*^{2} (apart from an *autem* added after *Cur* in all three recensions): "Cur deus magis assumpserit hominem in unitatem persone filii, quam in unitatem alicuius aliarum personarum?" However, while the second sentence in *CDM* (as we shall subsequently call the text, after its incipit) begins with a factual response, "I think this reasoning should be given: (Hanc reddendam rationem existimo:)", Anselm begins the equivalent sentence in *DIV*^{2} with an apology for digressing from the subject matter of the treatise. He explains that another question had come to mind: "Quamvis in hac epistola nostrum hoc non fuerit propositum, tamen quoniam huius rei mentio se obtulit, aliquam reddendam rationem existimo." The remaining first half of *CDM* is identical to the text of ch. 10, as found in the Hereford MS, a passage radically revised in *VP* and then touched up slightly in the final version. The remaining part of *CDM*, although touching the same subject matter as ch. 11 in *VP* and the final version, is significantly different from Schmitt's published text of the chapter. Is *CDM* a disciple's modification of this part of the *De incarnatione uerbi*, or an authentic draft of chapters 10-11 by its author?

Before answering this question, we need to examine Schmitt's analysis of different recensions of the work. He thought that the scribe of *H* had copied out in continuous form fragments of three originally separate recensions, which he titled Rec. I, 2, Rec. II (indeterminate recension) and Rec. II, 1. respectively.[11] The second fragment he was inclined to think had been extracted from a complete text of *DIV*^{2}, even though the third fragment certainly

---

Bari in 1108 according to EADMER, *Historia novorum*, ed. Martin RULE, Rolls Series (London, 1884), p. 105. *V* also contains the *Liber Prognosticon* of Julian, the *Vita Johannis Eleemosynarii* of Leontius and the *Historia Lausiaca* of Palladius. *P* is from the first half of the 12th century, probably from Canterbury. In both *V* and *P DIV*^{2} is followed by Augustine's *De doctrina christiana; Catalogue général des manuscrits latins de la Bibliothèque nationale* 2 (Paris, 1940), pp. 479-480.

(10) Schmitt lists the manuscripts he used in his edition in the 1968 Prolegomena to *Opera* 1, 213*-225*. For description and bibliography of these three manuscripts, see below, pp. 68-81.

(11) "Die verschiedenen Rezensionen", pp. 79*-86* (see note 4).

60

contained a preliminary version of chs. 8-10. He did not explain why the copyist should wish to make such an apparently arbitrary selection from three different copies of *DIV*. Such an analysis seems unnecessarily complicated. For our discussion it is simpler to consider all three fragments in *H* as part of a single recension, transitional between *DIV*[1] and *DIV*[2], and a sketch for a future revision rather than a series of extracts from separate, larger wholes.

Taken on its own, the text of *CDM* reads as a separate essay on why God assumed manhood in the person of the Son rather than of any other divine person. There would be too many "inconveniences" if it were otherwise, compromising the evident equality of the three persons. *CDM* has no direct invective against the absurdity of Roscelin's trinitarian argument, as in ch. 9 of *DIV*[2]. In *H* this essay about the rationale for the incarnation in the Son occurs within a longer, although still incomplete text of the *De incarnatione uerbi*. Anselm is obliged to include an apology for diverting from the main subject matter of the treatise "because it had come to mind". Only at the end of ch. 11 in *DIV*[2]—to which there is no parallel in *CDM*—does Anselm abruptly return to Roscelin: "As to the writings of him to whom I am replying in this letter, I was not able to see anything beyond what I have mentioned above [i.e. the argument reported to him]".[12] In chapters 12-16, found only in *VP* and the final version, Anselm continues his earlier assault against any attempt to identify plural substances within the divine nature.

The second part of *CDM* continues with a version of ch. 11 quite different from that found in either *VP* or the final form of *DIV*[2]. It opens with an apology of touching honesty, for which there is no equivalent in other versions of *DIV*:

"Why however or by what beautiful and necessary reason or rational necessity did the supreme majesty—since he is capable of everything by will alone—assume our nature with our weakness and mortality without sin to conquer the devil and to free man? If I included this—which many are asking—within this letter, the digression would be too long. Sometime however, if divine grace gives any effect to my will, because it has deigned to show this to me, I want to write < on this >, driven by the prayers of the many who have heard this from me."[13]

---

(12) *DIV*[2] (2.30): "De scriptis illius cui respondeo in hac epistola, nihil potui videre praeter illud quod supra posui; sed puto sic rei patere veritatem ex eis quae dixi, ut nulli lateat intelligenti nihil quod contra illam dicitur vim veritatis tenere."

(13) *A* f. 107[v]-108[r], *B* f. 81[vb]-82[ra], *C* f. 147[va]: "Cur autem uel quam pulchra et necessaria ratione siue rationabili necessitate summa maiestas cum omnia sola uoluntate possit, nostram naturam cum infirmitate et mortalitate nostra absque peccato ad uincendum diabolum et liberandum hominem assumpserit, quod utique multi querunt, si huic epistole insererem, nimis longa esset digressio. Aliquando tamen si diuina gratia effectum uoluntati mee tribuerit, quod inde michi dignata est ostendere multorum qui hoc a me audierunt precibus compulsus, scribere desidero."

The voice echoes closely that of Anselm in the opening chapter of the *Cur deus homo*.[14] The author of *CDM* broaches an issue that he is anxious to talk about—why should God have assumed mortal nature—but realises that this is not the subject matter of the letter which he is writing. The reference to the present text as an *epistola* within *CDM* is as clear an indication as any that it is written as a draft for the *Epistola de incarnatione uerbi*. Having voiced this thought on a subject about which many people ask, the author of *CDM* then continues with another question about the incarnation—the adequacy of Boethius's refutation of the Nestorian argument that there were two persons in Christ.

If we compare the subsequent text of *CDM* with that of ch. 11 in the second recension in *VP* (not significantly modified in the final form), we see that much fairly tortuous technical questioning in *CDM* has been radically abbreviated when incorporated within the larger work:

CDM De unitate uero *persone* Dei et hominis *quam firmissime credimus esse non ex duabus personis sed ex duabus naturis in Christo; tamen quia potest* aliquid *dici, unde parum caute intuentibus uideri possit Christus ex duabus et in duabus personis existere, non inutile michi uidetur* questionem ipsam hic facere, atque id quod contra fidem nostram dici posse uidetur, adiuuante Deo dissoluere. Non enim sufficit cum aliquid quodlibet firmis argumentis probatur, nisi quod ex aduerso pari ratione obici uidetur dissoluatur. Quamuis enim Boetius probet contra Nestorium Christum non ex duabus personis existere, non tamen michi uidetur Nestorii ratio-

DIV[2] c. 11 *De qua unitate personae, quam firmissime credimus esse non ex duabus personis in Christo, tamen quia potest dici unde parum caute intuentibus uideri possit Christus ex duabus et in duabus personis existere, non inutile mihi uidetur* aliquid dicere. Dicunt enim quidam: Quomodo dicimus in Christo non esse duas personas, sicut duas naturas? *Nam Deus et ante hominis assumptionem persona erat nec postquam hominem assumpsit persona destitit esse; et homo assumptus persona est, quia omnis homo individuus esse persona cognoscitur*. Quare alia est persona Dei quae fuit ante incarnationem, alia hominis assumpti. Sicut igitur Christus est

(14) *Cur deus homo* I, 1 (2, 47.5-7): "Saepe et studiosissime a multis rogatus sum et verbis et litteris, quatenus cuiusdam de fide nostra quaestionis rationes, quas soleo respondere quaerentibus, memoriae scribendo commendem. < ... > (47.11-48.3) Quam quaestionem solent et infideles nobis simplicitatem Christianam quasi fatuam deridentes obicere, et fideles multi in corde versare: qua videlicet ratione vel necessitate Deus homo factus sit, et morte sua, sicut credimus et confitemur, mundo vitam reddiderit, cum hoc aut per aliam personam, sive angelicam sive humanam, aut sola voluntate facere potuerit. De qua quaestione non solum litterati sed etiam illitterati multi quaerunt et rationem eius desiderant."

nem qua duas uult in Christo asserere personas destruere. Potest itaque aliquis dicere sic: "Si persona est rationalis natura indiuidua, sicut Boetius ubi contra Nestorium disputat definit, et in Christo sunt due rationales nature, scilicet diuina et humana, et unaqueque indiuidua est Deus, indiuiduus est enim homo ille, et indiuiduus est Deus, ergo uidetur due persone in Christo esse, persona scilicet Dei, et persona hominis. *Nam Deus et ante hominis assumptionem persona erat, nec postquam hominem assumpsit persona destitit esse, et homo assumptus persona est, quia omnis homo indiuiduus esse persona cognoscitur.*" Que ratio per hoc aliam personam esse in Christo hominem, et aliam Deum probare nititur, quia duo rationalia indiuidua putat in illo esse, hominem scilicet et Deum.

Deus et homo, ita duae in illo videntur esse personae. Quae ratiocinatio per hoc videtur probare duas esse personas in Christo, quia Deus est persona et homo assumptus persona est. Sed non est ita.

CDM is not the work of a less sophisticated disciple amplifying the thought of Anselm, even though stylistically *DIV*² is clearly the superior text. A wordy, but thoughtful preamble about a possible question about Christ's nature "against our faith" needing to be dissolved rationally is reduced in *DIV*² to a terse: "it seems not without use to me to say something". The author of *CDM* explicitly criticises the adequacy of Boethius' reasoning in the *Contra Nestorium et Euticen*: "Although Boethius argues against Nestorius that Christ does not exist out of two persons, he does not seem to me to destroy the reason by which he [Nestorius] asserts that there are two persons in Christ." In *DIV*² this is turned into an unintimidating "Certain people say". While such explicit critical citation of a traditional authority is unusual in Anselm's published writing, it is complicated to argue that someone else has here made explicit the complex tissue of authorities to whom Anselm alludes so indirectly in the *De incarnatione uerbi*. *CDM* makes more clear what is only indirectly evident in the final text, namely that Anselm glimpsed an indirect parallel between the argument of Nestorius about Christ and that of Roscelin on the Trinity. His preferred solution went beyond that of Boethius by focussing on common semantic problems of unity and plurality.

2. The making of the *De incarnatione uerbi*.

The relationship of *CDM* to Anselm's treatise is so complex that it must be an authentic draft of ch. 10-11 of the *De incarnatione uerbi*. (While the numbering of chapters in *DIV* is Schmitt's device, they do correspond to authentic dividing marks in the manuscript tradition.) In this draft Anselm explicitly identifies the common ground of any discussion about unity and plurality as philosophical definition of an individual (in fact from Porphyry) as that which is distinct in its collection of properties: "Philosophi utique diffiniunt esse indiuiduum, cuius proprietatum collectio non est in alio eadem, id est non dicitur de alio."[15] Although the definition of an individual might suggest that as the properties of God are different from those of man, there have to be two individuals in Christ, there is such a connection of God and man in Christ that one cannot say that God and man are two individual things. One can only say of a tongue that it makes speech and of a hand that it makes writing (and not a tongue writing or a hand speech), even though only one person is involved. Apparently contradictory statements about Peter being buried in Rome and being in Paradise can both be true if one distinguishes whether each signifies *secundum spiritum* or *secundum se*. Anselm's argument in *CDM* relied on a strict application of the semantic principles articulated in the *De grammatico*. It was not so far removed from the argument Roscelin claimed to have heard Anselm use, that the three divine persons were predicated of God in the same way as *albus, iustus* and *grammaticus* were predicated of an individual man.[16]

In *DIV*[2] Anselm summarizes a rather long argument into a single brief paragraph. He also leaves out the reference to *philosophi* as the source of the definition of an individual as that which has a distinct collection of properties, perhaps as being too 'academic' in tone. He prefers instead to begin with a more concrete illustration that the proper name "Jesus" like "this man" or "that man" referred to a particular collection of properties. Only at the end of

---

(15) *Isagoge* 7.21, transl. Boethii, ed. Laurenzo MINIO-PALUELLO, *Aristoteles Latinus* 1, 6-7 (Bruges, Paris, 1966), pp. 13.24-14.2: "Individua ergo dicuntur huiusmodi quoniam ex proprietatibus consistit unumquodque eorum quorum collectio numquam in alio eadem erit."
(16) *DIV*[1] (282.10-15): "Dictum quoque mihi prius fuerat similiter, quia Francigena quidam—hunc autem novi, quia amicus meus est—assereret se a me audisse ita de Deo dici patrem et filium et procedentem a patre et filio spiritum, quomodo albus et iustus et grammaticus et similia de quodam individuo homine." In translating this passage GALONNIER considered that *Francigena* was the name of a friend different from that of Roscelin, in *L'œuvre de S. Anselme* 3 (see n. 1), pp. 175 and 193. The reading of this passage in *H* (omitting *Francigena... meus est*, as indicated in the apparatus on p. 202 of the Schmitt-Galonnier editiontranslation) makes clear that the *Francigena* is identical to the *quodam clerico in Francia*, as Richard W. SOUTHERN pointed out in *Saint Anselm and his Biographer* (Cambridge, 1963), p. 80 n. 1.

the paragraph does he conclude with a definition, seemingly his own but in fact based on Porphyry: "Diversarum vero personarum impossibile est eandem esse proprietatum collectionem, aut de invicem eas praedicari." As with so many Augustinian ideas, Anselm took a traditional thought (in this case of Porphyry), and presented it in his own words as a reflection evident to reason. Even though there is more explicitly philosophical semantic discussion in *CDM*, the revised form of ch. 11 in *DIV*² still stresses as an underlying theme that one must pay attention to the particular mode of signification of a phrase like "Son of God", different from that of "Son of Man", albeit expressed in more compact form. The smooth, deceptively simple philosophical style of Anselm did not spring automatically from his pen. It emerged only from careful pruning of initially elaborate and complicated reflections generated by a sophisticated and subtle mind.

If the draft *CDM* was incorporated into the longer text of *DIV* in the Hereford MS, why is the latter recension still so manifestly incomplete? Its text is too incomplete to make sense as another draft of a projected revision. In *H* Anselm sketches out a revised introduction, modifying or leaving out certain phrases. Thus instead of saying "I have recently been informed by a letter that...", he writes "It is known to many that..." His earlier admission that "I knew this man [Roscelin] because he is my friend", he left out altogether as too compromising.[17] Anselm did not include the remaining part of *DIV*¹ in his draft *H*, because he was reasonably satisfied with its substance. Only technical details would be modified in the writing out of *VP*. Chapters 8-10 in *H* are written to bridge what he had already written in *DIV*¹ to the new ideas sketched out in *CDM*, introducing the idea that it was quite possible for one divine person to be in man, and the other not in man.[18] That part of *CDM* which Anselm felt still needed revision (equivalent to ch. 11), he did not copy out into *H*. Only with the writing out of *VP*, very likely the recension sent to Urban II, did Anselm knit together a text based on *H* (introductory), *DIV*¹ (ch. 2-6.2-10), *H* (ch. 8-10) and *CDM* (ch. 10-11), simplifying ch. 11 significantly.[19]

He also added a new section to where *DIV*¹ left off (= ch. 6.10) recommending a reader who wished to understand by "necessary reasons" without scriptural authority how God was both a single nature and three person—a doctrine firmly taught by the Fathers and above all by Augustine—to consult his *Monologion* and *Proslogion*. Insisting that in those works—"neither teaching what our doctors did not know, nor correcting what they did not say well, but saying perhaps what they were silent about, which, far from disagreeing with

---

(17) *DIV*¹ (1, 281.4, 11-12; cf. apparatus on 2, 6).

(18) *DIV*² (2, 24.1-2).

(19) This construction of the text also explains Schmitt's observation that certain phrases in *VP* replicate those in *DIV*¹ (see his apparatus to 2, 12.8-11, 14.21, 16.16, 17.7).

their propositions, coheres with them"—he was only countering those who "deride believers". He wished to help those who "humbly seek to understand what they firmly believe". For those who did not want to trouble themselves with reading further, he then supplied a short summary of the ideas mapped out in those earlier works.[20] When writing out the complete text in *VP* Anselm also greatly simplified the subtle argument of *CDM*'s version of c. 11. He left out its criticism of Boethius' *Contra Euticen et Nestorium*, and then added chs. 12-16 to the text of *H*. Anselm's major new argument in this final part, was in fact adapted from an analogy suggested by Augustine in a relatively minor work, the *De fide et symbolo*, although he presented it as his own: that of the Trinity as like a spring from which flowed a river, which then became a lake. All might be called "the Nile", even though each was also something separate. Anselm emphasised the philosophical aspect of Augustine's analogy, not making any direct identification of one person with the spring or the river, rather making a point about predication, that things could be different while being the same. Only in one sentence did he extend Augustine's image to the Incarnation, in comparing the channel through which the water flowed from its source to the lake to the incarnate Son.[21] These new passages in the first complete text of the treatise *(VP)* give the impression of being written in a hurry. He concluded his rather brief discussion of how the Son was born of the Father and the Holy Spirit proceeded from both, as he had begun the section tagged onto *DIV*[1], by appealing to the authority of Augustine, whose *De trinitate* could be supplemented by what he had himself said in the *Monologion*.

Perhaps the most significant change which Anselm made in writing out the letter was to re-address it to Pope Urban II, submitting it for censure and correction if anything was to be found therein contrary to the catholic faith.[22] In no earlier treatise had Anselm offered such a dedication to the Pope. Neither Lanfranc nor any other writer against heretical opinions had ever before made such a direct appeal to papal authority, allowing a work to be corrected.[23] This act of personal submission needs to be seen in the light of another

---

(20) *DIV*[1] (20.11-21.10).

(21) *DIV*[2] (2, 31.2-33.8), alluding to Augustine's *De fide et symbolo* c. 8.17 (*CSEL* 41, p. 18).

(22) *DIV*[2] (2, 3.2-4.4).

(23) G.B. FLAHIFF, "The Censorship of Books in the Twelfth Century", *Mediaeval Studies* 4 (1942), 1-22 did not notice this example of voluntary pre-censorship in *DIV*[2]. He thought that the earliest known example of a writer to seek approval directly from the Pope (as distinct from any other patron) was Gerhoch of Reichersberg, who asked c. 1150 for Eugenius III to correct his commentary on the Psalms, as well as the archbishop of Salzburg and Otto of Freising (*PL* 193, 491); three others were Godfrey of Viterbo, Herbert of Bosham and Ralph Niger. Nonetheless such examples of voluntary pre-censorship are extremely rare, prior to the mid twelfth-century. The one earlier example Flahiff thought to be provided by the reason for Abaelard's condemnation at Soissons in 1121, as explained in the *Historia calami-*

change in tone in the introduction, emphasizing the orthodoxy of his position. In *VP* Anselm deleted his reference to Roscelin's specific charges against himself of doctrinal unorthodoxy (repeated in *H*), instead emphasising that everything he had said in the *Monologion* and *Proslogion* conformed totally to what Augustine taught. He avoided any hint that he (or Lanfranc for that matter) might ever have sympathised with any aspect of Roscelin's teaching. By appealing directly to the Pope Anselm was presenting himself as a totally loyal son of the Church, defending the catholic faith from a pernicious intellectual, one of a breed of "modern pseudo-logicians or rather heretics of dialectic, who do not think universal substances to be anything but the breath of an utterance, say they understand a colour as nothing other than a body, nor wisdom of man as anything other than the soul who had to be excluded from discussion of all spiritual questions".[24] In rhetorical language Anselm repeated such claims of a radical gulf between himself and Roscelin (never named explicitly except as "a certain cleric in France") to an audience which now included the Pope.

When he came to writing out this new version of the *De incarnatione uerbi*, Anselm had no further knowledge of why or how Roscelin had arrived at his

---

tatum 11. 848-854, ed. Jacques Monfrin (Paris, 1978), p. 87: "Dicebant [*scil.* emuli mei] enim ad dampnationem libelli [*scil. de unitate et trinitate divina*] satis hoc esse debere quod nec romani pontificis nec Ecclesie auctoritate eum commendatum legere publice presumpseram, atque ad transcribendum jam pluribus eum ipse prestitissem; et hoc perutile futurum fidei christiane, si exemplo mei multorum similis presumptio preveniretur." Flahiff assumed this passage to mean that "the legate was persuaded to condemn the book... solely, it is said, because he had taught this book publically and allowed copies to be made without its being approved by the Pope or by the Church" (*art. cit.*, p. 4 and n. 16). Flahiff's interpretation was cited by Hubert Silvestre as evidence against the authenticity of the *Hist. cal.* ("L'idylle d'Abélard et Héloïse: la part du roman", Académie royale de Belgique. *Bulletin de la classe des lettres et des sciences morales et politiques*, 5e sér., 71 [1985-5] 183, following John Benton's assumption in the Cluny volume *Pierre Abélard-Pierre le Vénérable. Les courants philosophiques, littéraires et artistiques en Occident au milieu du xiie siècle* [Paris, 1975], p. 484). In "Abelard's Mockery of St Anselm", *Journal of Ecclesiastical History* 41 (1990), 1-23, Michael Clanchy has followed the same assumption that Abaelard's failure to pre-censure his book provided sufficient grounds for its condemnation, arguing that his accusers cited this passage in Anselm's *DIV²* to persuade the legate. Yet the Latin of *Hist. cal.* 1.849 says that his critics thought his failure *ought* to be sufficient, not that it *was* sufficient. The charge made at Soissons which prompted the archbishop's sentence was that Abaelard had said only God the Father was omnipotent (*Hist. cal.* ll. 871-4). Flahiff's reading of *Hist. cal.* is undermined by his much more important general observation (ignored by Clanchy) that such rare examples as survive from the twelfth-century of submission to papal censorship are all *voluntary* and not legal obligations. Alberic may have thought pre-censorship should be accepted practice and have admired Anselm's precedent in *DIV²*, but this was not the grounds of the actual condemnation at Soissons.

(24) *DIV²* (2, 9.21-10.1): "illi utique nostri temporis dialectici, immo dialecticae haeretici, qui non nisi flatum vocis putant universales esse substantias, et qui colorem non aliud queunt intelligere quam corpus, nec sapientiam hominis aliud quam animam, prorsus a spiritualium quaestionum disputatione sunt exsufflandi." The passage is taken over from *DIV¹* (1, 285.4-7) with the addition in *H* and *DIV²* of *nostri temporis* and *immo dialecticae haeretici*.

conclusion about the three divine persons as three *res*.[25] He still thought that
it must be a consequence of inflated intellectual self-esteem and spiritual blindness. He was particularly upset by Roscelin's apparent failure to recognize
that the word "thing" had a different meaning dependent on its context. The
only extra information Anselm admits to (not present in *H*, but found in *VP*)
is that after he had been captured for the episcopate he had heard "the author
of the aforesaid novelty, persevering in his opinion, say that he had only
abjured what he used to say because he feared being killed by the people".
Roscelin apparently justified his approach by saying that "the pagans defend
their Law, the Jews defend their own Law; therefore we Christians ought to
defend our faith."[26] Yet, as the isolated promise in *CDM* to write a work
about the reason for the Incarnation makes clear, Anselm was already thinking about bigger issues than Roscelin's argument when he wrote out the
complete text of *DIV*[2]. His heart was set on the theme of why God should
have become man, an issue that touched on the very essence of the human
condition, not just on the language one should use about God.

Anselm touched up his letter to Urban II only slightly after finishing the
version *VP* (very likely that sent to the Pope). The biggest change was the title.
Only in this modified version, the one most widely diffused in the manuscript
tradition, is the subject matter of the letter to the Pope defined as *De incarnatione uerbi*.[27] The letter in fact says relatively little about the incarnation of the
Word, as Roscelin's argument concerned the nature of the Trinity. As late as
1097-98, perhaps four years after its redaction, Malchus, bishop of Waterford,
asked Anselm for that book "composed about the Holy Trinity and commended by apostolic authority."[28] One reason why Anselm gave the title *De incarnatione uerbi* to the revised final version is suggested by the draft *CDM*. Here
he was concerned with a question raised indirectly by Roscelin's argument:
why did God assume man in the Son rather than in any other person? Roscelin had maintained that it was logically necessary to distinguish the three
persons as three things; otherwise the incarnation would have involved the
whole Trinity.[29] After rejecting Roscelin's conclusion in *DIV*[1] as palpably
absurd, Anselm then tried in the draft *CDM* to explain why God became
incarnate in the Son and not in the other persons. We see in its second part

(25) *DIV*[2] (2, 30.7-9).

(26) *DIV*[2] (2, 10.19-21): "Dicit, sicut audio, ille qui tres personas dicitur asserere esse velut
tres angelos aut tres animas: "Pagani defendunt legem suam, Iudaei defendunt legem suam.
Ergo et nos Christiani debemus defendere fidem nostram."

(27) Schmitt notes (apparatus to 2, 3.1) that in *P* the treatise is just known as an *epistola* to
Pope Urban II; no titles occur in *W*, *H* or *P*. Only one MS (Munich, Clm 21248, from Ulm;
early twelfth century) adds to the title "contra blasphemias Ruzelini Compendiensis". The
title *De fide trinitatis*, retained by Migne in *PL* 158, 259-84, was first given by Gerberon in his
1675 edition without any manuscript foundation.

(28) *Epist.* 207 among the letters of Anselm (2, 101-2).

(29) John, *Ep.* 128 (270.8-271.11); *DIV*[1] (282.5-7), *DIV*[2] (2, 4.6-9).

that he was here groping towards a way of explaining how God and man could co-exist in the Son, going beyond the arguments of Boethius in the *Contra Euticen et Nestorium*. As the apology added to the beginning of *CDM* in *H* makes clear, Anselm was aware that this was not the proper subject of the letter. Only in *CDM* does Anselm promise to write sometime in the future about the "beautiful and necessary reason and rational necessity" as to why God should have assumed human nature with its weakness and mortality. The promise confirms Southern's argument—based on comparison of passages in *DIV*² with Gilbert Crispin's *Disputatio Iudei et Christiani*—that Anselm was already starting to think about the reasons why God became man in the winter of 1092/93, spent in England prior to being appointed archbishop of Canterbury 6 March 1093.[30] After he had been consecrated archbishop (4 December 1093), he sent for Boso, his disciple at Bec since 1090, to come to Canterbury. Boso's stimulation was instrumental in writing the *Cur Deus homo*, a work he says he began in England at a time "of great tribulation of heart".[31] Anselm completed it in 1098 at Sclavia (modern day Liberi), in southern Italy, while staying at a mountain-top manor belonging to John, abbot of Telese, the Roman cleric and former monk of Bec who first informed Anselm about the dangerous opinions of Roscelin of Compiègne.[32]

3. The manuscripts of *Cur deus magis*

A PARIS, Bibliothèque de l'Arsenal 269, ff. 107ʳ-108ᵛ; s. xii² (dated to s. xiii by Martin, but written in a spacious hand more typical of s. xii²).[33]

---

(30) Shown by Richard SOUTHERN through comparison of the *De incarnatione uerbi* (for which he used *H*) and Gilbert Crispin's *Disputatio*, "St Anselm and Gilbert Crispin, Abbot of Westminster", *Mediaeval and Renaissance Studies* 3 (1954), 78-115.

(31) *De conceptu virginali et de originali peccato* (2, 139.5): "quem ut ederem tu maxime inter alios me impulisti"; *Vita Bosonis, PL* 150, 725D.

(32) *Cur deus homo*, Pref. (2, 42.6-9); EADMER, *Vita Anselmi* c. 30, ed. Richard W. SOUTHERN, *The Life of Saint Anselm* (Oxford, 1962, reprinted with corrections 1979), p. 107. While the traditional date for Anselm's beginning *CDH*, first suggested by Gerberon, has been 1094, René Roques thinks that it was begun closer to the first exile of Anselm from England in late October 1097; *Pourquoi Dieu s'est fait homme*, Sources chrétiennes 91 (Paris, 1963), p. 65. The period February 1095 - May 1097 was a relatively peaceful one for Anselm; cf. Sally N. VAUGHN, *Anselm of Bec and Robert of Meulan. The Innocence of the Dove and the Wisdom of the Serpent* (Berkeley, 1987), pp. 185-203. Schmitt is open on the question 1, 59*-60*. Eadmer tells us more about John in his *Historia novorum*, ed. Martin RULE, Rolls Series (London, 1884), p. 96. From Pope Urban II's first known letter to Anselm (*Ep.* 125 in the collection, 3, 265-6) we learn that John was a Roman cleric who came to France to study under Anselm, became a monk and priest at Bec (incurring some controversy in Rome), returned to Rome at the Pope's behest, but was released to France at the request of Fulco, bishop of Beauvais, to serve as his secretary for a year. John subsequently became abbot of Telese, cardinal-bishop of Tusculum by around 1100, and papal legate to England in 1101; SOUTHERN, *Vita Anselmi*, p. 106 n. 1.

(33) Henry MARTIN, *Catalogue des manuscrits de la bibliothèque de l'Arsenal* (Paris, 1885),

CDM occurs immediately after sermons 24-54 of St Bernard on the Song of Songs (ff. 1ʳ-107ʳ). Immediately after the final rubric to these sermons, *Finit sermo quinquagesimus primus* on f. 107ʳ, the scribe introduces his final text with: *Anselmus. Quod magis conueniat filio incarnatio quam patri uel spiritui sancto.* Directly following this text on f. 108ᵛ he continues with an unedited short discussion of the indissolubility of marriage *(Vinculum coniugale)*. On to the final leaves (ff. 108ᵛ-110ᵛ) are written miscellaneous notes on scripture and the vices and virtues of various peoples (with the exception of the Normans— perhaps a reflection of Norman provenance). The manuscript entered the Arsenal from the library of the Feuillants in Paris.[34]

B LONDON, British Library 5 E xiv, ff. 81ʳᵇ-82ᵛᵃ; s. xiii.[35]

This manuscript contains a complete collection of the works of St Anselm, including certain other works sometimes attributed to him in the manuscript tradition, as well as two texts commonly attributed to Hugh of St Victor. Its first gathering, which would have been numbered ff. 1-13ᵛ, is missing.

ff. 14ʳᵃ-30ʳᵃ, *De similitudinibus*, an authentic Anselmian treatise *De humanis moribus per similitudines* expanded with non-Anselmian treatises by his disciples.[36]

ff. 30ʳᵇ-31ᵛᵇ, *De triplici silentio*, two homilies on Wisdom 18:15-16 *"Dum medium"*.

ff. 31ᵛᵇ-35ʳᵇ, *De conflictu vitiorum atque virtutum*, attributed elsewhere to Ambrose (*PL* 17, 1149-68), to Augustine (*PL* 40, 1091-1106), to Isidore (*PL* 83, 1131-44) or to Leo IX (*PL* 143, 559-78).

ff. 35ᵛᵃ-50ʳᵃ, Hugh of St Victor, Commentary on the Lamentations of Jeremiah (*PL* 175, 255-322).

These initial gatherings conclude with various theological notes and texts, some from St Bernard, added in the fourteenth century. On a new set of gatherings the same scribe as responsible for the earlier works carries on with:

ff. 54ʳᵃ-69ᵛᵇ, *Monologion*.

ff. 70ʳᵃ-74ʳᵃ, *Disputatio inter Christianum et Gentilem*, incipit: "Maiestas divina..." (see below, p. 86-97).

ff. 74ʳᵇ-81ᵛᵇ, Letters, mostly of St Anselm (cited by Schmitt's numbering):

p. 158. *CDM* and *Vinculum coniugale* are noted without comment by H. ROCHAIS and E. MANNING, *Bibliographie générale de l'ordre cistercien; Saint Bernard,* La documentation cistercienne, 21 (Rochefort, 1979-82), no. 4282, in which Martin's thirteenth-century date is reproduced.

(34) On the important library of this order, founded in the late sixteenth century, see A. FRANKLIN, *Les anciennes bibliothèques de Paris* (Paris, 1870), pp. 281-6.

(35) G. WARNER and J. GILSON, *Catalogue of Western Manuscripts in the British Museum* (London, 1913) 1, 116-7.

(36) The expanded *De similitudinibus* occurs among the works of Eadmer in *PL* 159, 605-708. Southern and Schmitt argue convincingly for Anselm's authorship of the smaller treatise *De humanis moribus* on which it was based in their edition of the latter, *Memorials of St. Anselm* (London, 1969), pp. 4-104.

136 to Fulk of Beauvais; 1 to Lanfranc; 3 to Robert; 11 to Gerbert; 12 to Rodulph; 4 to Gondulf; 5 to Henry; 6 to prior Hugo; 38 to Arnulf; 45 to Frodelina; 61 to Fulk abbot of Saint-Pierre-sur-Dive; 41 to Gondulf; the text *Vinculum coniugale* also found in *A* and edited below (p. 72-73); 37 to Lanzo; 2 to Odo and Lanzo; 216 from Pascal II to Henry I; 300 Anselm to Gundulf, bishop of Rochester; 308 to Henry I; 224 Pascal II to Henry; 222 Paschal II to Anselm.

ff. 81rb-82va, *Cur deus magis* (draft of the *De incarnatione uerbi,* edited below, pp. 82-85).

ff. 82va-87vb, *Proslogion.*

ff. 88ra-99rb, *Meditationes* (nos. 9, 10, 2, 34, 50, 52, 63, 64, 65, 67, 68, 69, 72, 74, 75, 23, 24).

ff. 100ra-105ra, *De ueritate.*

ff. 105ra-109va, *De libero arbitrio.*

ff. 109va-118vb, *De casu diaboli.*

ff. 119ra-125va, *De incarnatione uerbi* (in the widely disseminated final recension).

ff. 125va-146rb, *Cur deus homo.*

ff. 146rb-148va, *Meditatio* no. 11 (on the redemption).

ff. 148va-156vb, *De conceptu uirginali et de originali peccato.*

ff. 156vb-167va, *De processione spiritus sancti.*

ff. 167va-169va, *De sacrificio azimi et fermentati.*

ff. 169va-170rb, *De sacramentis ecclesiae ad Walerannum.*

ff. 170rb-180rb, *De concordia praescientiae et praedestinationis.*

ff. 181ra-vb, *Oratio* to a guardian angel, incipit: "Sancte ac beate angele Dei..." with a note that it was to follow *Meditatio* 11 (ed. André Wilmart, *Auteurs spirituels* [Paris, 1932], pp. 544-551).

ff. 182ra-190vb, Hugh of St Victor, *De institutione nouitiorum* and *De modo orandi.*

Nothing certain is known about the manuscript's whereabouts prior to the seventeenth century, when it came into the possession of Walter Stonehouse, an antiquary with an interest in things Welsh and Celtic, and then into the collection of the Gloucestershire antiquary, John Theyer.[37] Nonetheless, a

---

(37) While Warner and Gilson note simply the inscription of "W. Stonehouse" on the opening leaf, it is the same signature as the "Walter Stonehouse" written onto B.L. Addit. MS 28, 696, a volume containing a 15th-century transcription of the foundation charter of Landaff Cathedral, a 17th-century copy of Bede's *Vita Cuthberti* and a 12th-century parchment copy of a moralizing poem, "Vicit Adam ueterem gula...". Stonehouse also owned Addit. MS 28, 791 and Egerton 2403; *B* subsequently passed into the possession of John Theyer, the antiquary who obtained the bulk of the library of Lanthony Secunda, and from there into the Royal collection.

constellation of factors suggests that *B* may derive from a collection of works
of Anselm assembled either at Llanthony Prima, an Augustinian Priory eighteen miles from Hereford or at Lanthony Secunda in Gloucestershire, to
where the fledgling community was forced to migrate in 1136 after a two-year
spell in Hereford.[38] Southern has already pointed to Llanthony Prima as the
original point of diffusion of the *De humanis moribus per similitudines*, on
which the *De similitudinibus* was based. Two very early manuscripts of the *De
humanis moribus* come from there, including one (now British Library, Royal
8 D viii) which was extended with additional passages by Robert de Braci,
third prior of Llanthony, 1131-7, to transform Anselm's notes into the work
now known as the *De similitudinibus*. No manuscripts survive from the Canterbury region. While most of these additional passages are from Alexander's
Dicta Anselmi and Eadmer's *Vita Anselmi* and *De beatitudine perennis vite,*
Robert de Braci also incorporated some other notes of a strongly Anselmian
character into the margin of his text, most of which subsequently entered into
the enlarged *De similitudinibus*. *B* was used by Southern and Schmitt for their
edition of these chapters "of unknown origin".[39] The rubrics to the *De similitudinibus* in *B* are the same as those found in the Hereford Cathedral MS P.2.i
and in the British Library MS Cotton Cleopatra C xi (both s. xiii) from Abbey
Dore, roughly equidistant to Hereford and Llanthony.[40]

The two homilies on Wisdom 18:15-16 which make up *De triplici silentio*
also occur in Robert de Braci's collection under the rubric *Anselmus, quomodo
intelligitur 'Dum medium',* as well as in the Cotton (Abbey Dore) manuscript
and another from Hereford Cathedral (O.I. xii; s. xii).[41] The prayer to the
guardian angel is not found in most collections of the prayers of St Anselm,
except in copies mostly of West country provenance: the oldest, from the late
twelfth century, comes from the Cistercian abbey of Buildwas, Shropshire
(Cambridge, Pembroke College 154), while a thirteenth-century copy comes
from the Carthusian abbey of Witham, Somerset. The prayer also occurs in

---

(38) See below, p. 75.

(39) *Memorials,* pp. 12-13, 296-303. The editors argue that the *De similitudinibus* must have
been compiled before 1130 when Robert de Braci added his notes "to bring the *De humanis
moribus* into line with the enlarged text". They doubt that the *De similitudinibus* was produced
at Canterbury as it was not used by Eadmer or Alexander. The possibility remains that
Robert de Braci was himself responsible for compiling the *De similitudinibus* from materials
available at Llanthony. A few fragments (edited pp. 300-303) he could have found after a
better transcription of the enlarged *De similitudinibus* had been made. Its manuscript tradition
still needs to be studied.

(40) Information gleaned from SOUTHERN and SCHMITT's introduction, *Memorials,*
pp. 11-16, 38.

(41) *Memorials,* p. 297 and n. 2; the authors note: "It is an interesting text which would
require to be studied in tracing the history of the *De similitudinibus,* but its connexion with
Anselm is too remote to justify its inclusion in this volume." They also mention its occurrence
in the Paris MS BN lat. 15686 (although not the Hereford MS).

VI

72

MSS of Oxford, Exeter College 23 (s. xiii), Cambridge, Corpus Christi College 284 from St Augustine's, Canterbury (s. xiv), Cambridge, Trinity College 59 (s. xiv) and Oxford, University College 16 (end of s. xv).

The letters within *B* are for the most part those written which Anselm wrote to monastic friends prior to becoming abbot at Bec in 1079, with certain significant exceptions that distinguish this anthology from the collections assembled at Canterbury and Bec.[42] At the head of the anthology stands letter 136 to Fulco of Beauvais about Roscelin, written c. 1091.

Inserted between letters 41 and 37 occurs a hitherto unknown text about the indissolubility of marriage, written in the form of an opinion or homily rather than a letter, and rather out of place among his early letters to monks when marital issues never arose. Its teaching about marriage is consistent with what Anselm said on the subject in his letter 427 to Muriardach, king of Ireland c.1100/1109, although is more specific.[43] Marriage could be dissolved only by the death of one partner. To someone who said that a husband who had never sinned with his wife but was separated from her, was unjustly condemned, he replied that even if she was removed by illness or for any other reason the husband had still to remain chaste and that these were the hidden judgements of God, always just. Perhaps God wanted people to suffer so that he could place them in paradise for their patience. He also thought that a common punishment should suffice for husband and wife since they were one body and one flesh. *Vinculum coniugale* differs slightly in its emphasis from that of the *De incestis coniugiis* written c. 1098 at Canterbury by Ernulf, from 1096 to 1107 prior of Christ Church. Ernulf had argued that marriage could be dissolved if a woman had fornicated with her step-son.[44] We edit the text here with the variants found in both *A* (f. 108v) and *B* (f. 77va):

"Vinculum coniugale nullo pacto dirrumpi licet, quod dicente apostolo nonnisi morte alterius solui potest. Semper enim et ille dicetur uir uxoris et illa

(42) On these letter collections, see SOUTHERN's introductory essay "La tradizione delle Lettere di Anselmo", in *Anselmo d'Aosta. Opere*, ed. Inos BIFFI and Costante MARABELLI (Milan, 1988), pp. 89-98, which takes issue with some points argued by Walter FRÖHLICH, "The Genesis of the Collections of St Anselm's Letters", *Anglo-Norman Studies: Proceedings of the Battle Conference* 6 (1983), 58-71 and "The Genesis of the Collections of St Anselm's Letters", *American Benedictine Review* 35 (1984), 249-66. None of these studies take into account the testimony of *B*.

(43) *Epist.* 427 (5, 374). G.R. EVANS' *A Concordance to the Works of St Anselm* (New York, 1984) reveals that he also used the word *coniugium* in letters 248, 168, 238, 243 and 364. He mentions it in passing fashion tending either to disparage or spiritualize the institution.

(44) *De incestis coniugiis, PL* 163, 1457-74. Ernulf had become a monk at Bec probably at about the same time as Anselm, but then moved to St-Symphorien, Beauvais, until 1077 when he transferred to Christ Church. In 1107 he became abbot of Peterborough; from 1114 until his death in 1124 he was bishop of Rochester; cf. Peter CRAMER's excellent study, "Ernulf of Rochester and Early Anglo-Norman Canon Law", *Journal of Ecclesiastical History* 40 (1989), 483-510.

uxor uiri. Hoc tantum modo audiant, ut a debito absolutii [-uti *A*] debitum non exigant, non reddant de cetero, uterque contineat, castus in incesti uita incestus in sua uita. Dicit aliquis (*B* 77vb) eum qui non peccauit iniuste dampnari, uidelicet ut separetur ab uxore, qui non peccauit cum uxore. Quod ille peccauit cuius uxor recens nupta infirmatur aut eripitur aut quolibet alio modo tantopere alienatur, ut ipse uiuente ea continere cogatur sine ea; occulta sunt Dei iudicia, sed tamen iusta. Ideo fortassis uoluit innocentem pati in hac uita, ut tali patientia probatum collocaret in eterna uita. Preterea etsi de coniugis reatu coniux innocens nulla sorde inquinatur, nonne id ei ad communem penam sufficere uidetur quod unum sunt corpus et una caro."

After two early letters of Anselm (37 and 2), the anthology then follows with Pope Paschal II's letter to Henry I, sent after Pentecost 1101. It does not occur among manuscripts containing the letters of Anselm, although it was quoted by Eadmer within his *Historia novorum* (no. 216 within Schmitt's edition).[45] While the next two letters in *B*, from Anselm to the bishop of Rochester (no. 300; c. 15 August 1103) and to Henry I (no. 308; December 1103) are found in the known Anselmian letter collections, its penultimate letter (no. 224) from Paschal II to Henry I is known only through its quotation by Eadmer.[46] He explains that Henry's episcopal envoys to Rome—Gerard,

---

(45) JAFFÉ-LOEWENFELD n. 5868 or no. 49 (*PL* 163, 70) among Paschal's letters. Edited by Schmitt (4, 115-118) from the MS (London, British Library, Cotton Titus A ix) of Eadmer's *Historia novorum*, pp. 128-131, and the Vatican MS, Vat. lat. 6024, ff. 156ᵛ-157ʳ (s. xii-xiii). This Vatican MS, not listed by Schmitt within his *Ratio Edendi* contains an important collection of the letters, including those of Hildebert of Lavardin, Arnulf of Lisieux, John of Salisbury and Ivo of Chartres as well as the Register of letters relating to Thomas Becket assembled by David of London, the canon of St Paul's who represented the case of Henry II to Pope Alexander III in the 1170s. According to the *Inventarium librorum latinorum MSS Bibliothecae Vaticanae*, vol. 6 (in manuscript, but now available within *A Corpus of Unpublished Inventories of Latin Manuscripts through 1600 A.D.*, prepared under the direction of F. Edward CRANZ [New London, Connecticut, 1988] reel 221) Paschal II's letter is preceeded on f. 155ʳ by a letter against clerical marriage, "Anselmus vita peccator, G. sacerdoti...". This letter, edited by F. Liverani within his *Spicilegium Liberianum* (Florence, 1863), pp. 559-63 but not mentioned by Schmitt in his *Opera Omnia*, relates to an issue at the forefront of Anselm's mind in 1102 at the Council of Westminster. Zachary N. BROOKE describes the manuscript as a small quarto volume written in different hands, probably all English in the thirteenth century; the small quire (ff. 155-7) containing the texts of Anselm and of Paschal II is sandwiched between quires containing the Register of Master David (ff. 140-154) and 134 letters of John of Salisbury (ff. 158-178), "The Register of Master David of London, and the part he played in the Becket crisis", *Essays in History Presented to R. Lane Poole* (Oxford, 1927), pp. 227-245. Christopher BROOKE has showed that John of Salisbury's letters in MS Vat. lat. 6024 were copied from the Paris MS, BN lat. 8625, *The Letters of John of Salisbury (1153-1161)* vol. 1 (2nd ed. London, 1986), p. lix-lx. The part of the MS relating to Arnulf was discussed by Frank BARLOW, *The Letters of Arnulf of Lisieux*, Camden, 3rd Series, 61 (London, 1939), pp. lxxiii and lxxxii. The association of Paschal II's letter with a text of "Anselm" perhaps prepared for the Council of Westminster as well as with the Register of David of London, suggests that these texts may have been preserved in or near the Palace of Westminster.

(46) *Historia novorum*, pp. 134-5; JAFFÉ-LOEWENFELD n. 5910; ed. SCHMITT 4; 129-130 (from Eadmer's text only).

newly appointed by the king (not by Anselm) as archbishop of York, Herbert
of Norwich and Robert of Chester—refused to show the Pope's letter to
Anselm, claiming that it confirmed the royal cause. However, someone very
highly placed in the royal court leaked the letter, embarrassing Henry's supporters by its clear statement of the papal position.[47] The last letter in *B* is one
(no. 222) which Paschal II sent at the same time to Anselm and which was
incorporated in other Anselmian letter collections. The draft chapters *Cur
deus magis* follow after a small space without any introductory heading.

The inclusion within *B* of two letters from the Pope to Henry I, known to
Eadmer but not otherwise found in collections of Anselm's letters (nos. 216
and 224 within Schmitt's edition) may not be unrelated to the presence in that
manuscript of other Anselmian documents with links to Llanthony. This
Augustinian house was initially established in 1103 as a hermitage on the
Welsh border by William, a household knight of the great Herefordshire
magnate Hugh de Lacy, and Ernisius, former chaplain to queen Mathilda
"and one of the foremost figures in the royal palace."[48] At Anselm's suggestion, the hermitage was turned into a community living under the Augustinian
Rule in 1108 through the benefaction of Hugh de Lacy. It was blessed by the
newly consecrated bishop of Hereford, Reinhelm, former chancellor to
Mathilda. Reinhelm had initially been appointed by Henry as a "safe" candi-
date to that see in 1102, but he then turned against the king by refusing to be
consecrated by the new archbishop of York, another royal appointee. As
Anselm went into exile on 27 April 1103, Reinhelm had to wait until
11 August 1107 to be properly consecrated bishop, only shortly after a
compromise had been reached with Henry, facilitating his return.[49] As the

(47) *Historia novorum*, p. 137: "Attamen quo tunc sollicitius sunt celatae, eo latius post
aliquot dies sunt divulgatae."

(48) William DUGDALE, *Monasticon Anglicanum*, revd. ed. (London, 1830), 6.1 569-70
with transcription of the *Historia Abbatiae de Lanthony* in the section on Lanthony Secunda,
128-34, p. 130; "Erat itaque vir iste Ernisius in curia Henrici regis primi, inter primos palatii
nominatissimus, capellanus videlicet venerandae Matildis reginae, uxoris eiusdem Henrici, qui
post inexplicabiles errorum circuitus, tandem ad suave heremiticae vitae sabbatum divina
miseratione respiravit." On the de Lacy involvement with Llanthony, see W. E. WIGHTMAN,
The Lacy Family in England and Normandy 1066-1194 (Oxford, 1966), pp. 183-4; see too
David KNOWLES, *Heads of Religious Houses in England and Wales 940-1216* (Cambridge,
1972), p. 172 and *Medieval Religious Houses in England and Wales* (London, 1971), p. 164.
The library was transferred to Lanthony Secunda, in Gloucestershire in 1136. A 1380 catalogue survives, edited by H. OMONT in *Zentralblatt für Bibliothekswesen* 9 (1892) and reprinted by T. W. WILLIAMS, "Gloucestershire Mediaeval Libraries", *Transactions of the Bristol
and Gloucestershire Archeological Society* 31 (1908), 139-78. Following the work of M. R.
James, Neil R. KER identifies many Lanthony MSS in the Royal and Lambeth Palace collections (but not *B*) in *Medieval Libraries of Great Britain* (2nd ed. London, 1964), pp. 108-112.

(49) *Historia novorum*, pp. 144-5, 187; see too VAUGHN, *Anselm of Bec and Robert of
Meulan*, pp. 248-9, 308-9.

former chancellor and chaplain to the queen, Reinhelm and Ernisius were in a key position to have divulged the letter so compromising to Henry. Mathilda was at the time affectionately close to Anselm, even though in 1101 he had initially resisted her arguments that she had worn a veil at Wilton abbey only under duress.[50] Was Ernisius' flight to the Welsh border prompted by his own involvement in making public the Pope's letter to the king?

As newly consecrated bishop of Hereford, Reinhelm was also in a good position to have bequeathed a whole set of Anselm's writings to Llanthony Priory at its re-foundation in 1108, as well as confidential letters from the Pope to Henry I from the early years of his reign. The small text about marriage may have been specifically written for the edification of Henry and Mathilda. Did Reinhelm collect what he could of Anselm's papers prior to the archbishop's departure in April 1103 and bequeath them to Llanthony for safe keeping? The last letters chronologically to be included in *B* were those Anselm sent from exile to the bishop of Rochester and to Henry in August and December of 1103. *CDM*, the draft of two chapters of the *De incarnatione uerbi*, was never intended as a text for wider publication. It may have been gathered up and later taken to Llanthony Prima at the same time as the *De humanis moribus per similitudines*, another work whose incomplete "draft status" character led to its being expanded with other material by disciples of Anselm into the *De similitudinibus*. The insecurity of the Welsh border eventually obliged Robert de Braci and his canons in 1134 to seek shelter at Hereford, where they were protected by Robert de Béthune, himself a former prior of the community, until they could establish a new foundation (Lanthony Secunda) near Gloucester in 1136.

The *De humanis moribus per similitudines* is not the only incomplete composition of St Anselm to occur in manuscripts from the Llanthony-Hereford region. His subsequent, though still incomplete sketch of the *De incarnatione uerbi* (based on *DIV*[1] and *CDM*) occurs immediately after the *Cur deus homo* in a Hereford Cathedral MS (P.I.i; s. xii).[51] This draft is followed on f. 158[r] by the *Explanacio super alas cherubin et seraphin* (Incipit "Prima ala est confessio"), of Clement, second prior of Lanthony Secunda (c.1150-78).[52] We do

---

(50) *Historia novorum*, pp. 121-5. Sometine c.1100/1103 she wrote to Anselm urging him not to follow excessively harsh personal austerities, eliciting from him a moralistic reply, *Epist.* 233-234 (4, 150-4).

(51) A. T. BANNISTER, *A Descriptive Catalogue of the Manuscripts in the Hereford Cathedral Library* (Hereford, 1927), p. 98. Rodney Thomson is currently engaged on a new catalogue of the Hereford Cathedral Library manuscripts.

(52) Clement succeeded to William de Wycombe (made prior in 1137, after Robert de Braci's death) after William was ousted by Roger Earl of Hereford; DUGDALE, 6.1, 133-4. The 1380 catalogue of Lanthony Secunda lists his commentaries on the Psalms (no. 49), on Acts, the Pauline epistles (= MS Royal 2 D V, possibly an autograph), Revelation (nos. 108-110), *De concordia IIII[or] Evangelistarum*, his *Summa de dyalectica et theologia*, his *Dialectica* and *Grammatica* (nos. 102-107).

not know where William of Malmesbury (d. 1143) found the copy of DIV^1 which he copied with other Anselmian letters into the Lambeth Palace MS 224; while he might have found it at Canterbury, this is not certain as no other Canterbury collection of Anselm's corpus includes the text.[53]

Another unique collection of Anselmian texts occurs in the Hereford Cathedral MS O.I.vi (s. xii), a manuscript initially given to the Augustinian abbey of Cirencester by a canon Joscelin sometime between 1131 and 1147. Besides a number of interesting arithmetical texts it includes on f. 81ᵛ under the rubric *Anselmi archepiscopi de dictis quaedam* (at the foot of f. 81) a version of chapters 2, 6-13, 15, 18-20 of the *Proslogion* which omits all passages in an Augustinian mode of direct address to God.[54] While it could be argued that a disciple may have made a host of small changes—deliberately removed chapters 3-5 on the so-called "ontological argument" questioned by Gaunilo (not so much a proof of God's existence as an extension of the meditation) and the final chapters 23-26, introducing Augustinian images of the Trinity—the Hereford *Proslogion* can also be read as Anselm's preparation for the final text. We have already seen that *CDM* differs from the finished version of the *De incarnatione uerbi* in being more of a debate with Boethius than the final version, which adopts—externally at least—a more Augustinian dress in the interests of greater acceptability to its audience. The Hereford *Proslogion* deserves further close study to see whether a "draft" hypothesis may illuminate its text.[55] While the Anselmian *similitudines* which follow the *Proslogion* on f. 83ᵛ at the marginal note *De rotulo* do not match exactly any of the other analogies assembled in other Llanthony-Hereford region manuscripts of the *De humanis moribus per similitudines,* they bear a similar character of being raw notes rather than being a careful adaptation of a disciple, like the *De similitudinibus.* Evans is probably correct in deducing that the source of the

---

(53) Montague Rhodes JAMES, *A Descriptive Catalogue of the Manuscripts in the Library of Lambeth Palace* (London, 1930-32), p. 5. See too Schmitt's Prolegomena, 1, 165*-171*. On William of Malmesbury's travels and involvement in this manuscript, see Rodney THOMSON, *William of Malmesbury* (Woodbridge, 1987), pp. 46, 87-89.

(54) Gillian R. EVANS, "The Hereford *Proslogion"*, *Anselm Studies. An Occasional Journal* 1 (New York, 1983), 253-73.

(55) Evans' preference for interpreting the text as a disciple's reworking of the *Proslogion* is based on her acceptance of established editorial assumptions, *art. cit.* 253: "Anselm seems to have taken care to ensure that his treatises were copied exactly. It is unlikely that any new discoveries will substantially alter the picture or throw seriously into question the work of A. Wilmart and F. S. Schmitt in establishing the text of his works." Her only textual argument against Anselmian authorship is based on the presence of one (unspecified) chapter heading in the final version in the Hereford text and her assumption that all the final chapter headings are inauthentic because they do not occur in the Oxford MS Rawlinson A 392 (s. xiᵉˣ). As the Rawlinson MS of the *Proslogion* contains the slightly revised recension of the *Proslogion,* namely with the rejoinder to Gaunilo, this fact cannot be used to disprove the draft status of the Hereford recension.

Anselmian material in MS O.I.vi were the texts available at Llanthony, an Augustinian house with which canon Joscelin could easily have had contact.[56] Southern and Schmitt's re-assertion of Anselm's authorship of the *De humanis moribus per similitudines* (against its rejection by Dom Wilmart) must serve to re-open the question of whether other texts of an "Anselmian vein" in *B* might also be re-considered as authentic. Wilmart noted the congruency of the prayer to the guardian angel with authentic prayers of Anselm, but did not come to any conclusion about its authorship.[57] The short draft *CDM* and the brief opinion about marriage share with the *De humanis moribus* the character of preparatory notes. The homily *De triplici silentio* found in *B* and attributed in other MSS to Anselm has a strongly Anselmian character, as does the most significant unpublished text in *B*—the *Disputatio inter christianum et gentilem.*

In this dialogue the Christian endeavours to explain to the Gentile, a philosophical non-believer, why an omnipotent God should have deigned to submit himself to mortal human nature in order to redeem man, on rational grounds rather than on those of any written authority that would not be accepted by the Gentile. The Christian's argument for the logical necessity for a God-man to take man's place in making satisfaction to God is similar to that developed in the *Cur deus homo,* except that it does not contain any specific refutation of the traditional argument about the devil's legitimate rights over sinful man. In this the *Disputatio* is similar to the discussions of the redemption in Gilbert Crispin's own discussion of the redemption in his widely-read *Disputatio Iudei et Christiani,* a work which bears the fruit of Anselm's own thinking on the Incarnation as it stood at the time of his re-drafting the *De incarnatione uerbi* in England 1092/93.[58] In not reproducing Boso's argument in the *Cur deus homo* about the rights of the devil, the *Disputatio* also resembles another treatise (in systematic rather than dialogue form) that is also attributed to Anselm in the manuscript tradition, the *Libellus Anselmi Cur Deus Homo.*[59]

(56) *Art. cit.* 255. Evans edits these *similitudines* on pp. 264-9 of this article.

(57) WILMART, *Auteurs spirituels et textes dévots du Moyen Âge latin* (Paris, 1932), pp. 544-51.

(58) See above n. 30.

(59) Edited by Eugène DRUWÉ under the title *Libri sancti Anselmi "Cur Deus Homo": Prima Forma Inedita,* Analecta Gregoriana 3 (Rome, 1933). Druwé's claim that it could be identified with the *primae partes* of the *Cur deus homo* which Anselm says were being transcribed without his permission (*CDH* Pref., ed. Schmitt 2, 42.2) met a hostile reception from Jean RIVIÈRE, who thought the work "unworthy" of Anselm, "Un premier jet du 'Cur deus homo'?", *Revue des sciences religieuses* 14 (1934), 329-69. DRUWÉ's reaction to these criticisms, "La première rédaction du 'Cur deus homo' de saint Anselm", *Revue d'histoire ecclésiastique* 31 (1935), 501-40 provoked an even more acerbic reply from RIVIÈRE, "La question du Cur deus homo", *Revue des sciences religieuses* 16 (1936), 1-32. This polemic, coupled with a negative reaction from Dom SCHMITT, then engaged on his own edition of the works of Anselm, "Zur Entstehungsgeschichte von Anselms 'Cur deus homo' ", *Theologische Revue* 34 (1935), 217-224, had the unfortunate effect of silencing investigation into a work that is still of great interest. While Southern rightly noted that Anselm's rejection of the rights of the devil

78

This treatise, whose authorship has been much contested, was included c. 1120 by Lambert of Saint-Omer within his *Liber Floridus*, an encyclopaedia that indirectly helped disseminate Anselmian theology in the Flanders region.[60] As in Gilbert Crispin's Dialogue between a Christian and a Gentile, the Gentile in the *Disputatio* becomes a Disciple to the Master for its last section, so that its author can deliver a homily on the sacraments of the Christian faith.[61] While Wilmart noted the evident similarity between this *Disputatio* and the treatise of Gilbert Crispin in a footnote, he did not consider the work authentic.[62]

Wilmart did not realize that the *Disputatio inter christianum et gentilem* in *B* occurs in a significantly fuller version within the Hereford Cathedral MS O.I.xii, ff. 32ʳ-107ʳ (s. xii; unattributed but in a MS containing on f. 1ʳ the Anselmian homily *De triplici silentio* found in *B* and other manuscripts) and in the Berlin, Staatsbibliothek MS theol. fol. 276, ff. 48ᵛ-55ᵛ (s. xii) from the

did not gain wide acceptance, he is not quite correct in implying that his opinions on the matter were adhered to by the author of the *Disputatio* and the *Libellus, Saint Anselm and his biographer*, p. 96 n. 1.

(60) Anselm stayed at the monastery of Saint-Bertin, outside the city walls of Saint-Omer during the first week of his exile from England (10-16 November 1097) but also dedicated an altar for the canons of Saint-Omer, within the city, *Vita Anselmi* 25 (ed. SOUTHERN 101-2). He had long discussions with Lambert, abbot of Saint-Bertin 1095-1125 (not the author of the *Liber Floridus*) which Lambert recorded within his *Tractatus de moribus* (MGH SS 14, 946-53), a work whose discussions of *bonum, malum* and *medium* are close to those of Anselm's *De humanis moribus* (cf. SOUTHERN's *The Life of St Anselm*, p. 101 n. 1). DRUWÉ noted that Lambert of Saint-Omer used the monastic library of Saint-Bertin to compile his *Liber Floridus* (*op. cit.*, p. 19), but not the combined testimony of Eadmer and Lambert of Saint-Bertin about Anselm's visit in 1097, which could be used to strengthen his hypothesis about the work's authenticity. Lambert's autograph (Ghent, Bibliothèque de la ville 92, ff. 144ᵛ-152ᵛ) has been reproduced in facsimile, *Liber Floridus: codex autographus Bibliothecae Universitatis Gandavensis*, ed. Albert DEROLEZ (Ghent, 1968). Independent copies of the work used by Lambert survive in Paris, BN lat. 16699, ff. 152ʳ-159ᵛ (from the Benedictine abbey of Notre-Dame-de-Pré, Rouen) and Brussels, Bibl. royale lat. 1384, ff. 1ʳ-17ᵛ (Notre-Dame, Cambe-ron). At least nine copies derive from the Ghent autograph, L. DELISLE, "Notice sur les manuscrits du 'Liber Floridus' composé en 1120 par Lambert, chanoine de Saint-Omer", *Notices et extraits des mss de la Bibl. nationale* 38.2 (Paris, 1906), 577-791. See now *Liber Floridus Colloquium, University of Ghent*, ed. A. DEROLEZ (Ghent, 1973). As SOUTHERN notes in *The Life of St Anselm*, pp. xvi-xviii, Eadmer's *Vita Anselmi* was much copied in abbeys of this region, as at Clairmarais (O. Cist. near Saint-Omer), Anchin and Tournai. The presence of Eadmer's *Life* at Clairvaux in a copy textually related to the Flanders group of MSS suggests that other works of Anselm could have reached Clairvaux from the Flanders region. Anselm's writings are not otherwise widely known in France and Burgundy; cf. SCHMITT's list of MSS in his *Ratio Editionis* (1, 213*-225*).

(61) Gilbert's *Disputatio Christiani cum Gentili de fide Christi* was edited by C. C. J. WEBB, "Gilbert Crispin, abbot of Westminster: dispute of a Christian with a Heathen touching the faith of Christ", *Mediaeval and Renaissance Studies* 3 (1954), 55-77 and again by Anna Sapir ABULAFIA and Gillian EVANS, *The Works of Gilbert Crispin* (London, 1986), pp. 61-87.

(62) "Les homélies attribuées à S. Anselme", *ADHLMA* 2 (1927), 11 n.4.

Abbey of Maria Laach.[63] In the Maria Laach manuscript (not used by
Schmitt) the *Disputatio* follows Anselm's late treatises, the *Cur deus homo, De
conceptu virginali et de peccato originali* and *De fermentato et azimo*, while
preceding the *Dialogues between a Christian and a Jew* of both Odo of Cambrai and Gilbert Crispin. As Wilmart noted, the incomplete form of the *Disputatio* as found in *B* also occurs in a family of fourteenth-century manuscripts
that contain the complete works of Anselm as well as a chain of other texts
clearly composed by disciples and imitators.[64] In the light of past fierce
controversy over the paternity of the *Libellus Anselmi Cur Deus homo*, we
supply a preliminary text of the *Disputatio* as presented in *B* (*not* a critical
edition) in the interest of provoking discussion among Anselmian scholars,
without making any claims to its authorship.

   B transmits a rich tapestry of Anselmian themes, even though it does not
emanate from those monastic scriptoria of Bec or Canterbury which have
been so influential in defining the known corpus of Anselm's writings. Southern and Schmitt have already pointed to the role of Llanthony in collecting
together unpolished notes of Anselm, the *De humanis moribus* into a bigger
work, the *De similitudinibus*. The letters in *B* have led us to suggest that either
Ernisius, first prior of Llanthony, or Reinhelm, bishop of Hereford, may
have sought to collect various writings of Anselm prior to his going into exile
a second time in 1103. The little draft *Cur deus magis* could have been one
such text copied out with other Anselmian writings certainly by the time of
Robert de Braci, third prior of Llanthony, 1130-37. In 1131 its second prior,
Robert de Béthune, a former pupil of William of Champeaux and Anselm of
Laon, became bishop of Hereford.[65] Four years later he welcomed Robert de
Braci and his canons to Hereford, where they stayed until they founded a

---

(63) BANNISTER, *Catalogue of Hereford Cathedral*, pp. 14-15; Valentin ROSE, *Die Hand-
schriften-Verzeichnisse der Königlichen Bibliothek zu Berlin* Bd 13. *Verzeichniss der Lateinischen Handschriften* Bd. 2.i (Berlin, 1901) no. 355, pp. 177-178. The Berlin MS had not been
noticed by Wilmart, but was mentioned briefly by Bernhard BLUMENKRANZ in the introduction to his edition of Gilbert Crispin's *Disputatio Iudei et Christiani et Anonymi Auctoris
Disputationis Iudei et Christiani Continuatio*, Stromata Patristica et Mediaevalia 3 (Antwerp-
Utrecht, 1956), p. 7. The Hereford MS has not hitherto been noted in the scant literature
relating to the *Disputatio*; cf. the comment of ABULAFIA and EVANS, *The Works of Gilbert
Crispin*, p. xxxii n. 7 which simply refers back to the comment of Blumenkranz and Wilmart's
initial footnote.

(64) WILMART, *loc. cit.*, noting its presence in the following fourteenth-century collections
of Anselm's works: Oxford, Lincoln College lat. 18, ff. 86[rb]-89[ra], Magdalen 56, ff. 136-,
Bodleian Laud. Misc. 264, ff. 122[rb]-125[va] (all now housed in the Bodleian Library); Cambridge, Peterhouse 246, ff. 101[va]-104[rb] (housed in C.U.L.) and University Lib. Dd 1.21,
ff. 181[ra]-183[ra], Worcester F 132, ff. 194- and a fragment only in Paris, BN lat. 1769, f. 131[r].
On the non-Anselmian works in the collection, see the description of *C* that follows.

(65) On Robert's education see the *Vita domini Roberti de Betune* in Henry WHARTON ed.
Anglia Sacra (London, 1691) 2, 293-300 and Frank BARLOW, *The English Church 1066-1154*
(London, 1979), pp. 88, 229, 249-50.

80

more permanent priory at Lanthony Secunda. As an Augustinian canon, he was undoubtedly interested in making the reflections of a great monastic thinker available to a wider audience at the cathedral of Hereford. The evidence suggests that the various texts found in *B* derive from documents possessed by the canons of Llanthony from a very early date in their history. The manuscript itself may have belonged either to Lantony Secunda or to another community in the Hereford-Gloucestershire region.

C CAMBRIDGE, University Library, Dd.I.21, ff. 147[rb-vb]; s. xiv.[66]

Nothing is known of the provenance of this manuscript other than that it belonged to one William Berier in the fifteenth century. The draft *Cur deus magis* occurs without title immediately after Anselm's *Proslogion* in this manuscript, which combines a large collection of Anselm's writings with a number of works attributed to him. It also contains Augustine's *City of God*, his *Enchiridion*, the *Liber de ecclesiasticis dogmatibus* attributed to him (in fact by Gennadius) and the *De miseria condicionis humanae* of Innocent III. Like *B*, *C* contains the *Disputatio inter christianum et gentilem* (ff. 178[r]-180[r]), here sandwiched between Anselm's *De concordia praedestinationis et gratiae cum libero arbitrio* and his *De veritate*. Similarly it contains the *De similitudinibus*, though here at the end of the manuscript.

Unlike *B*, *C* does not contain any of Anselm's letters. However, in common with other related fourteenth-century compilations which include the *Disputatio*, it includes on ff. 163[v]-172[v] a series of texts which were quite certainly composed by disciples of Anselm. These are Eadmer's *De conceptione beate Virginis*, the *De excellentia beate Virginis* (*PL* 159, 301-8 and 557-80), the *De antichristo* (attributed variously to Augustine, *PL* 40, 1131-34 or Alcuin, *PL* 101, 1089-1098), *De corpore et sanguine Christi* (*PL* 159, 255-7), *De occupatione bona* (the last part of which is among the works of Hugh of St Victor, *PL* 177, 185-88) and Ralph d'Escures' homily on *Intrauit Iesus* (*PL* 158, 644-9).[67] While the collection in *C* may have been modelled on an exemplar close to *B*, these non-Anselmian texts have also been added to *C* (or its exemplar) from other sources. That none of these six non-Anselmian works occur within *B* serves to strengthen the respect with which we should consider the other hitherto unpublished texts in this manuscript, here as elsewhere attributed to Anselm either explicitly or by association. Those monks who endeavoured to compile lists of Anselm's writings, mostly from Canterbury or

---

(66) *Catalogue of Manuscripts preserved in the Library of the University of Cambridge* (Cambridge, 1856) 1, 27-33.
(67) A. WILMART, "Les homélies attribuées à S. Anselme", 8-16.

the continent, did not have access to manuscripts from the Llanthony region which only became widely known in the thirteenth and fourteenth centuries.[68] While *C* does not contribute much to the text of *CDM*, it shares some variants in common with *B*. *A* belongs to a separate tradition that is not totally reliable. As the first part of *CDM* is incorporated into the draft *H* of the *De incarnatione uerbi*, we observe that *B* generally contains the best text, although it cannot be followed in every case.[69]

(68) Cf. ROBERT DE TORIGNY, *Chronicon,* ed. L. DELISLE (Rouen, 1872), pp. 135-136; SIGEBERT OF GEMBLOUX, *Chronicon Sigeberti* (*PL* 160, 429, 568); a monk of Bec (*PL* 150, 775); HONORIUS AUGUSTODUNENSIS, *De luminaribus ecclesiae* 4.15 (*PL* 172, 232).

(69) This study was completed before publication of R. W. SOUTHERN's major rewriting of his earlier biography, a work that will become a classic in its own right, *Saint Anselm. A Portrait in a Landscape* (Cambridge, 1990). He identifies another text, *Sententia Anselmi archiepiscopi de motione altaris*, as authentic in the MSS Hereford Cathedral O.I. VI, f. 43 and Oxford, Bodleian Library, Digby 158, f. 91 (from Cirencester), *op. cit.*, p. 257. Schmitt rejected this letter because it did not occur in the standard Bec and Canterbury collections of the correspondence.

82

A

<CUR DEUS MAGIS>

A Paris, Bibliothèque de l'Arsenal 269, ff. 107r-108v (s. xii2).
B London, British Library 5 E xiv, ff. 81rb-82va (s. xiii).
C Cambridge, University Library Dd.I.21, ff. 147rb-vb (s. xiv).
For the first part of *CDM* the text of the *De incarnatione uerbi* c. 10 (ed.
Schmitt 2, 25.6-28.4) in the Hereford Cathedral MS P.I.i, ff. 154v-155v (*H*;
s. xii2) has also been used.

Anselmus. Quod magis conueniat filio incarnatio quam patri uel spiritui
sancto.a

Cur Deusb magis assumpserit hominem in unitatem persone filii, quam in
unitatem alicuius aliarum personarum? Hanc c reddendam rationem existimo.
Nempe si spiritus sanctus incarnatus esset, sicut filius est incarnatus, esset
spiritus sanctus filius hominis. Essent igitur duo filii in trinitate Dei, filius
scilicet Dei et filius hominis. Quare quedam fieret confusio cum de Deo filio
loqueremur; et fieretd quasi quedam inequalitas diuersarum personarum,
secundum hoc quod filiie essent, que omninof equales esse debentg; cum alter
filius maioris parentis dignitate excelleret, alter minoris parentis humilitate
subesset. Quanto enim maior est natura Dei quam hominis, tanto dignius est
esse filium Dei quam esse filium hominis. Si ergo spiritus sanctus natus esset ex
uirgine, cum filius Dei haberet excellentiorem natiuitatem solam que est ex
Deo (*B* 81va) et spiritus sanctus minorem tantum que est ex homine, alia persona esset maior, et alia minor secundum dignitatem natiuitatis. Quod si pater
in unitatem sue persone hominem assumpsisset, easdem faceret in Deo pluralitas filiorum inconuenientias, et adhuc aliam. Nam si pater esset filius uirginis,
esset homo pater Dei sicut nunch est filius Dei. Esset igitur filius Dei filiusi
hominis qui uere esset filius uirginis. Quare filius Dei uirginis esset nepos. Si
autem filius Dei nepos esset uirginis, ergo et illa auia (*A* 107v) negari j non
posset. (*C* 147va).

Quoniam ergo quamlibet paruum inconueniens in Deo est impossibile, non
debuit alia Dei persona incarnari quam filius. Cum enim una persona sit filius

(a) Anselmus... sancto *om. BC*   (b) Cur] autem *add. H*   (c) Hanc] quamuis in hac
epistola nostrum hoc non fuerit propositum, tamen quoniam huius rei mentio se obtulit,
aliquam *H*   (d) fieret] sicut *C*   (e) filii *bis BC*   (f) omnino] omnes *C*   (g) debent]
deberent *A*   (h) non *H*; deus *proposuit Schmitt 2.26*   (i) dei filius *B H*; *om.*
AC   (j) negare *H*

Dei et filius[k] hominis, non sunt propter incarnationem filii in trinitate, filii plures quam erant ante incarnationem, nec ipse filius alii persone in dignitate natiuitatis excellit, sed idem ipse filius se ipso maior et minor existit. Sed nec alie persone maiores sunt filio secundum generationem, quia nullam habent maiorem uel digniorem natiuitatem uel generationem. Nam quod[l] modo patre dicitur[m] minor filius et spiritu sancto secundum humanitatem, non tamen ideo ille due persone excellent filio, quia eandem maiestatem qua maiores sunt humanitate filii, habet et filius qua et ipse preest cum illis sue humanitati.

Est et aliud cur magis conueniat filio incarnatio quam patri. Qui enim erat incarnandus, maturus erat pro humano genere, et conuenientius satis suscipit mens humana filium patri supplicare quam patrem filio, quamuis hec supplicatio non fiat a diuinitate, sed ab humanitate ad diuinitatem. Quam idcirco filius Dei facit, quia homo per unitatem persone filius est Dei[n].

Amplius qui[o] hominem erat assumpturus, uenturus erat ad pugnandum (*B* 81[vb]) contra diabolum et ad intercedendum sicut dixi pro homine. Qui ambo, diabolus scilicet et homo, per rapinam se uoluerunt[p] facere similes et equales Deo, cum propria sunt[q] usi uoluntate, et quia per rapinam uoluerunt[r], non nisi per falsitatem potuerit. Solius[s] enim Dei est, propriam habere uoluntatem. Sola autem uoluntas Dei omnibus debet[t] preesse, et nulli subesse. Quicumque igitur propria uoluntate utitur, ad equalitatem et similitudinem Dei nititur, et Deum propria dignitate et singulari excellentia priuare quantum in ipso est conuincitur. Si enim est alia aliqua uoluntas que nulli subdita sit, non erit uoluntas Dei omnibus prelata, nec erit sola cui nulla alia possit. Ex[u] propria uoluntate omne malum est rationalis creature, siue quod dicitur peccatum seu quod uocatur incommodum. Si enim uoluntas rationalis creature semper subesset uoluntati Dei, nullum umquam fecisset peccatum, et si numquam peccasset, nullum aliquando pateretur incommodum. Nulla igitur trium personarum Dei congruentius «semetipsam exinaniuit[v], formam serui accipiens» ad debellandum diabolum et intercedendum pro homine[w], qui per rapinam falsam similitudinem et equalitatem presumpserant, quam filius qui splendor lucis eterne et uera patris imago «non rapinam arbitratus est esse se equalem Deo»[x], uerum per ueram equalitatem et similitudinem dixit : «Ego et pater unum sumus»[y]. Et : «Qui uidet me, uidet et patrem»[z].

Cur autem uel quam pulchra et necessaria ratione siue rationabili necessitate summa maiestas[a] cum[b] omnia sola uoluntate possit, nostram naturam[c] cum

---

(k) dei et filius *om. BC*   (l) quod] quodam *A H*   (m) dicitur patre *A*   (n) dei est *A*   (o) qui *uacat C*   (p) uoluerunt] uoluerit A   (q) sunt] sit *A*   (r) uoluerit *A*   (s) Melius *C*   (t) diebus *C*   (u) Et *C*   (v) existimet *C Phil.* 2:7   (w) per hominem *A*   (x) *Phil.* 2:6   (y) sumus *hic deficit H*   (z) *Ioh.* 10:30, 14:9   (a) magestas *A*   (b) cum *BC*   (c) naturam nostram *A*

84

infirmitate et mortalitate (A 108^r) nostra absque peccato ad uincendum diabolum et liberandum hominem assumpserit, quod utique multi querunt, si huic epistole insererem, nimis longa esset digressio. Aliquando (B 82ra) tamen si diuina gratia effectum uoluntati mee tribuerit, quod inde michi dignata est ostendere, multorum qui hoc a me audierunt^d precibus compulsus, scribere desidero. De unitate uero persone Dei et hominis quam firmissime credimus esse non ex duabus personis sed ex duabus naturis in Christo; tamen quia potest aliquid dici, unde parum caute intuentibus uideri possit Christus ex duabus et in duabus personis existere, non inutile michi uidetur questionem ipsam hic facere, atque id quod contra fidem nostram dici posse uidetur, adiuuante Deo^e dissoluere. Non enim sufficit cum aliquid quodlibet firmis argumentis probatur, nisi quod ex aduerso pari ratione obici uidetur dissoluatur. Quamuis enim Boetius probet contra Nestorium Christum non ex duabus personis existere, non tamen michi^f uidetur Nestorii rationem qua^g duas uult in Christo asserere^h personas destruere. Potest itaque aliquis dicere sic : « Si persona est rationalis natura indiuidua, sicut Boetius ubi contra Nestorium disputat definit, et in Christo sunt due rationales nature, scilicet diuina et humana, et unaqueque^i indiuidua est Deus^j, indiuiduus est enim homo ille, et indiuiduus est^k Deus, ergo uidetur due persone in Christo esse, persona scilicet Dei, et persona hominis. Nam Deus et ante hominis assumptionem persona erat, nec postquam hominem assumpsit persona destitit esse, et homo assumptus persona est, quia omnis homo indiuduus esse^l persona cognoscitur.» Que ratio per hoc aliam personam esse in Christo hominem, et aliam Deum probare nititur, quia duo rationalia indiuidua putat in^m illo esse, hominem scilicet et Deum. Vtrumque enim constat rationale esse et indiuiduum. Si ergo quamuis unumquodque de duobus rationalibus sit indiuiduum, possumus ostendere in Christo duo rationalia non esse duo^n indiuidua, sed unum indiuiduum, certum est quia eneruata erit predicta duarum personarum assertio. Hoc quidem constat quia in Christo Deus est rationale indiuiduum et homo similiter rationale indiuiduum^o. Nec hoc dubium est, quia aliud rationale Deus et aliud (B 82rb) homo, quam aliud Deus et aliud homo. Alia namque est^p natura Dei, alia hominis. Nam quamuis idem ipse sit Deus qui homo, non tamen idem ipsum est Deus quod homo^q. Consideremus ergo an alter^r ab altero sic sit aliud indiuiduum, sicut est^s aliud rationale, ut ita sint^t duo indiuidua, sicut sunt duo rationalia. Philosophi utique diffiniunt esse indiuiduum, cuius proprietatum collectio non est in alio eadem, id est non dicitur de alio^u. Ergo si in Christo aliud indiuiduum est homo, aliud Deus, que dicuntur de homine non

---

(d) adierunt C (e) deo] posse *add. Bac*   (f) michi *om. BC*   (g) qua] quam *BacC*   (h) asserere] rationes *Bac*   (i) unaqueque] una que A (j) deus *om. A*   (k) est *om. A*   (l) est *BC*   (m) in *inter lin. A*; *om. BC*   (n) duo *om. BC*   (o) et homo similiter... indiuiduum *om. C*   (p) est *om. A*   (q) non tamen... quod homo *om. C*   (r) aliter *BC*   (s) est *om. BC*   (t) sunt C (u) Porphirius, *Isagoge* 7-21 (n. 15 *supra*)

dicuntur eadem de Deo; neque ea que Dei sunt de homine dicuntur. Et si ea
que Dei sunt, et ea que hominis sunt communiter dicuntur de Deo et de[v]
homine, non erunt duo indiuidua sed unum, Deus et homo. At quia[w] tanta est
in Christo Dei et hominis conexio, ut que dicuntur de Deo secundum deitatem
(*A* 108[v]) et que de homine secundum humanitatem, dicantur communiter[x] et
de Deo et de[y] homine, secundum coniunctionis indiuisibilem unitatem. Deus
enim[z] dicitur homo, et filius uirginis, et mortalis et mortuus et resurrexisse, et
ad celos ascendisse, quod totum est hominis; et homo dicitur Deus[a] et filius
Dei, et claritatem habuisse apud patrem antequam mundus fieret, et quecumque facit pater eadem facere et similiter, que omnia ex deitatis natura
sunt. Si uero dicit aliquis, quia[b] collectio proprietatum hominis non est
dicenda esse in Deo, nec ea que Dei est esse in homine, quoniam nec ea que
Dei sunt nec ea que hominis sunt similiter dicuntur de Deo et homine, nam ea
que de homine dicuntur secundum se, de Deo dicuntur secundum aliud, et que
de Deo secundum se dicimus, ea de homine secundum aliud dici manifestum
est; consideret quoniam qui describit indiuiduum esse cuius proprietatum collectio non est in alio[c] eadem, non[d] addit similiter sed tantum non est in alio
eadem. Quare si non possumus negare que[e] hominis sunt dici de Deo, et que
dici sunt de homine quamuis dissimiliter, nullatenus ualemus probare aliud
indiuiduum esse hominem et aliud Deum. Nam quamuis per se nec lingua
scripturam nec manus[f] uocem faciat, tamen tunc cognoscimus manum et linguam unius esse indiuidui et unius (*B* 82[va]) persone, cum lingua dicit «ego
scribo» et manus scribit «ego dico». Similiter omnia membra uel partes
hominis probamus eiusdem persone uel[g] indiuidui esse, quando lingua dicit
uel manus scribit se facere quod illa faciunt. Si autem[h] membra singula uel
partes loqui uel scribere possent, omnia pro omnibus inuicem loquerentur uel
scriberentur, que eiusdem essent indiuidui uel persone; sic quoque dominus
quia Petrus qui Rome iacet, est in paradyso, quamuis corpus secundum spiritum in paradyso sit, non secundum se; et similiter qui est in paradyso iacet in
monumento, cum spiritus non secundum se sed secundum corpus in terra
iaceat. Quapropter non est alius indiuiduus homo, nec alius Petrus; nec aliud
indiuiduum rationale, aut alia persona corpus Petri quam anima[i].

   (v) de *om. BC*   (w) quia] *in margine Bpc*; atqui *ABacC*   (x) -muniter *A*   (y) de
inter lin. B; *om. C*   (z) enim *om. C*   (a) deus *om. BC*   (b) quia] quod *C*   (c) non
est in alio] in alia *BC*   (d) non] Si *C*   (e) quoniam *BC*   (f) minus *C*   (g) uel *om.*
BC   (h) autem] in *C*   (i) anima.] Amen *add. C*

B

DISPUTATIO ANSELMI CANTUARIENSIS ARCHIEPISCOPI INTER CHRISTIANUM ET GENTILEM

I include here a transcription of the *Disputatio inter christianum et gentilem* as it occurs in *B* (London, British Library MS Royal 5 E xiv, ff. 70ra-74rb; s. xiii). This does *not* pretend to be a critical edition of the work, but is offered in the hope of promoting discussion of its authenticity, prior to a genuinely critical edition, based on all known manuscripts (see above, pp. 78-79). I have checked the text of *B* against four other manuscripts, all of the fourteenth century, and have ascertained that they are all of inferior quality (*L* Oxford, Lincoln College lat. 18, ff. 86rb-89ra, *O* Oxford, Bodleian Laud Misc 264, ff. 122rb-125va; *P* Cambridge, Peterhouse 246, ff. 101va-104rb; *U* Cambridge, University Lib. Dd 1.21, ff. 181ra-183ra). I came across the two twelfth-century manuscripts of the *Disputatio, (H)* Hereford Cathedral O.I.xii, ff. 82r-107r and Berlin, Staatsbibliothek theol. fol. 276, ff. 48v-55v (Rose 354), too late to be able to compare their text closely to that of *B*. Cursory examination of the Hereford MS, however, suggests that *B* represents a reliable if incomplete text, certainly more reliable than the fourteenth-century versions cognate to *B*. Obvious errors have been silently corrected.

Incipit disputatio Anselmi Cantuariensis archiepiscopi inter christianum et gentilem.

< *Gentilis.* > Maiestas divina cur ad dolores mortalis nature insuper et usque ad opprobria crucis se humiliauit, uellem addiscere. Quod quidem ex auctoritate uestrarum scripturarum uolo michi probari, cui non credo, sed si rationabiliter factum est, huius rei rationem quero.

Christianus. Christus uere filius Dei et verus Deus incarnatus et crucifixus est, ut homines liberaret a peccato, a pena inferni, a potestate diaboli et ab ira sua.

Gentilis. Dic, rogo, quis hominem dampnauit pro peccato?

Christianus. Ipse Deus.

Gentilis. Bene dixisti. Et quis eum addixit pene inferni?

Christianus. Ipse Deus.

Gentilis. Dampnare et penis addiscere potuit, liberare autem non potuit nisi prius ipse dampnaretur tamque turpiter cruciaretur. Quis hoc de Deo crediderit? Quod dixisti ab ira sua fuitne tam amaricatus felle ire sue quod non potuit eam condonare, si non prius se faceret interficere? ut de potestate diaboli hominem abstraheret iniustum non erat. Quando enim diabolus qui seruus Dei erat, hominem tunc Dei amicum eiusque creaturam seduxit, et uelud fraudator rerum domini sui eum suscepit et in mortem secum traxit, non meruit ut super eum potestatem haberet, sed si ei augeri tormenta possent non dico duplicari, sed si dici posset « milleplicari » debuissent. Quare cum nichil inius-

tum fecisset, si salua sua maiestate hominem liberaret : quod per omnipotentiam suam sine difficultate facere posset? Quis patienter ferat, Deum non
solum corruptioni et mortalitati subditum sed insuper sicut uanitas christianorum predicat, tam ignominiose cruci affixum?

Christianus. Quoniam displicet tibi Deum per humilitatem superbum hominem redemisse, consilium tuum qualiter hoc facere debeat, uellem audire.

Gentilis. Quia bonus et pius est, nec gaudet de pena malorum atque diues in
omnibus (*O* 122va) non indiget ut eis reddant si quid abstulerit, uel debitum non reddiderit, quid dignius tante maiestati quam gratis condonare
miseris?

Christianus. Quoniam tale consilium dedisti ei, non modo non te debet
(*B* 70rb) redimere, uerum si absque alio esses peccato, pro isto te deberet perhenniter dampnare. Nam si absque uindicta sicut tu uis nequitia peccati rema-
neret, iam nichil differet iusticie an iniusticie obaudire [obedire *Bac*], id est
persuadenti iniusticiam, siue admonenti iusticiam adquiescere ; unde consequi-
tur equales esse, qui Deo uel diabolo seruiunt. Sed quod nequitia libera non
debet regnare, ore prophetico precatur psalmista dicens : *Domine non miserea-
ris omnibus qui operantur iniquitatem.* Ad hoc quod opponis audisse te christianos laudentes ac predicantes Christi misericordiam dicentis : *Si quid habetis
aduersus aliquem dimittite* ei et non reddetis malum pro malo ; ad hanc oppositionem respondeo : Quando precipitur hominibus ne uindicent quod in eis
committitur, non prohibentur a suo, sed ne presumant de alieno. Qui hoc eis
preciperit, ipse idem dicit *Mihi reseruate uindictam, et ego retribuam,* et alibi
Mea est ultio, et ego retribuam eis in tempore. Et cum nec debeat nec possit
nequitiam punire, vix enim scitur ab homine quid promereatur qui peccat ut
iuste ei retribuat. Si nequitia manum omnipotentis euaderet, nonne contra
iusticiam libera regnaret? Attende adhuc quam impossibile sit hominem de
miseria quam peccando incurrit, eo modo quo dicis liberari. Rationalem
hominem ad hoc Deus condidit ut seruata iusticia, quod sine ulla difficultate
tenere potuit, ad equalitatem angelorum promoueretur. Et quoniam peccato
prolapsus ad illorum equalitatem angelorum non potest ascendere, conside-
randum est quid sit peccatum, per quod ei prohibetur equalitas angelorum.

Sic homo creatus est, ut uoluntati creatoris sui per omnia obediret et si non
esset sua uoluntas nisi ea tantum que Dei est, contra quam nullus potest, et
sine qua nichil est, beatus sine dubio esset. Beatus namque est, qui ea que iuste
uult, absque contradictione adimplet. Sed iam sicut proposuimus uideamus
quid sit peccatum. Cum homo peccat iniuste agit. At quam diu uoluntati Dei
obtemperat, nichil iniuste facit. Non est ergo aliud peccare nisi uoluntati Dei
contradicere. Sed qui uoluntati Dei contradicit, quantum in ipso est omnipotentiam eius destruit. (*B* 70va) Non enim est omnipotens, si non ualuerit
adimplere (*O* 102vb) quecumque uoluerit. Qui uero omnipotens non est, Deus
esse non potest. Iam considera quid committat homo dum peccat, qui non
solum contradicendo Dei uoluntati eum inhonorat. Dicimus enim seruus iste
inhonorat dominum suum quia non obedit ei, sed etiam quantum in ipso est

88

facit ut Deus non sit Deus. Imputatur quippe iure ei pro facto quod faceret si posset; uerum quantum potest, uoluntati Dei resistit. Quantum igitur in ipso est, Deus non solum ab eo seruo suo inhonoratur, sed ut *insipiens dixit in corde suo,* Deus *non est Deus.* Si uero Deus non est, omnino aliquid aliud non est, quia sine eo nichil est. Videsne quoniam qui peccat non solum reus est mortis Dei, sed ut destructionis omnium quecumque sunt uel esse possunt? Quomodo ergo poterit homo ad equalitatem angelorum prouehi absque digna satisfactione tanti reatus et iusta recompensatione tanti honoris, quem cum per subiectionem sancte obedientie Deo offerre debuisset, minime reddidit? Licet enim condonatum ei esset, conscius tamen sue inobedientie atque angelorum perseuerantis obedientie nunquam eque beatus esse posset. Quoniam qui ibi remordetur ubi magis refulget claritas beatitudinis, id est in conscientia, non dico beatus, sed qualiter potest esse sine miseria? Quem uero conscientia non accusat etiam in tormentis est absque miseria. Et si obtenebretur cruciatu extrinseco in conspectu hominum, fulgore tamen iusticie exhillaratur intus, ubi uidet Deus. Sed iam uideamus quanti sit precii illud quod homo Deo abstulit ut digna eius recompensatio estimari possit. Dico « abstulit », quia non reddidit quod debuit, sed quia quanti sit honor Dei quem ei homo obedienter non reddit, plene non ualemus considerare, uel consideremus pro quanto ipse non debeat inhonorari. Vt iam ostendimus, qui peccat contradicens eius uoluntati Deum inhonorat. Ecce si ea necessitate constrictus essem, ut aut celum et terram cum omnibus creaturis periret, aut contra (*L* 86rb) uoluntatem creaturis facerem, deberem ne ut cuncta ista reseruarentur uel mouere oculum ad dedecus Dei hoc nolentis et contradicentis? Potest hoc fieri inter homines ut seruus contra uoluntatem incauti domini faciat, conseruans illi uel adquirens quod admitteret, si iste tunc ei obediret? (*B* 70vb) Set hoc Deus non indiget. Nullus quippe potest ei auferre, quod ipse uult seruare. Et omnibus destructis facilius ea repararet, quam quis oculum mouere posset. Iam animaduerti potest quantus honor proueniat Deo ex obedientia hominis, qui pro conseruatione totius creature, angelorum, hominum, et omnium quecumque sunt uel esse possunt non deberet non reddi : obedientia que sola ad Deum ascendit, omnemque creaturam transcendit. Vbi ergo inueniet homo quod pro hoc honore equa recompensatione reddere possit? Alioquin angelo equalis esse non potuit, hunc honorem qui Deo assidue reddit.

Gentilis. Si uerum est quod asseris, qui peccando cadit resurgere utique non potuit, quando enim inuenerit homo, minima pars creature, tale aliquid quod non solum supra hominem, uerum etiam supra omnem angelicam dignitatem, immo supra omnem creaturam maneat, quod pro honore quem Deo non reddiderit iuste recompenset?

Christianus. Verum quidem est impossibile esse homini per se resurgere, si peccando ceciderit. Verum tamen oportet ne homo in perpetuum iaceat, qui peccando corruerat. Nec tamen obstupescis, set rogo, patienter audias. Deus hominem creauit ut esset beatus, et quod de numero angelorum perierat, per illum repararetur. Quod nisi Deus propositum suum compleuerit, criminabitur uel quod nescire resolidare quod fractum est, aut si scit non posse, aut si scit et potest. Dicemus ne sic eum indignari contra delinquentem hominem, ut imperfectum remaneat quod incepit, et tunc de Deo dicetur quod in euangelio ad exprobacionem dictum est, hic homo cepit edificare et non potuit consummare. Verum quia hoc uel illud indignum est dicere de Deo, conuenit ut ipse perficiat quod incepit.

Gentilis. Quid ergo? Ex necessitate Deus hominem redimit?

Christianus. Est necessitas que magis debet laudari et amari, quam si libera sit. Si quis egrotanti promitteret potionem qua salus ei uere posset reparari, differens non quia dare nollet, sed expectans egrotum adhuc infirmiorem ad uirtutem potionis sustinendam (*B* 71ra), ut tempus ad salutem eius oportunum inueniret, sola karitate hoc faciens, non quod ab eo aliquid accepisset uel speraret. Dic si minus deberet beneficium illius amari, laudari, aut predicari, quia teneretur sub tali necessitate reddende promissionis; quod si quis intelligeret hoc solum est quod acceptabile facit omne beneficium, cum qui illud impendit non se superiorem ostendit, sed sponte inferior factus, debito se constringit. Prius namque se donat quam sua. Itaque huiusmodi debito Deus hominem redemerit. Nunc quoniam conuenit ut Deus restaurando hominem perficiat quod incepit, quod secundum tuum consilium non potest fieri, uidelicet gratis omnibus condonatis, audi iam, si potes, atque intellige (*O* 123rb) consilium Dei. Vt diximus, iuste non ualet homo recompensare quod abstulit, nisi id quod rediderit omni creature melius fuerit. Verum supra omnem creaturam non est nisi Deus. Oportet igitur (*L* 87ra) ut Deus sit per quod homo reconciliabitur Deo, nec laudabiliter atque perfecte reconciliabit eum nisi homo. Si enim alius reconciliaret eum quam homo, equari nequaquam posset angelo qui per se ad supereminentiam beatitudinis adiutrice gratia prouectus est. Et sicut non potest reconciliare hominem nisi homo, ita impossibile est illum reconciliari nisi de suo, quod suum; oportet ut non sit minus Deo ad hoc quod de suo non sufficit adoptiue coniungi Deo. Aliud quidem est Deum non ex alterius beneficio, nec quasi se superiorem sed in sua potestate habere; et aliud illuminari ab eo, quia uerum lumen est, iustificari ab eo, quia uera iustitia est, beatificari ab eo, quia uera beatitudo est. Suum dicimus alicuius quod libere potest dare, uel non dare cui uult, quod fieri nequit ubi possessor possessione minor fuerit. Verum omne quod non est Deus, minus est quam si esset Deus, sed Deo nichil est maius. Quare Deus summum non erit alicuius, nisi ille cuius erit fuerit Deus. Ex hiis ergo colligitur qui hominem Deo reconciliare uoluerit, ipse idem Deus et homo necesse est ut sit, sicut ostensum est (*B* 71rb), quoniam decet ut homo repararetur ne imperfectum remaneat quod Deus uoluerit esse perfectum. Pulsemus ad aures pietatis eius, quatinus nobis aperire dignetur, quomodo id uoluerit esse completum.

Gentilis. Vt uideo, noliris [moliris *B*] impossibilia ostendere. Nullo quidem modo potest fieri, ut creatura creator sit. Quoniam autem fabula non semper nocet sed aliquando sua nouitate delectat, persequere quecumque uis; ego aures prebebo.

Christianus. Si credere uolueris quod impossibile tibi uidetur, ipso Christo adiuuante in ueritate esse comprobabis. Scriptum est enim : *Nisi credideritis non intelligetis.* Volens igitur Deus redimere hominem per hominem Deum, quoniam deitas est tres persone, una patris, alia filii, alia spiritus sancti, que nullo modo uniri possunt, set homo in pluribus personis non assumetur, uidendum est cui illarum trium personarum ipse unietur. Equidem si persone patris homo uniretur, iam plures filii, quod non decet in deitate, esse uiderentur. Quod idem eueniret si persone sancti spiritus iungeretur. Vnitus uero homo persone filii nichil addit uel aufert deitati. Rursus conueniebat ut homo ad honorem Dei diabolum (103va) uinceret, a quo ad ipsius Dei dedecus prius uictus fuisset. Sed quis conuenientius expugnaret eum qui per falsitatem similem Dei se fecit, quam qui per ueritatem omnimodo similis atque imago Dei existit? Quidue potius uinceret falsitatem quam ueritas? Aut quid iustius prosterneret propinatorem mortis quam uita? Quidue clarius illuminaret stultitiam mundi quam sapientia Dei? uel quid rectius rediret homo ad patriam celestem de qua exultauerit [exulauerit *B*] quam per uiam? Sed ipse Christus ait : *Ego sum uia, ueritas et uita.* Nec non et sapientia Dei dictus est. Non ergo melius potuit homo ad Dei ymaginem reparari quam si uniretur ueraci eius similitudini.

Sed iam uideamus unde homo sit assumendus, qui persone Dei est uniendus. Alius quippe omnino erat, si non fuerit sumptus ex illo qui peccauit. Alius uero, ut iam diximus, reconciliare eum non potuit. Quia ergo Adam preuaricatus est, reconciliator de Adam assumatur necesse est. Verum omnes qui de Adam (*B* 71va) descendunt, foeditate peccati cum eo deturpati sunt. Fieri autem non potuit, ut foeditas peccati mundicie Dei uniatur. Est namque peccatum a Deo separatio. Itaque quoniam Deus a seipso separari non potest, ut uniatur peccatori impossible est.

Gentilis. Sicut iam predixi, ipsa ueritate compelleris fateri ea esse impossibilia que astruere conaris.

Christianus. Oro te, adhuc expecta paululum. Ille propiciator noster per omnes decursus temporis usque ad finem seculi quos elegit redempturus, quia non decebat ut in hiis miseriis nostris semper uersaretur uel per omnia mundi loca ipsemet discurreret. Vnde erat multitudo fidelium congreganda, atque nobis expediebat ad maius meritum fidei, ut auferretur a nobis ; hoc habuit consilii, ut qui in eum crederent, tam illi qui corporalem eius presentiam non uiderent quod qui uiderent, redemptionis eius participes fierent. Et quoniam non tunc accepit initium quando dignatus fieri homo — fuit enim ante mundi constitutionem per quem omnia facta sunt — ita mundati sunt a peccato qui ante aduentum eius in illum crediderunt, sicut hii qui postquam aduenit eum confitentur. Quamobrem illa plures Ade de qua filius Dei carnem assumpsit, per fidem a peccato mundari potuit. Videsne quoniam quod tibi impossibile apparebat propter infidelitatem, possibile factus sit per fidem, quod etiam non intelligetur nisi per fidem? Hoc est quod iam dixi, et nunc iterum dico : *Nisi credideritis non intelligetis.* Iam ergo si sapienter egeris, (*O* 123vb) incredulus non remanebis, uerum quoniam qualiter Deus hoc mundauit unde hominem assumpsit.

Nunc queramus quomodo illum assumpsit. Decet namque ut qui absque contagione aliqua aliud de aliquo debet assumere, et de mundo accipiat et munde accipiat. Si autem secundum consuetudinem humane generationis, uidelicet ex concubitu, homo iste nasceretur [-scetur *Bac*], munde utique non assumiretur. Quia etsi iam mundatur anima per fidem, sic tamen corrupta est humana natura quando preuaricata est, ut mundus esse non possit eius concubitus. Quod ex hoc facile percipitur, quia cum excitatu quis ad coitum si uult, non potest se dare carnis motum. (*B* 71vb) Et multotiens uolunt homines ad hoc excitari nec possunt. Verum quicquid agit homo, iustum aut iniustum est. Quod iustum est mundum uocatur. Quod uero iniustum ut immundum respuitur. Iustum enim non dicitur nisi quod libera uoluntate agitur. Sed in illo carnis motu, homo libera uoluntate non utitur; quare non iuste. Sed quia nil est medium in factis hominum, inter iustum et iniustum iuste homo hoc operatur. Quod enim iniustum est, ut diximus, immundum reputatur. Mundi etenim corde si alterum uitare nequirent, mallent in foedissimum sterquilinium demergi quam in mundicia iniusticie foedari. Puto ergo iam apparere neminem ex Adam per costam munde generari. Prosequamur igitur quia hoc modo non potest quemadmodum homo nasci mundus ex Adam posset.

Gentilis. Prosequere igitur quod uis. Licet quidem forte non sit uerum quod asseris, rationem tamen (*L* 87va) omnino non deseris.

Christianus. Si tantum fidem rationi non contempseris accomodare, confido in domino quia non solum non repugnabis ueritati, set te quoque gaudebis claritate ipsius illuminari. Sed redeamus ad rem.

Itaque quoniam mundissimus iste homo ex concubitu munde nasci non potuit, pulsemus ad ianuam pietatis ipsius ut dicat nobis quomodo hoc potuit. Natus quidem est de semine Ade. Quia uero ex coniunctione maris et femine non est, utrum ex uiro an ex muliere uidendum est. Quoniam igitur Deus noua operaturus erat, qui prius hominem creauerat non ex homine, postea uero feminam de masculo ac deinde ex uiro et muliere alius, nunc hactenus mundo inauditum ex uirgine fecit uirum. Et sicut dictum est, per fidem mundata dum mundam ageret uitam, destinato angelo ad eam salutante ac prenuntiante quod ex ea ille nasceretur per quem mundus saluaretur, in ipsa hora (*O*124ra) sic accensa est diuino amore quod eius mens sola mundicia iusticie credatur tunc repleta fuisse. Quapropter et de mundo et spiritu sancto cooperante, munde iste mundissimus homo assumptus est. Qui cum munde et sancte inter homines conuersaretur, quia et benedicebat et benefaciebat, solita inuidia diaboli ab eo et a membris eius, sicut euangelica (*B* 72ra) narrat historia, pro Dei seruitio crucifixus est. Cuius honesta conuersatio etiam a Iudeis interfectoribus eius nec reprehendi potuit dum apud eos moraretur, nec adhuc reprehenditur.

Gentilis. Sicut prosecutus es, munde genitus et sancte inter homines conuersatus et, ut putas, laudabili fine consummatus est iste. Sed si secundum assertio-nem tuam omnipotentie deitatis unitus est, ignominiam probrose crucis frustra perpessus est.

Christianus. Si non restiteris pertinaciter aperte ueritati, ex manifesta efficacia pie mortis quam ei ad ignominiam deputas, uere cognoscere poteris non omnimodo esse supra hominem, sed sic creature uniuerse dominari, ut manifestum sit quod ipse est qui per omnipotentiam suam de nichilo omnia fecit. Nunc uero si pacifice attenderis ad ea que dicuntur, mortem eius non ignominiosam estimabis, sed rationabiliter ac pie susceptam comprobabis. Etenim decebat, ut qui hominem reconciliare uenerat, quicquid ille turpiter deliquit, iste laudabiliter recompensaret. At homo ignominiose et, quantum in eo fuit, ad dedecus sui creatoris a diabolo deuictus est, quamuis propter aliud, per carnis tamen uoluptatem. Conueniebat ergo ut reparator hominum per eiusdem carnis passionem reuinceret diabolum ad Dei honorem. Nec ille uerus Deus et uerus homo dehonestauit suam maiestatem morte quam sponte suscepit; sed ex humanitate obedientiam quam debeat diuinitati persoluens, de diabolo qui eum uicerat in Adam triumphauit; profecto hec est sola laudabilis uictoria contra diabolum, quascumque per se occulte uel per membra sua aperte, uidelicet per prauos homines, infert molestias sustinendo, iusticiam (*L* 87vb) inuiolabiliter seruare. Quid enim magnum fuisset Christo mortem declinare quam si uoluisset non accepisset? qui ex ea quoque per sapientiam suam tot bona nobis attulit et per omnipotentiam suam quando uoluit in eternum uicturus tam gloriose surrexit? Insuper illud propter quod homo factus est moriendo consummauit. Nam cum crucis tunc ignominiose, nunc pro honore super capita regum exaltate asperrimam penam (*O* 124rb), quam non debebat liber ab omni peccato, omnis namque pena uindicta est peccati (*B* 72rb) cum, inquam, talem penam propter amorem conseruende ueritatis sustinuit, misericorditer nos a gehennali pena quam incurramus peccando redimit, in ipsa quoque passione preciosam uitam Deo offerens pro nobis, ut fraterna caritate sibi adoptatos faceret nos secum uiuere in eternum, regni sui coheredes. Denique quis daret perfecte iusticie exemplum si iste non dedisset, scilicet non debere separari ab amore Dei mortem? Si quis dixerit quod mortuus sit Ysaias et Iohannes Baptista propter iusticiam etiam priusquam iste pateretur, patet quod nec isti neque aliquis natus de Adam preter Christum potuit animam ponere propter Deum, quam non dico post unum diem, sed forte antequam hora tota illa transiret in qua passi sunt. Inuiti quoque erant disposituri. Christus uero quia solus peccatum non habuit, solus mortem pati non debuit. Rursus quantum homo hominem debeat diligere monstrauit qui uere homo iustus pro impio homine, id est mori non renuit. Hoc quoque factum quod diabolo ad iudicium, qui nunc uidet hominem per uiolentiam penarum non posse se moueri a ueritate, in qua ipse non stetit, non solum nullam passus molestiam, uerum etiam cum eam posset perhenniter seruare, summa delectatione perfruens. Credo non iam rationabiliter uocabis stultum crucis Christi supplicium.

Gentilis. Quamuis quod dicis possit fictum uideri credenti, tamen proximum est rationi.

Christianus. Aperta ueritas ficto non debet inculpari. Nunc sicut proposuimus, consideremus mortificatio huius generis quid fructificauit. Christo quidem in cruce suspenso, signum crucis ab omnibus adoratur, gentibus redemptis precio sanguinis eius, per quod etiam omnia templa ydolorum euersa sunt, nec usquam nisi uni Deo supplicatur. Si quidem pagani licet non prosit eis ad salutem, quia in hac redemptione non participant, nullum tamen preter unum Deum adorant, quem Deum maiorem uocant. Qua in re manifeste apparet, quod ipse est Deus qui de nichilo omnia creauit, qui suo dominio omnia subiugare potuit. Non ergo debet ficta uocari, quorum effectus non potest negari. Quod clamas te non intelligere quod dicitur : Christus redimit, Christus obediuit Deo, quia si uere Deus est non debet dici obedientia, quod ipse a se non discrepat, si (*B* 72va) incredulus non permanseris, petitioni sui satisfieri potuit. At cum effectum rei uelis non uidere, non potes, amodo incredulus dampnabiliter remanes. Licet quippe Deus et homo indiuisibiliter unus Christus existat, ex humanitate tamen obedientiam preparat, (*O* 124va) qui per diuinitatem super omnia omnipotens regnat. Vtrumque sane in Christo, deitas uidelicet atque humanitas, suam seruat proprietatem.

Quod uero postea queris, utrum hec eius obedientia tantum promereri potuit et qua ratione hoc ei retributum sit, patienter ausculta et tibi forsan intimari potuit. Dic queso, si tibi quis indebiti boni aliquid tribueret, deceret te ne ei retribueres cum opus haberet, aut si tibi non superesset quod illi retribuere posses, nonne te ille superior esset ? Vere quidem eo inferior pro debito esses, cui per retributionem equari non ualeres ? Indebitum tribuitur, quod si non daretur nullo pacto exigeretur. Et non solun quod a te manu accipio michi tribuis, sed quicquid in meo seruitio uel ad meum honorem expendis. Nunc hoc uideamus, si iste bonus homo aliquid indebitum tribuit Deo. At iam puto ex superioribus clausum esse, uitam penali fine non debere exigi ab aliquo qui nullo obligatus sit peccato. Christus uero nulli umquam obnoxius peccato, uitam suam ad honorem Dei eiusque in seruitio expendit. Iam tu iudica secundum quod te paulo ante interrogaui, si Deum deceat quod hominem non deceret. Quia ergo indecens nichil potuit habere Deo quod ab eo gratis accepit, retribuet Christo. Nec ipse iustissimus Deus uelle potest, ut iste homo quem tam magnum fecerat, frustra tantum laborem expendisset, sed quid potest dari Christo ? Omnia quippe sua erant. Verum quoniam Deus et homo erat, si contenderis de homine quoniam in seipso pro hac obedientia aliquid posset accipere quod antea non habebat, dico quod ex quo esse cepit, quecumque erant Dei, temporalia siue eterna, erant et hominis filio Dei compersonati. Itaque cum Christo pro hac (*B* 72vb) sua obedientia nichil in se retribui potuit quod antea non habuisset, atque incongruum est quod Deus aliquid irretributum ab aliquo accipiat, si cui uult dare hanc retributionem suam qua sibi non eget, ei iure negari non potest. Sed cum homo sit cui potius hoc dabit quam miseris hominibus [*H adds* : suis fratribus ? Et cum ratum sit non debere hoc subtrahi hominibus] ut detur lapsis angelis, scire debemus quod sicut homo non potuit redimi nisi per hominem, ita angelus nisi per angelum reparari non potest. Quare quia angelus Christus non est, redemptionis eius lapsus angelus particeps non est. Et cum duobus modis retributio fiat, scilicet uel dando quod ante non habetur, uel condonando quod iure pro aliquo debito exigitur, quod utrumque sicut satis dictum est, nequaquam Christo fieri potest, quoniam utrumque homini fratri Christi necessarium est, utrumque ut ei fiat profecto opus habet. Quapropter uice Christi (O 124vb) perhennis pena inferni que ab eo iure exigitur propter peccatum et tribuitur salus anime et corporis cum gloria perpetue uite in regno celorum. Verum, quoniam superius diximus quodlibet peccatum non debere fieri propter conseruationem uniuerse creature etiam si aliter seruare non ualeret, atque honorem obedientie Dei, quem per inobedientiam fraudatus est, tanti esse precii quatinus per omne quod sanctum est restauriri nequiret, queritur si hec obedientia (L 88rb) nostri redemptoris habetur tanti quod hoc totum potuit promereri. Sed cui certum est, Deum sic esse unitum homini in Christo quod iam nichil est Dei quod non sit hominis, neque hominis illius quod non sit Dei nec fieri ab homine quod non faciat Deus, neque pati illum hominem Deum cum puro homine, et opus hominis Dei cum facto puri hominis, cui inquam illud certum est, atque istud prudenter existimare ualet, non solum non debet magnum dicere quod in nostra redemptione agitur ad hoc quod fecit Christus, sed si esset etiam qui pro Christo plus acciperet, (B 73ra) hoc sufficere non deberet. Christus uitam suam in passione obtulit, sed uita Christi uita est Dei. Est passio Christi passio et Dei. At quicquid non est Deus, non solum ad uitam Dei non conparatur, sed ad illam quasi nichil habetur. Et hic perpendent quanti sit ponderis passio Christi, quoniam non modo propter omne quod factum est non debuisset occidi, nec quidem per maliuolentiam tangi.

Gentilis. Qui certum tenet hominem illum esse Deum non modo non debet tibi contradicere, sed quia ei tam rationabiliter salutem suam annuncias, sine fine gratias agere.

Christianus. Quod Christus Deus sit, sicut iam dixi, ex effectu huius operis sui manifestatur. Quis namque crucem que solebat esse inter omnia tormenta abiectorum, non solum ab omnibus gentibus adorari, verum etiam super capita regum et imperatorum exaltari fecisset nisi Deus? Quisne alius templa, cultus et sacrificia ydolorum in omnibus nationibus euertisset; aut quis preter eum tam innumerabiles populos contra uoluntatem omnium potestatum huius mundi, suis legibus subdire potuisset? Et hoc quoque infideles, nolunt uolunt, non uidere [H non] possunt. Alia ueroque soli fideles agnoscunt qui intra domum Christi, id est catholicam ecclesiam, etiam commorantur, quod manifeste Christum Deum esse protestentur, non apparet infidelibus. Si enim Christus tantum homo esset et non Deus, qua fiducia tot turbe religiosorum pauperum, monachorum, heremitarum, et aliorum multorum omni felicitate huius seculi relicta propter amorem eius, in sola spe fidelis promissionis ipsius, iam nichil aliud exspectant nisi huius uite finem, (O 125ra) quos certe nulla blandimenta, nulla aduersa a suo proposito ualent deflectere? Miracula quoque fiunt inuocato solo nomine Christi, uidelicet omnium egritudinum curationes, et quod super impossible fuit omnibus nisi Deo, id est mortuorum resuscitationes; nec ipsi inimici Christi ignorant. Non enim hoc facit uirtus ministrorum cum sepe fiat per manus periturorum, quibus in ultimo iudicio dicentibus : *Domine, nonne in nomine tuo demonia* (*B* 73rb) *eiecimus et multas uirtutes fecimus*, respondebit ipsa iudicatrix ueritas : *non noui uos, discedite a me, operarii iniquitatis*. Quia ergo que diximus ita manifeste sunt quod negari non possint, atque soli Deo conueniunt. Licet infideles ore negent Christum esse Deum, corde tamen fateri coguntur, si rationabiles sunt. Rursus ipse Christus se dixit esse Deum. Quod si mentitus est (*L* 88va) et per falsitatem sit similem equalemque Deo sicut diabolus fecit, protestatus est quomodo hec que diximus que non potest facere nisi Deus, cum ipso Christo cum inter homines moraretur, et nunc in nomine eius quasi deceptus Deus operatus est? His hactenus tractatis utrum uera salus in fide Christianorum sit requirenda, tu uideris.

Gentilis. Ad hoc unum, oro, respondeas. Meliusne fuit facere quod fecit Christus quod non facere?

Christianus. Melius.

Gentilis. Quid debet quisque facere potius? Melius cum possit an minus bonum?

Christianus. Melius.

Gentilis. Fecit ergo Christus quod debuit, et nichil indebitum Deo optulit. Vbi est iam illud tam magnum precium quod ei retribuebas pro indebito nescio quo?

Christianus. Obsecro, comprime clamorem tuum. Non enim tam pueri sumus ut pro solo clamore fugiamus. Quod dicitur : fecit quod decuit, nichil aliud est dicere quam fecit quod debuit. Secundum hanc formam loquendi dicitur de omnibus que facit Deus. Facit quod debet, id est quid eum decet, non quia obligatus sit ullo debito ab aliquo exigendo. Dic, tu etiam si quis bonus quem numquam autem uidisses tibi indigenti pallium uel aliquod tale preberet, diceres quod debitum tuum tibi soluisset? Non credo hoc diceres. Et tamen de illo diceretur : fecit quod debuit, id est quod decuit.

Gentilis. Fateor me hoc usque errasse, et Christum uerum Deum et uere salutis auctorem et reparatorem corde et ore contestor. Nunc enim ualde desiderarem, atque pernecessarium, credo, esset ad fidem meam confirmandam audire cur huius sacramentis et ceremoniis que in ueteri testamento leguntur, uoluit se Deus honorari. Quidue discrepent a gentilium sacrificiis, et quare hiis (*O* 125rb) sublatis ista quomodo in ecclesia geruntur (*B* 73va) instituta sunt?

Christianus. Deo gratias quod iam non loquimur infideli et contradicenti, sed ei qui etsi ualuerimus exprimere quod credimus a fide tamen Christi nullo umquam modo separabitur; sed aderit dominus qui linguas infantium facit desertas, ut aperiat nobis quod querimus, dum inuicem patienter interrogando et beniuole respondendo auctoritatem sanctarum scripturarum, quasi patronum adducem sequimur.

96

Fidelis. Rogo pater, ne me iam quasi alienum habeas, sed sicut pater filium, magister discipulum me familiarius salutem meam doceas.
Magister. Annuat Deus ut in fraterna caritate permaneamus, et quod queris tibi aperiatur. Creatus est homo, ut beatus esset. Sed per peccatum miser factus iusticia priuatus est. Beatus quippe non erit si iustus non fuerit. Soli uero et iusti sunt qui uoluntate Dei obediunt. Et quanto magis ei obediunt tanto iustiores fiunt. Et tunc perfecte iustus erit si omnino nichil uoluerit nisi quod Deus uoluerit, totumque rectum erit quicquid uoluerit. Vnde liquet quoniam ille tantum beatus est, qui uoluntatem Dei in omnibus quecumque uult sequitur. Est enim uere beatus qui uult nichil nisi rectum, et quicquid uult assequitur, (*L* 88vb) quoniam uera beatitudo est omnipotentia recte uoluntatis. Set qui nichil uult nisi quod Deus uult, quia non potest non esse quod Deus uult, et ille potest quicquid uult. Nunc quoniam homo ad beatitudinem creatus frustra redimeretur nisi beatitudini repararetur, conuenit ut omnibus uitiis radicitus mortificatis Deo semper et in omnibus offerat perfectam obedientiam, sine qua non uenitur ad beatitudinem. Sed dum infirmitati mortalis carnis impedimur, non dico omnia desideria uitiose carnalitatis penitus mortificare cum quibus nascimur, et que quasi naturalia nobis donantur; sed ex hiis pauca uix refrenare ualemus. Obedientiam perfectam quomodo semper et in omnibus Deo offeremus, qui uix per continuam horam in bona uoluntate durimus?
Discipulus. Si te modo prius audirem, de redemptione nostra forte dubitarem. Verum quoniam in pluribus iam sum expertus, quia quod impossibile uidetur, consilio pietatis Dei facile completur, non iam desperatione fluctuo, sed letitiam ex (*B* 73vb) consilio nostri redemptoris expecto.
Magister. Iam consideremus quod proposuisti de sacramentis. Quoniam homo de miseria huius exilii ad beatitudinem debet reparari, ad quod non peruenerit nisi is qui ab omnibus uitiis emundatus atque in iusticia perfectus, uoluntatem (*O* 125va) Dei persemper et in omnibus sequitur, quod impossibile est ab homine impleri dum hic uiuit; Creator noster ex temperamento pii consilii sui prouidit nobis ut hanc mortificationem uitiorum et iusticiam debite obediencie ei promitteremus, signumque aliquod inde facientes pacto confirmaremus, et sicut terrenus dominus homini qui ei potestatem sui et omnium operum suorum dedit, atque manus suas inter manus illius mittens pacto confirmauit, que tamen seruicium scilicet et opera dominus nondum acceperit, sed per hoc signum pacto confirmata iam tenet quasi accepta, sicut inquam in ipso die quo pactum firmauit impendit ei auxilium si opus habuerit, ita celestis dominus homini sibi reconciliato per misterium sacramenti in ipso die sue reconciliationis, si de hoc mundo migrauerit, et auxilium contra omnes aduersarios et in regno celorum amplissimas solidatas impendit, ac si totum ille compleuisset quod pepigit.
Discipulus fidelis. Quidem delectat quod dicis, sed si hoc per totum orbem audiretur, nescio utrum iam aliquis in infidelitate moreretur.
Magister. Videamus iam qualia fuerunt priora sacramenta et quare fuerunt

talia. Oportebat ut beatificandus homo postquam crederet in redemptorem
Christum per quem omnia peccata delentur, perfectam obedientiam debite
subiectionis in omnibus uoluntatibus suis et semper eo exhiberet. Quod nullo
modo ualent adimplere, qui omnes carnales motus non represserunt sub domi-
nante ratione. Quos dum sequimur [*H adds* quoniam nobis communes sunt
cum animalibus, animales dicimus,] non percipientes ea que Dei sunt, unde
dicitur in psalmo : *Homo cum in honore esset non intellexit comparatus est
iumentis insipientibus et similis factus est illis.* Et quoniam nemo potest hanc
bestialitatem carnalium motuum statim penitus mortificare, nec continuam
obedientiam Deo perfecte reddere, patres nostri ab Abel (*B* 74ra) cum reconci-
liabantur Deo, mortificationem bestialium motuum per mortem bestiarum
paciscebantur per quasdam oblationes Deo conuenientes, obedientiam
subiecte uoluntatis et promittebant et quantum sinebat humana infirmitas,
reddebant. Scio quidem morte humane carnis istam mortificationem debere
significari, nec magnum fore mactare carnem propter anime uitam que etiam
mortua, uiuificat carnem. At si homo carnem suam mactaret quando solueret
quod promittit, cum in hac uita amplius non uiueret, in qua profecto oportet
eum reddere quod promittit quantum ualet. Et quia morte sua id facere non
potest, illud recipit ab eo prius dominus quod potest, mactacionem scilicet
interim bestiarum, donec Christus adueniret qui per indebitam mortem suam
omnia peccata credentium in se deleret atque in eadem morte ad uniuersam
redemptionem nostram sufficienti, mortificationem nostre carnis significando,
pro nobis promitteret ipsiusque mortificationis fideiussor existeret. Eo igitur
attentius, et quantum ualemus, sine dilatione decet nos persoluere quod Christus spopondit pro nobis, quo nullum inueniemus preter eum uel redemptorem
uel fideiussorem seu aliquo modo reparationis nostre adiutorem. Quis enim
pro nobis penitus nichil habentibus, nostrimet quaque potestate priuatis,
sponderet, nisi ipse qui in omnibus diues est? Videns ergo diabolus huiusmodi
sacrificiis diuine maiestati oblatis Deo homines reconciliari, iterum diuinum
honorem usurpare uolens, ab illis quos seduxerat similiter bestias sibi sacrifi-
care fecit, ut scilicet dum eum pro deo colerent, numquam ad Deum perue-
nirent. Et hoc inter illius populi Dei atque gentium sacrificia distabat quod
gentes per sua sacrificia diabolo subdite a Deo penitus separabantur. Hii uero
qui in fide Christi Deo sacrificabant, in mactatione animalium mortificationem bestialium motuum uiciose carnis pollicebantur, in signum ueri sacrificii
hoc interim facientes[a].

(a) *The text continues complete in H on f. 104 v :*
donec ipse Christus adueniens, illud de seipso offerret, in quo uero Deo reconciliari possent.
Hec igitur exteriora sacramenta ab Abel usque ad Abraham manserunt. Appropinquantes hoc
tempore redemptionis, maius aliquid Deus ab homine requisiuit. Set quoniam propter hoc
quod diximus non oportebat ut homo se omnino occideret, qui illicite ac bestialiter mouet de
omnibus membris suis in signum totius superfluitatis abscidende aliquid recidere debuit. Quod
etiam pietas domini compatiendo nostre infirmitati in uno tantum membro fieri precepit. Et
hoc quidem in illo membro conuenienter actum est in quo homo magis dampnatus apparet,
quodque etiam contra uoluntatem bestialiter mouet. Hec atque alia instituta legalia per Abra-

ham et Moysen aliosque patres nostros sancita usque ad Christum durauerunt. Que quoniam umbra erant futuri, aduenienti cesserunt ueritati idem Christo. Qui manifestans quare ad nos uenerit, quidue gesserit pro nobis ac per se et per discipulos suos precepta uite salubreque doctrinam disseminans nobis, dum recesserit a carneis oculis nostris, ut ad maius meritum fidei felicius ac laudabilius illuc eum sequeremur spiritualibus oculis ubi regnat cum patre semper uiuens ad interpellendum pro nobis, nec ignoras quia humanum genus tanta cecitate et mortali obliuione deprimitur, ut uix ea que iugiter audit et uidet ualeat obseruare, misericordia solita prouidit nobis huiusmodi sacramenta, que nec grauia essent sicut iudaici fuerant, et dilectionem qua pro nobis mori uoluit ad memoriam reducerent, et hoc quod pro nobis promisit ipse idem promissor ac fideiussor iterum promitterent. Studiosius namque custodit humana negligentia quod per seipsum promittit, quam quod alius promittit pro ea. Hoc ergo quod Christus pepigit pro nobis morte sua carnis, scilicet mortificationem et renouationem spiritualis uite, rursus idipsum promittimus Deo in baptismate. Vnde apostolus : *Quicumque baptizati sumus in Christo Iesu, in morte ipsius baptizati sumus. Consepulti enim sumus cum illo per baptismum in mortem, ut quomodo surrexit Christus a mortuis per gloriam patris?* Ita et nos in nouitate uite ambulemus. Si enim complantati facti sumus similitudini mortis eius, simul et resurrectionis erimus, scientes quoniam uetus homo noster simul crucifixus est ut destruatur corpus peccata, ut ultra non seruiamus peccato. Qui enim mortuus est iustificatus est a peccato. Si autem mortui sumus cum Christo, credimus quia simul etiam uiuemus cum Christo. Si quis igitur hoc pactum quod Christus morte sua cum Deo firmauit pro nobis, mortificationem scilicet uitiorum et renouationem spiritus, non concedit et diligit atque in baptisma sepultus similitudinem mortis faciendo ablutusque inde resurgens renouationem spiritualium uirtutum ad uitam pollicendo non custodit, hic in redemptionem Christi partem non accipit. Martires uero qui sine lauacro baptismi moriuntur, hoc agunt dum carnem suam morti tradunt pro Christo, quod in baptismo significatur. Sacramentum corporis et sanguinis sui iste bonus dominus ac benignus frater noster ad reparationem anime nostre nobis instituit. Quod uerissime corpus et sanguis eius est, inestimabiliter socians atque uniens membra capiti, idem uere christianos Christo. Huius sacramenti exterior comestio interiorem quamdam significat refectionem, quod uidelicet sic hec uita temporalis nisi corporali cibo reficiatur non potest subsistere, ita perhenni uita non fruetur anima que non comedit atque delectatur in illis que Christus gessit in carne, scilicet passiones quas pro nobis tam misericorditer sustinuit, et nisi illa maxime seruauerit, que ad bene uiuendum nobis ipse precepit. De hac comestioni interiori ipse saluator ait *Qui manducat carnem meam et bibit sanguinem meum, in me manet et ego in illo.* Et *Nisi manducaueritis carnem filii hominis et biberitis eius sanguinem non habetis uitam in uobis.*

Discipulus. Qui intelligit quam misericorditer ac sapienter in redemptione hominum ista digesta sint, credens quod in eis confidit, puto eum maxima iam ex parte fore beatum.

Magister. Si in huius redemptionis dilectione atque obseruatione indeficienter perstiteris, experimento doctus, et ab ipso Christo qui lux ueritatis est frequenti uisitatione interius illuminatus, perspicue uidebis plus esse qui eos in sola spe pie mortis Christi humilibus corde quam putent homines angelos realiter habere in illa celesti beatitudine. Quod bene sentiebat qui dicebat : «Est et in hac uita iam multa quies data sanctis.»

H then continues : Quadratus lapis sex latera habet ...

(to be continued)

VII

Nominalism and Theology before Abaelard:
New Light on Roscelin of Compiègne

Roscelin of Compiègne is commonly remembered as one of those modern "heretics of dialectic" who, according to St Anselm, "do not think universal substances to be anything but the puff of an utterance (*flatum vocis*), who cannot understand colour to be other than a body, or the wisdom of man different from the soul."[1] Anselm accused Roscelin of blindly applying to the Trinity an inane logic that denied the real existence of universals. Roscelin reportedly argued that the Father, Son and Holy Spirit had to be three separate things in God if one was not to argue that the Father had become incarnate with the Son. Anselm considered such speculation both logically absurd and spiritually dangerous.

Anselm's savage summary, delivered *c.*1093, has been instrumental in moulding subsequent perception of Roscelin as an unspiritual logician—a "maverick" in the words of Richard Southern.[2] A more positive angle on his achievement was presented almost seventy years later by Otto of Freising, who remarked that Roscelin was the first person to establish the *sententia vocum* in logic.[3] Otto was comparing Abaelard's rash application of this doctrine to theology with the prudent reflection of Gilbert of Poitiers on the *voces* of trinitarian belief. Far from criticizing Roscelin's thought, Otto supported precisely that definition of the three divine persons as three things which Anselm

---

[1] Anselm, *De incarnatione verbi* [henceforward *DIV*], ed. F.S. Schmitt, *Anselmi Opera Omnia* VI, Rome-Edinburgh 1938-68, II 9.20-10.1. For a full discussion of Anselm's writing about Roscelin, see Mews 1991, 55-97. Fuller treatment of contemporary testimony about Roscelin, as well as arguments for his authorship of various writings mentioned in this paper will be put forward in a forthcoming study.
[2] Cf. Richard Southern, in *Saint Anselm. A Portrait in a Landscape*, Cambridge 1990, 176: "Roscelin made enemies wherever he went, but he was irrepressible, and he touched nothing that he did not exacerbate. Far more than either Berengar or Abelard, who—though they both brought execration and condemnation on their heads—were essentially sober and well-versed theologians, Roscelin was always a cause of dissension wherever he went."
[3] Otto of Freising, *Gesta Frederici* I 48, ed. G. Waitz and B. De Simson, Hannover-Leipzig 1912, 69.

had abhorred. In Otto's mind, Abaelard had blurred the substantial distinction between persons which he considered Gilbert to uphold. Unlike Anselm, Otto thought that there was nothing intrinsically wrong with the new emphasis on *voces* in logic.

Although John of Salisbury considered Roscelin a logician whose opinions on *voces* had fallen into oblivion, Otto's judgement has tended to prevail.[4] His comments about Roscelin and the *sententia vocum* inspired Aventinus in the early sixteenth century to identify Roscelin as founder of "a new way of philosophizing" that came to include Abaelard, Ockham, Buridan, and Marsilius of Inghen. Aventinus considered medieval philosophy to have been an inane civil war between realists and nominalists, initially instigated by Roscelin.[5] The mythology which subsequently developed around Roscelin as nominalist "hero and rebel" has shown no sign of abating, notwithstanding François Picavet's dissection of the legend.[6] In focussing on nominalism as a cohesive school of medieval thought prefiguring "modern philosophy", we are heir not only to Aventinus' reading of the history of philosophy, but perhaps to his misreading as well.

Anselm never claimed that Roscelin had established a new school of dialectic, only that he was just one of a new breed of "modern" dialecticians. The author of the *Historia Francica*, writing in the early twelfth century, noted in a less polemical vein that Roscelin, like Robert of Paris and Arnulf of Laon, was a follower of a certain John who taught dialectic to be an *ars vocalis*.[7] Robert of Paris may be the

[4] *Metalogicon* II 17 (ed. Webb 93).
[5] *Annales Ducum Boiariae* VI 3, ed. S. Riezler, Munich 1884, II 200-2 [initially published Ingolstadt 1554]. Gerald Strauss comments on his encounter with nominalist philosophers in Paris in *Historian in an Age of Crisis. The Life and Work of Johannes Aventinus 1477-1534*, Cambridge Mass. 1963, 33-5.
[6] See for example Heinrich Christian Meier, *Macht und Wahnwitz der Begriffe. Der Ketzer Roscellinus*, Aalen 1974, which adds little to Picavet's pioneering *Roscelin, philosophe et théolgien d'après la légende et d'après l'histoire*, Paris 1911[2], a much enlarged version of the 1896 edition. See too Eike-Henner W. Kluge, *Roscelin and the Medieval Problem of Universals*, in: Journal of the History of Philosophy, 14 (1976), 405-14. Medieval nominalism has its own not inconsiderable literature; for most recent views see Normore 1987, 201-17 and Courtenay 1991a. I am indebted to Courtenay for allowing me to see this article in typescript, as for the same reason to Yukio Iwakuma, who is preparing an article on *Vocales, or early nominalists*.
[7] *Historia Francica*, ed. A. Duchesne, *Historiae Francorum Scriptores* IV, Paris 1641, 89-90 and by M. Bouquet, *Recueil des historiens des Gaules et de la France* XII, Paris 1781, 3: "Hoc tempore tam in divina quam in humana philosophia floruerunt Lanfrancus Cantuariorum episcopus, Guido Langobardus, Maingaudus Teutonicus, Bruno Remensis, qui postea vitam duxit heremiticam. In dialectica quoque hi potentes extiterunt sophistae: Ioannes, qui eandem artem sophisticam vocalem esse disseruit,

Robert who, according to notes attached to the *Glosule* on Priscian in the Chartres MS Bibl. mun. 209, f. 86ᵛ, held that the substantive verb did not "have any substances" but signified substantial differences of a thing.[8] All we know of Arnulf of Laon is that his teaching about *voces*, like that of Roscelin, was satirised within a poem in the *Codex Udalrici*.[9] I will come back to the unknown John later in my paper. While scholars have often glumly lamented the paucity of documentary evidence relating to early nominalism, I want to suggest that our sources may not be so scarce, if we extend our gaze to theology and grammar.

The Trinitarian theology of Roscelin

Roscelin's dialectic and theology are known more through his critics than through his own words. Anselm was informed of his argument about the Trinity in 1090 by John, a highly placed Roman cleric and former monk of Bec sent by Pope Urban II to act as advisor to Fulco, the newly appointed monastic bishop of Beauvais. He reported that Roscelin argued that the three persons could not be one thing or otherwise the Father must have become incarnate with the Son.[10] We can

Rotbertus Parisiacensis, Roscelinus Compendiensis, Arnulfus Laudunensis. Hi Ioannis fuerunt sectatores, qui etiam quamplures habuerunt auditores.''
[8] Notes edited by Hunt 1941-43; repr. in *Collected Papers* 31: "Magister uero Ruobertus dixit hoc uerbum non habere substantias aliquas, sed potius substantiales differentias cuiuslibet rei significare de qua predicatur ipsum subiectum, et illas differentias esse actionem illius uerbi, ut cum dicimus 'Homo est', hic 'est' significat rationalitatem et mortalitatem, et in aliis similiter." On this Chartres MS, see below, p. 14.
[9] Ph. Jaffé, *Bibliotheca rerum Germanicarum*, Berlin 1869, V 187.
[10] Anselm reproduces the argument quoted by John in *Epistola 128* (ed. Schmitt III 270-71), almost verbatim in *DIV* (I 282, 285; II 4, 6-9): "Si < + in deo *DIV²*> tres personae sunt una tantum res et non sunt tres res < + unaquaeque *DIV¹⁻²*> per se < + separatim *DIV²*>, sicut tres angeli aut tres animae, ita tamen ut voluntate et potentia omnino sint idem: ergo pater et spiritus sanctus cum filio incarnatus est.' '' In *Epistola 136* (III 279) to Fulco, bishop of Beauvais, Anselm omits the syllogistic form of Roscelin's argument in order to make it seem even more absurd: "dicit in deo tres personas esse tres res ab invicem separatas, sicut sunt tres angeli, ita tamen ut sit voluntas et potestas; aut patrem et spiritum sanctum esse incarnatum; et tres deos vere posse dici, si usus admitteret." Gillian R. Evans' claim in *Anselm and Talking about God*, Oxford 1978, 98 that "Apparently Roscelin had been saying that Lanfranc and Anselm had both agreed that the Father and the Holy Spirit had been incarnate with the Son" is a considerable distortion of the argument reported to Anselm. Similarly inaccurate is Southern's claim (*St Anselm. A Portrait*, 176) that Roscelin "asserted that the three Persons of the Trinity must either be so separate that they could (if convention allowed) be said to be three Gods; or so united that all three must

only lament that Anselm was unable to find any of Roscelin's writings which might have explained this argument.

Roscelin's logic has similarly been made notorious by negative caricature. Abaelard mocked as "insane" his opinion that no thing was made up of parts, parts being only *voces* just like *species*, and that since a house was nothing other than wall, roof and foundation, if one of its parts was a thing, that thing would have to be part of itself.[11] Abaelard makes Roscelin look a fool by transforming obsession with *voces* into an atomised view of reality which failed to recognise that the parts were only a whole when joined together. In a letter to the bishop of Paris (*c.*1120) Abaelard similarly ridiculed his teacher for explaining the scriptural words "the part of a piece of fish" (Luke 24: 22) as referring to part of a *vox* rather than of a thing.[12] Like Anselm, Abaelard wanted to present Roscelin as an incompetent dialectician whose insistence on defining terms as *voces* led to conclusions that were patently absurd. In the face of such a bad press, can we make any sense of these ideas?

The only document so far confidently attributed to Roscelin is a long and angry letter to Abaelard, castigating his ungrateful pupil for a variety of offences, of which the most serious was to minimise the differences between the three persons of the Trinity. It was identified by Schmeller within a Benediktbeuern MS in 1849.[13] The malicious

have been incarnate in Christ." Roscelin was saying that they had to be three *things* (not three gods), if one was to avoid concluding that the Father became incarnate with the Son.

[11] *Dial.*, 554-5: "Fuit autem, memini, magistri nostri Roscellini tam insana sententia ut nullam rem partibus constare vellet, sed sicut solis vocibus species, ita et partes adscribebat. Si quis autem rem illam que domus est, rebus aliis, pariete scilicet et fundamento, constare diceret, tali ipsum argumentatione impugnabat: si res illa que est paries, rei illius que domus est, pars sit, cum ipsa domus nichil aliud sit quam ipse paries et tectum et fundamentum, profecto paries sui ipsius et ceterorum pars erit. At vero idem quomodo sui ipsius pars fuerit? Amplius: omnis <pars> naturaliter prior est suo toto. Quomodo autem paries prior se et aliis dicetur, cum se nullo modo prior sit?"

[12] *Epist. 14*, ed. E.R. Smits, *Peter Abelard. Letters IX-XIV*, Groningen 1983, 280: "Hic sicut pseudodialecticus, ita et pseudochristianus, cum in Dialectica sua nullam rem sed solam uocem partes astruat, ita et diuinam paginam impudenter peruertit, ut eo loco quo dicitur dominus partem piscis assi comedisse, partem huius uocis que est piscis assi, non partem rei intelligere cogatur." The text in PL 178, 358D is corrupt. This was possibly a veiled suggestion that Roscelin was skating near Berengarian heresy in his exegesis of a traditional "eucharistic" verse.

[13] J.A. Schmeller published the text with arguments for its authenticity from Munich, Clm 4643, ff. 93v-99r (s. xii) in the *Abhandlungen der philosophisch-philologisch Klasse der Königlich Bayerischen Akademie der Wissenschaften* Bd. 5.3 Munich 1849, 187-210; it was re-edited by Reiners 1910 as an appendix, 62-80.

insults in this letter have tended to attract more attention than its solid speculative reflection. Although Reiners re-edited the letter in 1910, he did not analyse its contents, presumably because it did not touch on what he believed to be the essence of nominalism—universals and the relationship between parts and whole. The letter is mostly about the argument that one had to respect the plurality of persons within the Trinity.[14] Roscelin was fascinated by Augustine's comment that what the Greeks described as one essence, three substances, that Latins called one substance or essence and three persons.[15] The identification of person and substance made sense in the light of Priscian's definition that a *nomen* signified substance and quality. In the case of names applied of God:

> any nouns do not signify one thing and another, whether according to parts or to qualities, but they signify only substance itself, neither divided into parts nor changed through qualities. We do not therefore signify through *person* anything other than through *substance*, granted that we are accustomed out of a certain habit of speech to triple *person*, not *substance*, as the Greeks are accustomed to triple *substance*. Neither indeed is it to be said that they err in belief in the Trinity because they speak differently from us, for they believe the same as us, since—as we have said—*person*, *substance* or *essence* signify completely the same thing in God. For in speech there is diversity, in belief unity; otherwise there would not be a Church among the Greeks. For if they themselves say one thing by speaking thus, I do not see why we lie by saying the same thing.[16]

Roscelin does not deny the unity of God (as Anselm maintained), but emphasizes that plural names are applied out of linguistic convention.

---

[14] Augustine's *De trinitate* is the most frequently cited work; there are extracts too from his *De baptismo, De agone christiano, De coniugiis adulterinis, De Genesi ad litteram, De anima et eius origine, In Iohannis euangelium tractatus 124, Epist. 147, De doctrina christiana*. Other extracts are from: Prudentius, *Peristephanon*; Gregory, *Epistolae, Moralia in Iob*; Leo, *Sermo 22*, Ambrose, *De fide, De spiritu sancto*; Isidore, *Etymologiae*; Jerome, *Contra Vigilantium*.

[15] Cf. *Epist. ad Abaelardum*, ed. Reiners 70, 72, 74, quoting Augustine, *De trinitate* VII 4 n. 7 (CCSL 50, 259). See too *De trinitate* V 8-9 (CCSL 50, 216-7).

[16] *Epist. ad Abaelardum*, ed. Reiners 72: "Sciendum est vero, quod in substantia sanctae trinitatis quaelibet nomina non aliud et aliud significant, sive quantum ad partes sive quantum ad qualitates, sed ipsam solam non in partes divisam nec per qualitates mutatam significant substantiam. Non igitur per personam aliud aliquid significamus, quam per substantiam, licet ex quadam loquendi consuetudine triplicare soleamus personam, non substantiam, sicut Graeci triplicare solent substantiam. Neque vero dicendum est, quod in fide trinitatis errent triplicando substantiam, quia licet aliter dicant quam nos, id tamen credunt quod nos, quia sicut diximus sive persona sive substantia sive essentia in deo prorsus idem significant. In locutione enim tantum diversitas est, in fide unitas. Alioquin iam non esset apud Graecos ecclesia. Si autem ipsi sic loquendo verum dicunt, quare nos idem dicendo mentiamur, non video."

Following Priscian's definition *persona* signifies a substance, although not—in God's case—a quality, as this would suggest mutability in God. The argument runs diametrically counter to Abaelard's identification of a divine person with an attribute like power or wisdom. We use either singular or plural names of God "only on behalf of the wish of speakers to whom such a convention of speech is pleasing". In language that recalls Abaelard's summary of his teaching on parts, Roscelin argues:

> When therefore we vary these names or proffer them in the singular or in the plural, we do this not because it might signify one thing rather than another, but by virtue only of the will of the speakers to whom such a habit of speech is pleasing. For if there were different parts there [in God] so as to speak of one person and another substance, perhaps there would be a reason why we speak of one thing in the singular, another in the plural as we say of a man—since a body is one part, the soul another—that there is one soul but many bodies because of the different parts of the body; but neither is there one quality signified through *person*, or another through *substance* or *essence*, because—as we have already said—in God there is completely no quality.[17]

There is an inexorable logic to his argument that the proper names 'Father', 'Son' and 'Holy Spirit' must each signify a substance if none signify a quality. This is not language about the substance of God, but discussion of three different *nomina*, each of which had its own identity, as the city of Rome was Rome and water was water.[18] The Greek definition of the Trinity as a plurality of substances appealed because it fitted with Priscian's definition of a noun, modified in only a limited way. All utterances used of God had to obey the rules of language. One of these rules was the every noun, even those used of God, signified a substance. Such "grammatical Platonism" (to use a term coined by Jean Jolivet) might be uncomfortable to those who prefer to believe with Anselm that modern logicians did not believe in

---

[17] *Ibid.* 73: "Quando ergo haec nomina variamus sive singulariter sive pluraliter proferendo, non quia aliud unum quam alterum significet hoc facimus, sed pro sola loquentium voluntate, quibus talis loquendi usus complacuit. Si enim diversae partes ibi essent, ut altera persona, altera substantia diceretur, fortassis ratio aliqua esset, cur unum singulariter, alterum pluraliter proferremus, ut hominis, quia alia pars est corpus, alia anima, unam animam dicimus, sed plura corpora propter corporis partes diversas. Sed neque alia qualitas per personam, alia per substantiam vel essentiam significatur, quia sicut iam diximus, in deo nulla prorsus qualitas est."

[18] *Ibid.* 74: "Quae ergo differentia in hac pluralitate personarum secundum nos, substantiarum vero secundum Graecos sit, perquiramus. Nihil enim aliud est substantia patris quam pater, et substantia filii quam filius, sicut urbs Romae Roma est, et creatura aquae aqua est."

universal substances.[19] Roscelin believed that words signified things at a very literal level. He wanted to respect the identity of every proper noun invented by man. His proper nouns are like the individualised reliefs of a Romanesque capital, each a human utterance signifying in its own way a substantial reality beyond. Astonishingly neither Schmeller nor Reiners noticed that immediately preceding Roscelin's letter in the Benediktbeuern manuscript occur two short theological essays closely related in literary style. The first explores both common ground and differences between God and creation, with particular reference to the Trinity, defined as a plurality of things. The second, inspired by a homily of Augustine on John, explains the contrast between Christ's special love for John and Peter's special love for Christ in terms of the contrast between the active life of this world and the contemplative life of the world to come.[20] These are the only theological items within an otherwise secular manuscript.[21]

The first essay, which we shall call *Notandum est* after its incipit, helps explain the argument criticized by St Anselm. In some things God and creation are similar: just as different accidents of the same substance cannot be identified with each other, so the Father cannot be identified with the Son or the Holy Spirit. In God however, unlike creation, the divine persons are not divided between substance and accident. There is a trinity in God, which can be described as three persons or three *res*. The authority cited for this claim is the Greek definition of the persons as three *ousie* or substances.[22] The underlying

---

[19] Cf. Jolivet, 1966 and, in relation to Abaelard, Jolivet, 1975a, 532-43. Jolivet examines the grammatical foundations of the teaching of Bernard of Chartres on substance within a wider survey of the problem in *Eléments pour une étude des rapports entre la grammaire et l'ontologie au moyen âge*, in: *Sprache und Erkenntnis im Mittelalter*, ed. A. Zimmerman, Berlin 1981, 135-64. All these papers have been reprinted within his *Aspects de la pensée médiévale. Abélard. Doctrines du langage*, Paris 1987.

[20] Augustine, *Tract. in Iohannem* 124 (CCSL 36, 680). I am indebted to Anne-Marie Bouché for this identification.

[21] These texts follow on from works of Seneca (copied in the same hand). The letter is followed by advice on casting a horoscope, a commentary on Boethius' *De arithmetica*, an excerpt from Hugh of St Victor on the division of learning and a late twelfth-century treatise of logic. The first part of Clm 4643, originally a separate manuscript, contains a variety of historical texts. For an edition of these two texts, and discussion of their authorship, see my study *St Anselm and Roscelin: Some New Texts and Their Implications II*, forthcoming (see n. 1 above).

[22] f. 91^v: "In istis conueniunt creator et creature. In aliis differunt. Nam in creaturis uel eru<n>t plures substantie, uel plures partes, uel plura accidentia eiusdem substantie, ex quo pluralitas est ibi. Hoc autem non est i<n> creatore. Nam in deo sunt

---

argument is the same as in Roscelin's letter: with each divine person there is no accidental quality, only a distinct substance. Human words inevitably suggest plurality. Such language is far removed from the eternal simplicity.

A similar antithesis is central to an anonymous essay found within a Durham Cathedral manuscript (A.IV.15) containing the first book of Abaelard's *Theologia christiana* in its earliest known recension.[23] This text, which we shall call *Est una* after its incipit, explains on rational grounds how there existed a "one and perfect unity in which there is a certain wonderful trinity." The images used to describe this trinity are unconventional. The standard Augustinian explanation, developed by Boethius, had been that the three divine persons were three relations within God. *Est una* describes each as differentiated by a *habitudo*—a term used by Aristotle in the *Categories* to describe an individual's disposition. 'Father', 'Son' and 'Holy Spirit' are names invented to signify three ineffable distinctions in God.

> Each is described singly as a person; according to the property of the Greek language they are described as three substances. For what *substance* is for the Greeks, this is sounded by Latins as *person*; and these three persons are found in certain manuscripts to be spoken of as *things*, but infrequently.[24]

The author then answers the conundrum "if the Father and the Holy Spirit are of the same substance, then the Son is begotten of the substance of the Holy Spirit" by identifying each attribute as a *proprium* of each person. The essay closes with an allusion to Romans 1: 19-20: "To such a thought you may say that the philosophers of the world rose through visible created things." One can arrive at the doctrine of the Trinity by reflecting on categories of the natural world.

---

quedam tria; homo dicere (f. 92ʳ) non potest, nec intelligere. Non sunt tres substantie, neque tres partes, neque tria accidentia eiusdem substantie. Tres persone uel tres res dici potest. Hoc enim dicit autoritas. Greci dicunt tres usie, id est tres substantie, sed accipiunt substantias pro personis. Quid autem sint ille persone uel ille tres res, explicari non potest. Nam neque sunt substantia neque accidens. Sed in deo non sunt inmediata substantia, et accidens. Ita aliut est in creatore, aliut in creaturis. Nec est mirum si factor a sua factura differat."
[23] I first noted this text within description of the Durham MS in *Peter Abelard's Theologia christiana and Theologia 'Scholarium' re-examined*, in: RTAM, 52 (1985), 113-5, although in this study I had not then realised that it was followed by three other patristic texts.
[24] *D* f. 66ᵛ: "*Persona* tamen dicitur de his et singulariter ut dicatur primo, *persona* secundo et tertio; et ita dicatur iii persone et etiam secundum proprietatem grece lingue dicuntur tres substantie. Quod enim est apud grecos *substantia*, hoc a latinis sonat *persona* et inueniuntur iste iii persone in quibusdam codicibus dici *res*, sed rare."

Its author imitates the method of Anselm's *Monologion*: initial reflection on divine unity is transformed into reflection on the necessary plurality in God, to which the names of 'persons' and 'substances' are variously applied by Greeks and Latins. This argument, which St Anselm reminded potential critics had been upheld by Augustine, is central to *Notandum est* and to Roscelin's letter to Abaelard as well as to *Est una*. Their common theme is that 'Father', 'Son' and 'Holy Spirit' are each proper nouns with an identity as distinct as plural substances or things. Roscelin picked up Anselm's perception (inspired by Augustine) that there were different possible ways of describing the ineffable truth of the divine trinity. However, where Anselm tended to emphasise the continuity between human and divine language, Roscelin focussed on the gulf between human language and divine simplicity.

Person-things and the "Glosule" on Priscian

Where did the idea come from, so reprehensible to St Anselm, that a divine person could be identified with a thing? Although these texts buttress their argument by quoting Augustine, the image is not to be found in his writings. Even Abaelard in his *Sic et Non* only raked up one, relatively obscure text by Rufinus, to support the claim.[25] Anselm's invective has tended to make us search for its stimulus in his dialectic, in particular his supposed belief that just as the world was composed of radically discrete entities, none of which shared a common or universal nature, so the three divine persons were also radically discrete. It is often assumed that Roscelin was not a serious theologian. Did not Abaelard mock his literalism in considering a whole (like a house) simply as its parts (a wall, roof and foundation) instead of recognising that the parts were only a whole when they were joined together? Such criticism can mislead us if we read it as a guide to Roscelin's ontology rather than as a comment on his analysis of every term, genus, species or part, as a *vox*. Roscelin's unstated authority in his letter to Abaelard was Priscian, the great analyst of *voces*. The names Father, Son and Holy Spirit, are *voces* each of which

---

[25] Only n. 37 of forty-two excerpts in q. 8 "Quod non sit multitudo rerum in trinitate...", of the *Sic et Non*, ed. B. Boyer and R. McKeon, Chicago 1976-77, 135 speaks of plural things, Rufinus, *Comm. in Symb. Apostolorum* (CCSL 20, 139): "Quomodo ignis caelestis generat ex se ipso splendorem lucis et producit vaporem, et cum sint tria in rebus, unum sunt in substantia, ita trinitas est una maiestas."

refers to something called either a person (by the Latins), a substance (by the Greeks) or a thing. As this kind of person could not signify a quality in God, it had to signify a substance. This theology derives from rigorous acceptance of the universal validity of Priscian's definition of the meaning of a noun.

Anselm classified Roscelin as one of those "modern dialecticians" who did not believe that universal substances were anything but a *flatum vocis*. According to the *Historia Francica* these dialecticians were inspired by John, "who taught dialectic to be a vocal art". The seminal author for any speculative discussion of *voces* in the eleventh century was Priscian, whose *Institutiones grammaticae* was beginning to outstrip in popularity the *Ars maior* of Donatus, so beloved of Carolingian schoolmasters. Was Roscelin inspired by contemporary dialectical discussion of Priscian's grammatical categories? Anselm refers rather disparagingly to such inquiry into Priscian's ideas at the end of the *De grammatico* when he complains to his disciple of "the extent to which dialecticians in our times are at loggerheads about the question which you put—whether *grammaticus*, classified by Priscian both as a noun and an adjective, was a substance or a quality.[26] The *De Grammatico* was his response to such debate. Are these the same dialecticians as he warns against in the *De incarnatione verbi*?

In no other eleventh-century composition is dialectical interest in grammar more evident than in the anonymous *Glosule* on books I-XVI of the *Institutiones Grammaticae*. Its author is concerned throughout with the *causae inventionum* of the individual *voces* discussed by Priscian.[27] The earliest complete witness is Cologne Cathedral MS 201, probably dating from the late eleventh century. Its text contains a recension different from, and possibly earlier than that found in four other manuscripts, all from the early twelfth century: Metz, Bibl. mun. 1224, ff. 1ra-110rb from eastern France; Paris, BN nouv. acq. lat. 1623,

---

[26] *De Grammatico*, ed. Schmitt I 168; cf. D.P. Henry, *The De Grammatico of St Anselm*, Notre-Dame 1964, pp. 88-91.
[27] The importance of the *Glosule* was first indicated by Hunt, 1941-43. See too: Fredborg 1977; id., *Some Notes on the Grammar of William of Conches*, in: CIMAGL, 37 (1981), 21-41; her chapter *Speculative Grammar*, in: *A History of Twelfth-Century Philosophy*, ed. Peter Dronke, Cambridge 1988, especially 177-86. For what follows on the manuscript and incunable tradition of the *Glosule* I am indebted to the pioneering discoveries of Margaret Gibson, *The Collected Works of Priscian: the Printed Editions 1470-1859*, in: Studi Medievali, ser. 3ª 18 (1977), 249-60 and *The Early Scholastic 'Glosule' to Priscian, 'Institutiones Grammaticae': the Text and its Influence*, in: ibid., 29 (1979), 235-54. I am grateful too to C.H. Kneepkens for comment on its text.

ff. 1ʳ-54ᵛ an abbreviated text from Saint-Benoît-sur-Loire; Brussels, Bibl. roy. 3920, ff. 12ʳᵃ⁻ᵛᵇ (the prologue). The now destroyed Chartres MS, Bibl. mun. 202, ff.1ʳ-68ᵛ, contained additional passages not found in the other MSS. None of these MSS identify an author to the *Glosule*. Our only attribution is to a "Iohannes de aingre" mentioned in the colophon to the 1488 incunable edition of Arrivabenus, a printer of Mantua who relied on a good manuscript very like that now in Metz.[28] An impossible form in Latin, *de aingre* could well be a printer's corruption of *dei gratia*, the traditional interpretation of the name John. The device "by him whose name means the grace of God" is used to indicate the author of another very influential *glosule* on the Pauline epistles written in 1102 and closely related to those attributed to Bruno of Rheims (also concerned with the causes of words, in this case of St Paul).[29] Whether these two *glosule* are by the same author still has to be investigated. There is a dry irony in the author of a Priscian commentary so concerned with the causes of words being identified as "John by the grace of God".

One word whose cause the *Glosule* is much concerned with, is 'person', defined by Priscian in relation to a verb: the first is one who speaks about himself, either alone or with others; the second is the one

[28] 1488 unfoliated (reset in other editions, e.g. 1492 f. 226; 1511 f. 204): "Iohannis de aingre: summos qui inter expositores grammaticae arcem [*al.* artem] possedit: commentum super magno Prisciani uolumine omnibus desideratissimum finit." Cf. Gibson, *The Collected Works of Priscian* 253 n. 14. The Arrivabenus text of the *Glosule* is accessible through a microfilm reproduction of the 1496-97 Venice edition of Priscian's *Opera*, published by the General Microfilm Company within their series *Italian Books Printed Before 1601*, Cambridge, Mass. 1980-, Roll 463 item 2. Subsequent references are to the Venice 1511 edition, held in the Rare Books room of Rutgers University Library, to whose staff I am most grateful. Unfortunately not all editions share the same foliation.

[29] The information comes from the inital rubric to Paris, BN lat. 14442: "In nomine patris et filii et spiritus sancti. Incipiuntur glos[u]le epistolarum pauli ab illo videlicet cuius nomen gratia dei interpretatur in anno quo cons[u]l pictaviensis de iherusolima rediit." A. Stoelen notes that this could only refer to William VII of Poitou, duke of Aquitaine 1086-1126, who left for Jerusalem in 1101, but was present at Poitiers in 1102, *Les commentaires scripturaires attribuées à Bruno le Chartreux*, in: RTAM, 25 (1958), 177-247 at 186 n. 11. Stoelen edits a long passage from this author on the eucharist in *Bruno le Chartreux, Jean Gratiadei et la 'Lettre de S. Anselme' sur l'eucharistie*, in: RTAM, 34 (1967), 18-83.

[30] *Instit. Gramm.* VIII 101, ed. Keil II 448: "Sunt igitur personae verborum tres. prima est, quae de se loquitur sola vel cum aliis, ut 'dico dicimus', secunda, ad quam loquitur, de ipsa vel sola vel cum aliis, ut 'dicis dicitis', tertia, de qua extra se et illam, ad quam dirigit sermonem, posita loquitur prima, ut 'dicit dicunt'. et prima quidem et secunda verborum personae finitae sunt, praesentes enim demonstrantur, tertia vero infinita est itaque eget plerumque pronomine, ut definiatur."

spoken to about himself, and the third is the one spoken about apart from oneself and the person being addressed.[30] Applying the Boethian *res-vox* antithesis to the senses of 'person' as used by Priscian, the commentator considers 'person' as both *realis* (the thing being referred to) and *vocalis* (the word itself). He anticipates his explanation of Priscian's discussion in VIII 101, with a remark on VIII 66 about the relative priority of the first person over the other two persons. Here, he glosses a person as a thing.[31] Could this have been the point of departure for Roscelin's trinitarian theology? In the *Theologia 'Summi boni'*, Abaelard refutes Roscelin's definition of the Trinity as a plurality of things by explaining that Priscian's definition of 'person' referred to three properties.[32] He is here criticising an idea, not just of Roscelin but one laid down in the *Glosule.*

The commentator explains himself more fully when expounding Priscian's definition of 'person' in VIII 101:

> The word person can be taken in different ways: for it means a certain quality, which we can call personality adjacent to the things themselves, and this properly; it designates things participating in that quality which we call persons thanks to the thing which they receive; it [the word person] is also taken in designation of another quality, namely of signifying personal things—a quality adjacent to personal verbs: for when I say " 'I read' is a person" I do not say that in this verb is that thing "personality", rather the meaning of things subjacent to personality; so saying " 'I read' is a person" is "signifying a personal thing."[33]

---

[31] I cite the *Glosule* according to the 1502 edition (*e*), corrected where necessary by reference to the Cologne MS (*K*). *K* 35ᵛa *e* 114ᵛ: "Alia similitudo de ordine personarum, quod dicit sicut in dictis aliis modis praeponitur: *similiter prima persona praeponitur aliis* personis propter has causas: *quia per ipsam*, id est per primam realem significatam ab ipsa *ostenditur secunda* realis: quia ad ipsam loquitur prima et tertia realis: quia de ipsa loquitur, et uere *per* primam *ostenditur* secunda et tertia: nam *nisi sit prima* realis non erit secunda vel tertia; non dicit non esse res quae dicuntur (-unt *e*) secunda et tertia persona etiam destructa ea re quae dicitur prima; sed sub hac proprietate non remanere ut dicantur secunda et tertia siue (si non sit *e*) alia res sub hac proprietate ut dicatur prima et ideo etiam preponitur prima persona aliis, quia omnis (propriis *K*) *causa* efficiens *naturaliter* est *ante causatiua* id est ante suos effectus."
[32] *TSum* II 108, p. 153; *Tchr* III 175, p. 261.
[33] VIII 101 *K* 40ᵛb *e* 123ᵛ: [*Sunt igitur <personae uerborum tres>*] "Sciendum hanc uocem *persona* diuersis accipi modis: significat enim quandam qualitatem, quam possumus uocare personalitatem ipsis rebus adiacentem, et hoc proprie; designat etiam res illa qualitate participantes quas solemus uocare personas gratia rei quam suscipiunt; accipitur etiam in designatione alterius qualitatis scilicet significationis rerum personalium quae qualitas adiacet uerbis personalibus; nam cum dico "lego est persona" non dico huic uerbo inesse personalitatem rem illam immo significationem rerum personalitati subiacentium, et est dicere "lego est persona", id est significans rem personalem. Item accipitur persona significans uerba significationem rerum personalium participantia."

15

In identifying 'person' as both 'word' and 'thing', the commentator was trying to clarify the reason behind the imposition of this particular word. The first person was both "that thing which spoke about itself" and, as a word, "that which signified a thing speaking about itself". One had always to ask whether 'person' was being used as a thing or as a word. "A thing is the cause of the *vox*".[34] In this case the person-thing was the cause of the word 'person'. The commentator wanted to distinguish a word from that which it signified. By twelfth-century standards, this terminology might seem clumsy, but it was an attempt all the same.

The commentator did not accept some people's interpretation that "about oneself" in Priscian's definition had to enunciate an action or a passion about oneself, distinct from the first person of the pronoun.[35] He argued that the same person lay behind the pronoun as the verb. The comentator then proferred as the opinion of "certain people" (i.e. himself) the explanation he had already presented as his own, that Priscian was referring to 'person' both as a thing and as a word, imposed to designate something real. Expanding on Priscian's definition of the first and second persons as finite, he noted that "I read" represents the speaker as "You read" represents the one spoken to. This was true according to themselves "*ut reales*" or according to their meaning "*ut vocales*". The third person, being infinite needed to be defined by a pronoun to be a finite thing in itself.

The commentator's concern to distinguish the cause of 'person' (i.e. the thing) from the word itself is only one example of his desire to establish the causes of those *voces* analysed by Priscian. He was particularly interested in expanding upon those often brief passages in which Priscian tried to establish philosophical principles to different

---

[34] *Ibid.*: "Cum igitur his quattuor modis et sine dubio aequiuoce persona accipiatur: duas tantum significationes persone hic tractat Priscianus, scilicet agit de persona secundum significationem (*K* designationem) rerum personalitati subiectarum et in designatione uerborum quae duae significationes sunt ei secundarie: cum debet diffinire personam ut superius coniugationem diuidit eam per primam, secundam et tertiam: in qua dicerem (*K* 41ra) satis innuitur diffinitio personae. Nam personam dicimus realem *quae* uel *de se loquitur*, uel *ad quam* prima *loquitur de ipsa* uel de qua loquitur prima ad secundam, uocalem uero uocem hanc personam significantem. *Prima est*. Hic diffinit primam personam et secundum rem et secundum uocem: et competenter facit. Res enim est causa uocis: et sic dicit res illa est *prima* persona *quae loquitur*, id est quae profert sermonem de quocumque habitum siue *de se* siue de alio: ecce realis. Prima uocalis est quae significat rem loquentem *de se*, et hanc nobis innuit cum dicit *quae loquitur de se*, id est profert uocem se significantem."
[35] VIII 101 *K* 41ra *e* 123v.

16

parts of speech. Every noun had a 'thing' or *res* as its cause. This principle may help us understand the trinitarian argument St Anselm found so perplexing. While Priscian never explicitly identified a noun with a thing, he did say that it was "a part of speech which distributes a common or a proper (i.e. particular) quality of subject bodies or things to each" (II 22). Priscian's definition of a noun takes for granted the primary existence of subject bodies or *things*. A quality is what these bodies or things share. When explaining that it was proper to a noun to signify substance and quality [II 18], the commentator observed that here Priscian was not using substance in its customary sense of "a thing with subsisting accidents", but in a broader sense of all essence. In his lengthy gloss on the definition, he preferred to use substance to refer to the specific thing:

> [A noun] ... signifies that substance for which it was found to designate, either separate from another through any property or similar <through> the sharing of any property. For proper names are found and imposed so that they always signify some certain person separate from others through some certain properties. Proper nouns are found to designate substances in that they are separate in their properties. ... Similarly common names [*appellativa*] are found to designate substances similar to others in any quality, as man signifies many with one common property, namely rationality and mortality, because since man signifies that one as much as this one, it signifies a certain common property to be in all, in which they agree. Qualities, that is properties, are the especial cause of the finding of nouns. For if nouns were found only to designate substances, so many different nouns would be superfluous, since this name "substance" would suffice; but since substance signifies things in as much as they are or exist in themselves if taken strictly, it determines in these things neither corporality, animation, sensibility, rationality, whiteness or blackness or anything else of this kind. It was necessary to find different names which determined these and other different qualities in things themselves.[36]

[36] II 18 *K* 13ra *e* 24v: [*Proprium est nominis significare substantiam*] "... scilicet significat illam substantiam ad quam designandam est inuentum, uel discretam ab alia per aliquam proprietatem uel similem communionem alicuius proprietatis. Propria enim nomina sic sunt inuenta et imposita ut semper significent aliquam certam personam discretam ab aliis per aliquas certas proprietates; non enim sunt inuenta propter differentiam substantiarum, sed tantum ad discernendas proprietates in substantiis existentes, ut potest uideri in Socrate. Socrates significat certam (*K* 13rb) personam et discretam ab aliis non in substantia esse sed per has proprietates quod Sophronisci filius est, quod poeta et alia huiusmodi; cum enim eadem substantia sit in omnibus hominis indiuiduis, quia omnis homo est animal rationale mortale et non differant nisi in qualitatibus, inuenta sunt propria nomina ad designandas substantias in hoc quod sunt discretae in suis proprietatibus. Similiter appellatiua sunt inuenta ad designandas substantias similes aliis in aliqua qualitate, ut homo significat plures cum una communi proprietate, scilicet cum rationalitate, et mortalitate, quia cum homo tam bene illum quam istum significet, significat quandam communem proprietatem esse in omnibus, in qua conueniunt. Sunt ergo qualitates, id est proprietates

The commentator insists that substance and quality are not signified in the same way, as if both substance and quality are nouns. Rather a noun names a substance:

> because it [the noun] is imposed on it, while signifying a quality not by nomenclature, but by representing and determining in relation to a substance. For this reason every noun has two meanings, one through imposition on the substance, the other through representation of the quality of the substance, so that 'man' signifies the thing of Socrates or of other men, by naming it, determining rationality and mortality about it by representation.[37]

The commentator was aware that his interpretation did not please everybody. Some wanted nouns to name substance and quality joined together, so that "Socrates" was the name both of the substance and of the accidents which informed it: "which is proved not to be by many and various arguments".[38] The refutation of their argument

praecipua causa inuentionis nominum. Nam si propter solas substantias designandas inuenirentur nomina, superflue inuenta essent tot diuersa, cum solum hoc nomen substantia ad hoc sufficeret; sed quia substantia res tantum significat, in quantum sunt, uel per se existunt si proprie accipitur, nec determinat in ipsis rebus corporeitatem, animationem, sensibilitatem, rationalitatem, albedinem uel nigredinem uel aliquid aliud huiusmodi, necesse fuit inueniri nomina diuersa quae has diuersas qualitates, et alias huiusmodi in ipsis rebus determinarent."

[37] *Ibid.* [= De Rijk, *LM* II.1, p. 228 n.]: "Notandum est tamen quod nomen non significat substantiam et qualitatem insimul nuncupatiue, scilicet ita ut utriusque coniuncti sit nomen uel utriusque per se nomen sit, sed substantiam nominat tantum, quia ei fuit impositum, qualitatem uero significat non nuncupatiue, immo representando et determinando circa substantiam; propter quam tamen notandam substantiae fuit impositum. Quare omne nomen duas habet significationes: una per impositionem in substantia, alteram per representationem in qualitate ipsius substantiae, ut homo per impositionem significat rem Socratis et ceterorum hominum, id est nominando determinans circa illa rationalitatem et mortalitatem et hoc representando."

[38] *Ibid.*: "Similiter album per impositionem significat corpus id est nuncupatiue, quia qui dixit "dicatur haec res alba", non dixit "substantia et albedo dicantur alba", in quo notatur impositio, albedinem uero significat per representationem, ut principalem causam. Sed istud non omnibus aeque placet; uolunt enim quidam nomina utrumque coniunctum nominare substantiam scilicet et qualitatem. Verbi gratia, hoc nomen "Socrates" dicit nomen esse substantiae et accidentium quibus formatur substantia [*K*-antur-entie]; albedinem, lineam, Sophronisci filiationem, et cetera accidentia (*e* 25ʳ) quae informant Socratem dicunt esse partes componentes illam primam substantiam quae dicitur Socrates; quod non esse multis et uariis necessariis probatur argumentis. Si enim albedo esset pars constitutiua rei Socratis cum ipse Socrates sit prima substantia et ita fundamentum, albedo erit fundamentum, quod est inconueniens. Numquam enim aliquod accidens, uel per se uel cum aliis iunctum erit sustentamentum. Item si Socrates est nomen utriusque substantiae scilicet et accidentium, illud quod actualiter suscipit illas formas, id est ea accidentia in constitutione Socratis nihil esse probatur. Nam neque est res per se existens [*K* subsistens], nec accidentalis. Si dicatur esse res per se subsistens non est accidentalis. Si dicatur esse res per se subsistens non est accidentalis, quia homo species esse non potest; homo enim ens species nec albedinem nec aliud huiusmodi actualiter suscipit immo

forms an important part of his discussion of a noun. ''For if whiteness was a constitutive part of the thing of Socrates, since Socrates is a proper (or particular) substance, thus whiteness will be its foundation, which is inappropriate (*inconueniens*). For no accident can ever be a foundation either in itself or joined with another. Renouncing therefore this opinion, we say that Socrates designates a substance affected with qualities, which 'I' and 'you' signify, but they do not represent there qualities.''

The distinction between substance and quality distinguishes Priscian's approach to a pronoun from that of Donatus. Like most ancient grammarians, Donatus had taught that pronouns stood for a noun in general. Priscian on the other hand had insisted that a pronoun stood for a proper noun.[39] His commentator understood Priscian to teach that pronouns signified pure substance, unlike nouns which signified substance with quality.[40] It was not only 'person' that the commentator identified as 'thing'; any pronoun came under a similar category as it signified a thing or a substance, devoid of any quality.[41]

The commentator was fascinated by the implication of Priscian's distinction between subject and quality in the definition of a noun. Roscelin of Compiègne took this distinction for granted when discussing the three proper nouns 'Father', 'Son' and 'Holy Spirit' as three subjects. He defined them variably as things or substances, not signifying qualities because this would denote variability in God. While the *Glosule* is not concerned with theological issues, it does lay down very precise rules about the meaning of a proper noun. Glossing Priscian's

---

potentialiter tantum. Socrates iterum non potest esse quia est pars substantiae Socratis secundum hanc sententiam. Rursus si Socrates nominat utrumque et sic de ceteris nominibus pronominum significatio nulla esse conuincitur. Debent enim pronomina puram substantiam significare. Sed cum dicam in designationem Socratis ''Tu legis'' et Socrates designat substantiam et qualitatem, tu utrumque designabat; quod est inconueniens. Renunciando ergo huic sententiae dicimus Socratem designare substantiam quamdam qualitatibus affectam; quam ipsam significant ego et tu, sed non representant ibi qualitates; quod facit Socrates. Hoc autem in hac sententia attendendum quod Socrates ipse etsi plures habeat formas quam homo et quodlibet aliud superius, tamen non crescit ab illis in quantitate.''
[39] Irène Rosier and Jean Stefanini, *Théories médiévales du pronom et du nom général*, in: *De Ortu Grammaticae. Studies in medieval grammar and linguistic theory in memory of Jan Pinborg*, ed. G.L. Bursill-Hall, Sten Ebbesen and Konrad Koerner, Amsterdam-Philadelphia 1990, 285-303, esp. 288.
[40] See n. 36 above; see too *Glosule* on XIII, 31.
[41] *Glosule* on II 29: ''*Qui* habeat significare omnem illam rem ad quam proferatur. Habet significare et easdem proprietates quas determinat uox ad quam refertur''; cf. Rosier and Stefanini, 295.

comment about nouns applying to "subject bodies and things", the commentator suggested that Priscian could here be referring to two kinds of substance—corporeal and incorporeal.[42] One possibility was that incorporeal substance were things, while bodies were visible to the senses (alternatively *bodies* were substantial things, while *things* were accidental). When explaining Priscian's definition, the commentator preferred to explain "subject bodies and things" as "corporeal and

---

[42] II 22 *K* 14ra *e* 26^r [passages not in *K* are in small type]: "*Nomen est pars* <*orationis*>. Distinctis a se inuicem partibus orationis per proprietates earum breuiter annotatas de singularum proprietatibus sufficienter tractat, incipiens a nomine hoc modo. Substantiales enim eius prius ponit proprietates, deinde accidentales proprietates in quibus tractandis totus nominis tractatus pene uersatur. Tractat autem de nomine secundum primam inuentionem, id est secundum significationem quam habent ex prima inuentione, quod est in prima diffinitione et secundum eius ethymologiam et secundum formam uocis. Considerantur autem in nomine duo cum illo tertio ethymologia ipsius nominis secundum quae tria ipsae disponet illum totum tractatum de nomine: significationem scilicet et uocis compositionem, ex quibus duobus omnis eius proprietas nascitur tam substantialis quam accidentalis. Secundum significationem enim inest nomini illa proprietas substantialis quae in eius diffinitione notatur, scilicet significare substantiam cum qualitate. Secundum formam uocis tantum ualet secundum compositionem, et compositio sine forma ponet in nomine quod illud nomen uel non sit sumptum ab aliquo, id est an sit primitiuum an deriuatiuum ut ab album sumptum est albedo. Nomen hanc autem diffinitionem sub diuisione distribuit. Cum enim nomen diffiniens deberet dicere nomen significat qualitatem substantiae, diuidit qualitatem in communem et propriam et accedit per hoc ad diuisionem istam. Nomen aliud proprium, aliud appellatiuum. Diuidit etiam substantiam in corpoream et in incorpoream. Res uocat substantias incorporeas et omnes res aliorum predite propter substantiam; corpora uocat ista uisibilia quae sensibus corporeis subiacent: uel corpora uocat omnes res substantiales, res omnes accidentales. Nota iterum quia pro significatione ponit distribuit exequendo uocis aetymologiam. Nomen enim dicitur a tribuendo, modo pro singula uerba prosequemur diffinitionem, non est *pars orationis* id est significatiua uox. Nulla enim uox *pars orationis* ante debet appellari nisi significet, ut significando sensum orationis iuuare possit. Et partem uocat ut supra in dictione non quod semper in oratione consistat, sed quia aptum est ad hoc ut pars orationis cum aliis iuncta effici possit. Cum ergo nomen partem orationis dicat; ab huius diffinitionis terminatio syllabas et omnes uoces non significatiuas excludit. Sequitur quod *pars distribuit* id est diuersam scilicet communem uel propriam qualitatem tribuit; uel id est uidelicet significationem *communem uel propriam qualitatem* tributam *unicuique corporum siue rerum* hoc est siue illa subiecta sint res corporeae siue incorporeae. Sensus est: Nomen significat rem subiectam uel similem aliis per aliquam *communem qualitatem* uelut homo significat plures consimiles et unitos in eiusdem conuenientia qualitatis, scilicet rationalitatis et mortalitatis uel (*K* 14rb) dissimilem ab omnibus aliis per *propriam qualitatem*, ut Socrates per proprietatem accidentium quae nunquam erit tota eadem in alio significat illam *propriam* scilicet ab omnibus aliis dissimilem; ita tamen distribuit ut per se non dicat inesse qualitatem substantiae: sed per uerbum in quo differt a uerbo et parti quae dicunt inesse qualitatem substantiae: sed per uerbum in quo differt a uerbo et particulo quae dicunt inesse: quia uerba non principaliter corpus sed actionem uel passionem: et illam inesse significant uel ita distribuit ut nominet substantiam representando qualitatem circa eam per quod differt a uerbis quae nihil nominant."

---

incorporeal things''. *Grammatica* and *arithmetica*, two of the examples cited by Priscian, the commentator identified as appellative nouns of incorporeal things. He rephrased Priscian's definition: ''a noun signifies a subject thing or something similar to others through some common quality, as 'man' signifies several similar [men] united in the coming together of one quality, namely rationality and mortality.''

One question included in the printed version of the *Glosule*, found in all MSS except the Cologne recension, touches directly on universals: ''whether collective nouns, words of universals accepted in their universality, are appellative or proper.'' Its author concludes that they were appellative according to their initial invention, because when they were first found, they were found to signify individual things; therefore individual substances are said to be first substances because words were first imposed on them.[43] The inserted passage elaborates upon an existing theme of the *Glosule*, that the original purpose of a noun, as laid down by Priscian was to apply to individual things.

A sharp awareness of sensible reality informs the commentator's perspective on language. When 'man' signified that human species as a proper name, that universal nature which it designated was understood as a one and single man. This was quite separate from 'man' as an appellative, its original sense:

> He who found the word 'man' referred not to that unformed species, but to that thing (*res*) subjacent to the senses which he considered as sensible, rational, mortal and thus he imposed this name 'man' on all others agreeing in this nature. Therefore 'man' by its nature is an appellative. If afterwards a rational minded through some analogy with other things from all men to one certain common thing constant in itself, not in the nature of things, conceived it in the intellect alone, and designated it with this name 'man', 'man' ought not for this reason be called a proper [noun], since it designates neither a special substance nor special quality, rather [a quality] common to many.[44]

---

[43] *Ibid.*: [Text not in *K* in small type]: ''Et sciendum quod haec diffinitio data est quasi in collectione quia non singula (*e* 26ᵛ) nomina attribuunt *unicuique subiectorum qualitatem communem uel propriam*; uel potest dici de singulis omne nomen *distribuit qualitatem communem uel propriam unicuique subiectorum* scilicet si plura subiecta sunt pluribus, si unum uni quamuis improprie hoc modo distribuere accipiatur. Obicitur de plur<al>ibus nominibus quae substantiam et qualitatem significant. Item de collectiuis nominibus, de uocibus uniuersalium in sua uniuersalitate acceptorum utrum sint appellatiua an propria. Appellatiua sunt secundum primam inuentionem, quia quando primum inuenta fuerunt ad significanda indiuidua inuenta fuerunt, ideo substantialia indiuidua dicuntur primae substantiae quia uocabula prius fuerunt eis imposita. Item queritur de omnibus quod secundum diuersas appellatiuum et proprium, sequentia partim soluunt has obiectiones.''

[44] II 22 *K* 14ʳᵇ *e* 26ᵛ: *Et commune.* Posita nominis diffinitione exemplicat inde per partes dicens communem quidem corporum qualitatem demonstrat nomen, ut homo rationalitatem et mortalitatem quae in diuersis indiuiduis eadem reperitur. Nota quia

The commentator was interested in the way universal names were formed by the mind through an analogical process.[45] The conclusions he arrived at were quite different from those of Boethius in his commentaries on the *Isagoge* of Porphyry because he took Priscian's definition of a noun as his point of departure. Such a distinction between proper and appellative nouns is incidentally also pivotal to the argument of a small essay on universals attributed to *mag. R.* in a Compiègne MS which maintains that a species is a *vox*, as distinct from the universal thing platonically contemplated by the mind.[46]

Adjectives, Priscian had noted, derive from a quality and were common to many (II 25). His commentator understood this to mean that they were appellative because they signify a common quality or quantity, as in a white (or black or short) *grammaticus*. They derive from a quality, he explains because grammatically they do not come from a qualitative noun. Whiteness comes from white rather than vice versa. "If anyone asks what common property whiteness designates, we say that it signifies an incorporeal thing in that it is bright and contrary to black." 'White' signified not a substance, but a quality which could be increased or diminished without consuming the subject, "as when we say Socrates is whiter than Plato, we say this because of the several parts which he has occupied by whiteness, or when we say Socrates is less white than Plato, it is to be said because of the fewer parts of whiteness".

This account recalls St Anselm's rebuke that modern dialecticians could not consider colour to be anything other than a body, or a

---

quando homo speciem illam significat ut proprium nomen accipitur, cum autem uniuersalis illa natura quam designat uelut unus et singularis homo esse intelligatur; quidem tamen homo appellatiuum semper affirmant, arbitrantes iudicandum esse de nominibus secundum naturam inuentionis ipsorum nominum; non secundum quemlibet modum (*K* 14ᵛᵃ) significationis: qui autem inuenit prius hanc uocem homo, non respexit ad illam speciem informem, sed ad rem sensibus subiacentem quam considerauit sensibilem, rationalem, mortalem sicque illi praesenti cum omnibus aliis in hac natura conuenientibus hoc nomen homo imposuit. Itaque ex natura homo appellatiuum est. Si autem postea animus rationalis per quandam similitudinem [*K* quadam-dine] aliarum rerum ductus rem quandam unam ex omnibus hominibus communem quasi per se constantem [*K* subsistentem] non quantum [*K* numquam] in rerum natura, ita se habentem solo intellectu concepit, eaque hoc nomine homo designauit, non tamen propter hoc homo uidetur debere dici proprium, cum nec priuatam substantiam nec priuatam qualitatem, immo communem pluribus designet.
[46] Edited by Judith Dijs, *Two Anonymous 12ᵗʰ-Century Tracts on Universals*, in: Vivarium, 28 (1990), 85-117, especially 113-17.

universal to be a *flatum vocis*. Such ideas, I suggest, were inspired by the speculative aspects of Priscian's thinking about *voces*, in particular as interpreted by the *Glosule*. Its author's definition of a person or any other noun as a 'thing' flowed from his desire to distinguish the substance of any noun from the qualities with which it was informed. He did not deny that a common substance like 'man' was shared by different individuals, but he reserved the word 'thing' primarily for whatever was differentiated by some accident. He argued that if whiteness was a constitutive part "of the thing of Socrates", it would have to be part of the foundation of Socrates, an absurdity.[47]

Here I must voice disagreement with the suggestion of Reilly and Fredborg that the *Glosule* could be the work of William of Champeaux.[48] They suggest that the *Glosule*'s analysis of the substantive echoes William's understanding (according to Abaelard) that in "Socrates is white", grammatically there was a conjunction of the essence of Socrates and whiteness, even though this was different from the dialectical sense.[49] The *Glosule* does not make a distinction between

---

[47] See above n. 38.

[48] Hunt commented briefly (*Studies*, 219 n. 1) that there follows "rejection of a Nominalist view" in the sentence on II 18: "Iterum quando dicitur verbum significare ipsum inherere, perscrutentur verba sic: vel inherere istam vocem, quod nichil esset, vel significatum illius, quod iterum non potest esse propter supradictas rationes." The rejection here however is of any form of inherence, not of nominalism. The *Glosule* continues its rejection of any idea that with a verb like *currit, cursio* inheres in its subject, an opinion held by "magister noster V." and also rejected by Abaelard in *Dialectica*, 123. Hunt speculated that William might be its author, although misreading a passage in the *Historia calamitatum* to indicate that William lectured on Priscian (*art. cit.*, 209-10). L. Reilly, *Petrus Helias' Summa super Priscianum I-III: an Edition and Study* (D.Phil. Diss., Ann Arbor, Michigan 1978), 579-80 argued in favour of Hunt's suggestion on the grounds that *sum* "has a two-fold nature, signifying both action and substance". Yet the passage quoted in n. 49 indicates that the *Glosule* did not consider whiteness to inhere in its subject in this sense of *est*. Another argument raised by Reilly is that William is reported as saying that "humanity" is not the same, but is similar in two men, ed. O. Lottin, *Psychologie et Morale*, V, Gembloux 1959, 192, echoing the *Glosule*, (perhaps after being bested in debate by Abaelard?). Fredborg notes a connection between the doctrine of William of Champeaux (according to Abaelard's negative critique of his master) that there were two senses, dialectical and grammatical, to a proposition and the distinction between copulative and predicative functions of the verb *esse*, in *Speculative Grammar*, in: *Twelfth-Century Philosophy*, 178-88.

[49] Abaelard, *Super Topica*, ed. Mario Dal Pra, *Scritti di Logica*, Florence 1969², 272-3: "Dicebant enim quod cum dicitur *Socrates est albus*, alia est coniunctio rerum quam grammatici, alia quam attendunt dialectici. ... et hii [grammatici] tantum copulationem essentiae fundamenti albedinis ad Socratem attendunt. ... Hanc utique, secundum hanc sententiam, singulae propositiones sensus duos, unum dialecticum qui largior est et quodammodo superior secundum simplicem inhaerentiam, alium grammaticum qui determinatior est circa copulationem essentiae. ... Nolumus autem

two simultaneous senses, grammatical and dialectical, in a single proposition, only between different *possible* functions (copulative and predicative) of the substantive. It insists that one cannot interpret "Socrates is white" as "this thing [Socrates] is that thing [whiteness]" in the same way as "a dog is a barking animal". While William may have accepted certain ideas of the *Glosule*, Abaelard's explicit criticism of William—justified or not—is a more elaborate form of an argument already raised in the *Glosule*. It cannot be used to argue William was its author.

A newly discovered draft of two chapters of the *De incarnatione verbi*, less polished than the final version, shows clearly how Anselm countered Roscelin's literalism by applying principles developed in the *De grammatico* to plural words used of God.[50] One had to ask whether a word signified *per se* or *per aliud*. In imagining his adversary looked at everything as a collection of parts, Anselm was creating a straw man in order to demolish spurious arguments. The term *res* is not the central concept of Roscelin's thought. His theme is that all language, including that about the Trinity, had to obey grammatical rules and that every word is distinct from its meaning. Roscelin may have borrowed the term *res* from the *Glosule* on Priscian to refer to the meaning of that *vox* which was a proper noun, in this case 'Father', 'Son' and 'Holy Spirit'. Far from questioning the unity of God, he was only pointing out that in so far as these are proper nouns of human origin, they must refer to separate things.

In the *Monologion* Anselm had argued that there were three *nescio quid* in God that could be described as either substances or persons.[51] After the work had been criticized by Lanfranc (to whom he had submitted it for censure) Anselm included in its preface that passage of Augustine's *De trinitate* which justified the equivalence of the Greek definition with the Latin formula, even though it was strictly denied by the so-called "Athanasian Creed". What had most irked Roscelin's critic, John (then engaged in defending Fulco's recent and hotly contested appointment to the see of Beauvais), was that Roscelin was claiming Anselm's support for his argument.[52] The essay *Est una*

unquam ut in constructionibus alium sensum dialectici, alium attendant grammatici. Sed idem ex eadem constructione et dialectici intelligant et grammatici."
[50] See my *St Anselm and Roscelin I* (n. 1 above).
[51] *Monologion* c. 79, ed. Schmitt I 85-86.
[52] According to an entry added to an eleventh-century martyrology of Beauvais cathedral a *Roscelinus grammaticus* bequeathed to the chapter at his death (9 July of an unknown year) fourteen books, mostly texts studied grammar, logic and rhetoric,

reads as a deliberate attempt to demonstrate superficial continuity with the argument of the *Monologion*, with the addition of *res* to the *persona/substantia* identification. We know that Ivo of Chartres asked Roscelin to write such a palinode to clear his name.[53] Its unacknowledged authority is Priscian, as interpreted by the *Glosule*. Roscelin followed the commentary in emphasising the radical discreteness of every proper noun as a separate thing.

Anselm criticized excessive literalism in understanding the Trinity. While Anselm thought that the meaning of a word could change by being used *per aliud*, Roscelin rejected the notion that a word could change its meaning. His strict attitude to individual *voces* also earned the ire of Abaelard, who emphasised that Priscian's definition of the three persons as "he who talks", "he who is spoken to" and "he who is spoken about" related to properties and not things. Roscelin's thinking about *res* as what was signified by *voces* derived from application of the *Glosule*'s Boethian categories to Priscian. In engaging in

although with some theology: "Roscelinus grammaticus dedit libros suos Sancto Petro: Augustinum super Johannem, Augustinum de doctrina christiana, Prissianum, Macrobium, Arismeticam, Dialecticam, Rethoricam de inventione, Boetium de consolatione, Virgilium, Oratium, Juvenalem, Ovidium metamorphoseon, Statium Thebaëdos, et troparium." This Roscelin also bequeathed his house in the cathedral cloister and eight *arpenni* of vines at Hosdenc, eight kilometres from Beauvais. Léopold Delisle, *Notice sur un manuscrit de l'abbaye de Luxeuil copié en 625*, in: *Notices et Extraits des manuscrits de la bibliothèque nationale*, XXXI.2, Paris 1886, 149-64, at 160; see too Henri Omont, *Recherches sur la bibliothèque de l'église cathédrale de Beauvais*, Paris 1914, 2-3. A *Roscelinus*, cantor of the cathedral of Saint-Pierre, is mentioned in a charter of 17 May 1072 as having joined with a certain Nevelon, a canon of Compiègne, in requesting bishop Guy of Beauvais (1063-85) to establish a small community of canons in the church of Saint-Vaast, Beauvais, of which they had the care; cf. Pierre Louvet, *Histoire de la ville et cité de Beauuais*, Rouen 1613; repr. Marseille 1977), III 480-2 and *Histoire et antiquitez du païs de Beauvaisis*, Beauvais 1631-35, I 694-5; *Gallia Christiana* IX, Paris 1751, 709. The original (Beauvais, Archives municipales GG 251) is cited and commented on by Annie Henwood-Reverdot, *L'église Saint-Étienne de Beauvais. Histoire et Architecture*, Paris 1982, 9. Urban II confirmed their privileges only in August 1095, after the apparent deposition or death of Fulco. There was along history of rivalry between bishop Guy, patron of this Roscelin, and the family of bishop Fulco, Anselm's protégé. Much is explained about the political circumstances behind the desire to silence Roscelin of Compiègne, if he was one of those clerics of Beauvais opposed to Fulco's simoniacal appointment (cf. Anselm's *Epist. 124*).

[53] Letter 7 in *Yves de Chartres. Correspondence*, I ed. Jean Leclercq, Paris 1949, 26: "Restat igitur ut palinodiam scribas et recantatis opprobriis vestem Domini tui, quam publice scindebas, publice resarcias, quatenus, sicut multis exemplum fuisti erroris, sic de caetero fias exemplum correctionis. Sic enim bono odore praecedente et pristinum fetorem consumere, et a nobis et ab aliis diligi et colligi, et beneficiis poteris ampliari."

argument with Roscelin on the Trinity, Abaelard drew on the underlying concerns of the *Glosule*, while being impatient with its excessive use of the term *res*.

Roscelin's debt to the *Glosule* applies not just to his definition of 'person', but to his understanding of language as a whole. The commentator's explanation that 'person' was both *vox* and *res* is only one example of the way in which he expanded upon the tentative dialectical speculations in Priscian. He was particularly interested in the precedent Priscian had set of trying to re-establish the rules of correct Latin, free from corruption, on the pattern of the ancient Greek grammarians. Priscian's comment that younger grammarians were the more perspicacious prompted the commentator to reflect that linguistic knowledge had been expanding from its earliest days. The first "inventor" of words may only have established four letters in his life (presumably of the name of God). The next generation could learn them in one day and so find the other letters of the alphabet.[54] Not all subsequent changes were necessarily good, being done to please rather than for any rational reason.[55] One had to imitate the best the ancients could offer. Language was acquired gradually and thus had to be subject to rules of human origin.

The commentator wanted to understand the reasons behind the invention of words. The philosophical definition of a *vox* as the smallest unit of air sensible to the ear which opened Book I enabled him to launch into a long discussion of the nature of *vox* as distinct from *res*.[56] "Philosophers deal with the definitions of things, gram-

---

[54] I 2 *K* 1rb-1va *e* 2v: "*Cuius auctores quanto iuniores [quanto perspicaciores].* Arguitur inquam scilicet a iunioribus. Et bene a iunioribus potuerunt redargui, quia sunt perspicatiores, et uere sunt perspicatiores, quia et ingenio florent et diligentia, id est arte ualent, quia sicut fructus ex flore procedit, sic ex ingenio scientia. Ideo post *floruisse* addit *diligentia studii ualet,* quia nihil prodest per ingenium florere, nisi studium faciat florem ad maturitatem uenire. Et hoc, id est perspicatiores eos esse comprobatur omnium auctoritate. Non debet mirum uideri si iuniores grammaticae artis dicuntur perspicatiores in inuentione: cum primus inuentor per totam uitam suam in quattuor forsitan litteris elaborasset inueniendis: iuniores in solo die poterunt eas addiscere, et post ex sua parte alias reperire. Ita per additionem successorum ad perfectionem ista ars increuit, sed postquam consummata est non arbitror iuniores esse perspicatiores."

[55] *K* 1vb *e* 2v: "Sunt enim qui corrigunt pro solo placito et non pro aliqua causa rationabiliter prospecta."

[56] *K* 1vb *e* 3v: "*Philosophi definiunt uocem [esse aerem].* Priscianus de littera tractaturus, et in descriptione litterae uocem ut genus suum positurus: ne pro ignotum genus ignotam speciem diffiniret, uocis diffinitionem a philosophis datam conuenienter praemittit. Est autem philosophorum diffinitiones rerum; grammaticorum uero

26

marians with forming the etymologies of *voces."* Opinions differed among philosophers as to the nature of this small quantity of air. Some said that animals lived from this air which they breathe in and out; other *physici* said that animals got life not from this small quantity of air, but from that air which stretches up to heaven and which by

uocum aethimologias formare. Vel ad maiorem auctoritatem diffinitionis dicit philosophi diffiniunt uocem: ut auctores diffinitionis nominati commendabilem et autenticam reddant ipsam diffinitionem, dicentes *uocem esse aerem tenuissimum.* Ideo dicit *tenuissimum* quia aer naturaliter tenuis est respectu aquae et terrae; qui dum ab animali hauritur per arteriarum angustos aditus, et per illa interiora collatoria usque ad pulmonem attrahitur, fit tenuior, deponens in attractione si quam sordem sibi ab exterioribus contraxerat, ut sicut uinum post colationem liquidius quam prius in emissione uero per easdem arteriarum angustias regrediens si quid adhuc spissitudinis retinebat illam exuit, et tunc demum fit tenuissimus. Sed quia homo cogitans uel dormiens sine alicuius uocis informatione emittit spiritum, addit *ictum* id est percussum; et quia posset percuti digito in ore posito et non tamen esset uox, intelligendum est naturalibus instrumentis ad uocem formandam, uidelicet lingua palato labiis dentibus. De isto aere quem ita attrahunt et emittunt animalia, diuersa philosophorum opinio est. Alii enim dicunt animalia uiuere ex isto corrupto aere, qui nos undique circumscribit per attractionem et emissionem. Phisici tamen aliter sentiunt, quia dicunt animalia ex nostro aere qui adeo spissus est uitam suam continuare (K 2ra) non posse, sed ex illo superiori qui est extra globo lunae usque ad firmamentum qui nostri aeris consideratione tenuissimus est, et dicunt illum diuina dispositione per quasdam latentes uias et quosdam poros ad nos descendere, et animalia per arterias ad pulmonem illum attrahere. In primis quaerendum est an uox sic diffinita species sit aeris, id est significet aliquam rem uniuersalem quae sit species in praedicamento substantiae: quod dicimus non esse. Vox enim aeres in essentia sui, scilicet in hoc quod sunt aeres non significat, set potius ex quadam accidentali causa in hoc scilicet quod percussi sunt naturalibus instrumentis. Dicimus ergo hoc uocabulum uox accidentale esse, id est sumptum a quadam qualitate, percussione uel alia non secundum uocem, sed secundum significationem. Non est ergo substantialis diffinitio praemissa si uox aerem non significet. Hanc diffinitionem aliqui putant se infringere hanc hypoteticam in suae rationis exordio ponentes: si uox est aer et est corpus. Huic probationi duas regulas supponunt: unam Augustini qui dicit "nullum corpus indiuiduale in eodem tempore totum in diuersis locis reperitur"; alteram Boetii quae est, "idem sermo totus et integer, cum omnibus scilicet suis elementis ad aures diuersorum peruenit in eodem tempore, quasi in diuersis locis est." Inde inferunt: igitur uox non est corpus. Salua autem utriusque auctoritate uox poterit corpus remanere si quod Boetius dicit recte intelligatur. Est enim uerum quod uox formaliter eadem et non materialiter in eodem tempore diuersorum replet auditum ut puta iacto lapide in aqua fit orbis. Hic uero orbis iste uicinas undas impellens alium orbem facit, et ille alium et sic multi orbes materia quidem et loco diuersi: sed in forma idem a primo illo orbe formantur. Eodem modo aer in ore loquentis naturalibus instrumentis formatus uicinos impellit aeres, et in sua conficitur forma, et ita fit ut uox eadem secundum formam sit in orationibus diuersorum. Sed quantum ad materiam diuersorum, ut ita dicam, aerum diuersa. Potest igitur esse ut nullum corpus in eodem tempore totum in diuersis locis habeatur, et erit uox corpus, et ipsa secundum formam, id est soni similitudinem, eadem in eodem tempore in diuersis auditur locis. Et hanc similitudinem de aqua ponit Boetius in prologo quem praemittit in musica."

divine disposition descends into our lungs. The second interpretation fitted in with the bigger argument he sought to present, that a *vox* did not signify a universal substance, but was rather something accidental, so called from its percussive quality. While some argued that rules established by Augustine ("no individual body could be found in different places at the same times") and Boethius ("the same word comes complete to the ears of different people at the same time in different places") that a *vox* could not be a body (as distinct from a universal substance), these rules had to be interpreted correctly. When a word reached different people, it was a similar sound rather than the same sound which all heard.

The commentator's discussion of *voces* provides an excellent illustration of his thinking about parts and wholes. *Voces* were all quite distinct from each other. No individual thing could be the same in different places. Only God, who was truly incorporeal and underwent no change, remained the same in all places.

> Just as the continuous whiteness of a wall which rests on different things [i.e. walls] is said to be one, not because that whiteness adjacent to this part is individually the same as that of another part but because it is similar and judged to be called the same in the same species, likewise when I articulate 'man' once and I pronounce the same *vox* 'man' at another time, although they are essentially different, and materially *voces*, I affirm that it is as if I have articulated one *vox*, because of [their] similitude. We say as if informed by one because of similitude, and therefore one *vox*.[57]

There is a striking similarity here to the arguments Abaelard attributed to Roscelin about parts and wholes. The commentator insisted that the words of Boethius and Aristotle about *vox* and *oratio* had to be rightly construed:

[57] *Ibid.*: "Nulla enim res indiuidualiter (*e* 4ʳ) tota in diuersis locis esse affirmari potest, ut una essentialiter remaneat, nisi solus deus qui uerum incorporeum est, et qui nullam mutabilitatem recipere potest. Ad hoc respondeo quod sicut continua albedo parietis una dicitur quae in diuersis fundatur, non quia illa albedo quae huic parti adiacet sit illa indiuidualiter quae in alia parte fundatur, sed quia similis est et eadem specie iudicatur uocari eadem; ita cum profero homo semel et alia uice eandem uocem, id est homo pronuncio, et quamuis diuersae sint essentialiter, et materialiter uoces, tamen propter similitudinem quasi unam eandem uocem protulisse affirmo. Similiter cum in diuersis partibus aeris una forma uocis a diuersis audientibus suscipi uideatur, tamen illa qualitatiua forma, quae huic parti aeris copulata est indiuidualiter, esse illam unde alia pars aeris effecta est non potest probari. Nos tamen propter similitudinem quasi unam informationem uocamus et propterea unam uocem."

Others, armed by the authority of Aristotle, define a *vox* as a quantity...
Deceived by the ambiguity of *oratio*, they do not realise that the word signifies
one thing as a quantity, another as a substance.[58]

An issue raised very briefly by Priscian allowed the commentator to
bring ideas of Boethius and Aristotle to bear on the physical nature of
the words which grammarians analysed.

His key theme is that no *vox* signifies naturally. It is a physical object
on which meaning is bestowed by the one who forms it by striking air.
Priscian distinguished articulate sounds, in other words sounds "apt
to be spoken to show the sense of the speaker" from those "natural"
sounds which were inarticulate and not uttered from any intention to
signify. The commentator recognised that Boethius approached
language differently, in evaluating meaning by what was generated in
the mind of the listener. Priscian's physical analysis of sound attracts
the commentator's sympathy. Meaning is defined by what a speaker
wishes to say rather than any quality discerned in the language itself.

Roscelin extended the *Glosule*'s insight into language as an artefact
to words used of God. The message of *Est una, Notandum est* and the
letter to Abaelard is that the only underlying unity is that of God.
Roscelin's refusal to accept that the three persons of the Trinity constituted a common 'thing' was the result of applying litterally the
Glosule's grammatical definitions to trinitarian doctrine. He was
inspired by its perception of individual words as physical objects, each
with its own dimension, each radically different from the other.

---

[58] *Ibid.*: "Est alia sententia quae dicit omnes illos aeres simul acceptos simul unam
uocem et nullum eorum per se, sed hoc parum ualoris habet. Aliter quidam respon-
dent obiectionibus praemissis dicentes tantum uocem esse aerem plectro linguae for-
matum et nullum alium. Affirmant enim eandem uocem peruenire eodem tempore
ad aures plurium in diuersis locis existentium, non secundum sui essentiam, sed
secundum auditum, quemadmodum lapis in oculis plurium uel alicuius dicitur esse,
non secundum sui substantiam tantum, sed secundum uisum, et in hac sententia
oppositiones, quae sequentur cum praedictis quiescunt. Opponitur iterum praemissae
diffinitioni, quae dicit uocem esse aerem quod Boetius in secundo commentario
Periermeneias dicit uocem esse aeris percussionem per linguam, quod si aeris per-
cussio qualitati supponitur, uocem eidem supponi necesse est. Sed si quis diligenter
dicta Boetii consideret, inueniet uocem qualitati non supponi. Non enim dicit
simpliciter uocem esse percussionem, sed aeris percussionem, id est aerem percussum, et est dictum ad expressionem. Alii uero Aristotelica auctoritate muniti
uocem in quantitate ponunt; dicit enim Aristoteles in quantitate orationem esse. Sed
in quo praedicamento est species, ibidem oportet etiam esse genus illius speciei. Huic
obiectioni sic respondeo, quia isti aequiuocatione orationis decepti nesciunt illam
uocem quae est oratio, aliud significare in quantitate, aliud quando subiicitur uoci in
substantia. Voces enim eaedem saepe et significant substantiam quodam respectu, et
quantitatem alio respectu, ut corpus ista uox."

Anselm found this teaching, that a universal substances was nothing but a "puff of air", reprehensible. Rarely in the history of logic, has such weight been given to a single derisory and misleading remark. Like the commentator, Roscelin might have considered genus and species as *voces*. The *Glosule* author did not deny that a universal was a *res*, but insisted that the words we used of that universal were *voces* and had to be analysed as such. The accusation that "modern dialecticians" did not believe in the real existence of universals is a red herring distracting us from their concern with the nature and meaning of *voces*.

The *res-vox* distinction Roscelin used was too crude for Anselm and Abaelard when applied to the Trinity. Nonetheless, Roscelin shared with Anselm and passed on to Abaelard, a desire to uncover the "causes" of language about the Trinity. Whether one spoke of person, like the Latins, or substance, like the Greeks to refer to that which was plural in God, one was dealing with human attempts to define what was ultimately ineffable. While Anselm and Roscelin both accepted that such language was always subject to rules of signification, they disagreed on what these rules were. Anselm was perhaps the more original when it came to the interpretation of Priscian.

The *Glosule* illuminates the comment of the *Historia Francica* about Roscelin learning from the mysterious John that dialectic is an *ars vocalis*, a discipline founded on *voces*. To call this John "an early nominalist" is to fall into the same trap as Aventinus—reading into the past a school of thought which never had such a clear-cut existence. While the application to dialectic and theology of Priscian's reflection on nouns was taken for granted in the mid twelfth century by people like Gilbert of Poitiers and John of Salisbury, there was inevitably much disagreement as to the implications of this process. Polarisation between masters was an inevitable consequence of a fluid intellectual environment. The distinction Hermann of Tournai drew between those who taught dialectic *in voce* as against *in re* was between "empty talkers" unlike "real philosophers". We should be wary of interpreting such groupings as distinct philosophical schools with a "real" existence before the mid twelfth century. There is no evidence that Roscelin denied the reality of universal substances as Anselm claimed.

The interrelationship between study of *voces* and philosophy as a whole is explained within the prologue to the *Glosule*. Priscian's primary intention is teach people to speak grammatically:

I say grammatically as different from dialectic, which teaches speaking according to truth and falsehood and from rhetoric, which teaches speaking according to the decoration of words and phrases. Of these arts grammar comes first, because one ought to know how to make appropriate joining of words before truth or falsehood or the decoration of eloquence is learnt.''[59]

Grammar was a part of logic, a subject which could be divided into what was *sermocinalis* (to do with language) and what was *disertiua* (to do with finding arguments). Through this "linguistic" (*sermocinalis*) part, grammar was led back to logic as if to its genus.[60] The three arts of logic, with those of ethics and physics, derived from the "Greek springs" of which Priscian spoke at the outset of his work.[61] This idea had been expressed in similar terms in an eleventh-century poem on the seven liberal arts found in a manuscript of Saint-Evroul.[62]

The tradition of the Glosule

Not all previous thinkers had agreed that grammar was an integral part of logic.[63] Alcuin and others who followed Isidore of Seville divided logic into the arts of analysing and finding arguments, dialectic and rhetoric. (Confusingly Isidore had also suggested that logic was another name for dialectic.)[64] By contrast Clement, teacher in the

---

[59] *Glosule*, ed. Gibson, Studi Medievali, 20 (1979), 249: "Grammatice dico ad differentiam dialectice, que docet loqui secundum ueritatem et falsitatem, et rethorice, que docet loqui secundum ornatum uerborum et sententiarum. Quibus artibus prior est grammatica, quia prius scire oportet facere conuenientem coniunctionem dictionum quam ueritas uel falsitas uel ornatus eloquentie addiscatur.''

[60] *Ibid.* 249-50: "Nec dubitandum quin *logice supponatur*, cuius est ipsa grammatica tercia pars. Logice alia pars est sermocinalis, alia disertiua. Disertiua partes habet inuentionem et iudicium, que solis dialecticis et rethoricis conueniunt. Sermocinalis uero grammaticorum est; ac per eam ad logicam uelut ad suum genus grammatica reducitur.''

[61] *Ibid.* 251: "*Celebrasse* dico *deriuatam a fonte Grecorum*; Greci enim fuerunt *fons* et origo omnium artium, quia earum inuentores fuerunt. Cum dicit *deriuatam* alludit metafore, quia dixerat *fontibus*; latine enim artes quasi riui sunt grece inuentionis. Et etiam *celebrasse omne genus studiorum*, per hoc uocat *studia* quia in naturis rerum inuestigandis uehementior animi applicatio exhibenda est; et ne *in omni genere studiorum* acciperemus pictoriam et sutoriam artem et alia seruilia officia addit *genus* dico *prefulgens luce sapientie*, quia seruiles artes mentis oculos non illuminant sicut philosophia.''

[62] Printed in PL 151, 729-32 from Alençon, Bibl. mun. 10.

[63] On early medieval classification of the *artes*, see Bernhard Bischoff, *Eine verschollene Einteilung der Wissenschaften*, first printed in: AHDLMA, 25 (1958), 5-20, reprinted in his *Mittelalterliche Studien*, I, Stuttgart 1966, 273-88.

[64] Isidore, *Etymologiae* (ed. Lindsay) II.xxiv.7, but cf. I.ii.1; Alcuin, *De dialectica*, PL 101, 952C.

court of Louis the Pious and author of an *Ars grammatica* included grammar as a subdivision of rhetoric, itself a species with dialectic of *logica*.[65] An interpolation into pseudo-Bede's *De mundi constitutione* explained that there were two definitions of *logica*, one strict that it comprised dialectic and rhetoric another loose, that it was a *sermocinalis scientia* embracing dialectic, rhetoric and grammar.[66]

The *Glosule*, like the didactic poem, adhered to the view that included grammar within logic.[67] Roscelin of Compiègne likewise absorbed from the mysterious John the idea that dialectic was "a vocal art". Abaelard reacted against Roscelin's literalistic interpretation of definitions of Priscian. For him logic and dialectic were synonymous. Grammatical issues he dealt with in the first tract of the *Dialectica*, the "book of parts". I have suggested elsewhere that his lost *Grammatica* or "reconsideration of the predicaments", to which he alludes in his *Theologia christiana*, was a reworking of the first tract of the *Dialectica* and that it contained new ideas about the relationship between substance and quality.[68] While Abaelard tended to present himself as a great innovator in dialectic and to be silent about his debt to past masters, he was in fact developing a speculative tradition rooted in grammatical reflection of the late eleventh century.

Further manuscript discoveries may well illuminate the extent of Roscelin's influence on this tradition further than I have been able to do here. I have not had time to discuss the fascinating commentary on Psalms 1-25, attributed to Roscelin (with good reason I would argue) by Stegmüller. This work, surviving in six twelfth-century manuscripts, suggest that Roscelin was one of the most philosophically

---

[65] *Clementis ars grammatica* 15, ed. Joannes Tolkiehn, *Philologus. Supplementband* 20.3 (Leipzig 1928), p. 10.

[66] PL 90, 908B: "Logica est diligens ratio disserendi, et magistra iudicii; sic definita stricte accipitur, comprehendens tamen rhetoricam dialectica. Large vero sic describitur: Logica est sermocinalis scientia, et dividitur in tria, in dialecticam, rhetoricam, grammaticam." See also Charles Jones, *Bedae Pseudepigrapha*, Ithaca 1939, 39. Charles Burnett notes that these interpolations do not occur in the surviving MSS of Pseudo-Bede, none earlier than the 12th century, *De Mundi celestis terrestrisque constitutione*, Warburg Institute Surveys and Texts 10, London 1985, 11.

[67] *Ibid.* ed. Gibson 251: "*Celebrasse* dico *doctrinam omnis eloquentie*, id est scientiam totius logice; et hic includit triuium, quod homines doctos et eloquentes reddit. *Doctrinam* dico *deriuatum a fonte Grecorum*; Greci enim fuerunt *fons* et origo omnium artium, quia dixerat *fontibus*; latine enim artes quasi riui sunt grece inuentionis. Et etiam *celebrasse omne genus studiorum*, per hoc comprehendit ethicam et physicam, in qua physica continetur quadriuium."

[68] Mews 1987.

minded scriptural exegetes of his generation.[69] Much remains to be explained about his precise contribution to the study of dialectic. I hope however to have suggested that he is not a thinker who springs out of nowhere. Roscelin studied at Rheims, a city with a proud tradition of classical scholarship since at least the time of Gerbert of Aurillac.[70] There is no better witness to this classical revival in the eleventh century than the *Glosule* on Priscian. Its author, I suggest, was the John who taught Roscelin that dialectic was an art that dealt with *voces*. It might be worth investigating whether its author could be John of Rheims, the famous *grammaticus* who came to Saint-Evroul in 1076/77, remaining a monk there until his death in 1125 and who, according to Orderic Vitalis, was continuously engaged in the study of the ancients.[71] The Chartres MS of the *Glosule* contained a list of twenty-eight books borrowed from Saint-Evroul.[72] Bec was not the only centre of philosophic discussion in late eleventh-century Normandy.

The *Glosule* indirectly exerted an enormous influence on twelfth-century thought, not least through its impact on William of Conches and Petrus Helias. It may be worth studying its influence on Gilbert of Poitiers and the whole Chartrian tradition. Otto of Freising may have exaggerated Roscelin's originality in initiating interest in the *sententia vocum*. John of Salisbury considered him to be someone whose opinions had long since been overtaken by the achievements of Gilbert and Abaelard. Nonetheless, Roscelin did play a significant role in emphasizing that both dialectic and theology had to be based on clear understanding of the meaning of individual *voces*. St Anselm was not wrong in recognizing the intellectual challenge which he presented.

Clayton, Victoria
Monash University

[69] Stegmüller, *Repertorium Biblicum* no. 7516. He is certainly mistaken however in attributing to Roscelin the commentary on Psalms 26-150 in the Troyes MS, Bibl. mun. 1750 (in which the entire collection is attributed to "magister Bruno". For full discussion of this commentary, see my forthcoming study, *St Anselm and Roscelin: Some New Texts and Their Implications II* (see n. 1 above).

[70] *Epist. ad Abaelardum*, ed. Reiners 65. John R. Williams documents the importance of the school at Rheims, perhaps without sufficient importance on its role prior to Gerbert, *The Cathedral School of Rheims in the Eleventh Century*, in: Speculum, 29 (1954), 661-77.

[71] On John of Rheims and intellectual life at St Evroul in this period, see the eulogy of Orderic Vitalis, *Ecclesiastical History*, ed. Marjorie Chibnall 6 vols., Oxford 1972-80, III 166-70, and the introductory comments of Chibnall in I 11-23.

[72] The Chartres MS contained on a flyleaf a list of books borrowed from this abbey to another, according to H. Omont, *Catalogue général des manuscrits des bibliothèques publiques de France* XI *Chartres*, Paris 1890, 108.

Abbreviations and Bibliography

AHDL	Archives d'histoire doctrinale et littéraire du moyen-âge
BGPM	Beiträge zur Geschichte der Philosophie des Mittelalters
CCCM	Corpus Christianorum. Continuatio Mediaeualis
CCSL	Corpus Christianorum. Series Latina
CIMAGL	Cahiers de l'Institut du Moyen-Age grec et latin
RTAM	Recherches de théologie ancienne et médiévale

Primary Sources

Abelard, *Dial.* = *Dialectica*, ed. L. M. De Rijk. 2ⁿᵈ ed., Assen, 1956.

Abelard, *TChr* = *Theologia christiana*, ed. E. M. Buytaert, *Petri Abaelardi Opera Theologica II*, CCCM 12. Turnhout, 1969.

Abelard, *TSch* = *Theologia Scholarium*, ed. E.M. Buytaert and C.J. Mews, *Petri Abaelardi Opera Theologica III*, CCCM 13. Turnhout, 1987.

Abelard, *TSum* = *Theologia Summi boni*, ed. E.M. Buytaert and C.J. Mews, *Petri Abaelardi Opera Theologica III*, CCCM 13. Turnhout, 1987.

John of Salisbury, *Metalogicon*, ed. C. Webb, Oxford, 1929.

Secondary Sources

Hunt, R.W., 1941-43, 'Studies on Priscian in the Eleventh and Twelfth Centuries, I. Petrus Helias and His Predecessors', in *Mediaeval and Renaissance Studies* 1, 194-231; repr. In his *The History of Grammar in the Middle Ages. Collected Papers* (Amsterdam Studies in the History of Linguistic Science, ser. III, vol. 5), ed. G. L. Bursill-Hall. Amsterdam, 1980, pp. 1-38.

Jolivet, J., 1966, 'Quelques case de "platonisme grammatical" du VIIe au XIIe siècle', in: *Mélanges offers à René Crozet*, vol. 1, ed. P. Gallais and Y.-J. Riou. Poitiers, pp. 93-9.

Jolivet, J. 1975a 'Notes de lexicographie abélardienne', in *Pierre Abélard–Pierre le Vééerable. Les courants philosophiques, littéraires et artistiques en occident au milieu du XIIe siècle*. Paris, pp. 532-43.

Mews, C. J., 1991, 'St Anselm and Roscelin: Some New Texts and their Implications. I. The *De incarnatione verbi* and the *Disputatio inter Christianum et Gentilem*' in *AHDL* 58, 55-97.

Reiners, J., 1910, *Der Nominalismus in der Frühscholastik. Ein Beitrag zur Geschichte der Universalienfrage im Mittelalter. Nebst iener neuen Textausgabe des Briefes Roscelins an Abaelard* (BGPM 8.5). Münster.

VIII

ST ANSELM, ROSCELIN AND THE SEE OF BEAUVAIS

We know for sure, venerable father, truly we know that your insight proceeds by solving even those knotty problems of scripture at which most others fail. Therefore your diligence should not be reluctant to write to me and certain others what faith, simple prudence and prudent simplicity thinks about the three persons of the godhead for the common good of catholic Christians.

With these flattering words 'brother John' begs Anselm to resolve a question which Roscelin of Compiègne had raised: 'if three persons are merely one thing and not three individual things like three angels or three souls in such a way that by will and power they are entirely the same, then the Father and the Holy Spirit *has* become incarnate with the Son.'[1] Roscelin claimed that Anselm had yielded this point in disputation, as had Lanfranc. John felt sure that this contradicted an image of the Trinity as like the sun, a single thing endowed with both heat and brightness, traditionally attributed to Augustine. Anselm replied to this letter after an unspecified delay, providing a preliminary answer to an issue which he promised to discuss more fully at a later date: 'Either he wants to set up three gods or he does not understand what he is saying'. Anselm apologized for being too busy to see John in person before John returned to Rome.[2] As is widely known, Anselm then set about writing the initial version of his *De incarnatione verbi*, addressed to those 'lords, fathers and brothers' who might read his open letter. He also asked Fulco, bishop of Beauvais, to reassert that he had never defended the argument attributed to him by Roscelin.

1. *Ep.* 128: Schmitt, III, pp. 270-71. On Roscelin's thought, see C.J. Mews, 'Nominalism and Theology before Abaelard: New Light on Roscelin of Compiègne', *Vivarium* 30.1 (1992), pp. 4-33. Much of my research on Roscelin was conducted at the Institute for Advanced Study, Princeton, where I benefited greatly from its magnificent resources and from discussion with Giles Constable.
2. *Ep.* 129: Schmitt, III, pp. 271-72.

VIII

St Anselm's argument with Roscelin has often been understood in doctrinal terms—the clash of a philosophical realist with an unspiritual nominalist. Anselm described his adversary as one of 'those heretics of modern dialectic who do not believe a universal to be anything more than the puff of an utterance'. The political context of the conflict has never been analysed, it being commonly assumed that we know nothing about Roscelin other than that he became the teacher of Peter Abelard. Yet there are other documents beyond the correspondence of St Anselm which shed light on the dispute.

It may be useful to begin by looking more closely at what Roscelin's critic, John, was doing at the time in France. John was a Roman cleric who had become a monk at Bec not long after Anselm became abbot there in late 1079.[3] In his first letter to Anselm, Pope Urban II observed that the abbot of Bec had caused some controversy in Rome by presuming to ordain John, 'a son of our Church', to higher orders.[4] The Pope nonetheless allowed John to assist another Bec monk, Fulco, to establish himself as bishop of Beauvais, on the proviso that he return 'within a year from this present Lent'. He seems to be writing in Lent 1089. Fulco had initially obtained the see of Beauvais directly from the king after the death of Ursio, probably in 1088.[5] After returning to Italy,

---

3.   Eadmer, *Historia novorum in Anglia* (ed. M. Rule; London, 1884), p. 96 and *Vita Anselmi* (ed. R.W. Southern; London, 1962), p. 106 n. 1; William of Malmesbury, *De gestis pontificum Anglorum* (ed. N. Hamilton; London, 1870), p. 98. The name 'Ioannes episcopus' occurs relatively early among those received under Anselm's abbacy, while 'Fulco episcopus' was one of the last to be received prior to Herluin's death in September 1078, according to the list of Bec monks in Vat. Reg. 499; A. Porée, *Histoire de l'abbaye de Bec* (Evreux, 1901), I, p. 630.

4.   *Ep.* 125: Schmitt, III, p. 266.

5.   There is no firm evidence that Ursio died in 1089, as assumed by L.-H. Labande, *Histoire de Beauvais et des institutions communales jusqu'au commencement du XVe siècle* (Paris, 1892), p. 52 n. 5. All we know of him is that he signed a royal privilege at Compiègne in 1085 (M. Prou, *Recueil des Actes de Philippe Ier, Roi de France [1059–1108]* [Paris, 1908], p. 299, no. 117). The martyrology of Beauvais indicates only that he died on 18 April. No bishop of Beauvais was present when the king confirmed a prebend of Saint-Quentin in 1089 (Prou, *Recueil des Actes*, pp. 303-304, no. 119 [with a corresponding document from Saint-Quentin edited at n. 1]). Ewald argued that Fulco's submission to the Pope, recorded in the *Collectio Britannica*, took place before the council of Melfi, September 1088, like other events it recorded ('Die Papstbriefe der Britischen Sammlung', *Neues Archiv* 5 [1880], p. 360). In his edition of the notice, D. Lohrmann (*Papsturkunden in Frankreich. VII. Nördliche Ile-de-France und*

John was appointed abbot of San Salvatore, Telese by Urban II; by 1100 he had become John IV, cardinal bishop of Tusculum, and was papal legate to France and England.[6] John's deposition of Hugh, abbot of Flavigny, in 1100–1101 on behalf of Norigaud, bishop of Autun, provoked Hugh to comment sarcastically about John: 'I am amazed that the seriousness of such a man, famous for his unbounded goodness and honest reputation, whose constancy the Gallican Church reveres, could be deceived by one person [Norigaud], with the result that he now holds, watches over and protects its regions with his hand, yet is the only person in our world who thinks good and right things about that man, since general opinion even of the absent and the ignorant is hostile to his judgement.'[7] Hugh, already disillusioned by what he saw as the hypocritical reform rhetoric of Roman cardinals, then berated John's high-handed attitude in excommunicating canons of Aûtun and reports otherwise unknown information about Roscelin's critic: John had been a regular canon at Saint-Quentin, Beauvais, but had abandoned his religious habit for the world; only after he had been unable to make some unspecified accusation did John become a monk of Bec.[8] This detail helps explain why Fulco asked Urban II for John's help: Fulco wanted someone who knew Beauvais.

John was wanting Anselm to assert himself as an authoritative Christian teacher at a time when there was no clear spiritual leadership in the city. He was assisting a monastic bishop then facing widespread

Vermandois [Göttingen, new edn, 1976], p. 23 n. 17 and pp. 246-47, no. 13, following JL 5046) notes that the date cannot be established more exactly than between March 1088 and July 1089. He suggested July 1089 as the most likely date for Fulco's submission on the authority of the 1 August date appended to Urban's letter of indulgence in Paris, BN *lat.* 14146 f. 164ᵛ. However, as M. Horn ('Zur Geschichte des Bischofs Fulco von Beauvais [1089-1095]', *Francia* 16.1 [1989], pp. 176-84 [179]) points out, the rubric is contradicted by Urban's statement that he was writing during Lent. J.R. Somerville queries the 1088 date for Fulco's submission without realizing that the 1089 date for Ursio's decease was only approximate ('Mercy and Justice in the Early Months of Urban II's Pontificate', in *Chiesa, diritto e ordinamento della 'Societas christiana' nei secoli XI e XII: Atti della nona Settimana internazionale di studio, Mendola, 1983* [Milan, 1986], pp. 138-54 [50-1], reprinted in *Papacy, Councils and Canon Law in the 11th-12th Centuries* [London, 1990]).

6. R. Hüls, *Kardinäle, Klerus und Kirchen Roms 1049–1130* (Tübingen, 1977), pp. 141-42. John IV died in 1119, MGH SS 20.74.

7. *Chronicon*, MGH SS 8.494.

8. *Chronicon*, MGH SS 8.494.

opposition to his authority. Anselm complained to the Pope that 'the canons and priests of his diocese, with very few exceptions, and certain laymen are so angry with him and so inflame any strangers they can by whatever means, that they curse not only him [Fulco] but also those who offer him some consolation'—presumably an allusion to John.[9] Anselm blamed this resistance on hostility to Fulco's efforts to prohibit clergy from associating with women and promoting their sons to prebends (in other words for enforcing the canons of Melfi).[10] He claimed that Fulco was resisting lay appropriation of ecclesiastical property.

A letter from the Pope to Rainaud of Rheims chiding the archbishop for his continued hostility to Fulco in 1090–1091 suggests a different picture: widespread suspicion that Fulco's father had bought the bishopric from the king.[11] Lancelin I was an ambitious Beauvais *miles* who had married his eldest son, Lancelin II, to Adelaïde, daughter of Count Hugh of Dammartin.[12] Another son, Radulfus, had been cathedral treasurer of Beauvais in 1078 before becoming a monk at Bec.[13] Anselm supported Fulco's appointment to Beauvais with the approval of the king, even though Fulco had then to renounce his position and receive it back directly from the Pope, at the same time as Henry of Soissons, an 'ecclesiastical adventurer' similarly tainted by irregular appointment.[14] Fulco was not reinstated with full episcopal rights on this first visit to Rome.[15] He had to make a second trip to Rome to swear on the Gospels

9. *Ep.* 126: Schmitt, III, p. 267.

10. *Ep.* 126: Schmitt, III, pp. 267-68. If the *Collectio Britannica* is correct in implying that Fulco submitted to the Pope before the council of Melfi, then Fulco is likely to have been present at this council in September 1088 if he did not return to Beauvais until the following Lent.

11. JL 5522; *PL* 151, 388B-389. A. Lohrmann corrects to 13 May 1090 Jaffé-Loewenfeld's dating of this letter to this date in 1094 (*Papsturkunden*, VII, p. 23 n. 19). Horn distinguishes two visits of Fulco to Rome, and assigns the Pope's letter to 13 May 1091 (n. 5 above).

12. O. Guyotjeannin, *Episcopus et comes. Affirmation et déclin de la seigneurie épiscopale au nord du royaume de France (Beauvais-Noyon, X^e-début XIIIe siècle)* (Geneva, 1987), pp. 73-74, 102-104 and 263.

13. *Ep.* 117: Schmitt, III, p. 254; see too *Ep.* 99 and *Ep.* 115: Schmitt, III, pp. 229-30 and 251.

14. Lohrmann, *Papsturkunden*, VII, pp. 246-47; see C. Clark, '"This ecclesiastical adventurer": Henry of Saint-Jean d'Angély', *English Historical Review* 34 (1969), pp. 548-60.

15. Horn, 'Zur Geschichte des Bischofs Fulco', p. 179.

with his father that no simony had taken place, bringing with him Anselm's letter of recommendation. Fulco also had the support of Ivo of Chartres, who blamed the hostility towards him on jealousy and thought it wrong for Fulco to be criticized when already pardoned by the Pope.[16]

The archbishop of Rheims nonetheless remained hostile to Fulco. The council of Soissons was called some time between 1090 and 1092 not just to judge Roscelin of Compiègne's orthodoxy, but to settle Fulco's legitimacy within the archdiocese and resolve complaints about his father's behaviour.[17] Before the assembled bishops, the elderly Lancelin I had to restore to the church of Beauvais the properties of Longueil and Berthecourt. Helinand of Laon reminded Lancelin of his excommunication on that account and of a submission he was supposed to have effected at a council in Paris, and challenged him to a duel.[18] Because Roscelin was present at Bayeux on 7 May 1092, before embarking for England, the council of Soissons must have taken place before this date.[19]

By December 1093 Fulco's position at Beauvais had deteriorated so much that Anselm asked Urban to relieve him of his bishopric.[20] In February 1094 Urban charged Fulco with complicity in no less than murder and treason.[21] Fulco had imprisoned the brother of the bishop of Sens for financial gain, delivering him as a captive to the king, and had ignored the judgment of his fellow bishops; he had also usurped possessions of Odo, castellan of the church of Beauvais, guaranteed by Pope Gregory in the time of his predecessor, Bishop Guy. Fulco had acted in

---

16. *Ep.* 3 (b), *PL* 162, 13C-14B.

17. P. Louvet, *Histoire de la ville de Beauvais* (Rouen, 1614), pp. 487-89; and M. Hermant, *Histoire ecclésiastique et civile de Beauvais et du Beauvaisis*, BN fr. 8579, pp. 448-50.

18. Guyotjeannin, *Episcopus et comes*, pp. 72-74, 103; and Labande, *Histoire de Beauvais*, p. 53; see a notice copied from the cartulary of St Pierre, Paris, BN Duchesne 22, ff. 249-50.

19. *Antiquus Cartularius Baiocensis*, no. 22 (ed. V. Bourrienne; Rouen-Paris, 1902), I, pp. 30-31: 'Rotselino Compendiensi'.

20. *Ep.* 128: Schmitt, III, p. 269. While Schmitt dates this letter to 1091, Lohrmann (*Papsturkunden*, VII, p. 23) dates it to about May 1094. Horn ('Zur Geschichte des Bischofs Fulco') notes that the letter must be before Anselm's consecration as archbishop (4 December 1093), and that it must have been written between 1091 and 1093.

21. *PL* 151, 378B-379C (JL 5509; Lohrmann, *Papsturkunden*, VII, p. 23 n. 20).

concert with his brother, Lancelin II, to try to seize Odo, snatching from him the keys of the city, which Odo held by right, and had encouraged members of Odo's household to betray their master. The Pope required Fulco to submit himself either to the archbishop of Rheims within a fortnight or to himself within three months.[22] Ivo of Chartres counselled Fulco not to resist the edicts of the papal legate, Hugh of Die.[23] Although Anselm wrote to Urban once again on Fulco's behalf after 27 May 1095, Fulco must have either died, renounced his position or have been suspended, since a new bishop of Beauvais, Roger, obtained a papal privilege for the collegiate church of St-Vaast, Beauvais, at La Chaise Dieu on 19 August 1095.[24] Recalling the establishment of canons at this church by Bishop Guy in 1072 at the request of Roscelin and Nevelo of Compiègne, the charter permitted its expansion, explicitly protecting St-Vaast from any depredation of the bishop of Beauvais.[25] This was the only known action of the bishop who replaced Fulco.

Is this Roscelin the same person as Roscelin of Compiègne? It is not a common name. Much is explained about the opposition from canons and priests in Beauvais that Fulco and John faced in 1089 if this is so. Despite the accusations against Fulco, Anselm stayed loyal to his protégé through the next five years, either not knowing or deliberately ignoring the fact that he was effectively providing spiritual legitimacy for an ambitious Beauvais family. Anselm saw nothing wrong in supporting Fulco's accession to the see, one of the most lucrative and sought after positions within the Ile-de-France. Bec had acquired some significant properties in France since 1080. Anselm's interests coincided with those of Fulco's family. The bishopric conferred effective government of the

---

22. In another missive to the clergy and people of Beauvais, Urban II confirmed existing privileges of Odo, castellan of Beauvais, against the ambitions of Fulco, *PL* 151, 379D-380A (JL 5510; Lohrmann, *Papsturkunden*, VII, p. 33 n. 5). Lohrmann's assumption that this was sent at the same time as the letter to Fulco (i.e. 14 February 1094), is questioned by Horn ('Zur Geschichte des Bischofs Fulco', p. 183); he thinks that it might belong to early in Fulco's career because it does not mention Fulco's actions. The original confirmation of Odo's possessions, then disputed by Bishop Guy (1075–79), is edited by Lohrmann, *Papsturkunden*, VII, p. 244.

23. *Yves de Chartres. Correspondance*, no. 30 (ed. J. Leclercq; Paris, 1949), pp. 127-29.

24. *Ep.* 193: Schmitt, IV, p. 82; A. Becker, *Papst Urban II (1088–1099)* (Stuttgart, 1964, 1974), II, p. 436.

25. Edited by Lohrmann, *Papsturkunden*, VII, pp. 251-52.

city and its surrounding countryside in the name of the king of France.[26] Through his two sons, the elderly Lancelin had effectively taken power over Beauvais at the same time as Bec was consolidating its position in the Ile-de-France.

The bitter antagonist of Lancelin I was Guy, bishop of Beauvais from 1063 until 1085. Guibert of Nogent remembered Guy fondly as an aristocratic figure who relished the intimate company of close companions.[27] Unlike Lancelin, Guy was an outsider to Beauvais. A former dean of Saint-Quentin-en-Vermandois and archdeacon of Laon who had been consecrated by Archbishop Gervaise of Rheims in 1063–64 (during the minority of Philip I), Guy continued Gervaise's policy of establishing collegiate churches outside the cathedral's jurisdiction to serve an expanding urban community.[28] The most famous of these was Saint-Quentin, named in honour of his former church in the Vermandois, where canons followed the Augustinian Rule, introduced by Gervaise in Rheims in 1067. In a solemn ceremony attended by many French bishops and a large crowd from the city, Guy transferred the relics of St Romana from the cathedral to the new church in 1069, deliberately weakening the monopoly of the cathedral chapter by directing popular devotion to a church outside the *urbs*.[29] Guy used the occasion to humiliate Guarinus, the treasurer of the cathedral, whom he

---

26. Guyotjeannin, *Episcopus et comes*, pp. 3-31, 62-66. On properties of Bec in France, see V. Gazeau, 'Le domaine continental du Bec. Aristocratie et monachisme au temps d'Anselme', in *Les Mutations socio-culturelles au tournant des XIe et XIIe siècles* (Paris, 1984), pp. 259-71.

27. *Autobiographie* I.15 (ed. E.-R. Labande; Paris, 1981), pp. 120-22.

28. *Vita S. Romanae virginis* 10, *Acta Sanctorum* (Paris, 1866); October 2, p. 138 and *Recueil des historiens de la France* 14.29; see A. Fliche, *Le Règne de Philippe Ier* (Paris, 1912), pp. 338-39; and Guyotjeannin, *Episcopus et comes*, pp. 70-72. J.-F. Lemarignier documents the increase of collegiate foundations during the eleventh century, often with royal support in 'Aspects politiques des fondations de collégiales dans le royaume de France au XIe siècle', in *La Vita Comune del clero nei secoli XI e XII. Atti della Settimana di studi: Mendola, settembre 1959* (Miscellanea del Centro di Studi Medievali III, Pubblicazioni dell'Università Cattolicà del S. Cuore III. 2; Milan, 1962), pp. 19-40, with discussion pp. 41-49. He observes that the strongest concentration of collegiate churches, standing up to the monastic federations of Bec, Cluny and Marmoutiers, was in the archdiocese of Rheims.

29. *Acta Sanctorum* Oct. 2, pp. 138-39, with valuable introduction on pp. 134-37.

accused of purloining half the tithe of the city of Beauvais for personal advantage.[30]

In 1072 Guy increased the number of canons at the church of Saint-Vaast, 'at the request of Roscelin, cantor of Saint-Pierre and Nevelon, canon of Compiègne so that by an increased number of ministers, the service of religion might be multiplied'.[31] His charter described this ancient church, now called Saint-Etienne, as 'by its antiquity in the burg of Beauvais like the mother and head of the other churches placed both in the city and the suburb'. It assured them 'the same liberty and dignity as other canons in the city as in the suburb'. The bishop's anathema against anyone who removed the stipends of these canons suggests resistance from the cathedral chapter to the development. Leading the signatories to this charter, after the Benedictine abbots of Saint-Lucian and Saint-Symphorian, was Ivo, described here as abbot of Saint-Quentin.[32] Ivo's presence at Saint-Vaast, hitherto unnoticed in discussion of the

30. Labande, *Histoire de Beauvais*, p. 260, pièce justificative no. 2. By 1072 a new treasurer had been appointed, named Gualterius.

31. The original foundation charter of Saint-Vaast was edited by Louvet, *Histoire de la ville de Beauvais*, pp. 480-82 and *Histoire et antiquitez du païs de Beauvaisis* (Beauvais, 1631–35), I, pp. 694-95: 'Guido Dei gratia Belvacensis Episcopus omnibus tam futuris quam praesentibus notum sit. Quod nos considerantes Domini Roscelini Cantoris Ecclesiae S. Petri et Nevelonis Compendiensis Ecclesiae Canonici religiosam devotionem collaudamus, et sicut dignum est comprobamus. Hi siquidem Ecclesiam B. Vedasti quae in Belvacensi Burgo sita pro antiquitatis dignitate quasi mater, et caput et coeterarum Ecclesiarum tam in urbe quam in suburbio positarum sub nomine personae possidentes cum duo tantum in ea presbyteri deservirent nostrae mansuetudinis licentiam postularunt, ut in praedicta Ecclesia plures apponi Canonicos concederemus: quatinus augmentato numero ministrorum multiplicaretur quoque religionis obsequium. Quorum laudabilem petitionem libenter amplectentes in praedicta B. Vedasti Ecclesia Canonicos institui decrevimus, id etiam constituentes ut Canonici illi iam dictam Ecclesiam, necnon et Ecclesiam S. Salvatoris sine calumnia possideant, cum omnibus quae ad utramque Ecclesiam pertinentia in ea die qua Canonici constituti sunt, Roscelinus et Nevelo possidebant. Id etiam decernimus et praesenti pagina sancimus ut iam dictae Ecclesiae Canonici ea dignitate et libertate vigeant quam caeteri qui vel in suburbio sunt Canonici obtinent. Ut autem haec Canonicorum institutio rata in posterum et stabilis permaneat illam cartae praesentis attestatione et sigilli nostri assignatione corroboramus. Illud postremo adiicientes ut si quis Canonicorum redditus et stipendiae vel Ecclesiae ornamenta violenter aut fraudulenter et perperam detrahere, corrumpere aut alienare praesumpserit anathema sit.'

32. The dozen clerics who signed included Hugh (dean of Saint-Pierre), Walter (treasurer), Roger and Goscelin (archdeacons); among the dozen lay signatories was the castellan Odo, with whom Fulco entered into conflict.

date of his arrival in Beauvais, confirms that he had already been invited by Guy to introduce a reformed canonical life at Saint-Quentin at its foundation (not in 1078, as had been thought).[33] One of the twelve prebends of Saint-Vaast was controlled by Saint-Quentin.[34]

Guy's sense of the educational role of his collegiate foundations and outrage at clerical malpractice is clarified by his charter for Saint-Nicolas in 1078. Its establishment had been prompted not just by certain clerics, but by 'helpers of the lay order'.[35] Its prebends could not be acquired by an outside cleric who simply paid for a deputy (reported to be a common practice). To avoid the pernicious practice of able clergy being driven out of the church by poverty at the expense of the idle rich, the canons of the cathedral had to grant a prebend without cost to maintain a treasurer, charged with educating boys and maintaining the fabric of the church.[36] Saint-Vaast would have had a similar educational role. Standing at the heart of the commune of Beauvais, the church came to be endowed by the burghers, often textile merchants, of the city.

Guy's patronage of collegiate churches brought him into conflict with the cathedral chapter. Only a year after establishing canons at Saint-Vaast, Guy was accused of despoiling episcopal property for the sake of his new foundations.[37] Gregory VII insisted that the canons receive Guy back to the city.[38] Guy was also in conflict with Lancelin I, whom he had excommunicated for seizing episcopal properties at Longueil and

---

33. The 1078 date for Ivo's invitation to Beauvais is based on a Beauvais version of Sigebert's *Chronicon, PL* 160, 388B; MGH SS 6.461-2: 'Ab hoc tempore coepit reflorere in ecclesia beati Quintini Belvacensis canonicus Ordo, primum ab Apostolis, postea ex beato Augustino episcopo regulariter institutus, sub magistro Ivone, venerabili eiusdem ecclesiae praeposito, postea Carnotensium episcopo.' The date is debated in the Bollandist introduction to the *Vita S. Romanae, Acta Sanctorum* Oct. 2, p. 135.

34. Confirmed in 1116; see Lohrmann, *Papsturkunden*, VII, p. 266.

35. Louvet, *Histoire et antiquitez*, pp. 689-90 (*Histoire de la ville de Beauvais*, p. 492).

36. *Histoire et antiquitez*, pp. 690-91 (*Histoire de la ville de Beauvais*, pp. 493-94).

37. *Acta Sanctorum* Oct. 2, p. 139. The editors suggest (p. 136) that Guy's expulsion may have been provoked by his generosity to the newly founded church of Saint-Quentin, for whose sake he despoiled existing churches, a point reiterated by Labande, *Histoire de Beauvais*, p. 48.

38. Gregory VII, *Registrum* I.74-75 (JL 4854-5), *PL* 148, 347C-8D, dated 13 April 1074; *Papsturkunden*, VII, pp. 23 n. 12 and 32 nn. 1-2.

VIII

Berthecourt.[39] In 1074 Gregory VII had urged the archbishops and bishops of France to protest against the king's harassment of merchants and pilgrims, and singled out Lancelin of Beauvais as a brigand for taking hostage a pilgrim from Rome, Fulcher of Chartres.[40] Lancelin's son, Radulfus, had become cathedral treasurer by 1078, when Guy was accused by the papal legate, Hugh of Die, of selling prebends (probably alienating cathedral prebends for collegiate foundations).[41] In January 1079 Guy succeeded in obtaining royal confirmation at Gerberoy that Saint-Quentin fell under his jurisdiction alone. Radulfus was still treasurer when he attended that august assembly, which gathered the kings of England and France, as well as Anselm of Bec, Ivo of Saint-Quentin and Lancelin.[42] Not much later Radulfus left Beauvais for Bec. Fulco's future assistant, John, also left Saint-Quentin for Bec about this time. According to Guibert of Nogent, Guy's subsequent ousting in 1085 was engineered by those he had promoted within his diocese.[43] After Guy was officially deposed by Hugh of Die in 1085, he became a monk at Cluny, where the prior was Ivo, a monk from Saint-Quentin-en-Vermandois who had been with him in Beauvais.[44] It is difficult to avoid surmising that Lancelin I, Radulfus and John were all involved with Hugh of Die in the conspiracy against Bishop Guy. An alliance between Bec and a local Beauvais dynasty was forged.

After the short spell of Ursio as bishop of Beauvais (1085–88?), the accession of Fulco marked a clear victory for the elderly Lancelin.[45] It

39. Gregory lifted Guy's excommunication against Lancelin according to a document printed by Louvet, *Histoire de Beauvais*, pp. 486-7 (*PL* 148, 658BC); Lohrmann (*Papsturkunden*, VII, p. 32 no. 3) notes Jaffé's opinion (*Bibliotheca rerum Germanicarum*, II, p. 520 n. 1) that this was a forgery, presumably on the grounds that Lancelin was still excommunicated on his deathbed in 1092. See Guyotjeannin, *Episcopus et comes*, p. 74 n. 29 and Labande, *Histoire de Beauvais*, pp. 48-49, 53.

40. *Registrum* II.5 (*PL* 148, 363A-365D).

41. Hugh of Die, MGH SS 8.419; Lohrmann, *Papsturkunden*, VII, p. 23 n. 15. Anselm's earliest letter to Hugh, E100 (Schmitt, III, pp. 131-32), written soon after 1082, when Hugh was appointed archbishop of Lyons, indicates that they were already friends.

42. Prou, *Recueil des Actes*, no. xciv, pp. 242-45. Lancelin was described as *casatus* of the church of Beauvais, having taken over the role from Odo, castellan in 1072.

43. *Autobiographie* I.14 (ed. Labande), p. 100.

44. Guibert de Nogent, *Autobiographie* I.15 (ed. Labande), p. 118.

45. *Lancelinus senex* witnessed an undated judgement of Fulco (Paris, BN

was advantageous for Bec to have such high-placed contacts in France. Either the older or the younger Lancelin witnessed a royal privilege for possessions of Bec in France in 1077. One or other is likely to be the Lancelin who was *buticularius* to the king some time between 1086–90/91 when Bec monks were granted exemptions from tax in Paris, Pontoise, Poissy and Mantes.[46] The first and only known action of Roger, Fulco's successor at Beauvais, was to obtain from Pope Urban II at La Chaise-Dieu in 1095 papal confirmation of the privileges of Guy's foundation at Saint-Vaast from episcopal interference.[47] Roger's charter specifically recalled the initiative of Roscelin and Nevelon of Compiègne in establishing the community. The privileges of another foundation of Guy, at Bury, were also confirmed by Urban II at this time, with the support of the canons of Beauvais.[48]

Given that John was in Beauvais for less than a year, engaged in controversy with 'nearly all' the canons and priests of the diocese and that Anselm subsequently addressed his letter about Roscelin to Fulco, it seems logical to assume that John argued with Roscelin of Compiègne in that city. After the council of Soissons, Roscelin made contact with

Baluze 71, ff. 19-19ᵛ) cited by Prou, *Recueil des Actes*, p. cxxxvii n. 9. On the date of Lancelin I's death, see Labande, *Histoire de Beauvais*, p. 53 n. 4.

46. Guyotjeannin, *Episcopus et comes*, p. 102 n. 153; and J.-F. Lemarignier, *Le gouvernement royal aux premiers temps capétiens (987–1108)* (Paris, 1965), p. 157 n. 95 and appendix; Prou, *Recueil des Actes*, nos. xc, pp. 232-34 and cxxii, pp. 308-10; the latter privilege for Bec was extended by Philip and Louis conjointly some time between 1092 and 1108, Prou, *Recueil des Actes*, no. clxvii, pp. 410-11 (no witnesses cited), and J. Dufour, *Recueil des Actes de Louis VI*, I (Paris, 1992), no. 18, pp. 31-32. Lancelin is mentioned as *pincerna regis* in 1086, Prou, *Recueil des Actes*, no. cxvii, pp. 301-302, and as *buticularius* to the king in 1089 in a charter granting privileges to the canons of Sainte-Croix of Orléans, *Cartulaire de Sainte-Croix d'Orléans (814–1300)* (ed. J. Thillier and E. Jarry), no. xlvii, pp. 95-96.

47. Ivo did not officially relinquish his position at Saint-Quentin until 1094, even though he was elected to the see of Chartres in November 1090, *Yves de Chartres. Correspondance* (ed. Leclercq), no. 31, pp. 126-28.

48. Guy's last major action had been to confirm the establishment of a community at Bury in 1084–85, originally established in 1079–80 at the request of a certain Albert for more canons to serve the needs of the local community. It was then transformed into a monastery belonging to Saint-Jean d'Angély, *Le Cartulaire de l'Abbaye Royale de Saint-Jean d'Angély* (Archives Historiques de la Saintonge et de l'Aunis XXX; Paris, 1901), no. xv, pp. 36-38, confirmed by Philip I in 1085, no. xvi, pp. 39-40; for the confirmation by Pope Urban II, see no. xiv, p. 35. See Guyotjeannin, *Episcopus et comes*, p. 71.

VIII

Ivo of Chartres, formerly dean of Saint-Quentin, Beauvais, but was warned by Ivo that a visit to Chartres would be compromising for himself. He suggested Roscelin issue a retractation to clear his name.[49]

Roscelin was a native of the region of Compiègne, not a canon of that town.[50] In a letter to Abelard, Roscelin rejected the claim that he had been exiled by the churches of Soissons and Rheims 'where I was born and brought up'. He boasted of holding canonries at Loches, Tours and Besançon, even of being received favourably in Rome (perhaps a reference to reception by Urban II, formerly of Rheims, during his travels in France 1095–96, rather than to any visit to Rome).[51] Roscelin was an old man when he wrote that letter to Abelard (c. 1119–20). He could have been a young cantor at St-Pierre in 1072, invited to the post by a reforming bishop from outside Beauvais, eager to employ a promising teacher.

According to an entry added in the early twelfth century to an eleventh-century martyrology of Beauvais cathedral a *Roscelinus grammaticus* bequeathed to the chapter at his death (9 July of an unknown year) fourteen books, of grammar, logic and rhetoric, with some theology: 'Roscelinus grammaticus dedit libros suos Sancto Petro: Augustinum super Johannem, Augustinum de doctrina christiana, Prissianum, Macrobium, Arismeticam, Dialecticam, Rethoricam de inventione, Boetium de consolatione, Virgilium, Oratium, Juvenalem, Ovidium metamorphoseon, Statium Thebaïdos, et troparium.'[52] This Roscelin also bequeathed his house in the cathedral cloister and eight *arpenni* of vines at Hosdenc, eight kilometres from Beauvais.[53] The

---

49. *Yves de Chartres. Correspondance*, no. 7 (ed. Leclercq), pp. 22-24.

50. *Ep. ad Abaelardum*, in *Der Nominalismus in der Frühscholastik* (Beiträge zur Geschichte der Philosophie der Mittelalters 8.5; ed. J. Reiners; Münster, 1910), pp. 64-65.

51. *Ep. ad Abaelardum* (ed. Reiners), p. 65.

52. L. Delisle, 'Notice sur un manuscrit de l'abbaye de Luxeuil copié en 625', *Notices et extraits des manuscrits de la bibliothèque nationale* 31.2 (Paris, 1886), pp. 149-64 (160); see also H. Omont, *Recherches sur la bibliothèque de l'église cathédrale de Beauvais* (Paris, 1914), pp. 2-3. I am indebted to Françoise Gasparri for confirming an early twelfth-century date (c. 1120), rather than eleventh-century, as judged by Delisle.

53. Delisle, *Notices*, p. 160: 'Nonis julii. Obiit Roscelinus gramaticus, qui dedit nobis suam domum in claustro, et octo arpennos vinearum in hosdenco, et libros suos numero quatuordecim.' Delisle suggested that this Roscelin was the same person as the cantor Roscelin, but repeated the confused statement in *Histoire*

presence of the book of tropes points to this being the same Roscelin as was cantor in 1072.

Roscelin the grammarian did not leave any identifiable annotation to the most precious item in his bequest to Beauvais, an uncial exemplar of Augustine's homilies on the Johannine epistles copied at Luxeuil in the seventh century (our earliest extant copy of the homilies). Also among his books was a tenth-century Horace.[54] The collection reminds us that a late eleventh-century *grammaticus* was expected to teach not just grammar, but dialectic and rhetoric as well as theology. It is particularly valuable because the books seem deliberately chosen to cover the whole curriculum. This collection would have been available later in the twelfth century to Ralph of Beauvais, who used classical authors extensively in his grammatical teaching and quoted approvingly the opinion of *nominales* that 'man' denoted the status of being a man, both special and general.[55] From his books, *Roscelinus grammaticus* seems to have been a master of great learning and erudition.

In his letter to Abelard, Roscelin insisted that he remained in good standing with the churches of Rheims and Soissons.[56] If, as Abelard implied, Roscelin had become unpopular at Tours, then it is not implausible that he should have wished to bequeath some of his books to the cathedral where he spent his first twenty years as a teacher. There is no reason for him to have lost whatever property he owned in the archdiocese of Rheims after the accusations raised at the council of Soissons.

While the evidence for identifying Roscelin the grammarian and Roscelin the canon at Saint-Vaast (and ally of Nevelo of Compiègne)

---

littéraire de la France, IX (Paris, rev. edn, 1868), p. 364, that Roscelin and Nevelon founded a community of canons regular in Saint-Vaast, Soissons. He cites Mabillon's authority for distinguishing the cantor of Beauvais from Roscelin of Compiègne, but I have been unable to identify the passage to which he alludes.

54. New York, Pierpoint Morgan Library no. 334 (see E.A. Lowe, *Codices Latini Antiquiores*, IX [Oxford, 1966] no. 1659, p. 23) and Leiden, Universiteitsbiblioteek, Bibl. pub. lat. 28; there is extensive grammatical commentary in this, according to a communication from J. Dijs, but it remains as yet unstudied.

55. On Ralph of Beauvais, see the pioneering discussion of R.W. Hunt, 'Studies on Priscian in the Twelfth Century', *Mediaeval and Renaissance Studies* 2 (1950), pp. 1-56, reprinted in his *Collected Papers on the History of Grammar in the Middle Ages* (ed. G.L. Bursill-Hall; Amsterdam, 1980), pp. 39-94, and Ralph's *Glose super Donatum* (ed. C.H. Kneepkens; Nijmegen, 1982), p. 21 (with comment on p. xxv).

56. *Ep. ad Abaelardum* (ed. Reiners), p. 63.

VIII

with Roscelin of Compiègne is inevitably circumstantial, it is hard to believe that the political arguments with Beauvais clergy in which Fulco and John were involved were not related to their doctrinal dispute at exactly this time with Roscelin of Compiègne. John's accusation that Roscelin was preaching heresy makes sense as an attempt to counter criticism raised about himself and Bishop Fulco. By supporting Fulco, Anselm was drawn unwittingly into an acrimonious local dispute. Both Roscelin and John claimed the authority of Anselm in their argument about the Trinity, an argument sharpened by bitter controversy surrounding Fulco's appointment. Roscelin of Compiègne's zeal for reform, notably his attacks on the ordination of sons of priests, provoked criticism from Theobald of Etampes, when he travelled briefly in England in 1092–93.[57] New collegiate foundations, much more numerous in the archdiocese of Rheims than in Normandy or England, provided a vital educational resource for prosperous towns, but their influence could be resented by monks as too sharply committed to new ideas about theology. Roscelin of Compiègne, who had studied at Rheims in the reform-minded atmosphere encouraged by Archbishop Gervaise, issued from such a world.

---

57. Theobald, *Epistola ad Roscelinum*, in T. Boehmer (ed.), MGH *Libelli de lite* (Hannover, 1897), III, pp. 603-607 (*PL* 163, 767-70); *Defensio pro filiis presbyterorum* (ed. Boehmer), in *Libelli de lite*, III, pp. 579-83.

IX

The Trinitarian Doctrine
of Roscelin of Compiègne and its Influence:
Twelfth-century Nominalism and Theology Re-considered

Roscelin of Compiègne is an enigmatic figure, remembered largely through second hand report. Otto of Freising described him as "the first in our times to institute in logic the teaching of words (*sententiam vocum*)"[1]. Anselm of Bec considered him to be simply one of a new generation of dialecticians:

> ... who do not think universal substances to be anything but the puff of an utter-ance, who cannot understand colour to be other than a body, or the wisdom of man other than the soul – they are to be completely blown away from discussion of spiritual questions. In their minds, reasoning, which ought to be the prince and judge of everything which is in man, has thus been enveloped by bodily imagin-ings, that it cannot free itself from them, nor is it able to discern from them those things which it ought to contemplate pure and alone. For who does not yet under-stand how several oxen are one ox in species: how can he understand how, in that most hidden and lofty nature, several persons, of which each individual one is perfect God, are one God? And how can he whose mind is confused in judging between his donkey and its colour, distinguish between one God and his three-fold relation[2]?

---

1. Otto of Freising, *Gesta Friderici I Imperatoris*, I 48, ed. G. Waitz and B. von Simson, MGH Scriptores rerum germanicarum in usum scholarum separatim editi 46, Hannover-Leipzig, 1912, p. 69. The ideas in this paper have benefited greatly from discussion with Jean Jolivet over many years, ever since I first participated in his seminars on Abelard and then Gilbert of Poitiers at the Vᵉ section of the ÉPHÉ in 1980. I am also very grateful for the opportunity to discuss these ideas at the ÉPHÉ during January 1993, in particular with Irène Rosier. I presented an earlier version in 1991 at the Madison conference on medieval nomi-nalism, "Nominalism and Theology before Abaelard: New Light on Roscelin of Compiègne", *Vivarium* 30, 1992, p. 4-33.
2. Anselm, *De incarnatione verbi*, ed. F.S. Schmitt, *Anselmi Opera Omnia*, 6 vol., Roma-Edinburgh, Thomas Nelson, 1946-1968, vol. 1, p. 285 (expanded in *DIV*² c. 1093, vol. 2, p. 9-10): "illi utique dialectici <+ immo dialecticae heretici>, qui non nisi flatum vocis putant universales esse substantias, et qui colorem non aliud queunt intelligere quam corpus, nec sapientiam hominis aliud quam animam, prorsus a spiritualium quaestionum disputatione sunt exsufflandi. In eorum quippe animabus ratio, quae et princeps et iudex debet omnium esse quae sunt in homine, sic est in imaginationibus corporeis obvoluta, ut ex eis se non possit evolvere nec ab ipsis ea quae ipsa sola et pura contemplari debet, valeat discernere. Qui enim nondum intelligit quomodo plures boves in specie sint unus bos: qualiter in illa secretissima et altissima natura comprehendet quomodo plures personae, quarum singula

Anselm was implicitly accusing such dialecticians of not living up to the philosophic ideal of rising from the particular to contemplate what was universal, defined by Boethius in the fifth book of the *Consolation of Philosophy*[3].

Anselm made these claims in 1090 when responding to a request put to him by John, a monk of Bec helping another Bec monk, Fulco, establish himself as bishop of Beauvais, in the face of considerable opposition from local clergy[4]. Roscelin of Compiègne had advanced an argument which John thought to be dangerously innovative[5]:

> If the three persons are only one thing, and not three things in themselves, like three angels or three souls, in such a way, however, that they are completely the same thing by will and power, then the Father and the Holy Spirit has become incarnate with the Son[6].

Anselm subsequently learnt that Roscelin had insisted that Christians had to defend their faith, just as pagans (*i.e.* Muslims) and Jews defend their law, perhaps vaguely aware of Muslim and Jewish thinkers like Ibn Sīnā (980-1037)

---

quaeque perfectus est deus, sint unus deus? Et cuius mens obscura est ad diiudicandum inter asinum suum et colorem eius: qualiter discernet inter unum deum et trinam relationem eius?"; see too vol. 1, p. 289 (vol. 2, p. 17-18): "Quod si iste de illis dialecticis modernis est, qui nihil esse credunt nisi quod imaginationibus comprehendere possunt, nec putat esse aliquid in quo partes nullae sunt...".

3. Boethius, *Philosophiae Consolatio*, V 4, 27-39, ed. L. Bieler, "Corpus Christianorum" Series Latina 94, Turnhout, 1957, p. 97, an allusion commented on by J. Jolivet, "Trois variations" (n. 15 below), p. 125.

4. *Epist. 128*, following an exchange between Urban II and Anselm about John and Fulco, *Anselmi Opera Omnia*, ed. Schmitt, vol. 3, p. 270-1; on John, see also Hugh of Flavigny, *Chronicon*, MGH SS 8, p. 494. The council of Soissons (1091/92?) not only considered the case against Roscelin, but the case against Fulco's father, Lancelin I (who was forced to abjure his acquisition of certain ecclesiastical lands); *cf.* O. Guyotjeannin, *Episcopus et comes. Affirmation et déclin de la seigneurie épiscopale au nord du royaume de France (Beauvais-Noyon, Xᵉ-début XIIIᵉ siècle)*, Geneva, Droz, 1987, p. 73-74, 102-4 and 263 and M. Horn, "Zμr Geschichte des Bischofs Fulco von Beauvais (1089-1095)", *Francia* 16.1, 1989, p. 176-184.

5. Anselm's adversary may have been the Roscelin, cantor at Beauvais cathedral who established canons at St Vaast with the help of bishop Guy (long hostile to Fulco's father and eventually ousted from Beauvais in 1085), P. Louvet, *Histoire de la ville et cité de Beauvais*, Rouen, 1613 (reprinted Marseille, 1977), p. 480-482. He may also have been the *Roscelinus grammaticus* who left fourteen books to Beauvais in the early twelfth century, including an uncial copy of Augustine's *In Iohannis epistulam*, *De doctrina christiana*, Priscian, Macrobius, an *Arismetica*, a *Dialectica*, *Rethorica de inventione*, Boethius' *Consolation of Philosophy*, Virgil, Horace, Juvenal, Ovid's *Metamorphoses*; see H. Omont, *Recherches sur la bibliothèque de l'église cathédrale de Beauvais*, Paris, 1914, p. 2-3. While Roscelin was born in Compiègne, there is no evidence that he was ever a canon of that town. Roscelin only took up canonries at Loches and then Tours after 1092; see "Nominalism and Theology before Abaelard", p. 24 n. 52, and "Anselm, Roscelin and the see of Beauvais", *Anselm. Aosta, Bec and Canterbury. Papers in Commemoration of the Nine-Hundredeth Anniversary of Anselm's Enthronement as Archbishop, 25 September 1093*, ed. D.E. Luscombe and G.R. Evans, Sheffield, Sheffield University Press, 1996, p. 106-119.

6. Anselm reproduces his report of Roscelin's argument almost verbatim in *DIV*[1] (ed. Schmitt, vol. 1, p. 282, 285) and *DIV*[2] (vol. 2, p. 4, 6-9): "Si <+ in deo *DIV*[2]> tres personae sunt una tantum res et non sunt tres res <+ unaquaeque *DIV*[1,2]> per se <+ separatim *DIV*[2]>, sicut tres angeli aut tres animae, ita tamen ut voluntate et potentia omnino sint idem: ergo pater et spiritus sanctus cum filio *incarnatus est* [my italics]."

and Rashi (1040-1105)[7]. John was perturbed that Roscelin was claiming that his argument had been conceded both by Lanfranc and Anselm himself. He thought the argument flatly contradicted the opinion he attributed to Augustine, that the trinity was a single thing, like the sun, a single thing, emitting heat and light[8]. Anselm never repeated this particular argument in his *De incarnatione Verbi* against Roscelin. Rather he considered Roscelin's argument to be the fruit of failure to grasp the most elementary principles of dialectic, which led directly to tritheism[9]. Just as he misunderstood the nature of a universal substance, so he misunderstood the unity of God. Such rhetoric has been of enormous influence in moulding subsequent perception of Roscelin as a nominalist who considered universals as "just" words, implicitly denying that individuals shared anything that was universal.

In the early sixteenth century, Aventinus (Johannes Turmair) relied on the authority of Otto of Freising to assert that Roscelin was

> the founder of a new school, who first founded the knowledge of utterances or words, finding a new way of philosophizing, from which two kinds of Aristotelians and Peripatetics have emerged, an older way rich in creating things, which they call for themselves the knowledge of things (for which reason they are called realists), the other a new one, which removes this knowledge, called nominalists because they seem to be expositors hungry for things, but prolix in names and notions of words; and between these two kinds there is dissent and civil war[10].

He thought that Ockham, Buridan, and Marsilius of Inghen all advocated this new way. Turmair was looking for the historical roots of the factionalism he had encountered within the university of Paris. His classification of philosophers into realists and nominalists indirectly owed much to the efforts of Gerson to impose order on a turbulent intellectual environment in the late fourteenth century, as well as to more distant echoes of debate from the twelfth-century schools[11].

---

7. *DIV*[1-2] (vol. 1, p. 285; vol. 2, p. 10): "Pagani defendunt legem suam, Iudaei defendunt legem suam. Ergo et nos Christiani debemus defendere fidem nostram."
8. The passage alluded to by John occurs in *Sermo 245* among the spuria of Augustine, PL 39, 2196-97, *Clavis Patristica Pseudepigraphorum Medii Aevi*, ed. J. Machielsen, CCSL 1A, Turnhout, 1990, p. 210, no. 1030.
9. *Epist. 136* (vol. 3, p. 279) to Fulco, bishop of Beauvais.
10. *Johannes Turmair's genannt Aventinus Sammtliche Werke* III, *Annales Ducum Boicarum* VI 3, ed. S. Riezler, München, 1884, [first published Ingolstadt, 1554] vol. 2, p. 200: "Hisce quoque temporibus fuisse reperio Rucelinum Britonum, magistrum Petri Abelardi, novi lycei conditorem, qui primus scientiam vocum [transforming Otto's *sententiam vocum*] sive dictionum instituit, novam philosophandi viam invenit; eo namque authore duo Aristelicorum Peripateticorumque genera esse coeperunt, unum illud vetus, locuples in rebus procreandis, quod scientiam rerum sibi vendicant, quamobrem reales vocantur, alterum novum, quod eam distrahit, nominales ideo nuncupati, quod avari rerum, prodigi nominum atque notionum verborum videntur esse adsertores; in hisce duobus generibus dissidium et bellum civile est." Aventinus also incorporated the satirical poem about Roscelin's attachment to *voces* in the *Codex Udalrici*, ed. Ph. Jaffé, *Bibliotheca rerum Germanicarum*, Berlin, 1869, vol. 5, p. 187.
11. Brilliantly exposed by Z. Kaluza, *Les querelles doctrinales à Paris. Nominalistes et réalistes aux confins du XIVe et du XVe siècles*, Bergamo, Perluigi Lubrina Editore, 1988. On

350

There is a long and venerable literature on nominalism as an innovative philosophy, quite different from an older realist tradition, which identifies Abelard as leading representative of a nominalist school of thought assumed to be Aristotelian and hostile to an ill-defined, supposedly Platonic philosophical realism [12]. Paradoxically, Roscelin has attracted little critical attention. The first serious study was that of Picavet, who questioned whether Roscelin had established a coherent nominalist philosophical system, but thought that he had recognized that "one could not apply categories of the physical world to the intelligible world" [13]. Picavet was fascinated by what he saw as an unresolved tension between Roscelin's neoplatonist trinitarian theology and his Aristotelian philosophical interest in the categories of the sensible world. The few subsequent studies that have since appeared on Roscelin have focussed more on his doctrine of universals than on his theology, and have been essentially reliant on the same small body of mostly hostile testimony as known to Picavet [14].

Turmair's encounter with nominalist philosophers in Paris, see G. Strauss, *Historian in an Age of Crisis. The Life and Work of Johannes Aventinus 1477-1534*, Cambridge Mass., 1963, p. 33-35.

12. V. Cousin influenced much subsequent perception of Abelard's contribution to medieval philosophy, above all to dialectic, by considering Abelard's "conceptualisme" to be a refinement of Roscelin's nominalism, which he assumed to mark a radical break with the philosophic realism of the past. Cousin looked for French precursors to Kant, whose "conceptualisme" he considered to have been idealized "jusqu'au système le plus réaliste et le plus objectif qui ait été depuis Platon"; cf. *Fragments philosophiques. Philosophie scolastique*, Paris, Ladrange, 2nd ed. 1840, p. 279. His categories of nominalism and realism derive from an earlier German enlightenment tradition, exemplified by J. Brucker, *Historia critica philosophiae*, Leipzig, 2nd ed. 1767, vol. 3, p. 709-731, indirectly stretching back to Aventinus. An alternative to the view that nominalism was essentially about universals was voiced by W.J. Courtenay, who suggested its roots may derive from grammatical discussion of the unity of meaning of nouns in propositions, "Nominales and Nominalism in the Twelfth Century", *Lectionum varietates. Hommage à Paul Vignaux (1904-1987)*, ed. J. Jolivet et al., Paris, Vrin, 1991, p. 11-48. These ideas, as also of C.G. Normore, "The Tradition of Medieval Nominalism", *Studies in Medieval Philosophy*, ed. J.F. Wippel, "Studies in the Philosophy and the History of Philosophy" 17, Washington, Catholic University of America, 1987, p. 201-217, were debated in a conference on twelfth-century nominalism, whose proceedings were published within *Vivarium* 30.1, 1992, including a valuable repertory, "Logico-Theological Schools from the Second Half of the 12th Century: A List of Sources" (p. 173-214) compiled by Y. Iwakuma and S. Ebbesen. While Courtenay in his introduction to the volume (p. 1) rightly comments on the longevity of the established focus on universals, his claim that Jolivet's "non-realism" is simply a substitution for "nominalism" fails to appreciate the significance of Jolivet's effort to direct attention away from universals to semantic theory (p. 1; see n. 15 below). For an overview of intellectual developments in the twelfth century, see my chapter, "Philosophy and Theology 1100-1150: The Search for Harmony", in *Le douzième siècle: les années tournants 1120-1150*, ed. F. Gasparri, Paris, Ed. Léopard d'Or, 1994, p. 159-203.

13. *Roscelin, philosophe et théologien d'après la légende et d'après l'histoire. Sa place dans l'histoire générale et comparée des philosophies médiévales*, Paris, F. Alcan, 2ᵉ éd. 1911 (a much enlarged version of a 26 page study of the same title published in 1896, but without *Sa place dans l'histoire...*).

14. H.C. Meier, *Macht und Wahnwitz der Begriffe. Der Ketzer Roscellinus*, Aalen, Ebertin Verlag, 1974; L. Gentile, *Roscellino di Compiègne ed il problema degli universali*, Editrice Itinerari Lanciano, 1975; E.-H.W. Kluge, "Roscelin and the Medieval Problem of Universals", *Journal of the History of Philosophy* 14, 1976, p. 405-414.

In 1992 Jean Jolivet published a comparative essay on Roscelin, Abelard and Gilbert of Poitiers which looked at their semantic theories rather than their teaching about the existence of universals[15]. Drawing on Abelard's discussion of Roscelin's ideas on *totum* in the *Dialectica* and the (hitherto neglected) *Sententie secundum M. Petrum*, Jolivet concluded that an essential feature of Roscelin's dialectic was a "sémantique de la référence", whereby each utterance was imposed to refer to a specific thing[16]. He contrasted this with Abelard's "sémantique de la signification", which emphasised the role of a universal as a name that generated an *intellectus* or understanding generated of an individual subject, but which never abandoned completely a Platonic sense that language did somehow relate to reality. Gilbert of Poitiers similarly reflected on individuality, but whereas Abelard stressed that a universal predicated of individuals had no real existence, Gilbert distinguished that which is (*id quod est*) from that by which (*id quo est*) it is informed. By drawing attention to the common concern of three very different thinkers to understand individuality, Jolivet was questioning the usefulness of realist / nominalist labels, based on a theory of universals.

Jolivet's arguments appeared too late for me to consider them in a paper in which I suggested that Roscelin's ideas were influenced by the semantics of the anonymous *Glosule* on books I-XVI of Priscian's *Institutiones Grammaticae*, a speculative commentary which enjoyed considerable influence in the late eleventh and early twelfth centuries[17]. Its avowed intention was to re-invigorate the Latin grammatical tradition by reference to its Greek roots, so continuing a task which Priscian had begun. Its prologue proclaimed that grammatical study of *voces* lay at the foundation of the study of Logic, which also embraced dialectic and rhetoric. Its recurring concern was with the *causa* behind an individual *vox*. Most significant for subsequent semantic reflection was the commentator's use of Aristotelian insight to refine of Priscian's definition of a noun signified as that which named a substance, while signifying a quality[18].

15." Trois variations médiévales sur l'universel et l'individu: Roscelin, Abélard, Gilbert de la Porrée", *Revue de métaphysique et de morale* 97, 1992, p. 111-155, developing themes already present in *Arts du langage et théologie chez Abélard*, Paris, Vrin, 1969, and subsequent studies assembled in *Aspects de la pensée médiévale: Abélard. Doctrines du langage*, Paris, Vrin, 1987.

16. *Dialectica*, ed. L.M. De Rijk, Assen, van Gorcum, 2nd ed., 1970, p. 554-555. The second part of the *Sententie*, ed. L. Minio-Paluello, *Twelfth Century Logic. Texts and Studies II*, Rome, Edizioni di Storia e Letteratura, 1958, p. 111-121, discusses propositions used against the author by those who profess *totum* to be only an utterance.

17. The *Glosule* was identified in the version of *Prisciani Opera Omnia* printed by Georgius Arrivabenus, Venice, 1488 (reprinted seven times until 1519) and its significance assessed by M. Gibson in "The Collected Works of Priscian: the Printed Editions 1470-1859", *Studi Medievali* ser. 3ª 18, 1977, p. 249-260 and "The Early Scholastic 'Glosule' to Priscian, 'Institutiones Grammaticae': the Text and its Influence", *ibid.* 29, 1979, p. 235-254 (including edition of the *Glosule*'s accessus, not printed by Arrivabenus). See also R.W. Hunt, "Studies on Priscian in the Eleventh and Twelfth Centuries I", *Mediaeval and Renaissance Studies* 1, 1941-43, p. 194-231, reprinted in his *Collected Papers on the History of Grammar in the Middle Ages*, Amsterdam, J. Benjamin, 1980, p. 1-38.

18. L.M. De Rijk cites this passage of the *Glosule* on *Institutiones Grammaticae*, II 18, ed. M. Herz *Grammatici Latini* 2, ed. H. Keil, Leipzig, 1855, vol. 1, p. 55, noting its influence on William of Conches, *Logica Modernorum. A Contribution to the History of*

The *Glosule* had distinguished between understanding an utterance like "person" as a word (*persona vocalis*), and the specific person-thing (*persona realis*), its original cause, to which it referred [19]. If Roscelin was influenced by the *Glosule*, our picture of his nominalism needs to be radically revised. His vision of the world may be crudely defined compared to Abelard's, but it may not be as inconsistent as Abelard would have us believe. Through detailed study of unpublished glosses on Porphyry, Iwakuma has shown that the label *vocales* was already in use by the early twelfth century to refer (often critically) to dialecticians who analysed categories as utterances. His re-assigning a vocalist *Dialectica* to the younger Gerland in the early twelfth century also provides us with valuable insight into vocalist influence at Besançon, where Roscelin was also a canon [20]. Like Abelard's earliest glosses and Gerland's *Dialectica*, these early glosses do not always discuss universals at any length, but they do analyse categories as *voces* or utterances. According to an early twelfth-century chronicle, Roscelin was one of several masters who followed the teaching of John that taught dialectic was an *ars vocalis*. Rather than invoking a special theory about universals, this phrase may be simply be about dialectic depending on study of *voces*. This emphasis on *voces* is a central theme of the introduction to the *Glosule* (attributed in the Arrivabenus edition to a *Iohannes*) [21]. Its author was passionately interested in exploring the roots of the vocabulary which named everything in the world.

Early Terminist Logic, Assen, van Gorcum, 1967, vol. 2, p. 228 n. 1; cf. *Categoriae*, 5, transl. Boethii, ed. L. Minio-Paluello, *Aristoteles Latinus* p. 11.

19. *Glosule* on VIII 101 (Köln, Dombibl. 201, fol. 41ra), ed. Arrivabenus, *Institutionum Grammaticarum...*, Venice, 1511, fol. 123ᵛ, quoted more fully in "Nominalism and Theology before Abaelard", p. 16 n. 34: "Nam personam dicimus realem *quae uel de se loquitur*, uel *ad quam* prima *loquitur* de ipsa uel de qua loquitur prima ad secundam, uocalem uero uocem hanc personam significantem. *Prima est*. Hic diffinit primam personam et secundum rem et secundum uocem: et competenter facit. Res enim est causa uocis: et sic dicit res illa est *prima* persona *quae loquitur*, id est quae profert sermonem de quocumque habitum siue *de se* siue de alio: ecce realis. Prima uocalis est quae significat rem loquentem *de se*, et hanc nobis innuit cum dicit *quae loquitur de se*, id est profert uocem se significantem." The whole section on Priscian's definition of person in VIII 101 (fols. 123ᵛ-125ᵛ in the 1511 edition) is of great relevance.

20. Y. Iwakuma, "Vocales, or early nominalists", *Traditio* 42, 1992, p. 37-111, esp. p. 40-54 on glosses and the *Dialectica* edited by L.M. De Rijk as *Garlandus Compotista, Dialectica*, First Edition of the Manuscripts with an Introduction on the Life and Works of the Author and on the Contents of the Present Work, Assen, van Gorcum, 1959. Iwakuma also edits certain *disputata porphirii* (p. 74-102), attributing them to Roscelin. They are so closely related, however, to Abelard's literal glosses on Porphyry, that they seem more likely to report early lectures of Abelard, as suggested by J. Marenbon, "Medieval Latin Commentaries and Glosses on Aristotelian Texts, Before c. 1150 AD", *Glosses and Commentaries on Aristotelian Logical Texts. The Syriac, Arabic and Latin Traditions*, ed. C. Burnett, "Warburg Institute Surveys and Texts" XXIII, London, 1993, p. 117 (77-127). Iwakuma has since conceded this likelihood in private communication.

21. *Historia Francica*, ed. M. Bouquet, *Recueil des historiens des Gaules et de la France*, vol. 12, Paris, 1781, p. 3. In "Nominalism and Theology" (n. 1 above) I argue that this John wrote the *Glosule*, attributed in the colophon to the incunable edition to a certain *Iohannes de aingre* (probably a misreading of *Iohannes dei gratia*, a play on the *causa* of the name John; cf. n. 13 above and Gibson, "The collected works of Priscian", p. 253 n. 14.

Anselm of Bec was also interested in defining the meaning of language, exploring it "from reason alone", in other words from an inner authority, rather than from the written word, be it scripture, Aristotle or Priscian. His preferred interlocutors were intimates, like those in Augustine's dialogues, rather than outsiders. In his one major work theorizing about non-theological language, the *De grammatico* (written probably in the 1080s), he used this strategy to deal with a question raised by contemporary dialecticians, whether *grammaticus* signified substance, as Priscian's definition demanded, or, as Aristotle had declared, a quality[22]. Avoiding rigid application of the Porphyrian *res / vox* antithesis, he focussed instead on the importance of appreciating the way a noun was used, either through itself (*i.e.* the quality of being a grammarian) or through something else (so signifying the substance of a grammarian). Although a response to an issue raised by the *Glosule*, the *per se / per aliud* distinction was not sufficient to cope with plurality, the issue that concerned Roscelin. When forced to confront Roscelin's argument as applied to the trinity, Anselm did not have a convenient answer to hand. Not used to a polemical situation, he mocked Roscelin's arguments without offering a single clear solution of his own. In a draft of part of the *De incarnatione Verbi*, he experimented with a distinction *secundum se / secundum aliud* when commenting on Boethius' justification of the doctrine of two natures in Christ, but did not include these ideas in his final version[23]. All he could offer was an Augustinian image disguised as his own of the trinity as like the Nile, at the same time a source, a river and a lake[24]. Long meditation on divine unity made Anselm uncomfortable with the evidence of plurality, even though required by the doctrine of the incarnation. He concluded uncharacteristically by referring his reader to Augustine's statement about the equivalence of Latin and Greek definitions of the trinity. He had once cited this reflection to counter criticism that he had been too loose in his comments about the equivalence of the terms person and substance when speaking in his *Monologion* about three "I don't know what" in God[25]. Now he was using it to refute someone else's attempt to interpret Christian doctrine.

22. *De grammatico*, ed. Schmitt, vol. 1, p. 146, 162; cf. *Categoriae*, 8, ed. L. Minio-Paluello, *Aristoteles Latinus* I.1-5, Paris-Bruxelles, 1961, p. 29.
23. For a previously unknown draft of one section of *DIV* in which Anselm reviews Boethius' argument in *Contra Euticen et Nestorium* about two substances within the person of Christ, see my study, "St Anselm and Roscelin: some new texts and their implications. I. The *De incarnatione uerbi* and the *Disputatio inter christianum et gentilem*", *Archives d'histoire doctrinale et littéraire du Moyen Age* 51, 1991, p. 82-85 (55-98). This criticism of Boethius is not retained in the final version.
24. *DIV²*, 13, ed. Schmitt, vol. 2, p. 31-32, alluding to Augustine, *De fide et symbolo*, 8, ed. I. Zycha, CSEL 41, p. 18-19; on Abelard's criticism of the image, see n. 48 below.
25. *DIV²*, 16, ed. Schmitt, vol. 2, p. 35; cf. *Monologion* 79, vol. 1, p. 85-86: "Unam quidem et unitatem propter unam essentiam, trinam vero et trinitatem propter tres nescio quid... Potest ergo hac necessitatis ratione irreprehensibiliter illa summa et una trinitas sive trina unitas dici una essentia et tres personae sive tres substantiae." He justifies this argument by quoting Augustine (see n. 29 below) in the *Monologion*, Prologus, ed. Schmitt, vol. 1, p. 8, ideas re-iterated in *Epist*. 77 (vol 3, p. 199-200), answering criticism by Lanfranc; in *Epist. 83*, vol. 3, p. 208-9, to Rainald, abbot of St Cyprian, Poitiers, he reveals that he had been criticised for seeming to permit use of plural substances to describe the divine persons.

ROSCELIN'S LETTER TO PETER ABELARD

For a firmer picture of Roscelin's thought, we must turn to the only text so far reliably attributed to him, a letter to Peter Abelard, written in old age *c.* 1119-20. Found anonymously within a twelfth-century manuscript from Benediktbeuern, in the diocese of Freising (München, Bayerische Staatsbibl. Clm 4643, fols. 93v-99r), the letter was first identified as his by Schmeller in 1849[26]. It began with a vitriolic accusation that Abelard had been "forgetful of the benefits, so many and so great which I showered on you in the name and act of being a teacher, as a boy to being a young man"[27]. Roscelin rejected Abelard's aspersions on his character and claim that he had been convicted, become notorious and exiled as a heretic, promising to show him that this was false "by the testimony of the churches of Soissons and Rheims..., where I was born and educated"[28]. He boasted that even Rome had willingly listened to him. How could he have been expelled "by the whole world", when he was eagerly honoured by the churches of Tours and Loches, where Abelard had sat for so long at his feet as the youngest of his disciples, and of Besançon, in all of which he was a canon? Responding to an accusation of Abelard, he maintained that he had never persecuted Anselm or the preacher Robert of Arbrissel, but had only exposed weaknesses in their teaching and behaviour. Had not even St Peter needed to be corrected in his faith? Robert of Arbrissel, whom Abelard had defended as "an outstanding preacher of Christ", had encouraged women to abandon their husbands. Anselm's argument in *Cur deus homo* that God could only have redeemed man in the way he did, contradicted the authority of St Augustine.

26. *Abhandlungen der philosophisch-philologisch Klasse der Königlich Bayerischen Akademie der Wissenschaften* Bd 5.3, München, 1849, p. 187-210, reprinted by V. Cousin in *Opera Petri Abaelardi*, vol. 2, Paris, 1859, p. 792-803 and in 1885 by J.-P. Migne, PL 178, 357-372. It was re-edited by J. Reiners as an appendix to *Der Nominalismus in der Frühscholastik. Ein Beitrag zur Geschichte der Universalienfrage im Mittelalter*, Beiträge zur Geschichte der Philosophie und Theologie des Mittelalters Bd 8.5, Münster, 1910, p. 62-80. The summary description in *Catalogus codum latinorum Bibliothecae regiae Monacensis* 1.i, München, 1892, p. 222-223 gives the clearly erroneous date of s. xiii for the whole manuscript. M. Grabmann, looking at the MS with particular reference to the *Fallacie*, dated it to the late twelfth century, "Bearbeitungen und Auslegungen der aristotelischen Logik aus der Zeit von Peter Abaelard bis Petrus Hispanus. Mitteilungen aus Handschriften deutscher Bibliotheken", *Abhandlungen der Preussischen Akademie der Wissenschaften. Phil.-hist. Klasse*, 1937, no. 5, p. 41-44, rept in *Gesammelte Akademie-Abhandlungen*, Paderborn, 1979, p. 1401-1404. The occasional use of a cedilla in the second section as of the ampersand, alongside the tironian *et*, points to an earlier date in the second half of the twelfth century, preferred by L.M. de Rijk (who cites the authority of B. Bischoff in a personal communication), *Logica Modernorum*, vol. 1, p. 127.

27. *Ibid.*, ed. Reiners, p. 63: "... et beneficiorum, quae tibi tot et tanta a puero usque ad iuvenem sub magistri nomine et actu exhibui, oblitus...".

28. *Ibid.*, ed. Reiners, p. 65.

These accusations were only a prelude to his major argument that the writings of Ambrose, Augustine and Isidore supported his claim that singularity could not be attributed to the divine substance. He cited a host of texts which insisted that the divine persons were plural and could not be identified with each other. Of particular significance were comments of Augustine in Book VII of his *De trinitate* (which Anselm had himself used to justify his comments about the meaning of plurality in God):

> Therefore, for the sake of speaking about ineffable things, so that we can speak in some way what we cannot say any way, it is said by our Greeks: one essence, three substances, but by the Latins, one substance or essence, because, as we have already said, *essence* in our speech, namely Latin, is accustomed to be understood no differently from *substance*. ... It was allowed by necessity of speaking and arguing to say three persons, not because scripture spoke thus, but because it was not contradictory [29].

Linguistic convention required recognition of this plurality.

The kernel of Roscelin's argument was rooted in a particular semantic theory: strict application of Priscian's definition that a noun signified substance with quality to the three most venerable names applied to God. The only difference with applying such a noun to God was that it could not signify a substance changed in any way by quality.

> Indeed it is to be known that in the substance of the holy trinity, any nouns do not signify one thing and another, whether according to parts or to qualities, but they signify only substance itself, neither divided into parts nor changed through qualities. We do not therefore signify through *person* anything other than through *substance*, granted that we are accustomed out of a certain habit of speech to triple *person*, not *substance*, as the Greeks are accustomed to triple *substance*. Neither indeed.is it to be said that they err in belief in the trinity because they speak differently from us, for they believe the same as us, since – as we have said – *person, substance* or *essence* signify the same thing in God. For in speech there is diversity, in belief unity; otherwise there would not be a Church among the Greeks. For if they themselves say one thing by speaking thus, I do not see why we lie by saying the same thing. Ambrose on faith and Augustine on the trinity speak thus about the diversity of the divine substance either through qualities or parts. ... When therefore we vary these names or proffer them in the singular or in the plural, we do this not because it might signify as much one thing as another, but by virtue only of the will of the speakers to whom such a habit of speech is pleasing. For if there were different parts there [in God] so as to speak of one person and another substance, perhaps there would be a reason why we speak of one thing in the singular, another in the plural as we say of a man – since a body is one part, the soul another – that there is one soul but many bodies because of the different parts of the body; but neither is there any quality signified through *person*, or another through *substance* or *essence*, because – as we have already said – in God there is no quality at all. From this multitude of holy writings, the attentive reader understands that the saints who wrote them never at all under-

29. *Ibid.*, ed. Reiners, p. 70, quoting *De Trinitate*, VII 4, 7-8, ed. W. Mountain, CCSL 50, p. 255-258.

356

stood such singularity to be in God that he was called one thing alone and one singular substance with those three names, lest they fall into that Sabellian heresy. ... That you say that I have recognized the singular substance of the holy trinity is in any case true, but not that Sabellian singularity in which it is called one thing only, not several, with those three names, but in which the triune or three-fold substance has such unity that no three things have such <unity>[30].

Augustine's remark about the comparability of the Latin *persona* with the Greek usage of *substantia* was interpreted by Roscelin as evidence that such nouns were instituted by human agency to refer to that thing which was the Father, that thing which was the Son and that which was the Holy Spirit. Rather than questioning the essential unity of the divine nature, Roscelin was insisting on the distinct reference of nouns applied to God, namely *pater, filius* and *spiritus sanctus*. The term *persona* was itself only another device of human construction imposed on some thing. To assert that the three persons constituted a single thing was to confuse the three persons. Anyone who wanted the three names to signify a single thing necessarily argued that the Father became incarnate because he was also the Son. This plurality was proclaimed by the Greek Church.

Let us inquire into what is the difference in this plurality, of persons according to ourselves, of substances indeed according to the Greeks. For the substance of the Father is nothing other than the Father, the substance of the Son other than the Son, just as the city of Rome is Rome, and the creation of water is water. Because the Father begot the Son, the substance of the Father begot the substance of the Son. Because the substance of the generator is one thing, the generated another, one thing is different from the other[31].

Roscelin cited the authority of the *De doctrina christiana* to support his position:

In all things therefore are those alone which are to be enjoyed which we have called eternal and unchangeable. For he had said before: The things which we enjoy, the Father, Son and Holy Spirit. Again, *De agone christiano*: We believe in the Father and Son and Holy Spirit; these are eternal and unchangeable things[32].

---

30. *Epist.*, ed. Reiners, p. 72: "Sciendum est vero, quod in substantia sanctae trinitatis quaelibet nomina non aliud et aliud significant, sive quantum ad partes sive quantum ad qualitates, sed ipsam solam non in partes divisam nec per qualitates mutatam significant substantiam. Non igitur per personam aliud aliquid significamus, quam per substantiam, licet ex quadam loquendi consuetudine triplicare soleamus personam, non substantiam, sicut Graeci triplicare solent substantiam. Neque vero dicendum est, quod in fide trinitatis errent triplicando substantiam, quia licet aliter dicant quam nos, id tamen credunt quod nos, quia sicut diximus sive persona sive substantia sive essentia in deo prorsus idem significant. In locutione enim tantum diversitas est, in fide unitas. Alioquin iam non esset apud Graecos ecclesia. Si autem ipsi sic loquendo verum dicunt, quare nos idem dicendo mentiamur, non video."

31. *Ibid.*, ed. Reiners, p. 74: "Quae ergo differentia in hac pluralitate personarum secundum nos, substantiarum vero secundum Graecos sit, perquiramus. Nihil enim aliud est substantia patris quam pater, et substantia filii quam filius, sicut urbs Romae Roma est, et creatura aquae aqua est. Quia ergo pater genuit filium, substantia patris genuit substantiam filii. Quia igitur altera est substantia generantis, altera generata, alia est una ab alia."

32. *Ibid.*, ed. Reiners, p. 76, paraphrasing *De doctrina christiana*, I 39 and I 10, ed. W. Green, CSEL 80, p. 18 and 10 (= I 20 and I 5, ed. J. Martin, CCSL 33, p. 16 and 9), cited

Roscelin concluded that the three persons were eternal like eternal things. "Let him speak better who can. I am not able to do better, but neither do I defend insistently what I say [33]."

In the *De doctrina christiana*, Augustine had defined all teaching as about either things or signs, which were signs of things. Words were signs customarily used for signification. This semantic terminology, employed by the *Glosule* with renewed focus on *voces* as signs of human imposition, provided Roscelin with a crude way of exploring the names "Father", "Son" and "Holy Spirit" as each a sign of something else. Taking seriously Priscian's definition that a noun was an utterance signifying a substance with a quality, he excluded the possibility that such a divine name referred to an accidental quality in God. Therefore it applied to a substance, or, following Augustine, a thing. Roscelin's claim *sive persona sive substantia sive essentia in deo prorsus idem significant* stretched traditional vocabulary to an unusual degree. Augustine had identified *essentia* and *substantia* when used of God as one, but not when used of a person [34]. When citing his final authority on the trinity, Isidore of Seville, Roscelin modified an unexceptional definition *tres hypostases, quod resonat in latinum vel tres personas vel tres substantias* to read *vel tres essentias* [35]. Unlikely to be a scribal error (no such variant is indicated in Lindsay's apparatus), the variant reflects an idiomatic sense of divine plurality as relating to the names we have to use rather than any fundamental division in divine essence.

In the last part of the letter, Roscelin countered the slurs Abelard had been propagating with malicious innuendo of his own, based on twisting a word or an image with devastating effect. Abelard had been justly punished for his recent fornication. Roscelin had heard rumours from the monks of St Denis that Abelard was still visiting "his whore", taking her in person the money he had earned from his teaching without being able to fulfil his lustful desire. Roscelin turned to a grammatical analogy to reinforce his point that Abelard was neither a cleric, nor a layman, nor a monk. A masculine noun, if it falls from its gender, will refuse to signify its customary thing, as any noun loses its proper meaning when what it signifies falls from perfection. Just as a house without a roof or a wall will be called an imperfect house, so Peter himself was incomplete [36].

---

more fully on p. 71: "In omnibus igitur rebus illae solae sunt, quibus fruendum est, quas aeternas atque incommutabiles diximus. Praedixerat enim: Res, quibus fruimur, pater et filius et spiritus sanctus [omitting *eademque trinitas una quaedam summa res communisque omnibus fruentibus ea, si tamen res et non rerum omnium causa*, rendered as *et haec trinitas una quodammodo res est*]. Idem *de agone Christiano* [c. 13]: Credimus in patrem et filium et spiritum sanctum; haec aeterna sunt et incommutabilia."

33. *Ibid.*, ed. Reiners, p. 76: "Aeterni enim erant pluraliter, sicut plures res aeternae; et aeterni non erant, ut aeternitas in eis varia videretur. Dicat melius qui potest. Ego melius non valeo, sed neque quod dico importune defendo."

34. *Epist.*, ed. Reiners, p. 72; cf. *De Trinitate*, VII 4, ed. cit. p. 255.

35. *Epist.*, ed. Reiners, p. 76, quoting in abbreviated and not always accurate form, Isidore, *Etymologiae*, VII 4, 2-11, ed. W.M. Lindsay, Oxford, OUP, 1911.

36. *Ibid.*, ed. Reiners, p. 80: "Certus sum autem, quod masculini generis nomen, si a suo genere deciderit, rem solitam significare recusabit. ... Neque enim ablato tecto vel pariete domus, sed imperfecta domus vocabitur. Sublata igitur parte quae hominem facit non Petrus, sed imperfectus Petrus appellandus es." Reiners' rendering of the grammatical joke (hard to read in the manuscript) is not certain. It is also appended at the foot of the letter: "A<modo>

358

Roscelin could not resist a closing jibe about the two faces on the seal Abelard had used on his letter, interpreting them as evidence of his ongoing affection for a woman [37]. There was much else he could mention, but "Since I am speaking to an incomplete man, I leave this letter incomplete" [38].

AN UNNOTICED TRACT IN THE BENEDIKTBEUERN MS

When Schmeller identified the author of the letter in Clm 4643, he did not consider whether two short theological tracts immediately preceding, might also be by Roscelin. The first (fols. 92^v-93^r), which we may call *Notandum est* from its incipit, distinguishes the meaning of *substance* when applied to creation and to God. What is three-fold in God can be called persons or things – the very proposition reported to St Anselm as evidence of heresy. The second (fol. 93^{r-v}), about the apparent contradiction in scripture between Christ saying that he loved John more than the others (Jn 21:19-22) and Peter's affirmation that he loved Christ more than the others, is based on the last of Augustine's *Homilies on John*. [39] Following immediately after Seneca's *De beneficiis* (fols. 79^r-90^r) and *De clementia* (fols. 90^r-91^v), they lead directly into the letter to Abelard, all copied by the same hand [40]. The various texts in Clm 4643 could have been collected by Otto of Freising, the only historian to record that Roscelin was Abelard's teacher [41]. The text of *Notandum est*, although brief, helps explain the ideas in the letter to Abelard:

---

si a suo genere deciderit, rem solitam significare recusabit. Amodo enim neutri generis abiectione, sicut et suum significatum penetra<tur?>, et cum omnem hominem integrum consueverit, dimidium forsitan significare recusabit <*M* recusabis>."

37. *Ibid.*, ed. Reiners, p. 80: "Ad huius etiam imperfecti hominis ignominiae cumulum pertinet, quod in sigillo, quo foetidas illas litteras sigillavit, imaginem duo capita habentem, unum viri, alterum mulieris, ipse formavit. Unde quis dubitet, quanto adhuc in eam areat amore, qui tali eam capitum coniunctione non erubuit honorare? He may have misread images of saints Rusticus and Eleutherius, companions of St Denis, conventionally portrayed as bearded and clean-shaven respectively, a suggestion I owe to C. Waddell.

38. *Ibid.*, ed. Reiners, p. 80: "Plura quidem in tuam contumeliam vera ac manifesta dictrae decreveram, sed quia contra hominem imperfectum ago, opus quod coeperam imperfectum relinquo."

39." Dominus plus ceteris dilexit Iohannem. Cuius maioris dilectionis in iudicium est... Quod virgo est Iohannes convenit future vite ubi neque nubent neque nubentur." Cf. *Tractatus in Iohannem CXXIV*, Tr.124, ed. R. Willems, CCSL 36, p. 680-688.

40. On the dating of this part of the MS, see n. 26 above. Roscelin's letter is followed on fol. 99^v by instructions on how to forecast a horoscope from the sphere of Apuleius, L. Thorndike and P. Kibre, *A Catalogue of Incipits of Mediaeval Scientific Writings in Latin*, Cambridge, Mass., 1963, col. 1522, and on fols. 100^r-110^r, a commentary on Boethius' *De arithmetica* (Thorndike and Kibre, col. 1587, noting *M* as our only witness), introduced by Hugh of St Victor, *Didascalicon*, VI 14, on the place of the arts within philosophy. In different hands then follow notes on Martianus Capella (fol. 110^{r-v}), a treatise on fallacies, the *Fallacie Parvipontane* (ed. De Rijk, *Logica Modernorum*, vol. 1, p. 551-609) with evident affinities to the writing of Adam of Balsham on the subject (fols. 111^v-128^r), and an alphabetical list of nouns and verbs (fols. 129^r-157^r).

41. Otto was an enthusiastic admirer of Seneca, *Chronica sive Historia de duabus civitatibus*, II 40 and III 15, ed. A. Hofmeister, MGH Scriptores rerum germanicarum in usum

Notandum est quia creator et creature in quibusdam conveniunt, in quibusdam differunt. In hoc conveniunt: Sicut enim de diversis accidentibus eiusdem substantie, non potest dici "hoc est illud", ut de iusticia et albedine, que est albedo, vel e converso; sed bene potest dici "quod iustum est album est" propter idemtitatem subiecti; ita ideo qui est pater et filius et spiritus sanctus dici non potest, <sed> qui est pater est filius vel qui est filius est spiritus sanctus vel è [*M* est] converso. Quod enim ibi faciebat diversitas accidentium hoc facit hic diversitas personarum. Sicut autem ibi dicitur "qui iustum est album est", ita hic quod pater est filius est. Nam quod ibi facit idemtitas subiecti, hoc facit ibi idemtitas substantie. Item: sicut ab igne na<s>citur calor et splendor, et tamen illud quod nascitur, non est prius aut posterius eo a quo nascitur; ita a patre nascitur filius, ab utroque procedit spiritus sanctus, et tamen una persona non est alia prior aut posterior. In istis conveniunt creator et creature. In aliis differunt. Nam in creaturis vel eru<n>t plures substantie, vel plures partes, vel plura accidentia eiusdem substantie, ex quo pluralitas est ibi. Hoc autem non est i<n> creatore. Nam in deo sunt quedam tria; homo dicere *(fol. 92ʳ)* non potest, nec intelligere. Non sunt tres substantie, neque tres partes, neque tria accidentia eiusdem substantie. Tres persone vel tres res dici potest. Hoc enim dicit autoritas. Greci dicunt tres usie, id est tres substantie, sed accipiunt substantias pro personis. Quid autem sint ille persone vel ille tres res, explicari non potest. Nam neque sunt substantia neque accidens. Sed in deo non sunt inmediata substantia, et accidens. Ita aliut est in creatore, aliut in creaturis. Nec est mirum si factor a sua factura differat.

It should be noted that the Creator and creatures agree in some things and differ in others. In this they agree: for just as it cannot be said about different accidents of the same substance "this is that", as about justice and whiteness which is whiteness, or vice versa, but it can well be said "what is just is wise" because of the identity of the subject – thus clearly it cannot be said "who is the Father and the Son and the Holy Spirit", <but> "who is the Father is the Son" or "who is the Son is the Holy Spirit" or vice versa. For what made there [*i.e.* in creatures] diversity of accidents makes here [in the Creator] diversity of persons. For just as it is said there "who is just is white", thus here "what is the Father is the Son", for what makes there identity of subject makes here identity

---

scholarum separatim editi 45, Leipzig, 1912, p. 114 and 153. On Otto's knowledge of the new Aristotle, Rahewin, *Gesta Friderici*, IV 14, ed. Waitz-von Simson, p. 250. Otto praised Aristotle as a pupil of Socrates before studying under Plato, *Chronica*, II 8, ed. cit. p. 75 and 77; in a footnote to this passage, Hofmeister notes that this belief, revealing testimony to contemporary enthusiasm for Aristotle, was reported in a *De Vita Aristotelis*, ed. V. Rose, Leipzig, Teubner, 1886, p. 443. Rose's thirteenth-century date for the translation (based on the earliest MS he knew) is clearly erroneous. The first Parisian master known to use the *De sophisticis elenchis* was Adam of Balsham (*Parvipontanus*), of whom Otto speaks with some knowledge, "vir subtilis et Parisiensis aeclesiae canonicus recenter factus", *Gesta Friderici*, I 53, ed. cit., p. 75, prompting the speculation that Otto himself acquired the *Fallacie Parvipontane*. Otto left the schools of Paris to become a monk at Morimond by 1133, so could already have acquired knowledge of the new Aristotle. There is no firm evidence that he ever studied under Abelard. The first section of Clm 4643, copied in the first half of the twelfth century, contains mainly historical works, probably all known to Otto: a life of Alexander the Great (fols. 1ʳ-25ᵛ), histories of the Goths, Amazons, Huns and Lombard, based on the Chronicle of Frutolf of Michelsberg (fols. 26ʳ-60ᵛ), an excerpt from Widukind's history of the Saxons (fols. 61ʳ-67ʳ), a life of queen Matilda (fols. 68ʳ-74ᵛ) and a sermon of Augustine (fols. 75ʳ-78ʳ).

360

of substance. Again: just as heat and brightness is born from fire and yet that which is born is neither prior to or posterior to that which is born, thus the Son is born from the Father, the Holy Spirit proceeds from both and yet one person is neither prior or posterior to another. In others they differ. For in creatures there will be either several substances or several parts or several accidents of the same substance, from which there is plurality. Yet this is not so in the Creator. For in God there are a certain three things; man can neither say nor understand. There are not three substances nor three parts nor three accidents of the same substance. It can be said that there are three persons or three things. For authority says this. The Greeks say three essences [*usie*], that is three substances but they accept *substances* for *persons*. What however are these persons or these three things cannot be explained. For they are neither substance nor accident. But in God they are not mediated substance and accident. Thus it is one thing in the Creator, another in creatures. Neither is it surprising if the Maker differs from what he has made.

This exposition of trinitarian doctrine is evidently close to that formulated by Roscelin in his letter to Abelard. At issue is the application to the divine nature of categories relating to creation. The central difference is that in the Creator, no accidents can be present and therefore not a plurality from several substances or several parts as in the world. However, what applied to diverse accidents, impossible to identify with each other, was true of the divine persons, not distinguished by any accident. Just as Roscelin distinguished substance in a person from its quality in the letter to Abelard, so the distinction is made here between substance and its accident. In a much more sophisticated fashion, this is the distinction drawn by Gilbert of Poitiers as that between *id quod est* and *id quo est* from Priscian's definition that a noun was an utterance signifying a substance with a quality. As in Gilbert's writing, stress is laid on respecting the necessary distinction between areas of investigation. In God, one was not dealing with plural entities as in creation, but with something that could be called a person or a thing.

Essentially the same analogy of the trinity as heat and brightness coming from fire, as had been quoted against Roscelin in 1090 as Augustinian authority that God was a single thing, is interpreted as explaining that one person does not come before or after another. Authority is then invoked to support the claim that there are a certain three things (*tria*) in God which could not be spoken or understood in human terms, yet were called *usie*, or substances in Greek, which can be called persons or things. There is no passage in Augustine's *De trinitate* which supports such an erroneous explanation of Greek *substantiae*. Augustine knew of the formula *mian usian tres ypostasis*, but only used *usia* in the singular[42]. Isidore had defined *usia* as substance, the first of the ten categories, recognizing the accidents of quantity, quality and location as within *usia*. The little essay relies on Augustine's general comment about Latin/Greek equivalent, but takes the principle of looking for synonyms a stage further than Augustine had countenanced. One authority for such use of plural *res* could be

42. *De Trinitate*, V 10, ed. Mountain, p. 217; *cf.* V 2, p. 207.

squeezed out of *De doctrina christiana*, I 10, as Roscelin had explained in his letter to Abelard[43]. Given the intellectual affinity of the two texts in the manuscript, it seems logical to assume that Roscelin was author of both.

Roscelin's argument with Abelard eventually provoked his former student to write to the bishop of Paris to explain that he had written his treatise on the trinity "particularly against the above mentioned heresy [of confessing three gods] for which he has become notorious"[44]. The *Theologia 'Summi boni'* (or *De trinitate* as Abelard calls it in this letter) certainly contained much criticism of false dialecticians and Roscelin in particular[45]. Abelard was still profoundly influenced, however, by his teacher. Abelard shared Roscelin's sense that it was necessary to identify the individuality of the names of the divine persons, that because of which distinct names were applied to God. However, where Roscelin assumed that a divine name was like any noun, imposed on a pure substance, without accident, Abelard believed such a name was imposed on God to signify an understanding about the divine nature, to be specific, his power, his wisdom and his benignity. None of these attributes could be identified with each other, even though they were not things. In his *Theologia christiana* Abelard mentioned that he had often heard the comparison of the trinity to the sun, heat and brightness raised in criticism of attempts to distinguish what made one person of the trinity different from another, but then cited the opinion of certain *novi* who said that such analogies did not really pertain to the question, as they did not explain why only one person of the trinity became incarnate, not all three[46]. Roscelin had asked a legitimate question. Anselm's response had been deficient. Abelard went on to criticize the analogy used by Anselm against Roscelin of the trinity as like a river with water and a source (identifying its Augustinian source), as likely to lead to a Sabellian heresy[47]. Abelard did not want to describe persons as things, but, in the spirit of the *Glosule*, wanted to get back to their root cause.

---

43. See n. 32 above.

44. *Epist. 14, Peter Abelard. Letters IX-XIV*, ed. E.R. Smits, Groningen, 1983, p. 279.

45. *TSum*, II 4-27, ed. E.M. Buytaert and C.J. Mews, CCCM 13, Turnhout, 1987, p. 114-127, is directed against false dialecticians, as is II 75-80, p. 140-141: "Responde tu michi, astute dialectice seu uersipellis sophista, qui auctoritate peripateticorum me arguere niteris de differentia personarum que in deo sunt..."

46. *Theologia christiana*, IV 82, ed. E.M. Buytaert, CCCM 12, Turnhout, 1969, p. 303: "Vnde et nonnullos fidelium quasi irridentes murmurare saepe audiuimus, cum de his ad hoc similitudo inducitur quae non sunt eiusdem essentiae, ueluti cum in illo *Sermone natalis Domini* beatus Augustinus ad defendendum qod solus Filius sit incarnatus, similitudinem de cithara et sole sumpsit... Sed ad haec quid nonnulli murmurent noui, dicentes quidem haec nihil attinere ad uim quaestionis, quae de identitate unius substantiae in tribus personis orta est." Abelard subsequently identified the image in Cassiodorus (*Tchr CT* I 104, p. 115; see n. 8 above), prompting him to observe in *Theologia 'Scholarium'*, II 119, ed. E.M. Buytaert and C.J. Mews, CCCM 13, Turnhout, 1987, p. 466-7) that it had been used by Plato, according to Macrobius.

47. *Tchr*, IV 83, ed. Buytaert, p. 304 and *TSch*, II 119-20, ed. Buytaert-Mews. p. 466-468; cf. n. 24 above. In "Abelard's Mockery of St Anselm", *Journal of Ecclesiastical History*, 41, 1990, p. 1-23, M. Clanchy rightly identifies the importance of Abelard's criticism of St Anselm. Whether "mockery" is the right word is not certain. Rather than mocking Anselm at a personal level, Abelard was criticizing what he considered to be an inadequate response to Roscelin.

ROSCELIN, GILBERT OF POITIERS AND OTTO OF FREISING

Abelard's attempt to define the individuality of a divine person in terms of a divine attribute differed considerably from that of Gilbert of Poitiers. Whereas Abelard emphasised the function of any name in signifying an attribute of the subject of which it was predicated (in this case God) and had argued that this was the meaning of Priscian's definition of a person (implicitly challenging the *Glosule*'s discussion of the *res* which "person" named), Gilbert defined a person as *per se una*. He related this to Boethius' discussion in *Contra Euticen et Nestorium* of *hypostasis* as individual substance, developing the *Glosule*'s distinction between what was named and the quality signified into that between that which (*id quod*) and that by which (*id quo*) [48]. Gilbert's solution was less apparently subjective than that of Abelard, although it did preserve a sense of the distinctness of definitions of God that were ultimately of human imposition. While Abelard was very opposed to crude attempts to use Priscian's definition to define divine properties as separate from God, his polemic may not have accurately grasped what such a distinction was intended to achieve [49].

When Otto of Freising compared Bernard's hostile attitude to a clever, but arrogant Abelard, which he considered legitimate, with Bernard's action against the wise and respectful Gilbert of Poitiers, which he thought unjust, he agreed with Roscelin that Abelard had not sufficiently respected the difference between the three persons. Otto was not critical of the *sententiam vocum* in logic, only of its careless application to theology:

> Holding in a natural capacity the teaching of utterances or names, he applied it incautiously to theology. For which reason, teaching and writing about the holy trinity, he weakened too much the three persons, which holy Church has hitherto piously believed and faithfully taught to be distinct things, separate in their properties; using not good examples, he said among other things: Just as the same statement is a proposition, an assumption and a conclusion, thus the same essence is Father, Son and Holy Spirit [50].

48. E.g. Gilbert on *De Trinitate*, I 2, 12 and *Contra Eutycen et Nestorium*, 3, 5, *The Commentaries of Gilbert of Poitiers on Boethius*, ed. N. Häring, Toronto, 1966, p. 60 and 272; cf. Abelard, *TSum*, II 108-12, ed. Buytaert-Mews, p. 153-154, expanded to incorporate Gilbert's Boethian definition in *Tchr*, III 175-80, ed. Buytaert, p. 261-263. N. Häring, "The Case of Gilbert de la Porrée Bishop of Poitiers (1142-1154)", *Mediaeval Studies* 13, 1951, p. 19 (1-40), notes that Gilbert's *per se una* definition had been used by Godescalc of Orbais, whose ideas on grammar and theology were studied by J. Jolivet, *Godescalc d'Orbais et la Trinité: la méthode de la théologie à l'époque carolingienne*, Paris, Vrin, 1958, and whose potential influence on Roscelin deserves to be considered.
49. Cf. *Tchr*, IV 77, ed. Buytaert, p. 301 (directed against Ulger of Angers) and *Tchr*, III 166-170, responded to in IV, 154-158, ed. Buytaert p. 257-259 and 342-344.
50. *Gesta Friderici*, I 49, ed. Waitz-von Simson, p. 69: "Sententiam ergo vocum seu nominum in naturali tenens facultate non caute theologiae admiscuit. Quare de sancta trinitate docens et scribens tres personas, quas sancta aecclesia non vacua nomina tantum, sed res distinctas suisque propretatibus discretas hactenus et pie credidit et fideliter docuit, nimis

Otto claimed that he had been found guilty of the Sabellian heresy (*i.e.* identifying Father and Son) at Soissons. Abelard made no such statement in any version of his *Theologia*, originally written to refute Roscelin's doctrine that the three persons were separate things. He defined them as separate attributes. While Roscelin and Otto construed Abelard's definition as tending towards Sabellianism, the official accusation at Soissons reported by Abelard in the *Historia calamitatum*, later taken up by St Bernard, was that he attributed omnipotence to the Father alone, thus distinguishing unnecessarily the Father from the Son and Holy Spirit[51].

Otto's own critique of Abelard was very different from that of Bernard. Abelard extended necessary philosophical enquiry into the realm of levity. Gilbert's case was quite different. Gilbert rightly maintained the catholic doctrine that the three persons were separate things, with distinct properties. Otto answered the accusation that he denied that the divine essence was God, or that the property of a divine person was the person itself, by explaining that Gilbert followed the view of those logicians "who say someone who says *Socratem esse* says nothing"[52]. When asked why he distinguished persons so much in theology, he replied, according to Otto: "Because every person is one thing in itself" (*Quia omnis persona res est per se una*). Whether Gilbert did originally use *res* in his definition is not certain. Other Porretan writers also preserved this usage, even after Gilbert' death[53]. These writers were using *res* in the sense of the *Glosule*, Augustinian in origin, of what was named by a noun, but not in a way that permits a so-called "realist" classification.

The issue of plurality in the trinity that Roscelin had raised was ultimately of more importance than the particular solution that he had provided. In a certain measure, he was justified in trying to claim that he was only continuing a debate which Anselm had launched in the *Monologion*, itself a very original attempt to redefine the trinitarian nature of God. More work needs to be done on eleventh-century trivium glosses before we can be fully appreciate the origi-nality and influence of Roscelin in dialectic or of the *Glosule* on Priscian in

---

adtenuans, non bonis usus exemplis, inter caetera dixit: *Sicut eadem oratio est propositio, assumptio et conclusio, ita eadem essentia est pater et fiius et spiritus sanctus.*"

51. *Historia calamitatum*, ed. J. Monfrin, Paris, Vrin, 1959, p. 88. When revising his treatise immediately after 1121, Abelard took care to justify his attribution of omnipotence to the Father alone in *Tchr*, I 25-31, ed. Buytaert, p. 81-85. In 1121 Alberic had spread rumours that Abelard preached a tritheistic heresy, the same rumour as had been spread about Roscelin thirty years earlier, while Abelard counter-attacked with accusations of Sabellian-ism (ed. cit., p. 83, 84-85). William of St Thierry formulated the same charge that Abelard denied full omnipotence to the Son and Holy Spirit in 1139/40. William's presence at Sois-sons in 1121 is noted in a Saint-Quentin charter by J. Benton, "Fraud, fiction and borrowing in the correspondence of Abelard and Heloise", *Pierre Abelard-Pierre le Vénérable*, ed. J. Jolivet, Paris, CNRS, 1975, p. 486 n. 1. On the compilation of the final list, see my "The lists of heresies imputed to Peter Abelard", *Revue bénédictine* 95, 1989, p. 73-110.

52. *Gesta Friderici*, I 54, ed. cit., p. 76: "Erat quippe quorumdam in logica sententia, cum quis diceret Socratem esse, nichil diceret. Quos prefatus episcopus sectans talem dicti usum haut premeditate ad theologiam verterat."

53. For example, the *Liber de vera philosophia*, quoted by A. Dondaine, *Écrits de la "petite école" porrétaine*, Paris-Montréal, Vrin, 1962, p. 28-29, noted by Jolivet, "Trois variations", p. 154.

grammar. There is no doubt that even before the composition of the *Glosule*, scholars like Berengar of Tours were seeking to identify the *res* behind the outward, externally constructed signs of language and sacrament. Such enquiry was only part of a much wider movement in eleventh and twelfth century society to re-evaluate the meaning of traditional language, symbols and institutions. By raising the question of the meaning of the trinity, Roscelin indirectly provoked both Abelard and Gilbert to formulate in different ways a more sophisticated solution to a problem that could not easily be solved by ecclesiastical censure[54].

One implication of analysing the thought of Roscelin, Abelard and Gilbert of Poitiers in terms of semantic theory, may be, as Jolivet has suggested, that we should avoid using the categories of "nominalist" and "realist" to understand the thought of the twelfth century. Once it is appreciated that Roscelin was not denying the existence of universals, but rather examining universals through linguistic utterances, and that Platonic influences can exist on his thought quite legitimately alongside an Aristotelian focus (just as they do in Abelard and Gilbert), then other writings of Roscelin on dialectic may yet be identified. One text deserving re-consideration is a tract on universals in a Compiègne MS *de rebus universalibus* which Hauréau suggested might be Roscelin, but which has generally been dismissed as such because of the "realist" tone of its opening[55]. It takes precisely that passage of Boethius which St Anselm had used in his invective against modern dialecticians to show that the argument of the *Consolation of Philosophy* is fully compatible with analysis of universal things through utterances (*per voces*). If we follow through the implication of Jolivet's emphasis on semantic theory, then the history of philosophy should not separate itself from study of the evolution of theological doctrine, or for that matter of scriptural commentary. At issue in the twelfth century is not so much an attempt to break with the past, as a desire to re-interpret those signs and symbols by which Christian society had traditionally defined itself.

54. Criticism of Lombard's idea that God was a single *res*, attributed to abbot Joachim, provoked the IV Lateran Council to issue a condemnation (H. Denzinger, *Enchiridion Symbolorum*, Freiburg, Herder, 1942, p. 200-203) that was vigorously attacked in *Joachimi Abbatis Liber Contra Lombardum (Scuola di Gioacchino da Fiore)*, ed. C. Ottaviano, Reale Accademia d'Italia. Studi e Documenti 3, Rome, 1934.

55. B. Hauréau, *Notices et extraits de quelques manuscrits latins de la Bibliothèque nationale*, vol. 5, Paris, 1892, p. 328-333, re-edited by J. Dijs, "Two Anonymous 12th-Century Tracts on Universals", *Vivarium* 28, 1990, p. 113-117 (85-117); see n. 3 above.

X

ST ANSELM AND ROSCELIN OF COMPIÈGNE: SOME NEW TEXTS AND THEIR IMPLICATIONS.

II. A VOCALIST ESSAY ON THE TRINITY AND INTELLECTUAL DEBATE C. 1080-1120

Résumé

Suite d'une étude parue dans AHDLMA *58 (1991). Elle analyse la querelle entre s. Anselme et Roscelin, en rejetant l'idée d'une simple dispute entre réalistes et nominalistes. La théologie trinitaire de Roscelin est interprétée comme le prolongement d'une argumentation rationalisante mise au point par s. Anselme. Edition critique d'un texte anonyme sur la Trinité attribuable à Roscelin.*

Abstract

Continuation to a study published in AHDLMA *58 (1991). It analyses the dispute between St Anselm and Roscelin, rejecting the idea of a simple division between realists and nominalists. Roscelin's trinitarian theology is interpreted as an extension of a rationalising mode of argument established by St Anselm. With a critical edition of an anonymous essay on the Trinity, argued to be by Roscelin.*

Zusammenfassung

Weiterführung einer in AHDLMA *58 (1991) veröffentlichten Untersuchung. Hier wird der Streit zwischen St. Anselm and Roscelin besprochen und die Annahme einer schlichten Gegenüberstellung von Realisten und Nominalisten zurückgewiesen. Roscelin's trinitarische Theologie wird als ein rationalistischer Denkenansatz interpretiert, der von St. Anselm eingeführt wurde. Es folgt die kritische Edition eines anonymen Texts über die Trinität, das von Roscelin stammen kann.*

[Mots-clés: Roscelin de Compiègne, s. Anselme de Cantorbéry, théologie trinitaire, rationalisme au XIe siècle]

P ETER Abelard is silent about a great deal of his early life in the *Historia calamitatum*, a narrative very influential in shaping our perception of intellectual life in northern France at the turn of the twelfth century[1]. He creates the impression that soon after he arrived in Paris to study with William of Champeaux, he started to outshine his teacher through the brilliance of his own intellect, only to be denied the opportunities which were rightfully his. The teaching of his elders on divinity he found to be as barren as that on dialectic. Writing not long after 1131, Abelard claimed that he had been motivated to compose his treatise on the divine unity and trinity at the request of his students for human and philosophical reasoning for the basis of Christian faith, since nothing could be believed before it was understood[2]. Abelard's narrative has often been used to justify either enthusiasm for his originality or dislike for his intellectual arrogance, with little understanding of the circumstances which helped shape his rhetorical claims. By the mid 1130s, when John of Salisbury arrived in Paris, Abelard had succeeded in creating the impression among his admirers that little of significance had happened before his arrival in Paris. If we are to understand what was going on in northern France in the first forty years of Abelard's life, we need to consult anonymous writings on grammar, dialectic and theology as well as charters and other documents relating to the political context of intellectual debate. Minor figures, who never achieved the prominence of an Abelard or a St Anselm, need to be brought into view, as does the turbulent social milieu in which they operated.

Abelard's failure to mention Roscelin in the *Historia calamitatum* has to be related to the climate of acute political tension prevailing in Paris in the early 1130s. The hostility between Stephen of Garlande, dean of the abbey of Sainte-Geneviève, and Stephen of Senlis, bishop of Paris, closely allied to the abbey of Saint-Victor, reached such fever pitch that in 1132 the churches of Sainte-Geneviève were put under papal interdict, while in August 1133 the bishop together with the abbot and prior of Saint-Victor were physically attacked by

(1) This study is a long overdue complement to C. J. MEWS, «St Anselm and Roscelin: some new texts and their implications. I. The *De incarnatione uerbi* and the *Disputatio inter christianum et gentilem*», AHDLMA, 58 (1991), p. 55-97; «Nominalism and Theology before Peter Abaelard: New Light on Roscelin of Compiègne», *Vivarium*, 30 (1992), p. 4-33 and «The trinitarian doctrine of Roscelin of Compiègne and its influence: twelfth-century nominalism and theology re-considered», in A. DE LIBERA, A. ELAMRANI-JAMAL, A. GALONNIER (eds), *Langages et philosophie. Hommage à Jean Jolivet*, Paris, 1997, p. 347-364. I am indebted to Monash University, Australia, to the Institute for Advanced Study, Princeton, for enabling me to pursue this research, and to the staff of the IRHT (Paris), and to J. Jolivet, I. Rosier and Iwakuma Y. for discussion over the years of the texts and ideas in this paper.

(2) J. MONFRIN, *Historia calamitatum* [HC], ll. 690-701, Paris, 1959. I cannot accept the argument of H. SILVESTRE, «Pourquoi Roscelin n'est-il pas mentionné dans l'*Historia calamitatum*?», *Recherches de théologie ancienne et médiévale*, 48 (1981), p. 218-224, that Roscelin's absence from *HC* is evidence that this work is a forgery; see my comments in the introduction to *Petri Abaelardi Opera theologica* III, CCCM 13, Turnhout, 1987, p. 41-46.

nephews of archdeacon Theobald and vassals of Stephen of Garlande[3]. As someone whose career had been powerfully helped by Stephen, Abelard had a direct interest in presenting William of Champeaux, founder of the abbey of Saint-Victor, as having unfairly schemed to do everything to impede his career. It would not have helped Abelard's efforts to re-establish himself as a teacher on the Montagne-Sainte-Geneviève by tracing his intellectual debt to Roscelin of Compiègne, tarred as a heretic since the 1090s. Abelard had also become very critical of Roscelin, who accused him *c.* 1120 of being profoundly ungrateful for the many and great benefits he had absorbed as Roscelin's student « from being a boy to being a young man »[4].

The *Historia calamitatum* disguises the extent to which Abelard was profoundly influenced by controversies from the time of his early studies with Roscelin. One way of re-assessing his impact is through a short essay on the unity and trinity of God appended to a twelfth-century copy of Abelard's *Theologia christiana*[5]. Before considering this essay, we need to survey other documents relating to Roscelin and those vocalist dialecticians with whom he was associated.

THE ACCUSATIONS OF HERESY AGAINST ROSCELIN OF COMPIÈGNE

Roscelin of Compiègne has never enjoyed a good press. Accused by St Anselm of believing that the three persons of the Trinity were three separate things, Roscelin has always seemed a maverick figure. Richard Southern described him as little more than a trouble-maker « who caused dissension wherever he went » unlike even Berengar or Abelard, whom Southern qualifies as « essentially sober and well-versed theologians »[6]. Yet both Anselm and

---

(3) A. LUCHAIRE, *Louis VI le Gros. Annales de sa vie et de son règne (1087-1137)*, Paris, 1890; repr. Brussels, 1964, no. 420, p. 194. The attack was reported by Stephen of Senlis to Geoffrey of Chartres, PL 173, 1416B-1417D.

(4) J. REINERS, *Epistola ad Abaelardum*, in *Der Nominalismus in der Frühscholastik. Ein Beitrag zur Geschichte der Universalienfrage im Mittelalter*, BGPMA, Bd 8.5, Münster, 1910, p. 63 (62-80): « Si Christianae religionis dulcedinem, quam habitu ipso praeferebas, vel tenuiter degustasses, nequaquam tui ordinis tuaeque professionis immemor et beneficiorum, quae tibi tot et tanta a puero usque ad iuvenem sub magistri nomine et actu exhibui, oblitus... ». J. SCHMELLER published the letter from the sole manuscript, Munich Clm 4643, ff. 93v-99r (s. xii), in *Abhandlungen der philosophisch-philologischen Klasse der königl Bayerischen Akademie der Wissenschaften*, 5. Bd. 3. Abt., Munich, 1849, p. 187-210, reprinted by V. COUSIN, *Opera Petri Abaelardi*, vol. II, Paris, 1859, p. 792-803 and in 1885 by J.-P. MIGNE, PL 178, 357-72.

(5) See p. 86-90 below.

(6) R. W. SOUTHERN, *Saint Anselm. Portrait in a Landscape*, Cambridge, 1990, p. 176. W. J. COURTENAY sums up the common view in the entry on Roscelin in the *Dictionary of the Middle Ages*, 10, p. 531-532. More sophisticated, but still working within the same basic assumptions are E.-H. W. KLUGE, « Roscelin and the Medieval Problem of Universals », *Journal of the History of Philosophy*, 14 (1976), p. 405-414 and L. GENTILE, *Roscellino ed il problema degli universali*, Editrice Itinerari Lanciano, 1974. H. C. MEIER, *Macht und Wahnwitz der Begriffe. Der Ketzer Roscellinus*, Aalen, 1974, presents Roscelin as a valiant fighter against dogmatism, but has little detail on his thought.

Abelard considered Roscelin's ideas sufficiently important for both to seek to answer to them. Roscelin occupies a pivotal role in the evolution of both scholastic philosophy and theology. Otto of Freising considered Roscelin to be « the first in our times to institute the teaching of utterances (*sententiam vocum*) in logic »[7]. In his letter to Abelard, Roscelin rejected the accusation that he had been convicted of heresy and expelled from the whole world, through the testimony of the churches of both Soissons and Rheims « where I was born, brought up and educated »[8]. He insisted that he was willingly received and listened to by Rome itself, as well as by the churches of Tours, Loches « where you sat so long at my feet as the least of the students of your master» and Besançon, in all of which he was a canon[9]. While there is no doubt that St Anselm was the more creative thinker in applying Aristotelian logic to reflection on sacred discourse, St Anselm was not as isolated a figure as he has sometimes been imagined[10].

Sometime around 1089, John, a monk of Bec who was then assisting his fellow monk Fulco as newly appointed bishop of Beauvais, reported to St Anselm a theological argument he had heard Roscelin use, which he feared flouted orthodox Christian doctrine:

> If the three persons are just one thing and not three things in themselves, like three angels or three souls, in such a way, however, that they are completely the same in will and power, then the Father and the Holy Spirit *has* become incarnate with the Son[11].

John took exception to this particular argument of Roscelin because it seemed to contradict an image he attributed to Augustine of the Trinity as like the sun, the

(7) G. WAITZ and B. VON SIMSON, *Gesta Friderici I Imperatoris*, I 48, MGH in usum scholarum 46, Hannover-Leipzig, 1912, p. 69: «Habuit tamen [Petrus Abaelardus] primo preceptorem Rozelinum quendam, qui primus nostris temporibus in logica sententiam vocum instituit».

(8) REINERS, p. 65: «... apud quas [*scil.* Suessioniensis et Remensis ecclesiae] et sub quibus natus et educatus et edoctus sum...». On eleventh-century classical culture at Rheims and elsewhere, see C. S. JAEGER, *The Envy of Angels. Cathedral Schools and Social Ideal in Medieval Europe, 950-1200*, Philadelphia, 1994, p. 56-62.

(9) REINERS, p. 64-65: «Quod vero sequitur, quod summa haeresi convictus et infamis et a toto mundo expulsus sim, haec tria modis omnibus refello et testimonio Suessionensis et Remensis ecclesiae falsa esse pronuntio.... Quomodo vero stare potest, quod dixisti toto me mundo expulsum, cum et Roma, quae mundi caput est, me libenter excipiat et audiendum libentius amplectatur et audito libentissime obsequatur. Neque vero Turonensis ecclesia vel Locensis, ubi ad pedes meos magistri tui discipulorum minimus tam diu resedisti, aut Bizuntina ecclesia, in quibus canonicus sum, extra mundum sunt, quae me omnes et venerantur et fovent et, quae dico, discendi studio libenter accipiunt».

(10) J. MARENBON, «Anselm and the Early Medieval Aristotle», in D. E. LUSCOMBE (ed.), *Aristotle in Britain during the Middle Ages*, Turnhout, 1996, p. 1-19.

(11) *Ep.* 128, F. S. SCHMITT, *Anselmi opera omnia*, 6 vols., Rome-Edinburgh, 1938-68, 3, p. 270-271.

same thing holding together heat and splendor[12]. St Anselm responded immediately to John in Letter 129, insisting that if Roscelin was saying that the three persons are three things as each is God (rather than as three relations), his argument was absurd. Sometime later, Anselm asked bishop Fulco to make representations at the forthcoming council of Soissons (c. 1090-92) that Roscelin was quite wrong in claiming that either Anselm or Lanfranc had ever conceded in debate that it was necessary to describe the three persons as separate things. St Anselm composed the initial version of a treatise against Roscelin probably with this council directly in mind[13]. He was still sufficiently troubled by Roscelin's question about the logical necessity of distinguishing the Father and the Son after arriving in England in September 1092, to ask prior Baldric for a copy of that initial treatise, in order to revise some of its chapters[14]. Once raised to the see of Canterbury, Anselm issued a considerably revised version of his treatise, now called *Epistola de incarnatione Verbi* sometime in 1093, addressed to Pope Urban II himself. Anselm eliminated reference he had made in the first version to Roscelin as someone he knew as a friend[15]. He had been provoked by hearing Roscelin say that he had only abjured his heresy at the council of Soissons out of fear for his life. Roscelin, who had travelled to England sometime after May 1092, was justifying his arguments on the grounds that Christians had to defend their faith, just as Pagans [i.e Muslims] and Jews both defended their law[16]. During this visit to England, Roscelin also earned the enmity of Theobald of Etampes, a master at Oxford, for claiming that the sons of married clergy were

(12) The analogy does not occur in the genuine writings of Augustine, but was used by Quodvultdeus, *Sermo 2, De symbolo II*, c. 9 (R. BRAUN, CCSL 60, p.346), whose sermons were often attributed to Augustine, his friend and correspondent. It also occurs in *Sermo 245* among the spuria of Augustine, PL 39, 2196-97, *Clavis Patristica Pseudepigraphorum Medii Aevi*, ed. J. MACHIELSEN, CCSL 1A, Turnhout, 1990, p.210, no. 1030. The image was picked up by CASSIODORUS, *Expositio in Psalmorum* Ps. 50:14 (M. ADRIAEN, CCSL 97, p.464). A former pupil of Lanfranc c. 1060, GUITMUND, monk of La-Croix-St Leufroi, appointed bishop of Aversa in 1088, discussed this image at length in response to questions raised by another monk, Erfast, without citing any patristic authority, *Confessio trinitatis*, PL 149, 1495-1502, reprinted from L. d'ACHERY, *Spicilegium*, 3, Paris, 2nd ed. 1723, p.401-404.

(13) The initial version of the *De incarnatione Verbi [DIV¹]* is edited by SCHMITT, 1, p.281-290.

(14) *Ep. 147*, SCHMITT, 2, p.51. SOUTHERN, *Saint Anselm. A Portrait in a Landscape*, p.189 n. 32, suggests that Anselm requested his letter against Roscelin in autumn 1092 rather than after Christmas, as argued by S. N. VAUGHN, *Anselm of Bec and Robert of Meulan. The Innocence of the Dove and the Wisdom of the Serpent*, Berkeley, 1987, p.125. A hitherto unnoticed draft of certain chapters of *DIV* is found in MSS of Anselm stemming from the region around Gloucester, see my «St Anselm and Roscelin... I» n. 1 above. Anselm was staying in a Gloucestershire village in March 1093, when the king held court in Gloucester in Easter 1093.

(15) *DIV¹*, SCHMITT, 1, p.282: «hunc autem novi, quia amicus meus est»; cf. *DIV²*, SCHMITT, 2, p.4.

(16) *DIV²* 1, 2, SCHMITT, 2, p.3-4, 10. Roscelin of Compiègne signed a charter at Bayeux on 7 May 1092, along with a future antagonist of Anselm, Ranulf Flambard, V. BOURIENNE, *Antiquus cartularius Baiocensis*, no. 22, Rouen-Paris, 1902, vol. 1, p.30-31.

invalidly ordained[17]. Roscelin subsequently left England and sought refuge in the Angevin stronghold of Loches, in the Loire valley. Among his students there was the young Peter Abelard, then fourteen or fifteen years old.

Either before or soon after his visit to England in 1092/93, Roscelin tried to win support from Ivo, bishop of Chartres (1090-1116) after twenty years as provost of the collegiate church of Saint-Quentin, Beauvais. Ivo seems to have been on familiar terms with Roscelin, as he sympathised with Roscelin's situation of having been stripped of his assets by certain violent people, but thought that this was a divine test sent by God. Ivo did not want him to visit, because he feared that some citizens of Chartres would resort to stoning Roscelin and that he himself would be held in suspicion by the townsfolk. It was thus necessary for Roscelin to write a palinode or retractation by which he publicly professed his orthodoxy[18]. In this way, he could be embraced and welcomed both by Ivo and others, as well as gain rich reward. Until now, no such confession of faith has ever been identified.

The accusations against Roscelin at the council of Soissons cannot be separated from the political controversy then surrounding the appointment of Fulco, a monk of Bec, to the see of Beauvais in 1088/89[19]. The council of Soissons had to deal, not just with Roscelin, but with suspicions of the archbishop of Rheims that Fulco had obtained his position simoniacally from king Philip through the influence of his father, Lancelin I. Fulco's father had long been involved in a protracted campaign to oust bishop Guy (1063-85) from the see of Beauvais[20]. Guy, an outsider to the city, was active in founding collegiate churches, such as Saint-Quentin (1069), Saint-Vaast (1072) and Saint-Nicolas (1078) for an expanding city, but came into conflict with the cathedral chapter, which saw its privileges as being threatened. A Roscelin and Nevelo of Compiègne are mentioned in a charter of 1072 as petitioning bishop Guy to establish a community of canons at the major suburban church of St-Vaast, Beauvais « so that by an increased number of ministers, the service of religion might be multiplied »[21]. At the height of the campaign against bishop Guy,

---

(17) THEOBALD of ETAMPES, *Epistola ad Roscelinum,* ed. T. BOEHMER, MGH *Libelli de lite,* Hannover, 1897, 3, p. 603-607; PL 163, 767-770.

(18) *Epist.* 7, J. LECLERCQ, *Yves de Chartres. Correspondance,* Paris, 1949, p. 26: « Restat igitur ut palinodiam scribas et recantatis opprobriis vestem Domini tui, quam publice scindebas, publice resarcias, quatenus, sicut multis exemplum fuisti erroris, sic de caetero fias exemplum correctionis ».

(19) For further detail on the political circumstances relating to Beauvais, see my study « St Anselm, Roscelin and the see of Beauvais », in G. R. EVANS and D. E. LUSCOMBE (eds), *Anselm: Aosta, Bec and Canterbury. Papers in Commemoration of the Nine Hundredth Anniversary of Anselm's Enthronement as Archbishop, 25 September 1093,* Sheffield: Sheffield University Press, 1996, p. 106-119.

(20) On Fulco's career, see M. HORN, « Zur Geschichte des Bishofs Fulco von Beauvais (1089-1095) », *Francia,* 16:1 (1989), p. 176-184 and on his family, O. GUYOTJEANNIN, *Episcopus et comes. Affirmation et déclin de la seigneurie épiscopale au nord du royaume de France (Beauvais-Noyon. X^e-début XIIIe siècle),* Geneva, 1987, p. 73-74, 102-104, 263.

(21) P. LOUVET, *Histoire de la ville de Beauuais,* Paris, 1614, p. 480-482 and *Histoire et*

around 1079, Fulco's brother, Radulfus, left the chapter of Beauvais, where he had been treasurer, and became a monk of Bec. Roscelin's future antagonist, John, abandoned a canonry at Saint-Quentin at about this time to become a monk of Bec after making some unspecified accusation[22]. John returned to Beauvais in 1088-89 to help Fulco establish himself as bishop in the face of much local opposition. According to St Anselm, canons, priests and certain laymen of Beauvais were so incensed with Fulco that they were doing everything possible to make life difficult for the new bishop and anyone who helped him[23]. As John only spent a year in Beauvais before returning to Rome, following Pope Urban's criticism of Anselm for ordaining him to higher orders, it seems likely that John made his complaint about Roscelin of Compiègne while involved in this political struggle. The family and friends of Lancelin took advantage of the patronage of St Anselm, who was initially interested in extending the influence and possessions of Bec in the French kingdom[24]. The council of Soissons, held sometime between 1090 and 1092, witnessed not only a profession of orthodoxy by Roscelin, but also the restitution of property by Fulco's father to the Church. This was after bishop Helinand of Laon had challenged Lancelin I to a duel over some long standing grievance[25]. Fulco was subsequently charged by Pope Urban II with imprisoning the brother of the bishop of Sens for financial gain and ignoring the judgement of his fellow bishops, and of acting in treasonable association with his brother Lancelin II in a coup against Odo, castellan of Beauvais[26]. These events led Anselm to beg the Pope to release Fulco from his bishopric, because of the political difficulties he was confronting[27]. The theological accusations against Roscelin of Compiègne must be related to this wider struggle over monastic influence in society.

---

antiquitez du païs de Beauvaisis, Beauvais, 1631-35, vol. 1, p. 694-695.

(22) Guibert of Nogent speaks only of the involvement of the papal legate, Hugh of Die, and certain people whom Guy had promoted, in the claims against him, E.-R. LABANDE, *Autobiographie* I, 14, Paris, 1981, p. 100. Hugh of Flavigny, very hostile to John, is the only author to mention that John was a canon of Saint-Quentin, and gave up his religious habit, before becoming a monk at Bec, *Chronicon* MGH SS 8, p. 494. For further details on Radulfus, see my « Anselm, Roscelin and the see of Beauvais ».

(23) *Epist.* 126, SCHMITT, 3, p. 267-268.

(24) Lancelin (either the elder or the younger) was *buticularius* to the king sometime between 1086-90/91 when Bec monks were granted exemptions from tax in Paris, Pontoise, Poissy and Mantes, GUYOTJEANNIN, *Episcopus et comes*, p. 102 n. 153 and J.-F. LEMARIGNIER, *Le gouvernement royal aux premiers temps capétiens (987-1108)*, Paris, 1965, p. 157 n. 95.

(25) GUYOTJEANNIN, *Episcopus et comes*, p. 72-74, 103; see too a notice copied from the cartulary of St Pierre, Paris, BN Duchesne 22, ff. 249-50.

(26) PL 151, 378B-379C.

(27) *Epp.* 127, 193, SCHMITT, 3, p. 269 and 4, p. 82.

ROSCELIN AND VOCALIST TRADITION

St Anselm never understood the intellectual tradition from which Roscelin came other than as a new type of dialectic which questioned metaphysical realities without any good reason, and believed that a universal term like *homo* in *Socrates est homo* was simply «the puff of an utterance» (*flatum vocis*). He described them as

> heretics of dialectic of our times who do not think universal substances to be anything other than the puff of an utterance, who do not understand colour to be anything other than a body or the wisdom of man anything other than the soul, to be puffed away from discussion of spiritual questions. In their minds reasoning, which ought to be the prince and judge of everything which is in man, has thus been enveloped by bodily imaginings, that it cannot free itself from them, nor is it able to discern from them those things which it ought to contemplate pure and alone. For who does not yet understand how several oxen are one ox in species, how can he understand how, in that most hidden and lofty nature, several persons, of which each individual one is perfect God, are one God? And how can he, whose mind is confused in judging between his donkey and its colour, distinguish between one God and his three-fold relation [28] ?

Anselm ridiculed their theory that a universal like 'wisdom' or 'man', predicated of different individuals, did not refer to a substantive reality. Instead these people interpreted a universal simply as a *vox*, a voice or an utterance, with no real existence other than in individual things. He accused such teachers of being unable to ascend above a material particular to the sublime truth of universal reality, as Boethius had taught in the fifth book of his *Consolation of Philosophy* was essential for any philosophic soul [29].

Anselm's rhetoric has been persuasive in shaping the idea that in the late eleventh century a school of logicians emerged in northern France notorious for

---

(28) *DIV¹*, SCHMITT, 1, p. 285, expanded in *DIV²*, 2, p. 9-10: «illi utique dialectici <+ immo dialecticae heretici *DIV²*>, qui non nisi flatum vocis putant universales esse substantias, et qui colorem non aliud queunt intelligere quam corpus, nec sapientiam hominis aliud quam animam, prorsus a spiritualium quaestionum disputatione sunt exsufflandi. In eorum quippe animabus ratio, quae et princeps et iudex debet omnium esse quae sunt in homine, sic est in imaginationibus corporeis obvoluta, ut ex eis se non possit evolvere nec ab ipsis ea quae ipsa sola et pura contemplari debet, valeat discernere. Qui enim nondum intelligit quomodo plures boves in specie sint unus bos, qualiter in illa secretissima et altissima natura comprehendet quomodo plures personae, quarum singula quaeque perfectus est deus, sint unus deus? Et cuius mens obscura est ad diiudicandum inter asinum suum et colorem eius, qualiter discernet inter unum deum et trinam relationem eius?»; see too SCHMITT, 1, p. 289 (2, p. 17-18): «Quod si iste de illis dialecticis modernis est, qui nihil esse credunt nisi quod imaginationibus comprehendere possunt, nec putat esse aliquid in quo partes nullae sunt...».

(29) L. BIELER, *Boethius. Philosophiae Consolatio*, V 4, 27-39, CCSL 94, Turnhout, 1957, p. 97, an allusion commented on by J. JOLIVET, «Trois variations médiévales sur l'universel et l'individu: Roscelin, Abélard, Gilbert de la Porrée», *Revue de métaphysique et de morale*, 97 (1992), p. 125 (111-155).

rejecting the real existence of universals. While they are commonly referred to as nominalists, the collective label of *nominales* did not emerge until the mid twelfth century, to refer in particular to pupils of Abelard. Iwakuma has convincingly demonstrated that these teachers were originally called *vocales* or vocalists, generally by their critics[30]. The image of Roscelin as a philosophical revolutionary, who initiated a «civil war» in medieval philosophy can be traced back to Johannes Thurmair (Aventinus) in the early sixteenth century[31]. Thurmair was relying on the claim of Otto of Freising that Roscelin was the first person to institute the *sententia vocum* in logic. Only with the researches of Victor Cousin in the early nineteenth century did his name begin to be better known. Accepting at face value Abelard's unkind summary of his argument about parts and wholes, as well as St Anselm's negative assessment of the thinking of «modern dialecticians», Cousin assumed that Abelard learnt his nominalism from Roscelin, rejecting only «its extravagances»[32]. Cousin knew about Roscelin only through a single passage he discovered in Abelard's *Dialectica*:

> It was however, I recall, such an insane opinion of our teacher Ros. that he wanted no thing to consist of parts, but just as he assigned species to utterances alone, so he assigned parts [to utterances]. If anyone said that that thing which is a house consisted of other things, namely a wall and a foundation, he would attack such a person with an argument of this kind: if that thing which is a wall is part of that thing which is a house, since the house itself is nothing other than the wall, roof and foundation, clearly its wall will be part of it and of the other things? And further indeed how can it be part of itself? More fully: every part is naturally prior to its whole. How, though, can a part be said to be prior to itself and to others, when in no way is it prior to itself[33]?

(30) IWAKUMA Y., «'Vocales', or Early Nominalists», *Traditio*, 47 (1992), p. 37-111. That the nominalist rather than vocalist label was applied to pupils of Abelard emerges from the various papers on twelfth-century nominalism in *Vivarium* 30.1 (1992), containing the proceedings of a conference held on the subject in Madison, Wisconsin in September 1992, edited by W. J. COURTENAY. It includes a valuable bibliography on twelfth-century nominalism, and repertory of references to *nominales* and other such labels, «Logico-Theological Schools from the Second Half of the 12th Century: A List of Sources», p. 173-214, compiled by IWAKUMA and S. EBBESEN. Another very useful checklist of Porphyry and Aristotle glosses is provided by J. MARENBON, «Medieval Latin Commentaries and Glosses on Aristotelian Logical Texts, before c. 1150 AD», in C. S. F. BURNETT (ed.), *Glosses and Commentaries on Aristotelian Logical Texts. The Syriac, Arabic and Medieval Latin Traditions*, Warburg Institute Surveys and Texts XXIII, London, 1993, p. 77-127.

(31) J. THURMEIER (AVENTINUS), *Annales ducum Boicarum* VI 3, ed. S. RIEZLER, Munich, 1884, vol. 2, p. 200, initially published Ingolstadt, 1554.

(32) V. COUSIN, *Fragments philosophiques. Philosophie scolastique*, Paris, Ladrange, 2nd. ed. 1840, p. 57-60.

(33) ABELARD, *Dialectica* V.1, edited in part by V. COUSIN, *Ouvrages inédits pour servir à l'histoire de la philosophie scolastique*, Paris, 1836, p. 471, and by L. M. DE RIJK, *Petrus Abaelardus. First Complete Edition of the Parisian Manuscript*, Assen, 2nd ed. 1970, p. 554-555.

X

48

Taking Abelard's criticism at face value, Cousin assumed that Roscelin held that only individuals existed, and that the world was made up of radically discrete things, none of which had parts. Cousin had observed the opinion discussed in a Porphyry gloss, falsely attributed to Rabanus Maurus in a manuscript also containing early glosses of Abelard, that Porphyry's five distinctions, genus, species, difference, particularity and accident, were *voces*, but assumed that Roscelin had made a daring leap in asserting that universals were nothing but words[34]. As creator of nominalism, Roscelin became for Cousin the creator of scholastic philosophy[35]. A strong nationalist agenda underpinned this perception of the history of philosophy. French thinkers had anticipated the achievements of Hobbes, Dugald Stewart and, more recently, of Kant, whose ideas he feared were becoming dangerously objectified in Germany[36]. The fact that Anselm was a monk, while Roscelin was a secular cleric, has only reinforced the impression that the conflict between these two men was between two radically different schools of thought: one Augustinian, philosophically realist, and rooted in the past, the other influenced by Aristotle and looking forward to the future.

Barthélemy Hauréau was able to correct Duchesne's mistaken notions about his supposed Breton birth by reference to Roscelin's newly discovered letter to Abelard[37]. He also found a charter which confirmed that Roscelin of Compiègne held a senior position at St-Martin of Tours c.1100-10. Seduced by the same attribution to Rabanus Maurus of certain glosses discussing genus and species as *voces* as had intrigued Cousin, he presented nominalism as an anti-Platonic philosophical movement with a pedigree stretching back to the ninth century[38]. In

(34) *Fragments philosophiques*, p.16-25; on p.311-320, Cousin describes and transcribes extracts from Saint-Germain 1310 (Paris, Bibl. Nat. lat. 13368), including: f. 215r-223r (formerly f.86r-93v) *Rabanus super Porphyrium*; f. 223r-224r (formerly f.94r-95r) fragment of gloss on *De differentiis topicis*; f. 224r-229v [225r-231r] (formerly f.95r-100v) *Rabanus super terencivia* [*Periermeneias*]. Also cited in extract by COUSIN, *Ouvrages inédits*, p.613-616 and *Fragments de philosophie du moyen âge*, Paris, 1855, p.245-249. GEYER observes its significance and the evidently spurious attribution in *Philosophische Schriften*, p.595-6. MARENBON, «Commentaries and Glosses» P3 and H11. See n. 120 below.

(35) *Fragments philosophiques*, p.127-128.

(36) *Ibid.*, p.277-279: «Il y a un rapport si intime entre le conceptualisme et le nominalisme que, selon les temps et les circonstances, et le plus ou moins de force et de hardiesse des esprits, le nominalisme, sans se détruire, se réfugie et se métamorphose dans le conceptualisme, ou le conceptualisme se développe en nominalisme. Ainsi, après l'orage qui, au concile de Soissons, éclata sur Roscelin, le nominalisme, proscrit et couvert d'anathèmes, se réduisit au conceptualisme, perdant ainsi de sa rigueur, mais suivant ses principes, où sont déposées toutes ses conséquences.... Avancez dans l'histoire, entrez dans la philosophie moderne: le nominalisme y passe tour à tour par les mêmes métamorphoses. Il se montre dans Hobbes à visage découvert; mais Hobbes décrie le nominalisme au XVIIe siècle, comme Roscelin à la fin du XIe.... C'est ainsi qu'en Allemagne, nous avons vu le conceptualisme de Kant s'élever successivement jusqu'au système le plus réaliste et le plus objectif qui ait été depuis Platon. Au fond, Abélard est un nominaliste qui s'ignore ou qui si cache».

(37) *Singularités historiques et littéraires*, Paris, 1861, repr. 1894, p.216-30, correcting a remark of Duchesne in his commentary to the *Historia calamitatum*, reprinted in PL 178, 115CD, in turn based on Aventinus' misreading of Otto of Freising.

(38) B. HAURÉAU, *Histoire de la philosophie scolastique*, Paris, 1872, p.138-147.

Hauréau's eyes, Roscelin was heir to Berengar of Tours in doing battle with orthodoxy, worthy of congratulation, even though he fell victim to ecclesiastical authority.

In 1896 François Picavet published a small paper, re-issued in much expanded form in 1911, in which he questioned whether Roscelin was a «free-thinker and rebel», as Hauréau claimed[39]. Picavet considered Roscelin to have been a harbinger of philosophic progress, but with an unresolved contradiction in his thought between the «principle of perfection», Platonist in origin and the basis of Trinitarian orthodoxy, and an Aristotelian awareness of the need to distinguish the Father and Son as separate objects[40]. Where Hauréau identified a conflict between the empiricist Roscelin, at odds with dogmatic authority, Picavet located the same contradiction within Roscelin himself. Unable to relinquish the idea that nominalism was fundamentally at odds with ecclesiastical tradition, Picavet was unconsciously perpetuating the image of «nominalism» first propagated by St Anselm.

In the same year as Picavet published the revised version of his study on Roscelin, J. Reiners published his own critique of Hauréau's broader argument about the history of nominalism before the twelfth century. Although he appended to his study a new edition of Roscelin's letter to Abelard, Reiners relied mainly on the reports of his teaching given by St Anselm and Peter Abelard that Roscelin believed only in individuals, the report of John of Salisbury that Roscelin defined universals as *voces*, and the claim of Otto of Freising that Roscelin was the first to introduce into logic the *sententia vocum*[41]. Reiners was not seriously troubled by the witness of an anonymous chronicle which declared that Roscelin of Compiègne, Robert of Paris and Arnulf of Laon were all distinguished sophists, who followed the teaching of a mysterious John that dialectic was a «vocal» art. He saw Roscelin as the true initiator of medieval nominalism, and questioned the significance of the enigmatic «Rabanus» gloss on Porphyry, which he re-assigned to the first half of the eleventh century[42]. Reiners dismissed other texts, such as the authors of glosses on Martianus Capella or the *Categories* attributed to Augustine, as well as the figure of Berengar of Tours as nominalist, because they did not deal with universals *per se*. It was a traditional Boethian topos, he argued, to debate the relationship between words and things. Reiners contributed valuable insight in suggesting that the ideas about parts and wholes, ridiculed by Abelard

---

(39) F. PICAVET, *Roscelin, philosophe et théologien d'après la légende et d'après l'histoire. Sa place dans l'histoire générale et comparée des philosophies médiévales*, Paris, F. Alcan, 1911, a much enlarged version of a 26 pages study of the same title, but without *Sa place dans l'histoire...*, published by the Imprimerie Nationale in 1896 under the aegis of the Ecole pratique des hautes études. Section des sciences religieuses.

(40) PICAVET, 1911, p. 96.

(41) *Der Nominalismus*, p. 25-31.

(42) J. REINERS, *Der Nominalismus*, p. 32-33, repeating the claim made by C. E. BULAEUS, *Historia universitatis Parisiensis*, vol. 1, Paris, 1665, p. 443, and *Der aristotelische Realismus in der Frühscholastik. Ein Beitrag zur Geschichte der Universalienfrage im Mittelalter*, Aachen, 1917, p. 38.

X

in the fifth book of the *Dialectica*, echo a passage in Boethius' commentary on the *Topics* of Cicero that without a part, such as the roof or the wall of a house, the house could not exist, and that the whole was found later than its parts[43]. Reiners wished to deflate the exaggerated claims Cousin and Hauréau had made about nominalism. He considered Abelard's theological thought as not a deep system and not penetrated by ecclesiastical tradition.

With so few texts to hand, twentieth-century commentators on Roscelin have rarely transcended the caricatures of his critics. John Marenbon has suggested that Roscelin may have taken his physical analysis of words from Priscian, but confessed that «there seemed to be no evidence of his having produced a theory of language which would explain how, if universals are just words, they are nevertheless meaningful ones»[44]. His comment is an insightful one, because it suggests that Roscelin was concerned not primarily with universals, but with the meaning of words.

THE TWELFTH-CENTURY HISTORIOGRAPHICAL TRADITION

That Roscelin was a significant teacher in the late eleventh and early twelfth century, until overshadowed by his more famous pupil, is evident from a range of contemporary sources apart from the letters of St Anselm. Walter of Honnecourt, an unashamed traditionalist, never alluded to Roscelin's reference to plural things, but was shocked by Roscelin's use of unfamiliar words about the Trinity, comparing the three divine persons to the souls of three people[45]. He was concerned that Roscelin was sympathizing too much with Greek tradition:

> For the whole Church of the Latin tongue faithfully believes, piously confesses, constantly preaches that there are three persons in the deity, so that it is one substance of three persons. Certain of the Greeks, as blessed Augustine remembers in the seventh book of the *De trinitate*, speak according

---

(43) *Der Nominalismus*, p. 35-36, discussing BOETHIUS, *In Topica Ciceronis*, PL 64, 1105D: «Genus semper speciebus suis prius est, totum vero suis partibus posterius invenitur. Nisi enim partes fuerint, totum vero suis partibus posterius invenitur. Nisi enim partes fuerint, totum non potest coniungi. Quo fit ut, si genus pereat, species quoque perimantur, si species intereat, maneat genus; quod in partibus totoque contrarium est. Nam si pars quaelibet una pereat, totum necesse est interire; si vero totum, quod partes iunxerant, dissipetur, partes maneant distributae. Veluti si domus tecta et parietes et fundamenta a semetipsis extrinsecus postea intelligantur, domus quidem non erit, quia coniunctio destructa est, partes tamen manebunt».

(44) J. MARENBON, *Early Medieval Philosophy*, London, 1983, p. 110.

(45) G. MORIN, «Un écrivain inconnu du XIe siècle: Walter, moine de Honnecourt, puis de Vézelay», *Revue bénédictine*, 22 (1905), p. 173-175 (165-180). Morin used a manuscript of Metz, Bibl. municipale 1212 (Salis 65), f. 361r-361v; the letter to Roscelin also occurs in Erlangen, Universitätsbibliothek 176, f. 75, H. FISCHER, *Katalog der Handschriften der Universitätsbibliothek Erlangen, Neubearbeitung. 1. Band: Die Lateinischen Pergamenthandschriften*, Erlangen, 1928, p. 194. Walter is the only contemporary who addresses Roscelin as a canon of Compiègne.

to the property of their language of one essence and three substances – although we speak of one substance and three persons – expressing to themselves the unity of the divine trinity perhaps more aptly through essence than through substance, since for them these two names are not signs of the same thing. These Greeks, granted that they have used *substances* for *persons* and have said that they have the same understanding as us with different signs, are able if they wish, according to Augustine, to say three *prosopa*, just as they say three *hypostases*; and they would do so more appropriately if they were to put the word on an equal level with what it is in our language. We, therefore, who are Latins, when we speak about divine nature, should be content with the conventional sayings of the great and with <our> native tongue. Otherwise, according to the vulgar proverb while we fly far beyond names, while through lynx-like or, if you will, eagle gazing we are tempted to pry into the sphere of the invisible sun – then, suffering a just reverse, having burnt <our> wings, we fall blinded from on high; falling we die a first death, and in the second we live in inextinguishable hell. Far be from us such misfortune! Rather it enmeshes those Greeks who distinguish the essence of the one deity without discretion. If any contentious individual among us prefers to greekify, let him not categorize three substances in Latin, but let him barbarize three *hypostases* with the Greeks[46]!

This is followed by a string of excerpts from Jerome's letter 15 to Damasus bemoaning Greek corruption of trinitarian doctrine as three substances. Walter quotes the Augustine's *De Trinitate* in the light of an impassioned Latin patriotism, arguing vociferously that only the Latin definition was free of any tinge of heresy.

Roscelin tended to question traditional Latin sources of philosophical as well as theological thinking, by focusing on the meaning of *voces*. Conservative critics feared that this concentration on words was at the expense of awareness of reality. Around 1125 Udalric, scholasticus of Bamberg, included in his anthology

---

(46) MORIN, p. 177: «Nempe tota latinae linguae fidelis ecclesia firmiter credit, pie confitetur, constanter praedicat, ita tres in deitate personas, ut trium sit una substantia personarum. Quidam uero Graecorum, sicut beatissimus Augustinus in septimo De trinitate libro [c. 7] commemorat, iuxta proprietatem locutionis suae, unam essentiam, tres dixerunt substantias: quemadmodum nos dicimus unam substantiam, tres personas; unitatem trinitatis deifice aptius sibi forte per essentiam quam per substantiam exprimentes, quoniam apud eos haec duo nomina non eiusdem rei sunt signa. Qui Graeci licet posuerint substantias pro personis, et in diuersis signis eandem nobiscum intelligentiam habere se dixerint, possent tamen, praedicto Augustino testante, si uellent, sicut dicunt tres hypostasis, sic tria prosopa dicere; et commodius facerent, si aequipararent in sua uocabulum linguae nostrae. Nos igitur, qui Latini sumus, quando de diuina loquimur natura, usitatis a maioribus dictis et patria lingua decet esse contentos; ne iuxta uulgare prouerbium ultra nomina diu dum uolamus, dum per lyneos, uel, si libet, aquilinos obtutus speram solis inuisibilis rimari temptamus, iusta passi repulsam, pennas adusti, insuper excaecati cadamus, cadentes prima morte moriamur, et in secunda inextinguibili gehennae uiuamus. Fiat procul a nobis infortunium tale; illos potius Graecos inuoluat, qui unius deitatis essentiam indiscrete discernunt. Quod si apud nos contentiosus aliquis graecizare maluerit, non iam latine tres substantias cathegorizet, sed cum Graecis tres ypostasis barbarizet».

52

two satirical poems about Arnulf of Laon and Roscelin of Compiègne. The author of the poem about Roscelin had no doubt that dialectic was about things:

> The voices you teach, Roscelin, dialectic does not want,
> And already, mourning for itself, does not want it to be in voices;
> It loves things; it wants to be in things for all days.
> Let it be reconsidered in voice: it is a thing which is taught by a voice.
> Aristotle weeps, as he considers to be senile wrinkles,
> The things taken away from it, referred to through voices;
> Porphyry groans because the reader is taking things away from it;
> Boethius hates one who takes things away, Roscelin;
> You do not perceive with arguments or any sophism
> Things existing, remaining in voices[47].

This sort of poem testifies to a current of hostility towards vocalist teaching, influenced profoundly by the rhetoric of St Anselm, a figure much revered in German Benedictine circles[48]. Some thought that Roscelin's obsession with words was leading to the death of true philosophy.

There are no negative associations, however, in a passage in a chronicle from Fleury (St-Benoît-sur-Loire), completed around 1110 by someone who had himself witnessed events in 1108, when Philip I was laid to rest at that abbey. It asserts that at the time of the death of Lanfranc (d.1087), great developments were taking place in dialectic as well as in divinity:

> At this time there flourished in divinity Lanfranc bishop of Canterbury, Guido the Lombard, Maingauld the German and Bruno of Rheims who later led an eremitic life; in dialectic as well, these were powerful sophists: John, who expounded the same sophistic art to be vocal, Robert of Paris, Roscelin of Compiègne, Arnulf of Laon. These were followers of John and had many disciples[49].

(47) Ph. JAFFÉ, *Codex Udalrici, Bibliotheca rerum Germanicarum*, Berlin, 1869, vol. 5, p. 187:
> Quas, Ruzeline, doces, non vult dialectica voces,
> Jamque, dolens de se, non vult in vocibus esse;
> Res amat, in rebus cunctis vult esse diebus.
> Voce retractetur: res sit, quod voce docetur.
> Plorat Aristotiles, rugas ducendo seniles,
> Res sibi subtractas, per voces intitulatas;
> Porfiriusque gemit, quia res sibi lector ademit;
> Qui res abrodit, Ruzeline, Boetius odit.
> Non argumentis nulloque sophismata sentis,
> Res existentes in vocibus esse manentes.

(48) There is a long account of St Anselm and his writing, including the treatise against Roscelin, in the *Annales Sancti Disibodi*, MGH SS 17, p. 14-15, which I discuss in C. J. MEWS, «Hildegard and the Schools», in C. S. F. BURNETT and P. DRONKE (eds), *Hildegard of Bingen and the Context of her Thought*, London, Warburg Studies and Texts, 1998, p. 97-98.

(49) P. PITHOU, *Historia Francorum* [or *Historia Francica*], *Annales* 1588 [p 407-416], repr. in *Historiae Francorum ab anno Christi DCCC ad ann. MCCLXXXV scriptores ueteres*

X

While the theologians mentioned here are all outsiders to France, the dialecticians are identified as of 'French origin. The chronicler does not say that John introduced a new way of teaching dialectic, but that he taught that it was an *ars vocalis*, to do with utterances. This was not such a revolutionary notion. In his commentary on the *Categories* Boethius had defined every logical art as about discourse and had explained that the *Categories* principally dealt with *voces*[50].

A key text frequently cited as evidence for the existence of two philosophical schools is the account of Hermann of Tournai about how Odo or Odard of Orléans (*c*. 1050-1113) restored the abbey of St Martin, Tournai[51]. Writing around 1142, Hermann explained how, prior to establishing a community of canons at St Martin's in 1092, Odo had taught dialectic at Tournai in the traditional manner *in re*, unlike Rainbertus, who taught the subject *in voce* in the rival town of Lille. An exact translation of these terms is difficult to obtain:

> It should be known about the same teacher that he lectured on the same dialectic to disciples, not according to the way of certain moderns, relating to utterance (*in voce*) but in the way of Boethius and the ancient doctors, relating to the real (*in re*). Master Rainbert, who taught dialectic to his clerics at the same time in the town of Lille, also lectured thus, relating it to utterance; but several other teachers were not a little jealous of him, criticising him and saying that their lectures were better than his – for which reason several troubled clerics hesitated about who to believe more, since they saw that master Odard did not deviate from the teaching of the ancients; and yet some of them, like the Athenians keen to learn or listen to something new through human curiosity, praised others greatly because they said that their lectures were more

XI, ex bibliotheca P. Pithoei [ex veteri exemplari Floriacensi], Frankfurt, 1596, p.88, by A. DUCHESNE, *Historiae Francorum Scriptores*, vol. 4, Paris, 1641, p.89-90 and by M. BOUQUET, *Recueil des historiens des Gaules et de la France*, vol. 12, Paris, 1781, p.3: «Hoc tempore tam in divina quam in humana philosophia floruerunt Lanfrancus Cantuariorum episcopus, Guido Langobardus, Maingaudus Teutonicus, Bruno Remensis, qui postea vitam duxit heremiticam. In dialectica quoque hi potentes extiterunt sophistae: Ioannes, qui eandem artem sophisticam vocalem esse disseruit, Rotbertus Parisiacensis, Roscelinus Compendiensis, Arnulfus Laudunensis. Hi Ioannis fuerunt sectatores, qui etiam quamplures habuerunt auditores». On this chronicle, see J. HAVET, «Les couronnements des rois Hugues et Robert. Un document interpolé par Pierre Pithou», *Revue historique*, 45 (1891), p.290-294 and *Oeuvres de J. Havet*, vol. 2, Paris, 1896, p.68-72. This Arnulf may be the Ernulfus remembered in an epitaph saying that a thousand sophisms were of no use now that he had passed away: A. BOUTÉMY, «Recueil poétique du manuscrit Cotton Vitellius A XII du British Museum», *Latomus*, 1 (1937), p.310 (278-313).

(50) PL 64, 161CD, 162B: «Quare quoniam omnis ars logica de oratione est, et in hoc opere de vocibus principaliter tractatur (quamquam enim sit huius libri relatio ad caeteras quoque philosophiae partes), principaliter tamen refertur ad logicam, de cuius quodammodo simplicibus elementis, id est, de sermonibus in eo principaliter disputavi.... Namque (ut docuimus) non de rerum generibus, neque de sermonibus rerum genera significantibus in hoc opere tractatus habetur, hoc vero Aristoteles ipse declarat...».

(51) G. WAITZ, *Narratio restaurationis Sancti Martini Tornacensis*, MGH SS 14, Hannover, 1883, p.274ff. On the date of Hermann's treatise, as well as the records he used to construct the early history of St Martin's, see C. DEREINE, «Odo de Tournai et la crise du cénobitisme au XIᵉ siècle», *Revue du Moyen Age latin*, 4 (1948), p.137-154.

54

valuable for the exercise of disputation and eloquence, or rather of loquacity and slickness[52].

Like St Anselm, Hermann wanted to assert that there was a clear difference between «wordy» and «reality based» teachers. A number of teachers envied Rainbert's success in attracting students in the rival town of Lille. In Tournai, a canon by the name of Gualbert was so worried «by the variety of ideas and of wandering clerics», that he approached a local deaf-mute with a reputation for prophecy to ask which teacher to believe. Gualbert interpreted the deaf-mute's gesticulations to mean that Odo was a good teacher while Rainbert was all talk. Hermann then turned to the authority of St Anselm:

> I may say these things not to take thought for vipers or because I think they are to be believed against divine precept, but to refute the excessive presumption of certain proud people, who searching for nothing other than to be called wise, prefer to read new-fangled novelty in the books of Porphyry and Aristotle rather than the exposition of Boethius and the other ancients. Finally Anselm, archbishop of Canterbury, in a book which he composed *On the Incarnation of the Word*, calls clerics of this kind who think universal substances to be nothing but wind, not dialecticians but heretics of dialectic; he says they deserve to be puffed out from the number of the wise[53].

(52) MGH.SS 14, p. 275: «Sciendum tamen de eodem magistro, quod eandem dialecticam non iuxta quosdam modernos in voce, sed more Boetii antiquorumque doctorum in re discipulis legebat. Unde et magister Rainbertus, qui eodem tempore in oppido Insulensi dialecticam clericis suis in voce legebat, sed et alii quam plures magistri ei non parum invidebant et detrahebant suasque lectiones ipsius meliores esse dicebant; quam ob rem nonnulli ex clericis conturbati cui magis crederent, hesitabant, quoniam et magistrum Odardum ab antiquorum doctrina non discrepare videbant, et tamen aliqui ex eis more Atheniensium aut discere aut audire aliquid novi semper humana curiositate studentes, alios potius laudabant, maxime quia eorum lectiones ad exercitium disputandi vel eloquentie, immo loquacitatis et facundie plus valere dicebant».

(53) *Ibid.*: «Unus itaque ex eiusdem ecclesie canonicis nomine Gualbertus, qui postmodum monachus noster, deinde in episcopatu Catalaunensi abbas extitit, tanta sententiarum errantiumque clericorum varietate permotus, quendam phitonicum surdum et mutum, sed in eadem urbe divinandi famosissimum, secreto adiit, et cui magistrorum magis esset credendum, digitorum signis et nutibus inquirere cepit. Protinus ille, mirabile dictu! questionem illius intellexit, dexteramque manum per sinistre palmam instar aratri terram scindentis pertrahens digitumque versus magistri Odonis scolam protendens, significabat, doctrinam eius esse rectissimam; rursus vero digitum contra Insulense oppidum protendens manuque ori admota exsufflans, innuebat, magistri Raimberti lectionem nonnisi ventosam esse loquacitatem. Hec dixerim non quo phitonicos consulendos, vel eis contra praeceptum divinum arbitrer esse credendum, sed ad redarguendum quorundam superborum nimiam praesumptionem, qui nichil aliud querentes nisi ut dicantur sapientes, in Porphirii Aristotelisque libris magis volunt legi suam adinventitiam novitatem, quam Boetii ceterorumque antiquorum expositionem. Denique dominus Anselmus Cantuariensis archiepiscopus in libro quem fecit *de Verbi incarnatione* non dialecticos huiusmodi clericos, sed dialectice appellat hereticos: *Qui nonnisi flatum*, inquit, *universales putant esse substantias*, dicens eos *de sapientum numero merito esse exsufflandos*».

Like Walter of Honnecourt, Hermann was afraid that fascination with Greek authors was leading to contempt for Latin tradition. Hermann followed St Anselm, whose writings were well represented at the church of St Martin, in castigating teachers who taught dialectic *in voce*[54]. He had been an oblate at St Martin's from 1094, and was fifteen years old in 1105, when Odo left St Martin's to become bishop of Cambrai in 1105. Hermann described how Odo had originally been prompted to leave Tournai cathedral and establish a new community through his discovery of Augustine. Odo had written two books about sophisms as well as a third, *De re et ente*. When discussing the original sin of Adam, Odo had argued that individuals were distinguished from each other by accident rather than substance[55]. Hermann's understanding of teachers like Master Rainbert derived from St Anselm's hostile remarks about modern dialecticians who were so in love with novelty that they lacked the substance of tradition. To their critics, these dialecticians emphasised so much that universals were qualities predicated of individuals, but not substances, that they saw wholes as nothing more than parts, just as in theology they seemed to view God as a composite of three separate persons.

ROSCELIN'S LETTER TO PETER ABELARD

Roscelin's letter to Peter Abelard is probably more known for its malicious report of rumours about Abelard's private life than for its theological argument: his pupil was failing to respect the necessary difference between the Father, the Son and the Holy Spirit. Roscelin was reacting to certain accusations that Abelard had made in a letter to the canons of St Martin of Tours, in particular the charge of tritheism and were repeated in his *Theologia 'Summi boni'*[56]. Roscelin

---

(54) The community transferred to the Benedictine Rule in 1094, the year Hermann was consecrated by his parents at the age of four to the monastery, of which he became the abbot in 1127. Odo left the abbey in 1105 to become bishop of Cambrai. On the presence of St Anselm's writings at Tournai, see A. BOUTEMY, «Odo d'Orléans et les origines de la bibliothèque de l'abbaye de Saint-Martin de Tournai», in *Mélanges dédiés à la mémoire de Félix Grat*, vol. 2, Paris, 1949, p. 179-222.

(55) Although Odo's *De re et ente* is lost, Odo's philosophic ideas are evident in his *De peccato originali* (PL 160, 1071-1102), discussed by J. J. E. GRACIA, *Introduction to the Problem of Individuation in the Early Middle Ages*, Munich-Vienna, 1984, p. 135-141 [mistakenly identified as Odo of Tours] and I. M. RESNICK, «Odo of Tournai on Original Sin», *Medieval Philosophy and Theology*, 1 (1991), p. 18-38. G. R. EVANS, *Anselm and a New Generation*, Oxford, Clarendon Press, 1980, p. 139-147, discusses the influence of St Anselm on both Odo and Hermann. The *De peccato originali* has been identified within the surviving fragments of Chartres, Bibl. mun. 205, f. 300r-309r, followed on f. 315v by a fascinating, and to my knowledge unedited treatise against religious doubt; see C. S. GALE, «Saint against Simoniac: A Tract of Ecclesiastical Reform attributed to Anselm of Canterbury», *The Journal of Religious History*, 17 (1993), p. 293-294 (290-296).

(56) E. M. BUYTAERT and C. J. MEWS, *Theologia 'Summi boni'* II, 75-76, CCCM 13, Turnhout, 1987, p. 140 and Abelard's letter 14 to the bishop of Paris about Roscelin, E. SMITS, *Peter Abelard. Letters IX-XIV*, Groningen, 1983, p. 279-280.

responded to the charge of distinguishing too sharply the three persons of the Trinity by quoting extensively from the Fathers of the Church[57]. He was particularly interested in Augustine's argument in the *De Trinitate*: «It is said by our Greeks that there is one essence, three substances, by the Latins one substance or essence and three persons»[58]. Augustine thought that Latins should use 'person' rather than 'substance' (which he treated as a synonym for 'essence') if one was to respect the particularity of the Latin language[59]. The distinction was one of custom, rather than of truth versus error. Augustine was more flexible here than the more philologically conscious Jerome, who feared the potential for error in Greek usage[60]. These comments of Augustine provided an essential basis for Roscelin's argument that one had to distinguish the separate identities of the three persons of the Trinity, and that there were different ways of expressing this truth.

Roscelin was not denying the unity of the divine nature. His attention was directed to the fact that one could not identify the name of the Father with the names of the Son or of the Holy Spirit. In his terminology, each proper name had its own *res* or thing. He was particularly struck by the implications of Priscian's definition that a noun signified substance and quality to names applied of God,

(57) AUGUSTINE's *De Trinitate* is the most frequently cited work; there are extracts too from his *De baptismo, De agone christiano, De coniugiis adulterinis, De Genesi ad litteram, De anima et eius origine, In Iohannis euangelium tractatus 124, Epist. 147, De doctrina christiana*. Other extracts are from PRUDENTIUS, *Peristephanon*; GREGORY, *Epistolae* and *Moralia in Iob*; LEO, *Sermo 22*, AMBROSE, *De fide, De spiritu sancto*; ISIDORE, *Etymologiae*; JEROME, *Contra Vigilantium*.

(58) *Ep. ad Abaelardum,* REINERS, p. 70, quoting AUGUSTINE, *De Trinitate* 7.4, W. J. MOUNTAIN, CCSL 50, p. 259: «Quod enim de personis secundum nostram, hoc de substantiis secundum graecorum consuetudinem ea quae diximus oportet intellegi. Sic enim dicunt illi tres substantias, unam essentiam, quemadmodum nos dicimus tres personas, unam essentiam uel substantiam». See also AUG., *ibid.* 5.8-9, p. 216-217: «Dicunt quidem et illi ypostasin, sed nescio quid uolunt interesse inter usian et ypostasyn ita ut plerique nostri qui haec graeco tractant eloquio dicere consuerint mian usian tres ypostasis, quod est latine, unam essentiam tres substantias. Sed quia nostri loquendi consuetudo iam obtinuit ut hoc intellegatur cum dicimus essentiam quod intellegitur cum dicimus substantiam, non audemus dicere unam essentiam, tres substantias, sed unam essentiam uel substantiam». (Greek words spelt out in the form most frequently cited in the critical apparatus of CCSL 50).

(59) JOLIVET points out this synonymy with reference to Abelard in «Notes de lexicographie abélardienne», in R. LOUIS and J. JOLIVET (eds), *Pierre Abélard-Pierre le Vénérable. Les courants philosophiques, littéraires et artistiques en Occident au milieu du XIIe siècle*, Paris, 1975, p. 532-543, repr. in *Aspects de la pensée médiévale: Abélard. Doctrines du langage*, Paris, 1987, p. 125-137.

(60) AUGUSTINE, *De Trinitate* 7.5, CCSL 50, p. 261 prefers the greater suitability of the Latin term: «Fortassis igitur commodius dicuntur tres personae quam tres substantiae». Yet in the preface to book 8, CCSL 50, p. 268, he says that he is more concerned by the sense intended than the legitimacy of one or other word: «Ideoque dici tres personas uel tres substantias non ut aliqua intellegatur diuersitas essentiae, sed ut uel uno aliquo uocabulo responderi possit cum dicitur quid tres uel quid tria; tantamque esse aequalitatem...». JEROME, *Letter* 15.4, CSEL 54, p. 65 is much less precise: «Et quis unquam, rogo, ore sacrilego tres substantias praedicabit?... Sufficit nobis dicere unam substantiam tres personas...».

given that to speak of quality in God suggested something less than pure substance.

It should indeed be known that in the substance of the Holy Trinity any names do not signify one thing and another, whether according to parts or to qualities, but they signify only substance itself, neither divided into parts nor changed through qualities. We do not therefore signify through *person* anything other than through *substance*, granted that we are accustomed out of a certain habit of speech to triple *person*, not *substance*, as the Greeks are accustomed to triple *substance*. Neither indeed is it to be said that they err in belief in the Trinity because they speak differently from us, for they believe the same as us, since – as we have said – *person*, *substance* or *essence* signify the same thing in God. For in speech there is diversity, in belief unity; otherwise there would not be a Church among the Greeks. For if they themselves say one thing by speaking thus, I do not see why we lie by saying the same thing.... [Here follow brief excerpts from Augustine and Ambrose on the unity of the divine substance]... When therefore we vary these names or profer them in the singular or in the plural, we do this not because it might signify one thing rather than another, but by virtue only of the will of the speakers to whom such a habit of speech is pleasing... But neither is there any quality signified through *person*, or another through *substance* or *essence*, because – as we have already said – in God there is completely no quality[61].

The analysis turns on his assumption that divine names had to conform to Priscian's definition that of a noun as a name signifying substance with quality. As the name of a divine person could not signify an accidental quality, it had to signify a substance. He then went on to cite all those Fathers of the Church who insisted on respecting plurality in the Trinity:

Let us inquire what difference there is in this plurality of persons according to us, or of substances according to the Greeks. For the substance of the Father is nothing other than the Father, and the substance of the Son <anything other>

(61) *Ep. ad Abaelardum,* REINERS, p. 72: «Sciendum est vero, quod in substantia sanctae trinitatis quaelibet nomina non aliud et aliud significant, sive quantum ad partes sive quantum ad qualitates, sed ipsam solam non in partes divisam nec per qualitates mutatam significant substantiam. Non igitur per personam aliud aliquid significamus, quam per substantiam, licet ex quadam loquendi consuetudine triplicare soleamus personam, non substantiam, sicut Graeci triplicare solent substantiam. Neque vero dicendum est, quod in fide trinitatis errent triplicando substantiam, quia licet aliter dicant quam nos, id tamen credunt quod nos, quia sicut diximus sive persona sive substantia sive essentia in deo prorsus idem significant. In locutione enim tantum diversitas est, in fide unitas. Alioquin iam non esset apud Graecos ecclesia. Si autem ipsi sic loquendo verum dicunt, quare nos idem dicendo mentiamur, non video... Quando ergo haec nomina variamus sive singulariter sive pluraliter proferendo, non quia aliud unum quam alterum significet hoc facimus, sed pro sola loquentium voluntate, quibus talis loquendi usus complacuit... Sed neque alia qualitas per personam, alia per substantiam vel essentiam significatur, quia sicut iam diximus, in deo nulla prorsus qualitas est».

than the Son, just as the city of Rome is Rome, and the created element of water is water[62].

By substance Roscelin understands what makes one noun distinct from another. The Greek definition of the Trinity appealed to him because it fitted with what he had learnt from Priscian about the meaning of a noun.

While Roscelin is stretching a point in relating the 'substance' of a divine person to a specific material substance, we need to respect what he is trying to say: our language about God has to conform with that of everyday experience, which is one of plurality generated by our will. In his mind Priscian had touched on a fundamental truth, valid in secular and divine spheres. While a name signified a quality in this created world, there was no such potential for partiality or mutability in God. Only very gradually within the letter does Roscelin lead up to defining a person as a thing.

> Thus therefore it should here be said that he [Augustine] did not completely deny that there were three eternals, but in that way in which was affirmed by Arius, who varied the measure of eternity in the persons. For they were severally eternal, just like several eternal things (res) and they were not'eternals' so that eternity could be seen variously in them. Let him who can put it better. I am not able [to do] better. I do not have the strength <to put it> better, but neither do I unashamedly reject what I am saying[63].

He then returned to a passage from Isidore's *Etymologies* (VII.4.1) about the belief of the Greek Church that there was one *ousia*, as if saying one nature or one essence, and three *hypostases*, which means (*resonat*) in Latin either as three persons or three essences. No manuscript of Isidore cited by Lindsay reads *essentias* for the correct reading *substantias*, taken from Augustine. Roscelin's variant reading helped confirm his emphasis that each person had its own distinct identity.

Monks like Walter of Honnecourt feared that Roscelin's argument conflicted with the definition of the so-called Athanasian Creed, composed in Gaul in the fifth or sixth century and recited daily at the office of Prime[64]. An instrument for

(62) REINERS, p. 74: «Quae ergo differentia in hac pluralitate personarum secundum nos, substantiarum vero secundum Graecos sit, perquiramus. Nihil enim aliud est substantia patris quam pater, et substantia filii quam filius, sicut urbs Romae Roma est, et creatura aquae aqua est».

(63) REINERS, p. 76: «Aeterni enim erant pluraliter, sicut plures res aeternae; et aeterni non erant, ut aeternitas in eis varia videretur. Dicat melius qui potest. Ego melius non valeo, sed neque quod dico importune defendo».

(64) ANSELM, *DIV*[1], SCHMITT, 1, p. 283, reminded Roscelin of its daily recitation. See too the 12th-century liturgist JOHN BELETH, *Summa de divinis officiis* 40, PL 202, 50A, who mentions that many falsely attributed it to Anastasius. This evidence of daily recitation contradicts what A. HUGHES, *Medieval Manuscripts for Mass and Office*, Toronto, 1982, p. 38-39, says about its being chanted at Prime on Sundays. Commentaries on the creed become much more frequent in the twelfth century; see N. HÄRING, «Commentaries on the Pseudo-Athanasian Creed», *Mediaeval Studies*, 34 (1972), p. 208-252.

defining unity in the Latin West, it allows for no such synonymy between the Latin *persona* and the Greek *substantia* as Augustine had allowed within the *De Trinitate*. A theologian who strayed too far from this definition risked falling into heresy, the crime of breaking ecclesiastical unity. Roscelin was straying too far from the orthodox tradition of the Latin Church.

Roscelin was enamoured not only of the grammatical definitions of Priscian, but of the vocabulary of patristic tradition, which he analysed with acuity. His careful selection of passages to support a particular doctrinal argument anticipates Abelard's more systematic collection of authorities in the *Sic et non*, much of which was incorporated into the *Theologia christiana*. Roscelin justified his criticisms of St Anselm by pointing out that no wise man of the Church was immune from criticism. Did not Augustine observe that even St Peter was not always beyond reproach[65]? St Anselm may have been a holy person, but his argument in the *Cur Deus homo* that God could not save man other than in the way he did, contradicted a venerable tradition which taught that divine omnipotence was never constrained by any necessity.

Roscelin emerges from the letter to Abelard as a bitter old man, a stickler for grammatical rules with a gift for satire. He mocked Abelard for supporting Robert of Arbrissel, a preacher whom he accused of taking wives away from their husbands. A wife who refused her conjugal duty was guilty of adultery if her husband was then forced to divorce her. Abelard himself was a rogue who continued to visit his prostitute and bring her money from his teaching in payment for past pleasure[66]. The seal bearing an image of two heads which Abelard had attached to his letter, he interpreted as the representation of a man and a woman (probably misinterpreting traditional images of saints Rusticus and Eleutherius, one of whom was always bearded)[67]. Roscelin could not resist a final jibe about Abelard's recent misfortune. Nouns lose their strict meaning when what they signify falls from perfection. A house without a roof or a wall was an incomplete house. Removal of that part which made Abelard a man, left him incomplete. Roscelin could not have emphasised the priority he gave to the meaning of proper nouns to more cruel effect: «As I am speaking to an incomplete man, I leave this work incomplete»[68]. Roscelin not only loved the rules of grammar as a true basis for logic and theology, but he was no mean

(65) REINERS, p. 66.

(66) REINERS, p. 67, 79-80.

(67) REINERS, p. 78: «Ad huius etiam imperfecti hominis ignominiae cumulum pertinet, quod in sigillo, quo foetidas illas litteras sigillavit, imaginem duo capita habentem, unum viri, alterum mulieris, ipse formavit». I am indebted to Fr. Chrysogonus Waddell for this enlightening suggestion about the double headed seal.

(68) REINERS, p. 78: «Certus sum autem quod masculini generis nomen, si a suo genere defecerit, rem solitam significare recusabit. Amodo enim neutri generis abiectionem, sicut et suum significatum, penet... et cum hominem integrum consueverit, dimidium forsitan significare recusabit. Solent enim nomina propriam significationem amittere, cum eorum significata contingerit a sua perfectione recedere. Neque enim ablato tecto uel pariete domus, sed imperfecta domus vocabitur. Sublata igitur parte quae hominem facit non Petrus, sed imperfectus Petrus appellandus es».

60

exponent of the art of invective. It is not hard to understand why Abelard came to dislike him so intensely.

ROSCELIN, ABELARD AND THE *GLOSULE* ON PRISCIAN

We can gain some idea of the sort of ideas held by 'modern' dialecticians of the late eleventh century by looking at what Abelard has to say in his *Dialectica* about Guarmundus, the scholasticus who took over Odo's position at Tournai cathedral, praised in 1107 as «the honour of the whole world»[69]. This discussion was formulated early in Abelard's career, and may well have been written before 1117[70]. The issue under debate was that of the signification of universal terms like animal or man:

> For some want everything to which a voice is applied to be signified by the voice itself, others in truth [want to be signified] only those things denoted in the voice and contained in its teaching (*sententia*). Our teacher master V. favours the former, Garmundus in truth seems to agree with the latter; the former rely on authority, the latter in truth rely on reason. For Garmundus agrees with them rationally that only those things <are signified> which are held in the teaching of an utterance, according to the definition of signifying which is to constitute an understanding [Aristotle, *Periermeneias* 3, 16b20][71].

Guarmundus argued that a species was not signified by its genus, or a particular body by what was coloured or was white (*colorato vel albo*), while his teacher 'master V.' argued that a genus signified every substance to which it could be applied. The implication of the latter view was that a genus was a substance shared by its species. Abelard defended the position of Guarmundus that 'animal' did not express 'man', only something insofar as it was a living, sensitive subtance or informed by colour or whiteness. Nouns did not signify everything to which they could refer, but only those things which they specifically referred to

(69) R. W. HUNT, «Studies on Priscian in the Eleventh and Twelfth Centuries I», *Mediaeval and Renaissance Studies*, 1 (1941-43), p. 194-231, repr. in his *Collected Papers on the History of Grammar in the Middle Ages*, Amsterdam, 1980, p. 15 (1-38) and corrigenda on p. 11. Hunt notes that this master Guarmundus is mentioned alongside master Guy of Langres, archbishop Lanfranc, master Robert and master Durand of England within opinions on the substantive verb appended to the *Glosule* in the Chartres MS Bibl. mun. 209, fol. 86v, edited by HUNT, p. 31-32.

(70) I find the arguments of J. MARENBON, *The philosophy of Peter Abelard*, Cambridge, 1997, p. 40-45, convincing in this respect.

(71) *Dialectica* I.III.1, DE RIJK, p. 112: «Alii enim omnia quibus vox imposita est, ab ipsa voce significari volunt, alii vero ea sola que in voce denotantur atque in sententia ipsius tenentur. Illis quidem magister noster V. favet, his vero Garmundus consensisse videtur; illi qui<dem> auctoritate, hi vero fulti sunt ratione». DE RIJK's suggestion, p. xix-xx, that «our teacher V.» is Ulger of Angers, as distinct from William of Champeaux, which he admits is the person referred to simply as "our teacher" has been criticized by a number of writers, including recently J. JOLIVET, «Données sur Guillaume de Champeaux, dialecticien et théologien», in J. LONGÈRE (ed.), *L'abbaye parisienne de Saint-Victor au Moyen Age*, Paris-Turnhout, 1991, p. 239-241 (235-251); see too the references given by MARENBON, «Commentaries and Glosses», p. 116.

(*Unde manifestum est eos velle vocabula non omnia illa significare que nominant, sed ea tantum que definite designant...*). Abelard explained that opponents of this view, like his teacher, argued from literal application of Priscian's definition that a noun signified substance with quality that man was signified by 'animal', or Socrates by 'man'[72]. He insisted that in Priscian's definition the principal cause for the signification of a noun was the quality, not the subject. Abelard's analysis deserves to be compared to the comments of St Anselm about dialecticians who thought a universal was only a puff of air, or colour anything other than a body. St Anselm interpreted the essential feature of their thought as rejection of the real existence of a universal substance. Abelard saw the teaching of Guarmundus and his kind as based on appreciation that a noun signified a quality, not any substance to which it could be applied.

The argument Abelard attributes to Guarmundus and his kind is paralleled by remarks of the influential commentary on Priscian's *Grammatical Institutes* I-XVI (omitting books XVII-XVIII about syntax), known as the *Glosule*[73]. Its author was particularly concerned with the causes of words. In particular, he clarified Priscian's brief definition that a noun signified «substance with quality» by explaining that a noun *named* a substance, but signified a quality[74]. 'Man' in «Socrates is a man» names an individual man, but signifies a universal quality. This is not saying that universals do not exist, but that the universal quality signified by 'man' is not a universal substance. The insight drew on a comment of Aristotle in *Categories* 5 that *album* did not signify anything other than a quality. As a discussion of grammatical categories, rather than general classes like

(72) DE RIJK, p. 113: «Hi vero qui omnem vocum impositionem in significationem deducunt, auctoritatem pretendunt ut ea quoque significari dicant a voce quibuscumque ipsa est imposita, ut ipsum quoque hominem ab 'animali' vel Socratem ab 'homine', vel subiectum corpus ab 'albo' vel 'colorato' nec solum ex arte, verum etiam ex auctoritate gramatice id conantur ostendere».

(73) The complete text of the *Glosule* was identified in the 1488 Arrivabenus edition of Priscian (reprinted several times until 1520) by M. GIBSON, «The Collected Works of Priscian: the Printed Editions 1470-1859», *Studi Medievali*, ser. 3ª 18 (1977), p. 249-260 and «The Early Scholastic *Glosule* to Priscian *Institutiones grammaticae*: the Text and its Influence», *Studi Medievali*, 20 (1979), p. 235-254. Irène ROSIER, «Les parties du discours aux confins du XIIe siècle», *Langages*, 92 (décembre 1988), p. 37-49, examined its significance; see also MEWS, «Nominalism and Theology before Abaelard: New Light on Roscelin of Compiègne», *Vivarium*, 30 (1992), p. 4-33 and «Philosophy and Theology 1100-1150: The Search for Harmony», in F. GASPARRI (ed.), *Le XIIe siècle. Mutations et renouveau en France dans la première moitié du XIIe siècle*, Cahiers du Léopard d'Or 3, Paris, 1994, p. 164-7 (159-203).

(74) DE RIJK edits the passage in *Logica Modernorum: a Contribution to the History of Early Terminist Logic* vol. II, Assen, 1967, 1, p. 522-523 and further on p. 228 n. 1: «Notandum est tamen quod nomen non significat substantiam et qualitatem insimul nuncupative, scilicet ita ut utriusque coniuncti sit nomen vel utriusque per se nomen sit, sed substantiam nominat tantum, quia ei fuit impositum, qualitatem vero significat non nuncupative, immo representando et determinando circa substantiam, propter quam tamen notandam substantiae fuit impositum. Quare omne nomen duas habet significationes: unam per impositionem in substantia, alteram per representationem in qualitate ipsius substantie, ut homo per impositionem significat rem Socratis et ceterorum hominum, id est nominando, determinans circa illa rationalitatem et mortalitatem et hec representando».

X

genus and species discussed by Porphyry, the *Glosule* is not particularly concerned with ontological issues. Nonetheless, its author is fascinated by the implications of applying simple Aristotelian distinctions to Priscian's rather crude assumptions. He wanted to distinguish between an individual utterance and its cause or meaning. He invoked the idea that the cause of an utterance is its 'thing' or *res*, vocabulary shaped by the vocabulary of Augustine on signification[75]. He distinguished *persona vocalis* from the *persona realis* to separate 'person' as a word signifying a quality from the thing to which it refers.

The *Glosule* author was seized by a desire to imitate Priscian in providing an analytic framework for the Latin language by reference to the Greek roots of Latin culture. Elaborating upon Priscian's comment about Greek grammarians, « the younger they are, the more they are perspicacious », he taught that language was an acquired skill. Adam had spent his whole life inventing four letters, whereas the next generation could accomplish much more[76]. Commenting on Priscian's thoughts about the fount of Greek wisdom, « from whose springs the teaching of all eloquence and every kind of study derive », he reflected on the role of grammar in relation to Logic: « I say grammatically as different from dialectic, which teaches speaking according to truth and falsehood and from rhetoric, which teaches speaking according to the decoration of words and phrases. Of these arts grammar comes first, because one ought to know how to make appropriate joining of words before truth or falsehood or the decoration of eloquence is learnt »[77]. Grammar is part of Logic, a subject which embraced what was *sermocinalis* (to do with language) and what was *disertiva* (to do with finding arguments), and was itself part of philosophy, along with *physica* and *ethica*: « Through this linguistic part, grammar is led back to Logic as if to its genus »[78]. The process by which language was applied to things in the world deserved critical attention.

---

(75) MEWS, «Nominalism and Theology before Abaelard», p. 16 n. 34, citing *Glosule* on VIII 101 (Köln, Dombibl. 201, fol. 41ra), ed. Arrivabenus, *Institutionum grammaticarum...*, Venice, 1511, fol. 123v: «Nam personam dicimus realem *quae uel de se loquitur*, uel *ad quam prima loquitur* de ipsa uel de qua loquitur prima ad secundam, uocalem uero uocem hanc personam significantem. *Prima est.* Hic diffinit primam personam et secundum rem et secundum uocem: et competenter facit. Res enim est causa uocis: et sic dicit res illa est *prima persona quae loquitur*, id est quae profert sermonem de quocumque habitum siue *de se* siue de alio: ecce realis. Prima uocalis est quae significat rem loquentem *de se*, et hanc nobis innuit cum dicit *quae loquitur de se*, id est profert uocem se significantem».

(76) Cited by HUNT, «Studies on Priscian I», p. 19.

(77) This proemium was not included in the printed edition. *Glosule*, GIBSON, *Studi Medievali*, 20 (1979), p. 249: «Grammatice dico ad differentiam dialectice, que docet loqui secundum ueritatem et falsitatem, et rethorice, que docet loqui secundum ornatum uerborum et sententiarum. Quibus artibus prior est grammatica, quia prius scire oportet facere conuenientem coniunctionem dictionum quam ueritas uel falsitas uel ornatus eloquentie addiscatur».

(78) GIBSON, p. 249-250: «Nec dubitandum quin *logice* supponatur, cuius est ipsa grammatica tercia pars. Logice alia pars est sermocinalis, alia disertiua. Disertiua partes habet inuentionem et iudicium, que solis dialecticis et rethoricis conueniunt. Sermocinalis uero grammaticorum est; ac per eam ad logicam uelut ad suum genus grammatica reducitur».

While it would be erroneous to identify the *Glosule* on Priscian as nominalist, because the subject matter is that of grammar rather than dialectic, its sensitivity to the distinction between the common quality that a noun may signify, and the specific substances or things to which a noun may be applied helps elucidate the criticisms made by Peter Abelard of those who maintained that a general noun signified a common substance. The discussion of *vox* in the *Glosule* is of particular interest because it raises the question whether or not an utterance like *homo* is a universal substance[79]. Its author begins by considering Priscian's definition of a *vox* as a substance, the smallest unit of air sensible to hearing (*aer tenuissimus ictus sensibile auditu*). After mentioning some uncertainty as to whether or not this is the air from which animals draw their life, he advances to his main question, whether or not an utterance is a species of air, and therefore a universal thing. The *Glosule* author is clear in his conviction that an utterance signifies puffs of air (*aeres*) not directly, but accidentally as puffs of air shaped by natural voices[80]. He brings forward two arguments raised against the notion that air is an individual body, a comment of Augustine that no individual body could be found in different places at the same time and another of Boethius that speech arrived whole in all its elements to the ears of different people at the same time[81]. Their assertions could be used to support the idea that 'man' must be a universal substance, not a specific body, as it seems to be the same thing to different people. Yet while the commentator recognizes that the form of speech may seem to be the same to different people, according to the matter of the air, he insists that each word 'man' is different. People hear different things, in the literal sense of different voices. It was a single voice only if taken in its broader sense[82]. No single *res* could be individually in different places other than God himself, who is incorporeal. Although this utterance may be applied to individual men, these utterances are different essentially and materially: «I affirm that I deliver them as like one and the same utterance because of their similarity»[83]. When the same utterance is heard, the sameness is one of form, not of substance. He reported

---

(79) I. ROSIER, « Le commentaire des *Glosulae* et des *Glosae* de Guillaume de Conches sur le chapitre *De voce* des *Institutiones grammaticae* de Priscien», *Cahiers de l'Institut du Moyen-Age grec et latin* [Université de Copenhague], 63 (1993), p. 115-144.

(80) ROSIER, p. 120: « In primis quaerendum est an vox sic diffinita species sit aeris, id est significet aliquam rem universalem quae sit species in predicamento substantiae. Quod dicimus non esse. Vox enim aeres in essentia sui, scilicet in hoc quod sunt aeres non significat, sed potius ex quadam accidentali causa, in hoc, scilicet, quod percussi sunt naturalibus instrumentis».

(81) ROSIER, p. 121 n. 26, identifies the passages as a modified version of AUGUSTINE, *De musica* I, 1, and BOETHIUS, *De institutione musicae* I, 14.

(82) ROSIER, p. 122.

(83) ROSIER, p. 122: « Ad hoc respondeo quod sicut continua albedo parietis una dicitur quae in diversis fundatur, non quia illa albedo quae huic parieti adiacet sit illa individualiter qua in alia parte fundatur, sed quia similis est et eadem specie iudicatur vocari eadem, ita cum profero 'homo' semel et alia vice eandem vocem, id est 'homo' pronuncio, et quamvis diversae sint essentialiter et materialiter voces, tamen propter similitudinem quasi unam eandem vocem protulisse me affirmo».

another argument that declared all those puffs of air accepted at the same time to be one utterance and of no plurality, « but this has little value »[84]. Some argued from Boethius that the same utterance reached different people, not according to its essence, but according to its hearing. The commentator explains that this position had many weaknesses. Boethius did not say that an utterance was a quality like « percussion » but « the percussion of air », in other words percussed air. Those who argued from Aristotle that an utterance was a quantity because a phrase was a quantity were confused because the same utterances could sometimes signify both a substance and a quantity (as in length of a syllable), but this was strictly about syllables, not utterances[85]. The thrust of the argument of the *Glosule* is to question any argument from Macrobius, Aristotle or Boethius that an utterance is a single quantity. His point always comes down to recognition that each utterance is a distinct unit of air, sharing a common form, but not a common substance.

The criticism made in the *Glosule* of the notion that an utterance like « man » was a universal substance inspired Abelard's own criticism of his teacher's opinion that it was the air itself which created a sound and signified[86]. This division of opinion is part of a larger debate in the *Dialectica* about the nature of a phrase and of an utterance, conceived as a quantity. Some considered a phrase like *homo currit* as a unity, others as a collection of composite, signifying utterances[87]. Abelard's own position echoes that of the *Glosule* that the form of the air, like the colour of something, was heard and signified, but this was different from the material elements which sounded. A phrase was only a unity in its understanding, not in its diverse parts[88].

Abelard's critique of his teacher in the *Dialectica* draws without acknowledgement from the *Glosule* on Priscian, from where he draws the allusions to Boethius and Augustine[89]. In his *Introductiones dialecticae*, William of Champeaux does not demonstrate any familiarity with the arguments about signification of the *Glosule* on Priscian:

> A universal word is said to be that which signifies a universal thing, like the word 'animal' [in « man is animal »]; for 'animal' signifies that universal thing which is sensible, living substance, diffused in all animals. An individual word is said to be that which signifies an individual thing, like this word 'Socrates'[90].

(84) ROSIER, p. 123.
(85) ROSIER, p. 124.
(86) *Dialectica* I.II.2, DE RIJK, p. 67.
(87) DE RIJK, p. 65 : « Est autem de nomine 'orationis' hoc loco, cum uidelicet in quantitate accipitur, magna dissensio. Alii enim in ipso cuiuslibet prolationis tenorem contineri volunt, tam simplicem vocem quam compositam, tam significativam quam non, alii tantum compositas et significativas ut 'homo currit' etc. ».
(88) DE RIJK, p. 67-68 : « Neque etsi plures dictiones vel a diversis hominibus vel ab eodem inter ipsas quiescente atque aliqua intervalla ponente proferuntur, una recte poterunt oratio dici nec ad unius orationis intellectus detorqueri ».
(89) ROSIER, p. 116-117.
(90) Two versions of these *Introductiones* were identified by IWAKUMA, Y., « The

William of Champeaux's thought evolved over the course of time. In theological sentences composed after his debate with Abelard in 1108/1109, William came to define the humanity of Peter as the same as that of Paul «non-differently», although not in essence. William raised this point within a larger argument that although one thing could not be identified with another in the material world, the names of Father, Son and Holy Spirit named different persons, understood as properties of God, although they were one in substance[91]. After William was forced to modify his position in response to argument with Abelard, he became much more familiar with the distinction between nomination and signification in the *Glosule*. When he challenged his teacher, Abelard was not himself offering a new theory of universals, but was rather bringing to his teacher's attention the perspective of the *Glosule*, which explained that any noun signified not an individual substance, but a quality.

The perspective of the *Glosule* was also similar to that of Roscelin of Compiègne, who had insisted that Father, Son and Holy Spirit could not be a single thing. His letter to Abelard was an impassioned defence of the proposition that these three persons had to be separate things if one were not to argue that the Father became incarnate with the Son[92]. Abelard shared Roscelin's insistence that one had to distinguish between the three persons, but whereas his teacher identified them as three things, Abelard elaborated on an idea of William of Champeaux, that they were three properties or attributes of God. Whether or not we accept the claim of the *Historia calamitatum* that Abelard was the decisive influence on the evolution of William's thought, there is no question that the thinking of William of Champeaux about signification did evolve. By the second decade of the twelfth century, it was becoming impossible to hold the position of St Anselm that a universal noun signified some common substance. Although Abelard carried on criticizing William's definition of a universal as that which was «non-differently» the same, he used the idea of identity by non-difference in his early writings on logic, when defining the way in which Socrates the man was the

---

Introductiones dialecticae secundum Wilgelmum and *secundum G. Paganellum»*, *Cahiers de l'Institut du Moyen-Age grec et latin*, 63 (1993), p.45-114; cf.2.2, p.59: «Vox universalis dicitur, quae rem universalem significat, ut haec vox 'animal'; haec enim 'animal' significat illam rem universalem, quae est substantia animata sensibilis, quae diffusa est in omnibus animalibus. Singularis vero vox dicitur, quae rem singularem significat, ut haec vox 'Socrates' ». The epithet *Paganellus* (from *paganus*, of the country) used of William in one manuscript may be another version of his more familiar cognomen, *Campellus* (of the field, or "champeaux" in French).

(91) O. LOTTIN, *Guillaume de Champeaux. Sententiae*, in *Psychologie et morale*, vol. 5, Gembloux, 1959, p. 192-194.

(92) Defending his emphasis on the separateness of persons in the Trinity, Roscelin once reminded Abelard of a phrase of Boethius that the cause of this unity [of the three divine persons] was non-difference, *Ep. ad Abaelardum* (REINERS, p. 71): «Huius unitatis causa est indifferentia». He was quoting rather freely from Boethius, *De trinitate* c.1, «cuius coniunctionis ratio est indifferentia».

66

same as Plato the man[93]. In the liturgical expression «the woman who damned [us], has saved [us]», Abelard observed that two different women were involved, a theme he reiterated in his commentary on Aristotle's *On Interpretation*:

> just as when it is said «through woman came death, through the same one life» and «woman who has damned [us], she has redeemed [us]», we apply pronouns non-differently, not personally, as if one said «the woman has damned and the same one, that is the thing which is her sex has redeemed [us]», namely similarly, so that it is said according to the non-difference of sex rather than according to the identity of person[94].

His point was that Eve and Mary could not be identified with each other, even if the same term (*mulier*) applied to both. Like William of Champeaux, Abelard was developing an idea implicit in the *Glosule* that a noun did not signify a common substance, although two individuals might be the same through similitude[95]. Abelard's awareness that two individuals could not share the same substance derived was one drummed into him by Roscelin. The evident connection between the *Glosule* and William's mature reflections on identity and difference cannot be construed as an argument for William's authorship of the *Glosule*, which first circulated in the late eleventh century[96]. The common practice of describing William as a philosophical realist and Roscelin as a nominalist risks blurring the common ground which they shared. Although the *Glosule* is not nominalist in the strict sense of the word, it did force a generation of thinkers to reassess the signification of any noun.

(93) L. MINIO-PALUELLO, *Twelfth-Century Logic. Texts and Studies. II Abaelardiana inedita*, Rome: Edizioni di Storia e Letteratura, 1958, *Secundum magistrum Petrum Sententie* XXVI [sophisms about 'totum'], p. 118: «Similiter cum in ista argumentatione dicimus hanc enuntiationem 'Socrates est homo' enuntiare Socratem esse id quod ipse est, istud 'id' non secundum personam discrete proferimus, sed indifferenter tam secundum naturam quam secundum personam illud accipimus».

(94) B. GEYER, *Peter Abaelards philosophische Schriften*, BGPMA, Bd 21, Münster, 1919-1923, *Logica 'Ingredientibus'*, p. 397: «sicut et cum dicitur 'per mulierem intravit mors, per eandem vita' vel 'mulier damnavit, ipsa salvavit' indifferenter pronomina referimus, non personaliter, ac si dicatur: mulier damnavit et eadem, id est res eius sexus, salvavit, scilicet similiter, ut videlicet eadem secundum indifferentiam sexus, non secundum identitatem personae». The formulas come from the liturgy of Holy Saturday. This expands on the discussion in the *Sententie* XXIV, MINIO-PALUELLO, p. 118.

(95) C. H. KNEEPKENS discusses Abelard's interpretation at length, alongside that of his contemporaries in an invaluable study, presenting all the relevant texts, «'Mulier quae damnavit, salvavit': A Note of the Early Development of the Relatio Simplex», *Vivarium*, 14 (1976), p. 1-25.

(96) Rosier suggests on p. 117-8 and p. 123 n. 38 of her study, that the opinion attributed to William of Champeaux in *Dialectica* (p. 67.5) is like that in the *Glosule* (ROSIER, p. 123). K. M. FREDBORG suggests William of Champeaux as a possible author in her chapter «Speculative Grammar», in P. DRONKE (ed.), *A History of Twelfth-Century Western Philosophy*, Cambridge, 1988, p. 178.

Independent witness to the influence of a certain grammarian in the early twelfth century in the Parisian schools is reported by the biographer of Goswin, a monk of Anchin who had dared to confront Peter Abelard in debate at the school of Mont-Sainte-Geneviève in about 1110:

> At that time, a very famous grammarian had produced commentaries on the works of Priscian, seized on everywhere by everyone as much for the depth of meanings as for the elegance of its diction, particularly because many people accept new things more, throw out old things for the sake of the new things coming in, soak themselves in new things and preach novelty[97].

Goswin was recommended this commentary on Priscian by a *physicus*, master Azo, and started to share out copying the work with his brother, but then decided that it was ultimately more important to live a Christian life than to speak skillfully and correctly, and so entered the monastic life. This testimony is valuable because it suggests a rather different picture from that of the early twelfth century schools presented by Abelard's *Historia calamitatum*. Goswin was implying to his biographer that a work of grammatical commentary was the source of the fascination for novelty, rather than Abelard himself. The parallels that emerge between the theological argument in Roscelin's letter to Abelard and the ideas of the *Glosule* on Priscian suggest that Goswin was referring to the *Glosule* on Priscian. Its author may be the John whom the Fleury chronicler identified as a key influence on Roscelin, Robert and Arnulf in maintaining that dialectic was an *ars vocalis*.

The provenance of surviving manuscripts of the *Glosule* on Priscian suggests that the work originated in the French kingdom. Although most of the manuscripts of the work are French, the earliest known copy, from the late eleventh century, has always belonged to Cologne Cathedral (MS Dombibl. 201)[98]. Bruno of Rheims (c.1030-1101), who studied at Rheims under Herimann and then taught there until a political crisis in 1077, returned briefly to Cologne before eventually establishing La Grande Chartreuse[99]. One important copy of the *Glosule*, in the possession of either Chartres cathedral or the church of Saint-Père (Chartres, Bibl. mun. 209) may have come from Saint-Evroul, Normandy, as it included an appended list of books of Saint-Evroul being sent to another

---

(97) *Vita Goswini*, BOUQUET, *Recueil des historiens des Gaules et de la France*, vol. 14, Paris, 1877, p. 444. See MEWS, « Philosophy and Theology 1100-1150: the search for harmony », p. 182-183.

(98) GIBSON, « The Early Scholastic 'Glosule' to Priscian », also notes one manuscript of the prologue (Brussels, Bibl. roy. 3920, fol. 12ra-vb; s. XII[1]), belonging in the 15th century to Nicholas of Cusa (d. 1464).

(99) On the political conflict with archbishop Manasses which led to the departure of Bruno, and very likely also of John of Rheims from that city, see J. R. WILLIAMS, « The Cathedral School of Rheims in the Eleventh Century », *Speculum*, 29 (1954), p. 661-677; see also GUIBERT of NOGENT, *Autobiographie* I.11 (LABANDE, p. 64): « Bruno, in ecclesiis tunc Galliae opinatissimus, cum aliis quibusdam Remensium clericorum nobilibus, in famis illius odio excessit ab urbe ».

68

abbey[100]. Other important copies are from Fleury (Paris, BN nouv. acq. lat 1623, fols. 1-54v) and the East of France (Metz, Bibl. mun. 1224, fols. 1ra-110rb). None of these manuscripts identify the author of the *Glosule*. The only surviving attribution is to a *Johannes de aingre* within the colophon of the incunable edition (based on a lost manuscript that was related to the Metz copy), may be a distorted reading of *Johannes dei gratia*, « John by the grace of God », a subtle play on the traditional explanation of the name John[101].

OTTO OF FREISING, ROSCELIN OF COMPIÈGNE AND EARLY VOCALISTS

Intellectual debate had become much more polarised by the late 1150s, when Otto of Freising described Roscelin as having initiated the *sententiam vocum* in logic. Otto had studied in Paris in the years prior to 1133 and had a much greater knowledge than St Anselm of the new texts of Aristotle just beginning to be studied in the French schools[102]. Otto mentioned Roscelin's achievement in the context of an extended comparison between Abelard's incautious use of dialectical theory with its wise application by Gilbert of Poitiers. Otto was criticizing Bernard of Clairvaux for condemning both Gilbert and Abelard equally for their application of secular learning to theology. New developments in Aristotelian dialectic were not harmful in themselves for theology, only their misapplication. In subtle criticism of Bernard, he argued that Gilbert remained loyal to his teachers, but skillfully applied his ideas in dialectic to the doctrine of the Trinity. Gilbert safeguarded orthodox doctrine that the three divine persons of the Trinity were « distinct things with separate properties » (a definition recalling precisely that definition of the Trinity for which Roscelin had been

(100) Tragically the MS was destroyed in 1944, although a microfilm of the folios containing the *Glosule* is preserved at the IRHT, Paris. The list of books is mentioned in Omont's 1889 catalogue. Artistic connections between St Evroul and St-Père at Chartres are noted by F. AVRIL, « Notes sur quelques manuscrits bénédictins normands du XIe et du XIIe siècle », *Mélanges d'archéologie et d'histoire. Ecole française de Rome*, 77 (1965), p. 245 (209-48). I am indebted to P. Stirnemann for this reference. Early twelfth-century copies also survive in from the East of France.

(101) In the Venice 1496 edition on f. 204r: «Ioannis de aingre summos qui inter expositores grammaticae arcem [*potius* artem] possedit: commentum super magno Prisciani uolumine omnibus desideratissimum finit». See MEWS, «Nominalism and Theology before Peter Abaelard», p. 14.

(102) Otto's knowledge of the new Aristotle is mentioned by RAHEWIN, *Gesta Friderici* IV.14, WAITZ-VON SIMSON, p. 250. Otto believed that Aristotle was a pupil of Socrates before studying under Plato, *Chronica sive historia de duabus civitatibus*, II.8, A. HOFMEISTER, MGH in usum scholarum 45, Leipzig, 1912, p. 75 and 77; in a footnote to this passage, Hofmeister notes that this belief, revealing testimony to contemporary enthusiasm for Aristotle, was reported in V. ROSE, *De vita Aristotelis*, Leipzig, 1886, p. 443. Rose's thirteenth-century date for the translation (based on the earliest MS he knew) clearly needs correction.

condemned)[103]. The arrogant Abelard, on the other hand, antagonistic to his teachers, incautiously applied the *sententiam vocum seu nominum* to theology, with the result that he eliminated the differences between the three persons (the same accusation as Roscelin made in his letter to Abelard). Given that Otto studied in Paris in the years immediately before 1133, it is unlikely that Otto knew Roscelin personally, although it is possible he may have had access to Roscelin's letter to Abelard.

In a pioneering study of glosses on Porphyry from the late eleventh and twelfth century, Iwakuma has identified a number of texts which either present or discuss the teaching of masters identified at the time as *vocales*. The phrase *secundum vocales* is used to introduce Abelard's own glosses on Porphyry in the Milan MS Bibl. Ambrosiana M 63 Sup., f. 72v-81v, a revision of the *'Ingredientibus'* Porphyry gloss earlier in the same MS[104]. A treatise within the important collection of dialectic texts from Fleury (Orléans, Bibl. mun. 266), titled *Positio vocum sententia* presents the ideas of Abelard about genus as a *vox* as does the *Sententie secundum magistrum Petrum*[105]. In the latter work Abelard engages in a sustained debate with opinions about the whole and the part, quite certainly those of Roscelin of Compiègne. Other glosses Iwakuma has edited are so closely related to the known «literal» glosses of Abelard that it seems much more likely to consider them different records of the same basic set of lectures of Abelard, rather than, as he then supposed, of Roscelin of Compiègne. To explain Abelard's dialectic simply as the continuation of that of Roscelin does not account for the vigour of the argument between the two men, conducted on the levels both of dialectic and theology[106].

(103) *Gesta Friderici*, I.48, WAITZ-VON SIMSON, p.69: «Sententiam ergo vocum, seu nominum in naturali tenens facultate non caute theologiae admiscuit. Quare de sancta trinitate docens et scribens tres personas, quas sancta aecclesia non vacua nomina tantumdem, sed res distinctas suisque proprietatibus discretas hactenus et pie credidit et fideliter docuit, nimis adtenuans...».

(104) C. OTTAVIANO, *Glossae secundum vocales. Fontes Ambrosiani*, III, Florence, 1933, p. 106-127, MARENBON, «Commentaries and Glosses», P11 in p. 104-105; see MEWS, «A neglected gloss on the Isagoge by Peter Abelard», *Freiburger Zeitschrift für Theologie und Philosophie*, 31 (1984), p. 35-55.

(105) IWAKUMA argues for Abelard's authorship of *Positio vocum sententia*, which he edits in «Vocales», p. 54-57 and 66-73. The *Sententie secundum magistrum Petrum*, MINIO-PALUELLO, p. 109-121, is analysed at length for its report of Roscelin's teaching by J. JOLIVET, «Trois variations», n. 29 above.

(106) IWAKUMA, «Vocales», p. 57-62, 74-102 edits certain *Disputata Porphyrii* from München, Bayer. Staatsbibl. Clm 14779, fol. 30v-36v (MARENBON, «Commentaries and Glosses», P7) as possibly the work of Roscelin of Compiègne. Copied in the same hand are glosses on the *De interpretatione* on fol. 44r-66r as well as on Boethius' *De hypotheticis syllogismis* and *De differentiis topicis* on fol. 67v-86v and 87r-105v. Iwakuma has since observed the frequent use of *Petrus* in these glosses, and concedes that they are more likely early glosses of Abelard, MARENBON, «Commentaries and Glosses», H5, and «Anselm and the early medieval Aristotle», p. 14. IWAKUMA, «Two More *Instantia* Texts. An Edition», *Zinbun: Annals of the Institute for Research in Humanities, Kyoto University*, 24 (1989), p. 17-18 (13-88), has also observed that glosses on Boethius' *De divisione* and *De differentiis topicis* in Paris, Bibl. Nat. lat. 7094A show great similarities to those of Abelard on the *De divisione* in

Another set of vocalist glosses occurs in a manuscript of the late eleventh or early twelfth century from St Peter's, Erfurt (Pommersfelden, Gräflich Schönbornsche Bibliothek 16/2764). It explains that Porphyry was concerned with the *voces* signifying other utterances, not with what was signified by them[107]. The five predicaments are described as «those five properties according to which they are participated in by their subjects»[108]. The introductory comments of the Erfurt master seem to have been even more radical (or some might say simplistic) than the opening comments of Abelard in his literal gloss, in explaining that Porphyry was dealing with the predicaments as *voces* and what they signified. The great range of definitions being canvassed by contemporary masters is mentioned in late eleventh-century glosses from St Emmeram, Regensburg (München, Bayer. Staatsbibl. 14458, f. 83ra- 93ra): «It is said by some that genera are said to be *voces*, by some things, by some things and *voces*»[109]. Such a statement should not be interpreted as evidence for three distinct schools of thought. It is a rhetorical device serving to introduce the «wise» opinion of Boethius, that genera and species are both utterances and things. This was not a formula of great originality, but it tells us about the bewildering variety of expositions currently being offered, and the need felt by this master to impose a solution drawn heavily from Boethius, interpreted in a literal manner.

One of the earliest references to the range of explanations being offered about Aristotle's categories is attributed to Rabanus in the same Fleury manuscript (Paris, Bibl. Nat. lat. 13368, f. 214r-223r) as contains early, attributed glosses of Peter Abelard[110]. Its initial version (Oxford, Bodleian Library, Laud lat. 67, f. 97v-14v) defines categories as just about things, although in the Fleury version the opinion is raised of those who consider the categories as about the five *voces*. It explains that such people «do not deny that genus can be accepted as designating things». The interpolation was not offering a diametrically different perspective, «vocalist» as distinct from «realist». Rather it was deepening analysis of Porphyry's text by raising a perspective that could be suggested by

---

Paris, Bibl. Nat. lat. 13368, and to those on *De diff. top.* in München, Bayer. Staatsbibl. Clm 14779, worthy of observation. He describes the 7094A MS in his introduction. Comparison of these glosses, and of one on *De categoricis syllogismis* in the same MS with Abelard's *Dialectica* may establish whether these are all glosses of Abelard.

(107) IWAKUMA, «Vocales», p. 103-107. He has since observed that the name Arnulfus occurs within a commentary on *De differentiis topicis* in this MS, fol. 21v: «Saepius quippe determinationes subduntur quae diversae a suis significant determinatis, ut Arnulfus est habens librum. Nam librum aliud significat quod Arnulfus habens». This prompts inquiry as to whether all the glosses in this MS might be the work of Arnulf of Laon, the other teacher criticised in the *Codex Udalrici*, a poem which testifies to Arnulf's reputation in the region of Bamberg.

(108) IWAKUMA, «Vocales», p. 45.

(109) IWAKUMA, «Vocales», p. 44; MARENBON, «Commentaries and Glosses», P16, p. 106.

(110) IWAKUMA, «Vocales», p. 43-44. His edition of the ps-Rabanus Porphyry gloss will appear in *Grammatica speculativa*. He assigns the date of *c.* 1060-70 to its earlier version.

X

closer attention to what Boethius had said in other writings, such as on the *Categories* or (in this case) in his *De divisione*.

In some glosses the term *vocales* or *sententiam vocum* is used to refer to a perspective that is accused of being quite wrong headed, the same sort of attitude as inspired Alberic and others to criticize the opinions of *nominales* from the mid twelfth century[111]. Abelard may well have been responsible for the new label, through his own shift in description of categories from *voces* to *nomina* (part of his own strategy in the *Ingredientibus* gloss to distance himself from opinions of Roscelin), but we must be careful not to impute a greater objectivity to the «nominalist» label than the category can stand[112]. The terms *vocales* and *nominales* were generated by often heated debate between rival teachers and their students as they compared contrasting expositions of Porphyry and Aristotle.

Abelard was not the first teacher to challenge the opinion of his contemporaries, only the most controversial. The Fleury MS containing his «literal» glosses on Porphyry, Aristotle and Boethius provides one of the earliest explicit attributions to a living master in dialectic glosses from the period: *Petri Abaelardi iunioris Palatini summi peripatetici* «Peter Abelard the younger supreme peripatetic of Le Pallet [The Palace]»[113]. Whether such self-identification was his own idea or that of a disciple, the attribution marks a new attitude to the gloss, in which the authority of an ancient author is now balanced by that of a modern commentator. Earlier glosses tend to carry either no attribution at all, or one that is to a figure in the past, such as *Rabanus*.

(111) IWAKUMA, «Vocales», p. 38-40, citing glosses in Paris, Bibl. Nat. lat. 3237, fol. 125r-130r (c. 1120-40, according to Iwakuma); shorter version on fol. 123r-124v; Oxford, Bodleian Library, Laud lat. 67, f. 6r-7v (attributed to Guarinus Cantaber); Wien, ÖNB cvp 2486, fol. 45ra-60vb (a pupil of Alberic?); see MARENBON, «Glosses», P17, P19, P20, p. 106-107.

(112) GEYER, p. 2: «Quod autem quinque diximus, et ad haec nomina, genus, species et cetera, et ad eorum significata quodammodo referri potest». See MARENBON, «Vocalism, Nominalism and the Commentaries on the *Categories* from the Early Twelfth Century», *Vivarium*, 30 (1992), p. 51-61.

(113) Paris, Bibl. Nat. lat. 13368, fol. 146r, abbreviated on fol. 128r and 156r. On this MS, see B. GEYER, *Peter Abaelards philosophische Schriften*, BGPTMA 31.4, Münster, 2nd ed. 1970, p. 592-597; M. DAL PRA's introduction to these glosses, *Pietro Abelardo. Scritti di Logica*, Pubblicazioni della Facoltà di Lettere e Filosofia dell' Università di Milano XXXIV, Florence, 2nd ed., 1969, p. xvii-xviii and J. BARROW, C. BURNETT and D. E. LUSCOMBE, «Checklist of the Manuscripts Containing the Writings of Peter Abelard and Heloise and Other Works Closely Associated with Abelard and his School», *Revue d'histoire des textes*, 14-15 (1984-1985), no. 143. That these glosses are the earliest to carry accurate authorial identification is apparent from Marenbon's invaluable catalogue appended to «Commentaries and Glosses» (P5, C5 and H4 being Abelard's glosses on the *Isagoge*, the *Categories* and *De interpretatione* in this Fleury MS).

Abelard implies that Roscelin himself composed a treatise on dialectic[114]. He mocked Roscelin's claim that a part had no thing, being only a *vox*[115]. Although Roscelin's treatise has not been identified, the *Dialectica* of master Garland adopts a strict application of vocalist principles to dialectic. It considers a universal to be simply a word which signifies itself. Tweedale has observed that for Garland a substance signifies each thing in virtue of the pure being of the thing (*purum esse rei*), while quantity refers to its amount and quality to its being of such a kind[116]. Not unlike Abelard in his *Dialectica*, Garland argues that the substantive verb in «Homer is a poet» does not in itself imply that Homer exists, identifying the copula as about Homer's status as maker of poems[117]. A related opinion that the substantive verb *sum* did not «have any substances» but signified substantial differences of a thing, is attributed to master Robert in notes attached to the *Glosule* in the Chartres MS[118]. This may be the Robert of Paris, mentioned alongside Roscelin and Arnulf in the Fleury chronicle. Garland was also particularly interested in consequences and hypothetical propositions. Traditionally identified with the elder Garland of Besançon, «the Computist», its author has been identified by Iwakuma with the younger Garland (or Gerland) of Besançon. The script of the manuscript from Eastern France, once thought to be of the eleventh-century, displays features characteristic of the early decades of the twelfth[119]. Given that Roscelin held a canonry at Besançon, it is quite possible that he taught or influenced the younger Garland, who directed the cathedral school of Besançon between 1118 and 1131, before becoming prior of the canons of St Paul. In 1149 Garland travelled with Thierry of Chartres to Frankfurt in the company of the archbishop of Trier. The *Dialectica* makes use

(114) E. SMITS, *Peter Abelard. Letters IX-XIV*, Groningen, 1983, *Ep. 14*, p. 280: «Hic sicut pseudo-dialecticus ita et pseudo-christianus cum in Dialectica sua nullam rem sed solam uocem partes habere astruat...».

(115) JOLIVET, «Trois variations», p. 114-128.

(116) M. TWEEDALE, «Logic: to the time of Abelard», in DRONKE (ed.), *A History of Twelfth-Century Philosophy*, p. 200, referring to GARLANDUS COMPOTISTA, *Dialectica*, ed. L.M. DE RIJK, Assen, 1959, p. 22-23.

(117) GARLANDUS, *Dialectica*, p. 79; ABELARD, *Dialectica*, p. 136-137; TWEEDALE, «Logic: to the time of Abelard», p. 202. IWAKUMA, «Vocales, or early nominalists», p. 52-53, observes parallels between Abelard and Garland; see GARLAND, *Dialectica, DE RIJK*, p. 45-47, and ABELARD, *Dialectica, DE RIJK*, p. 163-165.

(118) Chartres MS 209, f. 86v, ed. R. W. HUNT, «Studies on Priscian I» p. 31 (1-38): «Magister uero Ruobertus dixit hoc uerbum non habere substantias aliquas, sed potius substantiales differentias cuiuslibet rei significare de qua predicatur ipsum subiectum, et illas differentias esse actionem illius uerbi, ut cum dicimus 'homo est', hic 'est' significat rationalitatem et mortalitatem, et in aliis similiter».

(119) IWAKUMA, «Vocales», p. 47-54, based on Gasparri's re-dating of the Paris MS Bibl. Nat. lat. 6438 to the early twelfth century, before 1130. The traditional confusion between the elder and the younger GARLAND of BESANÇON is discussed by B. DE VREGILLE, *Dictionnaire d'histoire et de géographie ecclésiastique*, 20, Paris, 1984, cols. 883-7. He notes Kuttner's argument that the *Candela* must be reassigned to the early twelfth century (n. 121 below), but still assigns the *Dialectica* to the elder Garland the Computist, bishop of Agrigentum from 1088 to his death in 1100.

of a passage in Aristotle's *Topics*, a work known to Thierry[120]. Celebrated for his learning in the trivium and quadrivium and once suspected of supporting a «figurative» interpretation of the eucharist, he collected often rare patristic documents in his *Candela*[121]. Detailed comparison of the two systematic treatises of Abelard and Garland on dialectic may well shed further light on the teaching of Roscelin of Compiègne, who may well have been a key figure in applying vocalist principles both to logic and theological questions. Otto of Freising may be less accurate however than the Fleury chronicler in claiming that Roscelin was the first person to introduce the *sententia vocum* to logic.

ROSCELIN AND PETER ABELARD

In the *Historia calamitatum*, written *c.* 1132/33, Abelard glides over his early studies, by stating only that he «left the court of Mars to be educated in the cradle of Minerva»[122]. There can be little doubting Roscelin's claim that he taught Abelard until he was a *iuvenis*, a term normally used of one who had survived his apprenticeship to become a warrior or knight in his own right. Roscelin taught him to fight not with the sword but with the arms of reason[123]. Abelard would have been just fourteen or fifteen years old when he first encountered Roscelin at Loches, sent to this well-fortified citadel of the counts of Anjou by Berengar, his Poitevin father, to be educated in letters prior to learning the skills of war[124]. Roscelin must have been given a position at Loches by Count Fulk in about 1093/94, after his short spell in England and confrontation with St Anselm. To the young Abelard, Roscelin would have seemed a brilliant master unjustly persecuted by a hostile world. Roscelin's subsequent bitterness towards

(120) I. ROSIER, «Note sur une surprenante citation des *Topiques* d'Aristote au XIe siècle», *Bulletin de philosophie médiévale*, 28 (1986), p. 178-184.

(121) The prologue to the *Candela* was published by MARTÈNE and DURAND, *Thesaurus novus anecdotorum*, Paris, 1717, vol. 1, p. 601. See S. KUTTNER, «Gerland of Besançon and the Manuscripts of his 'Candela': a Bibliographical Note», in *Paradosis: Studies in Memory of Edwin A. Quain*, New York, 1976, p. 71-84, repr. in his *Medieval Councils, Decretals and Collections of Canon Law*, London, 1980. Hugo Metellus addressed Gerland as *scientia trivii quadruviique oneratus et honorus* in his *Epistola ad magistrum Gerlandum*, but then upbraided him for his teaching on the eucharist, HUGO METELLUS, *Epist. 33*, ed. J. MABILLON (with certain doubts whether it was to Gerland), *Vetera analecta*, Paris, 1723, p. 475-477 and C. L. HUGO, *Sacrae antiquitatis Monumenta historica, dogmatica, diplomatica*, vol. 2, Saint-Dié, 1731, p. 372-374 (PL 188, 1273).

(122) J. MONFRIN, *Historia calamitatum*, ll. 19-25, Paris, 1959, p. 63.

(123) It was normal for a *puer* to leave home at about twelve years to learn to be a knight. G. DUBY notes that *iuvenis* could be used to the age of forty, «Les jeunes dans la société aristocratique dans la France du nord-ouest au XIIe siècle», *Annales: Economies, Sociétés, Civilisations*, 19, 1964, p. 835-846, repr. in *Hommes et structures du Moyen Age*, Paris, 1984, p. 213-225 and translated by C. POSTAN within DUBY's *The chivalrous society*, Berkeley-Los Angeles, 1980, p. 112-122.

(124) That Berengar was a Poitevin married to a Breton woman is mentioned by RICHARD of POITIERS, *Chronicon*, MGH.SS 26, p. 81. Since Richard was a monk at Cluny when Abelard came there in 1140 there is good reason to believe his testimony.

Abelard suggests that his influence had been decisive in turning him towards a life dedicated to philosophy.

At some stage, Abelard fell out with his teacher. A humorous anecdote within a manuscript from Regensburg recorded that Abelard had grown bored with Roscelin's lectures and had resisted his injunction to remain another year [125]. Abelard alluded to an « insane opinion » of his teacher about parts and wholes in the fifth part of his *Dialectica*, in which he had already started to comment briefly on theological issues [126]. Abelard had been educated by Roscelin in the *sententia vocum*, but he now turned its principles against his teacher, accusing him of not fully implementing the Aristotelian ideas to which he claimed loyalty. Abelard refused to accept that this *homo* could be a thing, if Socrates and Plato were separate things. Instead he offered his own interpretation of a universal as a utterance imposed as a predicate on individuals according to their nature, constituting a common understanding about them. « Being a man » was not a thing in itself [127]. Abelard was much more interested than Roscelin in the epistemological aspect of language. A universal constituted no more than an opinion about what was ultimately known only to God [128].

Conflict between Roscelin and Abelard became much more acute and politically sensitive when it started to touch on the doctrine of the Trinity. In a letter to the bishop of Paris, perhaps written around 1120, Abelard explained that he had written his treatise *On the faith of the holy Trinity* « particularly against that aforesaid heresy [of preaching three gods] by which he has become notorious » [129]. Playing on the image of Roscelin as a self-important dialectician initially created by St Anselm, Abelard repeated his assertion that Roscelin had been condemned at Soissons for preaching tritheism and had been punished by exile. Roscelin had been lobbying the bishop of Paris to have him accused of

(125) MEWS, « In Search of a Name and its Significance: A Twelfth-Century Anecdote about Thierry and Peter Abaelard », *Traditio*, 44 (1988), p. 171-200.

(126) *Dialectica* V.1, DE RIJK, p. 554-555.

(127) GEYER, p. 19: « Non dico in homine, cum res nulla sit homo nisi discreta, sed in esse hominem. Esse autem hominem non est homo nec res aliqua, si diligentius consideremus, sicut nec non esse in subiecto res est aliqua nec non suscipere contrarietatem vel non suscipere magis et minus, secundum quae tamen Aristoteles omnes substantias convenire dicit ».

(128) GEYER, p. 23: « In primo namque Constructionum Priscianus, cum communem impositionem universalium ad individua praemonstrasset, quandam aliam ipsorum significationem, de forma scilicet communi, visus est subiunxisse dicens "ad generales et speciales rerum formas, quae in mente divina intelligibiliter constituuntur... Deus vero cui omnia per se patent, quae condidit, quique ea antequam sint, novit, singulos status in se ipsis distinguit nec ei sensus impedimento est, qui [solam] solus veram habet intelligentiam.... Ita etiam credo de intrinsecis formis quae ad sensus non veniunt, qualis est rationalitas et mortalitas, paternitas, sessio, magis non opinionem habere" ».

(129) SMITS, p. 279: « Relatum est nobis a quibusdam discipulorum nostrorum superuenientibus quod elatus ille et semper inflatus catholice fidei hostis antiquus, cuius heresis detestabilis tres deos confiteri, immo et predicare Suessionensi concilio a catholicis patribus conuicta est et insuper exilio punita, multas in me contumelias et minas euomuerit, uiso opusculo quodam nostro De fide Sancte Trinitatis, maxime aduersus heresim prefatam qua ipse infamis est, conscripto ».

heresy. In his treatise on the Trinity, Abelard explored the significance of the three major names used of God, Father, Son and Holy Spirit. He developed the theme that they signified three separate attributes of God, power, wisdom and benignity, rather than three separate things. When revising his initial treatise on the Trinity, renamed *Theologia christiana,* Abelard continued to pillory Roscelin as a «worm-like sophist»[130]. By the time he was preparing the *Theologia 'Scholarium',* however, in the early 1130s, Roscelin was no longer the central focus of his criticism[131]. When Abelard described the circumstances surrounding his writing on the Trinity in a new prologue to the *Theologia 'Scholarium',* written in the early 1130s, he only spoke about his desire to resolve questions about Christian belief, not to counter Roscelin. This was exactly the same emphasis as in passage of the *Historia calamitatum* in which he described the genesis of his treatise on the Trinity[132].

By the mid twelfth century, Roscelin's reputation had been completely overshadowed in the schools of Paris by that of Peter Abelard. John of Salisbury reported that supporters of Roscelin's theory of universals as *voces* «had almost completely disappeared with its author»[133]. John had no particular sympathy with this notion or Abelard's definition that a universal was a *sermo.* In associating Roscelin with a discredited opinion about universals, John was repeating a caricature that St Anselm had promulgated and that Peter Abelard had turned to profit, for his own ends. Although John was aware that Abelard differed from Roscelin by defining a universal as a spoken word (*sermo*) rather than as an utterance, he rejected Abelard's solution, and claim for Aristotelian authority in refusing to predicate a thing of a thing. John of Salisbury thus helped seal the impression which Abelard sought to create, that Roscelin was a figure of minor significance, whose contribution to both dialectic and theology had been forgotten by the mid twelfth century.

---

(130) E. M. BUYTAERT, *Theologia christiana* III.131, CCCM 12, Turnhout, 1969, p. 244, resuming *TSum (Theologia 'Summi boni')* II.75, BUYTAERT-MEWS, p. 140: «Responde tu michi, astute dialectice seu uersipellis sophista, qui auctoritate peripateticorum me arguere niteris de differentia personarum que in deo sunt, quomodo ipsos doctores tuos absoluis secundum traditiones quorum, ut iam ostendimus, nec deum substantiam esse nec aliquid aliud cogeris confiteri?»

(131) *Theologia christiana CT,* III.132, BUYTAERT, p. 244, contains a new address to *fratres et uerbosi amici,* replacing III.131 in *Theologia 'Scholarium'* II.89, BUYTAERT-MEWS, p. 451.

(132) *TSch* 2-5, BUYTAERT, CCCM 12, p. 401-402, extended in *TSch* Pref. 2-5, BUYTAERT-MEWS, CCCM 13, p. 313-314; see also *Historia calamitatum* ll. 690-701, MONFRIN, p. 82-83.

(133) *Metalogicon* II.17, ed. J. B. HALL, CCCM 98, Turnhout, 1991, p. 81: «Alius ergo consistit in uocibus, licet hec opinio cum Rocelino suo, fere omnino iam euanuerit»; *Policraticus* VII.12, ed. C. C. J. WEBB, Oxford, 1909, vol. 2, p. 142: «Fuerunt et qui voces ipsa genera dicerent esse et species; eorum iam explosa sententia est, et facile cum auctore suo evanuit. Sunt tamen adhuc qui deprehenduntur in vestigiis eorum, licet erubescant auctorem vel sententiam profiteri, solis nominibus inhaerentes, quod rebus et intellectibus subtrahunt, sermonibus ascribunt».

"EST UNA": A LOST CONFESSION OF ORTHODOXY
BY ROSCELIN OF COMPIÈGNE?

While Roscelin's writings on dialectic still need to be identified with certainty, more progress can be made with his theological writings, given that his letter to Abelard provides us with a firm point of departure. Immediately following a copy of Peter Abelard's *Theologia christiana* on f. 66v-67v of the Durham Cathedral Chapter Library MS A.IV.15 (*D*), from the second quarter of the twelfth century, are four untitled texts, all of which discuss the doctrine of God as a trinity of persons. *Est una* differs from the three other tracts in being a complete essay on the divine unity and trinity rather than being an elaboration of an existing Creed, like the essays of Pelagius and Gennadius. Its author debates how we can legitimately speak of a trinity of persons within the sublime unity of the divine essence by analysing *Pater*, *Filius* and *Spiritus sanctus* as *nomina* that have been found in order to signify the ineffable property of three certain things. While the substance of its theological teaching does not veer from what is laid down in any of the catholic creeds, its emphasis on the meaning of *voces* used about God distinguishes the text from patristic tradition. The opening sentence amplifies part of the introduction to the *Symbolum 'Quicumque'* or so-called Athanasian Creed («Fides autem catholica haec est: ut unum deum in trinitate et trinitatem in unitate veneremur»), but whereas the latter begins with the name God, and then comments on trinity within unity, *Est una* does not mention the word 'God'. Only towards the end of the first paragraph is it stated that this unity is of the divine essence, while the word 'God' only occurs later in the text within allusions to *Symbolum 'Quicumque'* and to Wisdom 1:1. Its emphasis is on the meaning of the terms 'Father', 'Son' and 'Holy Spirit'. These are names that have been found (*inventa sunt*) to signify the property of three things (*trium*) that is the Trinity, in the same way that names like 'eternal', 'immense', 'good' have been found to signify the unity of the substance of the Creator.

Est una subtly modifies the teaching of the Boethian *De Trinitate*. Boethius had defined the divine substance as form without matter, beyond the conventional category of substance and thus without any inherent accident or substantial difference[134]. None of the ten Aristotelian categories (substance, quality, quantity etc.), universally predicable of all things could be applied to God who was beyond the realm of things. Boethius had concluded that God was a *trium unitas*, but that this plurality was one of relations, a concept appropriated from the fifth book of Augustine's *De Trinitate*. *Est una* similarly emphasizes the distance between divine and material substance, but then considers 'Father', 'Son' and 'Holy Spirit' as words of human construction. While it stresses that

---

(134) On the influence of Boethian theological reflection in the Middle Ages, see M. GIBSON, «The *Opuscula Sacra* in the Middle Ages», in the volume she edits, *Boethius. His Life and Influence*, Oxford, 1981, p. 214-234. Peiper's edition, the basis for the text provided in the Loeb volume, can be supplemented by the edition of N. HÄRING, *The Commentaries on Boethius by Gilbert of Poitiers*, Toronto, 1966, p. 369-377.

these names were neither substantial nor accidental (an echo of the Boethian comment about there not being such differences in God), it employs the term *proprietas* in a disconcertingly unfamiliar fashion. It is applied first to the attribute of the trinitarian nature of perfect unity, but then is used to refer to the Father's attribute of being unbegotten. In the same sentence the Holy Spirit is defined as the attribute of proceeding from Father and Son. The expression «of those three» (*quorundam trium... illorum trium*) leaves open exactly what is meant by «the three». His initial caveat about trinitarian names not being substantial or accidental notwithstanding, he uses the language of accidents to define what they mean. *Est una* then glides into the Aristotelian term *habitudo* or 'disposition' to identify what each divine name signifies. Its underlying argument is faithful to the Augustinian theme, pulled into centre stage by Boethius, that the names of the three persons are relatives, not substantives. While its author imitates Boethius in focussing on Aristotelian categories rather than psychological analogies to elucidate trinitarian theory, his use of *habitudo* suggests a conscious desire to find a new way of describing a familiar truth. Boethius had used the term in his translation of Porphyry's *Isagoge* when talking about two *habitudines* in substance, one relating to genus, the other to species, as well in his translation of Aristotle's *Categories* to mean ingrained dispositions within an individual[135]. 'Disposition' is both more concrete and more consciously secular as image of a divine person than 'relation'. An Augustinian and Boethian theme is reworked by applying a grammatical question about the meaning of divine name, considered as a *vox* like any other utterance.

To justify this rather innovative image, *Est una* moves from a conventional admission that reason has to give way to faith in grasping «the ineffable trinity in the unity of the divine essence, which cannot be said to be either substance or accident», to a counter-claim that it is not inconsistent to understand this substance (i.e. the divine essence) in creation, even though it is not to be found in any created things. Such a contrast between what creation was and what was not found among created things (an allusion to Romans 1:20) had been drawn by Augustine at the beginning of his own *De Trinitate* to justify a search for traces of the Trinity in the human soul[136]. This provides the pretext for an investigation inspired by reflection on Aristotelian categories.

The names Father, Son and Holy Spirit refer to distinctions which the author insists can only be used in terms of their *habitudo* or disposition towards another. Thus although one may understand the Holy Spirit to be the Son or the Father, one cannot legitimately say that either the Father or the Son is the Holy Spirit or even go so far as to claim «who is the Father is the Son» etc.; only «that which is the Father is the Son» etc. is acceptable. Following through this emphasis on Father, Son, and Holy Spirit as names, the author notes that the Trinity can be

(135) L. MINIO-PALUELLO, *Porphyry. Isagoge* 5.9-16, translatio Boethii, Aristoteles Latinus 1.6-7, Paris-Brussels, 1966, p. 10-11; *Categories* 9a4, in both the Boethian and the Vulgate translation, AL 1.1-5, Paris-Brussels, 1961, p. 10 and p. 64.
(136) AUGUSTINE, *De Trinitate* I.1, CCSL 50, p. 29.

predicated plurally in terms of person, but that each person can only be predicated as a person in the singular. The argument is a grammatical explanation for what is said in the Athanasian Creed about the necessary distinction between the three persons of the Trinity, but the stress on the linguistic nature of the distinction leads to a remarkable comment. What is defined in Latin as three persons «is said according to the property of the Greek language to be three substances, for what substance is in Greek is sounded as person in Latin; these three persons are said in certain manuscripts to be things, but this rarely» (*...in quibusdam codicibus dici res, sed raro*).

The information that while Latins define the Trinity as three persons in one substance, the Greeks speak of three *ypostasin* (as the word was often spelt in manuscripts) or *substantie* in one essence was widely known from the fifth and seventh books of Augustine's *De Trinitate*. This was a theme Roscelin developed extensively in his letter to Abelard and also referred to in the tract *Notandum est*, in which he explicitly identifies *persona* with *res*[137]. This identification, based, according to *Est una*, on the authority of certain manuscripts, is not dependent on Augustine's *De Trinitate*. In as full a repertory of patristic texts on the subject as one might find, question 8 of Abelard's *Sic et Non* (*Quod non sit multitudo rerum in trinitate uel quod non sit trinitas aliquod totum et contra*), only one of forty-two quotations uses the word *res* in the plural to describe the divine persons, a line from a commentary on the Apostle's Creed that Abelard attributed to Augustine, but was in fact by Rufinus[138]. *Est una* is an assertion of orthodoxy which manages to slip in the imagery of *Notandum est* as an aside.

By moving from a relatively familiar notion about the equivalence of Greek and Latin definitions to a much less familiar one about obscure authority for «things» the author of *Est una* hoped to provide his claim with a certain authority. His remark that *substantia* was the Latin word for the Greek *usya*, is drawn from Augustine's *De Trinitate*[139]. But whereas Augustine was uncomfortable with Greek terminology, *Est una* approaches trinitarian doctrine in terms of a variety of possible names to define that which a divine name signified, analysed like any other name. As we have already shown, Priscian's definition was central to Roscelin's analysis of the Trinity in his letter to Abelard. The name of each divine person signified a substance, like any noun. When he introduced *res* as a similar concept it was to identify that which was signified by the divine person. The difficulty with the term is that it also means 'thing' in a specific sense, denoting difference from something else[140]. The same ambiguity is true of his use of *essentia*. Abelard steered clear, however, from the suggestion of his

(137) Ed. MEWS, «The trinitarian doctrine of Roscelin of Compiègne and its influence», p. 359 (n. 1 above).

(138) RUFINUS, *Commentarius in Symbolum Apostolorum* 4, CCSL 20, p. 139: «Quomodo ignis caelestis generat ex se ipso splendorem lucis et producit uaporem, et cum sint tria in rebus, unum sunt in substantia, ita trinitas est una maiestas».

(139) AUGUSTINE, *De Trinitate* 5.8, CCSL 50, p. 216.

(140) JOLIVET, «Notes de lexicographie abélardienne» (see n. 59 above) notes a similar ambiguity of usage in the writing of Peter Abelard.

teacher that a divine person signified a thing. The deliberately vague reference in *Est una* to the authority of certain manuscripts may be a deliberate attempt to justify such grammatical reflection on names used of God.

Est una then raises questions which highlight the need to distinguish what is particular to each of the three persons. Its author moves from analysis of simple predication like « the Father is God», to criticism of faulty syllogisms like :

> Since the substance of the Father and of the Holy Spirit is completely the same,
> then if the Son is begotten of the substance of the Father,
> <therefore the Son is begotten of the substance of the Holy Spirit>.

and

> The Son is incarnate,
> but the Father and the Son are the same,
> therefore the Father is incarnate.

Both syllogisms are invalid because Son is a name only having meaning in relation to being begotten from the Father. Holy Spirit is not in itself a person, but the name of a relation. Arguments like those suggested are invalid because the strict grammatical reference of the names involved (Father, Son and Holy Spirit) is not respected in the context of the syllogism. The author justifies his point that they are names by re-iterating traditional Augustinian teaching that although names of the three persons signify substantives, they are not substantives but relatives and thus not names of a substance. A name of a divine person is distinguished from the thing which it signifies. The implication of this is that one cannot identify the name of one person with the name of the whole Trinity.

The final section of *Est una*, on the eternal nature of trinitarian relationships, begins in a similarly conventional Augustinian vein. The Father cannot exist without the Son, identified as the wisdom of the Father; since the union of Father and Son is eternal, the mutual love between both persons must be eternal. No scriptural or patristic authority is invoked to arrive at this conclusion. Instead emphasis is placed on the validity of rational thought even though the issues being dealt with are ultimately ineffable: « And in this way by some subtle reflection (*aliqua tenui cogitatione*) it can be considered that the Holy Spirit proceeds from both, even though this procession is ineffable». The statement connects back to the initial description of the Trinity as «the ineffable and incogitable property of a certain three» within the one and perfect unity. The author had already maintained that it was quite legitimate to seek to understand uncreated divine substance in the created world. He concludes the essay with scriptural authority for such an argument: « To such a thought you may say that the philosophers of the world rose through visible created things. Hence <says> the Apostle: « The invisible things... etc." ». Augustine had commented at length on these verses of St Paul at the end of his *De Trinitate*, but always to justify his own meditations, not those of philosophy in general [141]. By transforming the Pauline phrase *a creatura mundi*, silently understood by the lemma *Inuisibilia*

---

(141) E.g. AUGUSTINE, *De Trinitate* 1.1 ; 15.2.6, CCSL 50, p. 29 ; 50A, p. 462, 473 etc. See also the list of allusions to Romans 1 :20, CCSL 50A, p. 680.

enim (Rom. 1:20), into *philosophi mundi per uisibiles creaturas* the author subtly transforms the way the text of St Paul would be understood. He identifies himself with those past «philosophers of the world» in their effort to arrive at an understanding of the divinity.

"EST UNA" AND LATIN THEOLOGICAL LITERATURE 1080-1120

While *Est una* scarcely ranks as a great piece of theological literature, it is an unusual one. Not only is there no reference to scriptural authority until the very end of the essay, but even the word 'God' is not used except within discussion of legitimate linguistic statements at the end of the second paragraph and once in the fourth. The tract begins on a metaphysical rather than a religious note: «There is a one and perfect unity...»; only at the end of the first paragraph is it mentioned that this unity is of the divine essence. Similarly, the author interprets *trinitas* as a property of this unity, not as a substantive term or object of devotion. Only at the beginning of the fourth paragraph is reference made to *sancta trinitas* as an entity in its own right.

The tone adopted in the essay could scarcely be more different from that set by Augustine at the beginning of his *De Trinitate*: «Anyone about to read these things which we shall explain about the Trinity ought first to know how to be attentive to our approach against the calumnies of those who, despising the beginning of faith are deceived by an immature and perverted love of reasoning»[142]. The author of *Est una* emphasises that while the divine substance is beyond reason one can still ascend from rational principles to ineffable and transcendental truths.

Such a philosophical approach is quite different from that identified with Anselm of Laon and his disciples. In the widely read *Sententie Anselmi* the trinitarian nature of God is defined very briefly within the initial paragraph, the emphasis being overwhelmingly on the identity of the three persons, in terms scarcely more elaborate than those of the Athanasian creed[143]. William of Champeaux's discussion of the trinity is considerably more sophisticated than that attributed to Anselm of Laon, yet the divergences with *Est una* are too great for the essay to be attributed to his influence[144]. William pursues the Augustinian identification of the Son as the wisdom of the Father and the Holy Spirit as the charity or love of the other two persons at much more length, while not

---

(142) AUGUSTINE, *De Trinitate* 1.1, CCSL 50, p.26: «Lecturus haec quae de trinitate disserimus prius oportet ut nouerit stilum nostrum aduersus eorum uigilare calumnias qui fidei contemnentes initium immaturo et peruerso rationis amore falluntur [Eccli. 25:16]».

(143) F. BLIEMETZRIEDER, *Anselms von Laon systematische Sentenzen*, BGPMA 18.2-3, Münster, 1919, p.47: «... ubi qui gignit et quem gignit, quique ab utroque procedit, unum sunt, unum in substantia, tria in personis, pater ingenitus, filius genitus, ab utroque procedens ingenitus spiritus sanctus. Hec tria unum sunt, hoc unum tria, summe unum, ineffabiliter unum, unius essentie, unius potentie, unius voluntatis, unius operationis».

(144) O. LOTTIN, *Psychologie et morale*, vol. 5, no. 236, p.190-194.

identifying the words Father, Son and Holy Spirit as properties in God. The only name he recognises as admitting a plural is that of person – never that of substance. William's discussion concludes with a blanket statement about the impossibility of penetrating the mysteries of the trinity, in a fashion diametrically opposed to *Est una*: «What therefore we call those three persons, or how they differ among themselves, has not yet been revealed to us, just as how God the Father eternally generates the Son or how God the Spirit proceeds from both, has not yet been revealed. He will reveal it to his faithful, however, when it will please him, because this is life eternal» [145]. The *Sententie diuine pagine*, an anonymous work linked to the school of Anselm of Laon, includes a section on the trinity as well as on the identity of the three persons. It announces very briefly a theme extended in much more detail by Abelard, that the Son and the Holy Spirit are respectively the wisdom and the goodness of the Father, but does not go beyond very conventional statements about plurality of person rather than of essence [146]. The *Sententie divine pagine* concludes, as does William's discussion, with a warning about the impossibility of rational speculation on the subject. Internal relationships of the Son and Holy Spirit to the Father are ineffable; since one could not provide reasoning on this, only assent, one ought to avoid disputation on the subject [147].

Est una is closer in methodology to St Anselm's *Monologion*, which begins with the claim that if anyone did not know «the one nature, the summation of all things that exist» through either not hearing or not believing, he could be persuaded of it «by reason alone» [148]. Studiously avoiding arguments about God, Anselm dwells instead on a more overtly philosophical issue, the nature of supreme unchanging essence. He discusses what can be predicated substantially of this essence (c. 15), through which all things exist (c. 5-14) and yet which is beyond the normal categories of substance (c. 27). Only when he begins to debate the properties of this supreme nature does he introduce the idea of its speech or Word, related to this supreme nature as a Son to its Father (c. 29-46). Without explicitly acknowledging his debt to Augustine, Anselm compares this Father and Son to memory and intelligence (c. 48) and argues that there must be a spirit of love between them both (c. 49-61). It is not until the very final chapter – after reflection on the contrast between human reason and the transcendent nature of

(145) LOTTIN, p. 194: «Quid ergo uocamus tres illas personas, aut quomodo diuerse sint inter se, nondum nobis est manifestum; sicut etiam quomodo Deus pater eternaliter generet filium, aut quomodo Deus utroque procedat, nondum est manifestum. Cum autem Deo placuerit, reuelabit fidelibus suis, quia hec est uita eterna».

(146) BLIEMETZRIEDER, p. 8-10. Similar brief definition of the Son as wisdom and the Holy Spirit as goodness is found in a summary of doctrine in the Oxford MS, Bodleian Library, Laud Misc. 277, fol. 43vb-45rb, edited by LOTTIN, *Psychologie et morale*, 5, p. 338-340.

(147) BLIEMETZRIEDER, p. 9: «Cum autem nequeamus inde reddere rationem, solam credulitatem, non disputationem exhibeamus, ut de Abraham legitur *Credidit deo, et reputatum est ad iustitiam*, non sicut greci sapientes, qui hoc solum reputantes esse quod humana ratio inuestigare potest, pro insipientibus reputati sunt».

(148) SCHMITT, 1, p. 13.

82

his subject matter (c. 54-56) and on the way an individual can accede to this ineffable essence (c. 68-78) – that Anselm gives the name of God to this *summa essentia* (c. 80), whose triune nature he had so carefully explained in preceeding chapters.

Despite the obvious gulf in sophistication and thoroughness between the *Monologion* and *Est una*, the two works share a common desire to arrive through philosophical reflection at the doctrine of the trinitarian nature of God. Unlike the Augustinian *De Trinitate*, both works avoid arguments from Scripture or authority since they seek to lead the reader to acceptance of the same underlying truths as taught by Augustine, through a process of rational reflection. Only in the penultimate chapter of the *Monologion* does Anselm grope towards definition of the plurality in the supreme essence that has occupied him in previous chapters. It is in c. 79 that we see the closest parallels with the argument of *Est una* about the presence of three difficult-to-define elements within supreme unity:

> See how it is clearly appropriate for every man to believe in a certain ineffable triune unity and in one Trinity – one and a unity because it is one essence, triune and a Trinity because of three I-don't-know-what. Although I can say a Trinity on account of the Father and the Son and the Spirit of both, who are three: I cannot however say in one name that for which they are three, as if I said on account of their being three persons, just as I might say a unity because of one substance. One must not think of three persons, because all several persons subsist separately from each other, so that there must be as many substances as persons[149].

Even though he had already arrived at the words Father, Son and their common Spirit, this is the first time Anselm has introduced the notion of *person* and then it is to say what *person* is not. The conclusion to which he is moving is introduced as a hypothetical suggestion: that one could say that that wonderful Trinity is one essence or nature and three persons or substances. As usual, Anselm does not make explicit that he is here referring to Augustine's repeated allusion in the *De Trinitate* to «three persons or substances», in acknowledgement of the equivalence of Greek and Latin trinitarian definitions. He follows with an explanation:

> For these two names are chosen more aptly to signify plurality in the supreme essence, because 'person' is only said about an individual rational nature, and 'substance' principally about individuals which consist particularly in a plurality.... By this necessary reasoning that supreme and single Trinity or

---

(149) SCHMITT, 1, p. 85: «Ecce patet omni homini expedire, ut credat in quandam ineffabilem trinam unitatem et unam trinitatem. Unam quidem et unitatem propter unam essentiam, trinam vero et trinitatem propter tres nescio quid. Licet enim possim dicere trinitatem propter patrem et filium et utriusque spiritum qui sunt tres, non tamen possum proferre uno nomine propter quid tres, velut si dicerem propter tres personas, sicut dicerem unitatem propter unam substantiam».

X

triune unity can be called one essence and three persons or three substances [150].

The climax of the *Monologion,* like that of *Est una,* turns on a passage of Augustine that both authors thought were sufficiently familiar to avoid explicit acknowledgement. Yet in one way, the author of *Est una* is more precise. Unlike Anselm he explains that the difference in terminology is caused by different usage in the Greek language. He goes on to suggest that *res* sometimes is a synonym for person or substance in certain manuscripts. Anselm, by contrast, leaves the comment about «three persons or three substances» unexplained in order to dwell in the closing chapter on the divine nature of the supreme essence on which all things depend.

The argument of *Est una* is so close to that of Roscelin's letter to Abelard that we must consider it to be by Roscelin. Their common argument is that one must respect the plurality of persons within God and that one cannot simply identify one person with another. In both texts Augustine's statement about the Latin doctrine of a plurality of persons as basically identical to the Greek doctrine of a plurality of substances, is used to argue that it is legitimate to speak of plural things in God. In *Notandum est,* a short essay which follows Roscelin's letter to Abelard in the manuscript, the author has no qualm about stating the identification of *persona* and *res,* and states that his authority is that of the Greeks. *Est una* is more carefully constructed as a confession of faith in which most emphasis is placed on belief in divine unity, but in which it is explained that certain manuscripts justified description of a person as a thing. In his letter to Abaelard, Roscelin was concerned not so much with justifying identification of things (*res*) in the Trinity as with emphasising that one could not identify one person with another. Patristic texts which spoke of plural substances or essences served his purpose just as well. St Anselm distorted Roscelin's thinking about the Trinity by making it hinge on the assertion that there were plural things within God. His central focus was that just as one could not identify one thing with another, so one could not identify God the Father with God the Son or God the Holy Spirit. There seems little reason for doubting that *Est una* is a compromise document in which Roscelin defends his orthodoxy, quite possibly that which Ivo of Chartres asked him to write to clear his name.

---

(150) SCHMITT, 1, p. 86: «Nam haec duo nomina aptius eliguntur ad significandam pluralitatem in summa essentia, quia persona non dicitur nisi de individua rationali natura, et substantia principaliter dicitur de individuis quae maxime in pluralitate consistunt.... Potest ergo hac necessitatis ratione irreprehensibiliter illa summa et una trinitas sive trina unitas dici una essentia et tres personae sive tres substantiae».

X

CONCLUSION: ROSCELIN AND ST ANSELM IN A COMMON CAUSE

The document *Est una* supports Roscelin's claim that his arguments were not so fundamentally different from those of St Anselm. St Anselm's invective has customarily been interpreted as evidence that the two thinkers were radically different. Yet both were committed to finding rational arguments for justifying Christian belief. In the *Monologion* Anselm arrived through rational reflection at the conclusion that there must be three persons or substances within the perfection of divine unity. In *Est una* Roscelin may even have deliberately echoed Anselm's argument, extending it very briefly with the suggestion that there was also some manuscript authority for referring to three things in God. He does not explain, however, what is more apparent from his letter to Abelard, that he considered each name to have its own *res*. His theological terminology arose from direct application of his understanding what was signified by a noun to divine names.

Both Roscelin and Anselm were interested in what Augustine had to say about the Greek use of *substantia* for what the Latins identified as *persona*. Walter of Honnecourt was shocked not by Roscelin's specific use of the word *res*, but by the idea that Latin terminology could be exchanged for that of the Greeks. Some fourteen years earlier, Anselm of Bec had been criticised for using *substantia* interchangeably with *persona*, to describe the plurality of the Trinity within his *Monologion*. In a letter to Rainald, abbot of St Cyprian of Poitiers, sent *c.* 1077, Anselm admitted his fears that if the *Monologion* fell into the wrong hands, critics might say that it contained things «unheard of and contrary to the truth». He confided that he had already been criticised for having followed what Augustine had said about persons and the substance of God[151]. The controversial passage was the mention in the penultimate chapter of «three persons or substances». In the prologue, added after he had sent the *Monologion* to Lanfranc, he explained the Augustinian authority for his statement that Greeks used the word *substance* to mean what Latins understood by *person*. Anselm reiterates in the letter to Rainald that «three persons» like «three substances» did not belong properly to God, but were names reached at by someone «who, forced by want of a properly suitable name, chooses from those names which cannot be spoken plurally in the summation of essence, to signify that which cannot be spoken of with a suitable name». Anselm opts for two names, person and substance. Silently adapting the language of the fifth book of Augustine's *De Trinitate*, he says that these two names are chosen more aptly to signify plurality:

(151)*Ep.* 83, SCHMITT, 3, p. 307-308: «Qui tamen nunc cognoscunt se non considerate reprehendisse, et hac occasione quod prius non animaduertebant gaudent se cognoscere. Nesciebant enim sic non dici proprie de Deo tres personas quomodo tres substantias, quadam tamen ratione ob indigentiam nominis proprie significantis illam pluralitatem quae in summa trinitate intelligitur, Latinos dicere tres personas credendas in una substantia, Graecos uero non minus fideliter tres substantias in una persona confiteri». Anselm's allusion to *Monologion* 79, is not noted by Schmitt, who alerts the reader only to its prologue where Anselm makes the same point as in this letter.

«'person' because it is only said of an individual, rational nature; 'substance' because it is said of individuals which consist particularly in plurality»[152]. Anselm gives no indication in the *Monologion* that he was using a Greek word here (as he takes pains to point out in the preface). To anyone for whom the use of person was unquestionably the only correct way to identify the nature of the Father, the Son and the Holy Spirit, as defined by the Athanasian Creed, Anselm's comment that any such name was not used *proprie* of God might appear a dangerous innovation.

Anselm alludes rather more enigmatically to criticism of his own teaching in the letter he sent to Lanfranc, after the monk Maurice had brought back a draft of the *Monologion* with various comments and criticisms from the archbishop. He expresses surprise and a degree of hurt about certain things which had been read into the work, but which he insists had been taken directly from Augustine[153]. Lanfranc's criticism is normally taken to have been directed against Anselm's method in general. The comments which Anselm includes in a new prologue suggest that Lanfranc was particularly concerned at Anselm's suggestion in the penultimate chapter that the Greek definition was as valid as that of the Latins. After «frequent reconsideration» he could find nothing in the work inconsistent with the writings of the Fathers and especially of Augustine. He specified that when he had said that the Trinity was three substances, he was following the Greeks, as Augustine had done in his *De Trinitate*. Anselm concluded the prologue with an injunction that it always be copied with the rest of the work, and with an expression of hope that if anyone read this preface, he would not judge the author harshly if he finds something contrary to his opinion[154]. Anselm wrote this prologue after he had received Lanfranc's critical comments on the draft. The oldest manuscript of the *Monologion*, dating from 1077-82 and containing the most primitive version of the text (Paris, BN lat. 13413, from the abbey of Saint-Martin, Séez), is itself that which had been released by Anselm after those initial corrections. Anselm made a few other slight modifications to his text after sending this copy to Sées, but none of major import. Anselm included explicit allusion to the authority of Augustine to forestall criticism of the most controversial part of his argument, the penultimate chapter,

(152) SCHMITT, 1, p. 86, see n. 150 above.

(153) *Ep.* 77, SCHMITT, 3, p. 199: «Etenim ea quae ex eodem opusculo uestris litteris inseruistis, nulla mihi ratiocinatio mea. Ea enim ipsa sic beatus Augustinus in libro De trinitate suis magnis disputationibus probat, ut eadem quasi mea breuiori ratiocinatione inueniens eius confisus auctoritate dicerem. Quod dico non aliquid eorum quae dixi apud vos defendendo, sed ea me non a me praesumpsisse, sed ab alio assumpsisse ostendendo».

(154) The second half of the prologue, from «Quam ego saepe retractans nihil potui invenire me in ea dixisse quod non catholicorum patrum et maxime beati Augustini scriptis cohaereat... Puto etiam quod, si quis hanc ipsam praefationem prius viderit, non temere iudicabit, siquid contra suam opinionem prolatum inuenerit», SCHMITT, 1, p. 8, ll. 8-26, may have been appended to an original prologue which concluded with «... in longum memoriae commendare satagerent».

X

in which he suggested that one could speak equally of either three persons or three substances in the divine essence.

The criticisms which Anselm had to counter from Lanfranc were perhaps not so different from those which Roscelin faced from Walter of Honnecourt. Both Anselm and Roscelin wished to arrive at the doctrine of plurality within divine unity rationally rather than by simply reproducing the formula of the Athanasian Creed. Both men understood terms like *person* and *substance* to be words which the human intellect could arrive at to define an evident plurality within God, and argued their case from the legitimacy of both Latin and Greek definitions of orthodox doctrine. Anselm was certainly the more nuanced thinker. He was fully aware, however, of contemporary philosophical concerns, and was anxious not to fall into the trap of being obsessively concerned with individual words. *Est una* and the *Monologion* may be far from equal as compositions, but in both Roscelin and Anselm wanted to penetrate beyond the familiar words of Latin orthodoxy, to come up with an argument more in accord with reason. When Peter Abelard set out to deliver his own interpretation of the foundation of Christian belief, he wanted to transcend the polarities of the debate between St Anselm and Roscelin of Compiègne.

"EST UNA": A CRITICAL EDITION

Est una is one of four untitled texts appended to a copy of book I of Peter Abelard's *Theologia christiana*, in its earliest known recension, Durham Cathedral Chapter Library MS A.IV.15, f. 66v-67v (*D*)[155]. The *Theologia christiana* and these texts are copied onto a single section (f. 57-69), made up of two gatherings of eight and four leaves respectively. The copyist finished transcribing the first of the five books that make up *Tchr* near the foot of the first leaf (f. 65v) of the second smaller gathering. He left f. 66r free, but then copied the four subsequent texts onto f. 66v-67v. Part of the intervening space has been filled in with miscellaneous notes on the virtues, the causes which make men good, spirits created by God, the forgiveness of sins and the composition of man. The final leaves (f. 68r-69v) are left blank. Only the first section of this manuscript (f. I-III, 1-16), containing the Gospel according to St John, was definitely copied at Durham, at a later date than the second and third sections, sometime in the second half of the twelfth century[156]. Together the second and third sections

(155) The manuscript is described by R. A. B. MYNORS, *Durham Cathedral Manuscripts to the End of the Twelfth Century*, Oxford, 1939, p. 51-52, and in further detail by E. M. BUYTAERT, « An Earlier Redaction of the 'Theologia christiana' of Abelard», *Antonianum*, 37 (1962), p. 481-495 and *Petri Abaelardi Opera theologica*, CCCM 12, p. 11-14.

(156) John's Gospel is preceded by a prologue, listed by F. STEGMÜLLER, *Repertorium biblicum medii aevi*, 1, Madrid, 1940, p. 286, no. 624. Only the first section includes a Durham inscription on fol. 1r; Mynors dated the first section to the mid twelfth century, and later than the second and third sections; Buytaert dated it to the second half of the twelfth century, «An Earlier Redaction», p. 481-482 and CCCM 12, p. 11. As the second section (fol. 17-56),

provide eloquent witness to a range of theological discussion in northern France in the early twelfth century. Three of the four texts found on f. 66v-67v are patristic in origin[157]. Immediately after a text identifiable by its incipit as *Est una* (f. 66v) have been copied the *Libellus fidei ad Damasum*, a confession of faith widely attributed to Jerome, but in fact sent by Pelagius to Pope Damasus after his teaching had been publically condemned towards the end of the fourth century[158]. The third text (f. 67r-v) is mostly an abbreviated version of the last chapter of book six of Augustine's *De Trinitate*[159]. It also includes a short summary of Augustine's definition in the *De doctrina christiana* of the three divine persons as unity, equality and the concord of equality and other notes on plurality and unity in God[160]. The final text (fol. 67v) contains the beginning of the *Liber ecclesiasticorum dogmatum*, conventionally attributed to Augustine, but in fact by his fifth-century admirer, Gennadius of Marseilles. Abelard recognized the true Gennadian authorship of the *Liber* when correcting the original text of the

containing glosses on John's Gospel attributed elsewhere to Anselm of Laon, differs considerably from the third in its collation, ruling and generally more careful presentation (three gatherings of twelve leaves and one of four, ruled in two columns of 45 lines ruled with a hard point) we may presume it was copied separately from the third, comprising one gathering of eight leaves and another originally of six, but missing the fourth; its text is written in a single column of 42-49 lines ruled with a plummet.

(157) In C. J. MEWS, «Peter Abelard's *Theologia christiana* and *Theologia 'Scholarium'* re-examined», *Recherches de théologie ancienne et médiévale*, 52 (1985), p.113-115, I noted the text under discussion, although had not then realised that it was followed by three other patristic texts.

(158) «Credimus in Deum patrem omnipotentem... quicumque voluerit se imperitum uel malivolum vel etiam non catholicum, non me hereticum comprobat», *Confessio seu libellus fidei a Pelagio ex oriente Romam missus*, PL 48, 488D-491C. It is followed in PL 48 by a learned commentary of R. P. Garnerius on 491C-497B and reprinted in parallel columns with the version by Coelestius, disciple of Pelagius on 498D-505C. A modified version is printed as sermon 236 among spurious works of Augustine in PL 39, 2181-83. Abelard cites the text as *Hieronymus in epistola de explanatione fidei ad Damasum papam*, B. BOYER and R. McKEON, *Sic et Non* 8, 19-21, Chicago-London, 1976-77, p. 132.

(159) *De Trinitate* VI.10, CCSL 50, p.241-242: «Pater non habet patrem... propter singulorum perfectionem partes unius Dei non sunt». This quotation is also found in the Zurich, Zentralbibliothek MS Car. C 149, fol. 145, L. C. MOHLBERG, *Katalog der Handschriften der Zentralbibliothek Zürich. Mittelalterliche Handschriften*, Zurich, 1951, p.132, no. 315.

(160) *De doctrina christiana* I.12, CSEL 80, p. 11; I have not been able to identify any source for the subsequent notes, separated in the manuscript by paraphs: «Ex ipso sunt omnia quia fecit, non de ipso, quia non de eius substantia, sed de nichilo» and «Pater et filius et spiritus sanctus, hi tres quia unius substantie sunt, unum sunt, ubi nulla naturarum, nulla etiam diversitas voluntatum. Ergo hi tres, quia unum semper ineffabilem coniunctionem deitatis, [quia] ineffabiliter copulantur. Unus est Deus, nec pars trinitatis; quicumque de tribus unus. Sicut una persona est Christus gemine substantie, non tamen pars persone Deus, alioquin autem non erat totus et crevit cum ei homo accessit, nec hoc modo crevit, nec cum ei adheret iustus, nec recedente minuitur pater et filius et spiritus sanctus. Propter individuam trinitatem unus est deus; propter uniuscuiusque proprietatem tres persone; propter singulorum perfectionem partes unius Dei non sunt».

Theologia christiana, as represented in the Durham manuscript[161]. All three patristic works quoted or excerpted on these two leaves were proof texts to which Abelard frequently turned for authoritative justification of his theological arguments.

\<DE UNITATE ET TRINITATE DIVINA\>

1. Est una et perfecta unitas in qua etiam est quedam mirabilis trinitas: unitas quidem substantie, trinitas vero non aliquarum substantiarum in ipsa substantia nec aliquorum accidentium in ea, sed quorundam trium ineffabilis et incog[g]itabilis proprietas[162]. Ad significandam igitur unitatem substantie inventa sunt nomina opificis *eternus, inmensus*[163], *bonus* et similia – quorum nullum est accidentale. Ad significandam vero ineffabilem proprietatem illorum trium reperta sunt hec nomina *pater, filius, spiritus sanctus* – quorum nullum est substantiale uel accidentale[164]; et est proprietas patris quod est ingenitus, et ab eo gignitur filius; et spiritus sancti est proprietas ut sit procedens ab utroque. Et ita data sunt hec nomina, ut habitudo ingenite persone ad genitam dicatur *pater*, habitudo vero genite persone ad ingenitam *filius* et procedentis persone ad ingenitam genitamque habitudo *spiritus sanctus*. Et ita est quedam ineffabilis trinitas in unitate divine essentie que nec potest dici substantia nec accidens – in qua deficit ratio, sed fides est adhibenda.

2. Nec mirum est, nec ullatenus inconveniens dici debet[a] si in creatione substantia hec intelligitur quod nullo modo vere ratione comprehenditur, nec aliquarum creaturarum reperitur[165]. Itaque secure potest dici quod sunt nomina

(a) potest *ante corr.* D

---

(161) «Credimus unum deum esse patrem et filium et spiritum sanctum... sed homo in deo, et in homine deus», c. 1-5, C. H. TURNER, «The *Liber ecclesiasticorum dogmatum* Attributed to Gennadius», *Journal of Theological Studies*, 7 (1905-6), p.78-99 at 89-90. Its Gennadian authorship is discussed by TURNER, «Supplenda to The *Liber ecclesiasticorum dogmatum* Attributed to Gennadius», *ibid.*, 8 (1906-7), p.103-114. Abelard assumed the traditional identification of the *Liber* to Augustine in the initial Durham recension of *Tchr* I. 27-28, but corrected it to Gennadius in the recension of Vatican, Biblioteca Apostolica MS Reg. lat. 159; see BUYTAERT, CCCM 12, p.51 and MEWS, «Peter Abelard's *Theologia* Re-examined», p.122-123. Thomas Aquinas similarly only identified Gennadius as its author in the course of his theological writing, after 1263, M. ARGES, «New Evidence Concerning the Date of Thomas Aquinas' *Lectura* on Matthew», *Mediaeval Studies*, 49 (1987), p.517-523.

(162) Cf. *Symbolum 'Quicumque uult'* 3, CCSL 50A, 000: «Fides autem catholica haec est: ut unum deum in trinitate et trinitatem in unitate ueneremur».

(163) *Ibid.* 12: «nec tres immensi sed... unus immensus».

(164) Cf. AUG., *De Trin.* 5, 5, CCSL 50, p.210: «In Deo autem nihil quidem secundum accidens dicitur quia nihil in eo mutabile est; nec tamen omne quod dicitur secundum substantiam dicitur».

(165) *Ibid.* 1.1, CCSL 50, p.29-30: «Quae uero proprie de deo dicuntur, quae in nulla creatura reperiuntur, raro ponit scriptura diuina... Proinde substantia Dei sine ulla sui commutatione mutabilia facientem, et sine ullo suo temporali motu temporalia creantem,

trium distinctionum ineffabilium *pater, filius, spiritus sanctus*; et ad se habitudine referuntur, *pater* filii pater, *filius* patris filius, *spiritus sanctus* patris et filii. Non tamen dicitur pater spiritus sanctus, quia iam intelligitur spiritus sanctus filius, nec dicitur filius spiritus sanctus[b] quia posset intelligi spiritus sanctus pater. Nec possit commisceri ista nomina ut ita dicatur «qui est pater est filius» et «qui est filius est spiritus sanctus vel pater». Sed ita sane potest dici: «hoc quod est pater est filius et spiritus sanctus et e converso», et possit dici de ista mirabili trinitate nomina pluraliter tres persona ut dicatur «III[c] sunt numero, *pater*, *<filius>*, *spiritus sanctus*». *Persona* tamen dicitur de his et singulariter ut dicatur primo, *persona* secundo et tertio [166]; et ita dicatur «III persone» et etiam secundum proprietatem grece lingue dicuntur tres substantie. Quod enim est apud grecos *substantia*, hoc a latinis sonat *persona*[167] et inveniuntur iste III[d] persone in quibusdam codicibus dici *res*, sed raro. Quod vero apud nos sonat *substantia*, apud grecos dicitur *usya*[168]. Vnde *homousious*, id est unius substantie, et[e] illa vocabula que sunt substantie, de his tribus distinctionibus dicuntur singulariter, sed nullo modo pluraliter – ut *spiritus sanctus* bonus spiritus, et alia huiusmodi. Dicitur enim «pater est[f] Deus, filius est Deus, spiritus sanctus est Deus», et ita pater est sanctus, filius est sanctus, spiritus sanctus est sanctus[169]. Non enim tres dii, uel tres sancti. Et ita de ceteris nominibus divine substantie intellige.

3. Quod si quis perversus ita argumentetur «cum eadem penitus sit substantia patris et spiritus sancti, tunc si filius est genitus ex substantia patris, <ergo filius est genitus ex substantia spiritus sancti>», non tamen dicitur genitus esse ex substantia spiritus sancti, quia hoc nomen *filius* convenit solummodo eo respectu illi persone que est genita a patre. Eodem modo si dicatur «filius incarnatus, sed pater filius idem sunt, ergo pater est incarnatus», non sequitur quia hoc est proprium huius persone que est filius[170]. Et nota quod hoc nomen *spiritus* per se non est nomen persone, et est unum nomen relationis *spiritus*

(b) sanctus] sancti *D* (c) tres *add. s. l. D* (d) III *s. l. D* (e) et illa... substantie *mg D* (f) est *s. l. D*

---

intueri et plene nosse difficile est».

(166) *Ibid.* 5.8, p. 216: «Quidquid ergo ad se ipsum dicitur Deus et de singulis personis ter dicitur, patre et filio et spiritu sancto, et simul de ipsa trinitate non pluraliter sed singulariter dicitur».

(167) *Ibid.* 5.9; 7.4, 5, p. 217, 255, 259, 261; ROSCELIN, *Ep. ad Abaelardum* 9, REINERS, p. 70, 72, 74, 76.

(168) AUG., *De Trin.* 5.8, p. 216: «Essentiam dico quae usia graece dicitur, quam usitatius substantiam uocamus».

(169) Cf. *Symbolum 'Quicumque uult'*, 15-16.

(170) Cf. *Ep. ad Abaelardum*, REINERS, p. 74: «Personas confundit, qui patrem filium et filium patrem dicit. Quod necesse est eum dicere, qui illa tria nomina unam solam rem singularem significare uoluerit. Omnia enim unius et singularis rei nomina de se inuicem praedicantur. Ita igitur pater incarnatus et passus est, quia ipse est filius qui hoc totum passus est; quod quantum sanae fidei repugnat, attende».

sanctus[171]. Dicantur itaque hec nomina relativa[g] esse non substantiva, et quamvis substantiva significent, non sunt tamen nomina substantie[172]. Videndum est quod cum hec tria sit trinitas, unum eorum non potest dici trinitas. Non enim potest dici per se «pater est trinitas» vel «filius est trinitas» vel «spiritus sanctus trinitas».

4. Et sicut hec sancta trinitas aliquando esse non cepit, sed ab eterno quod est fuit[173], ante secula enim filius est genitus a patre, et ante secula spiritus sanctus est procedens ab utroque; ita ei nichil postea accrevit, nichil ei diminutum est, sed semper invariabilis eadem permanet. Si enim filius non esset coeternus patri, aliquando pater sine sapientia sua fuisset; filius enim sapientia patris est[174]. Quod si hoc esse potuisset, vel ipse pater ab aliquo sapientiam suam accepisset, vel ipse idem sibi dedisset, quod utrumque de deo sentire nefas est[175]. Cum autem utriusque conexio eterna est, amor utriusque eternus est. Sicut enim nec pater sine filio, nec filius sine patre aliquando esse potuit; ita utrumque sine amore utriusque aliquando minime fuit. Et secundum hoc aliqua tenui cogitatione potest perpendi spiritum sanctum ab utroque procedere, que tamen processio ineffabilis est[176]. Ad talem cogitationem dicatis philosophi mundi per visibiles creaturas ascenderunt. Vnde Apostolus: *Invisibilia enim* et cetera[177].

(g) relativa] relata *D*

---

(171) Cf. AUG., *De Trin.* 5.11, p.219, quoted by ROSCELIN, *Ep. ad Abaelardum,* REINERS, p.70: «Sed tamen ille spiritus sanctus qui non trinitas sed in trinitate intellegitur, in eo quod proprie ad filium refertur quia spiritus sanctus et patris et filii spiritus est. Sed ipsa relatio non apparet in hoc nomine; apparet autem cum dicitur donum dei».

(172) AUG., *De Trin.* 5.5, p.211: «Quamobrem quamuis diuersum sit patrem esse et filium esse, non est tamen diuersa substantia quia hoc non secundum substantiam dicuntur sed secundum relatiuum, quod tamen relatiuum non est accidens quia non est mutabile»; cf. *ibid.* 7.1, p.247: «Restat itaque ut etiam essentia filius relatiue dicatur ad patrem».

(173) *Ibid.,* 5.5, p.210: «Quod si aliquando esse coepisset aut aliquando esse desineret filius, secundum accidens diceretur»; *Symbolum 'Quicumque'* 24: «Et in hac trinitate nihil prius aut posterius... sed totae tres personae coaeternae sibi sunt et coaequales».

(174) I Cor. 1:24, discussed by AUG., *De Trin.* 7.1, p.244-246.

(175) AUG., *De Trin.* 1.1, p.27: «Sunt autem alii qui secundum animi humani naturam uel affectum *de deo sentiunt* [Sap. 1:1], si quid sentiunt, et ex hoc errore cum de Deo disputant sermoni suo distortas et fallaces regulas figunt».

(176) Cf. *ibid.* 5.11, p.219: «Ergo spiritus sanctus ineffabilis quaedam patris filiique communio...» etc.

(177) Rom 1:20; AUG., *De Trin.* 15.2, 20, p.462, 516, etc.

ADDENDA AND CORRIGENDA

I Orality, Literacy and Authority in the Twelfth-Century Schools

p. 485: The Council of Sens, I argue, took place on 25 May 1141; see my article, 'The Council of Sens (1141): Bernard, Abelard, and the Fear of Social Upheaval', in *Speculum* 77 (2002), 342–82.

p. 489: Patricia Stirnemann argues that the early manuscripts of the *Glossa ordinaria* may originally have been produced at Chartres, but that by the 1140s Paris, in particular the abbey of St Victor, had become a major centre for their diffusion, 'Où ont été fabriquées les livres de la glose ordinaire dans la première moitié du XIIe siècle', in *Le XIIe siècle: Mutations et renouveau en France dans la première moitié du XIIe siècle*, ed. Françoise Gasparri (Paris, Cahiers du Léopard d'Or, 1994), pp. 257-301. She argues that Gilbert of Poitiers may have played a key role in promoting reverence for the text, ideas also developed by Theresa Gross-Diaz, *The Psalms Commentary of Gilbert of Poitiers: From Lectio Divina to the Lecture Room* (Leiden: E.J. Brill, 1996).

II Philosophy and Theology 1100-1150: The Search for Harmony

General Bibliography: For further detail on the explosion of interest in Aristotle's dialectic, see the papers of John Marenbon reprinted in *Aristotelian Logic, Platonism and the Context of Early Medieval Philosophy in the West* (Aldershot, Hants: Ashgate, 2000), pp. 128-40, in particular his previously unpublished Supplement, to 'Medieval Latin Commentaries and Glosses on Aristotelian Logical Texts, Before c. 1150. For an overview of many of the twelfth-century masters described in this study, see Peter Godman, *The Silent Masters. Latin Literature and its Censors in the High Middle Ages* (Princeton, N.J.: Princeton University Press, 2000).

p. 165: On the *Glosule* on Priscian, see the additional notes to VII below.

p. 168: While I here followed the unsubstantiated claim of Bautier, 'Paris au temps d'Abélard', p. 77 that Stephen of Garlande withdrew to St-Victor and bequeathed his books to the library, the necrology of St-Victor mentions only that his anniversary occurred on 14 January, but says nothing about his books or withdrawing to the abbey, Auguste Molinier (ed.), *Obituaires de la Province de Sens*, vol. I.1 (Paris: Imprimerie nationale, 1902), p. 537.

p. 169: Iwakuma Y. identifies a series of largely unpublished glosses on Porphyry's *Isagoge*, the *Categories*, the *Perihermeneias*, and Boethius's *De topicis differentiis* as by William of Champeaux, 'Pierre Abélard et Guillaume de Champeaux dans les premières années du XIIe siècle: une étude préliminaire', in *Langages, sciences philosophie au XIIe siècle*, ed. J. Biard (Paris: Vrin, 1999), pp. 93-123, esp. p. 101. In 'William of Champeaux and Aristotle's *Categories*', forthcoming in *Acts of the Nijmegen Conference*, ed. C. Kneepkens, Iwakuma argues that Paris, BNF lat. 13368 contains a revision of William's commentary on the *Categories*, perhaps by Joscelin of Soissons, rather than by William himself. (Marenbon's helpful summary of Iwakuma's conclusions, needs to be modified in the light of Iwakuma's more recent research, *Aristotelian Logic* II 129-30 and 134.)

p. 169: I am now inclined to follow Marenbon in dating the *Dialectica*, at least in its inception to early in the second decade of the twelfth century. He points out that I had underestimated the extent to which Abelard in his *Theologia 'Summi boni'* modifies his early, harsh criticism of Platonists who identified the world soul with the Holy Spirit, made in the *Dialectica*, *The philosophy of Peter Abelard* (Cambridge: Cambridge University Press, 1997), p. 42, and 'Abélard, la prédication et le verbe "être"', in *Langage, Sciences, Philosophie au XIIe siècle*, ed. J. Biard (Paris: Vrin, 1999), pp. 200-202.

p. 173: On Bernard of Chartres and the tradition he inspired, see Peter Godman, 'Opus consummatum, omnium artium . . . imago: From Bernard of Chartres to John of Hauvilla', *Zeitschrift für Deutsches Altertum und Deutsche Literatur* 124 (1995), 26-71.

pp. 175-9: On Gilbert's thought in relation to his contemporaries, see some excellent studies: L. M. De Rijk, 'Semantics and Metaphysics in Gilbert of Poitiers: A Chapter in Twelfth-Century Platonism', *Vivarium* 26 (1988), 73-112; 27 (1989), 1-35; Jean Jolivet, 'Trois variations médiévales sur l'universel et l'individu:

Roscelin, Abélard, Gilbert de la Porrée', *Revue de Metaphysique et de Morale* 97 (1992), 111-55; Klaus Jacobi, 'Einzelnes-Individuum-Person: Gilbert von Poitiers' Philosophie des Individuellen', in *Individuum und Individualitat im Mittelalter*, ed. Jan A. Aertsen and Andreas Speer (Berlin: De Gruyter, 1996), pp. 3-21.

p. 180: Usages of the label *nominales* are documented by Iwakuma Y. and S. Ebbesen, 'Logico-Theological Schools from the Second Half of the 12th Century: A List of Sources', *Vivarium* 30 (1992), 173-210.

p. 182: A new edition of the *Scito teipsum*, prepared by Rainer Ilgner, has been published within the series Corpus Christianorum. Continuatio Mediaeualis 190 (Turnhout: Brepols, 2001). Rainer Ilgner argues that the correct title is *Scito teipsum* rather than *Ethica* in 'Scito te ipsum – Ethica nostra. Zu Herkunft und Bedeutung des Titels von Abaelards Ethik', in *Theologie und Philosophie* 76 (2001), 253-70.

p. 185: My assertion that William of Champeaux founded the abbey of Saint-Victor is widely found in secondary literature. To be precise, however, an impoverished church dedicated to St Victor already existed, when William of Champeaux installed himself there in 1108/9. Robert-Henri Bautier explains in 'Les origines et les premiers développements de l'abbaye Saint-Victor de Paris', in Jean Longère (ed.), *L'abbaye Parisienne de Saint-Victor au Moyen Age* (Paris: Brepols, 1991), pp. 29-35, how Louis VI accorded many privileges to regular canons at Saint-Victor in 1113 (after the death of bishop Hugh of Châlons-sur-Marne, but before the consecration of William of Champeaux as the new bishop). The necrology of Saint-Victor, however, recalls that Girbert, Galo's successor as bishop of Paris (1116-23) was the person who first began to build Saint-Victor, rather than William of Champeaux, who was remembered as a canon of Saint-Victor, but not as founder of the abbey; Auguste Molinier (ed.), *Obituaires de la Province de Sens*, vol. I.1 (Paris: Imprimerie nationale, 1902), p. 538. The fact that William chose to be buried at Clairvaux rather than at Saint-Victor similarly suggests that William was not as closely honoured at Saint-Victor as sometimes thought. Hugh of Saint-Victor is not known to have studied under William, and thus never absorbed the complexity of his teaching about dialectic and rhetoric, such as was familiar to Peter Abelard.

III An Excerpt from Guibert of Nogent's *Monodiae* (III, 17) as an Appendage to the *De haeresibus* of Augustine

General Bibliography: On Guibert of Nogent, see the new translation, with introduction, by Paul J. Archambault, *A Monk's Confession: The Memoirs of Guibert of Nogent* (University Park, PA: Pennsylvania State University Press, 1996). Steven F. Kruger writes about Guibert's revulsion for the body, in relation to Jews and Muslims, rather than to heretics, in 'Medieval Christian (Dis)identifications: Muslims and Jews in Guibert of Nogent', *New Literary History* 28 (1997), 185-203.

p. 121: A lost treatise of Roscelin against Robert of Arbrissel is mentioned in a list of books from an unidentified abbey, Paris, Bibliothèque Sainte-Geneviève, MS 1042, fol. 113v (s. xii/xiii): *Roscelinus contra Robertum liber I*. I am indebted to François Dolbeau for this reference.

IV In Search of a Name and its Significance: A Twelfth-Century Anecdote about Thierry and Peter Abaelard

General Bibliography: On Thierry of Chartres, see the edition of Karin M. Fredborg, *The Latin Rhetorical Commentaries by Thierry of Chartres* (Toronto: Pontifical Institute of Mediaeval Studies, 1988).

p. 175: On the title *Scito teipsum*, see the notes to article II above. A new edition of Abelard's *Collationes* (also known as the Dialogue between a philosopher, Jew and a Christian) has been published by John Marenbon and Giovanni Orlandi, *Abelard's Collationes* (Oxford: Clarendon Press, 2000).

V La bibliothèque du Paraclet du XIIIe siècle à la Révolution

General bibliography: On the distinctive features of monastic life at the Paraclete, of seminal importance are the editions and studies of Chrysogonus Waddell: *The Old French Paraclete Ordinary*, Cistercian Liturgical Studies [CLS] 4 (Trappist, KY: Gethsemani Abbey, 1983); *The Paraclete Statutes. Institutiones Nostrae.*

Introduction, Edition, Commentary, CLS 20 (Trappist, KY: Gethsemani Abbey, 1987); *Hymn Collections from the Paraclete*, *CLS* 8-9 (Trappist, KY: Gethsemani Abbey, 1987-89).

VI St Anselm and Roscelin: Some New Texts and their Implications. I. The *De incarnatione verbi* and the *Disputatio inter Christianum et Gentilem*

p. 58: On the Hereford manuscript, see *Catalogue of the Manuscripts of Hereford Cathedral Library*, ed. R. A. B. Mynors and R. M. Thomson (Cambridge: Boydell & Brewer, 1993), pp. 64-5.

p. 86: On the context of the *Disputatio inter Christianum et Gentilem* see Anna Sapir Abulafia, 'Christians disputing disbelief: St Anselm, Gilbert Crispin and Pseudo-Anselm', in *Religionsgespräche im Mittelalter*, Wolfenbütteler Mittelalter-Studien IV, ed. B. Lewis and F. Niewöhner (Wiesbaden, 1992), repr. in *Christians and Jews in dispute: Disputational Literature and the Rise of Anti-Judaism in the West (c. 1000-1150)* (Aldershot, Hampshire, 1998). Colin Gale discovered a further complete manuscript, from the twelfth century, of the *Disputatio*, matching those from Berlin (Maria Laach) and Hereford, in Cambridge University Library, Gg V 34 (from St Werburg, Chester), 'From Dialogue to Disputation: St Anselm and his Students on Disbelief', *Tjurunga: An Australasian Benedictine Review* 44 (1993), 71-86, especially 80. Sapir Abulafia also notes a fifteenth-century manuscript of the *Disputatio* in Venice, St Mark's Library, cod. Lat. (Valentinelli) III 49, ff. 168-171; 'Christians Disputing Belief', in *Christians and Jews* V 142 n. 52.

VII Nominalism and Theology before Abaelard: New Light on Roscelin of Compiègne

p. 5: Iwakuma points out that the name *Arnulfus* is used as an example in vocalist gloses on the *De categoricis syllogismis* and *De differentiis topicis* within the manuscript Pommersfelden, Gräflich Schönbornische Bibliothek 16/2764, suggesting that these might be by Arnulf: see X 70 and Iwakuma 'Pierre Abélard et Guillaume de Champeaux dans les premières années du XIIe siècle: une étude préliminaire', in *Langages, sciences philosophie au XIIe siècle*, ed. J. Biard (Paris: Vrin, 1999), p. 96.

p. 12: C. H. Kneepkens points out that the kind of discussion provoked by the *Glosule* on Priscian cannot be labelled either nominalist or realist, although its ideas on nomination could be used to lend support to nominalist positions, in: 'Nominalism and Grammatical Theory in the Late Eleventh and Early Twelfth Century: An Explorative Study', *Vivarium* 30 (1992), 34-50. Irène Rosier-Catach argues that many of the ideas developed in a second stage of the *Glosule* parallel those of William of Champeaux, criticized by Abelard in the *Dialectica*; see her study, 'Abélard et les grammariens: sur la définition du verbe et la notion d'inhérence' to appear in Pierre Lardet (ed.), *La transmission des textes entre Antiquité et Moyen Age. Mélanges en l'honneur du Pr. Louis Holtz* (forthcoming).

p. 33: I discuss the unpublished commentary of Roscelin on Psalms 1-25, not in the second part of my study on St Anselm and Roscelin (X in this volume), but in 'Bruno of Reims and Roscelin of Compiègne on the Psalms' in *Medieval Latin Literature in the Eleventh Century: Proceedings of the Third International Medieval Latin Congress (Cambridge, 9-12 September, 1998)*, ed. M. Herren and C. J. McDonough, Publications of The Journal of Medieval Latin 5 (Turnhout: Brepols, forthcoming). The Psalms commentary is attributed to Roscelin in Paris, Bibliothèque de l'Arsenal, 83, fols. 1-79v.

VIII St Anselm, Roscelin and the See of Beauvais

General bibliography: For further discussion of the Parisian context of the rivalries between Bec and Stephen of Garlande, who himself competed with Galo in wishing to become bishop of Beauvais, see C. J. Mews, *The Lost Love Letters of Heloise and Abelard. Perceptions of Dialogue in Twelfth-Century France* (New York: Palgrave, 1999), pp. 60-61.

IX The Trinitarian Doctrine of Roscelin of Compiègne and its Influence: Twelfth-Century Nominalism and Theology Re-considered

p. 351: On the *Glosule* on Priscian, see notes to VII above.

X St Anselm and Roscelin of Compiègne: Some New Texts and their Implications. II. An Essay on the Trinity and Intellectual Debate c. 1080-1120

p. 48: Iwakuma, who is editing the ps-Rabanus gloss, argues that this manuscript (Paris, BNF lat. 13368) contains a revision of a gloss by William of Champeaux (see notes to II 168 above).

p. 66: Rosier-Catach's observations that the parallels are between William and a second recension of the *Glosule* on Priscian are important in this respect (see notes to VII 12 above).

p. 67: On Bruno of Rheims, see notes to VII 33 above.

pp. 72-3: On Gerland (or Garland) of Besançon, see my article, 'Hugh Metel, Heloise, and Peter Abelard: The Letters of an Augustinian Canon and the Challenge of Innovation in Twelfth-Century Lorraine', *Viator* 32 (2001), 59-91, especially note 55.

INDEX

INDEX OF MANUSCRIPTS